A Guide to the UNDERSTANDING OF PAINTING

A GUIDE TO THE

Understanding of Painting

William Gaunt

HARRY N. ABRAMS, INC. *Publishers* NEW YORK

Library of Congress Catalog Card Number: 68–12936
HARRY N. ABRAMS, INCORPORATED, NEW YORK

Printed and bound in Great Britain

Contents

Foreword 7

CHAPTER ONE
Some Basic Considerations 9

CHAPTER TWO
The Qualities of Medium 63

CHAPTER THREE
The Painter's Aims and Problems 101.

CHAPTER FOUR
The Theme and its Treatment 129

CHAPTER FIVE
The Qualities of a Masterpiece 245

CHAPTER SIX
The Spectator's Involvement 253

Bibliographical Note 270

List of Illustrations 271

Index 284

Foreword

The purpose of this book is, essentially, to suggest ways of looking at paintings and gaining enjoyment from them. By 'enjoyment' I mean both the pleasure they are capable of giving to the eye and the endless interest they offer as revealing how artists have expressed themselves and their view of the world. It is not an outline history of painting, compendium of biographies or dictionary of terms but a study of the qualities that go to make up works of pictorial art as illustrated by great example. Reference to the mechanics or science of picture-making is made within such limits as a general public may find useful in appreciation. A survey of the painter's aims and the various modes of realizing them follows. The comparisons and contrasts of the illustrations have been designed to show the relations between paintings of different epochs and something of the unity that is to be found beneath their variety.

In some chapters I have made use of essays in appreciation which I have contributed on various occasions to the 'Things Seen' column of *The Times*, and my thanks are due to the Editor for permission to quote or adapt passages from them.

W. G.

1 Paul Klee *Young Tree (Chloranthemum)* 1932

Some Basic Considerations

Great paintings have many facets. The place, the person, the scene, the objects depicted may engage attention first. Looking at a tree-lined avenue painted by Hobbema you seem to walk straight into seventeenth-century Holland. The painting of an Infanta by Velazquez brings her vividly to life. *The Last Supper* by Leonardo is a sublime narrative in which each gesture tells part of the story.

There are associations of several kinds which are moving or informative. The character and thought of the painter can be studied. The self-portraits of Rembrandt are a biography in themselves. The hopes, the struggles, the despair of Van Gogh come out in his impassioned canvases. Paintings have much to tell also of history, of the periods in which they were produced, their climate of belief and mode of thought, social conditions and manner of life. A mosaicist at Ravenna describes for us the formality of a Byzantine Court; a Gothic miniaturist the seasonal round on a medieval estate; a Baroque ceiling painter the spirit of the Counter-Reformation; even the abstract painter, rejecting subject-matter, may convey the attitude of mind of an age of scientific and technological research and exploration.

In such instances the immense variety of painting appears. Yet a factor of the greatest importance, always to be considered, is the quality of art. We need not deny the interest of subject or the value of associations but these are only part of the impression a great painting makes. There is the element, more confidently referred to in the past than in recent times as Beauty – in what does this consist? And how is 'good' painting to be distinguished from what is called 'bad'? These are questions that have often been asked before and answered in different ways. It was once supposed by aesthetic philosophers that there is a fixed canon of ideal beauty by which all paintings can be judged, though the attempt to define this ideal led to some baffling verbal complications and purely philosophic argument.

It had a certain plausibility when Classical Greece and Renaissance Italy were the prescribed models to follow. Once Greek sculpture was seen, however, not as a limited number of statues of the Classical fifth century BC (or Roman copies of them) but as a long evolution comprising all the varieties of character from Archaic to Hellenistic, the fixed standard seemed due for revision. An attempt to define the ideal of the Italian Renaissance also would have to be flexible enough to allow for the wistful angularity of Botticelli's Venus and the dynamic force of a Sybil conceived by Michelangelo. 'Truth to Nature' is an alternative which has proved equally elusive and capable of many interpretations, and with the evident fallacy that Whistler pointed out in his Ten O'Clock Lecture: 'To say to the painter that Nature is to be taken as she is, is to say to the player that he may sit on the piano.' The artist selects from the infinity of suggestion offered by natural forms according to his purpose. Indeed no two artists, even if contemporary, see things in exactly the same way and the greater they are the more individually distinct they become, creating fresh canons rather than conforming to those that exist.

It is possible to regard the beauty of paintings as consisting in this individual character alone, in the completeness and originality of a painter's self-expression. This is a reasonable view which disposes of doubtful generalizations. But it is necessary to add that in painting, as in poetry and music, art is the expression of feeling. Just as without the stimulus of emotion poetry sinks to a prosaic level, painting without a similar intensity of feeling becomes either prosaically photographic or a lifeless copy of some prevailing style.

To speak of 'feeling', it may be thought, is to bring another intangible into discussion. But feeling pervades all the processes the painter who is also an artist employs. It is the concentration which selects, emphasizes and animates form and colour as the musician the arrangement of notes and the poet the rhythmic sequence of word-sounds. It can be appreciated therefore, not as a vague generality but as a vital principle in the painter's technique and treatment of his theme.

It is not necessary to be a painter in order to appreciate painting but the elements of the painter's language, the qualities he extracts from a medium, the way in which he carries out a particular function are means to a full understanding of his art. One can best enjoy it by seeing to some extent as the painter sees, observing the problems set and the manner of their solution. That there is an element of mystery, a strangeness in beauty, not to be explained away by analysis, is admitted. As Sir Joshua Reynolds remarked, 'The great end of art is to strike the imagination . . . the spectator is only to feel the result in his bosom.' In a work that is truly a creation the whole is greater than the sum of its parts. But the differences of quality have still to be assessed in terms of what we can see. We need not lose sight of the totality of effect in considering the means by which it is attained.

FORM IN PAINTING

The two essentials, form and colour, are sometimes inseparable especially in modern painting in which colour has come to play an increasingly functional part. The well-known definition of the French painter and theorist, Maurice Denis, that a picture 'before being a war-horse, a nude woman or any subject whatever is essentially a plane surface covered with colours in a certain order' implicitly includes the idea of form but is characteristic of French developments towards the end of the nineteenth century in making colour the key factor.

Artists at an earlier date would have reversed the order of priority to place form first. Leonardo da Vinci, the complete type of intellectual Florentine, regarded colour as no more than a pleasing accessory and remarked with a certain contempt that it reflected credit on the compounder of pigments rather than on the painter who used them. The 'certain order' of the Old Masters was so independent of colour, that is, so carefully planned in monochrome to begin with, that one can well appreciate the substance of their work in black and white reproduction. It is only when colour itself is a statement of form that such a reproduction loses much of its significance. Venice by Monet, taking shape in a splendid shimmer of hues, disappears into a grey fog when half-tone imperfectly translates it.

One idea of form is mathematical – and mathematics are certainly independent of the attractions of colour! Plato's conception of an ideal beauty to be distinguished from the beauty of the human figure or other organisms, identified with 'straight lines and curves and the surfaces or solid forms produced out of these by lathes, rulers and squares', was advanced as a philosophic inquiry without reference to painting. But painters, also, have been aware of the value of an absolute, the form that is valid in all circumstances and at all times, with an existence independent of the irregularities of nature and owing nothing to association with story.

The symbolic art of primitive peoples tends in this direction, though the symbolic form still has a suggestion of something else, the circle for instance standing for the sun. Yet when the Australian Aboriginal draws varying series of curved lines to indicate the leaping movements of a kangaroo it may be felt that he is instinctively finding his way towards complete abstraction (*Pl. 2*). The lines, it is clear, cannot be considered as a rudimentary attempt to portray the animal in motion but as the track of movement in itself.

Modern abstract painting in its formal or geometric aspect gives the most complete and conscious application of the Platonic idea. Thus Wassily Kandinsky in the 1920s and 1930s produced a whole series of paintings in which the circle in various relations and dimensions is the motif. The living painter Josef Albers has concentrated in similar fashion on the beauty of the square and all the subtleties of proportions that emerge in the relation of these rectangular figures (*Pls. 4, 5*).

It is not only the geometric figure in itself but geometrical progression that is a special feature of this mode of abstract painting, the ratio between its parts giving a calculated variety

2 Primitive abstraction: Australian 'bull-roarer'

3 Formal relationships: Ben Nicholson *Vertical Seconds* 1953

of interval. This ordered proportion has always been a concern of artists, even in compositions of a far from abstract kind. Studied in isolation in the abstract paintings of Ben Nicholson, it provides an effect of pure harmony (*Pl. 3*).

If an account of mathematical form begins with abstract painting in modern times it is because this is so much occupied with basic principles and in separating them from such other aims as the delineation of natural form. Piet Mondrian developed his system of rectangles on the basis that the rectangle was furthest from the accidental shapes of nature and was therefore art in its purest form. Many people are apt to look on his rigid verticals and horizontals as a cold purism or puritanism. This is a matter of personal preference, as between the deliberate isolation of a principle and painting of a naturalistic kind.

4, 5 Square and circle: below, Joseph Albers *Homage to the Square* 1960 right, Wassily Kandinsky *Variegated Circle* 1921

Whether or no the spectator has a bias in favour of the latter, the principle is a reasonable inquiry. It is pursued in the Dutch painter's work with what one is entitled to think of as a passionate puritanism. The blocks of colour and grid shapes of his *Broadway Boogie Woogie*, creating analogies with the layout of New York streets, the flicker of neon signs, the syncopation of Negro pianists, convey the power of abstraction to evoke a mood without resort to imitative matter (*Pl. 27*).

One may also find it as an element in the work of the past, noting for example an affinity with Mondrian in the use Vermeer makes of the rectangle of a picture frame, the tracery of a window and the black and white squares which pattern a floor, these giving a delightful sense of pictorial order to his *Gentleman and Lady at a Spinet* (*Pls. 6, 7*). William Hogarth

6, 7 Uses of the rectangle: above, Vermeer *Gentleman and Lady at a Spinet* c. 1662

Opposite, Piet Mondrian *Composition with Red, Yellow and Blue* 1921

16

Rococo curvature: 8 François Boucher *The Birth of Venus* 1740

pursued as abstract an inquiry as Mondrian in his *Analysis of Beauty*, an exposition of the value of a double curve ('line of beauty') and spiral ('line of grace') which indeed are elements to be appreciated in all the Rococo painting of his century. One may for instance compare the systems of curvature in Boucher's *Birth of Venus* (Stockholm, Nationalmuseum, *Pl. 8*) and Hogarth's scene of orgy in *A Rake's Progress* (London, Soane Museum, *Pl. 9*).

The mathematical basis of painting may be considered either in terms of the Euclidean plane geometry which Leonardo da Vinci discusses as a sort of ground-plan in two dimensions or

18

9 William Hogarth *The Rake's Progress c.* 1732

as the principle of structure in representing three dimensions. When Cézanne said that 'Everything in nature is modelled on the sphere, the cone or the cylinder; once one has learnt how to paint these simple shapes, one can do what one wants', he reaffirmed the importance of the traditional properties of the art classroom.

To interpret three dimensions is the greater end, because it introduces, as no flat pattern can do, the idea of infinity, of endless possibilities and subtleties of form. It is part of the pleasure to be gained from paintings to see how these qualities are attained, not by the attempt to reproduce the rich confusion

10, 11 Geometrical ratio: above, Uccello *The Battle of San Romano*
c. 1454–7; below, Piero della Francesca *The Flagellation c.* 1455

12 Sculptural form: Rogier van der Weyden *The Deposition c.* 1435

of nature but by bringing out an essential order. Italian painting in the Early Renaissance is especially fascinating from this point of view. Solid geometry, the geometrical ratio, perspective, had the attractions of a new science for painters. Consider for instance the varied intervals between the lances of the warriors in Uccello's *Battle of San Romano* (*Pl. 10*), and the geometrical simplifications of Piero della Francesca's *The Flagellation* (Urbino, Galleria Nazionale delle Marche, *Pl. 11*).

It is a return to this aspect of form that one finds in the nineteenth-century French master, Georges Seurat. A comparison of Piero's fresco at Arezzo *Queen of Sheba before*

Solomon (Pl. *13*) and the French painter's *A Sunday Afternoon at the Grande Jatte* (Chicago, Art Institute, Pl. *14*) reveals a most interesting affinity between the two in the severity of form that magically arrests a moment and gives it permanence. Painters of large and simplified form have also owed much to sculpture, as providing them with a ready-made, partial solution of what to select from nature and what to reject in the rendering of three dimensions. Some, like Tintoretto and Daumier, have made models of their own because of their explicit suggestion of light and shade, already at a clarifying remove from the complexity of nature. Carving by the nature of the hard material used made for a simplification which in turn suggested a monumental dignity of 'plastic form' to the painter.

From the time of Giotto to that of the masters of the High Renaissance in Italy, Classical sculpture and contemporaneous

Formally ordered composition: 13 Piero della Francesca *The Queen of Sheba before Solomon*, begun *c.* 1452

sculpture exerted an influence on painting which contributed much to its grandeur. There is another example in the distinctive manner the Flemish painters of the fifteenth century derived from Gothic sculpture in stone and wood, notable in the stiff folds of dress and the effect of relief – an example of great splendour being *The Deposition*, Rogier van der Weyden's masterpiece, in the Prado, Madrid (*Pl. 12*). A modern instance can be found in the impression made on Cubist painters by the sharply cut planes and geometrical contours of African sculpture.

What Sir Joshua Reynolds termed the 'Grand Style' is not limited in Italian painting to one superb and culminating age. The majestic generalizations of form, disregarding any triviality of detail extend from the time of Giotto to the time of Raphael. The two great artists may be compared in the timelessness of the dress with which they clothe their figures, the exclusion of

14 Georges Seurat *A Sunday Afternoon at the Grande Jatte* 1884–6

15 Dignity of generalization: Giotto *The Marriage at Cana*, probably between 1305 and 1313

any circumstance which has no bearing on the theme. The frescoes by Giotto in the Arena Chapel of Padua have the same sense of lofty drama in consequence as the frescoes of Raphael in the Vatican or the Cartoons now preserved in London at the Victoria and Albert Museum (*Pls. 15, 227*).

Yet in their encounters with nature artists have always something to discover, if, like Hazlitt, they look on it as a reservoir 'deep, obscure, infinite'. From this viewpoint form is a protean thing, capable of endless transpositions as Leonardo imagined it 'like the sound of bells in whose clanging you may find any name and word you choose to imagine'. He dwelt for the first time on the mysteries and possibilities of the accidental form in nature. 'When you look at a wall spotted with stains or with a mixture of stones, if you are about to devise some scene, you will be able to see in it a resemblance to various landscapes, rivers, rocks, trees, plains, wide valleys and various groups of hills; or again you may see battles and figures in action; or strange faces and costumes.' His geological studies and his sense of the natural forces operating on form to produce what we call its accidents of appearance evolved the fantastic and strangely impressive landscapes that lie behind the *Mona Lisa* and *The Virgin of the Rocks* (Pl. *16*).

16 Strangeness of form: landscape detail from Leonardo's *Virgin of the Rocks*, begun *c.* 1483

The proposition somewhat diffidently put forward by Leonardo as 'a new device for study . . . which may seem trivial and almost ludicrous' has several later parallels and sequels. A painter may for instance provide for himself this haphazard basis of form instead of studying the stains or cracks in some surface or objects seen, relying on his faculty for improvisation to turn it into a definite image. Thus the eighteenth-century English watercolourist, Alexander Cozens, according to his *New Method for assisting the Invention* . . ., would swiftly lay down on paper vague blots and smudges of the brush from which a complete landscape could be elaborated (*Pl. 17*). This was a method of 'controlled accident'. The blot was 'the product of chance with a small element of design' but a great power of suggestion. The form took shape in the mind. There are some parallels in Oriental painting. A translation of precepts representing Zen principles of art by the Chinese artist, Ching Hao (tenth century) defines 'spirit' as meaning 'that the mind follows the movements of the brush and seizes unerringly the shapes of things'. As examples of the 'controlled accident' in the West one might instance the way in which Turner causes watercolour on damp paper to streak into the sky with the effect of a rain cloud; or the way in which random shapes and lines revealed a subject to Paul Klee as he worked on them (*Pl. 19*). Form as an

18 Strangeness of form: Jerome Bosch *The Garden
of Delights c.* 1500 (detail)

17, 19 Controlled accident:
left, Alexander Cozens *Landscape*
right, Paul Klee *Heavily Pregnant* 1934

20 Fusion of form and colour: Turner *Interior at Petworth* 1837

unstable element can be used to deliberately fantastic effect. This appears in the wonderful grotesques of Jerome Bosch, the hybrid shapes of *The Garden of Delights*, anticipating the fantastic inventions of twentieth-century Surrealism (*Pl. 18*). In another aspect one may see form, as the scientist now views solid objects, in terms of energy rather than mass. Turner whose later works were once criticized as 'without form and void' does precisely this in the remarkable *Interior at Petworth* in which form is dissolved or held in solution in colour (*Pl. 20*).

Turner presents a Romantic way of fusing form and colour, suggestive of elemental infinities. Cézanne contrasts with him in his Classical sense of order newly applied in the translation of structure into colour. That each plane on the surface of a solid object had its own nuance to be given a colour value rather than

21 Colour interpreting form: Paul Cézanne *L'Estaque c.* 1885

a degree of shadow, that a like construction could define space itself were conceptions that gave colour increased importance but were also linked with the tradition of monumental form (*Pl. 21*).

One may distinguish, as in Turner and Cézanne, the Romantic from the Classical mind but the basic ideas of form discussed, varying as they are, have all been used by great painters with the sense of an ultimate order, the product of the creative intelligence. It is this which transforms the geometrical element from a dull mathematical exercise and inventive exploration of the seeming accident from the mere imitation of substance in which the original quality of mind is lacking.

RHYTHM AND MOVEMENT

The kinship suggested by the phrase 'all the arts aspire to the condition of music' and more specifically by Leonardo's description of music and painting as 'sister arts' is observable in the use of the same terms as applied to each. Rhythm, primarily belonging to music, is an example. It is also used of painting and often in a vague fashion. It cannot mean exactly the same thing, it is clear, when transferred from one art to another. In music it has to do with 'time' and the succession in time of beats, measures, phrases. But painting is an art of space and not of time (leaving out of account the 'kinetic' experiments of today).

Everything in a picture that may be represented by the words 'rhythm' and 'movement' stands still and can be instantaneously perceived, even though the eye may move at a more leisurely pace over the surface in studying its detailed aspects. Rhythm is to be appreciated as a relation of forms coherently united. This coherence is obtained by the repetition of kindred shapes throughout the work. The aesthetically moving effect thus produced is independent of the descriptive value of form in defining any one object. The rhythmic congruity may be found in a variety of dissimilar things – figures, landscape, folds of dress, still-life detail.

Movement is to be distinguished from the representation of figures or animals in motion. It is the flow of rhythm which

IOANIS BELLINI OP

22 Rhythm in design: Gentile Bellini *Fra Teodoro as St Dominic* 1515

23 Flow of movement: Michelangelo, detail of the Creation, Sistine Chapel, 1508–12

leads the spectator's gaze from one point to another with an impression of continued harmony. One may be no more than subconsciously aware of it or even disregard it when the painter has made it a subtle accessory to the interest of subject. For instance Gentile Bellini's *Fra Teodoro as St Dominic* might be regarded simply as the portrait of an austere churchman. But when one examines it further, it can be seen that a system of curved forms is repeated and echoed all the way through – in the halo, the skull-cap, the floral pattern on the curtain behind. The design of the stylized petals is picked up and emphasized by that of the brass-bound edges of the devotional volume Fra Teodoro holds. The lily in his hands gives the variant of nature to the formal design (*Pl. 22*).

In many great paintings the flow of rhythm is more insistent and emotional. It is majestic in the superb relation of gesture as between the outstretched arm of God and that of Adam in Michelangelo's conception of the Creation in the Sistine Chapel (*Pl. 23*). It is an ecstasy of movement in Botticelli's *Mystic Nativity* (London, National Gallery). Here a circular rhythm is affirmed and reaffirmed in a way that can scarcely fail to

24 Flow of movement: Botticelli *Mystic Nativity* 1500–1

25 Dynamic movement: El Greco *The Burial of Count Orgaz* 1586

identify the spectator's feeling with that of the artist. The circle of angelic figures above is repeated by a smaller group of angels, expanding again into the circle that forms round the Virgin and Child. The rapturous embraces of the figures in the foreground are individual repetitions of the larger scene of the composition (*Pl. 24*).

It may convey the stress of violent and dramatic action and in this respect Rubens is without a peer. In his *Raising of the Cross* in Antwerp Cathedral the feeling of strain, tension and lifting is produced by the diagonal line that traverses the composition and the series of taut lines that radiate from it. Though the heaving men are as muscular as Rubens well knew how to make them, they would not in themselves produce this vigorous effect without the abstract device that links their efforts (*Pl. 26*).

34

26 Dynamic movement: Rubens *Raising of the Cross* 1610

The passionate effect of rhythm pervades the 'flame-like' forms of El Greco and is seen in its most complex and dynamic form in *The Burial of Count Orgaz* (Toledo, S. Tomé). Here the intended contrast is part of the rhythmic unity. The sagging curve of the body of the dead nobleman has its obverse in the parting of the clouds above. Their forms are repeated in the bowed figures of the saints. The line of mourners serves to emphasize the passage from life now to hereafter and the great upward surge towards an opening heaven (*Pl. 25*).

Gracefulness as a quality of rhythm is a particular feature of Mannerist painting to be seen in the use of elegant elongations and long sweeping lines by Parmigianino. Many works incline one to think of rhythmic movement as systems of curves though it is not exclusively so composed. The analogy with music again appears in the importance of 'intervals', the spaces between forms which become interesting to the eye when they approximate to a geometrical progression, that feature of mathematics which gains visual beauty in providing both variety and order. A modern instance already referred to is Mondrian's *Broadway Boogie Woogie* (*Pl. 27*).

In the paintings of Old Masters the rhythm often derives from the conscious study which already appears in preliminary drawings. In result however it evades a crude analysis, is sometimes partly concealed by variations and seeming hesitancies of direction, lost for a while only to regain a decisive strength, a consciousness of the guidance of the master remaining throughout. A question to be considered is how far rhythm may be instinctive rather than a conscious plan, how far the physical action of wielding a brush makes for a rhythm corresponding to the pulse-beat of the painter himself. 'The style,' it is said, 'is the man', one may consider the action, the gesture of painting as the essence of style. It is so in the art of the Far East, though here it is a product of a traditional skill (*Pl. 28*). Yet the act of faith of what is now called 'informal abstraction' is not necessarily productive of a comprehensible harmony. One must distinguish even in the quality of gesture. A unity comes from the 'action painting' of Jackson Pollock (*Pl. 29*) but the reliance

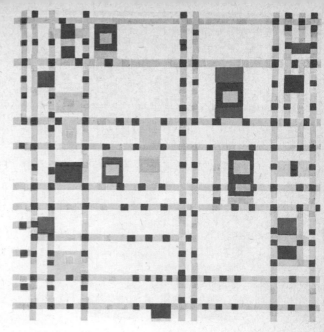

27 Formal relationships: Piet Mondrian
Broadway Boogie Woogie 1942–3

28, 29 Rhythm in the artist's gesture:
left, Ku An (active 1350) *Bamboo in
the Wind*; below, Jackson Pollock
Blue Poles 1953

on instinct may also lead to a mere chaos. Turning back to undoubtedly great works of painting one finds that as a beautiful repetition pervades the whole, it follows that no part of it can be dull. The rhythm that resides in every detail is part of the life and illimitable vigour of a truly great work. The film camera that nowadays scrutinizes each part of a master-work brings out the fact that all contribute to the profundity of result.

COLOUR: HARMONY AND DISCORD

Colour is the element in painting which probably gains the readiest response from most people. It offers the closest analogy with music in the purely sensuous reaction it causes. Again as with rhythm, a musical term, harmony, is used to denote the concord of colours. Their selection by the painter may be compared with the succession of notes that constitute the musician's melody and their combination with the simultaneous effect of notes – chords – of musical harmony. Just as the composer will retain all through a work the thread of some principal melody, so the painter will relate his combinations of colour to some main visual 'melody', appearing and re-appearing consistently, though in a number of variations.

The spectator may, as Reynolds put it, feel the effect 'in his bosom' and be content to leave it at that. Yet some consideration of the way it is achieved can only heighten the pleasure it provides, at the same time indicating that a difference does exist between good colour and bad – or between its sensitive and insensitive use. There is something in the idea that individual colours have emotional properties of their own though it is only applicable within certain limits. Red is a warm, exhilarating colour – but with some darkening of tone it may turn sullen and sombre. Blue is a cool, recessive colour, as conventionally suitable for rendering distant objects as warmer colour for the foreground, yet blue also can be warm and dominant. Yellow is cheerful, sunny, yet with a slight admixture it may turn sickly and livid.

The true colourist, it may be concluded, is not concerned with such simple definitions but with more subtle mixtures and relations. How much relation counts for is indicated by Degas' remark that if he had to use mud he could turn it into the purest of colours simply by its juxtaposition with others. An important factor first of all is the key or pitch of colour as corresponding to the theme or mood of a painting. A scheme of bright colours would be out of place in Rembrandt's dramatic and profound conceptions. His depth of tone would be equally out of keeping with some gaily decorative painting by Boucher. One can imagine a landscape in nature in which there is actually a good deal of bright colour though the impression the painter may wish to give is that of quietude and repose. He may elect to subdue his own colour to restful greys and a near-monochrome as the Dutch painters of the seventh century did so often.

One aspect of harmony then is fitness to the emotional purport of the theme; another is harmony in the relations of the colours used. This may be obtained by the repetition of the same colours in varying proportions and modifications of tone. In Vermeer's *Lady Standing at the Virginals*, for example, the melodic basis is a blue in relation with a golden tone. The blue of the lady's bodice is picked up in the blue of the sky in a picture to her left and again in the panel above her musical instrument and the seat of the chair in the foreground. The golden tone of a picture-frame is repeated and varied in the painted cherub of the central picture, the warm clouds in the panel of the virginals and has its fainter echo in the pale gold of the lady's skirt. The colours gain in value in this great picture by the subdued background against which they are set (*Pl. 30*).

Harmony is also connected with the idea of repose and completeness, requiring that certain colours should be balanced by others with different and compensating qualities. According to scientific theory the retina of the eye has three separate reactions to the radiations of light which give the sensation of colour, corresponding to the main constituents of white light. The eye has a physical tendency to complete a primary colour by its complementary which would explain why there is harmony in the balance and juxtaposition of red and green, yellow and violet or orange and blue.

30, 31 Harmony in blue and gold: above, Vermeer *Lady Standing at the Virginals* c. 1671; right, Whistler *Old Battersea Bridge: Nocturne – blue and gold* c. 1865

It would help to explain also why the landscapes of the French Impressionists are singularly harmonious in colour although they were not so much striving towards this result as trying to render the appearance of things in the open air with an objective accuracy. The method of translating daylight into pictorial terms by separate touches of spectrum colour tended towards harmony by its nature. Contrast however is not simply a scientific relation of colours but a needed balance which the artist may introduce in a number of ways. Whistler did not paint a rocket in the evening sky of his *Old Battersea Bridge* simply because there happened to be a firework display in Cremorne Gardens at the time when he looked at the river. The red and yellow shower repeated in the lights and reflections along the shore enhances the exquisite quality of the tones of blue (*Pl. 31*).

The conscious colour harmony, the deliberate selection of colours to an aesthetic end had a new aspect in the nineteenth century. There are of course effects of great richness and brilliance in the European Old Masters. Titian stands out among the Venetians for the contrasting splendour of orange warmth and deep blue as well as for the depth of quality obtained by successive thin glazes (*Pl. 33*). But speaking generally the Old Master picture was conceived in light and shade, i.e. gradations of monochrome. Brown was long favoured for its warmth and softness, heightened by the use of a mellowing varnish. This has become so accepted a feature of Old Master painting that the removal of darkened varnish from gallery masterpieces still creates periodical complaint even though it may be accounted an approach to the original appearance.

Colour was therefore 'local', that is descriptive of some particular object, a red dress for instance; or an ingredient of tone, the degree of darkness; in either case often an auxiliary rather than an essential. The development of colour in European painting and especially in France since the early nineteenth century has two aspects; as a scientific extension of realism and as an emotional factor in itself. The identification of colour with light was the point on which artists in the nineteenth century seized, either empirically or from their reading of such inquiries as that of the French chemist, Michel Eugène Chevreul. It implied that the colours which made up light, the colours of the spectrum should alone be used, that shadow should not be a degree of darkness but translation into some pure degree of colour. This decisively altered the function of colour, making it an omnipresent quality of atmosphere. Local colour was no longer seen descriptively but as a surface subject to various modifications by the incidence of light. Black as the complete exclusion of light was banned from the artist's palette. So too were the browns which had no place in the spectrum. This accounts for the remarkable freshness of French Impressionist painting compared with the work of earlier centuries (*Pl. 34*).

Yet the spectrum contained alternative suggestions. First, as Chevreul states, that colours 'may be reduced to such a state of division . . . that at the distance from which we view them together they appear a coloured surface continuous in all its parts', so presenting infinite nuances of vibration in which the separate effect of colours is merged. This is the union that Seurat's scientific systematization of the Impressionist method presents. Or it may suggest a bolder use of clear colour not necessarily in the small dots of Pointillism or Divisionism but in such emphatic brushmarks as Van Gogh made.

In the long run this was to divert colour from its realistic purpose to emotional and quasi-musical ends. Thus in the early twentieth century Robert Delaunay still influenced by Chevreul's conception of 'simultaneous contrast' (the modification in colour which objects appear to undergo when seen at the same time) produced chromatic 'discs' which presented 'colour as a function in itself. The artificial or non-naturalistic harmony in modern painting however has had another point of departure from Oriental art. The Japanese print indicated the value of colours rigorously selected; the Persian miniature the complex harmonies of bright colour in no way toned down to give a natural effect. Paintings by Whistler illustrate the influence of Japan, those of Matisse something gained from the sensuous richness of Persia (*Pls. 36, 37*).

32 The value of black: Brueghel *Peasant Dance c.* 1568

33 Venetian richness: Titian *Bacchanal c.* 1518

34 Colour translating light: Claude Monet *La Grenouillère* 1869

Oriental art brings into view the equivocal place of black and white in the colour scheme. These absolutes, the absence or fullness of light are avoided by the out-and-out realist as not found in nature as we ordinarily see it. Yet these absolutes are in a sense 'colours' which painters can turn to brilliant effect. The reds and ochres of Pieter Brueghel's *Peasant Dance* are held in gay and exhilarating concord by the black of a coat, the flash of a white cap or stocking (*Pl. 32*). A black picture-frame in Vermeer's *Lady Standing at the Virginals* enhances the delicate play of blue and gold (*Pl. 30*). Black and white in Oriental painting heighten the brilliance of bright hues.

45

35 Composition in light and shade: Rembrandt *Descent from the Cross*
c. 1653

What, then, is discord? It may be defined as the exaggerated vibration of one colour as compared with another, the result being irritable to the eye. But as this difference of vibration is always present in some degree it would seem to follow that there is no absolute distinction between discord and harmony. El Greco's oppositions of crimson, greenish blue and sickly yellow set up an insistent demand on the eye but their conflict generates an emotional force in keeping with the artist's deliberate distortions of form. This heightening of sensation is perhaps comparable with the deliberate use of discords in music.

They may be revealed as a kind of harmony as the eye develops tolerance for them. The emphatic colour of Van Gogh was once almost unbearable to many people. His paintings have mellowed not by time but by familiarity with his colour key. The same may be said of the French Fauves and the German Expressionists. The cleaning of certain old paintings gives a curious variant on this process of getting into key with an artist. The bright blue sky of a Koninck landscape in the National Gallery, London, emerged from behind its coating of yellowed varnish with a disturbing effect to which it was necessary to grow reaccustomed. Discord as an aesthetic device is to be distinguished from bad colour. Bad colour is that from which the emotional or musical character is absent. It is to be perceived in inferior works which strike one unfavourably because more colours were used than the painter could control. Alternatively in the dingy hues which have no vibration for the eye. Or in the tints of a coloured photograph. But how far the limitation of the palette to a few colours may give a rich effect, not in the least photographic, may be appreciated in the paintings of Daumier (*Pl. 147*).

COMPOSITION

Composition comprises all the means by which a painter arrives at a unity of total effect. Traditionally the general design comes first (using the word in the sense of the Latin verb *designare* – 'to plan or mark out'). A linear framework has often been the

East and West: 36 *The building of a castle*, a miniature from Nizami's
Khamsa c. 1494

37 Henri Matisse *Lady in Blue* 1937

38 Pyramidal composition: Raphael *Madonna and St John*

39 Energy of the diagonal: Delacroix *The Death of Sardanapalus* 1827

first step, taking the form of some geometrical figure though this basis is to be distinguished from the geometrical structure of individual forms. An arrangement of figures within a triangle or pyramid was a favourite device of the European Old Masters. Though of course it is only an underlying factor when the graphic skeleton is clothed with pictorial flesh and blood, it conveys to the spectator stability and repose, the weight of the composition resting firmly on the horizontal base. One does not need any diagrammatic analysis to see how the implied triangle contributes to the restfulness and dignity of Raphael's *Madonna and St John* (London, National Gallery, *Pl. 38*).

The painter has used other geometrical figures or broad divisions of shape to give a more dynamic result. A diagonal division of the canvas gives that energy which one can appreciate in Delacroix's *Death of Sardanapalus* (*Pl. 39*). An ellipse weaves together in movement the peasant dancers in Rubens' *Kermesse*. The double curve of Hogarth's aesthetic theory can be traced in the example given (p. 18).

Composition in light and shade has been another aspect of the general plan. As the balance of large and small areas in direct and dramatic contrast it was especially characteristic of the seventeenth century. Rembrandt's *Descent from the Cross* (Washington, National Gallery, *Pl. 35*) translates the triangular principle of arrangement into the illuminated area which is placed in emotional opposition to the surrounding darkness. The light and shade with which the painter has given the illusion in two dimensions of the rounded figure in a three-dimensional

40, 41 Space in composition: left, Tintoretto *Miracle of St Mark* 1548
above, Raphael *The School of Athens* 1509–11

world leads to consideration of composing in depth; of giving
space itself a material existence. It is not least among the
pleasures of looking at pictures that one can thus travel
imaginatively within them. The painter enables us to do so by
various means. By subtle gradations, ranging from the warmth
of foreground colour and definition of objects near at hand to
the cool blue and less determinate outline of distance Turner
leads the eye to a far horizon in *Crossing the Brook*. By the use of
perspective in architecture and the relative size of figures
Raphael introduces us into a space of classic grandeur in *The
School of Athens*. By emphasis on a dark contour and the light
behind it, by effects of foreshortening Tintoretto endows
figures with free movement in space to such miraculous result
as in the *Miracle of St Mark* (Pls. *40, 41*).

Composition in the past has naturally varied with the scale and medium used. The easel painting in oils has traditionally been a main vehicle of spatial illusion. It could be regarded as a stage with the action entirely contained within the rectangular boundaries of its frame. Any number of examples will readily come to mind but as a superb instance of symmetrical balance within the enclosed space one might select Velazquez's *Garden of the Villa Medici, Rome (Pl. 44)*. The effect of a theatre is heightened by the architectural background – indeed elements of architecture used somewhat in the fashion of theatrical properties are a feature of great interest in many imaginative compositions – the Italian Renaissance in particular providing balconies, columns and staircases the object of which is to emphasize dramatically the human action shown. *The School of Athens* is one great example. Veronese many times uses the sumptuous detail of the palace. The device is to be found elsewhere – Jan Steen makes striking use of the symmetrical framework in the *Young Woman at her Toilet (Pl. 43)*.

Mural decoration however may call for a different mode of composition from the illusionary focus on depth. The mosaics of San Apollinare Nuovo, Ravenna, are 'processional' compositions, the figures being arranged in a single rank and rigid stance, the object being a ceremonial dignity of design (*Pl. 42*). Decorative painting in general, 'decorative' implying an accordance with an architectural surface and setting, tends towards flatness for this reason as in the work of Puvis de Chavannes. Ideas of composition have altered in several respects

42 'Processional' composition: Mosaic of female saints, Ravenna, *c.* 561

The picture
as a stage:
43 Jan Steen *Young
Woman at her Toilet*

44 Velazquez *Garden
of the Villa Medici*
(detail)

45 Asymmetrical composition: Utamaro *Lovers*, early 1880s

since the mid-nineteenth century. The European discovery of the Japanese print influenced painters in two ways.

A comparison of Hiroshige and Whistler shows how the Japanese idea of simplified arrangement and carefully chosen colour added a new refinement to the work of a Western artist. But the Japanese print also suggested that an asymmetrical balance of forms offered as satisfying a unity as the Old Master scheme with its central placing of the features of most importance. Thus Degas derived from Japanese design the plan of deliberately placing the important figure on the outskirts of the picture area (*Pls. 45, 46*). The spontaneous and momentary effect of movement in his paintings and pastels of dancers was a calculated measure of spatial balance.

Degas' desire for natural effect led him further to consider a picture not as an artificial self-contained stage but as a 'slice of life'. Another source of compositional ideas was the photograph.

56

46 Asymmetrical composition: Degas *The Dancing Class* 1874

The objects seen in a photographic print only in part as they came within scope of the lens again suggested the seemingly accidental and natural result he valued. In other ways the Impressionist era to which he belonged raised new questions as theory logically excluded old recipes. Impressionist paintings do not depend on line, assuming on the contrary that there are no lines in nature but only distinctions of colour (*Pl. 34*).

Linear composition was therefore ruled out. Light as translated into colour and also what the eye may physically be supposed to see at any given moment were the unifying factors. For instance, in observing a foreground figure in actuality one would find surroundings and background somewhat out of focus. This is the effect reproduced in Renoir's *La Balançoire*, where the background behind the girl becomes a blur of colour such as no Old Master would have imagined. The coherence is that of the momentary impression (*Pl. 49*).

Similarly, black being banished from the Impressionist palette and gradations of shade converted into specific colours, chiaroscuro as a system of composition was automatically eliminated. To compose in colour became a primary concern. Some reasons have already been advanced for the remarkable harmony so many Impressionist pictures attain. Perhaps it seems all the more remarkable in view of the fact that they worked without premeditation in the open air. Yet here one must consider the coherence produced by working swiftly and directly, the key being at once set and sustained. The sketches of Constable offer their superb example not only of observation but of a tempo maintained at a high pitch of sensitivity (*Pl. 74*).

Nevertheless, all the nineteenth century's objective studies of nature entailed the abandonment of a preconceived pictorial idea. The 'researches' of Cézanne (who so often used the word) were incompatible with a set composition. Unity grew out of his effort to determine the planes of solid structure by means of colour. He made the significant remark that a painter 'must always follow the logic of his eyes. If his perception is right, his conception will be right too'. His paintings of groups of bathers have a singular place in his art as an heroic effort to combine the

47 Formal composition in modern guise: Cézanne *Bathers*

old method of formal composition with his individual inquiry into form (*Pl. 47*).

The painting of more recent times in its subjective and experimental aspects, is further removed from rules and recipes. In the relation of geometric forms it is possible to see a survival of old principles of composition simplified in some examples of abstract painting. But the cultivation of the experimental and the idea that the subconscious should be allowed to take charge obviate by their nature the considered process of planning and arrangement.

The avoidance of formula may be looked on as one condition of pictorial vitality. A contemporary painter mainly concerned with originality of expression has conducted unconventional departures in teaching. He would set his students first to give their notion of a good composition. Produced according to

48 Suggestion from photography: Degas *The Cotton Exchange, New Orleans* 1873

textbook principles, the results, he says, were dull. But then he told them, 'Now, make as bad a composition as you can.' This time there were some interesting productions. The young painters jolted out of reliance on rule were thinking for themselves. The 'bad' composition turned out to be original.

In looking at any painting without prejudice as to the style or school of thought it represents it is however still necessary to ask whether or no it makes visual sense. The language of painting which is basically one, whatever new idioms may be introduced, must be distinguished from gibberish. Construction, rhythm, harmony are not empty words but essentials at any time of great art.

49 The momentary impression: Renoir *La Balançoire* 1876

50 Sketchbook: Jacopo Bellini *Drawing of the Entombment*

CHAPTER TWO

The Qualities of Medium

The quality of the medium a painter uses is not entirely a technical matter which concerns the practising artist and no one else. It is an active ingredient in the effect on the spectator. Drawing may be considered first as the basic means of expression in which one can find the most personal contact with artists. Matisse has described it as 'not an exercise of particular dexterity but above all a means of expressing intimate feelings and moods, a means simplified to give greater simplicity and spontaneity to expression, which should speak without heaviness directly to the mind of the viewer'.

Drawing may be practised independently of painting and as a preliminary to any form of design but it has essential links with the painter's art. The great number of drawings by the European Old Masters is one magnificent testimony to the role of draughtsmanship. They can be classified under several headings. There are the careful studies of the figure and of details such as hands or the folds of drapery, which would appear in a finished painting. When painters had busy workshops and a number of pupil-assistants, the master would often give special care to these studies as guides for detail to be painted by subsidiary hands.

Another type of drawing was the complete design for a composition, ranging from the first sketch which indicated the general distribution of forms to the more detailed *modello* which gave the full conception of the painting in view. This amount of preparation was called for in works on a large scale, in fresco especially where the actual painting had to be carried out swiftly and there was the minimum of allowance for later correction.

52 Fresco: Masaccio *Head of St John* (detail from *The Rendering of the Tribute Money*) *c.* 1425–8

◀ 51 Tempera: Duccio *Christ healing the Blind Man* 1308–11 (detail)

Then there are sketchbook drawings, a file for possible future use of something that had made an impression on the artist, a landscape effect, a human type observed, a gesture, a detail of architecture. They might be compared to the notebook entries of a writer briefly recording an incident or scrap of

54 Pen: Rembrandt *Titia van Ulenborch* 1639

53 (*opposite*) Pen and wash:
Claude *Southern Port at Sunrise*

55 Silverpoint: Leonardo da Vinci
Portrait of a Warrior

conversation to be expanded at leisure. The figures and land-scape and architectural perspectives in the sketchbooks of Jacopo Bellini preserved in the British Museum and the Louvre were a store of pictorial ideas of which Bellini's painter sons, Giovanni and Gentile had benefit (*Pl. 50*). The faintest outline and written notation of colour preserved panoramas of nature in Turner's memory. Drawings have been carried to an elaborate stage to give the patron an accurate idea of what he was to get. The highly finished portrait drawings of Holbein and the *modelli* of the Italians give examples. Others are the end-product, topographical drawings tinted with watercolour for instance (*Pl. 53*).

The media of drawing are various, from those which provide a simple outline to those in which effects of tone and colour combine drawing and painting. The reed or quill pen, a favourite instrument of the Old Masters, was sensitively responsive to their thought. Here one has to distinguish refine-ment of feeling from fineness of line. Thus the thick pen lines of

67

56 Pastel: Chardin *Self–Portrait* 1775 (detail)

57 Oil: Jan van Eyck *Arnolfini Marriage Portrait* 1434 (detail)

Rembrandt's sketches, far from being coarse are full of delicate suggestion (*Pl. 54*). The pen line in Old Master drawings is often reinforced by washes of bistre, a dilution of wood soot, which has a later equivalent in the sepia originally derived from the ink of the cuttlefish. The pen and bistre drawings of Claude are superb examples of the result that could be thus attained (*Pl. 53*).

The delicate method of silverpoint, the grey outline produced by the mark of a silver or other metal point on a surface coated with zinc white has become obsolete with the popularity of the pencil. It preceded the pencil as a sketchbook medium unliable to rubbing, as in the work of Dürer. Its delicacy is exploited in such a drawing as that by Leonardo da Vinci, silverpoint on a

58, 60 Chalk: above, Holbein *Anne Boleyn*; below right, Watteau *Studies*

59 Charcoal: above right, Dürer *Head of a Young Man*

cream-coloured ground, the *Portrait of a Warrior* (British Museum, *Pl. 55*).

The pencil since the eighteenth century has been a universal tool, suggestive rather than complete, though how far it may go in completeness of effect is shown by the exquisite portrait drawings of Ingres. Chalk, black or red has a more emphatic effect and also an indication of colour. Chalk drawing first came into wide use in sixteenth-century Italy. The many Italian masters who employed black or red chalk or the two in combination include Carpaccio at Venice, Andrea del Sarto at Florence, Correggio at Parma and the Carracci at Bologna. The suggestion of flesh colour given by red as a reinforcement of black has attracted portrait painters. The Clouets in sixteenth-century France used sanguine with a simplicity that also gave a remarkably lifelike effect, the great collection in the Musée

Condé, Chantilly, showing their unique quality. They may be compared with Holbein whose drawings of members of the Tudor Court include such variations of the medium as black chalk on a flesh-coloured ground (*Pl. 58*).

The supreme example of the medium's capacity is given by Watteau in his studies of figures and figure details for his paintings in red or red, black and white on a toned ground (*Pl. 60*). Watteau's love of drawing and delight in his own precision and force of execution appear in numerous examples. From them he chose what seemed to suit a particular picture best, forming them into groups. A modern example of the depth of light and shade obtainable on a grained paper is provided by the drawings of Seurat.

Charcoal, used in the past for large-scale cartoons and to the present time as the outline for a painting on canvas, is easily rubbed, unless a fixative is used, and has not often been practised for its own sake, though a number of drawings by Dürer in the British Museum show the range of effect, from bold outline to delicate tone that a master could obtain from it (*Pl. 59*).

61 Watercolour: William Blake *Dante meeting Beatrice in Paradise* 1824

In brush drawing in monochrome, draughtmanship is fused with painting. It is an art of supple and nervous line in the ceramic decoration of ancient Greece, in dramatic alternation and contrast with dark silhouette. Closely related in China and Japan to calligraphy the use of the brush with ink has been a special skill of a synthetic kind summarizing form and in many classic examples more concerned with the suggestion of space than the solidity of objects. This can be appreciated as a sort of shorthand, its visual effect deriving from the swift decision and economy of the brush's movement. Though the realism of much of Western painting has made for a sharp contrast between East and West, masters like Rembrandt and Claude working in freedom with washes of bistre sometimes offer a remarkable parallel (*Pls. 62, 63*).

62, 63 Brush: above, Hu Ch'i *Peonies*, thirteenth century
below, Rembrandt *Woman sleeping*

64 Tempera: Follower of Duccio *Madonna and Child with Six Angels* thirteenth century (detail)

TYPES OF PAINTING

As coloured powder the pigments used are the same whether they are eventually prepared for oil, tempera or watercolour. The vehicle with which the pigments are mixed however creates a wide range of possible effect. The oldest and most geographically widespread form of painting was tempera, that is, pigments made into a paste with water and applied with an emulsion thinned with water. Various emulsions have been used, gums, wax, casein, the yolk or white of egg, producing a hard surface insoluble after a time in water. Tempera was used by the ancient Egyptians for painting on papyrus and also for mural painting. In some form, applied on a dry coat of plaster, it was anciently a universal method of wall painting, in West and East alike. It was similarly a universal method of manu-script painting. In Europe it was the general medium for painting. altarpieces and panel pictures until the fifteenth century.

The quality of tempera is that of opaque colour smoothly and fairly substantially applied on a ground of fine white plaster (*gesso*). The colours dry very quickly and this produces the limitation that the painter cannot work freely in wet colour but must gain effects of tone and modelling by separate touches laid side by side or superimposed. It is therefore denied the richness of depth obtainable in oil painting. This is made up for by a strongly designed linear composition and by brilliant contrast of colour or an exploitation of the delicate shades of colour to which the medium lends itself. Italian painting gives superb examples from Duccio (*Pl. 51*) to Botticelli (*Pl. 132*).

The modern use of tempera has been confined to a few enthusiasts. It has otherwise long ceased to answer to the painter's desire for free handling and variety of effect. The related form of watercolour given more 'body' by the addition

65 Fresco: Pintoricchio
Susanna and the Elders
1492–5 (detail)

of white, known as gouache, has had a long life. Dürer used it sometimes in conjunction with transparent watercolour in his wonderful nature studies. Turner obtained brilliant results with body-colour on a blue-tinted paper. The verve of colour in gouache freely used can be appreciated in the work of modern European artists who have especially cultivated it, among them, Rouault, Bonnard (*Pl. 66*) and Miro.

Tempera was adaptable to a small scale. The minuteness of the Gothic illuminated manuscript inclined the painters of panel pictures in northern Europe during the late medieval period to a similar fineness of detail. Fresco, though demanding a like quickness and decision of execution, was quite different in being essentially an art of wall painting (*Pls. 52, 65*). The colour was applied on a coat of lime plaster while this was still wet, becoming incorporated with it as it dried. Each piece had to be completed at one session. The predetermined design in the form of the 'cartoon' was of particular importance.

The technique was known to the Greeks and Romans but seems to have been used to provide a coloured wall surface rather than for pictorial design. As a medium for figure composition it seems first to have come into use with the extension of church building from the Romanesque period onwards. It was practised in Italy consistently until the sixteenth century. There was no similar development in more northerly Europe, partly because the climate was less favourable and also because the Gothic style of church architecture with its enlarged window space and restricted wall space gave preference to stained glass as a mural decoration (virtually a painting). The panel painting of the North was a development of the Gothic tradition of manuscript illumination. The fresco was different in principle. It made for a broader treatment of form to be seen at a distance rather than scrutinized at close quarters. The 'Grand Style' of the Renaissance was a product of fresco just as the detail of Van Eyck was a product of the Book of Hours.

Like tempera the fresco technique gave way to oil painting. It was possible to paint with oil colours on a wall prepared with plaster or on smooth stone. Giulio Romano and other Italian

66 Gouache:
Bonnard
The Rabbits c. 1893

artists of the sixteenth century did so successfully. A more convenient practice however was to paint on a large canvas which could then be fixed to the wall and this has been usual in modern times. Attempts in nineteenth-century Germany and England to revive the true fresco method showed how little it was possible to recapture the spirit or use the recipes of craft with any hope of permanence in result.

In its range and adaptability to various ends oil painting has the advantage over other media, so much so that nowadays the word 'painting' at once suggests oils to most people. It is applicable to a variety of surfaces from a wood panel to a rough grained canvas. It can be used in many different ways and is capable of the greatest richness and depth, as well as of the most delicate and transparent effect. It is part of the fascination of oil painting that there is no one method. The use of oils in painting was not unknown to the ancient world as references in Pliny indicate. In the early medieval period in Europe it was a method of decorating shields and armorial bearings. In picture painting however it first comes into prominence in the fifteenth century as a medium especially belonging to northern Europe. It was not the sudden discovery with which the brothers Van Eyck used to be credited but probably a gradual evolution out of tempera painting. Experience would show that oil and varnish gave a superior measure of protection against dampness of climate. Recipes may have been found in the medical and chemical treatises of ancient authors by German and Netherlandish painters. At first oil provided a final enriching glaze to a painting executed in tempera. By degrees tempera became simply an underpainting on which the main work was carried out in oils.

It is likely that the Northern artists were influenced by the luminous colour of stained glass and sought for a comparable result in transparent colour smoothly applied. Wood panels of oak, poplar or chestnut covered with a gesso ground provided an ivory-smooth and luminous surface. Paint thinly applied with a soft brush gained a gem-like brilliance from the luminous white beneath. The whole design was carefully drawn and the painting finished piece by piece. An enamel-like translucency was added to the clarity of colour that belongs to tempera. The magic that detail took on, the brilliance of apple-green and red wonderfully preserved through the centuries can be appreciated in Jan van Eyck's great pictures (Pl. 57).

No paintings have lasted in better physical condition than those of the early Flemish school. Their methods however had limitations. They were especially suited to portraits and interior subjects on a small scale. Paintings on a larger scale required a broader treatment. The rendering of varieties of texture, of

67 Oil: Antonello da Messina *Portrait of a Man c.* 1475

modelling in light and shade, of space and distance, called for changes of technique which become noticeable in the sixteenth century.

The innovations belong to Italy. Taught by Flemish artists, Antonello da Messina (*Pl. 67*) transmitted their method to the painters of Venice, in the fifteenth century. Oils provide a final glaze of colour over a tempera base in the work of Giovanni Bellini, but his followers in Venice adopted a different process. On a solid monochrome underpainting new use was made of both the transparent and opaque qualities of oil paint. Lights were modelled thickly reflecting the light in which they were seen and not the luminous quality of the ground. Shadows were painted thinly with successive glazes. The sumptuousness of Venetian painting in the sixteenth century as represented by Giorgione, Titian and Veronese derives from this technical elaboration.

68 Oil:
Correggio
Sleeping Antiope
c. 1525

69 Oil: Rubens *Landscape – Sunset*

Other Italian painters explored the possibilities of oil painting in giving gradations of shadow. This was its essential virtue in the eyes of Leonardo da Vinci, producing the subtle and mysterious effect of the 'Gioconda smile'. Correggio at Parma was in some ways parallel in aim. If one considers an allegorical painting with nude figures such as his *Sleeping Antiope* (Louvre) one can see how well his method was adapted to convey the voluptuously rounded form of the nymph and how impossible it would have been to do so with the clarity of the Netherlandish technique (*Pl. 68*).

The classic Old Master precept 'transparent shadows and *impasto* light' long provided main technical guidance. It is illustrated in the seventeenth century by the work of Rubens. He combined fluent and rapid brushwork in almost a water-colour thinness with thickly loaded lights. The small *Landscape – Sunset* (London, National Gallery, *Pl. 69*) shows this even more strikingly than some of his more famous pictures. The setting sun impinging on the horizon is made to blaze with a yellow so thickly applied as to stand out in relief. The late afternoon landscape has the sensitiveness of transparent shadow that is well adapted to convey the approach of twilight.

Individual masters however have always had their own variants on the interplay and counterchange of the transparent and the opaque. Rembrandt worked over a thickly modelled monochrome underpainting. The richness of light and shade was obtained by transparent glazes of a colour darker than the areas to which they were applied as well as extra touches of heavy impastos in the lights. The final effect as in the self-portraits of his later years or in the magnificent *Man with Golden Helmet* (Berlin-Dahlem) is not merely a dramatic device but a channel from the material to the spiritual, exploring the mysteries of being (*Pl. 70*).

70 Oil: Rembrandt
Man with Golden Helmet c. 1650

71 Oil: Vincent van Gogh
Self-portrait 1890

There are many aspects of paint quality which one can isolate for oneself and study with a sensuous pleasure in the great picture galleries; the creaminess of substance in a Chardin still-life or in the flowers of Rembrandt's *Flora*; the dry crumble of paint in Veronese's *The Family of Darius* (*Pl. 125*); the liquid fluency of brushstroke in Rubens' *Chapeau de Paille* (*Pl. 188*), the broken touches of colour on the dress of an Infanta painted by Velazquez. The later paintings of Cézanne, almost of a watercolour thinness, illustrate beautifully the value of an enamel-like translucency. On the other hand Van Gogh, whose work, if seen in enlargement becomes a relief map of brush-work, so heavily charged is it with paint, has a vitality of a different kind (*Pl. 71*).

In the evolution of oil painting there is one main transition from Old Master to modern practice in the growth of direct painting, that is, colour fulfilling all its purpose at one go (in the Italian term *alla prima* or French *au premier coup*), dispensing with

72, 73 Oil sketch: left, Frans Hals *La Bohémienne c.* 1625; right, Hogarth *The Shrimp Girl*

the leisurely process of underpainting and successive glazings. It accompanies the transition from the elaborate subject composition to the direct observation of nature and thence to the idea of direct personal expression.

Already in the seventeenth century Frans Hals exploits the spontaneous and lively character obtainable in the oil 'sketch' of individuals in the momentary animation of a smile or laugh. He draws with the brush (which can be distinguished from brush drawing), the direct stroke at once giving shape to features, indicating light and shade and mood at the same time. *La Bohémienne* (Louvre) is a masterly example. Hogarth in the eighteenth century paints a kindred masterpiece (*Pls. 72, 73*).

When artists began to work in the open air direct painting was a necessity. The oil sketches of Constable have a sparkling freshness to which his method of painting swiftly in cool colours on a reddish-brown ground contributed (*Pl. 74*). The brilliance

84

74 Oil sketch: Constable: *Brighton Beach with Colliers* 1824

of Manet and his influence on the painters of the Impressionist era in France resides to no small extent in the swift translation of light and form into simplified areas of colour. Painting with a uniform thickness, the French Impressionists sacrificed the varied resources of the Old Masters in obtaining a richness of paint quality but made up for this by the freshness of primary colour and the vibration of divided touches.

Twentieth-century painting in oils displays less concern than in the past with craft and paint quality as a product of skill, but oil painting has remained the principal vehicle of new ideas. Technically it retains a range which extends from the smoothly minute painting of Dali or Tanguy to the fierce impasto of Appel or Jorn. It is still the medium to which the artist most readily turns when he conceives some new idea and attempts to give it visual shape, though some modern artists have also found congenial qualities in such synthetic paints as ripolin and polyvinyl acetate.

85

75 Watercolour: Thomas Girtin *View on the Wharfe, Farnley c.* 1800

That one medium is better than another is a dubious assumption. In any the imprint of the artist is clear. Turner or Cézanne is no less the genius we admire in watercolour than in oil. Yet the art of painting with transparent colours diluted with water as compared with oil might be likened to the sounds of a flute as distinct from the varied combinations of an orchestra. While Cézanne's watercolours are of great beauty it is not from them but from the structure conceived by his oil brush that European art has since drawn inspiration. It is likewise only through oils that the painter has made us aware of his attempt to grapple with abstract forces. The idea of physical engagement which has so much preoccupied some modern painters in oils, an absorption in the material that in a mysterious fashion draws into and incorporates with it not only the consciously intended effect but something of the inward person, is not found in watercolour. The watercolourist is never so deeply embroiled in the technical and ideological struggle. His work is a skirmish rather than a major engagement.

86

76 Watercolour: Turner *Salisbury Cathedral, View from the Cloister*

Watercolour is an art of suggestion. It fails when it essays the completeness and brilliance of oils. It is not in the same sense a craft yet its advantages in swift notation and freshness are popularly appreciated. It has two aspects; as a slight tint applied to a careful drawing and as a complete work of the brush. Its rise as a distinct art form dates from the eighteenth century with the growing demand for topographical and architectural subjects. The tinted drawing not only satisfied the requirements of individual patrons but provided originals for reproduction by the engraver. Watercolour painting is to be distinguished as relying to a greater extent on colour without a graphic foundation. In the past it has been mainly associated with England and the English cultivation of landscape. In the early nineteenth century it was known specifically to Delacroix and others on the European continent as 'l'art Anglais'. This was the one period when it exerted an influence on art in the *avant-garde* sense. The watercolours of Girtin were a distinct influence on Constable as an oil painter. It was moreover not only the oil landscape of Constable that greatly impressed French artists at the famous Salon of 1824 but the works then shown by English watercolourists. What was new was the freshness of colour and the freshness of atmosphere that came of the then novel practice of working in the open air.

That the medium was one of facile and pretty effect is a conclusion that may be drawn from the work of that vast army of amateurs and drawing-masters that took up the medium in the early nineteenth century. But again we have to reckon with the fact that a medium's quality depends on that of the artist who uses it.

Assessing their place in the revival of landscape painting Constable spoke of Cozens and Girtin (*Pl. 75*) as 'possessing genius of the very highest order'. The later watercolours of Turner (*Pl. 76*) are unique in art in their poetry of colour and variety and grandeur of design. It was the vehicle also of great achievement in other fields than landscape. Blake's 'illustrations' of Dante bring watercolour into the service of magnificent imaginative conceptions (*Pl. 61*). Rowlandson creates a world

88

of town and country in which, apart from the caricatural element, he shows a mastery of composition and of delicate colours so perfectly related as to gain a completeness and force of their own.

In modern times it has been used with a renewed freedom and brilliance of result, beautifully luminous in still-life or landscape by Cézanne, boldly expressive in the work of the German painter Nolde, its accidents of spreading colour seized on with imaginative effect by Klee (*Pl. 1*).

Some artists, like Klee himself, have used watercolour as an element in a mixture of media. An historic instance of such use is provided by Gainsborough who sometimes freely combines watercolour, chalk, body-colour, and touches of oil paint in the same work.

Pastel is a more elaborate form of the chalk or crayon medium for drawing, distinct in the wider range of colour provided by powdered pigments bound with gum and made up into sticks which can be applied directly without the use of a liquid medium. The range of colour makes it appropriately described as painting. The word is a diminutive of the Italian *pasta* or paste and these dry paste colours began to be used by Italian artists, Jacopo Bassano for instance, in the sixteenth century; though it was in the eighteenth century that it became generally popular with European artists, the practice of the Venetian woman artist, Rosalba Carriera, having much influence in France especially.

The delicate effects obtainable were then much cultivated in portraiture. Painters could combine a linear directness of touch with the softer effect of the dry colour rubbed down into a tint. Some spontaneity is lost, the more the colour is softened into tone in this way. Yet the great artist could judiciously combine directness and subtlety. One might take as an instance the pastel self-portrait of Chardin (Louvre). The firmness of modelling is as complete as in an oil painting, the modifications of flesh tint as exhaustively examined, individual strokes have an interplay with smoothnesses of surface. In total there is all the warmth and personality of a living being (*Pl. 56*).

77 Pastel:
Maurice Quentin de La Tour
Mme de Pompadour 1755

Maurice Quentin de La Tour is the celebrated specialist in pastel portraiture who explored its capacity to convey facial expression and also used it with that completeness that appears in his full-length portrait of Mme de Pompadour (*Pl. 77*). With the end of the Old Régime in France the medium which had celebrated its elegance passed out of favour.

It was revived in the later nineteenth century by Degas and Toulouse-Lautrec who sought somewhat different qualities from those cultivated in the century before. They valued the swiftness of execution and spontaneity of expression it made possible. Some of the most beautiful of Degas' studies of ballet dancers and the most trenchant of Toulouse-Lautrec's delineations of character are in pastel. Separate touches of colour are left in their original vigour, related together with something of that vibrating effect that distinguishes Impressionist painting in oils.

78 Crayon and
watercolour:
Henry Moore *Shelter
Sketchbook c.* 1941

The drawback to the medium is its fragility, the ease with
which the grains of colour can be accidentally rubbed or
dislodged, though fixatives can be used and even without them
a pastel under glass can be regarded as permanent. The delicacy
and fragility are perhaps alien to modern art in so far as artists
have sought for emphasis of effect, but the delicacy still appears
in figure studies by Jules Pascin. A variant of pastel, waxed
crayons, in conjunction with watercolour and pen line completes
the impressiveness of Henry Moore's *Shelter Sketchbooks* of
wartime London (*Pl. 78*).

The various forms of painting without brushes or equivalents
of painting each have special qualities. There is the ancient
encaustic painting (literally 'burnt in') in which pigments mixed
with beeswax were heated and applied in melted form with a
spatula, brushwork being supplementary. Encaustic was used
by the Greeks and Romans on walls and panels but the existing

79 Encaustic painting: Portrait of a Woman on an Egyptian Mummy-case from the Fayum, first–second century

80, 81 Mosaic: below, *The Battle of the Issus* from Pompeii, before AD 79; above right, Christ in the Cathedral of Cefalù, c. 1155

evidence of the Classical technique is represented by the portraits painted on mummy-cases in Egypt during the Greco-Roman period and discovered in the cemeteries of the Fayum (*Pl. 79*). They show both the skill in portraiture of the artists and the singular incisiveness which their use of the method gave to the features. Dating from the first to the third century A D these remarkable portraits bear witness to the permanence of the medium. It has been little used in modern times except by way of experiment with an ancient technique, though wax emulsions have been employed in mural oil painting. Some equivalent of work with the spatula may be found in the practice of palette-knife painting.

Mosaic, consisting of cubes (*tesserae*) of stone or coloured glass laid down in plaster, has the advantage of being the most permanent of all forms of pictorial and decorative design. The painting by the Greek artist, Philoxenos, representing the Battle of Issus is preserved in the mosaic copy found at Pompeii (*Pl. 80*) and enables us to appreciate the highly developed skill in elaborate composition and the representation of vigorous action obtained some three hundred years B C. The Roman mosaic pavement, a purely geometric pattern of the type that still comes to light from time to time in excellent preservation, was a standardized luxury of the Empire. Roman mosaics are often of considerable pictorial interest in the representation of figures and objects.

Yet the great triumphs of the art and craft belong to the Byzantine period when mosaic became transferred from floor to wall and interior dome and apse. The development of the technique which gave the desired tone by the juxtaposition of patches of different colours calls to mind the Divisionist technique of the French 'neo-Impressionist' painters, Seurat and Signac in the late nineteenth century. It is well illustrated by the mosaics in San Vitale, Ravenna, which show the height attained by the art in the reign of Justinian, sixth century AD. The use of coloured and gilded glass irregularly set in such a way as to create a shimmer of light and shade about Christian images conceived in majestic simplicity on the largest scale contributes to the wonderfully impressive effect of works in the second Byzantine Golden Age, ninth to twelfth century AD, such as the Madonna of Torcello and the Christ with the Virgin, Angels and Apostles of the Cathedral, Cefalù (*Pl. 81*).

Historically mosaic was supplanted by the rise of fresco in Italy and the development of stained glass in Gothic Europe, though stained glass was in a sense its continuation. This too may be considered as a mode of painting without brushes (or at its best with a minimum of surface painting). The mosaic-like assemblage of pieces of coloured glass, the colour being obtained by the fusion of pigments, became a kind of painting in light from the effect of light streaming through. The changes of daylight produced changes of colour like those synthetically produced by some forms of 'kinetic' art at the present day. The leads which held the glass together gave definition also of design. The richness of stained glass in the twelfth and thirteenth centuries in the great Gothic cathedrals of northern Europe is unequalled. It was when glass came closer to an imitation of painting with detail applied in monochrome *grisaille* that it lost its original virtue, descending at last to the muddiness of nineteenth-century painted glass. From this at least it was retrieved in England by the glass of William Morris and Edward Burne-Jones, though the old richness of colour still seemed lost. Modern efforts to restore it are exemplified in the work of Matisse at Vence and the modern glass of Coventry Cathedral in England.

On a small scale enamel has some relation with both mosaic and stained glass and has provided a kind of picture, permanent and with a lustrous glow. It was anciently used as a kind of jewel-like decoration. In the Middle Ages it took the form of *cloisonné,* the fused coloured glass being laid down into beaten out areas of a thin gold plate, separated and outlined by boundaries of wire (*cloisons*). The nearness of the technique to that of stained glass in miniature can be appreciated in Byzantine work of the ninth and tenth centuries on such objects of ecclesiastical nature as reliquary crosses. Champlevé enamel was a Western development, similar in principle but set in areas cut out of the metal with thicker divisions between. The history of champlevé ranges from its appearance in Celtic art of the pre-Christian era to the production of church ornament in the Rhineland, France and north Spain from the twelfth century. A nearer approximation was made to the painted picture in the enamels produced in the Early Renaissance period (fifteenth century) in Italy and at Limoges in France, the enamel being applied with a brush or spatula over a design outlined on the metal plate. Masters of the art were Pierre Raymond, Leonard Limousin and Jean Pénicaud. Purely pictorial are the enamel paintings of George Stubbs who painted on a white flux fired on a copper plate. Fired a second time, the flux united with the film of colour, which had a clear, transparent quality. Examples were exhibited at the Royal Academy in 1781–2 but caused some dispute as to enamel's legitimacy as a painter's technique.

Greater dispute would then have been caused if the modern development of *collage* had been known. This use of varied materials stuck on a ground to form a composition originated with the antagonism of the early twentieth century to academic rules. 'You could paint with anything you liked,' said the poet-compère of the Cubist painters, Apollinaire, 'with pipes, postage stamps, post-cards, playing-cards, candelabra, pieces of sealing-wax, collars, wallpapers, newspapers.' It might sound the merely playful idea of one who was not a painter, though collage has become an extended practice with several aspects.

The use of ready-made materials in conjunction with a drawn or painted design was largely the invention of Pablo Picasso and Georges Braque about the year 1912 in the course of their development of Cubism. Though departing from the illusionary effect of the painted picture, the intention nevertheless was to introduce a reality of substance and texture, heightening by contrast the value of an abstract design. Or alternatively the simulated textures of materials in paint could be combined and contrasted with the real thing. Thus an actual newspaper front page with its bold title could be pasted on to a still-life suggestive of the café table.

82, 83 Collage: left, Kurt Schwitters *Opened by Customs* 1937–9, above right, Max Ernst *Here Everything is Still Floating* 1919–20

Different aspects of collage appeared when it was again taken up in the experimental fervour of the Dada movement. Kurt Schwitters carried farther the assemblage of discarded and trivial papers, wrappings, bus-tickets and fragments of solid debris in a way that gave a poetic dignity to their humble character (*Pl. 82*). On the other hand Max Ernst created fantastic surprises by cutting out and reassembling nineteenth-century popular illustrations (*Pl. 83*). Artists have continued to make use of the collage principle in various forms until the present day. Matisse gave an example of its decorative possibilities in the remarkable designs of cutout and coloured papers which he produced in his last years. Others have annihilated the distinction between painting and sculpture in assemblages which combine solid objects with some element of painting.

A great deal of unexpected visual interest is the result. The limitations are obvious. Collage easily becomes no more than a game with materials, offering no more satisfaction than the titillating effect of the unusual. A comparison with Rembrandt,

Titian or Velazquez might seem altogether too heavy-handed but at least it prevents confusion between the significance of a great art and a cleverly devised novelty. And it may be added between work that is meant to last and that which is often by the nature of the materials used impermanent and expendable.

It is one of the tests necessarily applied to painting that it should stand the test of time. While this is primarily a matter of the thought and feeling it represents, it involves the question of physical survival. Leonardo's *Last Supper* (*Pl. 118*) survives as a conception, a marvellous ghost in which the thought of the artist remains alive though the experimental nature of the oil medium he used on the refectory wall of Santa Maria della Grazie, Milan, as well as the effect of damp have left little of the original. Oil painting, while the richest, is of all media the most susceptible to chemical change, largely due to the amount and nature of the liquid vehicle used. The reason why some of Sir Joshua Reynolds' portraits are in a ruined condition is that he used bitumen as a varnish producing brilliance of effect, unaware that this is a radio-active substance with an unending and destructive chemical action. On the whole however the technique of the Old Masters has proved remarkably lasting and though this has often been due to elaborate preparation the same may be said of many paintings executed directly without retouching. The control of light and temperature are now recognized as external factors of importance. Air-conditioned rooms in galleries are safeguards against such an atmospheric change as the hard frost of January 1947 which caused the wood panel of Rubens's *Château de Steen* in the National Gallery to split from one end to the other; and only filtered air now reaches Raphael's great Cartoons.

As an extraneous factor, with some bearing on the effect of a painting which it may either enhance or detract from, it is not irrelevant to consider the picture-frame. It is a strange omission from the history of art that there is no book devoted to the subject. The frame of course is not intended to obtrude on the eye. One might enjoy seeing Manet's *Bar aux Folies-Bergère* where it hangs in the Courtauld Institute Galleries without

84 The frame: Style of Orcagna, Altarpiece with *Coronation of the Virgin and Adoring Saints* 1370–1

being aware that it is set off by an early-eighteenth-century French frame attributed to the master-craftsman, Robert de Cotte (*Pl. 85*). Yet it presents the painting to admirable advantage.

In a great picture gallery one can appreciate the many forms frames have taken. There is the carved Gothic structure that unites the painted altarpiece of the later Middle Ages (*Pl. 84*); the Renaissance frame which like other forms of decoration drew inspiration and ornament from the Logge of the Vatican; the sumptuous Venetian frames of carved and gilded wood which enclosed the huge canvases of the Doge's Palace and the Scuola di San Rocco, the Baroque and Rococo frames with their ornaments of scrolls and shells.

99

85 The frame: Manet's *Bar aux Folies Bergère* 1882, set off by a frame attributed to Robert de Cotte

A good or appropriate frame is however not necessarily of the artist's own time. The product of an age of furniture which otherwise belongs to the past, the Louis XIV frame has a sober magnificence which suits paintings of many different kinds. The eighteenth-century Rococo frame with its delicacies of curvature and light and shade falls into a happy relation with the Impressionist landscape of the nineteenth century. But such harmony depends on the kind of painting. The anti-illusionist tendency of some modern painting even dispenses with the frame as the suggestion of a window in the wall or else dictates the use of undecorated material with a plainness that accords with the modern tendency to eschew ornament.

CHAPTER THREE

The Painter's Aims and Problems

THE RENDERING OF NATURE

The relation in which the work of the painter stands to nature has always been a subject of discussion and varied opinion. So great an artist as Michelangelo could state that the imitation of nature was the artist's proper aim. This however is to be interpreted in terms of the philosophy of his time. God, in the phrase of Michelangelo's disciple Vasari, was 'the divine architect of time and nature'. In imitation therefore the artist worked towards the divine end. At the same time Michelangelo disregarded a great deal we now comprise in the word 'nature'. It was through the human form alone that he sought to give some correspondence to the work of the Supreme Artist. Imitation consequently resulted in the perfection sought in the human figure.

But imitation has been otherwise defined. To copy an object so that it 'looks real' could be regarded as a mechanical exercise of skill and the pleasure it produces of an inferior kind. There are painters who have interested themselves in reproducing the bloom on a peach or bunch of grapes, with a result pleasing to the eye but not demanding imaginative power in the artist or any corresponding faculty of taste in the spectator.

It is a reasonable view that nature is so much raw material which it is the proper function of the painter to refine and improve on in accordance with the rules of his art. The fact that a painter learns about painting from the work of others and not from nature has an importance sometimes overlooked. When Sir Joshua Reynolds remarked that great painting is 'in many points of view and strictly speaking no imitation at all of external nature' he was evidently thinking of those harmonies and rhythms of the Renaissance masters which belonged exclusively to art.

Many artists have been at pains to assert an independence of nature on either imaginative or aesthetic grounds. William Blake did so in defence of the spiritual character of art as opposed to materialism. 'No Man of Sense', he wrote, 'ever supposes that copying from Nature is the Art of Painting; if Art is no more than this it is no better than any other Manual Labour; anybody may do it & the fool often will do it best as it is a work of no Mind.' He attacked Correggio for the melting softness of chiaroscuro which conveyed the material rounded-ness of the body. Blake's figures on the contrary were the outlines of spiritual ideas. And from his point of view a still-life or a landscape was an idle reflection of the mindless 'vegetative universe'.

Blake's contemporary Fuseli also expressed the attitude of the imaginative artist when he said that nature 'put him out'. He could see no more in Constable than weather and his jesting remark that he needed an umbrella with him when going to look at one of Constable's landscapes was also a criticism. At a later date and on more strictly aesthetic grounds Whistler emphasized in witty fashion the necessity of selection from nature and the paramount role of the artist in this respect. The idea of 'truth to nature' was potent in the nineteenth century. Ruskin saw it in the work of Turner as an under-standing of the principles of growth in trees, of the formation of rocks, of the movement of sea and cloud in which he excelled the painters of the past. Turner was indeed keenly observant of natural effect but this does not alter the fact which Ruskin seemed to disregard that Turner, though he learnt about nature from nature, learnt about painting from painting and that an important part of his equipment as an artist was the study of the European masters. That entire fidelity to nature is not possible and that some measure of selection is inevitable may be gathered from a comparison of the Pre-Raphaelites and the Impres-sionists, both sufficiently enthusiastic for the idea of objective truth as to paint in the open air. The Pre-Raphaelites however found it in precision of detail, the Impressionists in the rendering of light and atmosphere. It is evident that they could not exist together, that one must be sacrificed to the other.

It is possible also to conceive the paradoxical situation envisaged by Gauguin in which he spoke of 'the truth in the lie'. For instance, to use the brightest green possible entailed a corresponding pitch in other colours and a form of untruth would result from the failure to maintain it. Thus the free use of bright colour in the pictures of the French Fauves is in no sense imitative but has its own veracity as a coherent scheme.

At the present time the independence of the painter from nature as instanced in abstract and 'non-figurative' work especially is often proclaimed and sometimes deplored. But just as Hazlitt viewed nature as a reservoir 'deep, obscure, infinite', so in a wider definition it may still be viewed. The seeming accidents of inorganic form are part of its endless variety. We are constantly confronted by visual chances. An old wall with its patched and peeling surface roughened and stained with grime and damp becomes strangely interesting to look at Sun and rain, the processes of decay have created a pattern in which one sees a natural drama in progress. The value of these accidental shapes and colours for Leonardo who discussed them was their suggestion of landscape or figures, though modern artists such as the Surrealists have attached a somewhat different value to them. It is part of the tendency to regard nature not as a matter of pleasant scenery but as full of unstable and unexpected elements, subject to mysterious pressures.

In another way science has contributed to this attitude of painters in revealing the infinitely small, the congregation of elements within the atom for instance or the minute forms a microscope brings into focus. At the other end of the scientific scale nature becomes the vast abstraction of outer space. Consciously or unconsciously a number of modern painters reflect this extended view of nature. It may be said they are still reacting to nature even though they find it impossible any longer to sit on a camp-stool in a field and copy the shape of a tree.

Influences: 86 Giorgione *Sleeping Venus*

In the various views that have been discussed the spectator cannot look for any absolute and objective truth but is perhaps best advised to remember that art is 'nature viewed through a temperament' and that nature has many aspects from which art selects. The differences of temperament at the same time create an endless variety of a subjective kind.

ORIGINALITY AND TRADITION

There is no such thing as absolute originality in painting. Some relation to what has been done before always exists, though to say that an artist is 'influenced' by someone else need in no way detract from appreciation of his work. On the contrary, the influences to which the criticism of painting so often calls our notice may bring out all the more strikingly the respects in which a painter individually excels and in themselves contribute a new element of beauty and interest to what he does. As the French painter, Boudin, sensibly observed, 'Perfection is a collective work . . . without one person another would never have achieved what he did achieve.'

The clearest instance of tradition is the handing on of a master's method to his pupil. The young Raphael is close in

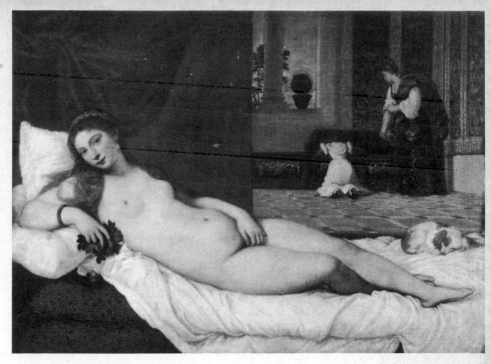

87 Titian *Venus of Urbino* c. 1538

88 Manet *Olympia* 1863

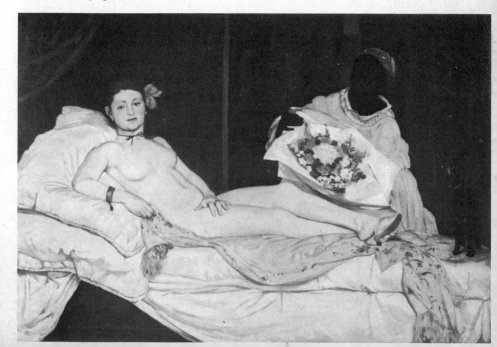

style to his master Perugino. But the influence of mind on mind has a wider significance than tradition as illustrated in this master-pupil relationship. Study of the work and example of Leonardo da Vinci and Michelangelo enlarges Raphael's more mature outlook, bringing him at a bound into a new sphere of action. Influence of this kind may be as personal as that of Manet on the circle of his young adherents in a Parisian café, or as distant as a colour reproduction in a modern book or journal. It is sometimes the suggestion of a technical method, seized upon and converted to fresh use or simply the inspiring memory of a master (to be distinguished from imitation) which in a strange way will leave its trace on the canvas of his admirer.

It is safe to say that the greater the artist the more pleasurable it becomes to see the influences in his work. They are a living and fruitful part of it. The delicate threads of communication with others form a new pattern. The personality of the artist loses nothing of its integrity. Thus the influence of Titian adds its beauty to the *Venus and Cupid* (*Pl. 89*) of Velazquez (London, National Gallery). Or again in the art of Rembrandt one can trace what he derived from Italy in the depth of light and shade that came to him via other Dutch painters from Caravaggio, which it remained for him to make 'Rembrandtesque'; or the value he gained from his study of gesture and character in Leonardo's *Last Supper*.

There are examples of many kinds. Titian seems to have derived much from Giorgione. They are close together in the sensuous quality of their art and in richness of colour. But while the static nature of Giorgione's *Tempest* (*Pl. 90*) is essential to its dream-like effect, Titian introduces his own feeling of movement in *Bacchus and Ariadne* (*Pl. 91*). The spectator may feel closer in sympathy to Cubism after considering the conception of structure in the painting of Cézanne and conversely, after looking at the work of the Cubist painters whom he influenced, be the more impressed by Cézanne's achievement. Seurat's *Grande Jatte* is not only a development of Impressionist technique. One can see him looking back among older masters than Monet and Pissarro for the idea of formal

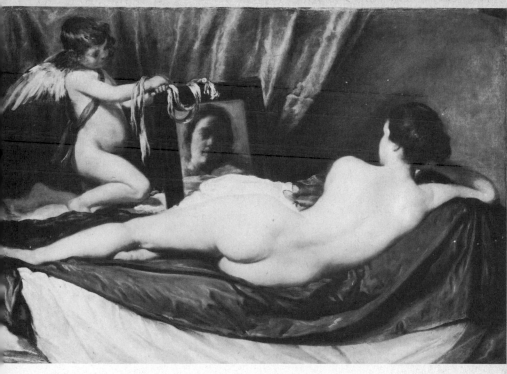

89 Influences: Velazquez *Venus and Cupid (The Rokeby Venus)* c. 1649–50

grandeur, he is close in spirit to Piero della Francesca (*Pls. 13, 14*).

The examples given suggest that if aesthetic beauty attaches to the influences we can perceive, it is because something emerges over and above what is to be found in the source from which they come. To borrow from others is of no value unless a creative and individual force is also at work. It is not sufficient to say that X was influenced by Y as if in a game of scholarly detection. 'To what purpose?' is a question to be answered. Mere borrowing leaves one cold, it is the transformation that counts. At the same time the influence of one artist on another may affirm in the work of both some underlying principle always valid and applicable.

Copying, by the same token, as a form of study and not simply as a reproduction, has not been beneath the attention of great painters. The refinement and consistency of Chinese painting through many ages are bound up with the artists' practice of copying the works of their predecessors. This aesthetic ancestor-worship was defended by the painter Ku K'ai-chih (c. 334–406) in the following words (as translated by Dr Sakanishi), 'If the brush and the eye travel boldly forward the copy will not be a mere reproduction but will contain something of the copyist's own.' In this spirit, one may imagine, the youthful Turner and Girtin developed their own approach to landscape from copying the Canaletto drawings and Cozens watercolours in the collection of their patron, Dr Monro.

It was with the humility of a giant that Rubens copied. Apart from impersonal replicas made to order, it was with a feeling that even he had something to learn that he made his free adaptations of Italian masters. He used Mantegna's *Triumph of Caesar* (Hampton Court) as a springboard for his imagination (*Pls. 92, 93*). His Flemish exuberance at once delights in and destroys the processional rigidity conceived by Mantegna in

90 Giorgione
Tempest

91 Titian *Bacchus and Ariadne* 1522–3

antique terms; lions snarl with all his sense of their superb fury;
elephants trumpet with a violence of fear and rage that is his
addition. Van Gogh had a not dissimilar aim in the copies he
made at Saint-Rémy of Delacroix's *Good Samaritan* and other
works by artists he admired including those he translated from
black and white into colour. An instance is the *Prison Yard* in
which he filled with his own sense of tragedy one of the wood-
engravings from Gustave Doré's *London* (Pls. *94*, *95*).

Originality and tradition are not simple terms. They are
complicated by the idea of self-expression and the idea of

92 Mantegna *Triumph of Caesar c.* 1486–94

progress. To express oneself in any art, clearly, freely and with sincerity of feeling is on the face of it an excellent thing, as valuable in painting as in writing or speech. The alternative is to be cold, stilted, conventional, dull. The style of a great painter is the man. In modern times it has come to be held that the painter's theme is himself, not necessarily as a display of egotism but in the sense that Rembrandt is Rembrandt and no one else.

Expression however has various facets. It is sometimes intellectual in painters who are especially interested in theory. They reason in a detached fashion almost as if concerned with solving an equation. In fact a quasi-mathematical truth seems to be part of their objective. It is a matter of record for instance that Piero della Francesca was much occupied by scientific

93 Free adaptation: Rubens *Triumph of Caesar*

theory and no painter perhaps ever constructed a picture with
more deliberate science. The beauty of geometrical progression,
of the mathematically disposed forms into which his subjects
resolved takes one into an intellectually detached sphere.
Modern instances may be found in the movements with a well-
defined basis of theory, such as appears in the Dutch De Stijl
movement, in the work of Mondrian particularly.

Here originality of expression, of set purpose, seeks to
exclude emotion personal to the artist. Another kind of
personality is involved when the painter signals an emotional
response to life and its problems with a vehemence of form and
colour. One might contrast Mondrian's precise rectangles with
Edvard Munch's *The Scream* (*Pl. 96*), it woeful figure so
intensely conveying the feeling of loneliness by which the

artist himself was oppressed. The agitation of Van Gogh's last days is manifest in the swirl and emphasis of brushstroke in his paintings of cypresses and cornfields (*Pl. 97*).

Many artists show the psychology of disquiet and this must be taken into account for a complete understanding of their work. It is moving to trace in Botticelli's painting the conflict between the delight in a physical beauty of *The Birth of Venus* and the pangs of religious conscience instilled by the puritanical exhortations of Savonarola. In the *Mystic Nativity* (London, National Gallery) he wished perhaps to return to the devotional spirit of Fra Angelico (*Pl. 24*). Yet the stress he laboured under produced other results apparent in the incoherent inscription which connects the troubles of Italy with apocalyptic prophecy, and in a composition which shows almost hysteric rapture.

Michelangelo gives a gigantic demonstration of the conversion of unhappiness into pictorial violence in his *Last Judgment* (*Pl. 98*). The difference of this tremendous wall from the earlier

94 Gustave Doré *Prison Yard* from the 'London' engravings

95 Free copy: Vincent van Gogh *Prison Yard* 1890

96 Disquiet: Edvard Munch *The Scream* 1895

97 Vincent van Gogh *Road with Cypresses* 1889

serenity of *The Creation of Man* in the ceiling of the Sistine
Chapel is one of psychology as well as design. Does not the
pent-up rage of a temperamentally angry man, beset by endless
frustrations, patriotically embittered by the distresses of Florence
and the havoc of foreign invasion, seem present in the painted
scene of ruthless vengeance?

The disquiet of a period can create an infectious and widely
felt unease as in the Romantic age with its unsatisfied longings
and avidity for sensation, such as may be perceived in Géricault's
Raft of the Medusa. The Expressionism of German painters
reveals another aspect of feelings shared by artists in an uncongenial society, perceptible in the defiant clash of colour and
such violence of hate as George Grosz infused into his satirical
drawings.

For completeness of view such elements of expression must be set in proportion. If we assume some part of Michelangelo's mind was concerned with ideas of retribution it should not be to overlook his originality in the conception of moving figures in space. Delacroix's *Massacre of Chios* is not only the 'terrible hymn' of calamity in Baudelaire's description but a beautiful scheme of colour (*Pl. 128*). A great work of art is indeed a complex thing.

Still another kind of expression is the instinctive and automatic process which artists since the advent of psycho-analysis have tried to induce as a means of bringing to the surface the inner depth of personality. At all times in the actual process of painting some part of the painter's conscious mind seems to be sealed off temporarily, leaving both acquired skill and the store of feeling in the unconscious to come freely into play. Masters have been able to paint while their mind was occupied with other things. Rubens could enjoy a reading from the classics while at work, El Greco, it is said, listened to music. The value of painting as therapy lies in the rest or holiday it gives to the mind.

A certain paradox is involved however, as in the work of the Surrealists when the 'psycho-automatism' (André Breton's definition of Surrealism) is consciously controlled and a product of theory. In a strict sense the automatic process is more limited than would appear from the works of fantasy the idea has suggested to such artists as Salvador Dali and Yves Tanguy. The limitation appears in the instinctive art of children, which, delightful as it is, is always of one type. The same remark applies to the work of the adult 'primitive'. The *naïveté* of expression gives pleasure but it is an art which allows no possibility of growth and development. Instinct in painting it is evident needs the balance of conscious purpose.

Tradition implies a continuity of method and intention. Such a continuity implies also a standard valid at all times and is consequently opposed to the idea that constant improvement in art is possible. For Renoir, painting was an ancient craft with unchanging rules and wisdom and this conviction eventually

98 Michelangelo
Detail of '*Mors stupebit . . .*'
from the
Last Judgement 1536–41

led him to suspect and depart from the Impressionist way of painting in so far as it was an innovation. A visit to Naples not only caused him to admire the paintings from Pompeii in the Museum but also to recognize a modernity in them. 'The priestesses in their silver-grey robes might have been nymphs painted by Corot,' he said. Here he gave an appropriate illustration of the French saying that 'the more it changes the more it is the same thing'.

Yet the need for change exists. That an advance is sought is nowadays indicated by the use of the term *avant-garde*. Progress however is not necessarily in a single forward direction. There are frequent examples of what might be called 'progress back-wards'. The Italian Renaissance looks back to Classical antiquity at the same time as it seeks new discovery. The Pre-Raphaelites of the nineteenth century looked back to the Middle Ages. The return to a primal model is even more emphatically evident in the art of the twentieth century. This can be seen in the new interest taken in primitive rather than naturalistic art, in Archaic Greek sculpture rather than that of the Classical period, in African sculpture, and every form of rudimentary expression.

Date, then, creates no barrier between one period and another. A free movement in history is possible. In appreciation this gives the inspiring sense of watching a great panorama in which there is unity as well as variety. The movement of painting is constant but this is to be distinguished from what are regarded as the improvements on the past made by material progress.

REVOLUTIONS OF PAINTING

Traditions in a more limited sense than that considered in the foregoing chapter are constantly subject to revision. Every school has its term of life. Artists appear who proclaim a new order and often enough seem opposed not only to the existing canons of art but to the society in which they live. The twentieth century has had its remarkable instances of the hostility of a State towards painting in the suppression of modern art in Germany during the Nazi régime as 'degenerate', and in Soviet Russia as a symptom of 'bourgeois decadence'.

The idea that an original artist is bound to be a rebel against authority has been often taken for granted. A contemporary painter, André Masson, states the view plainly, 'Whatever is scorned or despised or not understood by the society in which one lives has prospects for the future.' If the test of history is applied to this sweeping assertion it would seem only to become plausible in the nineteenth century. It would not apply to Rubens, a diplomat as well as a great painter, courted and favoured by society or to Titian and Velazquez who had a similar eminence. Their world treated them well and admired what they did. For their part they were able to adapt themselves to the conditions of their time without detriment to their originality.

The appearance of a new middle class in the nineteenth century knowing little of painting but with strong prejudices, the decline of enlightened patronage, the isolation of painters pursuing a course of their own and unable to provide a popular commodity give reasons for a changed position. But artists have usually played a passive role as far as society is concerned and have been rebels in spite of themselves or in being so labelled by others. It was the ambition of Manet and Cézanne to gain a conventional place in the Paris Salon. The nature of their work made them seem revolutionaries.

From a broad point of view the great rebellions of art are those of school against school, style against style, sometimes unintentionally directed by an outstanding individual who was a rebel primarily in having something of his own to say. Giotto in fourteenth-century Italy brings to an end a decaying tradition of Byzantine painting and opens the way towards the achievements of the Renaissance. Caravaggio brings a new and dynamic force into the age of Mannerism. Courbet supplants a wilting Romanticism with his Realism. The pace of change has become quicker in more recent times with the pace of life itself.

PAINTING: NATIONAL AND INTERNATIONAL

In threading a way through the history of painting due importance is to be allowed to both its national and international character. The idea expressed by Whistler and repeated more recently by the American painter, Jackson Pollock, that there is no more nationality in art than in mathematics is at best a half-truth. It may be agreed that form and colour in the abstract are not the property of any one race or country more than another. It is also true that great artists transcend time and place and belong to the world. But in a variety of ways differences of national history, geography, characteristics, beliefs, predilections appear. International styles have always existed when circumstances have produced the appropriate conditions. A religion held in common has in the past been a main factor. Thus the Romanesque and Gothic styles in medieval Europe are not confined by frontiers (*Pls. 99, 100*). There are illuminated manuscripts of which it would be difficult to say whether they were French or English.

Political institutions of a similar kind have also given rise to the wide distribution of a style distinct enough to have a name. The Baroque which had its origin in Italy and its main expansion in the seventeenth century was a form of propaganda for the Catholic Church in its efforts to counter the Reformation and

99 International Romanesque: Christ Pantocrator 1123

100 International Gothic: Gentile da Fabriano *Adoration of the Magi* 1423

for the political authority of despotically ruled states. In consequence it flourished in Italy, in the France of Louis XIV, in the various Courts of southern Germany and Austria. In the eighteenth century a more relaxed mood at a Court or patrician level encouraged the less oppressive and more elegant and decorative style known as Rococo.

The Rococo has its main focus in gay and luxurious Venice and in the pleasure-loving French Court of the eighteenth century (*Pl. 8*).

In these international styles from the Romanesque of the eleventh century to the Rococo it is to be noticed that architecture, whether of church or palace, had a key position and that sculpture, painting and the minor arts were designed to harmonize and combine with it. In many works the painter seems like the contributor to an orchestra rather than an

119

individual performer. A Baroque ceiling, for example, gains its full effect only in relation to its architectural and sculptural accompaniment (*Pl. 102*).

Though it can be considered as an international influence, the Renaissance of the fifteenth and sixteenth centuries is something of an exception in that the great works of Italian painting were dominantly individual and for that reason needed a considerable amount of translation by lesser artists before providing an acceptable idiom for general use. Thus the Italian Renaissance became international in the phase when this was accomplished by the painters known as Mannerists. They selected and laid stress on certain external characteristics of the art of Michelangelo and Raphael to grandiose or graceful purpose. Thus what is loosely termed 'French Renaissance', as represented in the sixteenth century by the School of Fontainebleau, was in fact the Italian Mannerism of such artists as Primaticcio and Il Rosso, invited to France by Francis I to decorate his palace at Fontainebleau (*Pl. 101*).

102 International Baroque: *The Glory of St Ignatius* ceiling of S. Ignazio, ▶
Rome, by Andrea Pozzo 1691–4

101 Italian Mannerism: Primaticcio *Bath of Diana* 1541–7

International styles from the end of the eighteenth century lost their coherent relation with architecture. They existed henceforward as aesthetic ideas transmitted by artists in one country to another or else as a reflection of a European attitude of mind. Romanticism at the beginning of the nineteenth century, with varied products in painting, English, French, German, American, was more a mood than a style, nostalgic, fevered, longing for the wild and stupendous. Impressionism, taking shape in the 1860s, was a method developed mainly by French painters but one which was not without its application elsewhere.

The twentieth century offers two aspects of internationalism in painting. There was in its earlier years the tendency of painters from all quarters to make for Paris where they formed an international school. The prestige of French art and the training and working facilities the French capital could provide caused this great assembly to gather, though not only to learn from France, but to share in the new ideas that seemed to generate in Paris, and to feel the stimulus of the prevailing atmosphere of experiment and discovery.

The result has been to create the international interest in what may be thought of as progressive ideas which has since become widely diffused. The expansion outwards since the Second World War coincides with the growth of communications and exchange. There is no one international style but an international exchange of ideas. It would be hard to distinguish the nationality of artists contributing to many exhibitions of modern painting by characteristics of their work especially in the abstract form which is without subject. Universal likenesses of buildings, transport, commodities, advertisement have a parallel in the world-wide similarities of painting.

In the past well-defined regional and national schools have had a separate existence though often parallel with and sharing in the character of the international movements. Cities have preceded nations as centres of art, Italy providing a great series of examples. While one can speak of the Renaissance as a general tendency, the city-states had their own life in art. Civic pride

103 Regional style: Ambrogio Lorenzetti *Good government in the Town*,
Siena, 1338–40

and rivalry gave a stimulus to architecture, sculpture and
painting alike, helping also to preserve an individuality.

Florence had its remarkable succession of painters from the
thirteenth to the sixteenth centuries, from Cimabue to Michelangelo. A general characteristic that appears is the scientific and
intellectual approach that involved so many Florentines in
research – Uccello into the science of perspective, Pollaiuolo
into anatomy, Leonardo raising the direction of endeavour to a
unique level of conscious exploration.

It is significant of the local spirit that Siena, also with its own
school, though not geographically far distant from Florence and
parallel in development, was distinct in painting, on the whole

123

milder and less intellectual, cultivating charm of colour and decorative linear qualities rather than the three-dimensional appearance of form. From Duccio in the thirteenth century to Simone Martini, Pietro and Ambrogio Lorenzetti (*Pl. 103*) in the fourteenth century and Sassetta in the fifteenth century the Sienese tradition is distinct.

Venice developed in its own way the sensuous richness of colour and sumptuousness of decoration, its great period being the sixteenth century in which Giorgione, Titian, Tintoretto and Veronese are pre-eminent.

Bologna, Ferrara, Parma, Padua, Perugia, Naples, Urbino, Vicenza all had an individual contribution to make. Rome was a kind of eventual synthesis that gathered to itself the best of what was produced elsewhere.

Similarly the cities of the Netherlands had their own periods of great production, Bruges, Ghent and Brussels sharing eminence in the first splendid epoch of Flemish painting in the fifteenth century, Antwerp succeeding them in the sixteenth and seventeenth centuries.

National schools have not necessarily coincided either with the appearance of nations or continued throughout their history but represent some period when circumstances tended to encourage a distinct form of expression. The great national period of Holland is the seventeenth century. Pride in the country's hard-won independence was strong. Holland, free and prosperous, delighted in the subjects that spoke of its way of life. Every subject was national, the landscape, the burghers in their spick and span interiors, the good things of the table, the harbours and canals. The painters may be said to have given in total a portrait of their country.

From the regional schools of the German-speaking lands in the fourteenth century, with centres at Cologne, Nuremberg and Prague, there came the great period of the fifteenth and sixteenth centuries when a German character in art is definitely proclaimed by the tragic and emotional power of Grünewald and the naturalism of Dürer. Britain had to wait for its national zenith until the eighteenth and early nineteenth centuries when

104 Regional style: French School: *The Avignon Pietà c.* 1460

portraiture, sporting pictures and landscape make the Georgian period so distinct.

France had the longest and most equably balanced tradition of European countries though a peak is certainly reached with the many brilliant developments of the nineteenth century. It has to be borne in mind however that in each instance it is the great individual who is the strength of the school. How far the national character may be concentrated in the single genius is shown with exceptional emphasis in Spain by Velazquez, El Greco and Goya who tower above their contemporaries.

A subdivision of the national art is produced by the affection for and choice of a region by painters. Thus the Barbizon School develops from the settlement of a group of French artists from about 1830 in the village of Barbizon on the edge of the forest of Fontainebleau. The Norwich School in England, somewhat earlier, was inspired by the local attachment of John Crome to East Anglia (*Pl. 106*). French Impressionism was virtually though not deliberately regional in being largely practised in Normandy and the Île-de-France.

Regionalism in the United States in the 1930s was an effort to give a more American character to painting by turning to American subject-matter (*Pl. 107*). Yet the modern trend in the United States as elsewhere has been towards the international currencies of abstraction and Expressionism. It has been said that it is impossible for regionalism to have any place in the modern world but this again depends on circumstances. The twentieth century with all its internationalism has witnessed the appearance of two national schools – in Mexico where the spirit of national independence and sense of national history were fostered by mural painting like that of Diego Rivera (*Pl. 105*);

105 Modern nationalism: Diego Rivera, detail of fresco

106 Norwich School: John Crome *Mousehold Heath c.* 1818

107 American regionalism: Thomas Hart Benton *Roasting Ears*

and in Australia where after the Second World War there came a great access of interest in the visual aspect of the country. Subject-matter from which modern art elsewhere was being divorced was here a determining factor.

Yet the logic of the present time – the logic of air transport for example which conveys the individual from one side of the Atlantic to the other in a few hours, of news which flashes instantly across the globe, of distribution which brings a surplus of North American wheat to some other country urgently in need of it – is also the logic of an international art. The artist, whose mind so often seems at each historical period like some complex radar apparatus, picking out significant messages from the void and charting the course of history, reflects the position more accurately than the barriers of menacing weapons, deep-seated prejudices and political enmities that contradict the ease of communication possible.

From this point of view one can see a reason for an *avant-garde* in art which may sometimes seem to have no very clear direction and to be divorced from life. The spectator may not necessarily like the version it gives of a swiftly moving age. It is quite likely that many new ventures are fated to be discarded as quickly as outworn machinery. The flimsiness of some modern techniques and of materials used suggest as much. Painting, it may be said, is not soothsaying (except in so far as 'sooth' means 'truth') but something to see with pleasure and refreshment of the mind and senses. There is a balance in favour of works that have a permanence, stability and profundity of their own, and are not only recording instruments of the general tempo of life. But the latter is inevitably a function of art. Appreciation that stops short of the contemporary position would make the unjustifiable assumption that at some arbitrarily established point the life-line of art has been cut.

CHAPTER FOUR

The Theme and its Treatment

How far subject-matter is of importance in the appreciation of painting is a question that has often been discussed with cautionary advice against making it the main consideration. It is beyond doubt that the spectator who thinks only of what a painting represents misses the essential point of its imaginative, emotional and visual appeal. Pictures likewise that have been produced with no other end than that of conveying fact or story and have no compensating beauty of treatment are of an inferior kind.

In the past – one might say throughout history until in the nineteenth century painters acquired a new independence – the subject more often than not was the demand of a particular kind of society or type of patron. It was in some way useful or considered to be so. A primitive society required the symbols of magic – the 'sympathetic magic' with which the Palaeolithic cave folk invested the paintings and drawings of the animals they hunted, the symbols by which an early agricultural community sought to define the unpredictable forces of nature. The link of painting, as of sculpture, with religion has been universal.

It could serve as a kind of sermon, speaking all languages and as readily understood by the unlettered as by the educated, giving its constant reminder of ideals and doctrine, of rewards and penalties. It could be an attribute of the authority and magnificence of the rulers of states. It could answer to some special taste such as the delight of the Renaissance prince in Classical mythology or of the Dutch horticulturist in minutely exact paintings of flowers.

The value of the subject as social evidence appears in these facts. From a purely historical point of view, it is a vast store of information about beliefs, modes and manners, character, events, pursuits and diversions at various periods in all parts of the world. From this reservoir the modern social historian can draw his most convincing reconstruction of the past. Though the works of minor artists will serve his purpose just as well as great works, often indeed much better, in being more distinctly of their own time. The informative value dwindles in importance when the quality of art is our study. Yet one may consider subject in the wider sense of 'theme', carrying with it the implications of the Greek term from which it derives, $\theta\varepsilon\mu a$, as a 'proposition' or problem to be solved. In many great paintings we are aware at the same time of the problem set the artist and the particular beauty of its solution. From this point of view the great variety of subject and the great variety of its treatment may be considered together. The fusion of 'form', that is to say, the aesthetic and purely visual qualities that have been considered in earlier chapters and 'content', the subject or idea a work presents, is one of the great goals of painting.

There is truth in the saying that the artist is, in one sense, the real subject of his works. It is the quality of his mind and personal mode of expression that count in the last analysis. In the classification of subjects one notes how certain types correspond to the length of life of a given order of society and the existence of a particular school of painting. But the vital point always is the individual transformation great artists effect.

PAINTING AND RELIGION

The connection between painting and religion, like that between sculpture and religion, is ancient and universal. Christian art extends from paintings in the Catacombs of the third century A D to the twentieth century. Buddhist art has its long history from the period of Asoka in India, the third century B C, its classic masterpieces of painting being those of the Ajanta caves produced between the second and seventh centuries A D (*Pl. 109*). The tomb paintings of ancient Egypt are found in the long span of time from the third to the first millennium B C.

108 Fowling on the Nile *c.* 1400 B C, represented in a Theban tomb-painting

The immense variety of belief, of race, of period would seem to make any generalization little worth while if not impossible. Painting in the service of religion is sometimes symbolic, as for instance in the conventional signs or specific objects which stood for some other and greater conception. Thus the fish in early Christian art stood for Jesus Christ, Son of God, Saviour being an anagram of the initial letters *IXΘYΣ* of the words in Greek. The peacock, the flesh of which was deemed incorruptible, represented the Resurrection. Or painting may be descriptive of ritual, as, to take a non-Christian example, in some of the Roman copies of Hellenistic paintings found at Pompeii. Or again it may give an account of historical or supernatural incident.

What is constantly of note is the variety of the artistic imagination, of solutions to the propositions set, the visual advantage taken which the mere statement of subject could in no way foretell. The description of what was hoped for in the

Art in the service of religion: 109 Fresco detail from the Ajanta caves, seventh century

110 'Carpet page' from the Lindisfarne Gospel, late seventh century

life to come gave the painter of the Egyptian tomb the opportunity of painting the life he knew. No pharaoh or priest could dictate the flutter and varied wing movement of the birds around the fowler's boat in the famous fragment from a Theban tomb in the British Museum (*Pl. 108*). The secular detail retains its pictorial value when the motives that brought it into being are among the extinct conceptions of the past.

In considering the amazing richness of Christian art which has enlisted the efforts of innumerable painters and sculptors from the third century onwards one must take into account the several purposes involved. What has been required of the artist can be stated simply enough. First, a kind of imagery which served as a constant reminder of unchanging principles. Second, pictorial narrative putting Biblical history into a form that could be generally understood. Third, the kind of painting which harmonized with and contributed to the impressive effect of a church interior.

These requirements have lent themselves to a great variety of style and pictorial interpretation. The first and earliest is a style of formal conventions which variously appear in mural art, the icon and the illuminated manuscript. Style has a continuity of its own to some extent independent of other factors. Thus it was inevitable that the early Christian artists should make use of the technical traditions of the pagan Classical world. The Greco-Roman portraits of the kind that has been found on Egyptian mummy-cases, with their concentration on essential features, the eyes especially, were the prototype of the icon, a characteristic product of Byzantine art (*Pl. 79*).

The history of style, from the foundation of Constantinople in A D 330, is intricately connected with the spread of Christianity. Constantinople, the centre of religious authority until the separation of the Western and Eastern Churches in the eleventh century, was also the missionary of art. Yet the Byzantine Empire of which it was the head was not only the heir of the Greco-Roman tradition but comprised also the eastern provinces of Syria, Mesopotamia, Anatolia and Egypt which added elements of their own to art. They appear in an Eastern wealth of colour and non-realistic decoration and ornament.

In the same way the countries of the West grafted some of their own pagan traditions of art in work of Christian purpose. Thus the beauty of the masterpieces of eighth-century manuscript painting, the Book of Kells and the Book of Lindisfarne, seems to derive from contacts with the eastern Mediterranean world adding a Byzantine richness of colour and conventionalization of the figure to the interlacing patterns which belonged to the pre-Christian Celtic period. The result is in some ways akin to the abstract geometric art of modern times (*Pl. 110*).

The problem of Byzantine art was how to encourage 'divine speculation' and reject the illusion of reality while conserving so much of physical aspect as perpetuated the supposed likeness of a holy person. This could only be done by formal means which make a link as it were between the spiritual and material worlds. The greatest Byzantine works are the mural mosaics which create this effect by majestic linear rhythms and the poise of the figure in transcendent space. This is extraordinarily moving in the tall figure of the Virgin rising in ethereal dignity above the smaller Apostles in Torcello Cathedral (*Pl. 111*).

A cleft can be seen gradually to open between the religious

111 Byzantine majesty: the Virgin (*c.* 1190) and Apostles (early eleventh century), Torcello Cathedral

art of Western and Eastern Europe. Constantinople stood for all that was conservative, unchanging and opposed to freedom of representation, although Byzantine art was not as entirely static as was once supposed. In its eleven hundred years there are two great periods, the Age of Justinian in the sixth century when the great mosaics of Ravenna were produced and a second Golden Age developing between the ninth and the twelfth centuries again noted for mosaics, wall paintings and a brilliant style of illumination. In between there is the period of Iconoclasm which represents a logical aversion from the human image as being associated with idolatry and as detracting from a purely spiritual ideal.

There is a certain likeness here to the sequence of ideas which in this century led Wassily Kandinsky to turn to an entirely abstract or non-representational form of art. It is not perhaps without significance that Russia which adopted the stylization of the icon, a moveable panel bearing the image of Christ, the Virgin, angels or saints, in its most rigid form should have developed still more abstract forms. In the work of the Russian painter, Alexei von Jawlensky, one of Kandinsky's associates one can see a reversion, albeit in a purely secular spirit, to a highly simplified icon-like image.

In the West at the period of Byzantine 'image-breaking' of the eighth century, there was no such ban of dogma but a great activity in manuscript painting under the Emperor Charlemagne. Portraits appear. Figures are set against landscape backgrounds. The Utrecht Psalter, a remarkable example of a free linear style, was copied at Canterbury and had much influence on manuscript painting in England. The mural paintings of the eleventh and twelfth centuries in the great period of Romanesque church building provide some parallel in France, England and northern Spain with the monumental aspect of Byzantine painting in being governed by iconographical conventions though with a new sense of vigour and movement in design. But a different form of art, given an unprecedented freedom in the narrative and interpretative sense begins in the thirteenth century.

112 Variety of interpretation: Hugo van der Goes *Nativity* from the Portinari Altarpiece *c.* 1475–6

This freedom accounts for the many differences of style and treatment in the religious subjects which occupied painters henceforward. The universal and timeless was no longer conveyed by rigid formula but in terms of a personal or period character. The religious subject is central in European painting, in Germany, the Netherlands, France, Italy and Spain, until the time of the Reformation. One can appreciate the differences between north and south, the changes from Gothic to Renaissance and Baroque in terms of the same subjects.

Thus the Nativity, together with the associated themes of the Adoration of the Shepherds and of the Astrologer-kings from

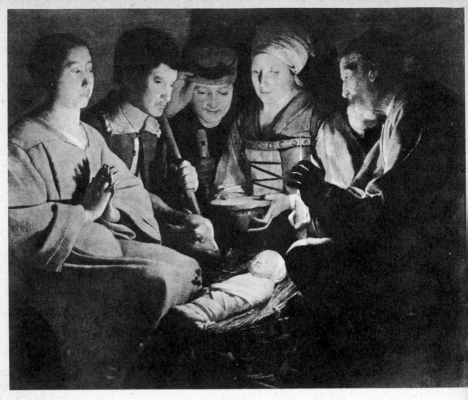

Variety of interpretation: 113 Georges de la Tour *Nativity*

the East, offered the painter endless visual suggestions of celestial harmony and light in contrast with the earthly and rustic picturesque, the homely and universal theme of mother and child intensified by the superlative drama of circumstances and setting; a range of character and dress from the rough features and apparel of the wondering herdsmen (*Pl. 112*) to the exotic magnificence of the regal and Oriental Magi, on whose robes, crowns and gifts the painter could lavish both fancy and skill.

'Celestial harmony' – how otherwise should one describe the pictorial effect of the famous Nativities of Piero della Francesca and Botticelli in the National Gallery, so much in consonance with St Luke's account of 'a multitude of the heavenly host' chanting praise. The expressions of Piero's angelic carol-singers are a beautiful aspect of a painting which is among the great triumphs of Italian art (*Pl. 114*).

Lighting provided effects more than natural. The double illumination of *The Nativity* in the National Gallery attributed to the fifteenth-century Dutch painter Geertgen tot Sint Jans, the pastoral figures lit both by their campfire and the rays from the flying angel which throw long magical shadows, gives an example. Even more moving is Rembrandt's *Adoration of the Shepherds* where the light is no more than that of lanterns struggling and bobbing in a cavernous darkness and touching with their gleam the most natural of peasant groups (*Pl. 116*). Artificial light in the same subject by Georges de la Tour holds serenity and drama in balance (*Pl. 113*). The strong shadows

114 Piero della Francesca *Nativity* (detail)

Variety of interpretation:
115 Jan Gossaert
Adoration c. 1507

116 Rembrandt
*Adoration of the
Shepherds* 1646

117 Emotional expression: Mathias Grünewald *Crucifixion* from the Isenheim Altarpiece *c.* 1515

accentuate the calm of the maternal figure, no longer a symbol of the religious story but a human being who re-enacts it.

The setting gave its pictorial licence. The stable where Mary and the Child lay 'because there was no room at the inn' sometimes has a ruinous grandeur as in Jan Gossaert's *Adoration* (*Pl. 115*) or is a decaying Netherlandish outhouse in paintings by Bosch with sagging thatch and broken timbers.

The expressiveness of gesture in narrative scenes taken from the New Testament is especially to be appreciated in Italian painting. Its purport and psychology is worked out to the last degree in *The Last Supper* of Leonardo (*Pl. 118*). It has been said that Christianity introduced pain into art. It gave opportunities for tragic expression which are realized in the great paintings of the Crucifixion (*Pl. 117*), the scene of mourning represented by

118 Leonardo da Vinci *The Last Supper*, recorded 1497

the pietà, the martyrdom of saints. Supreme among these emotional works is the Isenheim Altarpiece of the German painter, Mathias Neithardt Gothardt, known as Grünewald. Its panels preserved at Colmar are a wonderful illustration of the welding of form and content. Rejecting any obvious graceful-ness and facile harmony of colour, the artist ranges from the most sinister and sombre representations of torment to the unearthly flame of resurrection with an unfailing intensity. The keyboard of art has never been played on with more organ-like power.

Facial expression in the characters represented is another aspect of the religious subject inspiring to the painters. Rogier van der Weyden's masterpiece, *The Descent from the Cross* (Prado, *Pl. 12*), is a magnificent instance. The group of figures set against a gold background in a relief which gives the effect of naturalistic sculpture conveys every nuance of grief. It may be compared with the *Calvary* of Andrea Mantegna (Louvre) where the group of mourners is treated with more of the feeling of Classical tragedy.

142

A supreme challenge to the imagination is presented by the task of painting Paradise and Inferno. Paradise, the primal idyll, sadly concluded by the Fall, has its many interpretations. On the other hand it is the final rapture of ascent into space and spiritual reunion that Tintoretto conveys using every device of perspective, foreshortening and lighting in his conception of the subject in the Doge's Palace, Venice (*Pl. 119*).

The traditional eschatology of the Last Judgment in which, as a grim pendant to the ascent of the virtuous, demons appear at the foot of the composition and hustle away the condemned gave the Renaissance painter latitude to depict the human figure in every aspect of movement, contortion and emotional stress. Demonic physically in horns and claw feet – a distorted memory of the fauns and satyrs of Classical myth – the fiends painted by Luca Signorelli in his *Last Judgment* at Orvieto are athletes

Paradise: 119 Tintoretto *Paradise*

Inferno: 120 Luca Signorelli *Last Judgement* (detail) *The Damned* 1499–1504

(*Pl. 120*). The greater conception to which it led was Michelangelo's masterpiece in the Sistine Chapel. Its tumult of figures seems to have inspired Rubens as in the latter's *Fall of the Angels* (Munich, Pinakothek), a rival display of mastery though without that angry force which makes the work of Michelangelo so intensely the reflection of a mind.

The inclination of artists in northern Europe to the grotesque has resulted in the most fantastic of demons and infernal landscapes. The most remarkable of all are contained in the triptych by Jerome Bosch in the Prado commonly known from its central panel as *The Garden of Terrestrial Delights*. This is so personal a vision that one might wonder in what church it could have hung or what churchman would have sanctioned this supremely unconventional vision of earthly pleasures and

121 Jerome Bosch *Garden of Terrestrial Delights*

mysterious penalties. The symbolism is as subtle as elaborate. The fires he paints are a clean sweep of the material world, a way of entry into a psychological underworld. Here in an ashen twilight and an environment all of nightmare, the pale listless beings can be thought of as entrapped by their own follies. Instead of active and torturing fiends the gnomes and abnormal hybrids around them seem emblems of degenerate nature (*Pl. 121*).

The connection with liturgy and doctrine grew looser with the passage of time. The great masters of the Renaissance were not simply servants of the Church but individual in thought and expression. The Sistine Chapel ceiling of Michelangelo is the epic of humanity. *The Virgin of the Rocks* by Leonardo has a setting in which as a result of his geological researches he seems to convey his sense of the immense antiquity of earth (*Pl. 16*). The religious subject was no more than a pretext for Veronese whose answer to the questions of the Inquisition was, 'We painters take the same liberties as poets and madmen.' His *Marriage at Cana* (Louvre) with its opulent architecture, its one hundred and thirty figures including many contemporary likenesses, its sumptuous detail, is essentially a free product of art (*Pl. 122*).

The split of creed and countries at the Reformation made for different kinds of religious painting. Catholicism encouraged the dramatic fervour of the Baroque style in Italy, Spain, France and the southern Netherlands as a reassertion of the splendour and authority of the Church. In the Protestant countries many subjects became taboo. Holland provides an instance. It is humanity that interests Rembrandt in both Old and New Testament history. Executed for his own satisfaction and not to hang in any place of worship, his Biblical compositions portrayed Jewish types of the kind he was able to study in Amsterdam with the same richness of chiaroscuro and profound study of human character as appears in his other works. One hundred and sixty paintings, some eighty etchings and over six hundred drawings reflect his intense personal concern with the spiritual nature of man and the essential humanity of

122 Humanism: Veronese *Marriage at Cana*

the figure of Christ. One of his greatest works is *The Return of the Prodigal Son* (Leningrad, Hermitage) not merely telling a story but symbolizing in human guise, error and divine forgiveness (*Pl. 123*).

The close association of the religious subject with the international forms of painting consistently encouraged by church patronage ends with the seventeenth century. Henceforward the subject is the product of nonconformity, that is to say of an individual artist's free interpretation. It did not flourish in the sceptical and rational eighteenth century. William Blake, a great exception in the spiritual direction of his art, gives a purely personal interpretation of the internal conflict of the true and the false in the human mind. The Pre-Raphaelites in the nineteenth century painted for a while with great earnestness and detailed realism but outside the framework of organized belief.

123 Humanism: Rembrandt *Return of the Prodigal Son* c. 1668–9

124 The modern conception: Stanley Spencer *The Resurrection* 1923–7

There is the same individual freedom in the present century whether we consider the attempt to clothe the Christian story in the old fashion with the aspect of today, as in Stanley Spencer's *Resurrection* (*Pl. 124*), or the barbaric intensity of colour given to an interpretation of the Old Testament by the German painter, Emil Nolde, or the icon-like images of Georges Rouault. Such works find their destination in the museums of art rather than the buildings of religious purpose.

In contrast such painting and sculpture as the churches have latterly used has been on the whole of poor quality. Efforts made to enlist the services of the best artists of the day may leave the feeling that a revival of the narrative form has become difficult and that alternatively a purely abstract adornment of a religious building lacks something of ritual meaning. One may be forced to the conclusion that a revival of religious art without the purposes that originally brought it into being is artificial. Its span of life has been completed. Yet the solutions the past offers to the problems set live on by virtue of the imagination and the power to clothe an idea in magnificence of form and colour that the great artists of Europe have shown.

149

125 Grand opera of painting: Veronese *The Family of Darius before Alexander* 1573

HISTORY, MYTHOLOGY AND ALLEGORY

What is known as the 'history picture' was originally an aspect of the 'Grand Style' of the Renaissance. Its subjects were taken from Greek, Roman and Old Testament history. They allowed the painter freedom in an epic form of composition in which no historical accuracy of costume or setting was sought. Grandeur of effect, heroic action, a generalized interpretation of virtues and passions were the essence of this form of painting. A great example is Veronese's *The Family of Darius before Alexander* (London, National Gallery). Its general import is that of a conqueror's magnanimity. Its sumptuousness in architecture, dress and character is that of Venice. This is indeed the grand opera of painting (*Pl. 125*).

The course of the history picture is impressive from the sixteenth to the eighteenth century. The Baroque painter made it the vehicle of a dramatic energy of movement. Scenes of battle and rape – *The Defeat of Sennacherib, The Rape of the Daughters of Leucippus* – enabled Rubens to display all his powers of relating forms in a swirl of motion. Pictures of historic events, political or military, in the artist's own time

126 Contemporary history: Velazquez *The Surrender of Breda* 1635

127 Imagined drama: David *The Oath of the Horatii* 1785

belong to a different category, generalization giving way to concern with truth of circumstance. Yet a magnanimity like that of Veronese's Alexander still appears in the great *Surrender of Breda* by Velazquez (*Pl. 126*) and heroic action in Copley's *The Death of Major Pierson*. The last great history picture in the old sense was Jacques-Louis David's *The Oath of the Horatii* (Louvre). The appeal to antique virtue, the republican lesson for a France soon to embark on revolution, is contained in a composition of austere force (*Pl. 127*).

The Romantic period introduced two directions in history as a theme; violence and fatality in contemporary terms and a nostalgic feeling for the past. The deaths of Wolfe by Benjamin West, of Chatham and Major Pierson by Copley, of Marat by David, of Nelson by Turner follow in pictorial succession. Then the artist is moved to depict the waves of battle round the hero-figure of Napoleon. In the post-Napoleonic period the old attachment to the past was mingled in a dubious fashion with sentiment, anecdote and archaeology. Delacroix's *Death of Sardanapalus* (*Pl. 39*) and *Massacre at Chios* (*Pl. 128*) retain their value by reason of splendid colour and imaginative composition. But a decay into the false history of anecdote was a weakness of the nineteenth century in general. For illustration of the past the modern sense of reality calls for its actual relics rather than fancied pictures of incident. Photography gives a better record of contemporary events. How little of the 'drum and trumpet' aspect of history remains in modern art can be gathered from the work of the appointed war artists in the century's two greater wars.

The mythological subject has inspired many of the most beautiful works of European painting. The deities of ancient Greece, the stories woven around them and the ceremonies held in their honour appear in the highly developed form of painting of the Hellenistic Age which has come down to us in Roman copies, mainly at Pompeii and Herculaneum. In the grouping of figures, the rendering of three-dimensional space, sense of colour and emotional expression, the works that seem most nearly to correspond to the best of Hellenistic painting are

128 Imagined drama: Eugène Delacroix *The Massacre at Chios* 1824

prototypes of the achievements of the Italian Renaissance. The noble figure of Medea in a painting preserved in the National Museum, Naples, has a tragic tension appearing in the nervous clutch of the hands (*Pl. 129*). Complex action is depicted with mastery in the Pompeian wall painting also at Naples which shows Achilles discovered among the daughters of Lykomedes – a Roman copy of the first century AD after an original of the third century BC (*Pl. 130*).

A return to the ancient subject-matter in Italy was a product of the revived interest in the Classical world which marked the end of the Middle Ages. The development of the pictorial science of the Renaissance in anatomy, perspective, light and shade and spatial effect, applied equally to any subject. Yet in the fables that delighted his scholarly patrons the painter could give his imagination freer rein than in the solemnity of the religious theme.

The beauty of the human figure as in ancient sculpture was again the theme. The nude, instead of making its shamefaced appearance in the Garden of Eden or as one of the condemned thrown to the fiends, was triumphant in splendour. The artists in the great centres of the Renaissance in Italy – Florence, Venice and Rome – were able to produce a series of mythological and allegorical works parallel with their religious compositions but distinct in sensuous charm and poetic feeling.

They were variously inspired: by the ideal figure as re-presented in Greek sculpture or Roman copies of it; by the decorative bas-relief which was more distinctively Roman; by such fragments of ancient mural painting as were to be found in Rome in an age before Pompeian discovery. The stories contained in Homer, Ovid and Apuleius were a literary source. To these the Renaissance artists added their individual develop-ments of style.

Thus the Classical humanism of fifteenth-century Florence is interpreted with a linear grace and lyrical expression of personal feeling in Botticelli's *Birth of Venus* (*Pl. 131*). The allegory, giving shape to an idea by means of figure composition, is hardly to be separated from a mythology which was itself

Mythology:
129 *Medea Meditating*
Greco-Roman wall-
painting from Pompeii

130 *Achilles discovered
among the daughters of
Lykomedes* Greco-
Roman wall-painting

155

131 Classical allegory: Botticelli *Birth of Venus c.* 1486

allegorical. In Botticelli's *Primavera* (Uffizi), the sequence of
the seasons from spring to winter is represented by groups
which include the figures of Venus, Flora, Mercury and the
Three Graces (*Pl. 132*). The poetic feeling for the fabled world
of nymphs and fauns gains an individual touch of strangeness
and pathos in Piero di Cosimo's *Mythological Subject* (London,
National Gallery, *Pl. 133*).

Raphael, who was able to make superb use of many influences,
in his great works at Rome takes something from Michelangelo,
from ancient sculpture and from the painted mural decoration
to which he was directed by his interest in the ancient remains
of Rome. His cycle of paintings in the Stanza della Segnatura
of the Vatican is not least remarkable in its combination of the
Classical and Christian elements of thought typical of the neo-
Platonism of his time. Together with the majesty of the
Christian faith represented by his *Disputà* is the mighty vista of

156

132 Botticelli *Primavera, The Allegory of Spring c.* 1477–8

133 Piero di Cosimo *A Mythological Subject c.* 1482–*c.* 1515

scholarship and philosophy of *The School of Athens* (*Pl. 41*) and, purely Classical in its idea of beauty, the *Parnassus* with its central figure of Apollo and groups of poets and the Muses.

Venice envelops mythology in its own richness of colour and glorification of the flesh. The most sumptuous aspect of Titian's painting appears in what has been called *Sacred and Profane Love* (Rome, Borghese Gallery, *Pl. 135*), the *Bacchus and Ariadne* (London, National Gallery, *Pl. 91*), the sensuous *Bacchanal* (Prado). Feminine beauty has its apotheosis in the wonderful *Origin of the Milky Way* (London, National Gallery) by Tintoretto with its rapturous movement and metaphorical conversion of the milk from Juno's breast into stars (*Pl. 134*).

134 Tintoretto *The Origin of the Milky Way c.* 1575

135 Titian *Sacred and Profane Love c.* 1515–16

The technique of a soft gradation which Correggio learnt from Leonardo gives a voluptuous intensity to his *Mercury and Cupid* (London, National Gallery) and his *Io and Jupiter* (Vienna). Like other genres, mythology illustrates how many ways there are of interpreting the same subject, varying with the nationality and individuality of the artist. One may contrast with Correggio (*Pl. 68*) the sculpturesque Mannerism of Bronzino in his allegory *Venus, Cupid, Folly and Time* (London, National Gallery, *Pl. 219*). Poussin is as much the student of antiquity as Raphael, the student also of Raphael and Titian, but there is an intellectualization and harmony in his *Inspiration of the Poet* (Louvre) and in his *Bacchanal* in which his study of Titian appears, that proclaims the French master whose Classicism was later to take a more severely lucid form.

Rubens painted an immense number of mythological subjects though he was Classical only in the delight he took in the works of ancient authors and his examination of works of art in Italy. In his own painting he is entirely himself, investing fable and allegory with his own abundance of imagination and creating an ideal type from the buxom women of his own race.

A comparison of manner:

136 *The Three Graces*, a copy of a Hellenistic sculpture group in a wall-painting from Pompeii

137 Raphael *The Three Graces*

138 Rubens *The Three Graces c.* 1639

A constant factor in the appreciation of painting is the personality which presents the same subject in varying guises. *The Three Graces* as painted by Rubens can be appreciated all the better in comparison with the many versions of the subject since some Greek sculptor first conceived the interlaced harmony of the group of the three goddesses who were the bestowers and embodiment of beauty (*Pls. 136–8*).

An abstract beauty of rhythm links them in Botticelli's *Primavera* (*Pl. 132*). A youthful grace of poise distinguishes Raphael's version of the subject. Rubens is deliberately less formally rhythmic, more naturalistic, his genius presenting the ripeness of nature.

In northern Europe the artist did not so readily take to the genre as in the South where it was part of an inheritance. The Gothic aversion from the physical facts of life appears in the attenuated delicacy of a Venus by Lucas Cranach. Yet this German painter who turned away from religious subjects to satisfy the acquired taste for mythology of the Protestant

139 North European mythology: Lucas Cranach *Nymph of the Source*

140 Rembrandt *Danaë* 1636

princes of the Reformation adds a bizarre charm of proportion and refinement of sensuality that has never ceased to fascinate (*Pl. 139*).

Rembrandt shows a youthful contempt for myth as in his version of *The Rape of Ganymede* which converts the beautiful youth of legend borne aloft by Jupiter in the form of an eagle into an ugly squalling child. His mythological paintings were few but they include one of the great masterpieces of European painting, the *Danaë* (Leningrad, Hermitage). The golden shower in which form Zeus visited the daughter of Akrisios is absent. Other titles for the picture have been suggested. It is in effect a young Dutchwoman awaiting a lover. The humanity and mystery of the work are the miraculous product of light and shade (*Pl. 140*).

All that is playful and erotic in Classical fable is the especial feature of French art in the eighteenth century, summed up in the work of Boucher. The wrath of Olympus, the cruelty of the gods, the flaying of Marsyas, the labours of Hercules were set aside in favour of feminine charm. The change of mood from that of the Renaissance comes out with startling effect if one compares Boucher's *Birth of Venus* (Stockholm, National-museum) with that of Botticelli. The light-hearted fancy of the French painter and the shallow prettiness he gave to the nymphs of his water revel contrast with the idealization of Botticelli that reflects a sensitiveness of a more profound kind (*Pls. 8, 131*).

With Rococo art the pictorialization of Classical myth virtually reaches its end. The nude is a separate study if one considers it as the idea of the figure in itself and not as an element of the rhythmic and poetic composition to which mythology lent itself. Objectively viewed the human body is a complex structure which apart from the attraction of sex presents ever-varied relations of form and subtleties of modelling for the artist to make use of. By tradition, the figure is a necessary study for any painter, though as an academic exercise it is apt to make the dullest of pictures which not even a measure of sexual attraction in the model will mitigate. The great painter creates a type, declares an attitude and always produces, as well as the figure, idealized or realistic, a work coherent in design, form and colour.

European painters have been mainly concerned with the female nude, unlike the Classical Greek sculptors who were equally if not more interested in the proportion and co-ordination of movement in the athletic male. The Renaissance masters, it is true, occupied themselves with calculations of the ideal proportion of both sexes. Their anatomical science was displayed in representations of the male in vigorous action as in Pollaiuolo's *Battle of the Nude Gods* (*Pl. 141*) or in the violent movement and mighty exaggerations of Michelangelo.

141 Anatomical science: Pollaiuolo *Battle of the Nude Gods*

142 Modern rendering of the figure: Matisse *The Dance* 1910

It is however a new kind of painting of the female nude initiated by the genius of Giorgione in Venice that set a direction. There was now no story, no diverting fable, a thing so unusual that Vasari found it worthy of remark as a puzzling circumstance. The pose of Giorgione's reclining Venus (Dresden) allows of innumerable subtleties of form. The dreaming absorption of the model creates an atmosphere which makes the landscape background, void as it is of human life or Classical symbolism, in no way discrepant (*Pl. 86*).

Titian's *Venus of Urbino* (Uffizi) seems a sequel to or comment on the work of his contemporary though here there is more of probability in the interior setting and realism in the lively awareness of the beautiful model (*Pl. 87*). The same elements of composition have been used again and again by painters, how individually by the exceptional artist is strikingly shown in Manet's *Olympia* which so brilliantly translates Titian's Venus into a Parisian type of the Second Empire (*Pl. 88*).

While a broad distinction can be made between idealism and realism in painting the nude the European masterpieces show many individual differences of approach. The single nude painted by Velazquez, *Venus and Cupid* (London, National Gallery) shows artifice and reality in balance. Ostensibly mythological in subject it is a realistic painting of a Spanish model. More than this, however, it is a superb piece of pictorial planning in design and colour, the long fold of dark grey drapery emphasizing the exquisite curve of thigh, the contrast of warm and cool colours in the various fabrics bringing out the brilliant intermediary sparkle and delicacy of flesh tones (*Pl. 89*).

Rembrandt's *Bathsheba* (Louvre) is realistic in that humanity of feeling he always displayed, appearing not only in the un-glamourized sturdiness of body (which however in this instance he has not gone out of his way to stress) but in the expression of a mood of serious thought, consequence of the message in the letter Bathsheba holds.

Boucher's *Miss O'Murphy* (Munich) portrays a youthful voluptuousness of figure with the same enjoyment of rounded form that Renoir shows in the many *baigneuses* of his later years. The complex mind of Ingres is torn between an ideal of classic simplicity as in his back-turned *La Baigneuse* (Louvre) and the *bourgeois* sentimentality that produced the insipid prettiness of *La Source*.

The realism of the nineteenth century as displayed in French painting has two assumptions; firstly, the necessity of seeing truthfully – as Courbet looks at his thick-set models – and secondly, the need for some likelihood of circumstances or surroundings. Thus Degas sets his nudes in some relation to the bathtub and studies the unconventionality of movement involved in the various stages of washing and drying. Walter Sickert follows him in painting the glimmer of flesh in the half-light of dingy London bedrooms; Bonnard in his paintings of the figure in the bath or bathroom in narcissistic reverie (*Pl. 144*).

It was still possible in the twentieth century for an artist such as Amedeo Modigliani to combine a beauty perceived in the figure with an aesthetic beauty of line (*Pl. 143*).

143
Amedeo Modigliani
Seated Girl

The figure
vehicle of
expression:

144 Bonnar
Standing Nu

145 Picasso *Dryad* 1908

146 Francis
Bacon *Henrietta
Moraes* 1966

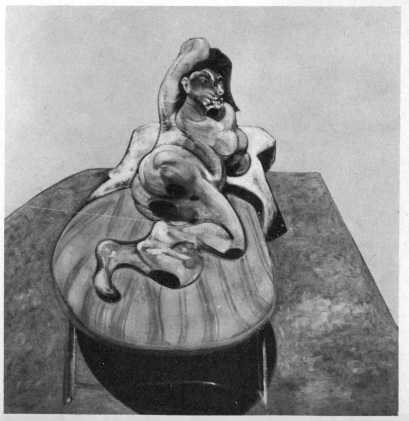

But more in evidence in modern times is a trend which is neither idealistic or realistic but makes use of the figure with a freedom that allows it neither more nor less value than any other kind of form and distorts it in any way an abstract aim suggests.

Music and *The Dance* (Leningrad, Hermitage) by Matisse are interpretations of rhythm in which the shape of the nude is secondary to the flow of line and brilliance of colour (*Pl. 142*). In the same collection the *Dryad* by Picasso is no graceful wood-nymph but a formidably geometric structure inspired by African carving and at the farthest remove from the spirit of the Renaissance (*Pl. 145*). Yet Picasso has had his own variety of Classicism and a study of the nude in his work is complex. One of his best achievements is the series of drawings in which with a sardonic humour he represents the academic artist and his inscrutable model.

It has been the lament of some critics, Bernard Berenson being notable among them, that artists should apparently be unable to set before modern society such models of physical excellence as those which the Greek artists gave to Athens and the Florentines and Venetians to Renaissance Italy. Modern painters have tended to treat the figure savagely or in an arbitrary fashion. A depraved ugliness sears the spectator's feelings in Rouault's paintings of prostitutes. Francis Bacon (*Pl. 146*) gives an unprepossessing animality to the gross and lumpish bodies he paints. Yet both are able to communicate an idea with singular force through the figure – in effect a criticism of society with more of truth of feeling than if they had attempted to revive classic beauties of proportion.

However viewed, the figure retains an advantage in painting in the capacity for 'communication' which 'non-figurative' painting cannot so obviously claim. Kandinsky dubiously states the case for abstract as opposed to figurative art in saying that 'the impact of an acute triangle on a sphere generates as much emotional impact as the meeting of God and Adam in Michelangelo's *Creation.*' An aesthetic sensation can be contained in the relation of geometric figures, but what Michelangelo conveys is exactly what triangle and sphere could not convey.

147 Character interpreted: Honoré Daumier *Don Quixote charges a platoon of sheep*

LITERATURE INTO PAINTING

Many things have been said in disfavour of the practice of taking subjects for pictures from literature. Whether the result is of value or sinks to the level of dependence on the written word rests with the artist. Sir Joshua Reynolds took it for granted that the painter's subject was 'commonly supplied by the poet or historian'. He assumed also that the 'invention' involved was the painter's affair. When we consider the religious subject and the mythological subject we can see the process in operation. Homer, Ovid, Dante, in addition to the many stories taken directly from the Bible provided literary sources for the Old Masters. Milton and Shakespeare inspired artists of the Romantic Age.

148 Imaginative
suggestion: Fuseli
*A Midsummer
Night's Dream*
1793–4

The greatest pictures are those in which the subject is a known
quantity that can be taken for granted or becomes transferred
from a particular to a general interest. Rembrandt takes his
Jacob Blessing the Sons of Joseph (Kassel) from the Book of
Genesis. Yet the episode as he treats it might belong to any age
and its riches of colour and light and shade owe nothing to a
text. Even without reference to the legend of Ariadne on the
island of Naxos one could appreciate Titian's *Bacchus and
Ariadne* as the flight of melancholy before joyous movement
and colour (*Pl. 91*). A remarkable instance of interpretation
rather than illustration is given by William Blake's watercolours for the *Divina Commedia*. The enchanted world of

Titania and Oberon in *A Midsummer Night's Dream* leaves full scope for Fuseli to people it with his own strange elves (*Pl. 148*). The descriptions of landscape in *Paradise Lost* and James Thomson's *Seasons* were a constant source of inspiration to Turner as can be gathered from the quotations which accompanied his exhibits at the Royal Academy. Yet Thomson's line, 'The rigid hoar frost melts before his beams', would not inevitably predict Turner's *Frosty Morning*. Words for great painters have been the means of releasing an image which has only an initial literary connection.

The weaknesses of illustration in painting have been forcibly described by Roger Fry. It stood for the 'sentimental commonplace', the 'secondhand drama', the 'horrible pictorial didacticism' which he found in many Victorian pictures. He pushed regard for the 'purity' of painting to the extent of asserting that Van Gogh 'was much more an illustrator than a plastic artist'. Very likely he was thinking of Van Gogh's attachment to the nineteenth-century graphic illustrators, a product of which was his famous picture of a pair of old boots (*Pl. 149*).

149 The implied story: Vincent van Gogh *Two Shoes* 1886

This particular picture impels the spectator, perhaps, to think of what stories those boots could tell, of weary tramping through all weathers and so on, though this suggested background of social life has little to do with the appraisal of the picture as such. It may be said that Van Gogh became truly great when he shed this illustrative element to achieve his triumphs of expression in colour.

A painting of a humorous scene from *Don Quixote* by C.R.Leslie may merit the criticism of 'second-hand drama'. But does this apply to Daumier's paintings of the Knight and his Squire? On the contrary, though they are sufficiently conformable to the accepted notion of what Cervantes' characters looked like, Daumier has appropriated them and made them his own (*Pl. 147*). These phantom figures, without commentary on the author's intentions, are infused with Daumier's own reflective melancholy and breadth of style. Here there is something beyond illustration in spite of the literary nexus. The imagination of the painter develops from it a painting that is complete and self-sufficient.

GENRE PAINTING

What is known as genre (a use of the word 'kind' which has narrowed down to one particular kind), the painting of scenes of everyday life unidealized, is the opposite of everything represented by the 'Grand Style'. By definition it excludes the generalized conceptions of the painter who seeks an ideal beauty and is concerned with the elevated matter, religious, tragic, philosophic that belongs to 'history painting', or the flight of the imagination into some mythical or past time, the propaganda of a régime or visionary and subjective expression in any of its forms.

It is an aspect of realism inasmuch as the artist paints what actually exists without seeking to invest it with a refinement it does not possess and not shrinking from its vulgar or unprepossessing nature. It may do so without any attempt to tell a story, as in the paintings of everyday Dutch life by Vermeer or Pieter de Hoogh, though there is always a story implicit in

150 Quentin Massys *The Banker and his Wife* 1514

the setting of a social stage. The tendency is t[o]
representation of 'low life', the subject has ofte[n]
peasant, the artisan, the kitchen and the alehouse [to]
the life of 'high society'. This has created also a lean[ing]
comedy or the representation of scenes and persons w[ith]
side or imperfections that may be so described.

For these reasons the traditional view of genre an[d]
art was that of a form inferior to the expressio[n]
thought such as the masters of the Italian Renaissance[.]
'The painters who have applied themselves more p[a]

racters and who express with precision
passion as they are exhibited by vulgar
in the works of Hogarth) descrve great
nius has been employed on low and con-
se which we give must be as limited as its

nt of Sir Joshua Reynolds which, however,
fallacy from a modern point of view in
eneral terms by their subject and not by the
or the perception of truth and intensification
eality. Pieter Brueghel the Elder is no less
cause he depicts the peasant life of the Nether-
sh and Dutch painters indeed give the first
Painters of many races have delighted in
emporary detail into their religious composi-
f types, dress, setting. This is especially marked
art. The glimpses of Flemish city life in the
paintings by Campin, the realistically defined
Portinari Altarpiece by Hugo van der Goes
ples (*Pl. 112*).

y towards genre may be associated with the
mocratic outlook. Quentin Massys illustrates a
for social reality in the subject which enjoyed a
eginning of the sixteenth century in *The Banker
hanger] and his Wife*. This gave scope for the
f character and a great amount of circumstantial
ail, as in the painting in the Louvre (*Pl. 150*).
example of genre with an implied democratic and
nd of thought is given by Pieter Brueghel. Some of
flects the religious and national unrest and schism
enth-century Netherlands under the despotism of
ontemporary scene appears under the guise of
ory in his *Census of Bethlehem*. His realism emerged
arly fantastic style of allegory in which he was
by Jerome Bosch. There is amusing incident and
in the two great works in the Kunsthistoriches
Vienna, *The Peasant Dance* and *The Village Wedding*

151 Realism in
genre:
Brouwer *Smokers*

but these are masterpieces in their power of design and resource
of form, colour and movement (*Pl. 32*).

The seventeenth century was the great age of genre in
Europe when it seems a necessary counter to, and relief from,
the art required by Courts and prelates. The peasant long
remained the hero of the realist. Painted in low tones of grey
and brown that match the dark squalor of bare rustic taverns,
the peasants of Adriaen Brouwer and David Teniers the
Younger, drinking, card-playing, quarrelling are studied with
a deliberate abstention from the beauty of colour and form. In
this way they gain intense veracity of effect (*Pl. 151*).

Realism in genre:
152 Louis Le Nain
Peasant Family

153 Murillo *Two Spanish
        Peasant Boys*

154 Ribera *Boy with a
        Club Foot 1652*

155 Velazquez *The
    Water-Carrier of Seville*

The influence of Caravaggio in Italy, as one who made a point of painting common types of humanity, spread elsewhere in Europe. In France the brothers Le Nain painted those peasants who seemed to aristocratic observers no more than beasts of the field. The masterpieces of Louis Le Nain, the *Famille de Paysans* and the *Repas des Paysans* in the Louvre have an unforced delicacy of style and discernment, a beautiful quality of grey enlivened by a touch of warm colour which belonged to the French tradition in particular (*Pl. 152*).

The interest of seventeenth-century painters in everyday life and the commonplace objects associated with it can be regarded as a liberation from the idealism of the Renaissance as well as from the religious and political rhetoric of the Baroque style. While the individual artist found refreshment in this new idea, it marked also the growth of a national and regional feeling in art independent of the international style. Genre had this role in the Netherlands, north and south, and also in Spain where it

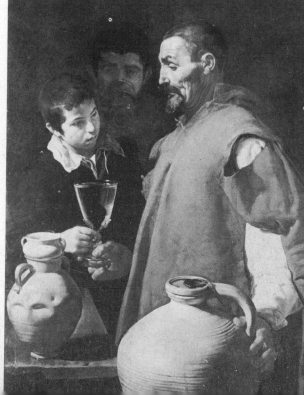

took the form of 'kitchen pictures' (*bodegones*) in which the homely figures of servants busied themselves among the pots and pans, the varied shapes and surfaces of which, the roughness of earthenware and the polished gleam of copper, were painted with a special delight in their honest substance.

A number of early paintings by Velazquez show this trend, a great example being *The Water-Carrier of Seville* (London, Wellington Museum), strong lighting bringing out a correspondence between the wrinkled visage of the man and the corrugated surfaces of the jars at his side (*Pl. 155*). Later, when Velazquez experimented with mythology, he used it as a pretext for what was essentially genre. In *Los Borrachos* (Prado) the presence of a semi-nude Bacchus is almost irrelevant to the merry group of tippling peasants whose expressions are depicted with magical skill.

A parallel tendency may be found in Murillo, an artist who now seems strangely divided between the softly sentimental style of his religious paintings and such studies of vagrants and urchins as *The Melon-Eaters* (Munich, Pinakothek) and *Two Spanish Peasant Boys* (*Pl. 153*). And in Ribera, whose *Boy with a Club Foot* is something more than a single portrait, a comment at once comic and tragic on life (*Pl. 154*).

Most clearly national, a social portrait, is the genre painting of seventeenth-century Holland, independent of foreign rule, proud of its liberty and its own way of life. Peasant humours are exchanged for *bourgeois* propriety. Instead of the squalid riot of the tavern the painter takes leisure to observe the well-ordered interior, the evidences of refinement of taste, the soberly-clad groups or single figures, often not engaged in any special activity. There is a certain amount of humorous story-telling, as in *The Idle Servant* (London, National Gallery) by Nicholas Maes and the scenes of domestic revelry in which Jan Steen excelled (*Pl. 156*). But in contrast, the paintings of Vermeer and Pieter de Hoogh of figures in interiors or in the courtyards of Dutch houses, ascend beyond the story and become superb arrangements of space, light and colour, even though every detail of fact is meticulously in place.

156 Humour in genre: Nicholas Maes *The Idle Servant* 1655

157 Middle-class life: Terborch *Woman Writing*

The music lesson and the reading of a letter are popular themes in which Terborch and Metsu are excelled only by Vermeer (*Pl. 157*). They show the Dutch tendency to specialize to which Rembrandt was an exception. Interested as his drawings show he was in the spectacle of contemporary life, his paintings reveal little concern with its everyday aspect. In the eighteenth century the painting of genre has its most notable examples in England, France and Italy. It is the achievement of Hogarth not only to depict a class of society but to set the whole of a nation's life in motion before our eyes in the great series of paintings and engravings which range from the palatial mansion to the hovel, from the comedy of fashion (*Pl. 159*) to the horrors of Bedlam. In the slighter medium of pen and watercolour Rowlandson gives an even wider view of life in country as well as

181

town. In France, Chardin with a dignity and simplicity of style all his own conveys the spirit of upper-middle-class domestic life in eighteenth-century France in paintings of which *Saying Grace* (Louvre) is a beautiful example (*Pl. 158*). The intimate Venice, with its masquerades, receptions, flirtations and entertainments is mirrored with charm in the paintings of Pietro Longhi.

Genre paintings as a setting of the social stage declined, in the merit properly belonging to art, in the nineteenth century. In English painting anecdote, sentiment and humour became reduced to triviality and were cultivated at the expense of aesthetic qualities. In France, on the other hand, the clear outline of what a genre painting is tends to dim as the artist becomes more concerned with a method of painting or a personal form of expression. When Degas for instance depicts laundresses yawn-

158 Middle-class life: Chardin *Saying Grace* (detail)

159 The view of society: Hogarth *Marriage à la Mode* 1744

ing at the end of a day's work, one may feel that here is a social remark, yet there is every evidence that the artist was more concerned with the transitory effects of human movement as movement and not because he wishes to inform us with that 'social realism' which in England in the later nineteenth century professed to investigate the lot of the working classes.

It might be said that genre has tended to disappear with the gradual disappearance of comedy and tragedy from art in terms of subject-matter, the decline of realism and the growth of a more subjective attitude. The levelling tendency of modern life and the abstract tendencies of art have both militated against it.

160 Poetic spirit in Chinese landscape: *Fishing in a Mountain Stream* eleventh century (detail)

LANDSCAPE

In landscape the painter has been faced with every phenomenon of the natural and visible world: space and light in the most general sense; the elements – in the old philosophic definition of the term – earth, air, water, fire; the seasons and their changes; effects of weather; day and night; all the variety of vegetable and mineral form; in addition and in more particular detail whatever indicates the presence of man – buildings, gardens, cultivated fields. Small wonder then that landscape painting provides an infinite store of wonder and delight.

For various reasons, however, it was only possible to an advanced civilization with a philosophic, poetic or scientific standpoint. For prehistoric man, concerned with his perpetual

184

hunt for food, it would have been meaningless to attempt to depict those terrifying wastes and jungles in which his quarry lurked. In early agricultural communities it was the business of the artist to give human or symbolic shape to the mysterious forces that caused their crops to grow or alternatively destroyed them – the sun-god, the rain-god. And at no time has landscape flourished in the extremes of heat and cold.

The first great landscape painters were the Chinese, whose masterpieces long antedated those of Europe. In the period corresponding to the early Middle Ages of Europe they were able to view the majesty of mountains and waterfalls with the philosophic detachment of the sage, expressing a sense of community with nature and conveying with a certain satisfaction the smallness of man in the presence of these immensities. The poetic spirit gave rise to meandering river journeys painted on the long scrolls in a 'moving picture' which conducts the eye past variegated rocks, swelling uplands, and picturesque gorges in a prolonged and constantly changing vista.

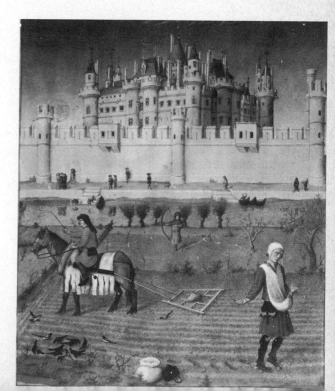

161
Rhythm of the seasons:
October from the
*Très Riches Heures du
Duc de Berri*, before 1416

Landscape as background: 162 Jan van Eyck *Madonna of Nicolas Rolin*
c. 1425

In the West the development is later and has a different motif.
The painters and sculptors of Classical antiquity were preoccupied with the doings of men and gods. The scenes from
the *Odyssey* of the first century A D now in the Vatican give in
effect no more than the stage-direction 'here is an island'. It
was not until the Late Gothic period and in the prosperous
Burgundian lands that the beauty of flowers and the rhythm
of the seasons evoked a visual response. Flowers became the

decorative pattern of tapestry. The calendar of the Book of Hours depicting the occupations proper to each season of the year had its appropriate backgrounds, as in the masterpiece of the early fifteenth century the *Très Riches Heures du Duc de Berri* (Chantilly, Musée Condé) by the brothers of Limbourg, Pol, Herman and Johancquin Malouel (*Pl. 161*).

Subsequently the landscape as a background, often a delightful extra for which there was perhaps no specific reason except as a diversion of the figure painter from his main duty, has a long history. Thus the eye is diverted in Jan van Eyck's *Madonna of Nicolas Rolin* (Louvre) to the neat little private flower garden of which there is a tempting glimpse between Romanesque columns and to the flourishing city and winding river beyond; the ideal city of the Netherlandish imagination with its towers and belfries, clustering roofs and arched bridge (*Pl. 162*).

163 Konrad Witz *The Miraculous Draught of Fishes* 1444

The distant glimpses of landscape as a delightful extra with no specific relation to the main theme provide an auxiliary pleasure in looking at many paintings. There was a gradual increase in the importance of its role from the fifteenth to the seventeenth century. Landscape was something more than a minor detail for the South German painter Conrad Witz, who worked at Basle in the first half of the fifteenth century. His masterpiece, *The Miraculous Draught of Fishes*, 1444 (Geneva), provides an elaborate setting for the religious subject, a view of Lake Leman believed to be the earliest representation of a landscape which is still identifiable (*Pl. 163*).

Landscape had a greater relevance in religious compositions as a vision of Paradise, the 'first garden' – a stretch of flower-spangled, tree-embowered parkland with a distant view of the Heavenly City in the Van Eyck *Adoration of the Lamb* (Ghent); another world of exotic vegetation, its strange luxuriance suggested perhaps by travellers' tales, in an altarpiece by Jerome Bosch. The miniature background of the early Flemish picture first expands into a subject in itself in the panoramic vistas of the early-sixteenth-century painter, Joachim Patenier (*Pl. 164*).

A number of minor Flemish painters of that time have left us attractive secular views of figures in rustic setting with much minuteness of detail (Joos de Momper, Roland Savery, Jacob and Abel Grimmer and others). Towering above them is Pieter Brueghel the Elder whose paintings of the Months (Vienna) give a more profound and dramatic view of the relation of man with nature than the medieval calendar. *February* with its hunters in the snow is one of the greatest landscapes ever painted, uniting the figures silhouetted against the white background in a marvellous design and somehow conveying the muffling of sound as well as the chill of the snow-blanketed scene (*Pl. 165*).

In this work Brueghel seems to combine aspects of Flemish and Alpine scenery. It is a reminder of the practice, growing in his century of travelling to Rome, the capital of art. Artists became aware of landscape through the new impressions they

164 Landscape as a main theme: Joachim Patenier *St Jerome in a Landscape*

165 Pieter Brueghel the Elder *February c.* 1565

received on their journey southwards. Dürer was thus incited to make those records in watercolour which have a unique place in his art. The Alpine view one sees through a window in his self-portrait in the Prado seems to draw the spectator's attention to the Italian journey from which he had not long returned and the transalpine direction of his thought (*Pl. 199*).

Flemish and German artists contributed much to the growth of what is known as 'classical' landscape. Rome and its environs and antique memories now had a *clientèle* of visitors for which artists catered during two centuries. There is a mixture of feelings and ideas in the work of the Northern settlers in Rome at the beginning of the seventeenth century. The recollection of Northern woods and meadows seems to fuse with their impressions of ruined villas and temples, the waterfalls of the Sabine Hills, the crater lakes of the volcanic region between Rome and Naples – Lake Nemi with its mysterious groves, sacred to Diana, and Avernus of unfathomable depth with Hades below.

The Frankfurt painter, Adam Elsheimer, who settled at Rome in 1610 was greatly influential in shaping landscape along

166 'Classical' landscape: Poussin *Landscape with a Snake*

167 'Classical' landscape: Claude: *Seaport – The Embarkation of the Queen of Sheba* 1648

these lines, mythological or religious subject-matter now having only a token presence. The desire to give landscape a separate existence can also be seen in the work of the Italian painters, Annibale Caracci and Domenichino. Yet the *tedeschi* (or foreigners) were, in being so, the more receptive to the poetic and elegiac associations of the ancient sites. They had perhaps something of that mood in which Gibbon mused pleasurably on time and vicissitude amid the ruins of the Capitol. The past was a romantic dream to Claude. The buildings in his great Sea Port paintings (*Pl. 167*) are entrancing impossibilities, the strangely garbed little figures might have been lifted from a masque at the Court of Louis XIV. His

Enchanted Castle leads us far from the imperial palaces to the 'faery lands forlorn' of Keats whom it inspired.

When examined from another point of view the 'classical' element in landscape was not a matter of historical retrospect but light and space treated with the maximum breadth in a carefully ordered composition. Claude is classical not in fanciful detail but in the radiance of dawn and sunset, his timeless and tideless expanse of sea, his splendidly massed foliage. His friend and contemporary in Rome, Nicolas Poussin, turning in majestic rather than romantic fashion from figure composition to landscape, achieves the feat of imposing the 'Grand Style' of Raphael on inanimate nature (*Pl. 166*). The breadth as opposed to particular detail, the serene glow, the calm certainties of design are the qualities that appeal to such a follower of the Classical tradition as Richard Wilson in the eighteenth century. 'Claude for air, Gaspar [Dughuet] for composition' was his precept.

A different motive for landscape may be found from the seventeenth century onwards in the affection for, the visual discovery of, a homeland. Rubens's pride in the Château de Steen, the manor-house he acquired in 1635 and the surrounding estate appears in the great picture now in the National Gallery, one of those landscapes he painted late in life for his own enjoyment, a marvellous combination of the Flemish panoramic style and detailed and sympathetic observation (*Pl. 168*). It is this feeling of local attachment that gives a distinct and national character to the landscape of seventeenth-century Holland, its shores, canals, windmills, stretches of lowland and expanses of sky being affectionately portrayed by artists from van Goyen to Ruisdael and Hobbema.

The local sentiment and style have their echo in the English East Anglian painters of the eighteenth century, John Crome at Norwich and Gainsborough and Constable who derived the impulse of their art from their love of Suffolk (*Pl. 171*). Again in France, in Théodore Rousseau and other painters who made Barbizon and the forests of Fontainebleau their special study. From the eighteenth century onwards landscape painting

168 (*above right*) Local attachment: Rubens *Château de Steen c.* 1635

169 (*below right*) The city view: Vermeer *View of Delft c.* 1658

170 Natural forces: El Greco *View of Toledo c.* 1604–14

however has a number of different motives. There is the place-portrait and the topographical record, in general assigned a subordinate place as being no more than a statement of fact. Yet how much more they may be can be gathered from such superb pictures as Vermeer's *View of Delft* (Pl. *169*) and Canaletto's *The Stonemason's Yard* (London, National Gallery).

In contrast with the homely landscape was that of the Romantic epoch of the early nineteenth century, exploiting effects of mystery and melancholy as in the work of the German painter, Caspar David Friedrich or of vastness and the violence

196

of the elements such as Turner gives in one phase of his immense achievement. His sense of nature's violence has few precedents, though among them is the unique tempestuous vision of El Greco in his *View of Toledo* (New York, Metropolitan Museum) (*Pl. 170*). Turner was supremely the painter of the elements, of storm, fire and flood arriving finally at the conversion of solid matter into the energy of pure colour (*Pl. 20*).

Eschewing extremes of drama or emotion the French artists of the nineteenth century created the last great phase of landscape. Realism was the dominant note. This implied the acceptance of any scene that lay before the painter's eyes, not necessarily for any conspicuous beauty or grandeur of effect but as being the vehicle of pervading light and atmosphere. In this respect, Constable was the first great innovator (*Pl. 171*). He may be said to have given the French painters their first impetus with the *Hay Wain*, exhibited at the famous Salon of 1824, though later the French development was self-contained. Corot,

171 Light and atmosphere: Constable *The Hay Wain* 1821

Boudin, Courbet lead to the Impressionists who in accordance with the scientific spirit of the nineteenth century found their special means of translating open-air light into terms of colour.

The scientific method of dividing colour had its final outcome in the neo-Impressionism of Georges Seurat. Colour as the expression of form in landscape reached its culminating-point in the work of Cézanne; as the expression of a personal emotion in the work of Van Gogh.

The twentieth century on the other hand has not found the same stimulus in nature. The attempt has been to convey a feeling of landscape without a direct rendering of it. Graham Sutherland and Nicholas de Staël are painters who have achieved this result (*Pls. 172, 173*). But in so far as landscape is an objective study it has dwindled in force in an age greatly concerned with the abstract and subjective.

The sensation of
landscape indirectly
conveyed:

◀ 172 Graham Sutherland:
Landscape with Estuary

173 Nicholas de Staël:
Roofs 1952

While it is of use in appreciation to have a general idea of historical development in mind, even in such condensed terms as are given above, it is necessary also to consider more precisely how the painter reduces the magnificent chaos of nature to some kind of pictorial order. How, for instance is a tree to be represented – as a number of individual leaves and branches; or as a solid on which light falls creating a system of light and shade; with or without an outline; as a recognizable type or a more or less freely imagined object? Each method has been used and has its value. To define each leaf separately is the 'primitive' solution, the opposite of the Classical generalization but it can be as beautifully decorative as in a Byzantine mosaic.

174–6 Trees: Corot *Road at Ville d'Avray* 1874; Hobbema *Avenue at Middelharnis* 1689 (detail); below, Henri Rousseau *The Dream* 1910

The detail as a symbol of the whole, in the painting of a jungle by the 'Douanier' Rousseau, is capable of summarizing all its imagined lavish and exotic growth (*Pl. 176*).

The Old Masters give us many fanciful trees – like the Tree of Life in Bosch's *Garden of Terrestrial Delights* with its bulbous trunk and radiating leafy crown. They often contain much of the artist's own character or thought. One might contrast the slender stems with their immature delicacy of leafage in the paintings of Perugino and the young Raphael, expressing that feeling of a virginal purity which was a main characteristic of their work, with the tortured trunks and decaying clusters of foliage which convey the sombre Romanticism of Salvator Rosa. The cypresses of Van Gogh quiver with the intensity of his emotion (*Pl. 97*).

The different patterns of growth have been studied and artists have their recognizable favourites. The oak seems the most painterly of trees, the ancient of the forest, heroic and venerable in the work of Ruisdael and of the Barbizon painters, in Gainsborough's *Cornard Wood* (London, National Gallery,

177 Thomas Gainsborough *Cornard Wood* 1748

Skies: 178 Constable *Study of Sky and Trees* 1821

Pl. 177), in Crome's *Poringland Oak* (London, Tate Gallery). Corot favours the trees of delicate form, the tremulous aspen, the silver birch (*Pl. 174*). The poplar, by reason of its vertical growth has been favoured as a decorative element of design, as in the trim uprightness of Hobbema's avenue at Middelharnis (London, National Gallery, *Pl. 175*) or Monet's paintings of the tall poplars lining the bank of the Epte. Turner uses trees with the same varied resource as other elements of landscape, from the homely picturesqueness of the pollard willow in *Hedging and Ditching* to the weird stumps amid which his Jason (London, Tate Gallery) ventures in search of the Golden Fleece; from the firs of the Alpine slopes to the pines of the Campagna.

In Constable's view the sky was the prime element of landscape, setting the key to any composition (*Pl. 178*). He shows his preference for the cumulus cloud. To the flat land of East Anglia (in itself suggesting a picture with a low horizon and a greater area above) the billowing cumulus adds a serenity and spaciousness. It links in sympathy Constable's *Cornfield*, Crome's *Mousehold Heath*, and the landscapes of such Dutch masters as Ruisdael and Koninck. It is a symbol of rural delight in *The Bright Cloud* of Samuel Palmer at Shoreham (*Pl. 179*).

It was left to Turner to investigate the upper regions of the sky, to weave into new pictorial patterns the delicate filaments of cirrus and to open fresh avenues of aerial perspective. Dawn and sunset – here Turner and Claude come together in splendid competition. For the sky as pure luminosity undisturbed by the dazzling source of light (either just withdrawn or yet to appear) Claude must be held unequalled, though the Turner sunset, inspired by the light imprisoned in the heavy air of the Thames, perhaps needs a revival of appreciation since the time when aesthetes began to laugh at the sunset as an instance of nature's 'vulgarity'. One may well refer again to Ruskin's description

179 Samuel Palmer *The Bright Cloud c.* 1831–2

of 'the cold deadly shadows of twilight . . . gathering through every sunbeam', of those deeply crimsoned skies which Turner always associated with some solemn or funereal subject. The sun itself, unless in some way veiled or close to the horizon is beyond the audacity of artists – but with what confidence Rubens in the National Gallery *Landscape – Sunset* (*Pl. 69*) thickens impasto on the glowing ball and darts its rays over the distant hills!

Storm has been inspiring, there is the lurid sky of Giorgione's *The Tempest* (Venice, Accademia) with its flicker of lightning, a drama apart behind the calm foreground figures (*Pl. 90*); the strangely rent and sultry sky that broods over El Greco's Toledo, the Alpine blizzards of Turner once more. It is in the Romantic period that effects not only of violence but of mystery are most eagerly sought. The moon and stars – moving always to the poetic spirit – took on new meaning for the painter as the visual art also claimed its right to poetry. The German Romantic, Caspar David Friedrich is irresistibly attracted by the magic of moonlight; the crescent moon is no less part of Kent's fascination for Palmer than its great clouds. The Nocturnes of Whistler distil the veiled beauty of twilight. The stars and moon which Van Gogh surrounded with catherine-wheels of light in *The Starry Night* and *Road with Cypresses* vibrate with the depth of his feeling.

The Impressionists admitted little incident into their skies. Only a little train of woolpack clouds occasionally breaks the placid shimmer they favoured. They were interested mainly in the effect on objects of an equable daylight and hardly at all, if we exclude the colour they found in the whiteness of snow, in the rarer phenomena of nature. The rainbow, for instance, (which considered as the spectrum is nature's own demonstration of Impressionist theory) is absent from their pictures though many other artists – Elsheimer, Rubens, Millet, Turner, Constable – have accepted its challenge to their capacity for design and delighted in its transient gleam.

The structure of land, the principles and complexities of movement presented by the sea have been represented by

180 Rocks: Giovanni di Paolo *St John entering the Wilderness*, mid-fifteenth century

painters both conventionally and scientifically. One may contrast the oddly shaped rocks which symbolized a mountain for an early Italian painter such as Giovanni da Paolo with the forms that resulted from Leonardo's study of geology (*Pls. 16, 180*). Or the system of interlaced triangles with which seventeenth- and eighteenth-century painters sought to convey the complex ripples of water with such representations of the force and volume of the sea as Turner gives in his *Calais Pier* and Courbet in *The Wave*.

181 Modern fantasy: Max Ernst *Europe after the Rain* 1940–2

One thing that emerges in the appreciation of landscape however is the universality of form. Artists at various periods of history have marked their awareness of this independence of scale or locality. Cennino Cennini thought a way of painting mountains was to copy the shape of a rough stone; this seems more a modern than a naïve piece of advice when one considers for instance a landscape by Graham Sutherland (*Pl. 172*). Some, like Gainsborough, have constructed landscapes from pieces of moss and other odds and ends in which to study general effects of light, mass and dimension. Degas could paint a cloud from a handkerchief made into a ball. In modern times however this idea of an essential basis of form has led to the extinction of landscape. Mondrian has demonstrated in a series of works how the search for underlying principles of construction in an apple tree may result finally in its disappearance, leaving only a geometric diagram behind. Similarly, the efforts of Cézanne to find the geometrical structure in nature led to the disappearance of landscape from Cubist art. Landscape has its most vivid modern form in the petrified forests, dream cities and endless perspectives of the Surrealist painters.

The art of the individual likeness has been so often deprecated in recent times as no more than a form of imitative skill which the camera has made an anachronism that there is some reason for reminding ourselves that it can be much more than what Hogarth described as 'phizmongering' and has in fact been one of the most richly productive forms of painting. It is one of the oldest, has passed through many phases, and there are few great artists who have not produced great examples. In spite of disparaging modern comparisons with photography, the painted portrait has the advantage in several respects. The artist can select essentials of feature, emphasize contour and synthesize many transient expressions into the most characteristic in a way no mechanical instrument can. In addition it is possible for the artist not only, as in other forms of painting, to create a work of visual beauty in composition and detail, but to convey psychological insight and his own reaction to the human presence.

In looking at the portraits of the past we are generally in no position to pronounce on the accuracy of the likeness except in so far as various artists or portraits of the same person seem to agree. There can be little doubt that an authentic Henry VIII emerges from the portraits by or after Holbein (though there is not the same unanimity about the features and aspect of Queen Elizabeth I). On the other hand the portraits of many unknown individuals are convincing and hold our attention simply because of an essential humanity.

This already appears in the portraits painted in encaustic on mummy-cases in Egypt in the first two centuries A D, the work of artists trained in the Hellenistic style, perhaps only a crude and provincial reflection of the portraiture of Greek masters now lost to us, but so full of character that you feel you might encounter any of these types in the Levant of today (*Pl. 79*). If one asks how it is that they so instantly convey patrician dignity, or the coarseness of a lower order, serenity or nervousness, intelligence or cunning the answer would not be through any subtlety of modelling, lighting or detail but in their grasp

182 Incidental portraiture: Jan van Eyck *Madonna of Canon van der Paele*

of general shape and main features, eyes, nose and mouth. The concentration on those large, dark, Levantine eyes brings to mind the later precept of the Elizabethan miniaturist, Nicholas Hilliard – 'the eyes for Life, nose for Proportion, mouth for Likeness'.

The art was lost in the Dark Ages and early Middle Ages of Europe. The portrait of a king was more a symbol of monarchy than a likeness, as in the painting of Richard II in state in Westminster Abbey. It revives as an incidental feature of religious compositions in the fourteenth and fifteenth centuries when it became usual for Italian and Flemish painters to introduce the portraits of themselves and their friends. Often one singles the artist out in a painted crowd by the sidelong glance towards the spectator that suggests the image studied in the glass. It is thus that Jan van Eyck appears among the Just Judges in the left-hand panel of the *Adoration of the Lamb* at Ghent; that the youth whom we presume to be Botticelli himself turns his head towards the spectator in the Uffizi *Adoration of the Magi* and Signorelli slants a look outward from the *Deeds of the Anti-Christ* in Orvieto Cathedral. Such masters might be said to sign their work by a portrait instead of or in addition to a written signature and perhaps gained a quiet satisfaction from leaving this clue to their identity.

Patrons required the commemoration of their piety in portrayal as donors. It is thus that Canon van der Paele, every wrinkle and vein on his elderly features exactly outlined, is seen kneeling before the Virgin in the painting by Van Eyck at Bruges (*Pls. 182, 183*); and Maria and Tommaso Portinari are placed devoutly before the saints in Van der Goes's altarpiece in the Uffizi. There is a whole family group in Holbein's *Madonna of the Burgomaster Meyer* (Darmstadt).

The independent individual portrait appears in both Flemish and Italian painting in the fifteenth century. Again one finds the concentration on essential features as in the mummy portraits though with a new appreciation of the value of a silhouette, of accessories and background. The two superb portraits of

183 Detail of Canon van der Paele

women by Robert Campin (London, National Gallery) and Rogier van der Weyden (Washington, National Gallery) show how each artist enhances the features by the pattern of the encircling white head-dress (*Pls. 186, 187*).

The Flemish portraits were usually full or three-quarter face. Probably influenced by the medallion portrait popular in the Early Renaissance period Italian painters often painted their sitters in profile, like the companion masterpieces by Piero della Francesca of Federigo da Montefeltro, Duke of Urbino, and his wife Battista Sforza (Uffizi), set against a distant Umbrian landscape (*Pls. 184, 185*).

A great development of portrait painting took place in the sixteenth century. It was encouraged by the development of the oil medium which gave increased possibilities of rendering structure and subtlety of expression; by the rise of powerful States, the heads of which required their image; and by the complete aesthetic equipment of the Renaissance artists. Raphael establishes an elegance of pose in his portrait of Baldassare Castiglione which became a model for others, among them Rembrandt (*Pls. 191, 192*). Leonardo explores the capacity of the oil medium to create those subtle gradations of expression in the mysterious half-smile of the *Mona Lisa* (*Pl. 189*). Titian, venerated by princes was capable equally of conveying the intense psychological indrawnness of Philip II of Spain and the youthful gaiety and charm of his daughter, Lavinia (*Pl. 194*). The portrait by El Greco of Cardinal Fernando Nino de Guevara, the Spanish Grand Inquisitor, indicates the tactics and tension of inquiry by the contrast between the relaxed right hand and the nervous clutch of the left.

One can consider the development of portraiture either as the requirement and iconography of types of society especially at the upper level of Court, aristocracy and the wealthy; or as the aesthetic and technical achievement of individual artists. From the latter point of view evolution is to be traced from the linear portrait to that in which the oil painter's brush freely indicates features by the incidence of light, shade and colour without being confined to determining outline. The genius of Hans

186, 187 The value of accessories: portraits by Robert Campin (*left*) and Rogier van der Weyden

184, 185 The profile portrait: Piero della Francesca *Federigo da Montefeltro, Duke of Urbino, and his wife* 1465–6

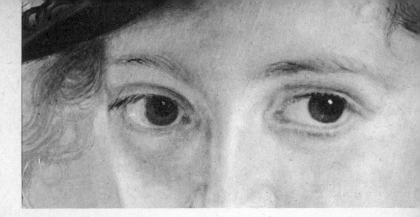

Variation of technique:
188 Rubens *Chapeau de Paille*
c. 1626 (detail)

189 Leonardo da Vinci *Mona Lisa*
c. 1503–6 (detail)

Holbein the Younger is even more conclusively shown than in his paintings in the superb drawings of members of the Tudor Court in which line unerringly defines facial structure (*Pl. 58*). The same remark would apply (with some necessary qualifications as to the difference of the artists' backgrounds) to the portraits of the Clouets in France. The loosening of the oil technique, giving more substance to modelling, appears in the work of the Venetians especially Titian, Tintoretto and Veronese. It is carried a stage further in the seventeenth century when Velazquez, Rubens, Van Dyck, Hals and Rembrandt give their classic examples. With a few colours, thin in shadow, more thickly brushed in the lights, Velazquez magically creates a living texture. Hals is a virtuoso of the brush, making each stroke tell and live and showing a unique facility in his freedom and directness of handling for catching the momentary animation of the features (*Pl. 72*). Rembrandt's weightier handling plumbs the more deeply into character (*Pl. 190*).

190 Rembrandt
Saskia as Flora
1634 (detail)

Rubens gives a pearly substance to flesh, a liquidity to the eye which again tells of the resource of the medium in the hands of a master (*Pl. 188*).

In great portraits at all times there seems an identification of artist and sitter rather than a conscious comment on character. The spontaneous movement of the brush traces out their conjunction in Goya's wonderful *Portrait of the Family of Charles IV* (*Pl. 193*). A moment of inspired vision preserves for ever the laughing countenance of Hogarth's *Shrimp Girl* (*Pl. 73*). A certain distinction remains, however, between the formal and the informal portrait. As general characteristics of the formal or state category one might consider the qualities of gravity, dignity and elegance, together with some suggestion of social standing and importance in accessories and dress. It is the special faculty of Van Dyck to impart something of his own refinement to his sitters. The lesson of his elegance was not lost on Gainsborough.

213

In the art of portraiture as cultivated in eighteenth-century England there are two factors to appreciate; the modifications of the formal portrait which derived from the models of the past and the development of an informal style. Reynolds studies both Titian and Rembrandt to good purpose as can be seen in his broad treatment of light and shade and richness of colour. Gainsborough studies the elegance of Van Dyck but adds a freshness of vision which prevents him from falling into those artificial conventions of grace which become mechanical in the work of Van Dyck's follower Peter Lely.

The naturalness of English painting appears in portraits of children as free and full of charm as Gainsborough's pictures of his daughters (*Pl. 195*). Also in the special development of the

A classic pose:

191 (*above*) Raphael *Baldassare Castiglione* c. 1516

192 Rembrandt *Self-portrait* 1640

193 Goya *The Family of Charles IV, 1799–1800, at Aranjuez*

'conversation piece', representing a family or group of friends in their normal everyday surroundings. Hogarth shows the trend away from grandiose convention in two ways. He adapts the formal portrait to middle-class level as in his painting of Captain Coram, in which symbolic objects, the globe and various documents indicate his life as a mariner and also his benevolent plans for the Foundling Hospital he initiated. In his conversation pieces Hogarth shows us for example an un-pretentious family at breakfast, exactly what a Georgian interior was like, what pictures hung on the walls, and a multitude of circumstantial details which, while they are beautifully painted, also compose a social document.

Portrait painting changes like other forms of art with the character of a period, partly as the sitter represents it and partly with the attitude of the painter to his work. Apart from satisfying requirements as to likeness, an artist is necessarily concerned with the picture as a picture and his own idea of how it should be composed. Thus Whistler emphasizes the fact that he regarded a portrait primarily as a design or 'arrangement', giving the title *Arrangement in Grey and Black* to the famous portrait of his mother in the Louvre, the essence of its effect residing in the simplified silhouette, balances of tone and relation of the figure to carefully placed details, selected not as items descriptive of an interior but as factors in design (*Pl. 194*).

Cézanne, equally regardless of psychology in likeness, approached a portrait in the same way as a still-life. His attitude appears in the celebrated remark, after many sittings given to the dealer, Vollard, that he was 'not displeased with the shirt-front'. The portraits of modern times which stand out are those in which the painter is least bound by photographic ideas. The Impressionist portrait is a vibration of light and colour, like Renoir's portrait of *Jeanne Samary* (Moscow, Pushkin Museum,

194, 195 Nineteenth-century portraits: Whistler: *Arrangement in Grey and Black* 1871; Renoir *Jeanne Samary* 1877

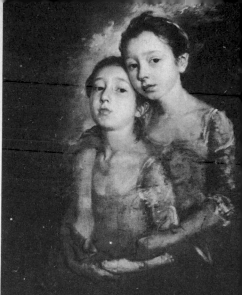

Pl. 195) or Manet's portrait of Mallarmé (Louvre). Van Gogh gives an intensity of his own to arbitrary contour and colour of fierce pitch in works such as *L'Arlésienne* and *The Postman's Son*. Modigliani exaggerates proportion to an impossible degree yet in a way that convinces us of his own truth of vision. The expressiveness of colour is a powerful factor in such twentieth-century portraits as those of Oskar Kokoschka. The Surrealist examination of the strange weathering of natural form seems to equip Graham Sutherland for such a penetrating study of character as appears in his *Portrait of Somerset Maugham* (London, Tate Gallery, *Pl. 198*).

196, 197 Portrayal of youth: above left, Titian's daughter Lavinia *c.* 1550; above right, Gainsborough *The Artist's Daughters teasing a Cat c.* 1759

198 Twentieth-century portrait: Graham Sutherland *Somerset Maugham* 1949 (detail)

199 Dürer *Self-portrait* 1498

200 Rembrandt *Self-portrait*, 1660

Historically, the freedom of portraiture is most distinctly seen in the way artists have painted themselves. They have been usually unceremonious before the reflection in the mirror, searching and unsparing in study of the essential man and for that reason providing the most moving of pictures. How dispassionately the aged Rembrandt studies his pitted and battered countenance and Goya his rough and sombre image. How objectively Van Gogh scrutinizes those bony contours which contain the fever of mind and spirit (*Pl. 71*). Dürer perhaps is a little vain in the self-portraits where he appears as a youth of delicate features and finely shaped hands, a foppish young man handsomely dressed with locks fastidiously curled, even finally as one conscious of a Christ-like appearance (as that had come to be interpreted in art); yet perhaps he, too, was objective in conveying an awareness of his follies (*Pl. 199*).

The self-portrait however is not merely so much autobiographical information but from the artist's point of view a process of discovery, a means of finding out something about this mysterious reflection of form which proves to be himself, the projection of which he seems sometimes to view with the curiosity and surprise evoked by the unknown. The revelation is probably more complete as the artist feels himself the more detached.

Among the greatest portraits are those produced late in life and in the detachment of age. The self-portrait of the aged Titian in the Prado, the head of Leonardo as he drew it, burdened with knowledge and saddened by experience and the later Rembrandts, have their affinity in lonely grandeur.

THE ANIMAL WORLD

The astonishing variety of organic form presented by the animal world, including the creatures of land, sea and air has inspired artists since the earliest times. In painting broadly surveyed there is the whole evolutionary story, first of a world in which animals were the main factor and man an interloper, the record of countless conflicts between man and beast and then the long process of domestication. An initial surprise of painting is the naturalism of prehistoric man or man of later times living in similar conditions, as represented by the cave art of south-west France and northern Spain and in Africa by the art of the Bushman.

201 Prehistoric art: the 'Chinese horse' of Lascaux

The hunter-artist may be assumed to have gained a sense of movement and character from constant and necessarily keen observation of the quarry; and of structure from the process of dissection – rather as the Renaissance artist perfected his knowledge of human anatomy. The great merit of this prehistoric art was the faculty it shows for abstracting the essential from the non-essential, for simplifying and emphasizing both outline and dimension. A few decisive strokes in red ochre made with some primitive brush were sufficient vividly to portray the woolly rhinoceros of a receding Ice Age (Dordogne, Font-de-Gaume). With limited means the Aurignacian artist (twenty to thirty thousand? years ago) depicted the shaggy force of the bison, the brisk movement of the wild pony in the wonderful caves of Lascaux (*Pl. 201*).

The animal was more important than the individual man who is pictured in relatively crude fashion. This again appears in the art of primitive southern Africa where antelope and giraffe are depicted with a delicate appreciation of their character in contrast with the rudimentary silhouette of the human being. A like power of expressing truth to type but with a more consciously decorative sense of pattern and silhouette is found in the more highly developed ancient cultures. The Greek vase painter could achieve such exquisite combinations of naturalism and stylization as are shown in the deer and cocks on two cups of *c.* 540–530 BC (Louvre, *Pl. 202*).

The ancient Mediterranean world was much aware of the rich variety of forms contained in the sea. A Cretan painter, 1500–1400 BC, transfers the waving tentacles of a squid to an amphora (Athens, National Museum) with no loss of realism. A Roman mosaicist depicting a diversity of marine fauna seems to have had as imaginative a feeling for form which brings to mind Paul Klee's *Golden Fish* (Hamburg, Kunsthalle, *Pls. 203, 204*).

203 (*above right*) Paul Klee *Golden Fish* 1925

204 (*below right*) Roman mosaic with deep-sea fish

202 Greek cup with deer

205 Albrecht Dürer
The Hare 1502

The artists of China, Japan, Persia and India have studied animals with a special subtlety and sympathy. The contemplative humour and calligraphic manner of the Chinese makes the reduction to essentials the finest of arts, as in a southern Sung painting by Mu-Ch'i (thirteenth century A D) of a wild goose in flight preparing to land. A sympathy which a European painter would perhaps be unable to show for an animal exotic from his point of view but familiar to the Indian can be appreciated in the elephant wallowing in a lotus pond, painted in the Ajanta caves (*Pl. 206*).

The medieval artist in Europe on the contrary was so far concerned with the spiritual as opposed to the animal world as to give only a crude notion of cattle ploughing or of an unnatural natural history in the Bestiaries containing many fabulous creatures. It was only with the new interest in science and desire for universal knowledge of the Renaissance that the animal world was again studied with the close attention that Dürer gives it in the studies preserved in the Albertina such as the famous watercolour of a young hare (*Pl. 205*).

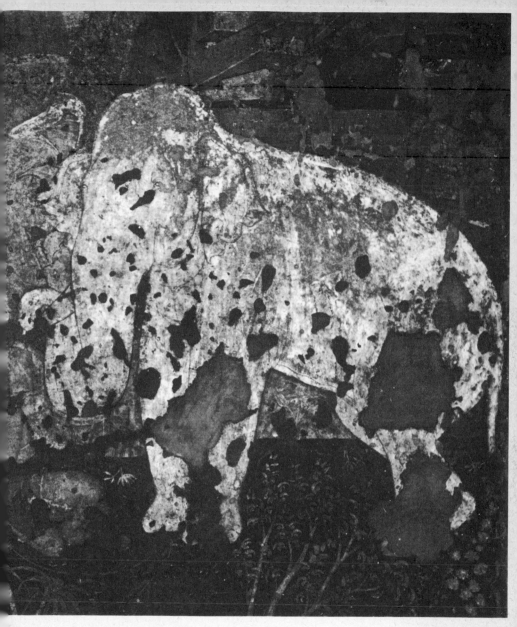

206 Ajanta fresco: *Elephant in a lotus lake* mid-fifth century

207 Stubbs *Horses and Foals* 1760–9

208 Pisanello *Vision of St Eustace* (detail)

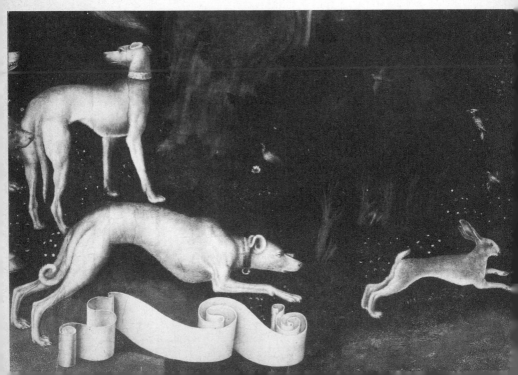

As a feature of European oil painting animals on the whole have been subsidiary, of interest as seen in a role secondary to that of human beings or sometimes as a delightful bonus of the artist's skill in a composition in which they have no necessary part. It is one of the pleasures of looking at Old Master pictures to single out these details – in the National Gallery for example the playful leopard that rolls over in Rubens's *War and Peace*, the cheetahs that draw the car of Bacchus in Titian's *Bacchus and Ariadne* (*Pl. 91*), the stag, greyhound and hare of Pisanello's *Vision of St Eustace* (*Pl. 208*). An anthology of horse, dog and cat would stretch from ancient to modern times and both East and West have lavishly contributed to it.

One must distinguish however the specialist interest of subject either for the sportsman or the student of natural history from that of the great work of art. Horse portraits have been produced primarily for the satisfaction or information of those engaged in horse-breeding. Paintings of cattle are of interest only as incidents in a composition. Among the British sporting painters, George Stubbs stands out as a great pictorial designer and not simply as an expert in equine anatomy (*Pl. 207*). The horses of Rubens, Géricault and Delacroix have an energy or violence in which the spirit of the artists themselves is to be traced. The horses of Degas are the vehicle for his unconventional rendering of movement. For any informative purpose animal life is nowadays best appreciated through photography.

STILL-LIFE AND FLOWER PAINTING

In representing at close range objects either natural or man-made – flowers, fruit, foodstuffs, glass, fabrics, pottery, musical instruments, earthenware, porcelain, objects of wood or metal – the painter is most intimately and exclusively concerned with the texture and colour of material things and the effect of light falling on their various surfaces, hard or soft, polished or matt, opaque or translucent. Without the distraction of more complex subject-matter the artist is free to give concentrated attention to form and colour and appreciation likewise is directed to these essentials.

As a separate art form it is largely the product of Europe from the seventeenth century onwards and oil paint, so apt to convey solidity of substance, niceties of gradation, richness of colour and light and shade and varieties of surface, has been the main vehicle. Yet great painters of earlier date have shown a manifest pleasure in the small accessories of still-life. The vases of myrtle by the window, the table with its hour-glass and open book are minutely detailed in Carpaccio's *The Dream of St Ursula* (Venice, Accademia), their very familiarity adding to the dream atmosphere in which the angel appears (*Pl. 209*).

Van Eyck's great Arnolfini picture (London, National Gallery) has its magic mirror (*Pl. 57*). Holbein's portrait of

209 Still-life in accessories: Carpaccio *The Dream of St Ursula* (detail)

210 Caravaggio *Basket of Fruit c.* 1596

George Gisze, merchant of the Steelyard, (Berlin) gives its various clues to the occupation of a man of business – scales, inkhorn, quill, ledgers, invoices. The popularity of the Banker and Wife pictures of Quentin Massys and Marinus van Weymerswael seems to have been bound up with the balances, the heaps of coin, the files of documents the artists so precisely painted (*Pl. 150*).

Caravaggio in the early sixteenth century was one of the first to give still-life a separate importance. This appears in a picture of a basket of fruit unusual in a time of elaborate figure composition (*Pl. 210*). His several pictures of musicians, such as the *Player on the Theorbo* (Turin), show also how the shape of the musical instrument interested him in itself.

229

211 Independent still-life: Pieter Claesz van Haarlem *Still-life c.* 1640

The cultivation of the independent still-life was however greater in the North than in Italy. In Holland, like portraiture, it was cultivated with the secularization of art following the Reformation. Though it was not confined to Protestant countries. The realism of Spanish painting produced a school of still-life in which Zurbarán, Sanchez Cotan and Luis Eugenio Meléndez are eminent. In England however the art gained no foothold. The Netherlands north and south were its main seventeenth-century centre.

Some trace of religious thought remained in the *Vanitas*, a form of still-life serving as a reminder of the vanity of human wishes in picturing a skull, a guttering candle and other symbols of the shortness of material existence. Still-lifes in which bread and wine were main features were perhaps a memory of the

Communion. Yet Dutch and Flemish still-life has different associations from these in its two main forms. The first speaks of the pleasures of the table and its luxurious appurtenances (*Pl. 211*). Specialists such as Claes Heda and Willem Kalf, temptingly rendered the pearly sheen of oysters, the vermilion lobster shell, the glitter of elaborately-chased goblets. Flemish painters depicted the spoils of the chase. Frans Snyders, in opulent still-lifes, derives a fractional part from the universal abundance of Rubens.

This materialistic form of art has a minor place when it gives no more than an imitation of inanimate matter. Standards of both design and feeling assign a superiority to the still-life of Zurbarán in which there is something of the austere simplicity that attaches to his paintings of religious zealots. Though inspired by Dutch and Flemish example, Chardin gives a new

212 Chardin *Bowl of Plums*

refinement and even grandeur to similar subjects, explicable only in the last analysis as a superior quality of mind (*Pl. 212*).

The painting of flowers, especially cultivated in the Netherlands has a long history. The miniaturist of the fifteenth century sets out in realistic fashion on his vellum page the humble flowers of the field, daisy, fennel, violet, columbine. The Flemish painters of the first great period included recognizable flowers in their religious compositions – the *Adoration of the Lamb* contains the herbal of a terrestrial paradise. Among its plants are the yellow flag, blue iris, celandine, watercress, milfoil, violet and lily of the valley. Saxifrage, clematis, poppy, wild narcissus and forget-me-not are to be found in the compositions of Van der Weyden.

The flowers of religious art were not only an addition of beautiful detail, they had their symbolic meaning: the lily, an emblem of purity; the violet, of modesty; the lily of the valley, of humility; the iris, of majesty. The rose in the numerous paintings of the Virgin of the Rose Bower seems at once the symbol of virginity and the dolour of the thorn. Symbolism lingers in the portraiture of the sixteenth century when the artist so often shows the sitter with a bloom between forefinger and thumb – a pink perhaps, not a sign of aestheticism but either a token of betrothal or of the medicinal protection its distilled essence was supposed to give against the plague.

At a later date the flower stood for the fleeting nature of all beauty – in the *Vanitas* still-life as practised by such seventeenth-century painters as A. van Nieulandt and Henri Andriessen. The religious association persists in the paintings by 'Velvet' Brueghel, Daniel Seghers and others who surround a religious subject with floral garlands as in the *Virgin of the Garland* (Louvre), the collaborative *tour de force* of Brueghel and Rubens (*Pl. 213*).

A main factor, however, in creating the flower-piece was the interest in floriculture. Its triumph was the tulip (a seventeenth-century exotic brought to northern Europe from Adrianople by an ambassador to Sultan Soliman). As Holland and Flanders vied in 'tulipomania' so did the Dutch and Flemish painters –

213 Brueghel and Rubens *Virgin of the Garland* 1621

Jan Brueghel, Roelandt Savery, Ambrosius Bosschaert and others – in their portrayal of prized and striking varieties, often grouped with other types of flower. Each is kept distinct as in a group portrait. A dark background and the subdued green of leaves bring out the brilliant colouring. The flower's insect

233

214 Paul Cézanne *Pomegranate and Pears c.* 1895–1900

court – bee, butterfly, caterpillar – remains a traditional detail
from the period of the manuscript miniature.

In Chinese and Japanese art flowers and plants have as
distinct a place as in the art of Europe. It is noticeable however
that the Oriental painter is concerned mainly with the idea of
growth and life in nature as represented for instance by blossom
on the bough and not the cut flower which has already become,
or is in process of becoming *nature morte*, the 'dead nature'
which is the French definition of still-life. In nineteenth-
century France, when the art of still-life was again brilliantly
cultivated, flowers were seen less and less either as botanical
specimens or as growing shapes with all the vitality these
contained but as incidents of light and colour. This more

215 Juan Gris *The Sunblind* 1914

generalized view applied also to paintings of fruit and objects of other kinds. Fantin-Latour is the last painter, perhaps, to make objective 'flower portraits'. Manet on the other hand paints a rose in a glass not so much as a rose but as an interception of light. Monet in the paintings of water lilies made in his old age carries the Impressionist aim of rendering the atmospheric effect of light to the point of almost complete abstraction.

The general course of still-life in France was that of the 'movements' of the time. The realism of Courbet leads him to concentrate on a massive contrast of light and shade. The Impressionists translate light into colour. Still-life for Cézanne was a profound study of the planes of which a solid object was composed and the nuance of colour attached to each. A plate of apples was enough to provide an intensity of research (*Pl. 214*). Van Gogh in contrast invests his sunflowers with a personal vehemence of feeling. In various ways still-life gained a new significance with the evolution of modern painting.

In the twentieth century it has been a main vehicle of the 'new way of seeing' represented by Cubism. The implication has been that our vision of objects in a fixed perspective is itself a convention, that objects may be seen in a different relation in space. Yet this radical conception has kept in view a relation with the familiar, as in the 'table-top' still-lifes of Braque, Picasso and Gris with their carafes, *compotiers*, newspapers and guitars reconstituted in relation, but recognizable still (*Pl. 215*). A quite different motive may be found in the attribution of 'magical' that is to say fantastic properties to form emerging from the minute imitation of detail. The American painter W. M. Harnett in the nineteenth century gives an instance of this 'magic' of illusion which has some modern examples also.

ABSTRACT AND NON-FIGURATIVE PAINTING

'Abstract' is a relative term. In painting it implies qualities of form and colour that have a value separate from that of imitating a specific object. They may however be found in conjunction or fusion with the forms that describe the visible world. All painting is abstract in some degree seeing that art is manifestly not nature but extracts something from nature, exercising the right of exclusion at the same time. The abstract may be said to consist in the general rather than the particular, just as in literature a work of philosophy deals with general ideas and a novel, in contrast, with the concrete instances of real life. A composition by Poussin with its generalizations of form is more abstract than the equivalent of a novel – a humorously detailed scene, for instance, by the genre painter, Jan Steen.

It is perfectly possible for the painter to arrive at an accommodation between nature and the abstract that actually increases the naturalism of effect. Whistler, perhaps the most abstract of nineteenth century artists, enables us to appreciate a phase of river twilight in what can alternatively be considered purely as an arrangement of colour and tone. Yet there are circumstances that lead artists to go further than selection from nature and to draw away from the recognizable image. The Muslim religious ban on the representation of human, animal and plant life was never strictly observed as witness the miniature painting and illustration of Persia and India which includes all these features. Nevertheless, it produced a strong tendency towards the abstract in calligraphy, pattern and the brilliance of colour used for non-naturalistic purposes. The Christian iconoclasm of the Byzantine Empire in the eighth and ninth centuries which for more than a hundred years banned the representation of figures in mosaics and paintings for churches made for a symbolic and non-representational art.

It is, however, with aims of their own that artists in modern times have not only cultivated the selective faculty and made more or less arbitrary use of nature but have isolated a completely non-representational or in the term now commonly used 'non-figurative' art. It results from several directions of thought converging. The idea that painting could 'aspire to the condition of music' and become equally free of imitation or description was one. The indifference of the French Impressionists to the scenic impressiveness of the landscapes they painted and the greater importance they attached to the colour in which they presented it also tended in this direction.

There was also the thought that art was or should be a spiritual expression coming from within, dissociated in its pure form from material conceptions. In this there is something of the iconoclastic outlook of Byzantium. It is not without historical relevance that Russia in whose art there was so much that was Byzantine and so little that was of the western tradition should have been the country of enthusiastic early exponents of non-figurative art such as Wassily Kandinsky and Kasimir Malevich.

The character of the modern age must also be taken into account as a factor shaping the forms of art. Scientific and mechanical development and the nature of modern urban life have had their effect. The movements that have been more particularly concerned with an expression of the age have tended to arrive at an abstract conclusion.

An example is Futurism which derived its impetus from the enthusiasm of artists for the liners, locomotives and automobiles of a new era of speed. Yet instead of pictures of these mechanical forms, in which they found beauty, the conception of speed or moving shapes produced a problem which straightforward portrayal would not solve. The attempt was made to represent simultaneously the various stages of movement as in Marcel Duchamp's *Nude Descending a Staircase* (Philadelphia Museum of Art, *Pl. 216*); or to give the idea of speed by showing the track of a racing-car. What in both cases resulted was an arrangement of abstract forms.

The De Stijl movement in Holland set the aim of finding a means of expression applicable to every kind of visual design. This attempt to set modern art in order was based not on abstraction as a process deriving something from nature but on the deliberate choice of the rectangle as entirely a conception of the human intelligence.

Much attention has been given to the process of reasoning that has produced a non-figurative art and in general it is not difficult to follow. Yet the results impose a severer test in appreciation than the painting which the world had so long been accustomed to regard as necessarily 'representational' that the adjective had hitherto never been regarded as necessary. There is still a division of view as to whether painting advances towards a liberation from 'impurities' in discarding subject-matter or whether it merely isolates certain phenomena thus sacrificing much that is humanly important or meaningful. It is probably best to consider what individual works stand out in more than a half century of abstract effort. A remarkable feature is the fact that though it has been international so much of individuality remains.

Kandinsky stands out as an innovator – one of the first to take the plunge into the deep end of abstract expression in the first decade of the twentieth century. He provides examples of its two main forms, the free improvisation of form and colour

216 Trend towards abstraction: Marcel Duchamp *Nude Descending a Staircase* 1912

and the geometrically conceived work in which circles, rectangles and triangles are variously assembled (*Pl. 5*). It is not so easy perhaps to establish his place as an artist as to admire his energy and audacity as a man of ideas. Considered from a purely aesthetic standpoint he may be thought (though this is a matter of opinion) often over-intricate in composition and without that sensitiveness of perception that appears even in a simple line or a touch of colour by his friend, Paul Klee (*Pl. 1*). These qualities in Klee seem the product of a mind less doctrinaire and a wider sympathy that springs from an interest in every aspect of the visible world.

It is the definiteness and austerity of Mondrian that compel admiration for his rectangular compositions of lines, creating panels like a heavily leaded and simple form of stained glass (*Pl. 7*). They make an uncompromising statement that allows no qualification but a special quality appears in the reminder of clarity and order they give. A similar refreshment may be gained from the elementary shapes of coloured paper which were a preoccupation with Matisse towards the end of his life.

A simplicity in which there are subtleties of vibration holds the attention in the coloured oblongs that partner each other with melting and uncertain edge in the work of the American painter, Mark Rothko (*Pl. 217*). In contrast is the free gesture of 'action painting' as practised by Jackson Pollock (*Pl. 29*). In principle this is an abrogation of all pictorial order but again one can appreciate the instinctive impulse of the true artist to create a work of beauty – from the chaotic procedure there emerges even a decorative unity.

Whether such works will be timeless in their interest and as rewarding to constant contemplation as the paintings of Old Masters is an open question. Yet in a concentrated form they give a tonic to appreciation and sharpen the eye.

A final product of the twentieth century's abstract inquiries and experiment is the research into movement. It has two aspects: firstly, the illusion of change in form as the optical result of certain arrangements of lines and abstract figures; secondly, as actual movement mechanically controlled. The illusion in its

217 Mark Rothko *Number 10* 1950

simplest aspect is like that most people have probably experienced when looking at the patterned flooring of black and white squares which seem alternatively to project and become hollow. The device is elaborated in the paintings of Victor Vasarely (*Pl. 218*) and in the black and white linear designs of Bridget Riley. Or again areas of line and colour on two planes may be so related that the effect changes as the spectator moves, as in the work of the Venezuelan artists, Soto and Cruxent.

The projection of moving shapes of colour is an extension of non-figurative painting. It has antecedents in the kaleidoscope of the nineteenth century and the 'colour organ', and a contemporary parallel in the colour film. It might be said that cinematography already has a highly developed technique which makes the artist's experiments seem elementary or superfluous. Yet there is a difference of aim inasmuch as the film is an illustrative form of entertainment and the projection of abstract colour a purely aesthetic idea.

How are these developments related to painting in the past? In one aspect they are a logical outcome of the conceptions of abstract art proposed by such painters as Kandinsky, and such other pioneers of the non-representational as the Czech painter František Kupka and the French painter Robert Delaunay. On the other hand they depart from picture painting as understood in the past in their 'instant' and 'expendable' nature. A dazzle effect of lines and squares is not one that the eye can study with physical comfort for more than a limited time. The changing colour lasts only as long as the motive power is in operation. It is the point of great pictures that they do not move but provide endless matter for contemplation. The idea of movement they offer (as has already been remarked) is not a physical but an intellectual property inherent in their static nature.

These are reasons for anticipating that any future extension of optic and kinetic experiment will separate it further from painting as hitherto understood and will link it with schemes of lighting and colour in architectural and urban use and the practical purposes of signs and advertisement. Another

218 Victor Vasarely *Cintra* 1955–6

criterion comes into being. Changes of light and colour in a stage performance can have a markedly emotional influence on the spectator and the skill with which they are contrived may well call for admiration. No doubt there are possibilities still to be explored to which chromatic experiment will contribute. But the attempt to compare the chromatic scheme of an opera with – let us say – a painting by Tiepolo would not only be far-fetched, it would force two entirely different things into relation.

There are some modern artists – Marcel Duchamp gives a celebrated example – whose attitude suggests that painting is an art form in process of being superseded by the solution of another variety of visual problems. This however is not to make one conclude that painting is finished, but rather that some who began as painters have not found the art to be their true *métier*.

219 Bronzino *Venus, Cupid, Folly and Time*

CHAPTER FIVE

The Qualities of a Masterpiece

Many of the works discussed may be called with good reason 'masterpieces' though this is a word often somewhat loosely used. In its original sense it applied to the painting which attested the apprentice's mastery of his craft. It refers us back to the time when painting was a workshop industry. The history of many great painters of the past begins with apprenticeship at an early age. After much routine work, the grinding of colours, preparing of canvases, and a measure of collaboration on the less important parts of the master's design, a youth would eventually produce a work to satisfy the mature practitioners and secure admittance to their guild.

The guilds of which Italy and the Netherlands offer main examples from the fourteenth to the seventeenth centuries declined with the rise of academies and the growing individual status of the painter. A more symbolic proof of mastery was required for instance by the 'diploma work' demanded of the newly elected member of the Royal Academy, though this was not a sign of graduation as the painter when elected might already have had years of success and distinction.

Alternatively it is possible to speak of the masterpiece of one particular artist as that which is better than anything else he did or most completely sums up the character of his work, though in comparison with other artists he may or may not be ranked high. There are instances of painters who have excelled themselves in one exceptional work. The Florentine painter, Bronzino, produced many able portraits but rises to an unexpected height in the beautiful allegory *Venus, Cupid, Folly and Time* (Pl. *219*).

The masterpiece which has most significance for those looking at pictures is naturally that with an absolute rather than a relative value, valid at all times and for all the world. It could be summed up as no longer 'abiding the question' or to put this in another way as a work on the great merits of which everyone is agreed. It may be regarded from various points of view. If we know nothing of painting technically it will still speak to us understandingly of human life. At the same time it will constantly reveal felicities of colour, brushwork, drawing that hold the more for the eye the more they are studied.

In the fusion of thought, feeling and technique, a great masterpiece is at once simple and infinite in its variety. The word 'creative' in modern usage tends to be spoilt by rather indiscriminate application, but the fusion is truly creative in imparting to the great painting a life of its own. In this there is an element of mystery, as all life is mysterious. The whole is something different from the sum of its parts. When we have analysed the craft and science of the painter, considered his aim and direction of thought and how it is expressed, the fascinating mystery of the whole work remains.

Among Titian's many masterpieces, *Sacred and Profane Love* (Rome, Borghese Gallery) is an instance of this completeness (*Pl. 135*). The title, which was not Titian's own but a later invention, may be set aside as offering no particular clue to his intentions. One might just as well accept the simpler title, *Beauty Clothed and Unclothed* by which it was known when in Cardinal Scipio Borghese's Collection. Pictorially the two figures provide quite simply a harmony of contrast. Contrast is emphasized by the different aspects of landscape in the background, hill and plain. The raised left arm of the nude figure offsets the right arm at rest of the clothed figure, the rich red of a sleeve balances the rich and larger area of a red cloak; the small area of white fabric round the right-hand figure's thigh balances the gown of the left-hand. The foreground plant, strongly silhouetted, unifies by leaning slightly in either direction. The arm of the little cherub dipping into the wellhead emphasizes its curve while the opposing curve of the figure on the stone relief directs the eye upward to the right. Light forms are cunningly opposed to dark; the dark bowl held by the nude against the sky, the rabbits behind the seated figure as a point of light against the dark ground.

All these factors contribute to the unity of the painting but the whole becomes a poem of warmth and ripeness alike in the flesh tones, the depth of green, the serene pink cloud of the sky. Analysis is secondary to the feeling of sumptuous idyll.

How many factors combine to create the profound impression that *Las Meninas* of Velazquez (Prado) makes? To see it as a picture of Court life in seventeenth-century Spain is obvious enough. The little Infanta Margarita Maria, suffering the tedium of having her portrait painted is being coaxed by one of the maids-of-honour and diverted by the presence of dog and Court dwarfs. It is also a wonderful presentation of space and dimension, seen as it were from every angle at once (*Pl. 220*).

The artist is in two places, unseen and outside the picture, looking in and also at his easel behind the group he had depicted. The King and Queen watch also from outside the picture but are reflected in the mirror at the back of the room, their image contrasting spectrally with the sharp silhouette of the Chamberlain at the open door beside them. An almost stereoscopic effect is contrived by the huge foreground canvas which suggests a long perspective to the open door at the far end. The bright sunlight beyond it emphasizes the dusky vastness of the interior. The abstract design composed by the canvas stretcher, the window-frames and the symmetrically placed paintings and mirror makes a foil to the varied incident of dress and gesture in the foreground group. The picture conveys at once the vivid sense of actuality and an infinite subtlety of vision.

Among Rembrandt's many masterpieces, the *Shooting Company of Captain Frans Banning Cocq* (Amsterdam, Rijksmuseum) which has acquired the misleading title *The Night Watch* from its strong oppositions of light and dark is a famous picture that never ceases to attract wonder as a composition of movement (*Pl. 221*). It is a great instance of the variety that may be contained within unity. One can take in at a glance the essential design radiating outwards from the advancing central figures.

220 Velazquez *Las Meninas* 1656

222 (*opposite*) Gerrit Lundens' copy of *The Night Watch*, indicating how ▶
Rembrandt's painting looked when complete

221 Rembrandt *The Night Watch* 1642

Then the eye is led into the amazing resource with which light is distributed, with which guns, pikes, the drum, the standard, the gestures of moving figures are so distributed as to build up the dramatic and orchestral effect.

It is unfortunate that the painting was cut down on all four sides early in the eighteenth century but the copy made of the original by Gerrit Lundens (London, National Gallery, *Pl. 222*), which enables us to see its complete state has a lesson to impart also in showing with what exactness a masterpiece is planned so that nothing can be altered without detriment. The copy shows us how essential to the total effect was the greater height of the original with the arch in itself dramatic (reminiscent of the arch in Raphael's *School of Athens*, *Pl. 41*), how the pike-bearer to the left and the drummer to the right become more dynamic factors in being closer within the picture space, how the rail to the left stresses the diagonal which is caught up on the right by the angle of a pike. The warm harmony of colour in the original with its greatest intensity in the contrast of black and yellow in the uniforms of the two advancing officers completes a universality of pictorial science that incorporates also the mysterious drama of human life.

Even a few examples from the great list of masterpieces of the first order define for us the idea of genius as a quality which distinguished an artist from all others, however much in some aspect of technique he may have been influenced by other painters. We can see also how 'beauty', a conception which has haunted the minds of so many philosophers of aesthetics, is not some one recognizable objective towards which all painters strive but is a fresh creation each time genius makes its unique combination of means to a personal end. Analysis enables us to see how they make use of means that are at the disposal of all painters but the order they impose on the infinite permutations possible of form, colour, light and shade and spatial effect is ultimately their own. Each masterpiece is a new world to explore, a fresh visual experience.

A question that may well come to mind however is whether the masterpiece does not now belong to the past. The value now set on instinctive expression may seem to upset the balance of thought, feeling and craft. A 'masterpiece of expression' may appear something of a contradiction in terms if we assume expression to be that which comes out spontaneously and is distinct from controlled and deliberate effort. Then again the tendency to isolate some particular factor in painting from others, as in abstract art, while it may bring out its visual interest to the full may entail also an impoverishment in other respects, a lack of the universality that is to be found in the greatest works.

The difficult problems which tested the full measure of a painter's abilities tend to be set aside in the entire freedom of painting. Without something to struggle against or to struggle towards art begins to atrophy or petrify into some easy convention, or lapse into a mere nihilism. In the second half of the twentieth century it can be seen there is a struggle to get away from inherited art forms though it is not possible as yet to make more than a tentative judgment of its value.

An inquiry as to the masterpieces of the last hundred years would provide more confident answers in the earlier rather than the later part of the period. If one takes as a standard the quality that makes a work distinct from all others and the deep general impression it has made or seems to have the capacity of making, the *Bohémienne Endormie* (New York, Museum of Modern Art) of Henri Rousseau, the *Portrait of Jeanne Hebuterne* by Modigliani (Edinburgh, National Gallery of Scotland), *The Melancholy and Mystery of a Street* by de Chirico (New York, Museum of Modern Art), the *Bride of the Winds* by Oskar Kokoschka (Basle, Kunstmuseum), *Guernica* by Picasso (New York, Museum of Modern Art, *Atelier* by Braque (Maeght Collection), *The Eye of Silence* by Max Ernst (Washington University, St Louis) are some of the works that stand out in the twentieth century, though any list offers room for opinion and opens up still controversial distinctions between what is currently exciting and what will last.

223 Georges de la Tour *St Sebastian attended by St Irene c.* 1631

CHAPTER SIX

The Spectator's Involvement

In the foregoing chapters the attempt has been made to describe essential factors, the varying circumstances and aims that go to the making of the painting as a work of art. A final question is how far a system of appreciation may be deduced from such particulars. The answer must be that no rigid system will serve. Some knowledge of the painter's methods and materials, the properties and potentialities of the media used are of value to the extent that they enable the spectator to see as the painter saw. Yet it is evidently not necessary for the spectator to have all the equipment of a practising painter or to be a painter also. The total result is what concerns him. Analysis, while it may enable us to admire some constructive aspect of the painter's work, is by its nature a process of dismembering and so necessarily incomplete.

There are canons of judgment which are serviceable in some applications but not in others. The idea of the 'Grand Style' is an appropriate measure of the achievement of the High Renaissance but it loses its meaning if we attempt to judge a realistic art by an idealistic standard. It would be absurd to complain that Goya does not give us the ideal human figures of Michelangelo or that the French Impressionists were more occupied with light and atmosphere.

As great painters are each unique and individual in what they produce it follows that appreciation has in some degree to be adjusted to their varying qualities. This which is obvious in other arts should be obvious also in painting. In poetry for instance Alexander Pope is clearly differentiated from Thomas Gray. The attempt to judge the author of the *Essay on Man* by the same criterion as the author of *The Bard* would result in as prejudiced a verdict as Dr Johnson gave in his *Lives of the Poets*.

William Blake trenchantly remarked that, 'Genius dies with its Possessor & comes not again till Another is born with it.'

It is of primary importance to like something but 'liking' is to be distinguished from a critical appraisal which will set aside a predisposition to assume that likes and dislikes have a necessary bearing on the question of what is good or otherwise. It may well happen that individuals who come newly to painting do not yet really know what they like or what is worth liking but find out as time goes on what paintings are of the first order and what, perhaps more appreciated to begin with, are in reality of a trivial kind. This, on a larger scale, seems to have been the tendency of history. Taste has constantly varied yet the good eventually comes to light and prevails even if this takes a considerable time.

It was long before the world recognized such great artists as Piero della Francesca, Vermeer of Delft and Georges de la Tour at their true worth. Georges de la Tour was a superb seventeenth-century French master who remained in oblivion until our own time. How could the author of those torch-lit or candle-lit groups which now seem so wonderfully original and to possess so much breadth of style and depth of feeling have been overlooked? Possibly because he painted no portraits of important personages; or perhaps because, though he painted religious subjects, they were pictures of a lay kind that did not gain the prominence of figuring in a church. At all events it was as an anonymous work that the writer on art, Louis Gonse, viewed the *Nativity* of the Musée de Rennes in 1900, a 'strange and delightful picture' to which he hesitated to attach a painter's name. The mysterious unknown was studied with the result that in the exhibition of *Painters of Reality in Seventeenth Century France* held in Paris in 1934, twelve paintings proclaimed the rank of Georges de-la Tour beyond doubt (*Pl. 223*).

Again some new line of thought in painting may at intervals throw sudden light on an old, a forgotten or underestimated master. They are seen with quickened interest and pleasure as 'modern' in having a kinship of feeling and aim with the present day. This applies not only to little-known painters

254

summoned from obscurity to confirm some aspect of modern experience but to those whom we might think always to have been known well.

Jerome Bosch had to wait four hundred years until modern interest in the curious workings of the mind investigated the whole subject of fantastic art. Surrealism which claimed Bosch among its forerunners contributed to the esteem in which he has come to be held.

It might appear far-fetched to say that Turner has been rescued from either obscurity or neglect but for a long time his later work was imperfectly understood. The bias of personal taste is evident in even so recent a critic as Roger Fry who applied the standard of 'plastic form' in which he found Turner sadly wanting. Abstract art more recently has helped to create the mood in which we can better appreciate Turner's gorgeous 'colour poems' and the elemental forces of the *Fire at Sea* (*Pl. 224*) and *Burning of the Houses of Parliament*. Claude Monet, too, fell in repute through the reaction in favour of solid structure in painting which followed the Impressionist triumphs of 1870–80. When he died in 1926 his last efforts to grasp every atmospheric nuance of his pool of water lilies at various times of day were regarded as pushing a theory to an eccentric extreme. In the light of abstract developments in art these paintings have again been admired as approaching the very essence of light.

A new line of thought has prejudices of its own and may obscure some aspects of a painter's art while it clarifies our view of others. A complete view of Turner or Monet is not the same as that inspired subjectively by some specifically modern interest. Of a many-sided artist's work there are always facets outside immediate focus though their existence becomes more apparent with each new direction of approach.

Thus a process of adjustment is constantly at work. It is strange now to think of the immense hostility that greeted the most original paintings of the nineteenth century. The *Déjeuner sur l'Herbe* and *Olympia* of Manet (*Pl. 88*) were greeted with fury when shown in Paris. The paintings of Cézanne were derided as the work of an incompetent or feared as the work of an ogre. If Van Gogh gained any attention at all it was as a madman. The outcry in Paris had its later parallel when Post-Impressionism and its sequels were presented to English eyes in the Grafton Gallery Exhibition of 1910–11, and when a large exhibition of modern art startled America in the Armory Show at New York in 1913.

Why, it might be asked, were painted canvases capable of producing so fevered a reaction? The idea for instance that Manet's nudes were an offence against morality, though part of the charge against him, was a mere fiction. It seems more likely that in this and other instances subject entered little into the matter and that the actual change of vision required to take in a new treatment of colour and form was a painful process. A later generation which looked with unprejudiced eyes found no difficulty in appreciation.

This is not merely a change of taste. It can be said with confidence that the good is durable. The changes of view, far from pointing to the non-existence of standards indicate that the standards affirm themselves by an almost inevitable action. The continued practice of looking at paintings tends to sift out the trivial and ephemeral from what is of permanent value as a work of art. We may return with a certain pleasure to some paintings characteristic of the period when they were produced for no other reason than the information they give about a type of society and its ways. From this point of view it could even be said that all paintings are equal. But a reference to works that transcend their period gives a sense of proportion of another kind.

It is only in comparatively recent times – and in this we are fortunate today – that the full wealth of the world's painting has come within the range of public vision. Admiration in the West was once confined to the centuries of European painting in which the Renaissance was the central fact. Admiration has extended at equal pace with knowledge.

The discovery of early Italian, Netherlandish and German painting was an aspect of the revived sympathy of the nineteenth century for the Middle Ages of principal importance in bringing

256

224 Turner *Fire at Sea c.* 1834

the so-called 'primitives' within the scope of appreciation. The discovery of Byzantine art which was once regarded as a sorry decline from Classical standards belongs to the twentieth century. The thousand years it covered were previously seen only politically in Gibbon's terms of decline and fall. The greatness of its legacy, the splendour of such a phase as its twelfth-century renaissance, have only recently been revealed.

The wonders of prehistoric art were unknown until the cave of Altamira was explored less than a century ago, bearing its message that picture-making was independent of time and material progress. The art of the Far East was not treated with any great seriousness in Europe until European painters in the

257

second half of the nineteenth century were inspired by the design and controlled colour harmonies of the Japanese print. Chinese painting has brought with it to modern eyes a fresh regard for the contemplative, poetic and calligraphic aspects of painting.

By virtue of this widening of interest there is an immense gain in the possibility it provides of seeing painting, like the other visual arts, independently of time and place and as a great legacy and testimony not of a few nations, within narrow limits of date, but of the human race. The language is essentially the same, though it has many dialects and offers an infinite choice from its resources. Assuming this, the spectator may approach works of very different origin with a pleasure undiminished by distances material or psychological that might seem otherwise to interpose a barrier.

The habit of looking at many pictures and pictures of different kinds is certainly a good one in cultivating a broad view and in keeping the vision alert and receptive to new experience. Yet this is not a matter of haste. A quick tour of a great picture gallery such as some people are apt to make is likely to produce no more than physical exhaustion and visual confusion. The great educators of painting are the paintings themselves. Theirs are the lessons to be heeded with care and allowance of time. It is more illuminating to spend a certain time with one master-work than with fifty. Indeed, one can visit such a work any number of times and still find it has something new to tell. The eye may be refreshed on such occasions by comparison between paintings of a comparable kind in school and period but would only be jaded by trying to take in too many impressions at once.

One can start anywhere. While chronology has an obvious importance in the study of art history and will certainly be referred to by the interested visitor to a gallery, a methodical study by date is not the first essential of appreciation. Historically, the spectacle is one of constant change but, as has been pointed out, not of consistent progress in the sense that painting proceeds from a crude beginning and 'improves' with the

225 Cimabue
Crucifixion
thirteenth century

material progress of civilization. This is a fallacy that in the past labelled Italian painters of the fourteenth to early fifteenth centuries and Flemish painters of the fifteenth century 'primitive' with a disparaging implication. When Sir Charles Eastlake proposed the purchase of early Italian masters by the National Gallery in the 1830s, Sir Robert Peel objected on the ground that 'we should not collect curiosities'. The term would now seem absurd as applied to Cimabue's *Crucifixion* (Pl. *225*) or the works of Giotto and his circle. It was once usual to regard European art as having two great peaks – in Classical Greece and Renaissance Italy. The progress of art was viewed as an ascent to a similar height or a descent from it to an inferior state. But the increased knowledge and understanding of modern times shows that each period has its excellence as represented by individuals who defy comparison in their own individual

259

expression. A great gallery therefore has a multitude of focal points, each having its special message to convey.

It is the great individual who counts for most and can most profitably be studied as such, even to the exclusion of 'period' considerations altogether. There are for instance Dutch painters of the seventeenth century who have more information to give about the taste and character of Holland and are more typical of the Dutch school than Rembrandt. In a number of respects he

Development of the individual: 226 Raphael *Vision of a Knight*

227 Raphael *Paul and Barnabas at Lystra c.* 1516

is untypical: in his very personal preoccupation with religious themes and his scant interest in painting those good things of the table that delighted his contemporaries. As a still-life his *Slaughtered Ox* was entirely unconventional and long considered revolting though it is a demonstration that any subject ceases to be 'ugly' when a great master invests it with the beauty of his paint and the quality of mind to which nothing is alien.

Change is to be found in the individual as well as in the periods of art. The great painter does not stand still. One of the adjustments the spectator must make is often to the remarkable difference between the works of a painter in youth and age. One might consider for example the great difference between Raphael as the pupil of Perugino and Raphael as he expanded in the stirring atmosphere and amid the powerful influences of Rome. A fascinating contrast is afforded by the delicate *Vision of a Knight* (London, National Gallery), painted when he was about the age of sixteen and the great Cartoons (London, Victoria and Albert Museum) that show him in the plenitude of his powers (*Pls. 226, 227*). There is a contrast, at first almost like that of two different beings, between the early topographical Turner and the Turner who converts the interior of Petworth into a gorgeous abstraction of colour, several stages of development intervening.

How can one best appreciate the many subtleties involved? Is there some special faculty required to distinguish not only the best from the second or third best but the authentic from the imitation? By what process does the innocent eye become the expert eye? An essential part of the answer to each of these questions is by training the eye and an essential part of this training is familiarity.

Some familiarity with the work of Rembrandt for example would show many a hopeful person with no especial interest in pictures that the old canvas found in an attic was not the work of that master. It needs only the briefest inspection by the trained eye of the gallery official to arrive at the conclusion that a picture submitted is or is not of any artistic value (the great majority of such works are usually to be found without). The expert of course has the advantage of long and close study backed by knowledge of the historical and documentary factors, though it has to be recognized that when style is the basis of judgment the expert also may encounter difficult problems, leaving room for differences of opinion.

There is an evident distinction between the assessment of qualities belonging to a good painting, whether or not its author is known, and the more specific task of deciding whether it is to be attributed to a particular artist. What, if indeed anything, Hubert van Eyck contributed to the great altarpiece at Ghent, which an inscription assigns to him jointly with his brother Jan van Eyck, is still a matter of debate. There has been much controversy about attributions to Giorgione. Bought for the National Gallery as his work, the *Scenes from an Eclogue of Tebaldeo* incited lengthy discussion. This exemplifies the speculative process, the various shots round the target which

228 Van Meegeren *Supper at Emmaus*, a Vermeer forgery

eventually narrow down to a likely and generally acceptable
conclusion, in this case a change of attribution to the lesser
talents of Andrea Previtali.

The history of the *Portrait of Don Adrian Pulido Pareja* (London,
National Gallery) formerly attributed to Velazquez and now to
Juan Bautista del Mazo is instructive. It was probably a copy
of a lost original by Velazquez. Its attribution to him was based
on a documentary reference which had little validity as proof.
The general design reflected that of the master but evidently the
purchasers in 1890 did not look as closely as the experts who
have since pointed out that the brushwork is 'clearly only a
feeble imitation' and the signature a palpable fake.

Material methods of examination such as micro-chemical analysis and radio-photography may tend to confirm or disprove authenticity but they cannot name a painter for us. The evidence of style and character is still of primary importance requiring in the specialist a feeling for painting, a measure of intuition as well as a familiar acquaintance with the methods of individual painters. An instinct often seems to come into play either in scenting out a 'find' or alternatively in the unease which first signals that a painting is somehow 'not right'.

There are paintings which give or should give the same amount of visual satisfaction whether we know who painted them or not, though the fact can scarcely be overlooked that an authenticated Rembrandt is worth a great deal more in financial terms than a painting that is simply 'School of . . .'. It seems likely that almost everything, old or modern, to which a considerable financial value is attached has been plausibly faked, not by the imitation of a known work which could easily be detected, but in manner of execution and type of subject. A canvas of the right age, colours of the right kind, cracks simulating the effect of age, the style of brushwork, may all be combined in an oil painting that may long deceive.

The work of the famous forger, Van Meegeren who took in the art world with his supposed discovery of a Vermeer, *Supper at Emmaus* (Rotterdam, Boymans Museum), is a case in point (*Pl. 228*). It is to be noted, however, that a forger, even one so highly skilled, could only imitate a lesser aspect of a great painter's work. Van Meegeren for instance copies the style of Vermeer at an early stage of his career when it was not fully distinct from that of others. There is, even so (though this may sound like being wise after the event), little enough of seventeenth-century feeling – an elusive factor however which was not pinned down at the time it was 'discovered'. What is certain is that the forger could not have produced out of his own imagination a 'Vermeer' with the mature mastery and originality of the *Allegory of Painting* (Vienna, Kunsthistorisches Museum, *Pl. 229*). This was not a stock subject but a unique conception which even the artist himself would not repeat. Such

265

229 Vermeer *Allegory of Painting c.* 1664 (detail)

works effectively demonstrate the difference between the skilled imitation and the genuine product of the original mind.

The approach to modern painting entails first some definition of the term 'modern'. If it refers to that living quality which the greatest works possess it may be thought of as independent of time. In a more specific sense it has no exact starting-point. The painting that seems particularly to belong to the twentieth century has emerged by an evolutionary process from that of the nineteenth century. A vast exhibition in Paris was needed to do justice to the complex origins of modern art from this point of view. This is something to give pause to the still not un-common tendency of those with an adverse prejudice of referring to modern art as if it were a sudden aberration.

As a rough guide to its appreciation in general terms one could point to two main threads. There is first a tendency to develop the means used to the end of giving a new intensity of expression. Colour claims the spectator's attention in being used not merely as a descriptive accessory but as a force calculated to affect the emotions in a fashion analogous to the effect of musical sound. Form has been subject to various kinds of emphases, distortions or simplifications which have an intensifying effect.

These tendencies have been abstract either in reducing subject-matter to a minor or nominal role or dispensing with it altogether. This is often a difficulty to a lay public which feels that a common ground, a way of 'communication' has thus been barred. The question of loss or gain has been earlier discussed. But instead of closing communication, the argument may be taken into account that painting of this kind opens the way to a greater degree of participation from the spectator. It is possible for instance in looking at some abstract works to bring to them figurative ideas of one's own – rather as Leonardo found his suggestions of figures and landscape in the abstractions of nature. Or more directly still, to follow and share the feelings of the painter in tracing a line or laying on colour without being diverted to associations which might obscure them.

One may prefer, on the ground of its richer content and

human significance, a composition by Veronese wonderfully replete with architecture, human figures, animals, and still-life detail to some simple juxtaposition of coloured threads by a contemporary; but if one were to consider the latter as the equivalent of a glass of clear spring water compared with a vintage wine one can see it as another kind of refreshment to the eye. Though there is evidently more to modern art than can be simplified in this fashion. Any historically well-defined period has always been distinct from others in its art. The twentieth century has been no exception.

Its opening years up to the First World War present an amazing spectacle of the formation of style in which the future development of the century is already forecast. The colour of the Fauves, the new translations of form in Cubism, the shaping of Expressionism in Germany, the appearance of non-figurative art, the Futurist effort to interpret movement, the imaginative symbolism of a painter such as de Chirico can be seen as history in the making, proclamations of the arrival of a new age. The artists' point of view has not always been as definite in paying tribute to the mechanical triumphs of progress as that of the Futurists. At a later date the Dadaists and Surrealists had no wish to identify themselves with a modern society, claiming on the contrary the timeless independence of the free and anarchic mind. Yet the interactions of all these movements have given shape to an art as distinctly of its period as 'International Gothic' or Baroque were of theirs.

If one chooses to extend the viewpoint to all the arts one may find a consonance between modern painting and modern architecture, music, drama, poetry. Its explorations parallel those of science. The swift succession of its phases, for which previous history offers little parallel, accelerating in recent years, correspond to the speed of social change. 'Period' characteristics are not necessarily a sign of quality in works of art. Like buildings of slight construction for which only a limited life is envisaged, there are contemporary paintings of which neither technique nor idea offers the prospect of permanence. These are an ephemeral aspect of public entertainment, in that they startle for a short while and are then likely to be forgotten.

They should not be the basis of a sweeping generalization, however. The abstract painting of today offers as many distinctions of quality as representational painting. The individual work rather than the school or labelled category is the proper subject of assessment. This can only be tentative because we are too close to the works in question to see them in the proportion that the perspective of time brings. It is scarcely possible for any age to see it as posterity will see it, though it is possible to say that one of the many exciting turning-points in the history of painting has been reached.

It is a history, in spite of all its changes, with a wonderful continuity. The superb extent of the panorama it offers to the spectator can be better appreciated in the exhibitions, reproductions and printed studies of the present time than ever before. As time goes on this continuity appears in additions tacitly made to the number of 'Old Masters' – a title once assigned only to European painters who lived at least three hundred years ago. The test of time and the consensus of the world's opinion admit, one by one, those of later date to join the select company that has ceased to abide the question.

Bibliographical Note

List of Illustrations

Index

Bibliographical Note

In a book designed to suggest ways of looking at pictures it might be said a bibliography is contained in the mentions made of those great works of reference, the museums and galleries themselves. But the direct experience of painting can be supplemented today by an unprecedented wealth of publications combining scholarship with the beauty of illustration. Histories of Schools, periods, styles, movements, accounts of the great collections, illustrated anthologies, monographs and biographies all have their particular bearing on the general theme of this book. A long list would be superfluous and unpractical considering the varied directions of taste and degrees of specialization that may be supposed in those interested in painting. Yet certain works and type of work may be singled out as particularly germane to the theme of appreciation.

Insight into the aims and ideas of painters may be gained from those who have set down their observations, published documents. They would include Leonardo's *Notebooks*, Hogarth's *Analysis of Beauty*, Sir Joshua Reynolds' *Discourses*, Delacroix's *Journal*, the *Letters* of Cézanne, Gauguin, Van Gogh, Whistler's *Gentle Art of Making Enemies* (especially for the Ten O'Clock Lecture), Maurice Denis, *Théories*, Kandinsky, *On the Spiritual in Art* and Klee, *On Modern Art* (both titles in English translation).

Books on method, the interest of which is not confined to the practising painter, include Sir Charles Eastlake, *Materials for a History of Oil Painting*, Sir Charles Holmes, *Notes on the Science of Picture Making*, W. G. Constable, *The Painter's Workshop*, Hilaire Hiler, *Notes on the Technique of Painting* and Moreau-Vauthier, *La Peinture* (translated as *The Technique of Painting*).

Modern critical views are set out in Roger Fry, *Vision and Design*, Bernard Berenson, *Aesthetics and History*, E. H. J. Gombrich, *Art and Illusion* and Sir Herbert Read, *The Meaning of Art*. Among many luminous general surveys are E. H. Gombrich, *The Story of Art*, André Malraux, *The Psychology of Art*, Bernard Berenson, *The Study and Criticism of Italian Art* and *Italian Painters of the Renaissance*, Sir Laurence Binyon's *The Art of the Far East*, Sir Herbert Read, *A Concise History of Modern Painting* and Lionello Venturi's *Modern Painters*. The painter's theme is deeply studied in Sir Kenneth Clark, *Landscape into Art* and *The Nude* and John Pope-Hennessy, *The Portrait in the Renaissance*.

List of Illustrations

Measurements are given in inches and centimetres, height preceding width.

1 KLEE, Paul
Young Tree (Chloranthemum) 1932
Watercolour on paper, $18\frac{1}{2} \times 14\frac{1}{8}$ ($47 \times 35{\cdot}8$)
Private collection, Berne

2 *'Bullroarer' with incised ornament*
Central Australia
(After Carl Stehlow, *Die Aranda- und Loritja-Stamme*, vol. 1, 1908)

3 NICHOLSON, Ben
Vertical Seconds 1953
Oil on canvas, 29×19 ($73{\cdot}7 \times 48{\cdot}4$)
Tate Gallery, London

4 ALBERS, Josef
Homage to the Square 1960
Oil on canvas, 40×40 ($101{\cdot}6 \times 101{\cdot}6$)
Gimpel Fils Gallery, London

5 KANDINSKY, Wassily
Variegated Circle 1921
Oil on canvas, $55\frac{1}{8} \times 39$ (140×99)
Kirchhoff, Wiesbaden

6 VERMEER, Jan
Gentleman and Lady at a Spinet c. 1662
Oil on canvas, $29 \times 25\frac{1}{2}$ ($73{\cdot}6 \times 64{\cdot}1$)
Buckingham Palace, London
Reproduced by gracious permission of Her Majesty the Queen

7 MONDRIAN, Piet
Composition with Red, Yellow and Blue 1921
Oil on canvas, $31\frac{1}{2} \times 19\frac{5}{8}$ (80×50)
Municipal Museum, The Hague

8 BOUCHER, François
The Birth of Venus 1740
Oil on canvas, $63\frac{3}{4} \times 51\frac{1}{4}$ (162×130)
Nationalmuseum, Stockholm

9 HOGARTH, William
The Rake's Progress, III, The Orgy c. 1732
Oil on canvas, $29\frac{1}{2} \times 24\frac{1}{2}$ ($74{\cdot}8 \times 62{\cdot}2$)
By permission of the Trustees of Sir John Soane's Museum, London

10 UCCELLO, Paolo
The Battle of San Romano c. 1454–7
Panel, $131 \times 71\frac{5}{8}$ (340×183)
Uffizi, Florence

11 PIERO della Francesca (1410/20–92)
The Flagellation
Panel, $32\frac{1}{8} \times 23\frac{1}{4}$ ($81{\cdot}5 \times 59$)
Galleria Nazionale, Urbino

12 WEYDEN, Rogier van der
The Deposition c. 1435
Panel, $103\frac{1}{8} \times 86\frac{5}{8}$ (262×220)
Prado, Madrid

13 PIERO della Francesca
The Queen of Sheba before Solomon begun *c.* 1452
Fresco, $298\frac{3}{4} \times 142\frac{3}{8}$ (757×364)
Church of San Francesco, Arezzo

14 SEURAT, Georges
A Sunday Afternoon at the Grande Jatte 1884–6
Oil on canvas, $41 \times 27\frac{3}{4}$ (104×70)
Courtesy of the Art Institute of Chicago (Helen Birch Bartlett Memorial Collection)

15 GIOTTO
The Marriage at Cana c. 1305–13
Fresco
Arena Chapel, Padua

16 LEONARDO da Vinci
Virgin of the Rocks (detail), begun *c.* 1483
Panel
National Gallery, London

17 COZENS, Alexander (*c.* 1717–86)
Landscape
$7\frac{1}{2} \times 5\frac{1}{2}$ (18·9 × 13·9)
Department of Prints and Drawings, British Museum, London

18 KLEE, Paul
Heavily Pregnant 1934
Crayon

19 BOSCH, Jerome
The Garden of Delights c. 1500
Detail from central panel of triptych
Prado, Madrid

20 TURNER, J. M. W.
Interior at Petworth 1837
Oil on canvas, 120 × 91 (305 × 231)
Tate Gallery, London

21 CÉZANNE, Paul
L'Estaque c. 1885
Oil on canvas, $28 \times 22\frac{3}{4}$ (71 × 57·7)
Collection Lord Butler

22 BELLINI, Giovanni
Fra Teodoro as St Dominic 1515
Oil on canvas, $24\frac{3}{4} \times 19\frac{1}{2}$ (63 × 49·5)
National Gallery, London

23 MICHELANGELO
Detail of *The Creation* 1508–12
Fresco
Sistine Chapel, the Vatican

24 BOTTICELLI, Sandro
Mystic Nativity 1500–1
Oil on canvas, $42\frac{3}{4} \times 29\frac{1}{2}$ (108·5 × 75)
National Gallery, London

25 EL GRECO
The Burial of Count Orgaz 1586
$191\frac{7}{8} \times 141\frac{3}{4}$ (487·5 × 360)
Church of Santo Tomé, Toledo

26 RUBENS, Peter Paul
Raising of the Cross 1610
Central panel of altarpiece,
Antwerp Cathedral

27 KU AN (active 1350)
Bamboo in the Wind

Ink on silk, $48 \times 20\frac{7}{8}$ (122·9 × 53)
United Museums and Libraries, Palace Museum Division, Taiwan

28 MONDRIAN, Piet
Broadway Boogie Woogie 1942–3
Oil on canvas, 50 × 50 (127 × 127)
Museum of Modern Art, New York

29 POLLOCK, Jackson
Blue Poles 1953
Oil, Duco and aluminium paint on canvas, $192\frac{1}{2} \times 83$ (488·9 × 210·8)
Collection Mr and Mrs Ben Heller, New York

30 VERMEER, Jan
Lady Standing at the Virginals c. 1671
Oil on canvas, 20 × 18 (50·8 × 45·7)
National Gallery, London

31 WHISTLER, J. A. McNeill
Old Battersea Bridge: Nocturne – blue and gold c. 1865
Oil on canvas, $26\frac{3}{4} \times 20$ (67·8 × 50·8)
Tate Gallery, London

32 BRUEGHEL the Elder, Pieter
Peasant Dance c. 1568
Panel, $64\frac{5}{8} \times 44\frac{7}{8}$ (164 × 114)
Kunsthistorisches Museum, Vienna

33 TITIAN
Bacchanal c. 1518
$76 \times 68\frac{7}{8}$ (193 × 175)
Prado, Madrid

34 MONET, Claude
La Grenouillière 1869
Oil on canvas, $39\frac{1}{4} \times 29\frac{3}{8}$ (99 × 75)
Metropolitan Museum of Art, New York
(Bequest of Mrs H. O. Havemeyer 1929, The H. O. Havemeyer Collection)

35 REMBRANDT van Ryn
Descent from the Cross c. 1653
Oil on canvas, $56\frac{1}{4} \times 43\frac{3}{4}$ (143 × 111)
National Gallery of Art, Washington (Widmer Collection, 1942)

Signers of the Declaration

Signers
of the
Declaration

JOHN and KATHERINE BAKELESS

1969
Houghton Mifflin Company Boston

Also by John Bakeless

The Adventures of Lewis and Clark

To Fyle Edberg

CONTENTS

TABLE OF DATES   xi

INTRODUCTION: The Glorious Fourth and the Men Who
              Made It Glorious   1

PART I   MASSACHUSETTS   15
           Samuel Adams   17
           John Hancock   33
           John Adams   45
           Elbridge Gerry   59
           Robert Treat Paine   64

PART II   VIRGINIA   69
           Thomas Jefferson   71
           Richard Henry Lee   79
           Benjamin Harrison   87
           Francis Lightfoot Lee   91
           Thomas Nelson   92
           George Wythe   96
           Carter Braxton   101

PART III   PENNSYLVANIA   105
           Benjamin Franklin   107
           Robert Morris   127
           Benjamin Rush   136
           John Morton   141
           George Clymer   143
           James Smith   146
           George Taylor   148
           James Wilson   150
           George Ross   155

PART IV   NEW JERSEY   159
               John Witherspoon   161
               Richard Stockton   166
               Francis Hopkinson   169
               John Hart   173
               Abraham Clark   175

PART V   NEW YORK   179
               Philip Livingston   181
               Lewis Morris   184
               William Floyd   187
               Francis Lewis   188

PART VI   CONNECTICUT   193
               Roger Sherman   195
               Samuel Huntington   202
               William Williams   204
               Oliver Wolcott   206

PART VII   RHODE ISLAND   211
               Stephen Hopkins   213
               William Ellery   216

PART VIII   NEW HAMPSHIRE   221
               Josiah Bartlett   223
               William Whipple   225
               Matthew Thornton   227

PART IX   MARYLAND   231
               Charles Carroll   233
               Thomas Stone   240
               William Paca   242
               Samuel Chase   244

PART X   DELAWARE   249

Caesar Rodney   251

Thomas McKean   255

George Read   259

PART XI   NORTH CAROLINA 263

William Hooper   265

Joseph Hewes   267

John Penn   270

PART XII   SOUTH CAROLINA 273

Thomas Heyward, Jr. 275

Arthur Middleton 277

Edward Rutledge 280

Thomas Lynch, Jr. 282

PART XIII   GEORGIA   285

Lyman Hall   287

Button Cuinnett   290

George Walton   296

BIBLIOGRAPHY   299

DATES

1760 OCTOBER 26   George III ascends the British throne.

1764 APRIL 5   The Sugar Act is passed by Parliament; the colonies protest.

      APRIL 19   The Currency Act forbids the colonists to issue paper money as legal tender.

      DECEMBER 22   Stephen Hopkins, Governor of Rhode Island, publishes "The Rights of Colonies Examined."

1765 MARCH 22   The Stamp Act becomes law. The Sons of Liberty organize throughout the colonies a resistance to its enforcement.

      MAY 15   The Quartering Act orders the colonists to provide barracks and supplies for British troops.

      JUNE 8   The Massachusetts General Court adopts a circular letter calling representatives from all colonies to a Congress in New York in October.

      OCTOBER 7   The Stamp Act Congress meets in New York.

      NOVEMBER 1   The Stamp Act goes into effect to the sound of the tolling of muffled bells and flags at half staff.

1766 FEBRUARY 13   Benjamin Franklin, examined before the House of Commons in London, declares the Stamp Act cannot be enforced.

      MARCH 18   England repeals the Stamp Act.

1767 JUNE 29   Charles Townshend, British Chancelor of the Exchequer, imposes in his Revenue Act duties to be paid on glass, lead, tea, paper, and painters' colors imported into the colonies.

      SEPTEMBER 4   Charles Townshend dies. Lord North succeeds him.

      OCTOBER 28   The Boston Town-Meeting renews its *non-importation* agreement; an action followed in other colonies to compel a repeal of the Townshend Acts.

1768	FEBRUARY 11	The Massachusetts House of Representatives adopts Samuel Adams's circular letter and orders it sent to the assemblies of other colonies, suggesting united opposition to Great Britain by discussion and petition.
	JULY 18	A "Song for American Freedom" by John Dickinson is published by the *Boston Gazette*.
	OCTOBER 1	Two regiments of British soldiers land in Boston to enforce the customs laws.
1769	MAY 18	Virginia agrees to non-importation of British goods.
1770	JANUARY 31	Lord North becomes Prime Minister of Great Britain.
	MARCH 5	The Boston Massacre takes place; five killed, six injured.
	APRIL 12	The Townshend Revenue Act is repealed, except for the tax on tea.
1772	NOVEMBER 2	Committees of Correspondence are first organized by Samuel Adams and Joseph Warren in Massachusetts and later followed by similar committees in the other colonies.
1773	DECEMBER 16	The Boston Tea Party takes place.
1774		Benjamin Franklin's articles, "On the Rise and Progress of the Differences between Great Britain and Her American Colonies," are published in London.
	MARCH 31	The Boston Port Act, first of Britain's coercive acts, receives the King's assent.
	MAY 12	The Boston Committee of Correspondence recommends suspension of trade with Great Britain by all colonies.
	MAY 13	General Gage arrives in Boston to command British troops quartered there.
	MAY 27	The Virginia House of Burgesses, meeting unofficially in Williamsburg, adopts a resolution calling for an annual intercolonial congress.

JUNE 1	Boston harbor is closed to exports and imports by the Boston Port Act of March 31.
JUNE 2	The Quartering Act is passed by Parliament. The colonists must house and feed the British soldiers.
JUNE 17	Massachusetts elects delegates to an intercolonial congress to meet September 1 in Philadelphia.
SEPTEMBER 1	General Gage seizes Massachusetts's stock of powder at Charlestown.
SEPTEMBER 5	The First Continental Congress assembles in Philadelphia with all colonies except Georgia represented.
OCTOBER 14	The Declaration of Rights and Grievances is adopted by Congress.
OCTOBER 26	The First Continental Congress adjourns to meet again May 10, 1775, if found to be necessary at that date.

1775

	The words of "Yankee Doodle" are written by Edward Barnes and set to an old English tune.
APRIL 18/19	Paul Revere takes his midnight ride.
APRIL 19	The battles of Lexington and Concord take place.
MAY 10	The Second Continental Congress meets in Philadelphia. All thirteen colonies send representatives.
MAY 24	John Hancock of Massachusetts is chosen president of this Congress.
JUNE 15	George Washington of Virginia is appointed by Congress to be Commander in Chief of the Continental Army.
JUNE 17	The battle of Bunker Hill ends in a British victory.
JULY 3	After traveling twelve days from Philadelphia, Washington takes command of the Continental Army on the Cambridge (Massachusetts) Common.
JULY 6	Congress adopts a "Declaration of the Causes and Necessity of Taking up Arms."

JULY 8   Congress adopts a petition to the king, of-
                      fering reconciliation. (Samuel Adams and
                      Benjamin Franklin think this a futile ges-
                      ture, but consent to yield to the "moder-
                      ates" of the middle colonies.)

SEPTEMBER 1   This petition of July 8 to the king from Con-
                      gress is refused.

1776 JANUARY 1   A Continental flag with thirteen stripes is
                      raised by Washington before his headquar-
                      ters in Cambridge.

APRIL 6   Congress opens the ports of all colonies to
                      all countries "not subject to the King of
                      Great Britain" and prohibits the importa-
                      tion of slaves.

APRIL 12   North Carolina is the first colony to instruct
                      her delegates to support independence.

MAY 15   Virginia instructs her delegates to propose
                      independence.

JUNE 7   Richard Henry Lee, chairman of the Vir-
                      ginia delegation, offers a resolution in Con-
                      gress: "That these United Colonies are and
                      of right ought to be free and independent
                      states."

JUNE 11   A committee is appointed in Congress to
                      draft a Declaration of Independence.
                      Thomas Jefferson is chairman.

JULY 2   Lee's resolution of June 7 is adopted by
                      Congress.

JULY 4   The Declaration of Independence, as
                      drafted by Thomas Jefferson, and amended,
                      is adopted by Congress and signed by its
                      president, John Hancock.

AUGUST 2   The Declaration of Independence, having
                      been engrossed on parchment, is signed by
                      the members of Congress then present.

The Glorious Fourth
and the
Men Who Made it Glorious

THE FOURTH OF JULY is the day on which Americans commemorate the independence of their country. Though there are several other days we *might* celebrate as Independence Day, the Second Continental Congress, in 1776, formally adopted the final revision of the Declaration of Independence on the Fourth of July. The United Colonies were already independent, for Congress had passed a resolution declaring independence two days before, on July 2, 1776. All the formal Declaration of Independence did was to state formally to the world, and especially to the British Empire, what Congress had decided and why.

We could celebrate July 2, the day independence was actually voted. We could celebrate June 7, the day Richard Henry Lee of Virginia submitted to Congress his resolution "that these United Colonies are, and of right ought to be, free and independent states, that they are absolved from all allegiance to the British Crown, and that all political connection between them and the State of Great Britain is, and ought to be, totally dissolved."

When Thomas Jefferson was writing the Declaration of Independence, some weeks after Lee's resolution, he took these words, almost without change, as the final, ringing paragraph of his immortal document. But Lee's resolution was only *submitted* to Congress on June 7. There was no vote. Congress took nearly a month to think it over, before formally and officially adopting it. John Adams expected July 2 to be the day formally celebrated. But there was only a vote of Congress that day. American independence was not officially announced to the world until July Fourth.

It wasn't really necessary to have a Declaration of Independence at all. If the Second Continental Congress was the legitimate government of the Thirteen Colonies, then the colonies became independent the moment Congress — when it finally passed Lee's resolution — said it was independent. But the delegates in Congress thought they ought to give reasons for so serious a step. That is what the Declaration means when it says that "a decent respect to the opinions of mankind requires that they should declare the causes which impel them to the separation" from Great Britain.

There was a great deal to do before Independence could be declared. Not every one, even among the delegates to the Second Continental Congress, favored it. They were good Americans. They were sound patriots. But they were mostly of British blood and they had been bred in a tradition of loyalty to King and Country. They knew the king and his government were treating them outrageously, but they still hoped the dispute could be settled peaceably.

Though Samuel Adams and a few others wanted to set up a new and independent country almost as soon as disputes with the royal government began, many leading American patriots — some of them among the greatest heroes of the Revolution — did not want to be independent at all, even after fighting had started. All they wanted was what every Briton back home in the British Isles had always wanted: self-government, the right to tax himself, protection against injustice in the courts of law.

In the beginning, both Washington and Jefferson had declared openly they did not favor independence. But they, like Franklin and many other moderates, began to change their minds not long after the fighting started. Within a year or two, the British were offering to concede nearly everything the patriots had ever demanded, except independence. But it was too late then. America had won independence by that time and meant to stay independent.

It was true, however, that a few Americans had been talking about independence long before the Revolution, though no one either in England or America took them very seriously. As early as 1764, Christopher Gadsden of South Carolina, later a delegate to the First Continental Congress in 1774, was discussing the possible independence of the colonies, though only among his friends. In 1766, Gadsden began to discuss the subject again. Samuel Adams apparently had made up his mind by 1768. When Patrick Henry, in 1773, also suggested American independence, the people who heard him "appeared to be startled; for they had never heard anything of the kind even suggested."

Jonathan Trumbull, the war governor of Connecticut whom Washington liked to address as "Brother Jonathan," wrote the Earl of Dartmouth, "We consider the interest of the two countries as inseperable, [sic] and are shocked at the idea of any disunion between them." Dr. Joseph Warren, not long before he was killed at Bunker Hill, declared that independence was "not our aim." The people of Portsmouth thought their delegates in the Provincial New Hampshire Congress should "totally disavow" any desire to separate from Britain. The New York Provincial Congress formally denied that it wished "to cast off the connexion and dependence of the Colonies on Great Britain."

Naturally, after fighting began, this loyalty to the old country swiftly cooled. The redcoats were now killing Americans. One of General Gage's spies in the American lines outside Boston reported on July 23, 1775: "A view to independence seems more and more general." This was less than a year before the Declaration of Independence. Yet even then all the spy could report was that the desire for independence was "more general." He didn't report any overwhelming demand for it. In late October, 1775, General Nathanael Greene wrote Washington that people were *beginning* "heartily to wish a declaration of Independence." But it was December before General Greene was willing to tell the commander in chief frankly: "We are now driven to the necessity of making a declaration of independence."

Because his wife was very seriously ill, Thomas Jefferson, soon to be the author of the Declaration, did not take his seat in the Second Continental Congress till May 14, 1776. Next day, he heard Congress adopt a resolution denouncing King George (in almost the same terms Jefferson himself would use in the Declaration of Independence a few weeks later) and recommending that Congress assume all the powers of government. This resolution did not go so far as to demand outright American independence but it did very nearly the same thing. If the American Congress assumed all the powers of government and made war on the King's army, the country would be practically independent.

On that same day, far away in Virginia, something else happened. In Williamsburg, the Virginia Convention (that is, the

state legislature) passed an official resolution, urging Congress
to "declare the United Colonies free and independent states."

It took some time for the news to reach the Virginia delegates
in Congress. In those days, people traveled on horseback or in
carriages, over roads that were sometimes stretches of log "cor-
duroy," at other times mere patches of mud and stone, crossing
streams by fords or clumsy ferries, for there were usually no
bridges. Hence it took time for news, even official news as important as this, to spread; and these instructions did not reach
the Virginia delegates in Philadelphia until May 27, 1776.

All through those first months of 1776, a good deal had been
happening to incline the thoughts of the patriots toward independence. Important among these events was the publication of a
little pamphlet called *Common Sense* by an English immigrant
who had come to America in 1774. His name was Thomas Paine.
He had hardly reached this country when he became an intense
patriot, ardent in the cause of independence. *Common Sense,* published January 9, 1776, is said to have sold 300,000 copies in its
first three months and another 200,000 copies immediately afterward. Even today, with our enormous population, any publisher
would be delighted with such a sale. In those days, amid the
thin populace of the eastern seaboard, it was almost a miracle.

It meant that, in the first few months of '76, as the idea of
independence took greater and greater hold of the people and of
Congress, practically every one was reading Paine's fiery arguments.

The scene was now set for independence. No matter how much
they might protest they were only loyal Britons demanding only
the rights of Englishmen, the colonists had refused to pay British
taxes, they had driven out British governors, they had been shooting British soldiers, and they had taken over the government. No
wonder Samuel Adams asked: "Is not America already independent? Why then not declare it?"

The Virginia delegates in Congress took their time about com-
plying with the instructions that state had sent them. The resolution for independence that they were to present had to be carefully
thought out and carefully worded. It was June 7, 1776, before
Richard Henry Lee, senior member of the Virginia delegation,
rose to propose it.

The New England advocates of independence were glad enough to see a Virginian make the first move. As John Adams said, long afterward, "the eastern members" had been viewed askance, "because they had been suspected from the beginning of having independence in contemplation." As a matter of fact, that was exactly what most of the "eastern" — that is, New England — delegates actually had favored for some time.

John Adams promptly seconded Lee's resolution. The two had probably fixed that little matter up beforehand. They knew well enough that this public co-operation of a Massachusetts Yankee democrat and a Virginian aristocrat would serve as a strong hint to the central Atlantic colonies that the most important New England colony and the most important Southern colony were working together to support independence. The delegates would also know that if the largest New England colony and the largest Southern colony felt that way, the rest of New England and the South would probably join them.

After it had heard the resolution, Congress did not rush matters. In fact, it did nothing at all until the next day. Then it decided to resolve itself into a "committee of the whole," to discuss what Richard Henry Lee had proposed. Legislative bodies often do that to make discussion easier and freer than it is under strict parliamentary procedure.

On June 7, 1776, the committee of the whole reported to Congress and there was a more formal discussion of the resolution. Among those who argued against independence were John Dickinson, James Wilson, and Robert R. Livingston. They felt sure that the middle colonies were not yet ready for so bold a move.

But there was one strong argument for not delaying the declaration of independence. The colonists would soon reach the end of their resources. They badly needed foreign arms, foreign soldiers, and foreign money. The only countries that might possibly give such help were England's enemies, France and Spain. Both had fought the British not many years before. Though no longer at war, both were still hostile to Great Britain. Both would be glad to do anything they could to cause the British trouble. Either one might be willing to supply arms, money, or soldiers. If America declared herself an independent nation, France and Spain might be willing to recognize her independence and aid her against Great Britain. But they certainly would not go openly to the aid of American rebels who admitted they were still subjects of King George. (In the end, France provided all three necessities and Spain went to war with Great Britain, which assisted the Colonies, even if there was no formal American alliance with Spain as there was with France.)

After debating till seven o'clock in the evening of Saturday, June 8, Congress decided to go back into committee of the whole on June 10. Following this second day of discussion, the committee of the whole at last decided in favor of Richard Henry Lee's proposal.

Congress decided, after hearing this report, to postpone any decision for three weeks, which meant until July 1. It seemed likely that the central colonies, which were still hesitating at the thought of complete independence, would soon change their minds. Hence, as Thomas Jefferson said later, "it was thought most prudent to wait a while for them." Edward Rutledge, of South Carolina, even thought that at this time "the sensible part of the House opposed the motion."

Though Congress postponed the vote and though there was certainly some hesitation, the delegates appointed a committee of five to decide on the wording of a future Declaration of Independence — in case Congress should ever pass it. Four members of this committee, Thomas Jefferson, Benjamin Franklin, John Adams, and Roger Sherman, favored independence. The fifth member, Robert R. Livingston, still had his doubts. In fact, he did not vote for the Declaration when it was finally submitted to Congress, and never signed it — though it was he who later, in 1789, administered the oath of office for President of the United States to George Washington. In 1776, however, Livingston was so doubtful about the whole thing that he left Philadelphia before the committee had finished revising the Declaration.

The rest of the committee had no doubt about independence at all. As soon as they met, they assigned Thomas Jefferson to write the first draft. Jefferson had been very silent during the debates, since he did not care for public speaking. John Adams later said: "During the whole time I sat with him in Congress, I never heard him utter three sentences together." But Jefferson was already known as one of the best writers in North America, or, as John

Adams put it, he had "a happy talent of composition."

Jefferson wrote the Declaration of Independence in the simple lodgings he had rented for himself — a parlor and a bedroom in the house of Jacob Graff, Jr., a Philadelphia bricklayer. Richard Henry Lee, though he had offered the original resolution for independence, had nothing to do with writing the Declaration that made his resolution effective. While Jefferson and his fellow-committeemen were busy with that task, Lee had gone back to Williamsburg to attend the Virginia Convention. This was not so odd as it seems today. To most of these men the affairs of their own colonies were quite as important as the affairs of America as a whole, especially since no one was then quite sure what was meant by America.

Many years afterward, when John Adams and Thomas Jefferson were both old men and both ex-Presidents, John Adams thought he remembered that the committee had made Jefferson and himself a committee of two to write the first draft. Adams was perfectly sincere when he said this, and a warm friend of Jefferson's, whom he greatly admired, but he was very, very old and was apparently confused. There is no doubt that Thomas Jefferson did write the Declaration of Independence, though the committee, especially Adams and Franklin, suggested certain verbal changes, and Congress eventually made some very important changes of its own.

Jefferson, in later years, had his own notes, made at the time, to prove his authorship; and the earliest draft of the Declaration now known (Jefferson may have torn up a good many sheets of paper while he was at work) is in his handwriting. Adams had no such record, only a very old man's memory of things long, long ago. No record, official or otherwise, suggests that there ever was a subcommittee to make the first draft of the Declaration.

As a literary composition, the Declaration of Independence is not particularly original. There is nothing surprising about that. Jefferson was not trying to say anything startlingly new. He was trying to state clearly some old but fundamental principles that justified the American fight for freedom. These had been stated many times before — by the English philosopher, John Locke; by the Swiss jurist, Jean Jacques Burlamqui; and by the Swiss diplomat, Emmerich de Vattel, years earlier. Tom Paine had repeated them vigorously in America in his best-selling pamphlet. *Common*

Sense stated the American case so vigorously that Washington had the whole pamphlet read aloud to his troops.

Practically every idea in the Declaration of Independence had also been discussed for a long time by speakers in Congress. John Adams, though himself on the committee to draft it, admitted long afterward that the Declaration contained nothing whatever that had not been "hackneyed over in Congress a hundred times."

Not only did Thomas Jefferson borrow the ideas in the Declaration of Independence, he also borrowed a good deal of the language. The list of wrongs the colonists had suffered from King George III was based on an earlier list of similar charges Jefferson had himself written for the new Virginia Constitution. From the Virginia Constitution Jefferson also borrowed part of the Bill of Rights, which George Mason had largely written in its original Virginian form, adding some new charges against the king. Everybody was discussing citizens' rights by that time and all these ideas were more or less familiar.

In writing the Declaration of Independence, Jefferson sometimes followed his models very closely. For instance, the first paragraph of Mason's Virginia Bill of Rights asserted "that all men are born equally free and independant." Mason also declared that every man had a right to "the Enjoyment of Life and Liberty, with the Means of Acquiring and possessing property, and pursuing and obtaining Happiness and Safety." Everyone knows the familiar sentences in which Jefferson repeated these ideas in the Declaration of Independence.

There is no reason for thinking that Roger Sherman did any of the drafting. If he did, it was very little. And Robert R. Livingston probably had as little to do with the Declaration as possible. Benjamin Franklin, who admired the Declaration of Independence as a literary production so much that he said he wished he had written it himself, wrote in a few changes in his own handwriting. A few others appear to be changes by John Adams; and Thomas Jefferson made some last-minute changes himself. All these alterations can easily be noted in the original manuscript, which still survives.

Since the other two members of the committee seem to have had no changes to suggest, the committee were able to lay their approved form of Jefferson's draft before Congress on June 28, 1776.

Congress merely received it formally and ordered it "laid on the table." For the moment, nothing could be done about a *declaration* of independence, since Congress had not yet voted in favor of independence. Richard Henry Lee's resolution had also been "lying on the table" ever since he had introduced it.

On July 2, however, Congress voted in favor of Lee's resolution and thus put itself on record as favoring independence. Congress went right on, that same day, to begin discussion of the exact wording of the Declaration. Thomas Jefferson's draft was now minutely scrutinized, line by line.

It was not very pleasant for Thomas Jefferson. His friend, John Adams, spoke vigorously in favor of the text of the Declaration, as the committee had submitted it. But, as usually happens, everybody else thought he knew exactly how to improve the manuscript; and, as also always happens, everybody had a different way of doing it. Jefferson, having done his best, had nothing whatever to say. He listened in unhappy silence.

Franklin, sitting beside him and seeing his annoyance, tried to comfort him with a funny story. (Franklin was a little like Lincoln in one respect: He always had a joke or a story to tell, especially when a touch of humor might relieve a delicate or difficult situation.)

While the other delegates were slashing various words, sentences, and whole sections of Jefferson's draft, Franklin told him about a hatter who asked a friend to write a sign advertising the hatter's business. The sign, as written, read: "John Thomson, Hatter, Makes and Sells Hats for Ready Money." On it was also a picture of a hat. Then the man's friends began to make suggestions. One wanted the word "Hatter" removed, because the words "Sells Hats" implied he was a hatter, anyway. Another thought the word "Makes" ought to be cut out. You can't sell a hat until it is made, he pointed out. Another struck out the words "for Ready Money." Another said: "Sells hats? Why no one would expect you to give them away!" Another thought the word "Hat" was needless. The picture was enough. In the end, all that was left of the original sign was the man's name and the picture!

The change that probably disturbed Jefferson most was Congress's insistence on striking out a passage denouncing King George III for continuing the African slave trade. Like all Southern land-owners, Thomas Jefferson owned slaves. But he treated them well and at least he wanted to end the dreadful practice of kidnaping free Negroes in Africa and shipping them — under the dreadful conditions existing on the slaving ships — to be sold in supposedly free America. Though most of the colonies had long since prohibited the slave trade, permitting only the sale of the Negroes already here (which was bad enough), South Carolina and Georgia still allowed importation of Negroes from Africa. Besides, many of the ships that were still bringing in kidnaped slaves belonged to ship-owners in "free" New England, who thus made a great deal of money. If Jefferson's denunciation was allowed to remain in the Declaration of Independence, South Carolina and Georgia might vote against it. It was also possible that the resentful Yankee owners of slaving ships might persuade New England delegates to oppose it. In the end, the passage denouncing the slave trade was cut out.

Congress also struck out Jefferson's last paragraph and substituted almost the exact wording of the resolution for independence that Richard Henry Lee had proposed in June. Other changes were largely verbal. Jefferson, who like many other patriots regretted leaving the British Empire, had said in his original draft, "We must forget our former love for them," and had added sadly, "We might have been a free and a great people together." Both these passages were struck out. The words, "a people who mean to be free" were changed to "a free people." The words "Scotch and other mercenaries" were dropped so as not to offend patriots of Scottish descent, especially Dr. Witherspoon, of New Jersey.

Jefferson's criticisms of the British Parliament were also eliminated. Congress did not want to annoy the members of Parliament any more than it had to. The delegates knew they might have to negotiate with them later on. Thomas Jefferson thought this great nonsense: "The pusillanimous idea that we had friends in England worth keeping still haunted the minds of many. For this reason, those passages which conveyed censure on the people of England were struck out, lest they should give them offense." Congress continued its discussion all day on July 3 and on into July 4, 1776, which was to become the most famous date in American history.

The vote was taken by states — or rather, by colonies, for the colonies did not become states until they had formally proclaimed their independence. Each had only one vote, no matter how many delegates it had sent. The delegates from each had to agree among themselves how they would cast the vote for their colony.

Secretary Thomson called the roll, from North to South, beginning with New Hampshire and ending with Georgia. Twelve colonies had voted in favor of independence and only twelve now voted for the text of the Declaration. In each case, the New York delegates abstained from voting because their Provincial Congress had instructed them to take no action, either for or against independence. Pennsylvania would not have voted for independence except that John Dickinson and Robert Morris purposely disappeared on the day the vote was taken, allowing the other members of the Pennsylvania delegation to cast an aye vote. Yet Dickinson later fought bravely for America and Morris became the financial mainstay of the War.

The Declaration of Independence was at first signed only by John Hancock, as President of Congress, and Charles Thomson, as Secretary. When all the revision was finished, the actual paper of Thomas Jefferson's draft was pretty well scratched up, and Congress ordered that the whole Declaration be written in a clear copy and engrossed on parchment for signing. This is the copy now shown at the National Archives, with the actual signatures. Not all the signatures were affixed at once, however. The engrossed parchment copy of the Declaration was not ready till August 2. Most of the fifty-six signatures were affixed then, but others were added later. Matthew Thornton, of New Hampshire, who had not been a member of Congress when the Declaration was passed, did not sign it until November, 1776.

There was no formal proclamation of America's independence on July 4, and it is very doubtful that the Liberty Bell rang at all that day. Congress had some other business to handle and it went right ahead. It ordered the Declaration printed and also ordered the printed copies sent to Washington's army, to all state assemblies, and to various churches.

A corrected copy of the Declaration of Independence was rushed off to John Dunlap, a Philadelphia printer. Dunlap worked all night to get the type set (by hand, of course) and, in the morning, was able to send a proof to Jefferson's lodgings. An hour later, the author of the Declaration of Independence returned it, after correcting a few typographical errors. Dunlap ran his press all day on July 5, but he did not wait to finish the press run before beginning to send forty or fifty copies at a time — as they came off the old, slow handpress — to Secretary Charles Thomson.

Late that afternoon, a delegation of chiefs of the Six Nations of the Iroquois appeared in Congress, were given seats and welcomed, listened to an explanation of the Declaration of Independence and what it meant, and were given the presents indispensable at all Indian councils. Chiefs and delegates then made speeches and John Hancock, the dapper Boston merchant, was formally adopted as a member of the tribe of the Onondagas.

Though the Declaration of Independence was published in the Philadelphia *Evening Post* on July 6, it was not officially proclaimed until July 8. Behind Independence Hall stood a large platform built for the Philadelphia astronomer, David Rittenhouse, to use in his observations. Here, on the eighth, the people gathered, while Colonel John Nixon, of the Committee of Safety, read the Declaration of Independence publicly and officially for the first time, though every one must have known for several days what Congress had done. July 8 was an appropriate date, for that was also election day in Pennsylvania — the first election as a free and independent state, no longer a British colony.

Post riders saddled their horses and rode off through the states in all directions, carrying printed copies of the Declaration, spreading the news as they went, and sometimes pausing to let the Declaration be publicly read before riding on.

People are likely to imagine that, as soon as the Declaration was adopted on July 4, 1776, the delegates went up, one by one, and affixed their signatures. That was quite impossible. All that Congress had, at the moment, was Jefferson's draft, much corrected and scribbled upon with all the changes Congress had made. The signed Declaration of Independence, now displayed in the National Archives in Washington, is a copy of Jefferson's manuscript as changed by Congress, beautifully engrossed on parchment, by a skilled professional penman.

It was not formally signed by the delegates until August 2, 1776. That is probably when John Hancock, affixing his usual big, bold signature, remarked that King George would have no trouble reading it — though he could have said the same thing when he signed Jefferson's draft, as amended. There is also a story that when Charles Carroll signed, someone remarked that there were so many Charles Carrolls in Maryland, no one would know which one it was. Then, the story goes, Carroll seized his pen and added "of Carrollton," so that there could be no possible doubt who the signer was. But a good many of Charles Carroll's signatures have survived, and they show that he often added "of Carrollton" for this very reason.

There was a certain solemnity as the signatures were affixed. All the signers knew that if the American army won and America became free they would be national heroes. They also knew that if America lost most of them would be executed as traitors. There would be no doubt about their treason. There were their signatures on the Declaration — enough to hang them, without other evidence. Indeed, if America had lost the Revolutionary War, the Signers of the Declaration of Independence would have been lucky to get off with hanging. The legal penalty for treason was still hanging, drawing, and quartering. That is, hanging the victim till he was half dead from strangling, then disembowelling him and cutting his body into four quarters while he was still alive.

Thinking of this, some one remarked that, after the signing there must be complete co-operation for victory:

"We must all hang together."

"Yes," replied Benjamin Franklin, who loved his little joke, even if it was a rather grim one. "We must all hang together or we shall all hang separately."

To make sure they were in earnest as patriots, new delegates elected to Congress continued to sign the Declaration of Independence when they took their seats, even if they had not been members when it was passed. This continued at least as late as November, 1776.

That is the story of the Declaration of Independence, to which our country owes its freedom and almost two hundred years of successful democratic living.

But what of the men who made the Declaration?

I

MASSACHUSETTS

Sam¹ Adams

John Hancock

John Adams

Elbridge Gerry

Rob¹ Treat Paine

Samuel Adams

Sam Adams

September 27, 1722 — October 2, 1803

THE GREATEST WORLD EVENT of the eighteenth century was the birth of a new nation. It was a hard struggle, and the new nation was long a-borning. But in the end the whole world benefited by ideals of human liberty that had been long developing and were now given practical application.

The first Signer's voice to give utterance to the profoundly stirring and revolutionary demand for American freedom was that of Samuel Adams, an unsuccessful businessman but an ardent talker and very persuasive reasoner in the town meetings of Boston. One of the Tories was quite correct when he remarked: "Independence, it is true, was declared in Congress in 1776, but it was settled in Boston in 1768 by Adams and his Junto."

For that reason we turn our attention to him first among the fifty-six representatives of the Thirteen Colonies in the Second Continental Congress of 1776, the Signers of the Declaration of Independence.

Like most of the 250,000 inhabitants of Massachusetts (which in those days included Maine), Samuel Adams's forebears were English.

Henry Adams of Devonshire was the first of the Adams family — which was to become both numerous and distinguished — to reach American shores. Arriving about 1636, with a family of eight children, he settled at Mt. Wollaston, in a part of Braintree, Massachusetts, which later became the modern town of Quincy.

This first Henry Adams had two grandsons. One, Joseph, became the grandfather of John Adams, a Signer and the second President of the United States. The second, John, became a sea-captain and the grandfather of Samuel, the other Signer bearing the Adams name. Samuel's father was another Samuel, a successful Yankee businessman who, with his wife Mary Fifield Adams, lived in a fine house on Purchase Street, Boston, overlooking the harbor.

The father Samuel was a prosperous brewer and merchant, a prominent man in Boston town — justice of the peace, deacon of the Old South Church, member of the Massachusetts Bay Assembly, landowner, a leader in public affairs.

His son, Samuel, born in the Purchase Street house on September 27, 1722, was given the usual education thought best for Boston's sons: the Boston Grammar School and then Harvard. He entered Harvard College when he was fourteen, studied Latin and Greek, and learned to admire the ancient classical heroes. Graduating in 1740, he took an M.A. degree three years later, then started to study law in spite of his father's wish that he become a theologian. Since in that harbor city business offered a more substantial career than law, young Sam Adams entered the counting-house of Thomas Cushing. This lasted only until his father gave him £1000 to start a business of his own. But that business did not last long either. After loaning one half of his £1000 to a friend who never repaid it, Adams lost the other half in his own operations. He then went into his father's brewery but even there he failed. Money simply got away from him. Generous to a fault, he was always loaning any money he had to others who never paid it back.

Actually, Samuel Adams did not have money on his mind. He did not care for clothes or style or fine living. He was no status-seeker, but a man of ideas, a dreamer.

Where could such a man succeed?

In the local taverns and clubs and town meetings, Adams was at his best. Night after night found him among groups of men discussing questions of the day, Boston's needs, and possible civic improvements. Though no one realized it, this was Samuel Adams's real training for his life work. In about twenty years serious questions were going to arise — not only for the town of Boston, but for the colony of Massachusetts and for all the colonies of America. Here already a great politician was in the making.

When his father and mother died, Samuel, at twenty-six, inherited a third of the family property, including the malt-house and the handsome estate on Purchase Street. The next year, 1749, he married Elizabeth Checkley, daughter of the "New South"

Church minister. Eight years later she died, leaving two children. Seven years passed before Adams married again. Elizabeth Wells became the second Mrs. Adams, a loyal, hard-working wife, and — what was especially good for Adams — a strict economist. It was she who managed to keep the household going, though there were times when neighbors' gifts of food and clothing were gratefully accepted.

Through all these years, Adams was an indifferent manager of the malt-house. Always in debt, a thinker and student, he was more interested in public matters than in private business, as was shown by the articles he wrote and sent to the papers. He was devoted to the discussions in the debating clubs, devoted to the welfare of his town. He was, his cousin John Adams once said, "a universal good character"; but John Adams qualified that by adding, "unless it should be admitted that he is too attentive to the public, and not enough to himself and his family." He served in various offices: on committees to see to the proper inspection of chimneys, and to take precautions against small-pox. His first official public duty was the modest one of keeping the town clean.

Though he seemed shiftless in managing the business in which his father had been successful, friends and townsmen apparently had faith in him, since they elected him a tax collector year after year.

Significant happenings in Sam Adams's life came in the year 1764. He was now forty-two, already turning grey. He had a peculiar tremor of hands and head that made him seem older still. But in spite of all that, he was vigorous enough to live on for almost forty years more, and his greatest work was still to come. He was of medium height, muscular and hardy, with grey, clear eyes and a prominent nose. His gaze was at times intense and stern, again genial and benign. He had been through hard times. His malt-house had failed, and everything else his father had left him had been gradually vanishing. He still lived in the Purchase Street house with its lovely harbor view, but it badly needed repairs. He owed so much that the Sheriff put it up for sale four times — though Adams managed to save it. Now, however, when Britain's arbitrary treatment of her American colonies was becoming increasingly annoying, Samuel Adams's great hour had come.

In April of 1764, the British Parliament passed a "Sugar Act," which laid a tax on sugar and molasses imported into the colonies. There had always been a tax on molasses, large quantities of which were brought into Massachusetts for distilling rum. The new law cut the tax on molasses in half. It may seem odd that the colonists should object to a law that reduced taxes. But under the older law, the tax on molasses had been so high nobody could collect it. Hence ship-owners made huge profits on smuggled molasses that paid no duty at all. The British hoped that if they reduced taxes, they might be able to collect them. They hoped smuggling would become less profitable and more cargoes would be brought in legally, if taxed at a lower rate.

The Sugar Act was, nevertheless, an objectionable law. A Yankee sea-captain had to give bond at a British customs house every time he loaded his ship for sea — whether his cargo included sugar and molasses or not! This was troublesome, especially as customs officials found the new law a profitable source of graft, frequently extorting tax payments that were not really due.

But the real grievance of the colonists was that they were being taxed in America by an English Parliament in which they were not represented. There was an immediate and violent protest against taxation without representation.

The Sugar Act marked the beginning of Samuel Adams's rise to fame. He and all the other Massachusetts Yankees reacted instantly and indignantly. In May, a Boston town meeting appointed a committee to instruct its representatives in the General Court (that is, the colonial legislature) to oppose the Sugar Act.

Town meetings, the freest and most democratic of all forms of government, were universal in colonial New England.* In a town meeting, all citizens appear in person to decide public questions — not through Senators or representatives, but by direct, free, public, open discussion among themselves. Each citizen has the right to speak and vote. He cannot be "silenced or brow-beaten by a richer or greater townsman than himself." In the perilous years before the Revolution, this gave citizens a splendid chance to speak out boldly against their tyrannical king.

*Town meetings still survive in some New England towns. The authors of this book live in a Connecticut town that still governs itself directly, by this completely democratic system.

Such a system of government is, understandably, possible only in rather small communities, but in the 1760's and 1770's Boston was still a small community. It was entirely possible for Bostonians to meet together in Faneuil Hall.

The free speech of these free citizens in these little New England town meetings probably did more than anything else in America to promote resistance to oppressive British rule. The British knew it only too well. As one of the Tories wrote: "The town-meeting at Boston is the hot-bed of sedition. It is there that all their dangerous insurrections are engendered; it is there that the flame of discord and rebellion was first lighted up and disseminated over the provinces." And the town-meeting voice in Boston was the voice of Sam Adams.

The committee which the Boston town meeting had selected to draft instructions to Boston's representatives in the General Court in turn chose Samuel Adams to do the actual writing. On old yellow paper, one may still read in his fine handwriting:

> "What still heightens our apprehensions is, that these unexpected Proceedings may be preparatory to more extensive Taxations upon us: For if our Trade may be taxed, why not our Lands? Why not the Produce of our Lands & everything we possess or make use of? This, we apprehend, annihilates our Charter Right to govern & tax ourselves. . . . If Taxes are laid upon us in any shape without our having a legal Representation where they are laid, are we not reduced from the Character of free Subjects to the miserable State of tributary Slaves?"

Here was a flat public denial of the British Parliament's right to tax colonists who were not represented in Parliament.

> "As His Majesty's other Northern American Colonys are embarked with us . . . we further desire you to use your Endeavors, that their weight may be added to that of this Province: that by the united Applications of all who are Aggrieved, All may happily attain Redress."

And here was a very early suggestion for a union of the colonies.

When England sent Commissioners of the Customs to Boston to collect the duties, Samuel Adams kept up a running fire of opposition in controversial articles in the *Boston Gazette* and other journals. He also wrote letters to official persons both in England and America.

But in spite of all these protests, the hated Stamp Act became law in March of 1765. Two months later, the Quartering Act ordered the colonists to provide supplies and barracks for British troops that were to be sent over. Indignation became so hot that delegates from nine colonies met in a Stamp Act Congress in New York in early October to prepare a "declaration of rights and grievances." Still, in spite of all protests, the Stamp Act went into effect on November 1. Flags were lowered to half staff, bells tolled mournfully.

In the Stamp Act year, 1765, Samuel Adams was elected to fill a vacancy as representative in the House. His influence spread until the royal governor, Thomas Hutchinson, became alarmed and described him as a dangerous "incendiary." Disapproval was mutual. Adams regarded the governor as an "enemy of liberty." Indeed, Adams's influence, which had started among the dock workers and "mechanics" of Boston where he had been a rabble-rouser, had during the years spread over the colony and into others.

After Benjamin Franklin patiently explained to the House of Commons in London in 1766 why the Stamp Act could never be enforced, it was repealed in March.*

But this was only one concession. The next year England imposed more duties on imported goods and the Boston town meeting decided to do without the imports. No one was to bring in any English goods. Other colonies followed suit.

Here was something to worry England, for trade with the colonies was important to British merchants, who made great profit out of it.

There was more trouble when, in the autumn of 1768, two regiments of British soldiers landed in Boston to help the Governor enforce the law in unruly Massachusetts, especially in Boston. The colonists had not yet completed arrangements to cut off British imports. Some British goods were still coming in, and there was much difficulty in collecting duty on them. The government in London hoped, by suppressing resistance in Boston, to end it throughout the colonies.

* See the chapter on Benjamin Franklin for the colonists' grievances over the Stamp Act.

Now the leader of a patriotic group called the Sons of Liberty, Sam Adams began to use his influence to stir up feeling against the redcoats. Eventually friction between the people and the soldiers grew so bitter that in 1770 soldiers fired on an American group who defied a British sentry. Probably without orders, the soldiers fired, killing four men and wounding seven. Two of the wounded Bostonians died later. This was the Boston Massacre. Some of the soldiers were arrested, though later tried and almost all acquitted, and the governor agreed to remove one regiment from the town.

After this, for about two years, disputes with the mother country cooled off. The most objectionable laws were repealed, though not the duty on tea. Sam Adams's cousin, John Adams, withdrew from politics for a time, disgusted because he was criticized for having done his duty as a lawyer by serving as attorney for the soldiers implicated in the Massacre.

But Samuel Adams, like an Old Testament prophet, kept steadfastly sounding the warnings of the wrath to come. In some forty articles in Boston newspapers, he warned the people of the "concealed conspiracy intended to deprive them of their liberty." He told them that the greatest danger was in thinking that there was no danger; that, though unaware of it, they were being made slaves.

At a Boston meeting on November 2, 1772, on Adams's motion, a committee of correspondence was appointed to state the rights of the colonists, "and of this Province in particular, as men, as Christians, and as Subjects; and to communicate the same to the several towns and to the world."

In London, Parliament passed the tax on tea the next day. Though it would take some weeks for this news to reach the American side of the Atlantic, the foresight of Samuel Adams caused him to begin at once to work for an assembly of the colonies, in other words, a Continental Congress. With his clear logic, he explained, persuaded, and wrote hundreds of articles, keeping his ideas before the public. Four months later, an article entitled "Observation," which was attributed to Samuel Adams, appeared in the *Boston Gazette*. It proposed that "a congress of American states be assembled as soon as possible; draw up a Bill of Rights — choose an ambassador to reside at the British

Court to act for the united colonies; appoint where the congress shall annually meet."

Adams knew the coming of the tea ships that very autumn would bring trouble, might even create a crisis. In early November, the Boston Committee of Correspondence voted that it would not allow the tea shipped by the East India Company (for whose benefit Parliament had imposed the tea tax) even to be unloaded. The next day, Sam Adams and others of the Sons of Liberty committee requested the resignation of the "consignees" — that is, the merchants who were to accept the consignments of tea when they reached Boston. The consignees refused to resign. Two days later, November 5, Adams drafted a resolution declaring all who helped in landing or selling the tea to be enemies of America.

The first of the tea ships, *Dartmouth,* arrived November 28. Next day there was a mass meeting in Faneuil Hall. Guesses were that from one thousand to five thousand people were present, either in the hall or in the square outside. Adams moved that the tea should be sent back to England, and the motion was carried. A meeting next day chose a directing committee, Sam Adams being included. During the next two weeks many meetings took place. All this time the tea remained on the ships. Finally the time was up. Under customs law, the cargo had to be either landed or confiscated by December 16.

Excitement was now at fever heat. A mass meeting of about seven thousand people filled the Old South Church, the adjoining streets, and Boston Common. It was like a swarming of bees. Nothing like it had ever been seen. Adams presided. The meeting lasted from ten in the morning until six in the evening. When a messenger came, saying that Governor Hutchinson still refused to have the ships return to England, Samuel Adams declared, "This meeting can do nothing more to save the country."

As if this had been a pre-arranged signal, a number of men rose and left the meeting. Presently a group, probably the same men, many now dressed as Indians, appeared on the wharf and dumped all the tea overboard. This was the famous Boston Tea Party.

In our coffee-drinking century, we may doubt that the rejection of the tea was very hard on the colonists. But tea had long been the favorite hot beverage of the English, and most New Englanders had come from the British Isles, or had English forebears. Some now tried to brew a tea from catnip and pennyroyal but it was not at all the same. They really missed their tea.

The Boston Tea Party had far-reaching effects. Philadelphia, New York, and Charleston also resisted the landing of tea. In England, the Parliament, King George, and his adviser, Lord North, were incensed. Retaliation was bound to come. The Boston Port Act, which would close the port entirely, was approved by the King at the end of March. Six weeks later, the Boston Committee retaliated by recommending that all colonies suspend trade with Great Britain entirely.

In the Massachusetts General Court, Adams moved to appoint delegates to a Continental Congress "to deliberate and determine upon all measures." Five delegates were chosen, Adams himself being one.

It was well that Samuel Adams, who never much cared how he looked, had some friends who did care. He could hardly go to Philadelphia and meet representatives from all the other colonies, looking the way he usually looked at home. Bostonians were used to his unkempt, slovenly personal appearance. After all, what did it matter? Sam Adams had brains, a wonderful singleness of purpose, spirit, and a capacity for indefatigable work — all for the cause of "the people," whose deep respect he commanded. He had education. They knew him; many loved him. Already in 1774, one friend had built him a new barn; another had repaired his house. Now, when he was about to take the first long trip of his life to attend the Congress for which he had labored so hard and so long, friends outfitted him with a new suit, new shoes, and several pairs of silk hose. People appreciated him, and when he needed help they helped him. Samuel Adams was now fifty-two, and he had never been outside Massachusetts, and never even far from home.

When the Massachusetts delegates reached Philadelphia, they were warned to keep themselves a bit in the background for a while. Some delegates from more "moderate" colonies felt that the Massachusetts patriots had been too rash. Pennsylvania, with her large Quaker population, was one of the moderate middle colonies.

In fact, the moderates and Tories believed that Samuel Adams "managed things both in and out of Congress." The Pennsylvania lawyer, Joseph Galloway, who had been Speaker of the Pennsylvania Assembly and was now a leader in Congress of the party who still wanted reconciliation with Britain, wrote later in his book on the rise and progress of the American Revolution that it was Samuel Adams who managed the expresses (mails) which were continually moving between Philadelphia and Boston during the seven weeks this first Congress convened. "These were," he wrote, "under the management of Samuel Adams . . . He eats little, drinks little, sleeps little, thinks much, and is most decisive and indefatigable in the pursuit of his objects. It was this man, who, by his superior application, managed at once the faction in Congress at Philadelphia and the factions in New England."

During the seven weeks session of the First Congress, the deliberators prepared a Declaration of Rights and Grievances, addresses to the king, to the people of England, of Canada, and of other British American colonies, as well as a letter to the agent of the colonies in England. Comparatively few men felt, as yet, that it would be impossible to deal with king and Parliament. Hence the colonies still begged Britain to understand their position, give them their rights, and allow them to be represented where their laws were made, that is, in Parliament. But Samuel Adams knew this would never be done, that Britain would never be conciliatory. Benjamin Franklin, in England at the time, also felt this way. Congress was adjourned October 26 to meet again May 10, 1775.

Returning to Boston in early November, these first Massachusetts congressmen were greeted with public demonstrations. Surviving letters of the time show the regard, even reverence, that Boston patriots felt toward Samuel Adams. Indeed, it was said that the uneducated people came to think he had a prophetic power and that even war and peace might rest with him.

Once back in Boston, Sam Adams had a busy winter in the Provincial Congress, which had now come into being. The redcoats under British General Gage were now all over Boston. Against this state of affairs, the colonists had been storing up guns and ammunition in secret. Adams led the local congress in making people aware of the ever approaching outburst of conflict. He pointed out the danger of allowing British soldiers to march into the country and recommended opposition if they went even ten miles from Boston. General Gage could not help realizing that Adams and John Hancock were two patriotic firebrands. He also was aware that the patriots were storing ammunition. He moved his regulars out to Lexington and Concord on the never-to-be-forgotten night of April 18/19, in order to seize those stores. That caused those first "shots heard round the world." He was hoping, too, to capture Hancock and Adams.

For some time tension in Boston had been tightening, what with the presence of British soldiers all through the streets, and more always coming. A silversmith named Paul Revere had already set up the first American intelligence net of about thirty "mechanics" * whose purpose, Revere reported, was to watch "the movements of the British soldiers" and keep a close eye on the Tories. That fateful Spring, these volunteers "frequently took turns, two and two, to watch the soldiers, by patrolling the streets all night."

On the evening of April 18, 1775, news spread around town that the British regulars were going out into the country. Samuel Adams and John Hancock were staying that night in the old parsonage at Lexington, at that time the home of the Reverend Jonas Clark.

Every American knows the story of Paul Revere's ride. When he galloped up to the Lexington Green, he found the parsonage dark, and every one asleep. A sergeant stationed at the house told Revere that the family did not want to be disturbed by any noise.

"Noise!" cried Paul Revere. "You'll have enough noise before long. The regulars are coming out."

The British infantry arrived about dawn and firing started. While the smoke was clearing away, Hancock and Adams escaped across the fields to Woburn. As the white sun of that Spring morning rose over the horizon, Adams exclaimed: "What a glorious morning is this!" Within the next few days, the Massachusetts representatives were again on their way to Philadelphia.

The Second Continental Congress convened May 10, 1775. Samuel Adams was now fifty-four, and he had travelled a long, hard road. Through all those years of persuading, discussing, debating,

* John and Katherine Bakeless, *Spies of the Revolution,* J. B. Lippincott Co., Phila., and New York, 1962, p. 44. "Mechanics" was the term for men who "made" things.

writing articles, getting poorer all the time, while trying to open people's minds to the danger of an increasing British tyranny, and showing them the desirability of American independence he had been a true servant of the people. Long after the war, Dr. Benjamin Rush, a Pennsylvania Signer, wrote in a letter to John Adams that "Samuel Adams once told me that the independence of British America had been the first wish of his heart seven years before the commencement of the American Revolutionary War in 1774." At the time of the Second Congress, Dr. Rush supposed Adams to be "near sixty," but he wrote that Adams "possessed all the vigor of mind of a young man of five and twenty." He said Adams "loved simplicity and oeconomy [sic] in the administration of government, and despised the appeals which are made to the eyes and ears of the common people in order to govern them . . . Ambition and avarice, the usual vices of politicians, seem to have no place in his breast."

One of the most important acts of the Second Continental Congress was the appointment of George Washington as commander in chief. And for this perfect appointment Americans must always feel grateful to the "brace of Adamses," for it was John who nominated the tall Virginian and Samuel who seconded the motion. This was a long and busy period for Congress. Two days after this appointment was made in Philadelphia, the Battle of Bunker Hill took place outside Boston. This was a British victory in which Samuel Adams's beloved friend, General (and Doctor) Joseph Warren was killed. Two weeks later, Washington, having traveled twelve days from Philadelphia, took command of all American armed forces in Cambridge.

Even after these clashes of arms, there were still insistent demands from the moderate middle colonies that Congress should send still more petitions to the king. Samuel Adams was out of patience with the Pennsylvania Quakers for such delays when war had already begun. Benjamin Franklin, now sitting in Congress after many years in London, also knew that further petition was useless; that Lord North, the king's prime minister, would concede nothing. But in July, Congress decided to send still another petition to George III. When it arrived in London, it was refused at once. Adams had been right. Franklin had been right. It had been of no use.

This Congress adjourned August 1 until September 5, and Adams returned home for a few busy weeks. But the Massachusetts delegates took back with them $500,000 for Washington's army.

Soon, however, Sam Adams was in the saddle on a horse loaned him by his cousin John for the three-hundred-mile ride back to Philadelphia. Some historians call this September, 1775, session of Congress the Third Continental Congress, while others refer to it as the Second. The confusion no doubt arises because there were no elections for representatives such as we have today. Instead, they were chosen by the state assemblies.

Adams was in favor of immediate independence. But a declaration of independence was a declaration of rebellion, and the middle colonies still could not bring themselves to accept this appalling idea. Persuasions, discussions, debates increased. The various committees in Congress were busy day and night. At the end of November Congress founded an American Navy. On January 1, 1776, Lord Dunmore, royal governor of Virginia, bombarded and burned Norfolk. And on that same day, in Cambridge, Massachusetts, Washington raised the Continental flag with thirteen stripes before his headquarters. Ten days later, Thomas Paine published his famous pamphlet, *Common Sense*. In April, North Carolina definitely instructed her delegates to stand for independence. She was the first to venture upon this bold course. Congress buzzed with excitement. A month later, a second colony, Virginia, took the same stand, and went further. Virginia instructed her delegates to make a formal proposal of separation from the mother country.

By the end of the first week of June the Virginia delegates were ready. On June 7, Richard Henry Lee of Virginia took the floor and offered to Congress the resolution for independence. This must have been the sweetest of music to the ears of Samuel Adams. After all those years . . .

The next day the debate on the resolution began.

Long after, Elbridge Gerry told Samuel Adams's daughter that the success of Lee's measure was largely due to the "timely remarks" of her father arguing in favor of independence. Gerry added that in one unusually long speech, Adams won over two or three wavering members.

Edward Rutledge of South Carolina moved for a postponement of this all-important question for three weeks to enable the hesitating delegates to consult their constituents and gauge the feelings of the people in their respective colonies.

During those three weeks, Samuel Adams's peculiar powers were brought to the fore in personal conferences. He labored long hours stating his views clearly, logically, over and over again. Patiently, he "button-holed" the moderates and those less stout of heart. Hot July arrived and the steadily ripening sentiment of the country made itself felt in Congress. They were ready to vote.

Then some late arrivals, who had not heard the previous discussions, asked to have certain points clarified. All eyes turned to Samuel Adams's cousin John who had just finished a formal address to Congress on these very matters. Since he had every point clearly in mind, he was asked to enlighten the newcomers and he obliged.

In the end, Delaware's representatives needed the absent Caesar Rodney to complete that colony's vote in favor of independence. Congress would be voting the next day and a messenger was sent off to get him. All through the night of July 1, through thunderstorms and driving rain, Rodney rode back to Philadelphia. He arrived in time on July 2 when Lee's resolution declaring independence was adopted by Congress. On the Fourth, the Declaration of Independence, as drafted by Thomas Jefferson and subsequently amended, was adopted and signed by John Hancock, President of Congress.

At once, the atmosphere in the hall changed. A wave of relief washed away the tenseness of worry, apprehension, fear of not doing the right thing. Now it was done. The anguish of decision was past. The men laughed and joked.

This then was the career of Samuel Adams, America's first great genius in politics. This was the part of his life that has given his name an exalted place in American history. It began with the resistance to mounting British tyranny and ended, really, when the war began. Adams had been the foremost revolutionary agitator, but his talent did not lie in the direction of constructive statesmanship, although he remained in Congress until 1781, serving ably on many committees, the most important of which dealt with the Articles of Confederation.

In April of 1781, he returned home to his beloved Boston. He was a delegate to the Convention which drafted the Massachusetts Constitution. Under the new government he became a senator, and from 1789 to 1793 he was lieutenant-governor of his state. When Governor John Hancock died in 1793, Adams became governor and was elected again for three terms.

In 1796, during his last term as Governor of Massachusetts, Virginia cast fifteen votes for Samuel Adams for President of the United States. Thomas Jefferson had twenty votes. But Adams, now seventy-four, was soon to announce his retirement from public life. When Thomas Jefferson became President in 1801, he would have liked the old congressman in his cabinet. He wrote Adams: "How much I lament that time has deprived me of your aid! It would have been a day of glory which should have called you to the first office of my administration. But give us your counsel, my friend, and give us your blessing, and be assured that there exists not in the heart of man a more faithful esteem than mine to you, and that I shall ever bear you the most affectionate veneration and respect."

Samuel Adams was a strange combination of qualities rarely seen in one person. In religion he was the narrowest of Puritans; in manner easy and genial. Absolutely rigid in his opinions, he could express them with a flexibility that was often compliant. Most conservative of men, he was at the same time a vigorous revolutionary. At political maneuvering he was wily as a fox. With no foresight or push in business, he was a power of force and shrewdness in politics, where his foresight was keen and accurate. No one could be more skillful than he in the managing of men. So adroit was he that his followers were often not even aware that they were being managed. Though he was not considered eloquent as an orator and could not match his cousin, John Adams, as a debater, he could, when his deeper feelings were aroused, speak with a "purity, correctness and nervous elegance" of style that strongly impressed all who heard and saw him. John Adams said that Samuel had "an exquisite ear for music, and a charming voice when he pleased to exert it." But when Boston wanted a theatre Samuel Adams was Puritan enough to oppose it strongly.

Thomas Jefferson has told us that, as a speaker, Samuel Adams could not be compared with his cousin John, who, in Congress, was "our bulwark in debate. But Mr. Samuel Adams," he continued, "although not of fluent elocution, was so rigorously logical, so clear in his views, abundant in good sense, and master always of his subject, that he commanded the most profound attention whenever he rose in an assembly."

The last years of the old revolutionist were filled with honor and expressions of regard. Even the Federalists — the opposing party — honored him. In 1800, when the new Governor of Massachusetts, Caleb Strong, moved through Winter Street in a large procession which was probably his inaugural parade, old Mr. Adams sat at his window looking out at the pageant. The governor ordered a halt, stopped the music, got out of his carriage, and went to the door to shake the hand of the old hero. With head bared, the new governor expressed his reverence for the man who embodied the Spirit of '76. The soldiers presented arms. The crowd stood silent with uncovered heads.

Years later, in an oration in Lexington, Edward Everett described the beginnings of Samuel Adams's work in the 1760's.

"The throne of his ascendency was in Faneuil Hall," he said. These were the town meetings. "As each new measure of arbitrary power was announced from across the Atlantic, or each new act of menace and violence on the part of the officers of the government or of the army occurred in Boston, its citizens, oftentimes in astonishment and perplexity, rallied to the sound of his voice in Faneuil Hall; and there, as from the crowded gallery or the moderator's chair he animated, enlightened, fortified, and roused the admiring throng, he seemed to gather them together beneath the aegis of his indomitable spirit, as a hen gathereth her chickens under her wings."

During the summer of 1803, the old man grew more and more feeble. Early on Sunday morning, October 2, the bells of Boston tolled for his death. Samuel Adams had reached his eighty-first year.

The funeral procession, headed by the Independent Cadets and followed by many dignitaries and friends, moved through the streets as minute guns were fired from the old fort and muffled drums beat a dirge at Faneuil Hall. At the old State House, the cortège turned up Tremont Street toward the Old Granary Burying Ground.

Samuel Adams's unmarked grave is appropriately near that of the victims of the Boston Massacre, which had taken place thirty-three years before, and almost beneath the feet of passers-by along the busy modern thoroughfare of Uncle Sam's beloved Boston town.

John Hancock

January 23, 1737 — October 8, 1793

"I WRITE SO THAT George the Third may read without his spectacles," John Hancock is supposed to have said when he signed his name, in his big, bold, careful handwriting, to the Declaration of Independence. Infinitely relieved and happy that the Declaration was now an accomplished fact, he obviously felt like flaunting it before the king of England.

The first American Hancock was Nathaniel, the Signer's great-great-grandfather, who came from England. He probably came in 1633 — at any rate, he was granted two acres of land in Newtown (now Cambridge), Massachusetts, on January 5, 1634. He improved his two-acre patch and thrived as a small farmer. When his children came along, he was no doubt glad that a grammar school had started next to the first American college, Harvard, founded in 1636.

The early settlers' activities revolved about their church, in which succeeding generations of Hancocks became leaders. By the time John Hancock, the Signer, was born on January 23, 1737, a hundred years after Nathaniel Hancock's arrival as an immigrant, he had an ancestral background of ministers. He was born in Braintree, Massachusetts, where his father, the Reverend John Hancock, was minister of the Congregational Church. His mother had been Mary Hawke Thaxter when she married the minister. The Signer's grandfather was another John Hancock, pastor of the Congregational Church in Lexington. In that house, which had been his grandfather's parsonage, John Hancock and Samuel

Adams were sleeping on the April night of Paul Revere's ride in 1775.

John Hancock was only seven when his father died, leaving his mother almost penniless with three small children: Mary, John, and Ebenezer. His father's brother, the boy's Uncle Thomas, took his elder nephew, John, to raise in his own home in Boston. This made a great change in the boy's life. His Uncle Thomas Hancock was the wealthiest merchant in Boston and his house was a large mansion on Beacon Hill. Moreover, since he and his wife had no children of their own, Aunt Lydia lavished her affection on their nephew. She fussed over him, buying him the finest of clothes, and kept him home from school a year, probably because he was not a very strong child. From this time on, John Hancock grew up amid elegant and luxurious surroundings. At nine years of age, he was sent to the Public Latin School, now the oldest school in the country.

In the next five years he was required to cover much more than boys of today study in eight years. Recitations lasted from seven in the morning until five in the afternoon. There were one-week vacations at Thanksgiving and Christmas and three weeks in August. At first young John worked on grammar, spelling, penmanship (to good effect as we can see), and other familiar subjects, but then came Latin and Greek and studies we hear little of today, including the New Testament in Greek.

From the Latin School he was sent to Harvard, where he had to get up in time for six o'clock chapel, listen to Scripture reading in Hebrew or Greek, and report for his first recitation at 6:30. Students had six weeks' vacation in summer, five in winter. If they lived within ten miles of Cambridge, as Hancock did, they could go home for four days each month. Nevertheless, work was more intense than the study students complain about today.

Many other things were different: The college gave boys beer for their evening meal. They also drank wines and spirits. Rum punch was popular, and so was "flip," a horrid concoction of ale, beer, cider, "etc." — which apparently meant anything else they had at hand to pour in. It is no wonder Hancock began to suffer from gout in his fifties.

With an M.A. degree at seventeen, John Hancock was ready to take a job, but that was no problem at all, for the job was all ready. He had only to enter his uncle's counting-house and learn the business from the ground up. But it was a complex business, which included shipping, book-keeping, importing, buying and selling; and Uncle Thomas had built it up from scratch, without the advantage of a Harvard degree. From England, Thomas Hancock was importing tea, cloth, paper, cutlery, and sending back American codfish, whale oil, whale bone, and lumber. His merchandizing had spread to include Nova Scotia and the West Indies on this side of the Atlantic, and Holland and Spain besides Great Britain on the other. As there was very little money in New England, most of these deals had to be accomplished by trading. Shiploads of goods were not bought with money, but traded for something else, and this brought about a great deal of smuggling. It seems strange to us today that in the land of the Puritans smuggling was almost respectable, that it was rather taken for granted, and that many of the merchant princes of those days gained their great fortunes in illicit dealing. Four large Hancock ships were always sailing between Old and New England. It was a big business.

After six years of studying and working in the local part of the business, John went to England to meet business connections and to settle accounts for the House of Hancock. He was therefore in London when King George II died. He attended the great state funeral and remained to see the coronation of George III, because, as he wrote home, it would be "the grandest thing I shall ever meet with."

Back home in Boston in October, 1761, young Hancock found his uncle's health had badly deteriorated. Uncle Thomas, now suffering from frequent attacks of gout, took John into partnership; and when he died, three years later, John inherited the vast business. Though he was still only twenty-eight years old, he now possessed a fortune comparable to that of a modern millionaire.

The responsibility, however, was heavy and growing heavier because under George III British relations with the American colonies soon began to deteriorate. Times were getting worse for businessmen and especially so for merchants. The very next year the Stamp Act went into effect.

John Hancock's first political interests probably began when he joined several lodges. Men in those times spent their evenings with friends in various clubs, which met in taverns and coffee-houses. A man usually belonged to several — at all of which current events were discussed, and public questions were debated. In 1762, the year after he returned from England, John Hancock became a member of the Masonic Lodge of St. Andrews. He also joined St. John's Lodge, the Long Room Club, and the Merchants' Club. Influential citizens in business and the professions met monthly or weekly in these and other clubs, and, as time went on, they aired more and more grievances against mounting trade restrictions placed upon them by the mother country. "Out of these talks came some of the earliest rebellious ideas," writes Herbert S. Allan, John Hancock's biographer, "although most of the men who took part in them, including Hancock, had then no conscious thought of disloyalty to the Crown." In the Long Room Club were Paul Revere, Thomas Dawes, Samuel Adams, Dr. Benjamin Church (later found guilty of treason to America), and others who became the leaders of the Revolution.

Here was the beginning of colonial resentment of the heavy British import duties and other taxes that Parliament was forcing upon her American colonies. It was also the beginning of Hancock's political career. Association and discussion with these men led him to run for the office of selectman when the opportunity arose. He won and from then on, for the remainder of his life, paid more attention to his exhausting work as a statesman than to his profitable private business.

Then came the Stamp Act, which aroused such indignation as to bring the first show of violence against England by the Sons of Liberty. Samuel Adams is supposed to have inspired the gathering of a mob under the "Liberty Tree," a large elm at the corner of Washington and Essex streets. As yet, Hancock was opposed to violence, but Sam Adams was a rabble-rouser from the beginning. The mob destroyed the house and property of Thomas Hutchinson, the royal lieutenant-governor, and with it his library and collection of irreplaceable American historical manuscripts.

Hancock protested the Stamp Act not by violence but in letters to his English correspondents. In England, Benjamin Franklin was explaining to Parliament why the Stamp Act could not be enforced. But their efforts were fruitless. Though the Stamp Act was repealed, more oppressive acts of Parliament eventually convinced

Hancock that the colonists would have to resort to arms.

In the meantime, he was elected to the General Court, as Massachusetts still called its legislature.

In 1767 John Hancock gave Harvard £500 worth of books, fulfilling a promise his uncle had made, and adding some books of his own. The next year he was in difficulty over importing a large cargo of Madeira wine in his sloop *Liberty*. Accused of having smuggled some of the cargo ashore, he engaged John Adams to defend him. After some months the case was dropped (smuggling was common among the merchants of those times and not much frowned upon), but the *Liberty* was condemned, converted into a coast guard vessel, and later burned by a mob in Newport. The publicity made Hancock all the more popular with the common people. After a frightful fire in Boston in February, 1767, which destroyed more than twenty buildings, including some of Hancock's, he contributed a large sum of money to the relief of homeless families. He also gave many gifts to meeting-houses and churches — others as well as his own. People came to look upon him as a generous benefactor.

After the Boston Massacre, Hancock was chosen to head the town committee. Samuel Adams, ever active in keeping patriotic feelings stirred up, saw the great advantage in having Boston's wealthiest man on the side of the patriots. For if anything were to be lost in being a patriot, Hancock surely had the most to lose. To the British, the word patriot had come to mean those Americans who were disloyal to the Crown. But all most patriots wanted as yet was to have some say in the laws that governed them. Most of them were still loyal British subjects who were not thinking of separation from the mother country.

As Sam Adams's influence spread, he helped his friend Hancock become a local favorite, winning election to various minor offices. After the General Court became the Provincial Congress in 1774, he was chosen president.

Hancock was a militia officer himself. In 1772, he had been made "Captain of the Company of Cadets with the rank of Colonel," the cadets being a small military unit that served as honor guard to the governor. This he loved because he could dress up in a resplendent military uniform. For John Hancock was a vain little man. Slight of build, he had a dapper, neat appearance and, of course, he could afford the finest of clothing. Perhaps his Aunt Lydia had stirred this harmless vanity in him when he was a small child, for she took great pleasure in keeping the boy well dressed. However that may have been, Hancock was always generous and supplied uniforms and arms to his Cadets at his own expense. They loved him for it. He gave generously everywhere. He supplied Boston with its first street lamps, and also gave the town its first concert hall — stipulating that no British officers, whether of the army, navy, or revenue service, should ever be admitted!

Then, in the autumn of 1774, John Hancock cut himself off from the Crown. At this same time, Samuel Adams and other Massachusetts delegates to the First Continental Congress were on their way to Philadelphia. Hancock saw more excitement at home in Boston. Threats against his life were now being made. The Boston Port Bill had gone into effect. The British government had closed the harbor to all imports and exports. Whigs and Tories were more hostile than ever. Undaunted by all these signs that his life was in danger, Hancock accepted appointment as chairman of the provincial Committee of Safety and proceeded to provoke the redcoats still further. As chairman of the Committee of Safety, he had the power to call out the militia. When more British troops came to Boston, he suggested burning the city to get rid of them, though most of his own property would have been lost. But the patriots gave up this idea.

Early in the following March, a farmer visiting Boston was seized by British soldiers on false charges of having tried to influence a soldier to desert. They tarred and feathered him and paraded him on a wagon through the streets. A British regimental band led the procession, playing for the first time for the American public, an old English tune to which new words had been set. The military escort sang:

> *Yankee Doodle came to town*
> *For to buy a firelock;*
> *We will tar and feather him,*
> *And so we will John Hancock.*

Within a month, it was plain that events were mounting to a climax. Whig leaders were leaving town and sending wives and families away. Hancock and Samuel Adams went out to Lexington and spent the night of April 18/19 in the old Hancock parsonage. But at Paul Revere's warning they were forced to flee at dawn. These two most wanted rebels escaped through woods and swamps while the first shots were exchanged on the Lexington Common in front of the parsonage. The British went on to Concord hoping to seize the patriots' ammunition but were stopped by the "embattled farmers." Meanwhile, Hancock and Adams were making their way safely to Woburn.

About two weeks later, chosen a delegate to the Second Continental Congress, Hancock was on his way to Philadelphia. The British General Gage had for a short time permitted Boston inhabitants to leave the city, and Hancock's Aunt Lydia and his fiancée, Dorothy Quincy, had gone to the home of an old friend of the family in Fairfield, Connecticut. From New York, Hancock sent letters back to his "Dolly," describing the rousing reception he was given in New York. The reception was meant for all the delegates, naturally, but Hancock was vain enough to make it appear as if it were especially for him. Perhaps he wanted to impress Dolly. And perhaps a good deal of the homage was indeed meant for him, for Hancock was very popular and was now known throughout the colonies for his many defiant gestures toward the British government. While Samuel Adams, equally defiant and a devotee of complete independence long before Hancock, had always worked quietly, Hancock deliberately provoked publicity.

He wrote Dorothy that when he was within a mile of New York, his carriage was stopped by people who wanted to unhitch the horses and pull his carriage into the city. He begged off from that, but "when I got to the entrance of the city," he wrote, "the number of spectators increased to perhaps 7000 or more."

The delegates from New England, now numbering fourteen (those from Connecticut, New York, and probably Rhode Island having joined those from Massachusetts), were all greeted by groups both military and civilian. Silas Deane of Connecticut wrote: "A battalion of about eight hundred men in uniform and bayonets fixed, with a band of music, received us with a military salute — led us down the main street to the corner of Wall Street; up that and down the Broadway by the fort; then up to Fraunces'

Tavern." At ten o'clock that night, John Hancock sat down there to a supper of fried oysters. Fraunces' Tavern is still one of New York's most interesting landmarks — and still a restaurant.

Approaching Philadelphia on May 10, the delegates were met by about two hundred "principal gentlemen on horseback." Hancock and Adams — already famous not only because of their own achievements but also because they came from the center of revolution — rode, surrounded by this escort, in a phaeton drawn by a pair of horses. As they entered the Pennsylvania city, all the church bells were ringing to greet them.

There was to be no rest for the travelers. Having washed up after riding through "the greatest cloud of dust I ever saw," Hancock wrote there was just time to have dinner before these founding fathers had to be in Independence Hall for the opening of the Second Continental Congress.

Philadelphia was the largest city in the colonies in those days. Its houses and streets reflected the prosperity of the rich countryside surrounding it, where ideal farmlands produced food more abundantly and more easily than did the colder and stonier New England the Massachusetts delegation knew. Though it had a certain refinement due to its Quaker origin, all kinds of people were to be seen in the streets: Indians wrapped in blankets; Pennsylvania Dutch in wooden shoes; Germans, Swedes, and Welsh farmers from the surrounding countryside; hunters from the "back country" wearing leather shirts and carrying their long rifles. Slaves were still bought and sold at Philadelphia auctions. On top of all this was the silk-and-satin aristocracy.

Such a mixture meant also a mixture of opinion; much more so than in Boston, whose inhabitants were mostly of a kind and mostly of English ancestry.

John Hancock, now forty-five years old, was unanimously chosen President of the Congress. Though he was vastly pleased by this great honor, he soon found that he would have to earn it by laborious and discouraging endeavor. The next two and a half years were extremely difficult for him. The role of president was arduous, and the atmosphere uncongenial. A good many Philadelphians were far from enthusiastic about the approaching Revolution. Philadelphia businessmen were ultra-conservative and willing to put up with things as they were. They did not like British trade restrictions any more than the Yankees did; but because they had greater resources for export in their corner of fertile Pennsylvania, they could stand the higher import duties better than New Englanders could. Besides, the Quakers, who were the dominant part of the population and pacifist by religious principle, preferred to accept whatever restrictions were put upon them rather than fight. Pennsylvania was therefore unsympathetic to the bold, new, radical ideas that Samuel Adams most ardently urged. Hancock labored under a tremendous handicap as president of a dissident assemblage that was struggling with some of the most difficult problems ever undertaken by statesmen. Moreover, rich as he was, he was intellectually inferior to some of the other statesmen sitting in the Congress over which he was presiding.

A month later, in mid-June, he suffered a bitter disappointment. It was necessary to appoint a commander in chief for the new American Army.

Strange as it now seems, Hancock wanted this appointment for himself, although his only military experience had been as colonel of the Cadets. In addition to his lack of experience, he was not a strong man physically and could never have endured such a heavy military responsibility nor withstood the rigors of army life. Even his friends the Adamses did not favor this idea.

When this discussion came up, a tall, robust figure in uniform, who had been listening to congressional business, rose and left the room. This was Colonel George Washington of the Virginia Militia, who had fought in the French and Indian War, had saved Braddock's army, and had long defended the Virginia frontier. After the colonel left the room, John Adams moved that Washington be appointed. Samuel Adams seconded the motion. Hancock was so bitterly disappointed he could not keep from showing it, and it affected his friendship with the Adamses, at least for a time. His truly great service to the country was his ability to mediate between the antagonistic factions in the Congress, and keep its business moving smoothly, with an appearance of unity through all the heated arguments and debates that preceded the day of the all-important vote on independence.

It was his duty, too, to see that all the thirteen provincial assemblies back home were kept informed of what was going on in Congress; to persuade them to comply with congressional resolutions;

to appease them when their own pet projects were by-passed. This meant a vast amount of daily letter-writing.

Even after the first shots had been fired at Lexington and Concord, and at Bunker Hill, there were ultra-conservatives in the middle colonies who still insisted on trying one more time to settle peacefully with Britain for American self-government within the Empire, rather than war over complete independence. In July, John Hancock signed their "Olive Branch" petition, as did a majority of delegates. But it was useless — George III would not even read their petition when it was presented to him.

Then the committees in Congress began to work long hours, day and night, making plans for the needs of a new country. Besides an army, there would have to be a navy. There was the problem of friendly relations with foreign countries and with the Indians. If a long war came, the colonies would have to have money and they looked to France for loans. Constant communications had to be maintained between the delegates in Philadelphia and the thirteen provincial congresses.

In April, North Carolina sent instructions to her delegates to stand for independence, the first colony to do so. A month later, Virginia instructed her delegates to *propose* independence. The atmosphere grew more intense as the days became warmer. On June 7, the chairman of the Virginia delegation, Richard Henry Lee, offered the great resolution. Three weeks were given to its consideration. It was a hot July first when Lee's resolution was reopened in Congress.

The leaders of the independence movement asked for a delay in the vote, hoping that a little more time would win a unanimous or near-unanimous vote. They almost had it when Pennsylvania and South Carolina moved over into line, and when Delaware's Caesar Rodney arrived on the morning of July 2 after an all-night ride through heavy rain and thunderstorms. His vote carried Delaware for independence.

After the black night, the vote came *yea*.

It was unanimous — with twelve colonies voting. New York representatives abstained from the vote. They themselves favored independence; but they were bound by their instructions to keep the way open for reconciliation with Great Britain.

Two more days of impassioned oratory followed, until, about

two o'clock on the afternoon of the Fourth, "the great white paper was reported out of committee to the House with a recommendation for approval, and was immediately ratified."

It was done.

John Hancock and Secretary Charles Thomson were ordered to sign the paper. It was then that Hancock made the remark that opens this chapter.

After about two and a half years of arduous work in Congress, John Hancock resigned, feeling that his indifferent health required rest. For all the demanding, worrisome labor he had done, he never received a cent of pay, though he was given $1392 in repayment of his own personal loans to the treasury. Six years later he was reimbursed for his incidental and household expenses.

Simple good manners demanded a polite vote of thanks from that body of public men as a gesture of gratitude to a leader who had been faithful to his trust. But here Samuel Adams, with his fanatically narrow conception of democracy, intervened. Confusing gratitude with homage, he thought no special tribute should be paid to any person in a democracy. To him, that smacked of treatment given to royalty! Samuel Adams had great influence among the members of the Congress and when he raised the issue, a vote of thanks to their presiding member was opposed. Hancock was given no public thanks and no formal credit for his excellent work as mediator in what was perhaps the most agitated, unhappy, uncertain Congress we have ever had. Keenly hurt, he was never able to feel so friendly as before toward his boyhood friend. But his own farewell speech to Congress was a model of restraint and good will.

From this time on, though he was again elected to Congress, Hancock spent more time in Boston and, in the latter war years, became primarily interested in the politics of his own state. In 1778, he had brief military experience when he commanded the Massachusetts contingent of five thousand men who were to move against the British in Rhode Island. But as a major general in charge of troops, he was not a success and, besides, he was already suffering from the gout.

John Hancock was a great favorite with the people, though he had some severe critics among his associates. Part of their feeling was due to his vanity, obvious to those who knew him but unknown to the mass of the people who could not see this side of his character.

In 1780, he was a member of the Massachusetts Constitutional Convention, and in September was elected governor. After serving five years, he resigned during the post-war economic depression, but was later re-elected. He presided at the 1788 convention for ratifying the Federal Constitution. His prestige increased as the years passed until he died at the age of fifty-six, on October 8, 1793, while serving his ninth term as governor.

No one had ever been given such funeral honors in Massachusetts by the state's elect, and with such expressions of sorrow by the people. Governor Hancock, who in life had shown himself a vain lover of pomp, luxury, and flattering appreciation, had asked for a quiet funeral with no public display, no firing of the salute customarily given at the grave of a chief magistrate. But this time he was not granted his wish.

Instead, his body lay in state in the Hancock mansion on Beacon Hill for almost a week while thousands of mourners from all over the commonwealth filed by for their last view of this "founding father." At sunrise on the day of the funeral, the bells of Boston began tolling and continued for an hour. Flags flew at half-staff; all ships in the harbor flew flags at half-mast. At one o'clock all stores closed. Every military unit in Boston was assembled on beautiful Boston Common. Units from nearby towns, under the command of General William Hull, who had served in the Revolution, were also there.

When the procession marched out of the Common, all the state functionaries and various citizens of national standing followed the military units. In the center of these walked seventy-one-year-old Samuel Adams, now the acting governor. An artillery guard of honor followed the coffin, drawing a shining brass fieldpiece draped in black. This fieldpiece was named the *Hancock*. It had been stolen from the local British arsenal at the instigation of young John Hancock almost forty years before when war clouds were gathering.

Then came the family, in twenty-one carriages. Then the Vice-President of the United States, John Adams; the justices of the courts; ministers of foreign governments; Harvard College representatives; the city officers; churchmen; other notables. And after them the people — a column marching four abreast and stretching for half a mile, people who had loved, admired, trusted John Hancock.

At two o'clock they moved off to the dirge of muffled drums. Across the Common to Boylston Street (then called Frog Lane), to Washington Street, and around the State House. Here Samuel Adams had to drop out, too tired to go on and, perhaps, overcome with emotion and memories. On to the Old Granary Burying Ground — the last stop. All this long lugubrious time the boom of cannons sounded from nearby hills, until John Hancock was placed beside his uncle in the ancestral tomb.

As one walks today along Tremont Street and passes this truly hallowed ground, one may see on a stone, among other remembered famous names, the one who among those dreamers of a new nation was the real Yankee Doodle Dandy.

John Adams

John Adams

October 19, 1735 — July 4, 1826

To SIGNER JOHN ADAMS, second President of the United States, America is indebted for much more than his work during the critical years that saw the launching of a new nation. For John Adams was a man of multifarious achievement. We are indebted to him for his ceaseless writing — his diary, the numerous letters he wrote to his wife, his autobiography — all of which give us much information which we, today, would not otherwise have.

Like his second cousin, Samuel, John Adams was descended from the Henry Adams who came from England about a hundred years before John was born. On October 19, 1735, the Signer John was born in the old family farmhouse at Braintree. His father was another John who had married Susanna Boylston. Her more urban and sophisticated family, of Brookline and Boston, had already become prominent in medicine.

The Adamses had been hard-working Puritan farmers, and John,

Senior, was a prominent citizen — selectman for many years, lieutenant in the militia, deacon in the church, and a good father. His influence on his son was very great. John considered his father "the honestest man I ever knew," and wrote after his father died that he had managed almost all the business of the town for twenty years.

The elder John himself taught his son to read before sending him to one of the "dame schools" which little boys and girls customarily attended. The school mistress, a certain Dame Belcher, taught reading, writing, and arithmetic, and guided her pupils through the traditional *New England Primer.* Then young John was sent to a Latin School, taught by a sour and uninspiring schoolmaster called Joseph Cleverly, a teacher so dull that John Adams came to hate all Latin studies, preferring mathematics. But his father had set his heart on his son's going to Harvard, which required Latin for entrance. When the boy admitted to his father that he could not bear Mr. Cleverly and preferred another teacher, his father consented. Under a teacher he really liked, John Adams was ready to enter Harvard in less than a year, at the age of fourteen.

In those days, Harvard College had four tutors, each carrying one class through its four-year curriculum. The day began with prayers at six, every student taking his turn reading from the Bible. Breakfast, usually "bread, biscuit and milk," followed, and classes started with a lecture at eight. Then came study and recitations until a light lunch at noon, followed by more study until evening prayers at five and a thin supper at 7:30. Students who could afford it "lived out" and took their meals in a tavern. After supper the students were free to entertain themselves for about an hour, until the college bell rang at nine, when they had to go to their rooms.

Greek, Latin, logic, rhetoric, and ethics were John Adams's freshman studies. Later, he had natural philosophy (elementary physics and chemistry), more philosophy, metaphysics, and geography. Every Saturday during the whole four years was given over to theology.

Upon graduation in 1755, he became a teacher in Worcester, a larger town than Braintree, with a population of about fifteen hundred. But school teaching did not greatly appeal to this ambitious young man. His parents wanted him to become a Congregational minister, but he himself hesitated between medicine and the law. In the end the law won out and, while he was still teaching school, the young pedagogue began reading in the office of James Putnam, a Worcester attorney.

John Adams was never an idler. Beginning his second year of teaching, he wrote in his diary: "I am resolved not to neglect my time as I did last year. I am resolved to rise with the sun and to study the Scriptures on Thursday, Friday, Saturday and Sunday mornings, and to study some Latin author the other three mornings." This was before school opened for the day, of course. Then: "Noons and nights I intend to read English authors. . . . I will strive with all my soul to be something more than persons who have had less advantages than myself." Though he frequently fell short of these exceedingly strict hours, the young man was preparing for a distinguished career. One Friday his diary says briefly, "A very rainy day. Dreamed away the time." But some of this kind of day-dreaming was useful, too, for in it came ideas and plans for the future.

Teaching, studying law, reading the classics, engaging in conversations, debates, discussions with the best company in the town (for a school-teacher gets to know everybody), John Adams, by 1758, was ready for his bar examination in Boston. Admitted then to the bar, he decided to practice in his home town and returned to Braintree. But since practice came slowly in so small a place, and since there wasn't much of it, the twenty-three-year-old Adams helped in the fields on his father's farm and enjoyed it. He also took an interest in public affairs and began writing articles for the newspapers.

After six years, he married Miss Abigail Smith, daughter of the Reverend William and Elizabeth Quincy Smith of Weymouth. This marriage widened the young lawyer's connections with other prominent families. Abigail was to prove a true helpmeet and companion for her husband in the difficult periods of his career. Theirs was a marriage of real partnership. They were to have four children, a girl and three boys, one of whom would be John Quincy Adams, the sixth President of the United States.

The year after the pair were married, the colonists were infuriated by the Stamp Act. Adams considered the Stamp Act unlawful, since the colonists had not consented to it, but he disapproved of the riots that followed its enactment. He contributed essays to the *Boston Gazette* on various legal points concerning the act and prepared the resolutions of protest for Braintree which were imitated throughout the Bay Colony. This led to a long contest between him and the royal lieutenant-governor, Thomas Hutchinson.

Two years after the Stamp Act was repealed, the Adamses moved to Boston and lived in the "White House" on Brattle Square. But before long, Adams, considering city life unwholesome, became homesick for Braintree. Then, for about a year he found himself commuting between the two places.

When his boyhood friend John Hancock, now the wealthiest businessman in the city, was charged with smuggling, he engaged Adams to defend him. Other important legal cases drew him into patriotic causes. He was elected to the General Court as representative of Boston, and, though he devoted himself to the law and soon achieved a leading position at the bar, times and events were pulling him into public life.

By the time the Boston Tea Party took place, Adams considered it "the grandest event which has yet happened since the controversy with Britain opened." Tension mounted higher and higher. By mid-May, the Boston Committee of Correspondence recommended to all colonies a suspension of trade with Great Britain.

When the Massachusetts delegates were chosen for the First Continental Congress, John Adams was among the number, and when he took his seat in Carpenter's Hall, Philadelphia, where the first Congress met, he lacked about a month to his fortieth birthday.

He had anticipated the adventure of traveling so far with great pleasure. It was going to be most interesting to see other towns and cities; to meet the representatives of the other colonies; to take part in the greatest discussions and decisions that ever faced a group of men, who were about to lay the foundations for a new nation. But who knew what this near future might bring? War? Very likely. Failure? Who knew?

Pausing in his southward journey to go sight-seeing in various cities and meet local political leaders, Adams reported in his letters home on the welcome the Massachusetts representatives received in

Hartford, New Haven, Milford, and Stratford in Connecticut. He was enraptured by New York, where he and his companions stayed for a few days. They also visited Princeton and finally arrived in Philadelphia, "dirty, dusty, and fatigued." Seeing the rich New Yorkers and their great estates made him feel, as he wrote his wife, that he had not much to show for all his labors. He kept contrasting his simple Braintree life with that of the wealthy merchants in the larger towns and cities he passed through. But he made up his mind he was going to "enjoy good company, good conversation and — a fine ride and see a little more of the world than I have seen before."

If doubts and fears like those of John Adams ever troubled John Hancock and Samuel Adams, they seem never to have mentioned them. But John Adams was a man often assailed by doubts — though he always conquered them. Perhaps he had the kind of imagination that caused him to look inward. Perhaps this was because he had studied more than either of the other two. At any rate, he confessed his feelings to his Abigail in his letters.

After a short while in Philadelphia, Adams wrote her: "We have numberless prejudices to remove here. We have been obliged to act with great delicacy and caution. We have been obliged to keep ourselves out of sight, and to feel pulses and sound the depths, to insinuate our sentiments, designs and desires by means of other persons." He was disturbed because "great things are wanted to be done, and little things only I fear can be done." To Abigail he admitted, "I confess myself to be full of fears that the ministry and their friends . . . will prevail and crush the cause and friends of liberty."

Meeting the representatives of all the colonies, except Georgia, for the first time in Carpenters' Hall, John Adams saw in that body of men "a great spirit." Two committees were formed: One was instructed to "state the rights of the colonies in general, the several instances in which these rights are violated or infringed, and the means most proper to be pursued for obtaining a restoration of them." The two Adamses were the Massachusetts representatives on this important committee. The other committee was to examine and report on the regulations which affected the trade and manufactures of the colonies. And then began the tedious long hours of discussions.

There was little time now to write letters to his wife. He explained that he had "the characters and tempers, the principles and views, of fifty gentlemen, total strangers to me, to study, and the trade, policy and whole interest of a dozen provinces to learn." But some of his time was given to happier hours of relaxation, when the Philadelphia patriots were eager to entertain the Massachusetts delegates whom they lionized. After much wining and dining, Adams reported on the good food, the good company, and the fraternal spirit. When a false rumor spread that Boston had been bombarded by the British fleet, expressions of sympathy and support touched him to tears. He wrote his wife: "The spirit, the firmness, the prudence of our Province are vastly applauded, and we are universally acknowledged the saviors and defenders of American liberty."

When Congress adjourned after many seemingly endless sessions at which, Adams thought, too many men talked too much, John Adams was eager to go home.

No sooner was he back in Braintree than he was re-elected to the Provincial Congress. When articles written by a Tory using the pen-name "Massachusettensis," began to appear in the Boston paper *Post Boy*, attacking the patriot position, Adams wrote essays in rebuttal under the name "Novanglus," which were published in the *Boston Gazette*.

On May 10, 1775, John Adams was again in Philadelphia for the opening of the Second Continental Congress. There was much to do. The business of Congress, he wrote Abigail, was "as great and important as can be trusted to man, and the difficulty and intricacy of it prodigious. When fifty or sixty men have a constitution to form for a great empire, at the same time that they have a country of fifteen hundred miles in extent to fortify, millions to arm and train, a naval power to begin, and extensive commerce to regulate, numerous tribes of Indians to negotiate with, a standing army of twenty-seven thousand men to raise, pay, victual, and officer, I really shall pity those fifty or sixty men." Yet he was one of them.

While the thinkers and planners were hard at work in Philadelphia, fighting was breaking out in the north. John Adams often wished he could be a soldier and see some action instead of sitting in Congress listening to endless talk. However, according to his good friend, Dr. Benjamin Rush of Philadelphia, he was in the place where he was most needed and doing the most good. Said Rush: "He was a most sensible and forcible speaker. Every member of Congress . . . acknowledged him to be the first man in the House. . . . Dr. Brownson used to say when he spoke, he fancied an angel was let down from heaven to illumine the Congress. He saw the whole of a subject at a single glance, and by a happy union of the powers of reasoning and persuasion often succeeded in carrying measures which were at first sight of an unpopular nature . . . he was a real American in principle and conduct."

Often at work from seven in the morning until eleven at night, the forty-year-old Adams frequently complained of ill health, and his eyes bothered him. When Congress adjourned for the month of August, he hurried home for a short visit, to ramble "all alone, through the fields, groves, meadows . . . of peaceful, happy Braintree." Best of all was to be back with Abigail and the children. In those days, when forty miles a day was fast traveling, and Philadelphia and Boston were twelve days apart, Adams could have only a taste of home before he had to start off again on his third trip to Philadelphia.

For three autumn months congressional work occupied all his time until, in the first week of December, he asked for a short leave to return home. So eager was he to be on his way that he broke his rule about not traveling on Sundays. He had Christmas with his family, made a trip to Cambridge to inspect the army, saw George Washington, and talked with people to learn their opinions.

Before the end of the month he was on his way back to Congress. He stopped first in Framingham to inspect the artillery that was captured at Fort Ticonderoga by Ethan Allen, then continued traveling over what had become a familiar route until he at last reached Philadelphia after a cold journey of eighteen days during which he stopped all along the way to talk to patriots.

In Philadelphia he found the delegates in "deep anxiety." He himself was now eager for independence. He knew it had to come, though it meant all-out war. War, after all, had now been going on for more than a year, not only in Massachusetts, but in New Hampshire and Virginia. Norfolk had been burned and cannonaded on the order of Lord Dunmore, and the Virginians were ready to demand independence. Adams was impatient at the backwardness of the middle colonies. After the fighting at Dorchester Heights in early March, 1776, a letter from his wife told him how the house shook with the thunder of distant cannon fire even while she sat at her desk writing. Then Abigail had gone out to climb Penn's Hill near their Braintree home to watch the artillery fire between the American and British batteries. The middle colonies simply *had* to be brought round to Adams's views which were, by this time, the views of the majority.

When committees were appointed to prepare a declaration of independence and to plan treaties with foreign powers, Adams was on both. He was also appointed to the Board of War.

After Richard Henry Lee placed the motion for independence before Congress on June 7, the question was to wait for three weeks to "ripen." Most of the colonies were now in favor of it. South Carolina, Pennsylvania, Delaware, and New York were still definitely reluctant.

The day came. John Adams was up early that morning of July 1. He rehearsed his own remarks in case he should have to speak. He and Samuel Adams and Richard Henry Lee reviewed their plans for working the resolution through the Congress. He wrote a letter to the Governor of Georgia, Archibald Bullock, who had been a delegate, in which he said: "This morning is assigned for the greatest debate of all."

As leader of the opposition to independence, John Dickinson of Pennsylvania spoke first in the fight against the resolution. He spoke with "ardent zeal," with "politeness and candor," at great length "with all his eloquence." After he sat down there was a long pause. It became uncomfortable. Who should answer this "orator of reconciliation?"

John Adams could not let this great moment pass. He stood up and began by saying that he had not the talents of the orators of ancient times, that he was no Pericles, Cicero, nor Demosthenes, but since the issue to be discussed might be safely left to the guidance of "plain understanding and common sense," he launched forth and made the "most notable speech of his life."

He reviewed the legal and constitutional arguments. He pointed out the measures the British Parliament had taken to curtail the liberties of their American colonies. He described the deepening crisis over the recent past years, the tyranny which had led to armed conflict. He mentioned past efforts at reconciliation, which had been in vain. Then he said that independence was inevitable and spoke of the advantages to be gained by declaring it at once.

Just as the moment came for the final question, the New Jersey delegates entered the hall. Though their instructions gave them permission to vote for independence, they wanted to hear a summary of the arguments. During the pause that followed, every one looked at John Adams. Laughingly approaching him, Edward Rutledge of South Carolina told Adams he must "satisfy the gentlemen from New Jersey." For, he continued, "Nobody will speak but you upon this subject, Mr. Adams. You have the topics so ready." Adams hated to repeat what he had just been saying — what he had, indeed, said in Congress twenty times over; but, when Dr. Witherspoon of New Jersey pressed him, he yielded. Afterwards, another New Jersey delegate, Richard Stockton, wrote his son: "The man to whom the country is most indebted for the great measure of independency is Mr. John Adams of Boston. I call him the Atlas of American Independence. He it was who sustained the debate, and, by the force of his reasoning, demonstrated not only the justice, but the expediency of the measure." Now, at the very end of the long argument, it was John Adams who urged in Congress the case for freedom, just as another Adams — his older cousin, Samuel Adams — had first urged it in Boston, many years before.

After Adams's speech, a quick canvass made it clear that only nine states were strong for independence; and it was most desirable that an affirmative vote should show unanimity. Pennsylvania and South Carolina were opposed to independence. New York delegates said their instructions held them back and they would abstain from voting. The two Delaware delegates who were present, McKean and Read, were split, and Thomas McKean, the pro-independence delegate, sent at once for the absent Caesar Rodney, who was strong for independence. Before the day's session ended, Rutledge of South Carolina was prevailed upon to concede that his colony would fall into line if, for the sake of unity, Delaware and Pennsylvania supported independence.

The large, prosperous, central colony of Pennsylvania was the last stumbling block. Of her seven delegates, three were for independence; four opposed. After further arguments and exhortations, it was finally agreed that Morris and Dickinson, two opposed, would not officially attend the next day, and then the three for independence, Benjamin Franklin, John Morton, James Wilson, could outweigh the other two against. These two, Charles Humphreys and Thomas Willing, never signed the Declaration of Independence. In fact, because of changes soon afterward, several signatures on the Declaration are those of men who were not even present at the voting on July 2.

So passed July 1. The vote would be taken the next day.

July 2, 1776, dawned squally with showers. It had been raining, with thunderstorms, all night — a most disagreeable ride for a man on horseback. Yet Caesar Rodney, responding to McKean's summons, rode all that wet night to reach Philadelphia. Inside the hall in the morning, the atmosphere was tight with tension. When word came that Rodney was on his way, Delaware suddenly became very important. As the members reassembled after lunch, Rodney, mud-stained, soaked to the skin, exhausted, rode up on his dripping horse.

Then the voting began, colony by colony. Rodney brought Delaware's vote over to the side of independence. With South Carolina's decision for independence, Pennsylvania came into line. With New York still abstaining from the vote, twelve colonies voted for independence. There was no vote against it.

It had all taken a vast deal of "managing." But it was done at last: the final act of an idea first born in a room in Boston fifteen years before, Samuel Adams's great dream.

John's letter to Abigail told her that he felt sure July 2 would be "celebrated by succeeding generations as the great anniversary festival." He thought it ought to be commemorated "by a solemn act of devotion to God Almighty." It should "be solemnized with pomp and parade, with shows, games, sports, guns, bells, bonfires and illuminations, from one end of the continent to the other, from this time forward forevermore."

Adams had no time for rest or relaxation. More and more duties were heaped upon him, until, worn out by the hot summer months of constant and arduous labor, anxious about his family at home, and wishing to confer with his constituents in his own harrassed state, he was able to leave Philadelphia at last on October 13.

He spent the next three months at home, returning to Congress on February 1, 1777. By that time the British held Philadelphia and Congress had to meet in Baltimore. Committee work now obliged him to take part in the debates on currency, on the French loan, on price regulation. In late October, 1777, he left Congress and, though re-elected, he did not serve because he had also been chosen as Commissioner to France.

With his ten-year-old son, John Quincy Adams, he sailed for France in February, 1778, aboard the new twenty-four-gun frigate, *Boston*. It is interesting now to note what a traveler had to take with him on a sea voyage two hundred years ago. In addition to their clothing, Mr. Adams and his son had their own bedding and food for a six-week crossing. Their baggage included a bushel of Indian meal (for making johnny cakes and hasty pudding), a keg of rum, tea, chocolate, brown sugar, two bottles of mustard, six chickens to provide eggs until they were themselves eaten, two fat sheep, five bushels of corn, a barrel of apples, fourteen dozen eggs, wafers, pepper, two mattresses and bolsters — among other things! Adams had three reams of paper, two account books, 25 quills (for use as pens), a bottle of home-made ink, tobacco and a dozen clay pipes.

Though his long life had not yet reached its half way mark at forty-three, John Adams had now done the work for which we read about him here — the work that made him a Signer. This man who once, as newly appointed congressman, had happily anticipated the sights he would see on a journey between Boston and Philadelphia, was now to undertake several trips to Europe. He spent the war years in France as commissioner of treaties and of peace, with journeys to Holland to negotiate loans. After his first return to Braintree for an all-too-short reunion with his family, Congress again appointed him commissioner to France and, later, minister to Holland. On this second trip he took his second son, Charles, as well as John Quincy, the elder. On the first trip, John Quincy had done so well in school in Paris that his father was encouraged to try the experiment with Charles. Abigail stayed home and worked the farm. In 1784, however, Adams sent for her and the two younger children. Until 1785, John Adams served the new United States as diplomat in France.

After Cornwallis surrendered at Yorktown the war was practically won, but endless negotiations were still necessary to frame the peace. By this time John Adams was, next to Benjamin Franklin, his young country's most experienced diplomat. It became his heart's desire to be appointed America's first minister to the Court of St. James.

He achieved his wish and from 1785 to 1788 represented the United States in Great Britain. In February of 1789, when the presidential electors voted George Washington first President of the United States, they elected John Adams first Vice-President, and after serving two terms he became the second President. Adams commented on Washington's pleasant and friendly manner during the inauguration, but added slyly that he knew very well the old hero was delighted to lay down the burdens of his office.

Since the new White House was not yet finished, the President and his family remained in Philadelphia during most of his term but moved into the new (and still unfinished) White House late in 1800. Abigail wrote a friend that she did not arrive till October 16 and added, "This house is twice as large as our meeting house." Not a single room was yet completed, but six could be made comfortable though thirteen fires had to be kept going. Mrs. Adams found one comfort, however: the huge audience room made a fine place to hang her washing!

At last the chunky little boy from Braintree had reached the climax of a great career. His had been, on the whole, a happy life.

Although he suffered some severe illnesses, John Adams lived in harmony with a loving family and many friends. Like all great men in politics, he had his enemies, but even these — or some of them — became more friendly in his old age. With all his intense and lengthy working hours, he enjoyed periods of relaxation in country walks at his beloved old Braintree farm and, later, in the parks and gardens in France.

The active years flew by. Adams was growing old. When he was eighty-three he lost his dear Abigail after fifty-four years of an ideal partnership. Thomas Jefferson wrote him a consoling letter. In fact, one of Adams's greatest pleasures in his latter years was his correspondence with Thomas Jefferson. The two men had had serious differences when Jefferson, defeating Adams, became the third President of the United States; but that was now in the past. Jefferson also wrote to congratulate Adams upon the election of his son, John Quincy Adams, to be the sixth President of the United States. Corresponding with Jefferson became the old man's deepest satisfaction. "Every line from you exhilarates my spirits and gives me a glow of pleasure," he wrote Jefferson, adding, "I look back with rapture to those golden days when Virginia and Massachusetts lived and acted together like brothers."

Two cherished events of his last years were the visits of Hannah Quincy who had been a teen-age sweetheart over fifty years before, and of the Marquis de Lafayette whom he had known in wartime. Hannah Quincy was now Mrs. Ebenezer Storer and a widow, but the years fell away as she entered the room, and old Adams greeted her with a happy smile, saying, "What! Madam, shall we not go walk in Cupid's Grove together?" That was the name of the nearby lover's lane. Taken aback for the moment, the old lady replied, "Ah, sir, it would not be the first time that we have walked there."

And then, in 1824, the year which saw Adams's son nominated for President, the old General Lafayette returned with his own son to visit the United States. The Marquis was given a hero's procession in Washington, again in New York, and again in Boston. He was honored as the great French friend who had come, a young man, to help the cause of the thirteen colonies. Adams sent him an invitation, and from Boston the Marquis went to the Adams farm at Braintree. They sat and talked of their reminiscences, of the battles and glories of a half century gone. But the years had made their mark on each and, though delighted at meeting again, both were saddened by time's toll. Aware, too, that this would be their last meeting, each made the same comment afterwards: Adams said privately, "That is not the Lafayette I knew." The Frenchman said, "That was not the John Adams I knew."

One more summer: 1826 — the summer which began with great plans for the fiftieth anniversary celebration of American independence. The historic cities, most especially Boston, bustled with excitement. In June, a committee called upon John Adams, asking him to attend on the Fourth of July. What a thing to have the

Grand Old Man present and on view on this day! No one would ever forget it. But Adams regretted he could not undertake the carriage ride, and he couldn't sit still on a hard seat all that time in July heat. He dictated his message: the thirteen United States were "destined to date the periods of their birth and emancipation from the Fourth of July 1776."

As the time drew nearer, the days became hotter and Boston was in a fever of excitement over the approaching anniversary day. A half century had passed since those great events. Every one seemed to have gathered that day on the Common to hear the bands, to see the Ancient and Honorable Artillery Company and the Boston militia pass in review. Josiah Quincy, Senior, gave the oration. People were jammed together under a hot sun to hear him. He described the growth and progress of the country since that great day fifty years ago, when it cut the ties with England. He referred to "that ancient citizen of Boston, that patriarch of American independence." But the sole survivor of "New England's worthies" never knew what was being said, for out in the old farmhouse, with family and friends gathered about him, old John Adams was sleeping away his last morning on earth.

When he was conscious for a time, a servant by his bedside asked: "Do you know, sir, what day it is?" "O yes, it is the glorious Fourth of July," replied the dying man. "God bless it. God bless you all."

He fell into a coma but about noon revived for a few clear moments and murmured: "Thomas Jefferson survives." Then he became unconscious once more.

About six in the evening of that July 4, 1826, John Adams met "the great and solemn event" of death. He had written to Jefferson some time before that he was ready for it. Unknown to him, at beautiful Monticello, Thomas Jefferson had preceded his friend into history by a few hours.

It took almost a week for the word to spread throughout the country — a country that now extended west to the Mississippi and beyond. Astonishment grew into wonder, amazement, awe — that these two great figures in the cause of national freedom should have expired on the same day — and that day the fiftieth anniversary of the birth of the United States.

It seemed as if destiny had taken a hand in it.

Elbridge Gerry

Elbridge Gerry

July 17, 1744 — November 23, 1814

ELBRIDGE GERRY'S FATHER came from the village of Newton Abbot in Devonshire, a beautiful and balmy region in southwestern England. He left in 1730, about thirty years before the American colony where he settled began to have troubles with the mother country. Since Newton Abbot lies close to the sea in the mouth of the Teign river, Thomas Gerry grew up near the water. He arrived in New York as master of his own ship. He sailed on until, northeast of Boston, he found the place he wanted to live at Marblehead. It was a little point of land jutting out into salt water — the kind of locale where he could feel at home.

Before Thomas Gerry went on to Marblehead however, he met Elizabeth Greenleaf, a daughter of a wealthy Boston merchant, and promptly married her. They had twelve children, the third being their son, Elbridge. Settling permanently in Marblehead, Thomas built up a business in shipping, trading, and importing, in which he made a respectable fortune. He also became a militia officer, commanding the local fort.

His son Elbridge entered Harvard in 1758 at the age of thirteen, but this is not so astonishing as it seems now, for the Harvard of those days was not much more advanced than a modern preparatory school. Graduating four years later, he took a Master's degree and, about this time, began airing his views on the steadily mounting oppression the British Parliament was inflicting on the American colonies.

Though the young graduate wanted to study medicine after college, he gave up the idea and joined his father and two older brothers in the family business. The Gerrys exported, in their own fleet of vessels, shipments of dried codfish south to the Barbados and Spanish ports, from which their ships brought back Spanish goods to be sold in the colonies.

The fishermen and merchants of Marblehead lived on the

bounty of the ocean. It was principally a fishing town and stood next to Boston in the extent and value of its trade. Men and boys earned their living most of the year on or from the sea — a dangerous life that called for bold, adventurous men. Such men are lovers of liberty. Naturally, when controversy between Great Britain and the colonies began, the inhabitants of Marblehead were among the first to show attachment to their country's cause.

In May of 1772, Elbridge Gerry made a start in public life, which appealed to him more than work in the counting-house, by being elected representative to the General Court. On making the acquaintance of Samuel Adams, he was completely won over to the older man's political ideas; and, after two years of steady correspondence, Adams began to feel that in Gerry he had found a receptive mind and a willing worker against British tyranny.

When a circular letter sent out by Adams's Boston Committee of Correspondence brought about a town meeting in Marblehead on December 1, 1772, the Gerry family took a prominent part. Thomas Gerry was moderator, and his sons Elbridge and Thomas, Junior, were on the committee that drafted the resolutions adopted. To obtain unity of ideas and effort, local committees of correspondence were being organized throughout the colonies, and the Marblehead committee, chosen at this town meeting, included all three Gerrys. Unfortunately, two years later Gerry and the whole committee of correspondence resigned in disgust when the isolation hospital for smallpox, which Gerry and other prominent citizens had built and paid for, was burned down by an angry and ignorant mob. The incendiaries did not know how contagious smallpox was and resented isolation of patients.

When in the Spring of 1774 Great Britain closed Boston's harbor, Marblehead became the port of entry for shipments of provisions sent up from southern colonies to aid the harassed Massachusetts Bay Colony. For England's high-handed act had angered the other colonies and aroused their sympathy.

Massachusetts now set up its First Provincial Congress. This was an assembly of delegates from all the towns in Massachusetts. It convened, after Boston harbor was closed, at Salem in October, 1774, with Gerry as member from Marblehead. This first convention adjourned to Concord and assumed the form of a legislative assembly by choosing John Hancock president. It had no legal justification under any provision of King George's provincial charter. It was supported wholly by voluntary consent and approbation of the people in their first attempt to organize resistance to the British. Since it assembled without royal authority, the royal governor of the province was excluded. He had no connection with it and no knowledge of its deliberations, except what he learned by espionage. These angry patriots simply assumed authority over Massachusetts, thereby in effect deposing the governor and ignoring the royal charter. They had decided to meet high-handedness with the same kind of medicine.

"From the day of their first meeting the royal authority within the province of Massachusetts was forever at an end," wrote James T. Austin, Elbridge Gerry's biographer. The mere assembling of these distinguished citizens in provincial congress really was the revolution, for by this act the province threw off its allegiance to the Crown.

Gerry, re-elected in 1775, worked with John Hancock and Samuel Adams in making last preparations in that never-to-be-forgotten April of '75. The British wanted to get their hands on the rebel leaders, Adams and Hancock, and their spies had learned that the Americans had stores of ammunition which they also wanted to capture. On the eighteenth of April in '75, the night of Paul Revere's side, when Adams and Hancock were sleeping in Lexington, Elbridge Gerry was at the Menotomy Tavern on the road the British took to Lexington. He and two American colonels were in bed when a detachment of redcoats came down the road to search the house. All three escaped in their nightclothes and hid in a cornfield until the search was over. (Corn high enough to hide anyone in the month of April would have had to be last year's cornstalks the farmer had left standing.)

Gerry spent the rest of the year raising troops, procuring munitions and supplies for the provincial army, and collecting material for fortifications. His business connections and shipping activities made him an ideal man for the supply department in which he labored efficiently until he departed for Philadelphia, January 25, 1776, as delegate to the Second Continental Congress.

Massachusetts members of the First Continental Congress had been the two Adamses, Robert Treat Paine, Thomas Cushing, and James Bowdoin. When Bowdoin declined re-election, John

Hancock took his place; and when Cushing retired at the end of the year, Gerry succeeded him. The other three remained. Elbridge Gerry traveled to Philadelphia in company with John Adams, and they became friends.

A week after taking his seat in Congress, Gerry was appointed one of five members of the standing committee for superintending the Treasury. During the Spring of 1776, the question of independence steadily moved to top place in the deliberations of Congress. Mr. Gerry made several speeches in which, a colleague said, "he laid out his whole soul" and "poured out his reasons with an energy and fervour that spoke the honest convictions of his mind."

After the long debate on June 10, the question of independence was postponed until July 1 in order to give the assemblies of the middle colonies, who were holding back, an opportunity to take off their restrictions and let their delegates unite in the measure. In the interim, Congress proceeded with plans for confederation and foreign alliance.

An early believer in the separation of the colonies from the government of Great Britain, like all the representatives from the particularly aggrieved province of Massachusetts, Elbridge Gerry voted for independence when the roll was called in early July. Then, worn out from the arduous and constant work and nervous tension of the past few years, he hastened home and wrote the Adamses later that month to sign his name for him on the Declaration of Independence, when it was engrossed and ready for signatures. But they did not have to sign for him; he was back in Philadelphia and signed for himself on September 3. He was thirty-two at this time, one of the youngest of the Signers.

Elbridge Gerry was a slight, dapper little man, with a long nose, a rather stern expression, and an aristocratic air, but with pleasant manners that made him a favorite of the ladies. He apparently looked down his nose at the "common man," with whom he did not care to come in contact in public meetings — an attitude wholly different from that of Sam Adams. But a good many prominent Bostonians were like that; and, besides, not unusual to find in men of small stature a cocky attitude and a pronounced sense of personal dignity, compensating for their slight physique. As he grew older, this characteristic became so noticeable that

Gerry came to be considered a snob and was naturally not very popular.

Some of his other qualities also made him difficult: He changed his mind so often that it was not easy to count on his views. He lacked a sense of humor, which is deplorable and deadening in human relations. He was prone to be suspicious of other people's motives. There were some who felt that sometimes, through obstinacy, Gerry would "risk great things to secure small ones."

He was, however, industrious and conscientious both in business and in Congress. His integrity was never questioned and his attention to detail was helpful to all with whom he worked. He was always the gentleman, and this, too, was appreciated by his co-workers, for it is always easier to deal with persons of good manners.

Gerry's work in supplying the army was invaluable. As a private merchant, he was able to show his brothers how to route their ships and to tell them what the army needed. He sent instructions about the manufacture of tents and gunpowder. The Gerry brothers shipped fish to Spain for the account of the colonies and received army supplies in return. A Marblehead man, he took more interest in fisheries than other congressmen. As the war went on and older congressmen retired, Gerry remained as one of the most experienced.

At the age of forty-two, Elbridge Gerry married Ann Thompson, daughter of a New York merchant. This was ten years after Independence, when he no longer had to devote all his time and effort to work. He now retired from business with a very fair fortune invested in government securities and real estate. He bought the beautiful house and grounds in Cambridge, Massachusetts, now known as "Elmwood," where James Russell Lowell lived in later years. This fine estate had been confiscated from a Tory family.

In 1797, our second President, John Adams, sent Gerry with John Marshall and Charles Pinckney on a mission to France as, after the war, French-American relations were greatly strained. France demanded a cash payment from the United States and tried to force the Americans to pay a personal bribe. The Americans refused and the mission failed, but Gerry, still hoping for an agreement, remained. When he returned later, he found himself snubbed by the Federalists and praised by the Republicans.

Loyal as he was to his country and able as he was in business, Elbridge Gerry nevertheless lost friends through mistaken efforts and through his inconsistent opinions. Though several times defeated for the governorship of Massachusetts, he ran again in 1810. He was now sixty-five and still not popular, but since his opponent, Christopher Gore, was a man of "even stronger aristocratic traits," Gerry won. In 1812 he was elected Vice-President of the United States with James Madison as President and took his oath of office in his Cambridge home, May 4, 1813.

Though he was then in his seventieth year and rather frail, he joined happily in the social life of Washington. But he had not long to enjoy it. Driving to the Senate chamber on the morning of November 23, 1814, he was seized with a hemorrhage of the lungs. He died in a matter of minutes.

Gerry suffered many losses in his last dozen years of life, and though he had once had a considerable fortune, left large debts which consumed his entire estate save for the lovely house. Congress paid for his burial in the Congressional Cemetery.

His wife lived on until 1849, the last surviving widow of a Signer. Their daughter, Emily Louise, lived until 1894, the last surviving child of a Signer.

Though Gerry's personality did not draw warm friendships, he had a genuine devotion to his country. Dr. Rush considered him "a genuine friend to republican forms of government." Gerry himself declared, "I hold it to be the duty of every citizen, though he may have but one day to live, to devote that day to the good of his country."

Robert Treat Paine

March 11, 1731 — May 11, 1814

"THE OBJECTION MAKER," as Robert Treat Paine was later to be called in Congress, was born on Beacon Hill's School Street, Boston, March 11, 1731, son of the Reverend Thomas and Eunice

Treat Paine. He had many notable forebears as befits one born in Yankeeland's core and on the hallowed ground of her blue-blood aristocrats. The first Paine in America was Thomas, who was a freeman of Plymouth Colony as early as 1659. An ancestor on the mother's side, Major Robert Treat, had been a governor of Connecticut colony. The Signer's father left the ministry to engage in the more financially rewarding mercantile business in Boston and Halifax, Nova Scotia. When Robert Treat Paine was born, he was carried down to the foot of Beacon Hill to be christened in Boston's Old South Church. By family tradition, he was expected to become a minister.

After winning high marks at Boston Latin School, the boy entered Harvard with the class of 1749, taught school for a short time after graduating, and then began to study theology. But since his health was frail, he sought a more robust life and went to sea, visiting the southern colonies, Spain, the Azores, and England, ending with a voyage on a whaler to Greenland.

Upon his return home, young Paine decided to pursue an earlier interest in law. He was admitted to the bar in 1757 and began practice in Portland, Maine, then a part of Massachusetts. A few years later he moved his office to Taunton, about thirty miles from Boston.

Paine was interested in the patriots' cause from the first. By the time of the Boston Massacre, March 1770, he was associate prosecuting attorney at the trial of the British soldiers who had fired upon American civilians. His argument on the basic question — whether the British Parliament had the right to quarter a standing army on a town in her American colony *without its consent* — sent his name throughout the other colonies, where eyes were eagerly turned upon all news from Boston. For what happened there could happen anywhere else in the colonies. How would the colony of Massachusetts accept this act of violence?

Now thirty-nine years of age, Robert Paine married Sally Cobb, the daughter of General David Cobb, lieutenant-governor of Massachusetts under the Royal Charter. Soon afterward, he was elected to the Provincial Assembly, where he served for several years. When the first call came for delegates of all the thirteen colonies to meet in Philadelphia in 1774, Robert Treat Paine was chosen one of the five from Massachusetts. His name was now known outside his own province, not only because of his Massacre trial speech, but because he represented the most important town in southern Massachusetts.

In the first Congress he was placed on committees for drafting the rules of debate, and for fasting and prayer. After the battle of Bunker Hill, June 17, 1775, Paine was made chairman of the committee charged with providing gunpowder for an army that had to be created quickly.

The next month, July, 1775, the colonies made their second and final appeal to the Crown for the preservation of goodwill. This was called the Olive Branch Petition and carried the signature of Robert Treat Paine. But, as Benjamin Franklin had thought, the Crown would not even consider it.

Re-elected to Congress in 1776, Paine, now forty-five years old, sat among the debaters on a declaration of independence. The Philadelphian, Dr. Rush, considered him "a firm, decided, and persevering patriot, and eminently useful in Congress, particularly upon committees, in which he was remarkable for his regular and punctual attendance." In conversation, he could be droll and amusing. Dr. Rush said, "His temper was amiable, and his speeches and conversation often facetious." But there was another side to Paine, for Dr. Rush also said that he "had a certain obliquity of understanding which prevented his seeing public objects in the same light in which they were seen by other people. He seldom proposed anything, but opposed nearly every measure that was proposed by other people, and hence he got the name of 'The Objection Maker' in Congress."

But, in spite of that, Paine had positive talents. He was one of the commission sent to negotiate a treaty with the upper New York State Indians. In 1777 he was elected attorney-general for Massachusetts. As the war came to an end, he was on the legislative committee which had to prepare a draft for a state constitution. And when the Tories fled, many of them to Canada, Paine helped to confiscate their estates. He also helped suppress Shays's Rebellion against the state of Massachusetts.

He continued to win honors. After he moved to Boston in 1780, he helped found the American Academy of Arts and Sciences. His life-long friend, Governor John Hancock, twice appointed him to the new Supreme Court of Massachusetts. Paine declined the first time, 1783, in order to retain his larger salary as attorney-general.

The second time, he accepted. Since Maine was still a part of Massachusetts in those days, Paine's work as judge required much travel into those then remote regions where life was severely regulated. At one time, he was arrested for traveling on Sunday! Once he was fined by a little cross-roads court for violating a law which he himself helped to frame years before.

After fourteen years he retired from the bench, since he was getting old and was bothered by increasing deafness. He died on May 11, 1814, at eighty-three, a ripe old age for those times. The man who had, when young, probably traveled farther than any other patriot "Father," was laid to rest in the Old Granary Burial Ground in Boston, along with other patriots and Signers, and near the very spot where he had been born and christened.

II

VIRGINIA

Th Jefferson

Richard Henry Lee

Benj Harrison

Francis Lightfoot Lee

Th Nelson jr.

George Wythe

Carter Braxton

Thomas Jefferson

Th Jefferson

April 13, 1743 — July 4, 1826

THOMAS JEFFERSON IS UNIQUE among the Signers of the Declaration of Independence, for he did more than sign it. Jefferson also wrote it — and this was one of only three among all his achievements that he wished inscribed upon his tombstone. Any other man who had accomplished half as much as Jefferson would have wanted a great deal more in that inscription, for Jefferson's career was one of the most brilliant any man — of his own day or of modern days — has ever made for himself.

Twice President of the United States, Vice-President before that, Minister to France, Governor of Virginia, first Secretary of State, Jefferson was also a successful lawyer, a scholar, an inventor, a musician, a man of science, and a book collector — one of the three libraries he assembled for his own use became the basis for the present Library of Congress. (By his own secret marks of ownership, you can still distinguish the books that once were Jefferson's from the others in that great collection.) But to Jefferson all the distinguished posts he held were more or less tiresome tasks. It was his duty to undertake them and in that duty he did his brilliant best; but his heart was always with his books, his tools, his garden, and his fields at Monticello. If he could have had his own way, if he had not had so keen a sense of duty, if he had not always answered to his call, he would have spent a long, happy life as a country gentleman of intellectual tastes. He would never, in that case, have become world famous. But Thomas Jefferson wouldn't have minded that in the least. He once referred to the presidency as "a splendid misery."

Born into an old and wealthy Virginian family, Jefferson grew up on the estate of his father, Peter Jefferson, near Charlottesville, Albermarle County. This was a plantation of four hundred acres — small for those spacious days — which a friend had sold to

Peter Jefferson at possibly the lowest price ever paid for real estate anywhere. The price was a bowl of punch, and that land is still called "the Punchbowl Tract" in Albemarle County. It was, of course, only a part of Peter Jefferson's land holdings but it was the part where he built his house, to be near the friend who had "sold" it to him.

Thomas Jefferson was born here April 13, 1743. Peter Jefferson, who liked to name his lands for places in the Old World with which his family had been associated, had called his plantation "Shadwell," because that was the London parish in which his young wife had been baptized twenty-three years before. He called another plantation "Snowdon," after a mountain in Wales near which he thought his Welsh ancestors once had lived.

In addition to being born into a good family with plenty of money — a blessing by no means to be despised — Thomas Jefferson had two other advantages. He was born with iron health and lived a long life with almost no illness. Best of all, he was born with a fine mind which, by constant study all through a busy life, he kept improving to the very end.

Though his own tastes inclined him to a quiet home life, he gave the best years of his life to his country's service. Even when he had completed two terms in the presidency and could at last go home, Jefferson spent endless hours planning the new University of Virginia, designing the beautiful buildings that are still its pride, and supervising their erection. To this day, it is a custom at the university to refer to him always as "Mr. Jefferson." People still talk, a surprised visitor once remarked, "as if he were in the next room."

His aristocratic and luxurious background spared Jefferson many of the hardships and struggles other great men have sometimes had to endure. He was not a poor boy, fighting his own way from poverty to fame and fortune, like Benjamin Franklin. The young Jefferson, when he was still only a boy, inherited thousands of acres of land, with many slaves to farm it for him. In the end he owned large estates and several beautiful plantation houses — though Monticello was always the place he loved most. The young widow whom he married brought him a second fortune, equal to his own.

In colonial days there were no public schools in Virginia. The sons of poor people usually received no education — or none worth mentioning. Very wealthy families sometimes employed private tutors and later sent their sons to the great English universities. Other prosperous families often sent their children to small private schools kept by local parsons. Some of these clergymen did not have churches at all, but devoted themselves entirely to education.

As a boy, Thomas Jefferson was sent to a private school of this sort, kept by the Reverend Matthew Maury — probably the only American schoolteacher who educated three Presidents of the United States, for both James Madison and James Monroe also studied under him. Captain Meriwether Lewis, another of his pupils, was one of the two leaders of the Lewis and Clark Expedition.

From the Reverend Mr. Maury's school, the boy went on to the College of William and Mary, in Williamsburg, then the capital of Virginia, and after only two years there, to the law office of George Wythe in Williamsburg. Wythe, who also became a Signer of the Declaration that his pupil wrote, was one of the most distinguished lawyers of the day. Jefferson studied in his office for five years.

Young as he was, during this period he regularly made one of the group of four who dined together at the Palace of the Governor. Lieutenant-governor Francis Fauquier, then acting as governor, was, of course the host. Professor William Small, of the William and Mary faculty, and George Wythe himself were the others. Although these men were much older and were among the most prominent in Virginia, they made the young man from Albemarle County one of themselves. In spite of his youth, they recognized his brilliance.

When the five years of study in Wythe's law office were over, Jefferson was admitted to the bar and at once established a legal practice of his own. He had begun to make a success of it as the Revolution approached, but became so much involved in public affairs that he closed his law office, turned over his remaining cases to a friend, and never practiced law again.

Jefferson's public service had begun long before the Revolution. In 1770, he became county lieutenant of Albemarle County, the official in general charge of county affairs, including the militia.

He was county surveyor in 1773. A year later, as disputes with the British grew more serious, he was chosen for the Virginia Convention, which was to become the state legislature. Unable to attend, he nevertheless sent the members his *Summary View of the Rights of British America.* Not yet in favor of separation from the Mother Country, Thomas Jefferson nevertheless expressed in this paper many of the ideas he was to use, two years later, in the Declaration of Independence.

In 1772, he married Mrs. Martha Skelton, a young widow of twenty-three, to whom he remained intensely devoted throughout the ten years of their marriage. She was to die in 1782 after bearing numerous children, all of whom, except two daughters, Martha and Maria, died in infancy. Married in midwinter, which can be cold even in Virginia, Jefferson bore his bride away to their new house at Monticello which he had designed and built himself and for which he had especially leveled off the top of the "little mountain" on which it stood. He was to modify and refinish this beloved home, in one way or another, throughout the rest of his long life.

The midwinter snow was so deep that the bridal couple, unable to get up the steep slope of Monticello in their carriage, unhitched two of the horses and rode up. (Any Virginia girl of that period was perfectly familiar with horses.) When they reached their new home, however, their problems had not ended. The slaves, not expecting them in such weather, had all gone to bed; and, since the house was still unfinished, only one room was ready for them. Gaily they built a fire, and there is a legend that Jefferson played the violin for his bride.

Thomas Jefferson's services in the Second Continental Congress and his authorship of the Declaration of Independence have already been discussed in the opening chapter of this book. That trying period was made agonizing for Jefferson by the difficulty of getting news from his wife, who lay ill at Monticello. Postal service was slow and bad in those days and often he had no news from her for long periods. She died as the Revolution was drawing to a close.

After her death, Jefferson was appointed one of the Peace Commissioners to meet with the British in Paris; but Benjamin Franklin and the other commissioners, already on the scene, had finished negotiating the treaty before Jefferson could sail. He remained in America.

Jefferson did go to Paris in 1784, however, to assist Franklin and John Adams in arranging treaties of commerce; and when Franklin, first American Minister to France, wanted to return, Jefferson became our second Minister to France. Some one asked him one day whether he was replacing Dr. Franklin. Jefferson, a modest man, replied: "I succeed him. No one can take his place."

He remained in Paris until 1789, traveling widely in Europe and Great Britain, observing agriculture, industry, the lives of the people, inventions, and the fine arts. There has probably never been another American diplomat who knew so much about the country to which he was accredited.

During this period, Jefferson made the designs for the present Virginia State Capitol in Richmond, based largely on a reproduction of the Maison Carrée at Nîmes, and sent them home to guide the workmen. It is believed that these designs were the real start of the classical revival in American architecture.

Jefferson returned in 1789 to become Secretary of State in President Washington's first cabinet, a position that brought him into constant official association with Alexander Hamilton, Washington's Secretary of the Treasury. That meant inevitable friction and endless trouble. For — though both had brilliant minds and were devoted patriots — the two men's fundamental views of what the new American government should become were poles apart.

Hamilton, a West Indian immigrant of the humblest possible birth, was a Federalist. That meant he favored a government by "the wise and good," in other words, the wealthier, better educated upper classes, with a rigid restriction of the right to vote and a powerful central government. Jefferson, born a wealthy Virginian aristocrat, called himself a "republican." This did not mean that he belonged to the Republican Party as we know it. This party did not yet exist. We should call him a "democrat" (with a small "d") today. He favored government by almost all the people, or at least by all property holders. He also favored the utmost freedom in thought, speech, and religion, and complete freedom of the press. Hamilton favored restriction and control.

Jefferson at first tried to co-operate with him but did not succeed. Some years of bitter disagreement followed, which President Washington could not smooth over.

In July, 1794, Jefferson resigned as Secretary of State, though he remained in office until the end of the year. After that, weary of political life, he returned to Monticello, hoping to settle down at last to his plantation, his garden, his books, his music, his scientific studies. But when Washington left the presidency in 1797, Jefferson and Vice-President John Adams were both candidates. Jefferson did not really want the office and can hardly have been disappointed when John Adams won by three electoral votes. Jefferson thus became Vice-President, under the original provisions of the Constitution, whereby the candidate with the second highest number of electoral votes received the second highest office.

Very likely the coolness that developed in Adams's friendship for Jefferson dates from this election — which is a pity, considering how little Jefferson wanted the presidency. If so, the election of 1800, in which Adams lost entirely, did not strengthen whatever was left of their friendship. This was the only presidential election that has ever resulted in a tie, though Rutherford B. Hayes in 1876 won the presidency by the margin of one electoral vote and John F. Kennedy won by one tenth of a per cent of the popular vote.

In 1800, the Federalists had nominated John Adams for a second term as President and Thomas Pinckney for Vice-President — hoping that Adams would get a majority of the electoral votes and Pinckney would have the second largest vote, making him Vice-President. The Republicans nominated Jefferson for President and Aaron Burr for Vice-President, hoping for a similar distribution of the vote on their side. But when the electoral vote was counted, Jefferson and Burr had exactly seventy-three votes, Adams sixty-five, Pinckney sixty-four, while somebody had cast one vote for John Jay.

This situation made it necessary for the House of Representatives to choose between Jefferson and Burr. The count of the electoral vote had been announced February 11, 1801. It took thirty-six ballots before, on February 17, the deadlock was broken and Jefferson was elected, only for two weeks before the inauguration. Realizing the danger of such a situation, Congress immediately passed the Twelfth Amendment to the Constitution, providing for the present method of voting separately for President and Vice-President.

This defeat embittered John Adams more than ever. Intent on getting his own men into office despite Jefferson's success, he spent the last few hours of his administration busily signing commissions for judges and other high U. S. officials, to keep out the men Jefferson would have appointed. He is said to have kept on signing till about nine o'clock that night — till midnight, it is sometimes said. As a result, Jefferson, as President, had to deal with a great many hostile subordinates, instead of with men of his own choice.

After that, President Adams left the capital at once, not waiting for Jefferson's inauguration. From that day to this, no outgoing President has ever shown such rudeness to his successor. Yet the two men had been good friends and, when a few years had sweetened John Adams's disposition, became warm friends again. It must be said for President Adams that as he was only the second man who had ever been President, the now familiar ride of the outgoing and the incoming President to the Capitol together had not become an established custom.

Matters grew worse when Jefferson removed Adams's son from a government job and replaced him with another man. Jefferson explained later that he had merely made a new presidential appointment, not knowing that this would deprive the younger Adams of his office.

During his two terms as President, Thomas Jefferson practically transformed the United States, though the far-reaching effect of some of the things he did could not be fully realized until many years had passed. Unquestionably his most important achievement was the Louisiana Purchase, which extended the territory of the United States at least to the summit of the Rockies. (The exact boundaries of the Louisiana Purchase were not very clearly defined in that wild country.)

Actually, this meant extending American territory to the far Pacific. The United States already had a claim to the Columbia River Valley, beyond the mountains, for the river had first been entered by an American ship. Lewis and Clark, whom Jefferson sent out, ensured the American territorial claim and brought back so much information about the Great West, that the fur-trade and then white settlement swiftly followed.

Jefferson also fought the "Barbary pirates," small Mohammedan countries on the north coast of Africa that had been attacking American ships passing their coast. His success made the Eastern Mediterranean safe for American shipping and before long the Barbary pirates became helpless little nations no one feared any longer. His efforts to keep out of the Napoleonic wars in Europe succeeded so long as Jefferson himself was President, though we did eventually have to fight the War of 1812, which was directly related to the conflict overseas.

When the second term of his presidency ended in 1809, Jefferson was at last able to retire permanently to Monticello, as he had so long wished to do. But he never wholly ceased serving the public. During this period he created the new University of Virginia, made suggestions for its curriculum, served as a member of the Board of Trustees, became the new university's first Rector, and designed some of the beautiful buildings that are still the university's pride.

But Jefferson had devoted too much time to his country's service to give his own estates the attention they needed. He had been compelled to leave his rich plantations in the hands of overseers, and lands rarely prosper save in the hands of the owner himself. To make matters worse, the British had carried off thirty of his slaves. The various offices he had held paid salaries and some of them must have included expense accounts, but expenses were almost always larger than salary and expense account combined. Martha Jefferson once remarked that the vice-presidency was the only office her father ever held that paid the cost of holding it. In other words, the patriotic Jefferson had for years been paying for the privilege of placing his tremendous talents at his country's service.

Though Jefferson did his best to build up such estate as he had left, it was a difficult task, which had been postponed too long while he was in his country's service. The fame he had achieved added to his financial difficulties. Hundreds of people, from far and near, came calling. With the usual hospitality of the Southerner, Jefferson gave food and lodging to all comers — and they literally ate him out of house and home.

One consolation of these later years, however, was reconciliation with his old friend, John Adams. In the end the Yankee statesman forgot his defeat for a second term as President and forgave their political struggles. As for Jefferson, it is doubtful if he ever had any resentment toward Adams. After the reconciliation, they wrote each other lengthy letters for years, on all sorts of subjects — literature, art, politics, philosophy. Until the very end, the two elder statesmen found a continual delight in this correspondence.

When, on July 4, 1826, Adams lay dying at his Massachusetts farm, he was heard to murmur that Jefferson still lived. But Adams was wrong. Jefferson had died only a few hours earlier. For some days both he and the devoted Dr. Dunglison — who had lived at Monticello for a week to be sure he would be at hand when needed — had known there was no hope. But at seven o'clock on the evening of July 3, the physician heard the sick man murmur: "Is it the Fourth?" He replied: "It soon will be."

At eleven o'clock that night, the sick man asked again: "This is the Fourth?" Rather than disappoint him, Nicholas Trist, husband of a granddaughter, nodded affirmatively.

"Ah," murmured the dying man, and an expression came over his face that seemed to say, "Just as I wished." He did die on the Fourth, a little before one o'clock in the afternoon.

It was the fiftieth anniversary of the Declaration of Independence.

Richard Henry Lee

Richard Henry Lee

January 20, 1732 — June 19, 1794

JOHN ADAMS BELIEVED the Virginia Lees had produced more "men of merit" than any other family. Whether he was right or not, the Lees well deserved their reputation for brilliant service to their colony, to their state, and to the cause of Independence.

The first Lee to come to America was Richard, great-grand-father of the two Signers, who left his home at Stratford Laughton in Essex County, England, during the reign of Charles I. He made several voyages back to England afterward, each time returning with a number of followers to settle in the New World. Since he was granted a tract of land as "Head Rights" for each man he brought, he acquired vast land holdings. With these, he grew wealthy as a tobacco planter, and left his offspring "considerable fortune, high standards of culture, morality, and a sense of public service." This first Richard Lee finally settled in Northumberland County in Virginia's "Northern Neck," between the Rappahanock and Potomac rivers.

His grandson, Thomas, married Hannah Ludwell, a daughter of Colonel Philip Ludwell of Green Spring, near Williamsburg, then capital of the colony. Ludwell had been a member of the King's Council, and the Ludwells as a family had become conspicuous for public service. Thomas and Hannah Lee were the parents of the two Signers and of other sons and two daughters. It is interesting to note that Hannah Lee's mother was a Harrison, of the famous Harrison family which also produced a Signer and two later Presidents of the United States. High quality of character marked both sides of the Lee family.

Richard Henry Lee was born on the family estate called Stratford, no doubt after the old home in England. He was educated by private tutors and, while still in his teens, was sent to England to round out his education at the academy of Wakefield, in Yorkshire. Before returning to America, young Lee spent some months traveling. By the time he was nineteen, he was home again, now a young man well read in Greek, Latin, and English literature, and possessed of an attractive, polite manner. His candor, charm, and complete lack of pride made him popular. He seems to have had everything required for success in public life.

Though his father had died during his absence, he did not at once make plans for his future. In fact, he never needed to think of living by a profession, since he was heir to rich plantations. He stayed at home, read, and studied by himself from the books in his father's fine library, while enjoying a congenial home life on his flourishing and beautiful Virginia estates. He made a special

study of the laws of his own country, of the principles of civil law,
and of history, especially that of England and her colonies. He
was a thorough student, who, after reading a work, liked to write
a digest or synopsis of its contents. In this way he learned a con-
ciseness of style of which, in later life, he was esteemed to be a
master.

It was only natural that Richard Henry Lee should follow his
father and more distant ancestors into public life. He was about
twenty-five when he was appointed justice of the peace for his
county. Diligent in this office, which involved more important
duties at the time than it would later, he was presently elected to
the House of Burgesses, where his father had also served. Richard
Henry Lee served in the House for thirty-three years.

At first, the shy young member was so concious of his youth
that he was hesitant about standing up to speak before that
august assembly of his elders. But with each attempt, the ordeal
became easier, and he seems to have begun to enjoy public
speaking by 1776, when he went to Philadelphia as one of Virginia's delegates to Congress. By that time he had acquired such
"harmonious" gestures while speaking that one of his colleagues
suggested that he practiced them before a mirror. However that
may have been, young Richard Henry Lee was soon winning
friends, admiration, and even the respect of his opponents.

In 1757, the year in which he began to hold public office, he
also began married life. His bride was Anne Aylett, daughter of
William Aylett of Westmoreland County. The young newlyweds
resided at "Chantilly" — an estate near Stratford.

About a year after becoming a member of the House of Burgesses, young Lee made a very important speech in opposition
to slavery. All Virginia planters had slaves to work in the fields.
But as early as 1759, Lee saw the coming dangers and, in his
speech, proposed that a duty be paid on the importation of slaves
— a duty so heavy that it would "put an end to that iniquitous
and disgraceful traffic within the colony of Virginia." He advised
the House to give serious attention to the debate on this subject,
as the consequence would "greatly affect posterity." Foresighted
though he was, Richard Henry Lee could not then have imagined
that a descendant of his uncle — who would be born at Stratford,
his own birthplace — would grow up to be General Robert E.

Lee, leader of the Confederate Army, in a war caused by slavery just about a hundred years later.

By 1764, Lee was speaking against the parliamentary plan to tax the colonies. He wrote to a friend in England that "free possession of property, the right to be governed by laws made by our representatives, and the illegality of taxation without consent" were principles of the British Constitution. His firm stand places Richard Henry Lee in the front rank of the defenders of colonial rights.

When the House of Burgesses registered a protest against the Stamp Act, Lee was the committeeman chosen to draw up an address to the king, another to the Lords, and a remonstrance to the Commons. He was absent from the House on May 30, 1765, when Patrick Henry astonished the assembly by his proposal of five resolutions denouncing the Act. But Lee and Patrick Henry were in agreement, and the eloquence of both these orators caused Silas Deane of Connecticut to describe them as the Demosthenes (Henry) and Cicero (Lee) of America. Deane wrote: "God grant that they may not, like them, plead in vain for the liberties of their country."

In February, 1766, Lee formed a Westmoreland Association of citizens from his own county, who bound themselves not to import any British goods until the Stamp Act was repealed. This was the first of many boycotting measures the colonists tried in order to convince the British government of the seriousness of interfering with the colonists' rights and liberties.

Though the Stamp Act was repealed, matters grew worse. When the New York legislature was suspended in 1768, Lee wrote that this "hangs like a flaming sword over our heads." In that same year, he began to urge the colonies to set up inter-colonial correspondence, in order to unite their counsels. This was the start of what would eventually be a Congress of representatives from all the colonies — today, from all the states. In February of that same year, the Massachusetts House of Representatives adopted a circular letter prepared by Samuel Adams to be sent to assemblies of other colonies, suggesting *united* opposition to Great Britain by discussion and petition.

It was in 1768, too, that Lee's wife died, leaving him with four young children. The next year, he married a widow, Mrs. Anne

Pinckard. From this year until 1773, Lee was also engaged in shipping tobacco to his brother William in London. Both his brothers, William and Arthur, had gone to England to engage in mercantile enterprises, and during these years, Arthur's letters from London kept Richard well informed on British opinion.

Sometime during the 1760's, Lee had a bad accident. A gun exploded while he was hunting, and he lost all the fingers of one hand. Thereafter, he always wore a close-fitting black silk scarf around what was left of his hand, with an opening for the thumb.

In 1769, a new voice for liberalism came to the Virginia House of Burgesses when Thomas Jefferson was elected. Jefferson, Lee, and Patrick Henry were soon working cordially together for the American cause. It was these men who, in May, 1774, "cooked up" — as Jefferson said — a resolution to make the day when the port of Boston was to be closed, a day of "Fasting, Humiliation, and Prayer." Lee prepared a set of resolutions, which included a call for a general congress of all the colonies to secure their rights and liberty. But before the Virginia convention assembled and announced its demand for a general congress, Massachusetts had already sent out the call, naming Philadelphia as the place.

Of Virginia's seven delegates, the conservative Peyton Randolph, speaker of the House of Burgesses, was named first; Richard Henry Lee second. The other five in the first Congress were George Washington, Patrick Henry, Benjamin Harrison, Richard Bland, and Edmund Pendleton.

In Philadelphia, Lee now came in contact with kindred spirits from other colonies, especially the two Adamses of Massachusetts, the colony which had suffered the most marked British spite. A lifelong friendship began between him and Samuel Adams, while John Adams, though never a close friend, thought Lee "a masterly man." Silas Deane of Connecticut (who was later to suffer grave injustice at the instigation of Lee's brother Arthur) said that Lee was regarded as Patrick Henry's equal in eloquence. Lee was active on many committees in Congress — always in favor of strong measures, always against any weak remonstrances that lacked spirit. His speeches were polished, easy, and "inspired with more than mortal powers of embellishment," according to one admirer — the kind of oratory people like to listen to.

Lee was now forty-four, tall and slim, with reddish hair, bold striking features, a deep, melodious voice, and the commanding manner of the real aristocrat. Well-read not only in history, Latin, Greek, French, but also in politics and various branches of science, he was competent to discuss almost any topic of the day. Dr. Benjamin Rush observed of Lee: "I never knew so great an orator whose speeches were so short." They were also convincing. As Dr. Rush said: "He conceived his subject so clearly, and presented it so immediately to his hearers, that there appeared nothing more to be said about it."

Perhaps Richard Henry Lee had been thinking of an independent American union of states as early as November, 1775, when he agreed with John Adams that it was time the colonies adopted their own government. Samuel Adams had certainly believed that for a long time, and the idea was steadily being forced upon Americans by the stubborn attitude of the British. In March, 1776, Lee joined George Wythe, another Virginia Signer, in proposing a resolution that the king, rather than the ministry, was the "Author of our Miseries." Before long, Lee was advocating independence, not so much as an end in itself but rather as a "necessary prerequisite" to a foreign alliance. Others were coming to entertain the same views, but it was Lee's insistence which brought the Virginia convention to adopt, in May, 1776, its resolution favoring independence, foreign alliances, and a confederation. It was, therefore, appropriate to choose Lee to move these resolutions in Congress the next month.

He wrote them and on June 7, on the floor of Congress in Philadelphia, made the first formal declaration "that these United Colonies are and of right ought to be free and independent states."

Much as Lee was admired, he had adversaries, even among Virginians. Benjamin Harrison, Pendleton, and other conservatives of the "cold" party, were still trying to make themselves believe reconciliation was possible.

Having offered the resolution for independence, Lee did not remain in Philadelphia for the final vote on the Declaration, though he eventually returned to Congress to sign it. By this time he had devoted himself so whole-heartedly to the patriot cause for so many years that his private affairs were suffering, and his plantation needed the owner's personal attention. Lee also wanted to go back to Virginia to help form the new state that would replace the old colony. He left Philadelphia in the middle of June. That is probably why he was not appointed to the committee that drafted the Declaration of Independence.

Troubles now arising in foreign relations caused serious disputes in Congress and badly strained Lee's reputation as a statesman.

To give a brief outline of this unfortunate affair we go back to the year before, when Silas Deane of Connecticut had been a delegate from his colony to the First Continental Congress. In March, 1776, Deane was selected to represent the colonies abroad. If war came, they would need foreign aid. In the following months, he secured eight shiploads of French military supplies, which arrived in time for the Saratoga campaign of 1777. He also sent over a large number of European military officers. Later, desiring to strengthen relations with France, Congress appointed a commission of three — adding Benjamin Franklin and Arthur Lee, a brother of Richard Henry, who was already in Europe — to continue the work originally undertaken by Deane alone. Franklin was the best choice, and Arthur Lee the worst choice, they made. The commissioners succeeded in signing treaties with France in February, 1778. Soon afterward, Congress called Silas Deane home.

Arthur Lee, an erratic and unreliable individual, had made grave accusations against Deane. He charged that he was dishonestly trying to get money for himself, because Deane and the French dramatist, Beaumarchais, who was also a businessman, requested payment for the supplies the French had turned over. Arthur Lee "supposed" these supplies had been a gift from the French government! During the ugly controversy that ensued, Richard Henry Lee vehemently took his brother's side. A rift, dividing Congress into two hostile factions, produced most unhappy difficulties in American foreign relations for at least two years. Arthur Lee was at fault; his brother in Congress in grave error. By his devoted service to the American cause, Silas Deane had lost so much that he lost faith in the cause; and being rewarded with ill will, suspicion, and slander, he left America entirely and spent his last years in exile. Long after all his accusers were dead, Congress tried to make it up, in 1842, by voting to give Deane's heirs the sum of $27,000, and by admitting that the original inspection of Deane's account, which had been made under Arthur

Lee's direction, was "erroneous and a gross injustice to Silas Deane." Deane had long since passed away, and so had the Lees, but Richard Henry, in standing up for his troublesome brother, lost stature as a statesman. Had he known the truth, he might have known much remorse.

In May, 1799, Lee resigned his seat in Congress. The next year he was elected to the Virginia House of Delegates. In 1784, once more elected to Congress, he was gratified at being chosen its president for a year. In 1787, though a Virginian, he favored the veto on slavery north of the Ohio river.

The American government had thus far operated under the Articles of Confederation, which had at length been formally adopted in 1781. Though these provided for a "perpetual union" of the states, they did not provide a strong central government. Congress was the whole government, but it had no way of collecting taxes or establishing a strong central government. But after his experience with King George, Lee was extremely suspicious of a too much centralization. He especially feared giving Congress power over "both purse and sword." Congress obviously had to have power over the sword — that is, it had to possess the right to make war. Hence Lee opposed giving it the right over the purse — that is, the right to tax — even the right to collect a five per cent tax on imports.

When it became clear to everybody that the government could not go on under the Articles of Confederation, a convention met in Philadelphia in 1787, with George Washington as president and with Benjamin Franklin and many other Signers as members. Richard Henry Lee was not among them, however. Though chosen as a Virginia delegate, he declined to serve.

Though called only to amend and improve the Articles of Confederation, the convention eventually cast them aside and prepared the Constitution of the United States, under which we live today. Even to this Lee objected, largely because it did not yet contain the first ten amendments, usually known as the Bill of Rights; but when the Constitution was adopted, he became one of the first two Senators from Virginia. The Bill of Rights, which was soon adopted, met most of his objections.

He had for some time been suffering from attacks of gout. By October, 1792, realizing that his health was broken, he resigned as Senator and spent his remaining two years at Chantilly, where he died June 19, 1794.

Benjamin Harrison

c. 1726 (day and month unknown) — April 24, 1791

Two of the signers, Benjamin Harrison and Carter Braxton, were first cousins. Both these "founding fathers" belonged to the First Families of Virginia.

The first Benjamin Harrison in America came to Virginia Colony in the early 1630's — or at least before 1633. The Signer was the fifth of the name in the direct line of descent. All these Harrisons were important to their Colony, holding high offices in their province or sitting in the House of Burgesses. Benjamin, the Signer, had a son, William Henry Harrison, who became President of the United States. And he had a great-grandson, another Benjamin Harrison, who also became President — a remarkable record for any family, equaled only by the Adamses and Roosevelts.

Benjamin, the Signer, was born at "Berkeley," the family seat in Charles City County, in 1726. He entered the College of William and Mary but, while he was a student there, his father and two sisters were killed by lightning. The nineteen-year-old Benjamin had to leave without graduating, as the charge of the great estate fell upon his young shoulders. Plummeted into a man's responsibilities while hardly more than a boy and needing a helpmeet badly, he married his second cousin, Elizabeth Bassett.

Still in his early twenties, Benjamin Harrison was elected to the House of Burgesses (as the Virginia legislature was called) and served in it, sometimes as speaker, for twenty-six years, until it was dissolved in 1774.

Harrison labored mightily as the head of a great estate, whose duty it was to build up the property he had himself inherited, for the benefit of his children. It was not an easy task, for in addition to managing his plantation, growing tobacco and breeding horses, he erected extensive mills, established a large shipyard, and built his own ships. Like Washington and Jefferson and all wealthy Virginians of his time, he owned slaves as a matter of course.

Since John Rolfe, husband of Pocahontas, had shipped the first experimental crop of tobacco to England in 1613, the tobacco trade had grown to the point where it was not only the chief income of the Maryland and Virginia colonies, but a source of great prosperity to the mother country. It is no wonder that these able planters and businessmen were incensed and offended when members of Parliament in faraway London began to enact laws for the colonists overseas, though they did not understand what life was like here nor how the tobacco business was run.

In 1764, Harrison sided with those who protested the Stamp Act. But, a man of conservative nature, he at first considered the extreme attitude of the radicals to be unwise. As the political storms broke with ever more frequency, however, Harrison stood for Virginia as a member of the Committee of Correspondence.

In August, 1774, the Virginia convention elected him delegate to the First Continental Congress. He was in Carpenter's Hall in Philadelphia on the opening day, when his brother-in-law, Peyton Randolph, was chosen first president of Congress. When Harrison first went to Philadelphia, he shared a house with Peyton Randolph and Colonel George Washington.

Washington, chosen by Congress to lead the new Continental Army, took command in Cambridge in June of 1775. The following September, Benjamin Harrison, Benjamin Franklin, and Thomas Lynch were the congressmen sent to Cambridge to confer with the general and with delegates from the New England states with regard to the support and regulation of the army. Soon after this conference, one of the first of the six small armed vessels that were the beginning of a United States Navy was named the *Harrison*.

Benjamin Harrison was a large, impressive-looking man. He stood six-feet four-inches tall and weighed two hundred forty pounds when he signed the Declaration of Independence at the age of fifty. In Congress, Harrison did not indulge in high-flown oratory. He preferred making short speeches in plain words which, it was said, often had more influence than the long and windy speeches of some of the others. He was among the first in advocating decisive and energetic action. Even critical John Adams observed that "these gentlemen of Virginia appear to be the most spirited and consistent." The tubby little Massachusetts patriot also recorded some unflattering opinions of Harrison.

This worked both ways of course, and Dr. Rush noted that though Harrison well understood "the forms of public business," he had strong state prejudices and was hostile to the leading men from the New England states. This is understandable when we read that Benjamin Harrison was an open, generous, vivacious and liberal host, enjoying the pleasures of dining with convivial company. Even then the warm Southern hospitality and the colder, more reserved New England frugality were at odds. Nevertheless, Harrison was a man of good humor and a master of repartee. Thomas Jefferson thought that he had made the "readiest and most successful remarks ever heard in Congress."

But John Adams was really impressed when Harrison said that he would have come on foot (from Virginia to Philadelphia) to be in Congress, rather than not come at all. For here was a loyal man who would set aside his own interests to help his country. Devoted to his own Virginia, he showed equal devotion later to the Union for whose establishment he had worked most diligently.

After the signing in early August, 1776, a new delegation from Virginia presented their credentials in Congress, their number reduced from the seven — who had signed the Declaration — to five. Harrison was not included. He left Philadelphia in late August and returned home. He had been away so long that ugly suspicions about him had begun to circulate and dissension had arisen in the Virginia delegation. Therefore, when the Virginia legislature convened that fall, Harrison demanded a hearing. The result showed his wisdom in not allowing malicious gossip to go unchallenged. The air was cleared, and that same month the Virginia legislators re-elected him to Congress, entering in their Journals the resolution that "the thanks of this House are justly due to the said Benjamin Harrison for the diligence, ability, and integrity with which he executed the important trust reposed in him as one of the delegates of his country in the General Congress."

Upon his return, Harrison was appointed to a committee to consider the establishment of a War Office. This was the beginning of an effort, heartily sponsored by Harrison, to free General Washington from the continual interference of "Congressmen who were supremely ignorant of military matters." By this action, Washington was no longer hampered in the direction of his armies in the field, as he had been before 1777, when he had to await orders from a congressional Board of War. While in Congress, Harrison was the man upon whom Washington depended for guiding the legislative measures that pertained to the army.

Harrison was the first member named for the Committee of Secret Correspondence, created in November, 1775. Later, he was appointed to the marine committee and to the Board of War and Ordnance. He thus had a share in establishing three of the great departments of the American government: State, War, and Navy.

As chairman, when Congress met as a committee of the whole, he usually presided over the momentous debates which determined the text of the Declaration of Independence. He presided, too, over the first debates concerning the Articles of Confederation. He was noted for his fairness, his ability to make decisions, both in Congress and in his own state's assemblies.

When the traitor Benedict Arnold captured Richmond in 1781, he made his headquarters at Westover, the plantation adjoining Harrison's Berkeley. At the time, Harrison himself was in charge of the state militia. The British, who destroyed so much property of American patriots, seized his house and burned his collection of paintings in the back yard.

After the war, Harrison was elected Governor of Virginia several times, and when his last governorship terminated, he was again elected to the House of Delegates, remaining a member until his death.

In the Spring of 1791, he suffered a severe attack of gout. But the day after his unanimous election to the legislature, he invited a party for dinner and happily received congratulations upon his popularity. The day passed pleasantly. During the night, however, he had a relapse and died the next day.

Over a period of two hundred and fifty years, from 1634 to 1889, when a Benjamin Harrison became the twenty-third President of the United States, the Harrison family of Berkeley furnished more men distinguished in public life, in an unbroken male line, than any other American family.

Francis Lightfoot Lee

Francis Lightfoot Lee

October 14, 1734 — January 11, 1797

THE TWO LEES OF VIRGINIA were the only two brothers among the Signers. Francis Lightfoot and his brother Richard Henry, older by two years, belonged to the fourth generation of Virginia Lees. All these wealthy Lees were owners of vast plantations, inherited and then enlarged by diligent sons. They lived pleasant lives as country gentlemen, many of whom, like Francis and his brother, interested themselves in politics.

Francis was born at the family plantation, Stratford, a lovely spot in Westmoreland County on the Potomac river, where his brother also was born. Both boys were educated by private tutors, as was the custom among families that could afford it. He was still a young man when he inherited from his father an estate in Loudon County where he lived for a long time. It was that county that he represented in the House of Burgesses from 1758 to 1768. While he was a member of the House, Francis did not hesitate to sign the protest against the hated Stamp Act.

In the Spring of 1769, Francis Lee married Rebecca Tayloe, and moved farther south to a plantation called "Menokin" in Richmond County. By this time, he already had some reputation as a man in public life, and his marriage brought him new connections in his wife's county, where he was again elected Burgess, serving during the critical period preceding the War of Independence.

Though Francis Lightfoot Lee was not so well known as his older brother Richard Henry, he attained great political influence, was perhaps as able, and was certainly the more ardent revolutionist. He took part in every measure of defiance to the government of Great Britain. Like his brother, he was shy about speaking in public, but unlike his brother, he never did become a good speaker. Nevertheless, he was one of Virginia's boldest spirits in taking a stand against the British.

In 1773, Francis became one of the committee who formed the Virginia Committee of Correspondence. Having signed the call for the Virginia convention of 1774, he became a member of the convention, too, the following Spring and was chosen as one of the Virginia delegates to the First Continental Congress. He was thereafter re-elected until 1779. He was forty-two when he signed the Declaration.

In Philadelphia, he was active on many committees in Congress, being especially eager to win free navigation of the Mississippi River for American citizens — something America did not secure for a long time. Had he been a man of political ambition, he could doubtless have remained longer in Congress, but he preferred quiet country life on his plantation. Though he did his part for his colony and for independence, he was not a leader in the revolution. He did not have the ambition for that.

After his period in Congress, Lee served in the Virginia state senate for a time, but the later years of his life were uneventful. In the winter of 1797, he passed away at the age of sixty-three at his home, Menokin.

Thomas Nelson

Th.³ Nelson jr.

December 26, 1738 — January 4, 1789

IN THE 1690's, from Penrith on the English side of the Scottish border, came one Thomas Nelson, called "Scotch Tom," to settle in Virginia. His chosen locality was to become Yorktown, where Cornwallis would surrender almost a century later.

Scotch Tom amassed a large fortune as a merchant and incidentally built the first custom house in the colonies. His son, William, who inherited the fortune, bought up large amounts of land and became even wealthier as a merchant and planter. He married Elizabeth Burwell, who bore him five sons. The eldest, named Thomas for his grandfather, was born the day after Christmas, 1738, into the most luxurious style of living in early colonial Virginia.

Since there was plenty of money, education was no problem.
When he was fourteen, Thomas went to school at Hackney, England. At nineteen, he entered Christ's College, Cambridge, for
three years.

His father, now President of the Council and acting Governor
of Virginia, had also served as Presiding Judge of the General
Court, and the esteem in which the father was held helped the
son's career. While Thomas was still on the vessel bringing him
home, before he had even landed, York County voters chose him
to represent them in the House of Burgesses, though he was only
twenty-three.

The next year, in 1762, Thomas married Lucy Grymes, a daughter of Colonel Philip Grymes of Middlesex County. Father William gave the happy young couple a fine big house, almost opposite his own. Here the young Nelsons lived a delightful social life,
entertaining frequently, while Thomas rode out over his plantation
daily to keep an eye on everything. He kept a pack of hounds on
a farm near town and during the winter he and his friends and
neighbors went dashing off on a foxhunt twice a week. It was the
southern gentleman's ideal existence. But nothing stays ideal forever.

As the 1760's moved fatefully into the 1770's and as black clouds
of war gathered on the horizon and the dreadful storm of revolution drew near, Thomas Nelson — for all his formative years in
England — felt keenly the injustices imposed by King George III
upon the American colonies. He was one of eighty-nine members
who met at the Raleigh Tavern in Williamsburg, after the royal
governor had dissolved the House of Burgesses, to protest this
invasion of their rights and to plan a provincial congress to replace their dissolved House.

Nelson was a member of this first Virginia convention, which
met on August 1, 1774, in Williamsburg and chose seven delegates
to the First Continental Congress.

The second convention of the Virginia colony met the following
Spring in the old church in Richmond. By that time, England's
vengeance upon Massachusetts for the Boston Tea Party had
aroused the sympathies of all the colonies, and Virginia's feelings
were intense. The excitement in that March, 1775, convention in
Richmond is revealed in the ringing words of Patrick Henry, when

he prophesied: "The next gale that sweeps from the north will bring to our ears the clash of resounding arms."

He was right. The very next month, Paul Revere and William Dawes made their "midnight ride," and the "clash" Patrick Henry had predicted occurred at Lexington. There was no turning back after that.

Four months later, in July, 1775, there was a convention in Richmond, at which Patrick Henry was elected colonel of the First Virginia Regiment and Thomas Nelson colonel of the Second. The next month, Nelson and George Wythe were elected delegates to the Philadelphia Congress to take the places of Patrick Henry and George Washington, the latter being now commander in chief of the American Army. In mid-September, the new congressmen took their seats in the Second Continental Congress, the body that was to decide the great question of independence in the following July.

For most personal appraisals and first-hand descriptions of our founding fathers we are indebted, as we have seen, to Benjamin Rush and John Adams. Adams was not always kindly in his comments. He noted that "Nelson is a fat man — he is a speaker, and alert and lively for his weight." Dr. Rush's comment on Nelson is more sedate — and duller: "a respectable country gentleman, with excellent disposition in public and private life."

"He informed me," Rush added, "that he was the only person out of nine or ten Virginians that were sent with him to England for education that had taken part in the American Revolution. The rest were all Tories."

The emotional attitudes and political loyalties of Americans changed swiftly through 1774 and 1775. Before that, most of them had been loyal subjects of the king. But by 1776 Thomas Nelson was writing to a friend that it was absurd to suppose Americans could have "any affection for a people who are carrying on the most savage war against us." Lord Dunmore had ordered the burning of Norfolk, Virginia. No wonder Virginians were changing their minds!

During the early months of 1776, the members of the various provincial assemblies throughout the colonies were busy debating, arguing, endeavoring to foresee all aspects of the problem. On May 6, Virginia convention delegates took over authority from the king's government. A week later, Nelson moved for independence and, when the Virginia resolution for final separation from Britain was finally passed, Nelson rode off to Philadelphia carrying it to the Continental Congress.

Thomas Nelson was only thirty-eight when he signed the Declaration in early August, but he had felt the strain of these arduous years and in the following May he withdrew from Congress because of ill health. In August, when Virginia feared invasion by the approaching British fleet, which actually invaded Pennsylvania, he was appointed brigadier general and commander in chief of the state's forces.

When, in the Spring of 1778, Congress appealed for volunteer troops of light cavalry "to serve at their own expense," Nelson raised a company of about seventy emergency soldiers, who marched to Philadelphia. In August, after the enemy had withdrawn to New York, the company disbanded, but the thanks of Congress went to General Nelson and his volunteers for their patriotic effort. Nelson had also advanced large sums of money for other purposes.

The next year, again in Congress, Nelson was once more forced to retire because of illness. In June, 1780, when the Virginia assembly asked for $2,000,000 to help the Continental Treasury pay for the French fleet, Nelson himself tried to raise the money and on his own personal security did raise the larger part of the loan. Later, he was forced to redeem the security at a great sacrifice, and the government never compensated him for his loss. He also paid two whole regiments who refused to march south until they had received the back pay due them; and when Benedict Arnold led British troops into Virginia, Nelson's plantations were exposed to the traitor's raids.

Nelson was elected Governor of Virginia in June, 1781, and at the siege of Yorktown, it was he who commanded the Virginia militia. In his orders of the day for October 20, Washington expressed his deep appreciation to Nelson to whom, he said, "the highest praises are due" for activity and bravery.

Again poor health forced Governor Nelson to resign. Thereafter, having spent his fortune for his country, he lived very modestly in Hanover County until he died in 1789, at the early age of fifty-one. He was buried in an unmarked grave at Yorktown.

His courage, his zeal, and his generosity marked him as a man of "true religion" in the minds and memories of many who had known him and worked with him.

George Wythe

George Wythe

1726 (day and month unknown) — June 8, 1806

"ONE OF OUR BEST MEN," George Wythe, was born in 1726 on his father's prosperous plantation on Back River, Elizabeth City County, Virginia. His father, Thomas, was the grandson of Thomas Wythe, who came to Virginia from England about 1680. For three generations, the Wythes had increased their property in America and become prosperous. George Wythe's father was also a justice for the county and its delegates in the House of Burgesses for three terms.

His mother was Mary Walker Wythe, daughter of Quaker George Walker, reputed to have been a man of considerable learning. A firm believer in the education of women — an idea not generally accepted until more than a century later — he had given his daughter such excellent schooling that she was able to teach her son Latin, Greek, grammar, rhetoric, and logic. She began teaching the boy when he was three years old immediately after his father died. She must have been a devoted teacher, filled with ardent love for the subjects she presented to him; for though he was given very little formal education later, the boy pursued his studies eagerly in later life, spurred on by the incentive she had given him. On this foundation he was able to build a successful career and win a great reputation. He never ceased to study and in later life became known as a proficient scholar in Greek and Latin literature.

George was the middle one of three children, with a brother many years older than himself, who inherited the family estate, and a younger sister, Ann. When he was still a mere child, his widowed mother died, and after that no one seems to have taken any interest in the boy's further education. The lack of such a mother's care and advice must also have been a sore misfortune for the growing Ann. Later, she was to marry one Charles Sweeney, who was probably not a man of the same quality as the Walkers and Wythes, and probably not the type of person Mary Walker Wythe would have liked her daughter to marry. At any rate, Ann's grandson was to bring tragedy and death to his great-uncle George, the Signer.

In his teens, George Wythe entered the College of William and Mary, but his stay was very brief since he was a poor boy who had to earn a living. He soon left college to study law at the office of Stephen Dewey, a connection of the family. He was so successful in his studies that he was admitted to the bar at the age of twenty and began to practice in association with a prominent attorney, John Lewis, in Spottsylvania County. He soon fell in love with Lewis's sister, Ann, whom he married the following year. But death robbed the young lawyer of his bride in less than eight short months.

In that same year Wythe, now twenty-two, began his first service in public office as clerk of the Committee on Privileges and Elections in the House of Burgesses. His efficiency surprised his elders. Six years later Governor Dinwiddie appointed him Attorney General of the Colony, during the absence of Attorney General Peyton Randolph in England. After his friend Randolph returned, Wythe courteously resigned.

By this time he was twenty-nine and upon the death of his much older brother, the large family plantation, with its usual population of animals and slaves, became his responsibility. However, as he was representing Williamsburg in the House of Burgesses, he continued to reside there. This same year Wythe was married again, this time to Elizabeth Taliaferro of Williamsburg. They had one child who died in infancy.

He was admitted to the bar of the General Court when he was thirty-two. Serving in the House of Burgesses for ten years, he built up a brilliant career. In 1761, he was elected to the Board of Visitors of the College of William and Mary, his alma mater, and, though he had never had money enough to graduate, he joined the faculty eight years later — the first man to hold a chair of law in an American college.

As a teacher, George Wythe gave some of the most effective service of his useful career. He loved teaching. He loved to direct the studies of young men and he had some remarkable students, among them Thomas Jefferson, Henry Clay, James Monroe, John Marshall, and others who became governors, United States senators, congressmen, and state and federal judges. A pioneer in American jurisprudence, Wythe brought honor to the college.

George Wythe was a man of middle height with a good figure, and remarkable for his courteous manners. He dressed conservatively, with his long hair combed straight back and curled up at the neck.

The mid-1770's brought special troubles with the mother country for Virginia tobacco planters. Virginia and her great tobacco trade which made fortunes for her planters was also extremely profitable to the London businessmen who bought and sold tobacco. In fact tobacco was so important that, under Virginia law and with the approval of the Crown, the churches paid their ministers in tobacco, which was better than money, for if the price of tobacco rose the clergy made a profit. When Virginia commuted these salaries at a fixed monetary rate without royal consent there was trouble, for now the clergy would receive only cash and there would be no chance of profit. Law-suits followed, and the Virginians' troubles with tobacco made them very sympathetic with Boston's tea trouble and the closing of her port.

When war threatened in 1775, Wythe recommended that Virginians set up a full-time regular army instead of relying on a part-time citizen militia, as the colonies had always done. Upon the opening of hostilities, he himself volunteered for service as a soldier, but he was sent instead to the Continental Congress in Philadelphia, where he took his seat in September.

Following the hot debates, discussions, and arguments that swayed Congress in the spring and early summer of 1776, he voted in favor of Richard Henry Lee's resolution for independence, and signed the Declaration the following September. Two months later, in November, 1776, Wythe was appointed by the Virginia legislature to the committee to revise the laws for the new state. His former pupil, Thomas Jefferson, was also on this committee.

In 1777, George Wythe became speaker of Virginia's House of Delegates and next year was chosen one of the three judges of the new Chancery Court, a post he held for the rest of his life. During these decades, Chancellor Wythe earned the appellation of "the American Aristides," an allusion to an ancient Athenian with a high reputation for fairness, known in Athens as Aristides the Just. Wythe, too, was known to be "scrupulously impartial," erudite, and logical. Dr. Benjamin Rush considered him a "profound lawyer and able politician."

"I have seldom known a man possess more modesty," he wrote, "or a more dove-like simplicity and gentleness of manner."

Like all large land-owners, Wythe suffered great losses during the Revolution and his income as chancellor was most welcome. When he received that post in 1789, he terminated his connection with the college and moved to Virginia's new capital, Richmond.

His political theories agreed substantially with those of Jefferson and Madison. He favored a representative republicanism — the kind of government we have today. Opposed to slavery as were other eminent Virginians, he freed his own servants, though he was well aware that he would have to support them until they learned how to take care of themselves. And this led to tragedy.

In his will, Chancellor Wythe made his sister's grandson, George Wythe Sweeney, the principal beneficiary. But he also left legacies to provide for three of his freed slaves. After Wythe's death, the income from the rental of his Richmond house and from his bank stock was to be used to support "my freed woman, Lydia Broadnax, and my freedman Benjamin and freed boy Michael Brown." Later, when Benjamin died, Wythe provided that Michael was to have half the bank stock and his grand-nephew Sweeney the other half. But if Michael should die before coming of age, Sweeney was to have it all. Sweeney decided to hasten his legacy by getting rid of his uncle and of Michael Brown at the same time.

While the Chancellor was in court on May 25, 1806, young Sweeney came to the house and went to his great-uncle's room. Lydia, the cook, saw him at the desk reading the will, but she believed him when he said his uncle had told him to do so. Next morning he came to the kitchen, asked for coffee and toast, and explained he could not wait to breakfast with his uncle. He took the whole coffee-pot to the table while Lydia was making his toast, and poured himself a cup. Lydia saw him toss a little white paper in the open fire but thought nothing of it.

Sweeney had poured a cup of coffee for himself and had then dropped yellow arsenic into the coffee-pot, and burned the paper that had contained it.

After Sweeney had left the house, Chancellor Wythe appeared, took some coffee with his breakfast, and told Lydia to get some breakfast for herself and Michael. Lydia was taken very ill, seized with a violent cramp. The Chancellor and the mulatto boy, Michael, died.

No one had any doubt what had happened — least of all the Chancellor, who as a lawyer had a lifetime of dealing with crime. He lingered on in agony for two weeks but he was able to change his will in time to keep Sweeney from profiting by his crime. Watchers by his bedside heard him say: "I am murdered."

Sweeney was arrested and given a preliminary hearing before magistrates. They had no doubt of his guilt and held him for trial on six charges — the murder of Wythe, the murder of Michael Brown, and the forgery of checks. But the only murder witness was Lydia Broadnax, the Negro cook. And under Virginia law of that day, the testimony of a Negro could not be received against a white man. Though Sweeney could not be convicted of the murder of which every one knew he was guilty, he was brought to trial for forgery, and convicted. But he was granted a new trial and the district attorney decided not to prosecute. Again the rascal went free!

Wythe died in great agony, both of mind and body. He said of the grand-nephew who had poisoned him: "I shall die leaving him my forgiveness." But it was an anguish, too, for him to realize that law suits would follow and that large expenses were to be caused by his death. He died on June 8, 1806, at his home in Richmond.

Years later Wythe's ardent admirer and erstwhile student, Thomas Jefferson, made notes with the idea of writing a biography of George Wythe. But he did not live to complete it. He noted, however, that "no man ever left behind him a character more venerated than George Wythe, whose virtue," he said, "was pure, whose integrity inflexible, whose justice exact." He considered his old teacher, "the honor of his own, and model of future times."

Carter Braxton

Carter Braxton

September 10, 1736 — October 10, 1797

THOUGH MANY OF THE PATRIOTS who survived the war suffered heavily in loss of health or lands or fortune because of the time and energy they devoted to their country, Carter Braxton was among the most unfortunate of all. Born into one of the First Families of Virginia with an inherited background of wealth and culture, he suffered heavier losses than most other patriots just because he had so much to lose.

Carter Braxton was the son of a wealthy planter, a member of the House of Burgesses, whose estate lay at Newington, in King and Queen County, Virginia. His mother, Mary Carter Braxton, was from an equally proud and wealthy family, but her son never knew her, for she died soon after September 10, 1736, the day when he was born.

The boy was educated at the College of William and Mary. He was only nineteen when he married Judith Robinson, who died two years later, leaving him with two small daughters. Perhaps it was this sad experience that caused him to go to England for over two years. Some time after his return, he married Elizabeth Corbin, and in the same year he was appointed, at the age of twenty-five, to represent King William County in the House of Burgesses.

The unhappy 1760's were beginning; and in the disputes between Great Britain and her Virginia Colony, Braxton, though a conservative, took Virginia's side, never at this time dreaming of such an extreme notion as American independence.

In 1769, however, he joined Washington, Jefferson, and other prominent Virginians in resolutions supporting the sole right of the House of Burgesses to tax Virginia. He also represented his county in the conventions of the early 1770's, and, when the House of Burgesses was dissolved in 1774, became a member of the patriots' Committee of Safety.

Peyton Randolph, Virginia's most popular leader during the decade before the war, had been representing his colony in the First Continental Congress in Philadelphia. When, in October, 1775, he died suddenly, Carter Braxton became his successor. It was said that the Virginians were "so alarmed with the Idea of Independence that they have sent Mr. Braxton [to Congress] on Purpose to turn the Vote of that Colony, if any Question on that Subject should come before Congress."

Braxton took his seat on February 23, 1776, four months before Richard Henry Lee introduced his resolution for independence. Many minds had had to change in those months, and Braxton's was one of them. He was just under forty when he voted for Independence and signed the Declaration.

Dr. Benjamin Rush, who recorded so many comments about his colleagues in Congress — not all of them favorable — thought Braxton an agreeable and sensible speaker and an accomplished gentleman, but strongly prejudiced against New Englanders.

When discussions came up later as to the form of government the new American states should have, Braxton doubted the success of a democracy, and he advocated a more conservative form of government for Virginia. In those days democracy was considered the most extreme radicalism.

(National attitudes have changed much in the last two hundred years. It is amusing now to reflect that Russia would have nothing to do with so radical a country as the new United States. The Tsar would neither send a minister, nor receive one from us in the early days of the United States!)

Braxton's expressed doubts about democratic government may have been one reason why he was not reappointed to the Continental Congress, but he did continue to serve in the Virginia Assembly. Here, in 1785, he supported an act to establish religious freedom. The next year he moved to Richmond because his losses during the war had been on such a gigantic scale that he could not continue living on his elaborate country estate.

While he was still possessed of great wealth, Braxton had loaned £10,000 sterling to "our Suffering country." It was never paid back to him. He had been engaged in merchandizing and shipping throughout the war, but some of his vessels had been captured by the British, others had been lost in unfortunate enterprises.

Vast debts due him were worthless in the depreciated Continental currency. All these misfortunes left him bankrupt at the end of the war.

Weighed down by the endless litigation in which these financial troubles involved him, and by the hopelessness of recovering from his misfortunes, Carter Braxton died in Richmond at the age of sixty-one. He lived only long enough to see the first few years of the new nation for which he had sacrificed so much.

III

PENNSYLVANIA

Beny. Franklin

Robt Morris

Benjamin Rush

John Morton

Geo Clymer

Jas. Smith

Geo. Taylor

James Wilson

Geo. Ross

Benjamin Franklin

January 17, 1706 — April 17, 1790

OF ALL JOSIAH FRANKLIN'S seventeen children, his youngest son, Benjamin, was, from early childhood, the most promising. He was born with something the others never had. Even as he was the "different" member of his family, so was his career different from those of all the other men chosen for the Second Continental Congress. Of the Signers of the Declaration of Independence, Benjamin Franklin was the oldest, being seventy at the time, and also the most famous, both in his own country and in Europe. Several of the Signers were exceedingly able and talented men, two became President of the United States; but Franklin was the one possessed of genius — a quality that cannot be achieved, something that, like lightning, strikes no one can tell where.

Benjamin Franklin's forebears were of lowly British stock: farmers and blacksmiths, of Ecton, Northamptonshire, a county in central England. His father, Josiah, was a dyer in Banbury, Oxfordshire, who already had a wife and three children when he decided to cross the ocean to the colony of Massachusetts. Having broken away from the Church of England and become a dissenter, at a time when that was difficult and even dangerous, he hoped that his work would prosper better and his life be more agreeable in the new land, where there were fewer restrictions than in the rigid, class-conscious Old World.

He was right. His favorite brother, Benjamin, also a dissenter, remained in England and had a hard time of it. But Josiah, settling in Boston and finding that a dyer was not needed there, became instead a busy maker and seller of soap and candles and, as a tallow-chandler, flourished to a ripe old age. His wife, however, did not survive the birth of their seventh child. Then Josiah married young Abiah Folger, only twenty-two, the daughter of Peter Folger of Nantucket, and by her had ten more children, the seventh of whom was Benjamin. Josiah was nearing fifty when Benjamin was born on the first Sunday in January, 1706. The Franklins were then living in a house on Milk Street, opposite the Old South Church, and the new baby was carried across the street and baptized there the same day.

Benjamin was, of course, the favorite nephew of the English uncle for whom he had been named. Eight years older than his brother in Boston, the lonely uncle, who had lost his wife and all nine children, began to write letters in verse to his nephew Benjamin when the child was only four years old. At seven, the boy was writing verses in answer. Two years later, Uncle Benjamin came to visit the Boston Franklins, and he was much pleased with his namesake, for there was something about young Benjamin that usually drew marked attention from older men. Perhaps it was because he learned so easily and grasped ideas so quickly — more easily than the average child of his years. He could read at a very early age.

When he was eight, his father sent him to the grammar school (now the Boston Latin School), where, in less than a year, he advanced from the middle of the class to the top. At first, his father thought to have him educated for the Church; but seeing how expensive a college education was and how poor ministers were, he took Benjamin from the grammar school and sent him to a school for writing and arithmetic kept by a schoolmaster named George Brownell. Though the boy did well in writing, he failed in arithmetic, and after he was ten his father kept him home to help in the business. From this time on, Benjamin Franklin taught himself.

For two years, his father tried to get him to learn the tallow-chandler's trade. But candle-making was one thing that did not interest young Benjamin. In summers he spent his free time in, or on, the water, which he loved; and, as the Franklins lived right on the shore in Boston harbor, he learned early to swim well and to handle boats. He was so adept at sailing that the other boys let him take charge, "especially in case of difficulty," as Franklin recorded when he wrote his autobiography. With all this, he grew strong, not above average height, but with a stocky, sturdy figure and powerful muscles.

Seeing that Benjamin was not enamored of candle-making and so fond of the water, his father was afraid his son might run away to sea, as one of his older sons had already done. It was not an uncommon thing in the days of the sailing ships for a son to go off to sea without consulting his parents. But Benjamin Franklin stayed ashore because, mindful of his love of books, his father turned him over to James Franklin, his older brother, to serve as an apprentice in James's new printing shop. After learning the trade in London, James had returned to set up a shop of his own in Boston. He was twenty-one and Benjamin was twelve when the apprenticeship agreement was made. The father paid James £12 for teaching Benjamin the "art of a printer" and providing the boy's lodging, meals, and necessities. The sturdy young apprentice, as quick with his hands as he was with his mind, was soon a skillful printer. The elder Franklin had done exactly the right thing, for eventually his son Benjamin made a fortune as head of his own printshop.

Boston was then a small provincial town with a number of other printers, and the Franklin brothers, who were not burdened with orders, had to do all sorts of odd jobs, printing pamphlets and ballads (which young Benjamin began to write) and even designs on linen, silk, and calico. After his young brother had been in his shop for a year, James was engaged to print a newspaper, the *Boston Gazette*. He had printed forty numbers when the job was given to another printer, whereupon James started his own competing newspaper, the *New England Courant*.

An example of Benjamin's early wisdom was his recognition of the value of his own time. He liked people — if they were not boring — and made friends easily. He liked certain games and boating; he was an expert swimmer. But he never had any use for loafing around taverns, drinking, or gambling. At fifteen, he couldn't get enough time to read. With any money he could save he bought books, and when he finished these books, he sold them to buy others. He read history, travel, fiction, science, and biography — Plutarch's *Lives,* essays by Defoe, Cotton Mather, and Locke. By himself, he now mastered the arithmetic he had failed a few years before. He read to learn, not just to pass the time. He studied prose style, argument, and discussion. When he came upon a volume of the *Spectator,* he was delighted. This, he decided, was a style he wished to emulate; and he went about it cleverly, choosing one essay for study, jotting down the hints contained in each sentence, then rewriting it himself to compare his own work with the original.

Benjamin Franklin had a goal. While still young, he had considered the kind of man he wanted to be. He felt he must refine his taste constantly, and this led him to copy the literary masters. Like most adolescents, he loved to take part in serious discussion, but after reading Plato's accounts of Socrates, he "gave up the disputatious habits" he had formed when engaged in discussion, and assumed a manner more persuasive, agreeable, and modest in argument. Aiming constantly to improve his mind, he also considered his manners. All these were useful and most desirable achievements for a boy who was to become in later life his country's ablest diplomat.

Realizing that he needed time and money for making himself the kind of person he wanted to be, young Benjamin went to the printing house early in the mornings, stayed late on week-days, and went back on Sundays, in order to be alone to read and study. Wanting a little money to buy books (we must remember that there were no public libraries), he conceived the idea of asking his brother to give him half the money that his board cost and let him feed himself. Then he saved money by not eating meat. He found he could save half of the amount his brother paid him by making a meal of a biscuit or a slice of bread and some raisins. This gave him three advantages: he could have his light snacks alone in the office while the others went out for their meals and thereby have time to study; he discovered that he had a clearer head after one of his light meals than after a hearty one; he had more money to buy books and so feed his hunger for knowledge.

With a mind so inquisitive and acquisitive came a disposition to experiment. He liked to invent new things and new ways of doing things. Combining kite-flying with swimming, he gave himself a glorious experience one day by holding to the string of his kite while the wind pulled him across the pond. What strange experiments might not this young boy try in the future!

As printer's apprentice, his brother's newspaper brought him in touch with local affairs, current events, contemporary ideas. The *New England Courant* first appeared during a smallpox epidemic in the hot summer of 1721. Some doctors upheld the new idea of inoculation — a kind of early vaccination — while others denounced it as a "doubtful and dangerous practice."

When James Franklin invited his friends, through his newspaper, to send in short pieces to enliven the news, young Benjamin accepted the general invitation without telling his brother. He decided to submit a short "epistle" twice a month, hoping it would appear among the letters to the editor. But, because he knew his brother would not use anything written by his fifteen-year-old apprentice, he signed his pieces "Mrs. Silence Dogood." Slipping his papers under the printing-house door at night, the unknown correspondent soon had the pleasure of seeing himself in print. In his first contribution, he started out by describing the writer as a widow and gave a short and entirely imaginary account of her life. This and later Dogood letters entertained and amused the readers of the *New England Courant*.

Then James Franklin made the mistake of printing a fictitious letter from Newport, in which was a sarcastic jibe at the royal governor of Massachusetts. James found himself clapped in jail for ridiculing the authorities and, during his forced absence, young Benjamin had to print and edit the paper himself.

In time the real author of the Dogood articles was discovered, and James became intensely jealous when he found that the writer who had been so highly praised was really his younger brother. Resentfully, he now accused young Benjamin of being vain, which was most unfair. Benjamin Franklin may have had his faults, but vanity was never one of them. Inevitably, with all this ill feeling, an uncomfortable atmosphere crept into the printing office. Probably neither brother quite understood what was really wrong. The truth was that Benjamin was outgrowing his position and would soon be ready for bigger things. James had already reached his limits.

Presently young Benjamin was in more trouble. Having ventured upon what he later called "indiscreet disputations" about religion, he found himself denounced as "an infidel or atheist."

Strict, narrow-minded, and Puritanical, many people of eastern Massachusetts of those days were quick to form suspicions of other people's religious beliefs. This was ironical, since their own fathers had come to the New World seeking for themselves the very religious freedom which their descendants now refused to others. It had not been very many years since the more fanatical Puritans had hanged innocent women, calling them witches. One trouble was that Benjamin had not been a steady attendant at church because he wanted the time for study. His father, of course, disapproved, and apparently others made it their business to disapprove also. Benjamin Franklin later recorded in his autobiography that he believed in God, but he could not believe that God was as narrow-minded as many of the New England preachers.

Troubled by this petty public criticism and gossip, and by his uncomfortable relations with his jealous brother, and with his father who sided with James, the seventeen-year-old Benjamin decided it was time to seek broader horizons. Borrowing a little money from a boyhood friend, he secretly boarded a sloop for New York. Fearing his father would prevent him, he did not tell his family. This was to be a permanent break — with family, home town, and familiar ways.

Becalmed off Block Island, the sailing vessel took three days to reach New York, at that time a smaller city than Boston, though less provincial. Calling on the town's only printer, William Bradford, Benjamin was told that a new hand was not needed. However, the printer's son, Andrew Bradford, in Philadelphia, might be able to use him.

Benjamin arrived in the Quaker City on a sunny September morning, tired, hungry, and dirty. The first thing he needed was food. Inquiring of a passing boy who was carrying bread, he learned where to find the baker. Unaware of the differences in the price of bread between Boston and Philadelphia, he simply asked for three pennyworth and was surprised to be given "three great puffy" rolls. With one under each arm while nibbling the third, he walked on up the street. As he passed a house where a young girl was standing at the door, she watched him go by, amused because he looked "most awkward" and ridiculous. He found this out some years later when this same girl, Deborah Read, became his wife.

Following many "cleaned-dressed people" all walking in one direction, he came to the Quaker Meeting-house. Every one else went inside. So did he and, during the quiet service, fell asleep. Out in the street again afterward, he inquired of a young Quaker where to find lodging. The next day, making himself as neat as he could, he went to see Andrew Bradford, the printer. This was the beginning of Franklin's Philadelphia career.

It was not easy at the start. Though Bradford welcomed the teen-age runaway, he could not offer steady work, and for some time Benjamin was a "journeyman" printer, working at odd jobs of printing wherever he could find them. Eventually, he rented a room in the house of Mr. Read — the house where the girl stood on the stoop that first Sunday morning. Even as journeyman printer he soon began to earn more money than he ever had earned in Boston.

In Philadelphia that first winter, Benjamin made friends and enjoyed his new freedom. He liked the Quakers and their tolerant views of their fellow men. It was a great relief not to be under the domination of his older brother and the criticism of his father. Though he probably did not realize it yet, he already had a more active brain, more wit, imagination, common sense, and industry than any one of his relatives. In the spring, he visited his family in Boston and told them about his life in Philadelphia.

Seeing his young son dressed in a good new suit, wearing a watch in his pocket, with more money than he himself had ever accumulated in Boston, Josiah Franklin gave up all hope that Benjamin would ever work again with James and consented to his return to Philadelphia. This eased Benjamin's mind, of course, for he was still a minor. His father could have forced him to come home.

By this time Benjamin Franklin had grown to be a well-built, vigorous young man, about five-feet nine- or ten-inches tall, with a large head (which accommodated a good brain), and strong, deft hands. His hair was light brown, his eyes gray, and his regard steady and honest. His unfailing sense of humor was revealed by a humorous mouth and easy smile. He could be quick and prompt to act, but his speech was hesitant and slow. He was at his best in small groups of chosen friends in the clubs he formed, or others which he joined.

Evenings spent in discussions, listening to and criticizing poems written by each other, sharing their opinions on the books they read, Sunday walks in the beautiful countryside around Philadelphia — these were the pleasant ways in which Benjamin and his young friends, mostly clerks, used their free time. Generous and disposed always to help others, young Franklin more than once had the unpleasant experience of loaning his hard-earned money to "friends" who never repaid him. He believed too easily in the word of people who, having nothing else to give, airily gave promises and forgot them.

It was this trusting disposition that presently left Franklin stranded in London whither he had sailed relying on the promises of no less a personage than Sir William Keith, royal governor of Pennsylvania. Sir William had been impressed by a letter that Benjamin had written to his own brother-in-law, who was master of a sloop that operated between Boston and Delaware. Sir William took the trouble of looking up the young man, liked him, and made elaborate plans for setting him up in a printing shop of his own. He was to go to London to select the stock he would need, and Sir William would advance the necessary credit.

This offer came when Benjamin, now eighteen, was courting Deborah Read, whose parents wanted the marriage delayed until his return. With his friend, James Ralph, Benjamin boarded a ship for London. Until the last moment, he was expecting Sir William's promised letters of credit and of introduction. They did not come. Then he hoped to find them on his arrival in London. But Sir William's promises were but air. The papers never came, and once more Benjamin Franklin found himself in a strange city with no friends and little money. He had, however, his trade and his will to work. He soon found his chance in the printing house of Samuel Close.

He also had on his hands James Ralph, who now proved to be less than a friend. Ten years older than Benjamin, he had left behind a wife and baby and now declared he was not going to return to them. Nor did he even try to support himself, but proceeded to live on Benjamin's earnings, borrowing steadily while planning to be a poet, then an actor, then an editor of a weekly paper "like the *Spectator*." Their ways parted when Ralph went to Berkshire to be a schoolmaster, leaving only an unpaid debt. Benjamin was well rid of a knave.

For a year and a half, the young printer lived in London during one of its most brilliant periods. At the beginning of manhood, Franklin was eager to drink in the advantages of this center of luxury, fashion, and wit. A poor young American printer of twenty had no way of meeting the great writers and artists there — Lord Chesterfield, Fielding, Defoe, Swift, and a refugee from Paris named Voltaire; but he had his own intellectual interests which led him to good reading, and he made good use of his time. He soon moved to a larger printing-house, and among the printers, his strength and speed distinguished him. At this time he published his first pamphlet: *"A Dissertation on Liberty and Necessity, Pleasure and Pain."* A printer friend suggested they travel through Europe as journeymen printers together, but Benjamin's thoughts were turning toward home. He sailed for America in July, 1726.

With plenty of time for reflection during the long voyage, Benjamin drew up a plan for his future conduct in life. His first aim, he decided, was to be extremely frugal, pay his debts and save money "for some time." Second, he must "endeavor to speak truth in every instance, to give nobody expectations that are not likely to be answered," (was he thinking of Sir William's vain promises?), "but aim at sincerity in every word and action; the most amiable excellence in a rational being." Third, he must apply himself industriously "to whatever business I take in hand, and not divert my mind from my business by any foolish project of growing suddenly rich; for industry and patience are the surest means of plenty." Fourth, he decided "to speak ill of no man whatever, not even in a matter of truth; but rather by some means excuse the faults I hear charged upon others, and upon proper occasions speak all the good I know of everybody." In his autobiography, the old Franklin wrote that he followed these resolutions, on the whole, "quite through to old age."

Upon his return, Franklin first kept store for his friend, Thomas Denham, a Quaker merchant whom he had met on the homeward voyage. Denham set up the store with stock he had brought from England. But after some months, Franklin returned to his own trade and became foreman for the printer Samuel Keimer.

Through his twenties, Benjamin Franklin's advancement was rapid. Keimer employed him to print paper money for New Jersey, and for this work Benjamin contrived the first copperplate press in the country. The New Jersey Assembly liked his work and they liked him. It was he — not Keimer — whom the assemblymen invited to their houses while the printers were working in Burlington,

New Jersey. Franklin was now making friends for life. Older men were attracted by his innate charm and simplicity of manner, his conversation, and his marked ability. Success came swiftly now. Within four years Benjamin Franklin was his own master, the proprietor of a printshop, and the best printer in America.

Always, somehow, he found time to write, and now he began writing articles, which he signed "Busy-Body," for the *American Weekly Mercury*. Before long, he was planning a newspaper, the *Pennsylvania Gazette*, which he started with the issue of October 2, 1729. For many issues he was the writer as well as the printer; and after two years, as the *Gazette* became profitable, he became part owner of other *Gazettes* in South Carolina and Rhode Island.

An alert man of business, he was also deeply interested in public welfare, in good companionship, and in stimulating talk. He brought together a group called "The Junto," for Friday evening meetings to discuss civic improvements and the improvement of their own knowledge. Under his leadership, the Junto was a gathering of tradesmen and artisans for pleasure as well as for serious debate. It was a kind of brotherhood, whose members promoted each other's interests and businesses. At first they met in a tavern, sometimes in their homes. Young people always like to organize social groups, but few last as long as Franklin held the Junto together. It continued to meet for thirty years.

While he had been away in England, he had written only one letter to Deborah Read. As the months passed into a year and longer, still with no further word, she concluded he had forgotten her and married a potter named Rogers. But she was unhappy with him and learning, too late, that he already had a wife, she parted from him. Rogers ran away to the West Indies, leaving many debts. Finally the report came of his death. In 1730, when Benjamin Franklin was twenty-four, he "took her to wife" as he noted in his autobiography.

He set up a shop in a part of his house where his wife helped in selling books and stationery. Wanting more income, and needing more work for his active brain, the budding philosopher began writing the famous *Poor Richard's Almanac*. The first issue appeared in December, 1732, and a new annual number was forthcoming for many years thereafter. *Poor Richard* was translated into French when Franklin achieved international fame, and his amusing nuggets of wisdom have afforded entertaining reading now for over two hundred years.

There seemed to be no limit to the intellectual curiosity of this man. He studied languages by himself till he could read books in Italian, French, and Spanish. He enlarged his shop to offer all kinds of goods that he could sell through advertisements in his own *Gazette*. The business broadened until Franklin became a general trader; he even operated a kind of employment agency, offering for sale (again through his paper) the unexpired time of indentured servants.

Ever eager for more books, he conceived the idea of what we call today a lending library, an idea which he suggested to the Junto. They agreed, and Franklin worked out the details: fifty subscribers paid for membership, and the Library Company was formed. It is still operating in Philadelphia!

Concerned about the town's fire protection, Franklin formed the first volunteer fire company in December, 1736. He also helped establish the "City Watch," thus providing better police protection for the city.

As the years passed, Franklin's reputation as a helpful citizen increased and put him into various offices. He was appointed clerk of the Pennsylvania Assembly and, the next year, postmaster for Philadelphia.

Working with the newspapers and trade of other colonies, Franklin's affairs brought him in touch with ideas in other colonies. He was about thirty-seven when he conceived a kind of intercolonial Junto. This resulted in his founding of the American Philosophical Society. It, too, is still operating in Philadelphia.

Busy at his work six days a week and studying with his friends evenings and Sundays, Franklin had, by the age of forty, made enough money to be able to indulge in some leisure. But to a man of his lively mind, leisure did not mean idleness. It meant time for new ideas, and a very big new idea soon came his way.

Visiting Boston in 1746, Franklin met "a Dr. Spence, who was lately come from Scotland, and showed me some electrical experiments." Electricity interested Franklin so much that he soon wanted to make his own experiments. When the doctor visited Philadelphia, Franklin bought Spence's apparatus and was soon engrossed in experiments.

Some of those experiments were more dangerous than Franklin quite realized. When he drew lightning from a cloud with his electrical kite, he escaped injury, but he was really playing with fire. Later he did receive a severe shock when he tried to kill a turkey by "electrical fire." He described his experiments in pamphlets and articles, one of which — his account of his electrical kite — was read before the Royal Society in London. In November, 1753, the Society awarded him a gold medal for his scientific observations on electricity and some time later made him a member. Already known as printer, publicist, philanthropist, philosopher, tradesman, journalist, Franklin was now becoming famous as a scientist and inventor. In the six years from the time he first saw those experiments in Boston until he flew his electrical kite in Philadelphia, he made fundamental contributions to the scientific use of electricity. One of the most important of these was the lightning rod. He put the first one ever used on his own house, "fixed to the top of my chimney." He always refused to patent his lightning rod, though every one knew he had invented it and it was often called the "Franklin rod."

One writer says that Franklin "found electricity a curiosity and left it a science." To the public, who knew nothing of these strange things, he seemed to be a magician. To scientific men, who did know, he appeared to be a master; and though he had never attended college, both Harvard and Yale gave him the honorary degree of Master of Arts.

Never ambitious for fame, and wise in the knowledge of human nature, Franklin well knew that petty people — even among scientists — easily become jealous of another's success. He was careful not to stir them up by emphasizing his inventions. Himself free of jealousy and of vanity, he would not risk raising envious emotions in others if he could help it. With all his ability, he was a modest man.

At the age of forty-two, Franklin retired from business, turning the management of the printing-house over to his partner, David Hall. The firm, known as Franklin and Hall for many years, continued to bring its founder a steady income.

As time went on, Franklin, now free from business, was drawn more and more into public affairs.

His public interest, like his intellectual interest, blossomed out in every direction. Though he was given so little formal education as a boy, he was the man who proposed and helped organize the Pennsylvania Academy because he felt that his province should have a college. He also helped to organize the Pennsylvania Hospital, the first fire insurance company, the first voyage — or one of the first voyages — for Arctic exploration.

On the other side of the Atlantic wars were going on. England and Spain were at odds over British smuggling in Spanish America. England and France were at odds over Austrian affairs. Here, the English and French were both stirring up the Indians and, as a result, Pennsylvania, like other colonies, suffered from Indian trouble.

In the late 1740's raiding privateers — both French and Spanish — came dangerously close to Philadelphia, entering the bay and plundering two plantations just below New Castle, Delaware. They captured a ship and murdered the captain. Franklin, concerned for the safety of the city itself, called meetings to organize self-defense, and wrote and published pamphlets to awaken the people to their danger. But it was difficult to persuade the large Quaker population — all pacifists — to organize military defense.

Franklin's career as a public official began with his election to the assembly — the Pennsylvania state legislature. His remarkable career in diplomacy began with his mission to Carlisle to make a treaty with the Indians.

Franklin liked and respected the Indians, regarding the tribes and their customs with kindly curiosity. He had a real admiration for the Iroquois Confederacy. If the Six Nations of "ignorant savages" were able to form a successful union, the colonists, he thought, ought to be able to do it, too. Franklin had had this idea long before the Revolution.

As representative in the assembly, Franklin had sounded his first warning to the British governor on England's crude disregard for her American colonies in getting rid of her felons by shipping them to America. He proposed sending American rattlesnakes back to England and trading them for the British convicts, saying that the rattlesnakes were better! In spite of this criticism, however, the British government appointed him Deputy Postmaster-General two years later, thus giving him prestige as an officer of the Crown. In reorganizing and improving the postal service, he traveled through the New England colonies, and through Maryland and Virginia; he visited post offices, acquainted himself with the local postmasters, studied their various problems, road conditions, and the fords and ferries the mail carriers had to use. He instituted the Dead Letter Office. By improving the speed and safety of the mails, he caused an increase in their use and thus provided easier communications which helped to draw the colonies closer together. No one had done so much to improve the mails as Franklin.

As early as 1751, Benjamin Franklin outlined a plan for the union of the colonies; and, as a defense against Indians, he proposed an intercolonial council on Indian Affairs. Though the colonies' resistance to the king would not grow serious for another decade, Franklin was already looking forward to a larger and ever-growing America. The population had increased greatly in the hundred and thirty years since the first settlers came to Virginia and Massachusetts. It was reasonable to conclude that the spread of the American frontier and colonial growth could not long be regulated from distant London. It would have to be controlled by Americans who were there and understood American conditions.

In 1755 the frontier was not far from Philadelphia. Less than a hundred miles away, Indian raiding parties from the Ohio slipped through Pennsylvania's dark forests, scalping and killing settlers in the "back country." Franklin himself visited the frontier, and when the Assembly resolved to send commissioners to London to explain these problems, Franklin was chosen to go as agent of Pennsylvania, with a petition to the Crown.

For safety's sake, Britain and France being at war, it was necessary for the small packets to sail in a convoy. As the convoy approached European shores, the packet Franklin was on was chased several times by French privateers. But the ship escaped each time and, three and a half months after leaving Philadelphia, he reached London on July 27, 1757, little thinking that London was to be his home for several years to come.

After being abroad for five years, he returned to America with an honorary degree from St. Andrew's University in Scotland. After that, he was always known as Dr. Franklin. But little more than a year later, he was back in London, the official voice for the colonies in England. He wrote a pamphlet on the value of the American colonies to the Empire. When he attended the coronation of George III in October, 1760, Franklin regarded him as a generous and virtuous young king, but he learned better five years later when the king's government imposed the outrageous Stamp Act. Franklin's enemies blamed him for allowing it to be passed at all! "I took every step in my power to prevent the passing of the Stamp Act," he wrote; and he added that he might as well have "hindered the sun's setting." Nevertheless, after the Act had passed the House of Commons and the House of Lords and had received the king's assent, Franklin thought it wiser to submit to it temporarily, while working for its repeal.

Nobody could have worked harder than Dr. Franklin to explain the American attitude on the Stamp Act to the British, who seemed unable to grasp the viewpoint of the colonists and were angered by the Americans' outcry against the Act. During the following months, Franklin received much news from home about American opposition; and when he was summoned to the House of Commons for questioning, he had the answers on the end of his tongue. No question could surprise him. He attempted no eloquent speech, but simply replied to anything the members asked, clearly, unhesitatingly, and brilliantly. The House of Commons was the most influential audience he had ever faced.

The *Examination* — the report of what Franklin said — was published in London, in five American cities, and later in Strasbourg, France. And when the Stamp Act was repealed the next year, Franklin was the hero of the jubilant colonists.

The reason for all taxes is that the government needs money. Great Britain had been carrying on wars — in part for the defense of the colonies — and the wars had to be paid for. Feeling that American colonists were growing rich and owed something for British protection, Parliament passed the act requiring a stamp on every legal paper, on marriage licenses, on newspapers, advertisements, office appointments, college degrees, liquor licenses. The last three required expensive stamps. Commodities were also taxed. The stamp for a pack of cards was to cost a shilling; a pair of dice, two shillings; and many other commodities were similarly taxed.

It was impossible to enforce this act, especially in the back woods. Dr. Franklin explained to the House of Commons that it might cost four or five times the price of the stamp for a back-woods man to travel the distance to the tax office where the stamp was obtainable. The colonists had no objection to helping pay for their own defense. The taxes they had imposed themselves were already heavy because of wars, even as were those of the British. But Franklin explained that the colonists should be represented in any vote that imposed *internal* taxes on the colonies.

During these periods of ticklish diplomacy when, as one writer says, Franklin was walking on eggs, he nevertheless enjoyed London life. He had many friends among scientists, writers, economists, with whom he could converse on his many different interests. He enjoyed the sophisticated, urbane society of an ancient city. The Royal Society became a kind of club house for him. Artists wanted to paint his portrait. Priestley, the discoverer of oxygen, was his friend. Life in London was much more stimulating than it had been in provincial Philadelphia for a mind such as his. He wrote timely articles for British newspapers. He traveled to other countries, and enjoyed finding presents to send to his wife and his daughter Sally. His wife was his best correspondent during all those years of separation, but in 1774 she died of a stroke. Some time passed before Franklin even heard of it; it took weeks for news to cross the ocean.

When, long after they had happened, Franklin heard about the Boston Massacre (1770), the Boston Tea Party (1773), and the establishment of Committees of Correspondence, he knew that England and her colonies were drifting apart. And, after the stubborn Lord North became the king's prime minister in 1770, he lost all hope of reconciliation. To help the British understand, Dr. Franklin, in 1774, published in London an article explaining all the trouble. He called it "On the Rise and Progress of the Differences between Great Britain and Her American Colonies." But it was too late.

The First Continental Congress was called together in Philadelphia.

Through all these troubled times in his own country, Franklin was kept busy in London until, disappointed and disgusted, having lost all hope that Lord North's disastrous ministry could be overthrown, he sailed for home. The last news from the colonies he had read with eyes filled with tears. It was only too plain that war was coming nearer.

Arriving in Philadelphia early in May, 1775, he learned that the battles of Lexington and Concord had been fought the month before. The very next day, Dr. Franklin was chosen by the Assembly as one of Pennsylvania's members to the Second Continental Congress, which was to meet within four days to carry further the dispute with Great Britain.

Franklin was the oldest, as well as the most famous, member of that most famous Congress. He was seventy when he signed the Declaration of Independence, and was chosen as one of three commissioners to the Court of France who were expected to secure French aid against the British. In the autumn of 1776, Dr. Franklin again crossed the Atlantic to play his part, now on the international stage, to persuade France to acknowledge the American colonies as an independent nation. The new country needed French soldiers, arms, and money.

It was a perilous voyage. Had the American armed sloop *Reprisal*, on which he traveled, been captured, Franklin would surely have been hanged for high treason, or perhaps beheaded. Yet the indomitable traveler took two grandsons with him: Temple Franklin, almost seventeen, the son of Franklin's Tory son, William, and the seven-year-old Benjamin F. Bache, the son of Franklin's daughter Sally.

The sage from Philadelphia was greeted by the French with an outburst of enthusiasm. Having lived thirty years in the society of scientists, scholars, politicians, clergymen, merchants and men of fashion, Dr. Franklin was no backwoods philosopher. He was at ease anywhere. His manner was urbane. He could speak French, though not always correctly. But he retained his simple dress — almost Quakerish, though he was not a Quaker. The French were charmed to see the stocky figure in the long brown coat, wearing the fur cap he had brought along to keep his head warm on the cold November voyage. His spectacles were the only ones to be seen in Paris. His long hair, straight and gray, was a contrast to the powdered wigs of fashion. The very plainness of his appearance made him conspicuous in a Parisian salon of Louis XIV's reign, when men dressed in lace-trimmed silks and satins of all colors. The Parisians regarded him as a kind of hero, "a combination of Voltaire and Rousseau, in a plain American package."

Soon it became the fashion to have a medal or an engraving of his likeness on every French mantelpiece. He wrote his daughter Sally that his portrait was appearing on the lids of snuffboxes, even tiny ones in finger-rings "and the numbers sold are incredible." These and other busts and prints "have made your father's face as well known as that of the moon," he told her.

Dr. Franklin was the perfect diplomat. His country profited by the French passion for this plain but brilliant American. The ladies, in whose salons he was quite the rage, adored him. In the spring, Louis XIV received him in the great palace at Versailles. Even here, where the other envoys wore formal court dress as prescribed by the chamberlain, Franklin appeared without wig or sword, in his dark brown velvet, his own gray hair hanging loose, spectacles on nose, white stockings, and a white hat tucked under his arm — the plainest and most conspicuous figure present and, among the envoys, the most eminent.

Franklin's last years in France, as the Revolution drew to its close, were taken up mainly with peace negotiations and, after the war, with peace treaties. He enjoyed his life in France and the warm friendships he made there. But he was growing old, becoming infirm and uncomfortable and plagued with "the stone" (kidney or gallstones). He was almost eighty when he made plans to leave. Several of his French friends begged him to stay and spend the rest of his life with them.

To save him from a rough carriage journey, which would have been painful to him, he was furnished with a royal litter swung between two Spanish mules to carry him from his home in Passy, a suburb of Paris, to his ship at Le Havre. This last voyage home in midsummer proved the most pleasant and cheerful of all his eight Atlantic crossings, partly because his two grandsons were with him.

Nine days before he landed in Philadelphia, a ship preceding his carried the news of his coming, and his home town prepared a great welcome for her most famous citizen. Dr. Franklin's landing was announced by a boom of cannon at the Market Street wharf — the very wharf where, as a runaway from Boston, he had first set foot in the city over fifty years before. Bells rang as he moved up the four blocks to Franklin Court, his house which the British had plundered, where his daughter and grandchildren, those he had never seen, now lived.

The reception continued for a week. People gave him the next day to rest from his voyage and see his family, then began calling in droves, representatives from all the various activities with which Benjamin Franklin had had to do. Members of the Constitutional Society called and saluted Dr. Franklin as the "father of our free and excellent constitution." Less than a month after his return, he was voted President of Pennsylvania, or Governor, as we should say today.

Having spent almost thirty years in Europe on public business, he had had no time to attend to his private interests. But he was more fortunate than Jefferson, who was ruined by his public services. Franklin found his estate more than tripled in value since the war. Money was due him for service as agent in Europe from colonies as far away as Georgia, and he obtained a right "to take up three thousand acres of Georgia land." He had a large tract on the Ohio River, and several properties in Philadelphia. The old man now amused himself by improving these city properties, building houses and designing gardens with gravel walks and flowering shrubs, perhaps remembering the charming gardens of England and France.

Now he was old and his memories went back to friends of other years. Looking through his son-in-law's papers, he discovered a letter written to him in 1775 and never forwarded. It was from Mrs. Polly Hewson. She had been the little daughter of the lady in whose house he had taken rooms when he was a young stranger in London, over sixty years earlier! He answered the eleven-year-old letter:

> The companions of my youth are indeed almost all departed, but I find agreeable society among their children and grandchildren. I have public business enough to preserve me from ennui, and private amusement besides in conversation, books, my garden, and cribbage. . . . Cards we sometimes play here, in long winter evenings; but it is as they play at chess, not for money, but for honour or the pleasure of beating one another. . . . I have indeed now and then a little compunction in reflecting that I spend time so idly; but another reflection comes to relieve me, whispering: "You know that the soul is immortal; why then should you be such

a niggard of a little time, when you have a whole eternity before you?" So, being easily convinced and, like other reasonable creatures, satisfied with a small reason when it is in favor of doing what I have a mind to, I shuffle the cards again and begin another game.

But games and time were soon to end for this lovable old philosopher and "friend to mankind." Tormented by "the stone," he now had to be given opium to relieve the pain. This caused him to lose appetite until "little remains of me but a skeleton covered with skin," he wrote his sister, Mrs. Jane Mecom. He spent most of the last year in his bedroom. Pain seemed to have no effect on his memory or wit, or even on his cheerfulness. He continued to do a little work: he composed the inscription for the corner-stone of the Library Company's new building. He listened to his nine-year-old granddaughter Deborah, who came to him every day to recite her next day's lesson from the Webster spelling-book. He answered letters with his usual grace and wit.

After Thomas Jefferson returned from France and was on his way from Virginia to New York to take up his new duties as President Washington's Secretary of State, he stopped in Philadelphia to call "on the venerable and beloved Franklin," whom he found in bed. It was to Jefferson that Franklin wrote his last letter, just nine days before he died on April 17, 1790, at the age of eighty-four.

The *Pennsylvania Gazette* announced his death on a black-bordered page. The funeral cortège, forming at the State House, was made impressive by the presence of Pennsylvania's leading men in all fields. Twenty thousand people were estimated to have followed or watched the funeral. Muffled bells tolled, and in the harbor flags flew at half-mast. James Madison moved that the House of Representatives wear mourning for one month. The National Assembly in Paris wore mourning for three days.

Benjamin Franklin seemed to have been one individual in whom there was a harmonious combination of many men, his life and works had touched so many people in different walks of life.

His grave is in the churchyard of Christ Church in Philadelphia beside that of his wife, Deborah. When it was too late, he expressed the wish to see Boston again, perhaps to rest his bones there, but he could no longer undertake the journey.

Robert Morris

[signature: Rob Morris]

January 31, 1734 — May 8, 1806

WITHOUT ROBERT MORRIS, financier of the American Revolution as well as Signer of the Declaration of Independence, General George Washington could not have held his army together and history would tell a different story of America's fate.

Morris was another of the Signers not born in the colonies. He came, instead, from Liverpool, England, where he was born January 31, 1734, the son of Robert Morris, an iron worker. His mother, Elizabeth Murphet Morris, died young, and when his father came to America, he left the boy under the care of his grandmother Murphet. Only after he had become well established as an American tobacco importer, did the father send for young Robert, who arrived in Oxford, Maryland, on the Eastern Shore of Chesapeake Bay, when he was about twelve or thirteen.

For a time, Robert was tutored by the Reverend William Gordon, who had himself come to America as an indentured servant, until one day he told his father he had learned "all that the master could teach me." Deciding that his son was right, the elder Morris sent him to the leading school-master in Philadelphia, but after a year the boy's formal education came to an end, and he was placed in the counting-house of Charles Willing, one of the city's most important business men. This sudden curtailment of his education may have been due to the father's early death in an accident.

When he entered business life at fifteen, Robert Morris was a tall, strong boy with a round fair face under a thatch of sandy red hair. Good-humored, with a pleasant personality, he was also a diligent and conscientious worker, whose industry, integrity, and common sense won him the high respect of his employers.

With its own ships and its own banking business, the Willing firm was engaged in importing British goods and exporting American goods. Much of the firm's trade was with the British colonies in the West Indies, and young Morris asked permission to go on one of their ships to visit the "Sugar Islands," as they were called. The older Willing, who had taken on young Morris, had died; and the son, Thomas Willing, only three years older than Morris, was now head of the firm. Morris was given the responsibility of selling the ship and cargo in Jamaica, a job which he accomplished successfully.

While he was in the West Indies on a second voyage, a merchant of Jamaica invited Morris to become his partner. The decision was to be made by Morris himself, as the merchant had already written to Thomas Willing about it, and Willing had replied that he held Morris "in great esteem" and hoped to see him "advantageously engaged anywhere." Robert Morris pondered the offer. A partnership looked attractive. But he finally declined it and decided to stay with the House of Willing.

While he was returning, however, his business career very nearly ended for good. The brig on which he was traveling was captured by French privateers, who robbed the passengers of everything. But Morris, the captain, and the American crew escaped and managed to reach the shore of Cuba. Here they wandered through fields and forests, half-starved, until they finally reached Havana, a city ruined by the French three years before.

They had saved their lives, but they had lost their money and baggage and were stranded. One day Morris, seeing a man trying unsuccessfully to make his watch run, suggested that he might be able to repair it. He did, and this first customer not only paid the stranded American boy, but sent him other customers who wanted repair work done. In this way, Morris managed to buy food and necessities until an American vessel arrived and took him home.

Thomas Willing, delighted by his safe return, offered him a partnership not long afterward, when Robert Morris was only twenty-two. The firm became Willing, Morris & Company, later Willing & Morris. Though he had been in America only about a decade, Robert Morris had already achieved remarkable success as a businessman. To be a partner in one of the most important Philadelphia firms was a very real achievement. For Philadelphia, until 1830 the largest city in the country, was naturally the largest business center and also a busy port, with ships constantly sailing in and out. The merchant aristocracy, of which Morris now became a part, could boast of the greatest prosperity and gayest society in all America, even though it was established in a sober Quaker city.

Prosperous though they were, however, the merchants and ship-owners were soon to find themselves in serious trouble. After the French and Indian War (1754–1763), the British government, in an effort to "regulate trade," began to pass laws that seriously hampered colonial businessmen. At first these may have been mere emergency measures, but the British government found these so-called "regulatory acts" so profitable that they were kept permanently. Most annoying of all was the law that required ships returning home with cargoes from Europe and Africa to stop in an English port on the way. This round-about route meant needlessly long voyages, cost time and money, and encouraged smuggling to escape English import duties. Customs officials, knowing that smuggling was going on, began annoying investigations of merchants and shipping, and British naval vessels began prowling about to enforce the revenue acts.

Though the firm of Willing & Morris, with its huge foreign shipments, remained above reproach, all this governmental interference made trouble for them. Any financial or other business difficulty worried the senior partner, Willing, a timorous man who became very gloomy and pessimistic at such times. But Robert Morris rose to meet these problems with such optimism and determination that, as time went on, Willing, with ever-increasing trust, began to place greater responsibilities upon his partner. The two were great friends as well as partners. Finally, when Willing was elected Mayor of Philadelphia in 1763, at the end of the French and Indian War, Morris took over management of the business alone and remained the active head for almost twenty years.

When Parliament passed the Stamp Act, twenty-nine-year-old Morris took part in a meeting in Davenport's Tavern, at which four hundred Philadelphia merchants, including Willing & Morris, signed the Non-Importation Resolutions. Though this was a serious blow to their business, it seemed a patriotic duty to resist British encroachments on American rights. The next year, Morris entered public life as Warden of the Port of Philadelphia.

An eligible young bachelor, a wealthy and successful merchant, a dashing man-about-town, Morris was invited everywhere. The most elegant social events were the Assembly dances, managed by Willing for some years, to which only Philadelphia's elect were invited. When thirty-five-year-old Robert Morris met the charming nineteen-year-old Mary White at one of these balls, his bachelor days were soon to end. Though he had no "family," he had achieved a position in society by his own ability and personal charm. Mary's father consented, and the wedding took place in Christ Church under crystal chandeliers sparkling with candles.

Mary Morris was to prove her husband's greatest blessing, the perfect partner. She was the gracious hostess for Robert Morris's generous hospitality in their fine house on Front Street, facing the river in Philadelphia, and later at "The Hills," their three-hundred-acre estate overlooking the Schuylkill River, eight miles from Lancaster, Pennsylvania. Here, in the years to come, they would entertain the most important Americans and Frenchmen of revolutionary times, General Washington and the Marquis de Lafayette among them. When prosperity fled from Morris at last and he was betrayed by the jealousies of lesser men, Mary stood by him. Apparently the only real fault in this able and generous man was his too easy trust in his associates. A man of integrity himself, he did not suspect others of jealous machinations and treachery.

The Stamp Act had been passed and then repealed a few years before Morris's marriage. Within a few years, still graver events were taking place. In the early summer of 1774, Paul Revere rode to Philadelphia with news of the closing of the Port of Boston and of Parliament's action in quartering British troops upon Boston's citizens. Philadelphia's businessmen closed their offices on the first of June in sympathy with the Bostonians. Flags on the river boats were lowered to half-mast. The bells of Christ Church and other churches were muffled and tolled mournfully. On June 18, a meeting in the Pennsylvania State House, over which Thomas Willing presided, passed a resolution declaring that the Boston Port Act was unconstitutional and that the cause of Massachusetts was a common cause to all the colonies. The meeting further decided that a Continental Congress ought to be called. The

Committee of Correspondence soon had messengers riding swiftly from colony to colony.

In September, 1774, the delegates to the First Continental Congress met at City Tavern in Philadelphia and walked to Carpenter's Hall to begin their deliberations. The colonies were pulling themselves together. "Meatless days" were ordered. Companies of infantry, artillery, and cavalry had to be formed, outfitted, trained. Pennsylvania's newly appointed Committee of Safety — with Benjamin Franklin as chairman, Robert Morris as vice-chairman — met every morning at six o'clock. Their tasks were heavy: They must devise plans for the fortification of the Delaware river, which still lay open to attack, organize militia, issue bills of credit, purchase arms and ammunition, create defenses for the city and port of Philadelphia, and raise funds. And who could know better than Morris, long-experienced businessman and ship-owner, how to manage all these practical matters?

Morris's successful labors for defense led to his appointment to the Second Continental Congress, November 3, 1775. He was immediately detailed to find two swift sailing vessels to carry dispatches and two weeks later was put on a committee on naval armaments. Early in 1776 he was on the committee that drew up instructions to Silas Deane, American envoy to France, then put on the "ways and means" committee to help raise funds, and on another to fortify seaports.

Meantime, Willing & Morris imported supplies for the army and at times did banking for Congress. Like any other businessmen, they charged commissions for their services. This led his enemies to accuse Morris of what would today be called "conflict of interest." But his fellow-congressmen, who knew all about it, had every confidence in him. John Adams remarked that Morris "no doubt pursues mercantile ends," but thought him "an excellent Member of our Body," a man with "an honest Heart."

Robert Morris worked hard at his duties in Congress, and at the same time he and gracious Mary Morris were hospitable and lavish hosts to many of the congressmen and others who had occasion to visit Philadelphia. In July of 1776, however, Morris was not in favor of independence. He was one of Pennsylvania's "moderates." Voting against Independence on July 1, he did not attend the following day when the "violents" voted Independence, since he considered the vote premature. Benjamin Rush later explained Morris's stand. Morris, he wrote, "was opposed to the *time* (not to the *act*) of the Declaration of Independence, but he yielded to no man in his exertions to support it, and a year after it took place he publickly acknowledged on the floor of Congress that he had been mistaken in his former opinion as to its time, and said that it would have been better for our country had it been declared sooner."

Morris had no hesitancy in signing the Declaration the next month, and he always worked for the American cause, living his belief that it was "the duty of every individual to act his part in whatever station his country may call him to in hours of difficulty, danger, and distress." This, he said, was the only thing a gentleman could do.

When the struggle grew desperate the following winter, and Congress was slow in supplying food and money for the army, it was to Robert Morris that General Washington appealed — and not in vain. On Christmas night, when Washington crossed the Delaware and captured over a thousand Hessian soldiers, the British suffered their first stinging defeat. Back of all the fighting and planning was Robert Morris, working day and night to raise the funds to pay the soldiers, to procure food, clothing, and ammunition. General Washington never forgot how he had relied on the faithful financier.

On committees that dealt with commerce, supplies, and foreign affairs, Morris was a most valuable man. Often he served as banker and middleman. If he made large profits, he took great risks. Timid merchants considered him "bold and enterprising," his own self-confidence inspired confidence in those who dealt with him. This was a period when Morris was popular.

When, in the autumn of 1777, the British occupied Philadelphia and Congress had to move, Morris stayed in the city with (British) General Howe's permission. This must have been galling itself, aside from the appalling difficulty under which he then had to work. He had sent Mrs. Morris with the children to Maryland to stay with her step-sister, Mrs. Hall. "Having got my family and books removed to a place of safety," he wrote, "my mind is more at ease, and my time is now given up to the public, although I have many thousand pounds' worth of effects here without any prospect of saving them."

In March, 1778, he signed the Articles of Confederation on behalf of his state, and retired from Congress at the end of his term, November 1. But five days later he was elected to the Pennsylvania State Assembly.

In January, 1779, the editor and writer, Thomas Paine — who was not a businessman and not without a temper — attacked Morris and Silas Deane in the newspapers, charging them with handling "private commercial enterprises" while holding public office. Since everyone knew that Morris was director of the firm of Willing & Morris and that the firm was carrying on its legitimate business, this had little effect. Paine's accusation was petty, ignorant, and absurd. But it showed that the wealthy, clever, and successful Robert Morris was drawing envious eyes upon himself. A later member of Congress, Henry Laurens, even charged Willing & Morris with fraudulent transactions. Morris thereupon invited examination of the firm's books by a congressional committee. Their opinion was that Morris had "acted with fidelity and integrity and an honorable zeal for the happiness of his country."

But all this had been bad publicity. Though Morris was cleared, ugly rumors had spread. His political opponents, especially the ones who were not rich and consequently were jealous of his wealth, continued to criticize him. With his popularity weakened, Morris was defeated at the polls in November, 1779. The next year, however, he was again elected to the Assembly.

The year of 1780 saw the American cause at its lowest point. The Treasury was empty. Credit was gone. "Paper money was not worth the cost of printing it." The condition of the army was deplorable, and there were two serious mutinies. Though Morris had warned Congress for years against currency inflation, nothing was done to head it off. When prices sky-rocketed and Congress, having exhausted its own resources, could not meet the soldiers' demands, it had to turn to the man who had never yet failed his country. It appointed Morris Superintendent of Finance. Never has anyone since held such a position. On his shoulders, Congress placed all the responsibility for America's finances.

The task that now confronted Robert Morris was herculean. He was the only man on the continent who could possibly have pulled order out of such financial chaos as now existed. He received many letters from generals, congressmen, and financiers, expressing their enthusiasm over his appointment and the deep satisfaction and renewed hope that his acceptance had given them.

The financial wizard became the nation's banker and pulled his country through its financial doldrums. Yet his salary as Superintendent of Finance was only $6000 a year. Of his private fortune he had given a million dollars for the Yorktown campaign, and half a million for mustering out the army.

But envious tongues wagged. Acrimonious and ignorant critics of Morris, observing his sumptuous hospitality, were not bright enough to realize how much it contributed to the profit of the country. His enemies, not understanding the intricacies of high finance, sneered at what they called Morris's "financial sleight-of-hand." They did not credit him with the enormous risks he had taken, or the tremendous services he had performed. Often, when the credit of the nation was almost gone, it was Robert Morris's signature alone — which stood for business integrity, stability, and commercial honor — that made it possible to borrow money for the public cause.

After years of struggling because the states, unwilling to accept their obligations, let him down by not paying their required revenue, Morris despaired at last. He resigned January 27, 1783, saying, "To increase our debts, while the prospect of paying them diminishes does not consist with my ideas of integrity. I must therefore quit a situation which becomes utterly insupportable."

Then Morris was violently abused in the press. Ingratitude is universal, and if a man allows himself to be imposed upon, there are always those who want to go on imposing upon him. As there was no one else who could even undertake the work, Morris consented to stay in office until the army was paid and demobilized. John Adams succeeded in obtaining a loan in the Netherlands which carried Morris through until he was free from his grave responsibility in September, 1784, and free from what had always been a thankless task. A few men, General Washington among them, understood what the financier had accomplished and were grateful.

Unfortunately, Robert Morris, like many another, was caught up in the epidemic of land fever that swept the country after the

war. Many rich men who wanted to be richer still began land
speculation. Investigating carefully before purchasing, Morris
traveled through inhabited Pennsylvania, Virginia, and Georgia,
buying lands and forming partnerships to buy more lands. He
bought lands also in western New York State. With a partner he
acquired a large part of the site on which our present city of
Washington, D.C. now stands. Then a swampy wilderness, ten
years later it was to become the site of the capital city. But
unfortunately, Morris could not hold his purchase as long as that.

Then, as usual, the unforeseen happened. The Napoleonic Wars
paralyzed Europe and cut off much of the immigration to America.
As it was the immigrants who bought land, when their numbers
diminished, so did the sales of land — and land values, too.

Rich as he was, Robert Morris had borrowed to make many of
his larger land purchases. Now, when he had to meet taxes and
interest on his loans, he did not have the money. And when he
tried to sell some of his properties to meet these costs, he could
not raise enough money from sales. Thus the great financier lost
everything. His beautiful town house, his other city properties,
and, eventually, his beloved estate The Hills, all had to go.
When the crash came, he had been in the process of building a
marble mansion in Philadelphia, designed by the French architect L'Enfant, who had run up more expenses than Morris had
intended.

Retreating to The Hills, he was arrested by a *small* creditor.
The great financial wizard of wartime was taken to the Prune
Street debtors' prison where he was confined for three and a
half years. How could a man, imprisoned, pay off his debts?

Now he knew who his friends were. George Washington went
to the prison to dine with his unfortunate friend. Mary Morris
proved staunch and true. The erstwhile gracious hostess, accustomed to elegant and rich surroundings, was her husband's support in these years of poverty and disgrace. She lived on an
annuity from the Holland Land Company obtained for her by
Gouverneur Morris (no relation), and this supported Robert
Morris when he was released August 26, 1801, under the federal
bankruptcy law. The prison, on Walnut and Prune (Locust)
streets was a large stone building, neat, well-kept, and considered
an ornament to the city. But, ironically enough, while confined for

debt and thereby denied the chance of earning money to pay his debts, Morris had to pay a high price for the rent of his room! Courageously, he remarked, "a man that cannot bear and face misfortune should never run risks, but I have been too adventurous and therefore it is a duty to meet my fate with fortitude." His comfort came from his wife and his loving sons and daughters.

Morris was sixty-six when he was released, a penniless man, dependent upon his sons and his wife's annuity for subsistence. He tried several times to find something to do to earn money. He went to Washington by stagecoach to confer with President Thomas Jefferson and enjoyed a bit of social life such as he had been used to in bygone days. He dined with the President, and visited the ex-President, George Washington, at Mount Vernon.

During his last years, the Morrises lived modestly in a small house on Twelfth Street, the house in which he died on the eighth of May, 1806, aged seventy-two. He was buried in the family vault in Christ Church graveyard.

For years his will was sought, but not until 1939 was it discovered — with the wills of six other Signers — in a forgotten vault near the furnaces in the cellar of the Philadelphia City Hall. In his last testament this wise and shrewd man left a message "to the inhabitants of the United States of America," prepared about the time when he retired as Superintendent of Finance. Stressing the need for a sound economy, he wrote: "How soon we may be plunged into another, a longer or more expensive contest, is known only to Him from whom no secrets are hidden, but . . . the only moral surety for peace is a state of constant preparation for hostilities."

Benjamin Rush

Benjamin Rush

January 4, 1746 — April 19, 1813

Dr. BENJAMIN RUSH was the best known physician practicing in America during the Revolutionary period. He was born on a farm in the community of Byberry, near Philadelphia, the day before Christmas, 1745 (old style), which would be January 4, 1746, by our modern (new style) calendar. His father, John Rush, was descended from the first American John Rush, who had once been a soldier in Cromwell's army, and had come to Pennsylvania from Oxfordshire, England, in 1683. When Benjamin was five, his father died at the early age of thirty-eight, and his mother, Susanna Harvey Hall Rush, now twice widowed, kept a grocery store to earn a living and provide education for her children.

At the age of eight, Benjamin was sent to a country school at Nottingham, taught by his uncle, the Reverend Dr. Samuel Finley. West Nottingham Academy was later situated in the country at Colora, about two miles south of where it was in Rush's day, and a memorial arch was placed there to commemorate its two alumni who became Signers of the Declaration of Independence: Richard Stockton and Benjamin Rush.

Seven years later, at fifteen, Benjamin Rush entered the junior class in the College of New Jersey (now Princeton) and received his B.A. degree in 1760. He had been advised by friends and by the head of the college, the Reverend Dr. Samuel Davies, to study law. But the young graduate consulted his old teacher, Dr. Finley, who insisted that the law was not the profession for him. Rush ought to study medicine. Accordingly, he became the pupil of Dr. John Redman, then Philadelphia's leading physician. He lived in his teacher's house for four years, studying medicine under his direction, with only eleven days absence the whole time. He also attended lectures at the College of Philadelphia.

Finishing this study in July, 1766, Rush again took his former teacher's advice and sailed off in August to continue medical study at the University of Edinburgh, whose medical faculty was then the most celebrated in the world. While in the Scottish city, Rush met the Reverend Dr. John Witherspoon.

Dr. Witherspoon had been invited to come to America to be President of the College of New Jersey in 1766. But he had declined because of his wife's fear of crossing the ocean. Richard Stockton had presented the invitation. In another decade, these three men would all be together in Philadelphia and all three would sign the Declaration of Independence!

The next summer, 1767, Benjamin Rush visited the Wither-spoons at Paisley. The young twenty-two-year-old medical student must have described his own ocean crossing and persuaded Mrs. Witherspoon that it was not to be feared. At any rate, when in 1768 Princeton sent Dr. Witherspoon a second invitation to become President, he accepted, and the Witherspoons sailed for the New World.

Medicine was not the only subject that interested Benjamin Rush while abroad. He studied French with a tutor, and Italian and Spanish by himself, until he was able to read in all three languages. Then, upon graduating at Edinburgh, Rush went to London to train in St. Thomas's Hospital, and to attend lectures on medicine. Another Philadephian, Benjamin Franklin, had been in London since 1764 as agent for the Province. Young Rush at once wrote Franklin asking for letters of introduction. The older man responded generously, and with these letters, the young doctor's introduction to English life was most agreeable.

After visiting Paris, Benjamin Rush returned home to begin his medical career. Two months later, he was given the professorship of chemistry at the College of Philadelphia — the first man to hold such a chair in any of the colonies — while at the same time he opened a doctor's office. For some time most of his practice was among the poor; and though his office, which he called his "shop," was soon filled with patients, he treated many of them without charge. Others he visited, walking through all the streets and alleys of the city, sometimes climbing ladders to reach the upper rooms. But within five years his practice grew to the point where he was making a good income, in spite of his generosity to the poor.

Rush was one of those rare persons who knew the value of using every bit of his time. In spare moments, he began to jot down notes on his observations, ideas, and conclusions until, before long, he had enough material to write articles and essays. His first publication was the first American textbook on "A Syllabus of a Course of Lectures on Chemistry." In 1773, his newspaper articles on behalf of the colonists' cause brought him into public affairs, and he also became a member of the American Philosophical Society, which still exists in Philadelphia.

In September, 1774, Rush and some of the other Sons of Liberty, rode a few miles out from Philadelphia to meet the first congressional delegates who were coming down from New England. He now had an opportunity to become acquainted with the great patriot leaders who came from the other colonies to attend the First Continental Congress — such men as Samuel Adams, Thomas Jefferson, and Thomas Paine. As he listened to their views, the young doctor became more and more inflamed with the colonists' indignation against mother England.

In January, 1776, he married Miss Julia Stockton, the eldest daughter of Richard Stockton of Princeton, another Signer. He had admired Julia ever since she was fourteen years old.

The following June, Dr. Rush was elected to the Provincial Conference. As a member of this body, he at once took his stand for independence. A month later he was sent to the Second Continental Congress. He was only thirty when he signed the Declaration.

When George Washington received his appointment as commander in chief, Dr. Rush attended the party given in his honor. Later, he offered his services to the patriot cause and in April, 1777, was appointed surgeon-general of the armies of the Middle Department. Investigating the army medical service, he found it in such poor condition that he protested to General Washington, accusing Dr. William Shippen, another important Philadelphia physician, of bad administration. Washington referred the matter to Congress, which decided in Shippen's favor, whereupon young Dr. Rush angrily resigned. Not long afterward, General Washington met his discouraging defeats at Brandywine and Germantown — not far from Philadelphia — and Rush took this opportunity to raise questions as to Washington's ability as a commander. It is a sorry thing to have to report that Rush even wrote an anonymous letter to Governor Patrick Henry of Virginia, urging that Washington be replaced by either General Gates or General Conway. Had this been done, the Americans would surely have lost the war, but the iniquitous plot to get rid of Washington — the so-called Conway Cabal — soon collapsed, leaving Washington still in a command that only he could fill.

Governor Henry sent the letter on to Washington who, recognizing the handwriting, accused Rush of personal disloyalty. This contretemps ended Rush's military career, of course.

Clever, industrious, studious, and socially agreeable though he was, Benjamin Rush had some less admirable traits, as this regrettable incident shows. He could never believe or admit that he might have a wrong opinion; and as he kept no records of his cases or opinions, it was easy for him to forget that he had ever been wrong. He did not examine facts and was often therefore in the center of professional jealousies and arguments. He had an able, versatile, but not a critical mind.

John Adams, with whom he had a friendly correspondence for years, described Rush as being "an elegant, ingenious body, a sprightly, pretty fellow." But, Adams added, "too much of a talker to be a deep thinker; elegant, not great."

Two years after the opening of the new University of the State of Pennsylvania in 1778, Rush began to lecture there. Three years later, he went on the staff of the Pennsylvania Hospital, where he remained for the rest of his life, and in 1786 he established the first free dispensary in America.

Interested in social reforms, Dr. Rush condemned capital punishment and worked to improve education for girls. He argued against overemphasis on classical training, that is, on Latin and Greek, and advised more training for children in science and utilitarian subjects. After urging in the newspapers the acceptance of the new Federal Constitution, he was elected to the Pennsylvania Convention, in which he and James Wilson, another Pennsylvania Signer, led the movement for its adoption.

Dr. Rush was also treasurer of the United States Mint from 1797 to 1813.

When the College of Philadelphia merged with the University of the State of Pennsylvania to become the University of Pennsylvania in 1791, Dr. Rush became professor of medical theory and clinical practice, and this is probably where he achieved his greatest distinction. His students adored him. His classes became very popular and increased enormously in size. He thus probably contributed more than any other man to making Philadelphia the main center for medical training in America during the first half of the nineteenth century.

Unfortunately — since he was more given to ideas than facts, and a doctor, like any scientific man, is always up against facts — Dr. Rush came to believe that all diseases and physical ailments were practically the same, and therefore one cure sufficed for all. Thinking as he did, Dr. Rush saw diagnosis and treatment as simple matters. All he had to do, he thought, was administer his "cure," which was the bleeding and purging of the patient. Dr. Rush was even willing to remove as much as four-fifths of the body's blood. The average doctor of the period, when giving a treatment by bleeding, rarely took more than ten ounces, for bleeding a sick man could be dangerous. George Washington's last illness was laryngitis, caused by exposure to rain and cold; but it is now believed that he would have recovered had he not been weakened by the amount of blood taken by the physicians who were trying to cure him. Other medical men proclaimed Rush's "system" fanciful, declaring that he carried bleeding to dangerous extremes. During the yellow fever epidemic of 1793, he became involved in another serious medical controversy, thus making many new enemies among medical men. But, by this time, he was America's most widely known physician, for he had had a great deal of publicity, and he remained influential.

There were times, however, when Dr. Rush's cures were effective. During the Lewis and Clark Expedition, when Thomas Jefferson was President, the two leaders kept journals recording everything. From these Journals we learn that they carried with them some of "Dr. Rush's pills," which they administered freely, and with excellent results when all their men were exhausted after crossing the Rockies.

At the age of sixty-eight, after only a few days' illness, Dr. Benjamin Rush passed away after a busy, full life. He was buried in Christ's Church graveyard, in Philadelphia.

John Morton

John Morton

c.1724 — April, 1777

THE FIRST AMERICAN of John Morton's line was his great-grandfather, Morten Mortenson, who sailed from Gothenburg, Sweden, in 1654, a member of the Tenth Swedish Expedition, and settled along the banks of the Delaware River, not far from Philadelphia. The Signer's father was another John Morton, who married Mary Archer when he was very young and died before his child was born, some time in 1724, though the exact date is unknown. Mary Morton then married again, and John's step-father, John Sketchley, took a fond interest in the boy.

Sketchley was a surveyor who had come from England and was a man of some education. He taught his step-son at home, instructing him in the common branches and also in surveying. John had a quick mind and an industrious nature. He studied, helped in surveying, and worked on the home farm.

He was thirty before he married Ann Justis, a young woman who also descended from early Swedish settlers in Delaware.

Interested in public welfare and affairs, John Morton was elected to the Provincial Assembly from Chester County in 1756 while he was still in his early thirties, was re-elected for the next ten years, and was appointed speaker of this assembly in 1775. He also served as justice of the peace and as high sheriff. Though he had no formal legal training, Morton was appointed President Judge of the Court of General Sessions and Common Pleas and in 1774 he became an Associate Judge of the Supreme Court of Pennsylvania.

In 1765, Judge Morton was one of the four Pennsylvania delegates to the Stamp Act Congress. He was definitely not one of the Pennsylvania moderates but stood boldly for freedom in a province where opinion had long been divided.

Though Morton made no spectacular contributions to the cause of independence, he felt strongly about the patriot cause. So little is really known about him that it is interesting to read passages from a letter he wrote to Thomas Powell, a merchant in London and a friend to whom Morton felt able to speak freely. As early as June 8, 1775, Morton was writing that "we are really preparing for the worst that can happen, viz. a Civil War. We have nearly 2000 Troops now under Arms in this City, and very well disciplined. I suppose the Province will raise 20,000 effective Men determined to support the Noble Cause of Liberty." Congress had turned out in a body on June 8 to see soldiers drilling and Morton had been impressed by the spectacle.

He pointed out that General Gage was now so closely besieged in Boston that he "cannot penetrate 500 Yards into the Country, were he supported by all the troops now in England." The letter concludes: "You have declared the New England people Rebels, and the other Provinces Aiders and Abettors. This is putting the Halter about our Necks, and we may as well die by the Sword as be hang'd like Rebels. This has made the People desperate." This gives an idea of the determination with which Congress was meeting its problems.

A delegate to the Continental Congress from 1774 until early 1777, Morton cast one of the votes which placed Pennsylvania on the side of independence by a majority of one.

Morton served on many committees in Congress. He was chairman of the committee for the adoption of the Articles of Confederation, though these were not finally adopted until after his death, in the Spring of 1777.

Soon after the battle of Lexington, Morton had been offered a colonelcy of Pennsylvania volunteers, but he declined because of his other duties.

A man of strong character, Judge Morton was modest about his self-made career, but men discovered that his judgment was sound, his social manner pleasant.

Morton was buried in St. Paul's Churchyard in Chester County, the county in which he first entered public life.

George Clymer

March 16, 1739 — January 24, 1813

GEORGE CLYMER'S GRANDFATHER, Richard Clymer, came to America from Bristol, England. His son Christopher married a Philadelphia girl named Deborah Fitzwater, and these were the short-lived parents of the Signer. Both died the year after George was born, and the little boy's uncle, William Coleman, a prosperous merchant and a friend of Benjamin Franklin, became his guardian.

George grew up in the home of his aunt and uncle in Philadelphia, where he made good use of the large library his uncle had collected. His uncle seems to have provided the boy with a good schooling because when George was old enough to start work, he was prepared to enter his uncle's business as a clerk. He proved to be so diligent and competent that he was made a partner in the firm. Later on, William Coleman left the business to his nephew who, in his turn, became a well-known and successful Philadelphia merchant.

When George Clymer was twenty-six he married Elizabeth, daughter of Reese Meredith, another important merchant. He now enlarged his activities by working in association with other merchants. Taking his father-in-law and brother-in-law into partnership, he established the firm of Meredith and Clymer.

From early years, Clymer was an ardent patriot. Men engaged in the importation of goods from England and her West Indian colonies were, of course, among the first to feel the restrictions of British taxation. Included in this group were those southern planters who were sending cotton and tobacco back to England.

George Clymer attended all the first meetings of those men who were offended by Britain's insensitive high-handedness, and he also became a captain of volunteers in General Cadwalader's brigade. In 1773, there was a "Philadelphia Tea Party," very much like the Boston Tea Party, which forced the resignation of merchants who had been appointed by the British to sell tea. Clymer was chairman of the "Party." Like so many of the Signers, he became a member of the Council of Safety. This was a first step into a public career. Clymer, however, who was of a modest, retiring nature, never sought public honors. But as his diligence and faithfulness became known, he was repeatedly chosen for office, and he was elected to the Independence Congress.

With the New Jersey Signer Richard Stockton, Clymer was sent in September, 1776, to inspect the northern army at Ticonderoga. He also advocated broader powers for General Washington. In 1777, when the British drove Congress and the colonial government out of Philadelphia, Clymer went to Baltimore with Signers Robert Morris and George Walton as a committee for congressional business.

When he was re-elected to Congress in 1777, George Clymer was assigned to the Board of War and the Treasury Board. He was also on the local committee for the protection of Philadelphia. Here, his duties were so arduous that he was forced to take a rest, but by July he was back at work as one of the commissioners to investigate and remedy the food shortage in Washington's army. Then, in the autumn, he became commissioner of prisoners, his duty being to receive Hessian prisoners and send to Allentown all those who were able to travel.

After the British victory at the Brandywine, some of the British took the trouble to detour in order to raid Clymer's house. His family, fortunately, had left, but the raiders destroyed all his furniture, and seized whatever supplies they could use. The redcoats had a special hatred for the men who had signed the Declaration of Independence, and they found out from local Tories where Clymer lived.

In the winter of 1777, Clymer was sent to Fort Pitt with two other commissioners to investigate the Indian disorders that the British had instigated. He rode through Pennsylvania's dark forests all the way to the frontier fort at Pittsburgh. In Congress again, for the third time, he worked steadily on committees, then retired to Princeton to educate his children.

In the first Congress after the Revolution, Clymer supported his old friend, George Washington, as President, and later supported the economic policy of another old friend of the stirring days of '76 — Thomas Jefferson. President Washington appointed Clymer to serve in two commissions, after which he retired from national affairs. He was then fifty-seven, and he had spent over twenty years in the service of his country.

George Clymer now took a leading part in the development of his own community, serving as the first president of the Philadelphia bank, first president of the Academy of Fine Arts, and vice-president of the Philadelphia Agricultural Society. These honorary offices he was still holding when he died in 1813.

In Congress, Clymer had not been one of the orators. He had spoken only briefly, very seldom, but always to the point. One fine thing was said of him that can be said of very few people, he "was never heard to speak ill of any one."

James Smith

Jas. Smith

c.1719 — July 11, 1806

OF THE THIRTEEN COLONIES, Pennsylvania had the largest number of representatives in the "Declaration" Congress. With such well-known men as Benjamin Franklin, Robert Morris, and Dr. Benjamin Rush among her nine congressmen of the Revolution, it is not surprising that some of the others are known today only because their signatures are on the revered document.

One of these lesser-known men is James Smith, who was born in northern Ireland about 1719, the second son of a large family. His father, John, persuaded to come to America by James's uncles who had already settled in the new country, migrated when James was about ten or twelve. The family settled near the other Smiths in beautiful Chester County in southeastern Pennsylvania.

John soon became a successful farmer in this fine agricultural region and sent young James to the school in nearby Philadelphia that was taught by the Reverend Francis Alison.

In those early days in America, when congregations were not large enough to be able to pay their pastors an adequate salary, nor to require all of a pastor's time, it was common for a minister to "keep school." In most communities, he was the best educated man and so the man best equipped for teaching.

Thus James had the opportunity to study Latin and Greek, some knowledge of which was essential to any educated gentleman. He also studied surveying. Afterwards, he read law in the office of his brother George in Lancaster.

Admitted to the bar when he was about twenty-six, he moved to Cumberland County, near Shippensburg. At first he earned his living by surveying and practiced law when a chance offered. But after four or five years in this scantily populated region, almost on the frontier, he moved back east forty or fifty miles and settled in York, Pennsylvania, where he lived for the rest of his life. Until 1769, he was the only resident lawyer in town.

Even so, little legal business came his way during his first years there, and in order to earn a better living, he started to operate an iron furnace. Unfortunately, instead of making anything, he lost £5000 before he sold out seven years later, having employed two incompetent managers, who simply let the business fail. One, said Smith, was a knave, and the other a fool.

When he was forty-one or thereabout, he married Eleanor Armor, the daughter of John Armor of New Castle, Delaware.

Through the 1760's, the colonists' dissatisfaction and unhappiness under the ever-tightening rule of the mother country was spreading, and Smith became a leader in his part of the country. In 1774, he attended a provincial conference at which he read an article he had written, "Essay on the Constitutional Power of Great Britain over the Colonies in America." In this he urged an end to import of British goods and promoted the idea of a general congress of the thirteen colonies, where colonial grievances could be discussed and shared. Several thoughtful men in different parts of the colonies were now getting this same idea. Encouraged by this conference, James Smith raised a volunteer company in York in 1774 and was selected captain.

This company grew into a battalion later on, and Smith was given the honorary title of Colonel, though he turned over the active command to younger men. Having been appointed delegate to the provincial convention in Philadelphia in January, 1775, he was busy helping to draft the resolutions for independence and recommending improvement of provincial defenses.

James Smith sat in the constitutional convention of June, 1776, and was made a member of the committee to draft a new frame of government, which he had been advocating for some time. On July 20, in the first week of this convention, he was elected to Congress. As this was after the great Fourth, Smith was too late to vote for independence. But he was on hand to sign the Declaration. Re-elected in December, 1777, he served one year longer, but declined re-election thereafter. While Congress met in York, Pennsylvania, the meetings of the Board of War were held in Smith's law office.

After retiring from Congress, James Smith held few political posts. He served one term in the assembly, and for a few months he was Judge of the Pennsylvania High Court of Errors and Ap-

peals. In 1782 he was brigadier general of the militia and counselor for the Pennsylvania-Connecticut Wyoming Valley controversy.

Again, in 1785, Smith was elected to Congress by the assembly,
but he declined because of age. He was about sixty-five at this
time.

James Smith had a sharp wit and a lively manner. He was a
good conversationalist, equipped with a fund of amusing anecdotes.
He made good company and thus attracted to himself many
friends. It was remarked that he had a most surprising memory.
There were some who regarded him as rather an eccentric, but this
might be said of any real individualist.

A fire destroyed Smith's office and all his papers in 1805. But for
this we might now know more about his life and work. The next
year, he passed away on the eleventh of July, at the ripe old age
of eighty-six. He was buried in the graveyard of the English Presbyterian Church.

George Taylor

c. 1716 — February 23, 1781

LESS SEEMS TO BE KNOWN about George Taylor than any of the
other Signers. He is believed to have been born in northern Ireland about 1716 and to have had some education before he arrived in Pennsylvania at about the age of twenty. We first hear
of him in Chester County, where he became clerk in the Warwick
Furnace and Coventry Forge. Later he became the manager.

In 1742 Taylor married a widow, Mrs. Anne Taylor Savage.
When he was about thirty-eight, he moved to neighboring Bucks
County, Pennsylvania, where he and a partner leased an iron
furnace. This was his main business interest for the rest of his
life, though after 1763 he lived in the town of Easton, where his
political life began.

The next year, the ironmaster was elected to the Provincial Assembly, and he was re-elected for the following five years. Taylor was strongly opposed to the royal government, and when the Stamp Act was passed, he was on the committee that drew up instructions for Pennsylvania delegates to the Stamp Act Congress.

There is then no record of Taylor's appearing in politics for about four years, when he returns to the scene as chairman of a meeting of the important men of his county, called to protest the British order closing Boston harbor. Here, he spoke in favor of an intercolonial Congress and was one of six men named as a Committee of Correspondence. He attended the convention in Philadelphia in January, 1775.

The next July, Taylor was chosen colonel of the Bucks County militia; and, though he never saw active service, he retained the title.

In October, he was sent to the assembly again, served on many committees, and helped draft instructions for the delegates to the Continental Congress in November. Though he was a member of the second Committee of Safety from that same autumn to the following July, he rarely attended. After the great Fourth, George Taylor was appointed delegate to the Second Continental Congress to replace one of several Pennsylvanians who had refused to approve the Declaration of Independence. Taylor approved it, but as it was July 20 when he was sent to Philadelphia, he was not there for the voting. He was there for the signing, however.

After that, he took no further part in Congress other than to represent it, along with George Walton, at a conference with Indians at Easton, in January, 1777. Leaving Congress soon afterward, he was elected to the new Supreme Council of Pennsylvania, but served only six weeks because of illness. Soon after, he retired from all public affairs.

George Taylor was called a "moderate radical." He was a man of limited, provincial outlook, who never became absorbed in the broad, far-reaching questions of that great moment when a nation was being born. He probably had had only a little education, not enough to make him wish to follow it up in his own reading. His heart was not in politics, and this no doubt explains why so little is known about him. There was not much to know.

His wife died in 1768, and he himself passed away thirteen years later, at the age of sixty-five.

James Wilson

James Wilson

September 14, 1742 — August 21, 1798

AT THE AGE OF TWENTY-THREE, James Wilson was a newcomer to American shores, having arrived as late as 1765, the Stamp Act year, from Scotland.

He had studied at the University of St. Andrews for about two years, went to the University of Glasgow for a time, and then attended the University of Edinburgh. One does not know now why he moved from university to university, but he appears to have acquired considerable learning, a broad outlook, and rather more social polish than some of the other lesser known patriots who met together in Philadelphia in 1776.

However, when Wilson left Edinburgh University in 1765, he still had no degree. He began to study accounting, dropped it almost at once, and took ship for America, already equipped with a better education than most immigrants of the time. He carried with him letters of introduction to some prominent Pennsylvanians, among whom was Dr. Richard Peters, secretary of the Provincial Council, Episcopal rector in Philadelphia, and trustee of the College of Philadelphia. Through this contact, James Wilson secured a position as Latin tutor in the college in February of 1766, almost as soon as he arrived, and in May his petition for an honorary M.A. degree was granted. He was on his way up.

Though he always kept his scholarly interests, Wilson soon saw that advancement in America would not come through teaching. The law seemed to be the best and quickest way to power and position, and that was what he wanted most—that and wealth. A few months later, aided by his new influential friends, Wilson succeeded in entering the office of John Dickinson to read law. He applied himself to his legal studies for about two years and was admitted to the bar in November, 1767. The next summer, he began to practice law in Reading, Pennsylvania. This was near "Birdsboro," the home of Miss Rachel Bird, a young lady whom Wilson had met in Philadelphia.

His practice among the German farmers, who were the forebears of the people now known as the Pennsylvania Dutch, was lucrative indeed and as settlements spread westward, Wilson moved to Carlisle to practice among the Scotch-Irish settlers. His practice built up steadily until Wilson had the largest practice in the local bar. He was soon a rich man, thus achieving one of his great desires.

Then James Wilson bought a farm. Most properties in that sparsely settled region were farms, and even town lots were large enough to keep a few cattle, enough to supply milk for the family. He bought some livestock and a slave, and he married Miss Bird.

By this time, Wilson was handling almost half the cases tried in the county court and practicing in seven other counties as well. A man of unfailing energy, he was the go-getter of the region. Sometimes his work required trips to New Jersey and New York, over what seemed in those days considerable distances. During six of these busy years he even found time to lecture on English literature at the College of Philadelphia. Most of his law practice dealt with land disputes. Brought thus in touch with land titles, he was soon speculating in land himself and borrowing money to do so.

James Wilson was an early believer in the colonies' cause. In less than ten years after his arrival in America, he entered public life as a member of the Pennsylvania provincial meeting of July, 1774, and was asked to head the Committee of Correspondence at Carlisle. The next month, his pamphlet, "Considerations on the Nature and Extent of the Legislative Authority of the British Parliament," was published. In this he maintained that Parliament had no constitutional right to make laws for the colonies. This was an advanced position to take in 1774 and not many Pennsylvanians held it, but Wilson had already been arguing his points for four years. Of course, this was the opinion of the Adamses and Hancock of Massachusetts. His pamphlet was distributed among the first Continental Congressmen when they met and it made a considerable impression. Wilson was elected to the first Provincial Congress where, in January, 1775, he declared it was *possible* that the British Parliament *could* pass an *unconstitutional* act. But when he introduced a resolution declaring the Boston Port Act to be unconstitutional, it was not adopted.

The following May, Wilson was made colonel of the Fourth Battalion of Cumberland County, but he never saw active service because three days later he was elected to the forever famous Second Continental Congress. Assigned to serve on various committees, he attended faithfully for two years, though he found committee work burdensome. He was also on the Board of War.

On the question of independence — the question which steadily increased in importance, provoking more and more thought and discussion through 1775 and the first half of 1776 until the great decision in July — James Wilson, though favoring independence himself, was heedful of the wishes of his constituents, and, as we have seen, Pennsylvanians were seriously divided on that subject. Many thought a complete break with the mother country would be dangerous, perhaps disastrous, and they feared such an extreme move. Wilson, therefore, opposed Richard Henry Lee's resolution in June, 1776, arguing that a few individuals in Congress should not commit the whole province of Pennsylvania to such a step. It should be a decision of the people themselves. With three other congressmen, he thus succeeded in getting a three-week delay on the vote in order to ascertain the feeling of the Pennsylvanians. This debate on the Lee resolution occurred behind closed doors on the same day. When the debate ended, six states, including Pennsylvania, voted in the negative; seven states, affirmative. The matter was postponed to June 10, two days later. On June 11, a committee of five, with Thomas Jefferson as chairman, was chosen to prepare a Declaration.

Meanwhile, debates were hot and constant. The Independents had to use all their persuasive powers to win the luke-warm members to their side.

Wilson's stand, however, had caused a tempest of criticism. It looked to some as if he had gone back on his original views. He was so bitterly abused that twenty-two of his fellow congressmen felt it necessary to come to his defense. But on July 2, Wilson was one of three out of the seven Pennsylvania delegates who voted for independence. This was not to be the only storm of criticism he would have to face; others were to come in the future.

Dr. Benjamin Rush, to whom we are indebted for reporting his impressions of so many of the congressmen of 1776, regarded Wilson as an eminent lawyer, an enlightened statesman, a profound and accurate scholar. Wilson, he said, "spoke often in Congress and his eloquence was of the most commanding kind. He reasoned, declaimed, and persuaded according to circumstances with equal effect. His mind, while he spoke, was a blaze of light. Not a word ever fell from his lips out of time, or out of place, nor could a word be taken from or added to his speeches without injuring them. He rendered great and essential services to his country in every stage of the Revolution."

Wilson's personal appearance made his eloquence even more impressive. He stood six feet tall, with a large frame and erect bearing, and all his fiery energy went into his declamations. Though his voice was not melodious, it was powerful, and his blue eyes gleamed through heavy spectacles rimmed in metal.

The next storm that blew about him came when he fought the new constitution of Pennsylvania, which he thought "the most detestable that ever was formed." Even his close friend, Arthur St. Clair, considered Wilson "perhaps too warm" on the subject. His seat in Congress became precarious and he knew it. He was, in fact, removed in 1777 but reinstated after about two weeks because a successor could not be found. He continued to oppose the Pennsylvania constitution until he was finally removed from Congress September 14, 1777. Feeling ran so high that he could not feel comfortable in his own state and spent the winter in Annapolis; then he settled in Philadelphia.

Arrived at middle-age, the former frontier lawyer handling land disputes became a corporation counsel. The former congressman became a counselor for Loyalists, the former Whig became a leader of the Republicans, the former Scotch-Presbyterian became an Episcopalian. Wilson did not, however, change in his desire for wealth and love of speculation. Because he engaged in privateering — unlawful today but perfectly proper in those times — and various enterprises for making a quick dollar, some of his fellow citizens came to distrust him. When, in 1779, a food shortage developed in Philadelphia and there were riots in the streets against profiteers and Tories, Wilson found it necessary to barricade his house to defend himself and some of his friends against attack. A few were killed and wounded on both sides, but Wilson was rescued by the First City Troop and went into hiding for some days. In that same year, the French government appointed Wilson advocate general for France in maritime and commercial causes in the United States.

With the return of the conservatives to power in 1782, James Wilson was elected to Congress once more from 1785 to 1787. Through the 1780's, with his business and public interests taking up more of his time, he dropped his law practice. But he was legal adviser to Robert Morris, the Revolution's great financier, in the formation of the Bank of Pennsylvania and in drawing plans for the purchase of army supplies. In 1781, Congress chose Wilson as one of the original directors of the Bank of North America. In the Spring of 1782, General Washington paid Wilson 100 guineas for receiving Washington's nephew as a student in his law office. Later that year, Wilson defended Pennsylvania's claims against Connecticut's charter claims to the Wyoming Valley lands in Pennsylvania.

In May, 1784, James Wilson was one of eight Pennsylvania delegates to the Philadelphia convention to adopt a constitution for the United States, held in Independence Hall with George Washington as President. Only six of the thirty-nine members had been Signers of the Declaration of Independence: Benjamin Franklin, James Wilson, Robert Morris, and George Clymer of Pennsylvania; Robert Sherman of Connecticut; George Read of Delaware. The total number was small "but the quality was excellent." Students of constitutional history consider this "to have been as wise and capable a deliberative body as ever assembled in this country, perhaps the wisest."

Three years after the end of the war, in 1786, James Wilson's wife died, leaving him with six children. Seven years later, at the age of fifty-one, he married nineteen-year-old Hannah Gray of Boston. Four years later his speculations caught up with him, and he had to move to Burlington, New Jersey, to avoid arrest for debt.

Wilson was keenly disappointed in not being given a high office in the new federal government established under the Constitution. He had been mentioned as a candidate for Chief Justice, and even went so far as to suggest himself to President Washington who appointed him Associate Justice in September, 1789. That winter Wilson gave a law course at the College of Philadelphia.

More deeply involved than ever before, Wilson turned again from public interests to land speculation in 1792 and 1793, and, like most speculators, did not know when to stop. He involved the Holland Land Company in unwise purchases of hundreds of thousands of acres of land in Pennsylvania and New York. In the end, Wilson's own personal speculations ended disastrously, wiping out all of his accumulations, and led to his confinement for a time in a debtors' prison.

By 1798, when Wilson was fifty-six years old, he was in severe mental distress. He had too many worries. He wrote a friend, "I have been haunted — like a wild beast." In those days Supreme Court justices did not spend all their time in Washington, and Wilson arranged to be sent on a southern circuit of the United States Circuit Court of Appeals, and went to North Carolina to visit a friend. But his truly brilliant mind now lost its hold and gradually his lucid moments came at ever increasing intervals. He died that year at the home of his friend, of what was called a nervous fever. One hundred and eight years later, in 1906, his body was moved from North Carolina and re-interred in Christ Church, Philadelphia.

At last, the Signer had returned to the city where he had given the best of his life and work.

George Ross

May 10, 1730 — July 14, 1779

GEORGE ROSS WAS a Pennsylvania Signer with a persuasive manner, a liking for pleasantry and mild joking. He appeared always to be in good humor. He was born at New Castle, Delaware, on May 10, 1730, the eldest son of the Reverend George Ross and his second wife, Catherine Van Gezel Ross. The Reverend George had graduated at the University of Edinburgh and prepared for the Presbyterian ministry. But while engaged in theological study he came to feel that his church was censorious and hypocritical, and he took orders instead in the Church of England, came to America as a missionary, and became rector of Immanuel Church in New Castle, Delaware, where he remained for many years.

His son George, one of twelve children by his two wives, was given a classical education, studying Latin and Greek in addition to the three R's. Later, he read law in the office of his older stepbrother, John, in Philadelphia. At the age of twenty, he was admitted to the bar and opened his own office in Lancaster, Pennsylvania. The good humor, wit, and eloquence which Dr. Rush perceived in George Ross twenty-five years later in Congress, together with his ability, brought him a large practice.

Among his first clients was beautiful young Anne Lawler, whom he soon married. At twenty-one, with a good practice, a beautiful wife, an attractive personality, a cordial manner, a love of dining and wining among congenial companions, George Ross was on his way up.

He served twelve years as Crown Prosecutor (he would be called District Attorney today) in Carlisle, Pennsylvania, adding a political career to a legal one when he won election to the Provincial Assembly. During his seven years' service there, Ross became much interested in the steadily mounting disputes with the royal governor and stood boldly for the assembly and its rights. Gradually gaining political influence, he was elected to the Provincial Conference in Philadelphia in July, 1774, and was in the Pennsylvania delegation to the First Continental Congress in the same year.

At this time, Ross was still regarded as a Tory. But as tension with Parliament increased, he joined the Whigs in 1775, serving both in the assembly and on the Pennsylvania Committee of Safety.

Though he had been a Pennsylvania delegate to the First Continental Congress in 1774, Ross was not chosen as delegate to the Second Congress until the debates were over, the vote had been taken, and the Declaration of Independence had been adopted. He took his seat on August 2, 1776, when the new official copy of the Declaration, now engrossed, was ready for signing. He signed the "immortal instrument" on that day.

In those times a man might hold more than one high office at once. During his first two terms in Congress, Ross was also a member of the Pennsylvania Assembly, and in 1776 he was a colonel in the army while still serving as congressman. In that significant year, Ross, who had become much interested in Indian Affairs, helped negotiate a treaty with the northwestern Indians of Pennsylvania. He was also vice-president of the Pennsylvania constitutional convention of 1776, in which he helped to draw up the declaration of rights.

George Ross was elected to Congress three times. In 1777, the authorities of Lancaster County paid him a well-earned compliment by awarding him £150 as a testimonial "of their sense of his attendance on public business to his great private loss and of their appreciation of his conduct." But Ross declined to accept it. He said that it was "the duty of every man, especially of a representative of the people, to contribute to the welfare of his country without expecting pecuniary rewards." Ill health forced him to resign in January of that year.

Ross was at first in favor of the constitution establishing the new state government, but by 1779 he began to feel, as did other lawyers, that it was already time for a revision. In March, 1779, he was commissioned judge of the admiralty court in Pennsylvania. He became involved in a controversy between Congress and the new state of Pennsylvania — a controversy which dragged on for more than thirty years. But not for George Ross. He died, suddenly, four months later on a hot July day, from a severe attack of gout. He was only forty-nine.

He kept his good humor to the very end. On his deathbed, oppressed by midsummer's heat, he calmly observed that he was about to go on a "long journey to a cool place, where there would be most excellent wines." He might have added, "and no more gout!"

IV

NEW JERSEY

Jno Witherspoon

Rich:d Stockton

Fra:s Hopkinson

John Hart

Abra Clark

John Witherspoon

Jno Witherspoon

February 5, 1723 — November 15, 1794

ONE OF THE BEST educated among the Signers, John Witherspoon was a late comer to the colonies, having arrived in response to an invitation to become President of Princeton (then called the College of New Jersey) only seven years before the Declaration of Independence.

He was the son of the Reverend James and Anne Walker Witherspoon of Yester, near Edinburgh. In the early eighteenth century the clergy were the best educated men in Scotland, and the Reverend Mr. Witherspoon was no exception. He sent his son John to the first-rate preparatory school at Haddington, where he was prepared for the University of Edinburgh at fourteen. A precocious boy, endowed with a good mind and diligent in study, he was soon the best in his class. An important feature of Scottish university life outside of classrooms was the existence of literary clubs, which were common among the students and the professional men of Edinburgh. His activity in these societies made Witherspoon proficient in debate, which is valuable training for an alert mind, for clearness of expression, and for public speaking. Long years after, no doubt remembering the literary clubs of his youth, Witherspoon encouraged two famous literary societies at Princeton: Whig Hall and Clio Hall.

After his four-year classical course, John Witherspoon entered the divinity school, and by the time he was twenty had both a Master of Arts degree and a degree in divinity. In the autumn of 1743, he became Presbyterian minister of the parish of Beith, where he remained for twelve years.

Shortly after going to Beith, he married Elizabeth Montgomery, daughter of Robert Montgomery, of Craighouse, Ayrshire, a dis-

tant kinsman of the Earl of Eglinton, who had appointed Witherspoon to the parish.

After entering the ministry, the young preacher became engaged in a dispute between two factions in the church — the
Popular Party and the Moderate Party. Witherspoon was active
on the side of the conservative orthodox, or Popular, party, who
were opposed to what they considered the religious decadence
of the Moderate Party. While he was still at Beith, he published
an essay on *Justification*, a little book which had a wide sale in
Great Britain and among the English-speaking churches of the
continent as well as in the American colonies. The year of his
transfer to a church in Paisley, he published a more pretentious
book on *Regeneration.*

With this, Witherspoon won a high reputation as a theological
writer and as the foremost man of his party in the Church of
Scotland. In 1764, the University of St. Andrews conferred upon
him a degree of doctor of divinity as a mark of his leadership and
ability. Increased reputation brought him invitations to preach
on special occasions, one of which was the anniversary of the
Society for Propagating Christian Knowledge. The foremost place
for such work was, at that time, the American colonies, where
one could work among the Indians.

The Scotch society had, some twenty years before, sent money
for the purchase of books for the library of the new College of
New Jersey, and had granted an appropriation for the education
of two young Indians. It was to Scotland, then, that two Americans went in the mid-1760's to raise funds for the much needed
new "seminary of learning" in the middle colonies.

The two Americans who visited Scotland in the interests of the
New Jersey College were the Reverend Samuel Davies, later president of the college, and Gilbert Tennent. Dr. Davies was much
impressed by Witherspoon's new little book, *Ecclesiastical Characteristics,* considering the humor of it equal to Dean Swift's. It was
popular enough to require several printings. The far-reaching result of Witherspoon's rising publicity was a call for him to come
to America and accept the presidency of the College of New
Jersey.

The first letter of invitation was presented to him by Richard

Stockton, who was to be another New Jersey Signer nine years later. But Mrs. Witherspoon, fearing the ocean crossing, was very rude to Stockton, and her husband was forced to decline. Later, Mrs. Witherspoon regretted her bad manners and apologized, explaining that she had been ill at the time. When, not very long afterward, another American and future Signer, Dr. Benjamin Rush, who was in Scotland studying medicine, tried his persuasions, he succeeded in overcoming the lady's objections. Thereupon, the Reverend Dr. Witherspoon said he would accept if another invitation were forthcoming. The second invitation duly arrived, and in August of 1768, the Witherspoons entered upon the American scene.

From the beginning, Dr. Witherspoon was charmed with America and with the Americans. He was greatly impressed by the pleasant countryside, the fertility of the land — so far beyond that of his native Scotland — and by the many opportunities for future work and growth. The Scottish minister became a whole-hearted American.

Under his able administration, things began to change at Princeton. The new president introduced the study of history, oratory, French, and philosophy, together with the Scottish system of lectures. The college student body, faculty, and endowments increased. His students adored him. More and more came to Princeton until, less than ten years later, all these advances were destroyed by British invaders.

At first, Witherspoon thought that ministers should avoid becoming embroiled in political questions. But the treatment by the king and Parliament of their American colonies caused him to stand with his patriot friends. Though he refrained from touching upon controversial political ideas in his sermons, he wrote essays, arguments, and opinions on these matters, which were widely read. In Scotland he was now labeled a rebel and traitor.

The president of Princeton consented to act on committees of correspondence and to attend the provincial conventions called by the American patriots in their endeavor to organize resistance to British pressures. All the time he was involved with politics and the administration of the college, Dr. Witherspoon continued preparing long sermons for Sundays. In those days sermons lasted for hours and there were two a day — morning and afternoon. When John Adams spent Sunday in Princeton on his first journey to Philadelphia in 1774, he wrote home that he listened to Dr. Witherspoon all day and noted in his diary that Witherspoon was "as high a son of liberty as any man in America."

On June 22, 1776, Witherspoon himself was chosen as a delegate to the Second Continental Congress, the only minister among those "founding fathers" of a new nation. He arrived in Philadelphia just as Congress was getting ready to vote on Richard Henry Lee's resolution for independence. On July 1 came the greatest of the debates, when John Adams summed up the arguments for independence for the new members from New Jersey. The next day, Witherspoon stood up and spoke in favor of adopting the resolution without delay.

When one of the delegates who held back objected that times were not yet *ripe* for a declaration of independence, Dr. Witherspoon replied that, in his opinion, the country "was not only ripe for the measure but in danger of rotting for the want of it." His emphatic stand no doubt helped some of the waverers to vote for the Declaration on the Fourth.

John Witherspoon was fifty-three when he signed the Declaration and he had been an American for only seven of those years; but, with some intermissions, he served in Congress until November, 1782. He worked on more than a hundred committees, including two very important ones: the Board of War, and the Committee on Secret Correspondence. He debated on the Articles of Confederation, helped the new government form its foreign alliances, and helped in drawing up instructions for the American peace commissioners. Recognizing the dangers of inflation, he wrote an *Essay on Money* and fought against an issue of a large amount of paper money.

When the British drew near Princeton in November, 1776, the college could not carry on, and Dr. Witherspoon had to announce on the twenty-ninth that classes must be suspended. A week later, when the British arrived, they took over Nassau Hall and most of the private houses in the town, and Witherspoon had to flee for his life. In January, he wrote from Baltimore in a letter to his son: "We carried nothing away of all our effects but what could be carried upon one team. Benjamin Hawkins drove your mother in the old chair and I rode the sorrel mare and made John Graham drive the four young colts."

In little less than a month, however, General Washington drove the British out at the Battle of Princeton. College work was not resumed until the following August.

After the war, Dr. Witherspoon worked hard to rebuild the college, but Princeton did not recover from the war's disastrous effects in his lifetime. Twice in those intervening years, he returned to the state legislature. He was moderator of the first American General Assembly in May, 1789. In that year, his wife died.

Less than two years later, when he was sixty-eight, Witherspoon married Mrs. Ann Dill, a twenty-four-year-old widow. The marriage naturally caused much comment. But he was lonely and trying to find a little happiness in his last years. He had lost so much, and his beloved college was poor. The British had burned his own fine library, and the college's two thousand books were scattered everywhere. He had undertaken a trip earlier in the 1780's to England to raise funds for the college, but this was a foolish decision on the part of the trustees. No one was inclined to give money for an American college. His errand was without success. Moreover, he suffered a bad accident. During a storm at sea, he was thrown against the side of the vessel and received a blow which injured one eye. Some years later, the other eye was bruised by a fall from a horse while he was riding over land which he had bought in Vermont.

Blind the last two years of his life, Dr. Witherspoon lived on his farm "Tusculum," about a mile outside Princeton, enjoying the outdoors and gardening as long as he was able. He died there at the age of seventy-one and was buried in the President's Lot at Princeton.

He had been a powerful speaker and preacher. Someone said that his eloquence made one's blood "shiver along the arteries." But his voice was rather harsh and he spoke with a broad Scottish burr. John Adams said he could understand Witherspoon better after having conversed with him and hearing him speak in Congress. It is said that he coined the word "Americanism" in an article he wrote on the differences between English speech in the United States and Great Britain.

Richard Stockton

Rich Stockton (signature)

October 1, 1730 — February 28, 1781

THE FIRST AMERICAN Richard Stockton, the Signer's great-grand-father, came from England — probably in the 1650's — and settled in Flushing, Long Island, New York. Forty years later, in 1696, the next Richard, the Signer's grandfather, moved to New Jersey and acquired a large parcel of land, which included the spot where Princeton is now. On this land he built his house, called "Morven," now the property of the state of New Jersey. His son, John, became a presiding judge of the Court of Common Pleas in Somerset County. All this, of course, was while the colonies were under royal government. John Stockton was also a patron of the College of New Jersey at Newark, and he was influential in having the college moved to Princeton. John married Abigail Phillips, and these were the parents of the Signer, Richard Stockton, born at Princeton, October 1, 1730.

The boy was sent to school to the Reverend Dr. Samuel Finley, director of the West Nottingham Academy, after which he entered the College of New Jersey, graduating in 1748. He then studied law in the office of David Ogden, of Newark.

When he was twenty-two, he married Annis Boudinot. Their first child, Julia, was to grow up and marry Dr. Benjamin Rush, a Pennsylvania Signer.

Some years later, Richard Stockton was licensed as an attorney, and after that his advancement at the bar was rapid. In ten years he built up a practice so large that by 1766 a trustee of the college, the Reverend Dr. John Rodgers, was saying that Stockton was at the head of his profession in the colony. Dr. Rodgers also considered him a gentleman of learning and a man of probity.

Absorbed by his legal work, Stockton did not pay much attention to politics at first. As late as 1764 — the year before the infuriating Stamp Act — Stockton was writing to his friend and pupil, Joseph Reed, that "the publick is generally unthankful, and

I never will become a Servant of it, till I am convinced that by neglecting my own affairs I am doing more acceptable Service to God and Man."

It was not long, however, before "publick" affairs convinced him. First, as a trustee of his beloved alma mater, he was asked by the board to offer the presidency of the College of New Jersey to the Reverend John Witherspoon of Paisley, Scotland. This meant a trip abroad.

After his return, Richard Stockton entered politics the next year by being appointed to the council, remaining until the royal government came to an end. In 1774, he was commissioned a Justice of the Supreme Court. He spent much time making improvements at Morven, his grandfather's home, which he had inherited. It was a large estate where he bred horses and cattle, and collected books and works of art. Ever attached to his college, he was one of its financial advisers. He believed great changes for the better would be achieved when colleges sent "into the lower House of Assembly men of more foresight and understanding than they can now boast of."

On the differences that were fast forming between the colonies and the mother country, Stockton at first took a moderate stand. In 1764, he suggested that some able Americans be elected to Parliament. Of course, this representation where the laws were made was just what Americans wanted, but narrow-mindedness prevailed. The next year, when the Stamp Act was passed, Stockton held that the British Parliament had no authority over the colonies. Nine years later, he sent Lord Dartmouth a paper entitled, "An Expedient for the Settlement of the American Disputes," warning him that immediate measures would have to be taken or there would be an "obstinate, awful and tremendous war."

Elected to Congress June 22, 1776, Stockton arrived with his New Jersey colleagues to take his seat six days later in Philadelphia's Independence Hall just as the closing debate on Lee's resolution for independence was going on.

John Adams reported the scene in a letter. In many previous debates on the subject of independence, Adams wrote, the New Jersey delegates had voted against it. New Jersey constituents had been informed and had sent a new set of delegates "on purpose to vote for Independence." Judge Stockton and Dr. Wither-spoon were appearing for the first time. Chief Justice Stockton asked to have the whole question discussed. Though it had been gone over time and again, the newcomers did not wish to state their opinions until they could hear other members speak. Hearing that Judge Stockton in particular was so eager to hear other delegates' views, many began to say, "Let the Gentlemen be gratifi'd," whereupon all eyes turned upon John Adams. One delegate said, "Come Mr. Adams you have had the subject at heart longer than any of us, and you must recapitulate the arguments."

John Adams then made a speech that deeply impressed Stockton, who later reported to his friends at home: "The man to whom the country is most indebted for the great measure of Independence is Mr. John Adams of Boston." On the day of the vote, all five Jerseymen voted for independence.

When, in September, he was chosen first Chief Justice of his new state, he declined, preferring to remain in Congress. At the end of the month, he was appointed, with George Clymer of Pennsylvania, on a committee to visit the northern army. From Saratoga he wrote, toward the end of October, that the New Jersey soldiers were "marching with cheerfulness, but great part of the men barefooted and barelegged. . . . There is not a single shoe or stocking to be had in this part of the world, or I would ride a hundred miles through the woods and purchase them with my own money." While absent on this errand, Stockton was appointed in late November as one of a committee to consider ways to reinforce General Washington and to hinder the progress of the British army.

Before Stockton could return to Princeton, the British had invaded New Jersey, where Morven, his family estate, lay in their line of march. He hurried his family to safety in the home of a friend. But on the night of November 30, he himself and his friend were captured by Tories and cast into jail in Perth Amboy. Here he was exposed to bitter cold weather, then removed to prison in New York, where he was badly treated. Congress tried to have him exchanged, but his health was already seriously affected.

After his release, Stockton was able to give only occasional counsel to his country. His beautiful estate had been used as military headquarters by the British, who had then destroyed it, burning his library — one of the best in the country — his furniture, his clothes, and his writings. Reduced to the point where he had to ask help from friends, Stockton, overwhelmed by losses and deteriorating health, passed away in Princeton on February 28, 1781, at fifty-one.

The following October Cornwallis surrendered at Yorktown, and how Stockton would have rejoiced, could he have known.

His widow, Mrs. Stockton, wrote a poem celebrating the capture of Lord Cornwallis and sent it to General Washington. He wrote her a letter of thanks. Later, when he rode through Trenton on his way to New York for his inauguration as first President of a new nation, the young ladies of Trenton threw flowers in his path, and sang Mrs. Stockton's composition, "Welcome, Mighty Chief, Once More!"

Francis Hopkinson

October 2, 1737 — May 9, 1791

IN A LETTER to his wife, John Adams described Francis Hopkinson as:

> . . . one of your pretty, little, curious, ingenious men. His head is not bigger than a large apple. I have not met with anything in natural history more amusing and entertaining than his personal appearance, yet he is genteel and well bred, and is very social.

This delightful, dainty little man, whose small features harmonized with his short stature and general appearance, was a gentleman of many attainments. The small head contained a lively and curious brain, as was shown by his animated countenance, by his fluent speech and quick motions, and by what he achieved, as lawyer, statesman, musician, and author. Like Thomas Jefferson and Benjamin Franklin, he was interested in scientific invention.

Possessed of a curious mind, he was interested in many subjects, and being "very social," he was undoubtedly a most entertaining conversationalist.

Though Signer Hopkinson represented New Jersey, he was born in Philadelphia in 1737. His father, Thomas Hopkinson, was an Englishman who came to America in 1731 and settled in Philadelphia. About five years after his arrival in the New World, Thomas married Mary Johnson, daughter of Baldwin Johnson, who had distinguished family connections in England. The next year Francis was born, the first of eight children. In the prime of life, Thomas died. Left with eight children to raise, the mother, realizing that her eldest son Francis was the most brilliant, made special sacrifices in order to give him a superior education.

When the Academy of Philadelphia opened in 1751, Francis, at fourteen, was the first pupil to enroll. Six years later, he received the first diploma granted by the College of Philadelphia. At the age of seventeen, he began to study the harpsichord and showed his musical talent by being able to play in public three years later. He loved music, composed tunes, and his song, *My Days Have Been So Wondrous Free,* and his publication, in 1763, of a collection of Psalm Tunes mark him as our first American composer.

After graduating from college, young Hopkinson studied law under Benjamin Chew, attorney-general of the province; and in 1761, at the age of twenty-four, he was admitted to practice before the Supreme Court of Pennsylvania. He was hardly more than a boy when he began to display literary, as well as musical, leanings. Many of his poems appeared in the *American Magazine.* This small, young man was intelligent, quick of mind, and versatile in his accomplishments.

In 1766, the year the Stamp Act was repealed, Francis Hopkinson went to England to visit the land of his fathers, and to seek a government appointment through the influence of relatives there. He was sent off with a public expression of respect and affection by the board of trustees of his college. In England, he was entertained at Hartlebury Castle by the Bishop of Worcester, who was his mother's cousin. While in London, he visited the artist Benjamin West, from whom he may have received some instruction in drawing and painting. At any rate, he was fond of drawing crayon portraits in his later years. Lord North, a relative by marriage, tried to help Hopkinson attain a preferment, but even he was unable to do so; such offices in America were by this time being reserved for those who had lost their jobs when the Stamp Act was repealed. Hopkinson returned home after about a year without the appointment he had hoped for.

Soon after his return, his thoughts must have turned to romance, for he married Ann Borden on September 1, 1768. She was the daughter of Colonel Joseph Borden, the leading citizen of Bordentown, New Jersey.

Francis Hopkinson then settled in his wife's town and opened a shop to sell drygoods imported from England. The mercantile and importing business did not fully satisfy him, apparently, because after a few years, he went to New Castle, Delaware, as collector of customs. But this lasted only about a year and a half; the work was even less satisfactory. He returned, then, to Bordentown to practice law, for which he had been trained; and in this work, he rose rapidly.

In 1774, Hopkinson was appointed member of the Governor's Council; and from this, two years later, he was elected to the Continental Congress of 1776. His speeches, marked by his special gift for satire, were most influential in arousing the feelings of the people.

Throughout all these years, however, he had amused himself with his music and writing. Essays and verses from his pen were to be read in the *Pennsylvania Magazine,* and when he published a piece called *A Pretty Story,* in which he presented the grievances of the colonists, he found himself launched upon a long career as a political satirist.

It was the latter part of June, 1776, when Francis Hopkinson arrived in Philadelphia, his native city, to represent New Jersey in Congress. He was thirty-nine when he signed the Declaration of Independence.

He now began to hold various offices of considerable responsibility. He served as chairman of the Continental Navy Board for two years. Following this, he held the office of treasurer of loans. In 1779, he became Judge of the Admiralty for Pennsylvania, and ten years later a United States District Judge, a position he held for the rest of his life.

But the successful always have their enemies, especially in wartime. The British had marked him as a prominent rebel. During their occupation of Philadelphia, the Hessians plundered his Bordentown house, and his family barely escaped. Because of a quarrel with the Treasury Board, a quarrel instigated not by himself but by an enemy or enemies, Francis Hopkinson suffered the embarrassment of an impeachment trial and resigned his position as treasurer of loans. But he was acquitted, and so cleared.

During the war he wrote much of the time, turning out pamphlets encouraging the Americans, deriding the British, and excoriating all Tories. In 1777, he protested brutality to noncombatants in *A Letter to Lord Howe* and in *A Letter Written by a Foreigner,* he satirized the character of John Bull. Some of his most effective writing appeared in verse which he called "political ballads." In the best known of these, a humorous piece called "The Ballad of the Kegs," he celebrated the early use of mines in warfare. In 1781, he composed a dramatic allegorical cantata, words and music, called "The Temple of Minerva," which celebrated the French alliance with our new nation. This dapper, clever little man even directed its performance.

Acquaintances observed that Hopkinson had a very animated countenance, that he was fluent in speech and quick in motion. He no doubt bubbled with enthusiasm for all his many interests — artistic, political, and scientific. He was the happy kind of creature who found it delightful just to be alive, with so many fascinating interests around him. This attractive and winning quality is probably what led to John Adams's amusing remarks.

There seemed to be no end to things that caught his interest. He is said to have designed the seals for the American Philosophical Society and for the University of the State of Pennsylvania, which was founded in 1778. He designed the Great Seal of New Jersey. Hopkinson amused himself, too, by inventing such little articles as a shaded candlestick and an improved quill or "pick" for the harpsichord. He took an active interest in his church, too, and was known for his kindly disposition.

Some of his best essays and social satires were written after the war when two new magazines, the *Columbian Magazine* and the *American Museum,* were glad to publish everything he wrote for them. They republished most of his earlier pieces, which shows that he had achieved a certain reputation as an author. In 1788, he published a volume called *Seven Songs,* which contained his best lyrical poetry, and which gave him the distinction of being the first American composer to publish a "book of music."

On May 9, 1791, at the age of fifty-four, he died suddenly of apoplexy. It is interesting to know that he imparted his love of music to his son, Joseph, who became the finest harpsichord player of his day in the new America, and was the author of *Hail Columbia.*

John Hart

c. 1711 — May 11, 1779

"HONEST JOHN HART," as his neighbors called him, was born in Stonington, Connecticut, but his parents, Edward and Martha Hart, moved to Hopewell, New Jersey, when John was only a year or so old. Though the year of his birth is uncertain, it was probably 1711.

Edward Hart, the father, had commanded a volunteer corps called the New Jersey Blues in the French-Canadian wars. At home, however, he was a farmer; and the vicinity of Hopewell is still beautiful, fertile country, better for farming than Connecticut.

Naturally, young John was raised to work on the farm with his father. Though this meant that he had very little schooling, he nevertheless grew rich enough in that excellent farming country to acquire, as he grew older, many acres of land for himself. Over the years, by diligence and good character, he won a reputation as "the most considerable man in his community."

When he was about twenty-nine, John Hart married Deborah Scudder of Ewing, New Jersey. His public life began when he was chosen justice of the peace. After that, in 1761, he was elected to the assembly and was re-elected until the assembly was dissolved in 1771, as matters grew ever more stormy in the colonies.

Hart opposed the Stamp Act in 1765. Three years later, he favored sending a message to the king bluntly saying that the right to tax the colonies lay with the colonies only — and not with Great Britain.

In 1775, he was appointed to the local Committee of Safety and the Committee of Correspondence, also serving as Judge of the Court of Common Pleas. Then he was elected to the First Provincial Congress of New Jersey. From this he went on to the scene of national politics in June, 1776, when the Provincial Congress elected him one of New Jersey's delegates to the Second Continental Congress, which in turn chose him as its vice-president.

We have Dr. Benjamin Rush's report that John Hart was "a plain, honest, well meaning Jersey farmer, with little education, but with good sense and virtue eno' [enough] to discover and pursue the true interests of his country." Hart was probably about sixty-five when he signed the Declaration of Independence.

In the autumn following the Declaration, the British invaded New Jersey. Since Hart's farm and mills lay in the path of the destroying armies, all his property was ruined by the Hessians. He himself had to hide in the area around the Sourland mountains, while British sympathizers hunted for him. He was exhausted by privation and, as if all this were not enough, he was further saddened by the death of his wife. These things took their toll of his health.

After the American victories at Trenton and Princeton, John Hart returned to find that the spot where his home had been was left in desolation. He tried to build up his farm again but there was not much left for him. Trying still to serve where he could, he became chairman of the Council of Safety for a while, until ill health forced him to retire in the autumn of 1778. The next Spring, he died.

Eighty-six years later, at the end of the Civil War, the New Jersey legislature erected a monument to his memory in Hopewell, in honor of their patriot father's services to his state and to his country.

Abraham Clark

February 15, 1726 — September 15, 1794

As EARLY AS 1675, a shipwright named Richard Clark was living in Southold, Long Island. He moved about three years later to Elizabethtown, New Jersey. His grandson, Thomas, a charter alderman and magistrate of the town, inherited from his father and grandfather the family farm between Rahway and Elizabeth, and here his only son, Abraham, was born. In after years, he was nicknamed "Congress Abraham" to distinguish him from other Abraham Clarks in the vicinity.

He was a frail child, consequently pampered by his family, and as a growing youth he was considered too slight for heavy farm work. He seems to have had little formal education as a child, but he was a born student and was probably taught at home. His liking for mathematics led him to study surveying. As an aid in this, he equipped himself to settle land disputes and to transfer property titles by studying a little law on the side. He rarely — perhaps never — charged for legal services, and there is a strong suspicion he was never admitted to the bar. But he enjoyed giving free whatever his slight knowledge of law permitted, and he enjoyed, it is said, the title he thus acquired: "The Poor Man's Counsellor." Whatever his legal status may have been, a good many people were glad to get his advice.

When he was about twenty-three, Abraham Clark married a girl named Sarah Hatfield, who came from a family the Clarks had known for more than a generation. The newly-married pair went to live in Abraham's father's house near Elizabeth. Eventually, they had a family of ten children.

About the time of his marriage, Abraham Clark was given two offices under the Crown. He became Clerk of the Colonial Assembly and also High Sheriff of Essex County.

This was his start in public life. His integrity had been early recognized during his first work with the poor, who had found they could trust him. By 1774, Clark was an avowed Whig, identified with the patriot cause, and soon became a bold advocate of independence. When Committees of Safety began to spring up throughout the colonies, Clark was placed on New Jersey's committee, later becoming its secretary.

In May, 1775, Clark was elected to the Provincial Congress of New Jersey. Since he was already supporting a break with Great Britain, he was by this body appointed to the Second Continental Congress on June 22, 1776.

Abraham Clark was much impressed by the men he met in Congress. Himself a man of few words, he was enthralled by the orators in Congress. On July Fourth, he wrote from Philadelphia to his own local people: "Our Congress is an August Assembly — and can they support the Declaration now on the Anvil, they will be the Greatest Assembly on Earth." Aware, however, of the great danger in which the colonies had now placed themselves, he added: "We can die but once. . . . We are now embarked on a most tempestuous sea. . . . It is gone so far that we must now be a free independent State or a Conquered Country."

Knowing law as he did, Clark was well aware of the penalties for treason which, under British law, all the Founding Fathers incurred when they put their signatures to the Declaration. To have been a Signer is a proud title now, but Abraham Clark wrote a friend: "As to my title, I know not yet whether it will be honourable or dishonourable; the issue of the war must settle it. Perhaps our Congress will be exalted on a high gallows." That is exactly what would have happened, too, if the British had won — unless the victors had preferred to behead them.

Though he was much of the time "in want of health" there was no absenteeism in Clark's record in Congress. He was a most energetic member, and the Library of Congress still contains many reports in his handwriting on many different subjects that concerned the patriots of 1776. But devoted to his duty though he was, he never wanted to go to Congress. As he wrote his friend, James Caldwell, he would have preferred to remain in New Jersey, where he thought he would have been of more service to his own province.

Elected to Congress in spite of his own desires, Abraham

Clark won the approval and respect of those with whom he worked, even as he had proved his worth in his own colony. He served on committees, wrote many reports, and was always present to vote. He was very active in keeping people of doubtful loyalty from being elected, and he labored mightily to gather the supplies that General Washington's army so badly needed. He opposed "commutation of pay" for army officers — that is, commuting retired officers' pay to a lump sum — and to the unlimited issue of paper money, thus acquiring numerous enemies in politics. But nothing affected his industry or his influence. Three times he was re-elected to Congress while giving interim service in the New Jersey legislature, and he was, in 1786, a delegate to the Annapolis Convention, which met to discuss interstate commerce. Chosen a representative of his state to the Philadelphia Convention that framed the great Federal Constitution in 1787, he was unable to attend because of ill health.

When the British forces landed on Staten Island, they were only a few miles across the water from Clark's New Jersey home — too near for comfort. Luckily, his estate escaped destruction at the hands of the British, but Clark had so neglected his private business affairs while on his country's service, that he nevertheless lost heavily from the Revolution. Two of his soldier sons were captured and confined on a British prison-ship. Clark knew so much of the cruelty and oppression of Great Britain that his hatred did not end, even with the treaty of peace.

He was a man of average height, slender, with dark hair and heavy eyebrows, moderate in all his desires, "very temperate," with no special ambition for wealth, and in manner reserved and thoughtful.

On September 15, 1794, he was out in one of his fields watching a bridge being built when suddenly he suffered a sunstroke. Realizing his danger, he stepped into his chaise and drove himself home. Two hours later, he died.

V

NEW YORK

Phil. Livingston

Lewis Morris

Wm Floyd

Fran! Lewis

Philip Livingston,
of Livingston Manor

Phil. Livingston

January 15, 1716 — June 12, 1778

PHILIP LIVINGSTON, one of the most distinguished, aristocratic, and wealthy of the Signers, was born in Albany, New York. By the time the decision for independence was made in Philadelphia, he was sixty and had already enjoyed almost a lifetime of distinction and wealth. He came by some of these blessings through inheritance, but being capable and energetic, he increased upon his gifts.

The first American Livingston was Philip's grandfather, Robert, who came to America in 1673 and settled in Albany. He had previously lived in Rotterdam, where he had been taken by his father who, as a Presbyterian minister in Scotland, had been banished for not conforming to the English church. Robert Livingston married Alida Schuyler, widow of a Van Rensselaer — two important names in the early Dutch settlement in New York. He received grants of large land holdings and, as the busy years passed by, he purchased more, so that by 1686, only thirteen years after his arrival, he was privileged to exercise his own jurisdiction as lord of his manor in the British colony of New York. His 160,000 acre estate extended north from Dutchess County about fourteen miles, along the east bank of the Hudson River — a glorious country. Robert's fifth son, Philip, became the second lord of the manor and was married to Catherine Van Brugh of Albany. These were the parents of Philip, the Signer who, born into all this wealth and feudal privilege, grew up on a princely scale uncommon in the colonies of early America.

The youthful Livingston took his A.B. at Yale in 1737. Nine years later when another Signer-to-be of New York, Lewis Morris, received his Yale A.B., these two were among the fewer than twenty men in the whole New York province who had a college education.

After graduation, Philip Livingston became an importer in New York City. When he was twenty-four, he married Christine Ten Broeck of Albany, and they began house-keeping in a fine house on Duke Street, New York City, while maintaining a country-seat in an ideal spot on Brooklyn Heights, overlooking the harbor. By the time he was forty, Philip Livingston had earned an excellent reputation. The British governor of the province, Sir Charles Hardy, wrote that "among the considerable merchants in this city no one is more esteemed for energy, promptness, and public spirit than Philip Livingston."

As he grew older, he became much concerned with civic affairs. Regretting the lack of an educational establishment in New York province (Massachusetts, Connecticut, and Virginia already had their colleges), Livingston was one of the first to advocate the founding of King's College, now Columbia University, and he contributed heavily to its support. He was only thirty when he set aside a sum to establish at Yale a professorship of divinity which still bears his name. He was interested in all kinds of public enterprises. He helped organize the New York Society Library; was president for a time of the newly formed St. Andrew's Society, the earliest benevolent institution in the city; and collaborated in 1768 in organizing the New York Chamber of Commerce. When the New York hospital was incorporated in 1771, he was a member of the first board of governors.

Civic interests eventually carried Philip Livingston into politics. He served on the Board of Aldermen for nine years. In 1758 he was elected to the assembly, where he came to disagree with the financial policy of the administrators of the Crown. In 1764, he helped to write the address of the assembly to the British lieutenant-governor, asking his aid in securing the rights of His Majesty's subjects everywhere, to be taxed only with their own consent. Though he deplored the rioting of the Sons of Liberty when the Stamp Act came into force the next year, he joined the lawyers and merchants in their protests and helped draft the protest to the House of Lords as a New York delegate to the Stamp Act Congress.

Livingston served on the Committee of Fifty-One, which

named the New York delegates to the First Continental Congress, and was himself one of the five selected. When he attended the Philadelphia sessions, he was very conservative, bearing in mind the terrible cost to colonial merchants that would follow a disruption of normal trade with the mother country. John Adams found Livingston unwilling even to listen to the ideas and proposals of the extreme patriots. Of course, many worthy Americans (who were, after all, transplanted Englishmen and subjects of the king) found it difficult to take a stand against the Crown. John Adams considered Philip Livingston a "downright, straightforward man" but a "great, rough, rapid mortal" with whom "there is no holding any conversation. He blusters away; says if England should turn us adrift, we should instantly go to civil wars among ourselves."

From reading the Adams chapters, we recall that the New England delegates, eager to meet the New York delegates in order to learn how they thought and where they stood on these vital questions, stopped over in New York on their way to Philadelphia. Some went to dine with Mr. Livingston at his elegant country house in Brooklyn Heights. These Massachusetts politicians felt that patriotism had "taken but shallow root in some places, particularly at New York."

An important man of business and commerce, Philip Livingston was drawn into much committee work in Congress for his province: on Indian Affairs, Marine, Commerce, the Treasury Board, and on the board of commissioners to inspect the army under General Washington. In his own state of New York, Livingston was a member of the Committee of One Hundred and of the Provincial Congress. Both he and his cousin, Robert R. Livingston, were chosen for the Second Continental Congress. But, as one had to be in New York while the other was in Philadelphia, it was Philip who signed the Declaration in early August although he could not secure an affirmative vote on the part of New York for Independence in July.

Livingston's duties in Congress were constantly being interrupted by the demands of his province. In 1777, he was chosen by the new state of New York as one of the senators to the new legislature. After attending these first meetings, he returned to Congress, which by that time was sitting in York, Pennsylvania, because the British were occupying Philadelphia.

This time his family did not want him to go because his health was poor. But he insisted on serving in public office until the end. He died in York, with only his son Henry at his bedside.

Philip Livingston had given much and lost much. His fine town house on Duke Street fell into the hands of the British invaders. His sumptuous country house, which had once been the scene of a conference between Washington and his generals, after being seized by the British and used as a naval hospital, was finally destroyed by fire. Not long before his death, he had had to sell some of his remaining property to preserve his credit. And he did not live to see the surrender of Lord Cornwallis, which made American victory certain and made heroes of the Signers.

Lewis Morris

Lewis Morris

April 8, 1726 — January 22, 1798

THE SIGNERS FROM NEW YORK COLONY were men of great wealth, either by inheritance or by their own industry. But both those who had inherited their wealth and those who had earned it had to work hard to keep it when war began. Patriotism does not buy bread, and serving the patriot cause often meant the sacrifice of much property.

Lewis Morris was the eldest son of Lewis and Tryntje Staats Morris, born in his mother's manor house, April 8, 1726. His father personally managed his early education, after which he took a Yale A.B. when he was twenty. That same year, his grandfather, another Lewis Morris, who had been the first royal Governor of New Jersey, died. He had been the first lord of the manor of Morrisania, a vast estate he had acquired in beautiful Westchester County, New York. The Signer's father then became the second lord of the manor.

Returning from Yale to this attractive homestead to help his father manage the family estates, the younger Morris found that he enjoyed this so much that he preferred to go on collecting quitrents and produce from the family's vast acres rather than devise new ways to increase the family fortune. Most people never have enough, but Lewis Morris was not the go-getter that his forebears had been; and, of course, didn't have to be, thanks to them. He felt it was better to use wisely what they had accumulated, while himself taking time to enjoy it. And he did enjoy the life of an aristocratic land-holder for sixteen years. But when trouble threatened, he was ready to work for the continued existence of the pleasant kind of civilized life he had always had.

On September 24, 1749, he married Mary Walton, daughter of Jacob and Maria Beekman Walton, who brought him additional wealth. The Beekmans were a prominent, wealthy, New York family, and Beekman Place, along the East River, is still one of the "best" addresses in New York City.

When his father died in 1762, the tall, handsome thirty-six-year-old Lewis became the third and, as it turned out, the last lord of Morrisania Manor. Coming into the inheritance of so vast an estate placed upon him a great responsibility, which turned his thoughts to politics, for on political questions depended his own future welfare. After serving a term in the Provincial Assembly, he began to realize where the British policy was leading.

Some of his Tory neighbors in Westchester objected to his resistance to British policy, saying that he was supporting the revolutionary movement only because he himself had not been given better offices. In fact, Morris simply had more foresight than they. But he was still representing only a minority in his county when he persuaded some local politicians to issue a call for a meeting in White Plains to choose Westchester's delegates to New York's Provincial Convention. Bearers of such wealthy New York names as DeLancey, Pell, Phillips, tried to defeat the aim of the meeting, but Lewis Morris and his side carried the day, and eight deputies were appointed to attend the Convention when it met in New York on April 20, 1775.

Morris was named chairman of the delegation instructed to support a resolution to send representatives to the Second Continental Congress. He was hoping to be chosen a delegate himself and he got his wish.

A little more than three weeks later, Lewis Morris took his seat in the Congress in Philadelphia. Here his services had to do mainly with administrative matters. He was put on the committee to select army posts in New York should trouble with England grow worse. Then he was assigned to the committee which was to supply ammunition and military stores. He was much occupied with the practical, business side of the Revolution, locating and purchasing tent cloth, gunpowder, or the sulphur and saltpetre used in making it. But, active though he was in practical affairs, Morris was not one of the debaters and speechmakers in Congress.

In September of 1775, Morris dealt with Indian affairs at Pittsburgh, and was later made a permanent member of the Indian Affairs Committee.

The following June he was home again as brigadier-general in command of the Westchester County militia, while his son was appointed brigade major. Believing that his military post would offer more opportunity for active service than proved to be the case, Morris secured a leave of absence from Congress and was therefore away from Philadelphia on the great day of decision in early July, 1776. Instead, he was attending the fourth New York Provincial Congress in White Plains which endorsed the Declaration of Independence. He went back to Philadelphia a short time afterward and signed the Declaration. He was then fifty.

In the autumn of 1776, Morris took part in the campaign in New York but after that his military service was interrupted by the responsibilities of his civil offices. He was county judge in Westchester for a brief time, and he served intermittently as member of the upper house of the new state legislature until 1790.

When the war ended, Morris retired with the rank of major-general and set about the heart-breaking task of rehabilitating his beautiful estates, which had been sadly plundered and burned by the British. Many of the fine houses and properties of American patriots were deliberately destroyed by the British, and Morris was one of their victims.

In his older years, Lewis Morris served as a member of the first Board of Regents of the University of the State of New York. His younger brother, Gouverneur Morris, played a prominent part in the drafting of the new Federal Constitution, and at the convention in Poughkeepsie in 1788, Judge Lewis Morris worked for its ratification.

Above everything, however, Signer Lewis Morris loved to preside over his beautiful Morrisania home and its fine grounds, and there he finally passed away at the age of seventy-two.

William Floyd

December 17, 1734 — August 4, 1821

WILLIAM FLOYD'S FAMILY had been in America since his great-grandfather Richard Floyd emigrated from Wales in 1654. The first Floyd settled at Setauket, Long Island, became a successful farmer, and interested himself in public affairs, serving as Judge of Suffolk County and as colonel of the militia. Richard Floyd was the founder of the family fortune and established the local reputation of the Floyds. By the time William, the Signer, was born in Brookhaven, Long Island, eighty years after his immigrant great-grandfather's arrival, the family was wealthy. Nicoll Floyd and his wife Tabitha Smith Floyd were the parents of the Signer.

Though William could have had the best of educations, he received only elementary schooling for when he was in his teens his father died, leaving him with the responsibilities of a landed proprietor. It is interesting to note that one of his daughters, Mary Floyd, became the first wife of Colonel Benjamin Tallmadge, chief of General Washington's secret service, who played an important part in catching Major André and uncovering the treason of Benedict Arnold.

William Floyd's family connections and the pleasure he took in extending generous hospitality naturally made him prominent in his community and, like his great-grandfather, he was active in both civic and military affairs. He served in Suffolk County's militia and eventually became a militia major general, though he was in Congress during most of the Revolution. Active resistance to British oppression had developed with especial strength among the settlers who had moved from the New England colonies to the eastern end of Long Island. Floyd was about forty when he aligned himself with the patriotic cause. Though this was against his interests as a large land-owner, such were his convictions and he stood by them.

In 1774, William Floyd was elected delegate to the First Continental Congress and took his seat on opening day. As a member of the Provincial Convention the next year, he was again elected and so was in Congress in 1776. He was one of those who, being neither aggressive nor brilliant enough to stand up and argue in the debates, "never quit their chairs" — as another delegate observed — but he served on many committees, and his independent judgment won the respect of his colleagues.

William Floyd and his family suffered severe hardships during the war. His property on Long Island was taken over by the British after the Declaration was signed, and his wife and family had to flee to Middletown, Connecticut. Difficult years followed, during which his duties separated him from his family. When he finally saw his home after seven years, it was in ruins.

At the end of the war, Floyd bought land in what is now Oneida County, New York, at the headwaters of the Mohawk River. He returned to Congress from 1789 to 1791 and was several times a presidential elector. In 1803 he finally moved to his new property and spent more and more time doing what he loved the most — cultivating his land. In 1808 he was elected state senator.

Floyd was a practical man of no special distinction, save for his stout and faithful patriotism. He was reserved, frank, independent, and well-liked, though he is known today only because his signature appears on the birth certificate of his country.

Francis Lewis

March 21, 1713 — December 31, 1802

No LONGER YOUNG, Francis Lewis had retired from a successful career in business, which included much travel and some high adventure, by the time he went to Philadelphia to attend the Second Continental Congress at the age of sixty-three.

Lewis was not a native-born patriot. He was a Welshman, born in Llandaff, Glamorganshire, March 21, 1713, only son of the Reverend Francis Lewis and his wife, Amy Pettingal Lewis. His parents died while he was still a child, and he was brought up by his aunt in Caernarvon until he went to Westminster School in London. This was the end of his formal education. He became apprentice to a London merchant, working in the counting-house and thus preparing himself for a career in trade.

At the age of twenty-five, Francis Lewis came to New York, bringing a cargo of goods which, it is said, he had been able to buy with money he had inherited. Some of this cargo he took on to Philadelphia, where he remained for a year. He returned to New York, formed a partnership with a man named Richard Annely, and established permanent residence there. His continuously successful business necessitated considerable travel to England, and two visits to Russia. While on these business trips, Lewis was twice shipwrecked on the treacherous coast of Ireland.

When he was thirty-two, he married Elizabeth Annely, sister of his partner.

Serving as clothing contractor for the British troops during the French and Indian War, Lewis was at Fort Oswego during Montcalm's attack. Upon the surrender of the fort, when its garrison of sixteen hundred men became prisoners of war, Lewis was one of the thirty captives given to an Indian chief assisting Montcalm, but after some time, he was sent to France and there exchanged. The British government granted him five thousand acres for his military service.

Lewis accumulated a considerable fortune and became a man of influence and importance in New York. As British treatment of the American colonies became more intolerable, Lewis showed active interest in the patriot cause, serving as a member of the Stamp Act Congress in his colony.

A few years later, wishing to establish his elder son Francis in the business, he took the young man to England to make commercial connections there. Returning with a quantity of dry goods, they set up the firm of Francis Lewis and Son. But when the son was well launched, he carried on so successfully that the father retired. He never again engaged in business, but occupied himself wholly with public affairs which, by this time, were becoming very serious. He was wealthy enough to leave the city and live on his country estate at Whitestone, Long Island. Inevitably, all this obvious success made him enemies among jealous competitors who had not done so well.

Like Philip Livingston, another New York Signer, Lewis was a member of the important committees which organized the beginning of the rebellion: the Committee of Fifty-One, which later became the Committee of Sixty and, later yet, the Committee of One Hundred. The Fifty-One were really a committee of correspondence. Eventually Lewis and ten others resigned from the Fifty-One in protest against their "excessive caution" in opposing the British. Lewis favored a stronger stand and in April, 1775, the provincial convention agreed with him enough to pick him as one of New York's twelve delegates to the Second Continental Congress.

Though New York sent twelve members to the Second Congress, they were directed to arrange among themselves that only five would be attending Congress at the same time. Thus it was a matter of chance who the actual New York Signers were. These five were in favor of Richard Henry Lee's resolution declaring independence, but because their constituents had not instructed them to vote separation from Great Britain, they believed that they were not justified in voting on either side. They asked leave to withdraw from the question. This Congress granted, and that is why New York did not vote on July Fourth. Happily for the New Yorkers, the Declaration was not signed, except by John Hancock, on that day.

On July 9, when the New York provincial convention met at White Plains, letters from the New York delegates in Philadelphia and the Declaration itself were laid before them. That same evening they

> Resolved, unanimously, That the reasons assigned by the Continental Congress for declaring the United Colonies Free and Independent States are cogent and conclusive; and that while we lament the cruel necessity which has rendered that

measure unavoidable, we approve the same, and will, at the risk of our lives and fortunes, join with the other colonies in supporting it.

When, therefore, the Declaration had been engrossed and was produced in Congress, the New York delegates were authorized to sign it, and gladly did so.

In Congress, Francis Lewis was a member of the committee of claims, of the committee to report a method of establishing a hospital, and of the committee to advise the best way of assigning persons of character as intelligence agents and couriers. He was also on the committee charged with inquiring "into the state of the army and the best means of supplying their wants." He was indefatigable in this endless committee work. He was not one of the congressional debaters, and Edward Rutledge considered him to be one of the quiet ones. Nevertheless, Dr. Rush called him "a very honest man, and very useful in executive business."

Lewis was again chosen a delegate to the Congress which had to flee to York, Pennsylvania, when the British took Philadelphia. Sometimes at that session, no more than nine members were present, and never more than eighteen. In January, 1777, Lewis wrote that for several months he had been the only member attending from New York, and this when Washington's army was in desperate need of food and clothing! But these congressmen at first all had their own businesses to attend to.

Some of them lost their businesses, their fortunes, their homes and their health as well, during the difficult years when they were laboring for their country. Lewis was one of these devoted but unfortunate men. After his staunch patriotism and hard work in the cause of American liberty, Lewis was naturally a target for British retaliation and suffered great losses. Less than a month after he signed the Declaration, the British deliberately destroyed his Long Island home, with all his books, papers, and furniture, and carried Mrs. Lewis off to a New York prison. Lewis was distracted. About two months afterward, General Washington had two Tory ladies placed under house arrest in their own Philadelphia houses until they could be exchanged for Mrs. Lewis. But the experience and the worry about her husband's losses injured her health and hastened her death, which occurred less than two years later.

During the disgraceful intrigues of the Conway Cabal against General Washington, when the plotters wanted to remove him and give General Gates the supreme command, Francis Lewis was Washington's strong supporter and played a part in defeating the plot.

In 1779, Lewis was elected for the fourth time to Congress but had to ask for leave of absence because of his wife's illness. He also endured the pain of having his only daughter married, clandestinely, to an officer of the British Navy. Thus lost to her father, she presumably went to live in England.

In December of this same year, Lewis became Commissioner of the Board of Admiralty; but after his wife died, he retired from public life.

In his ninetieth year he passed away, one of the few Signers to reach such an advanced age. His younger son, Morgan Lewis, who had been an officer in the Continental Army, was elected Governor of New York the next year.

VI

CONNECTICUT

Roger Sherman

Sam.^d Huntington

Oliver Wolcott

Wm Williams

Roger Sherman

Roger Sherman

April 30, 1721 — July 23, 1793

WITH NO EDUCATION save what he gained at home by his own efforts, Roger Sherman made himself, in the opinion of John Adams, "one of the most sensible men in the world. The clearest head and the steadiest heart." He was one of the five in Congress chosen for the committee to draft the Declaration of Independence. Thomas Jefferson, who composed it, recalled in after years: "I served with him [Sherman] in the old congress, in the years 1775 and 1776; he was a very able and logical debater in that body, steady in the principles of the revolution, always at the post of duty, much employed in the business of committees." Then he added: "I had a very great respect for him."

Roger Sherman was born in Newton, Massachusetts, just west of Boston. His parents were William and Mehetable Wellington Sherman, and his earliest American ancestor was John Sherman, who came from Dedham, in Essex, England, about 1636.

The boy was only two when his father moved to Stoughton, some twenty miles south of Boston and farther from the coastline. In those days, it was practically a frontier community, sparsely settled, with harmless Indian neighbors. Here Roger grew through boyhood and did not leave until he was a young man of twenty-two with responsibilities.

Schooling facilities were very poor in outlying communities like Stoughton. Young Roger was thirteen when the town built a schoolhouse and the boys were taught reading, writing, and arithmetic as far as fractions. The Stoughton school became a "grammar school." That meant Latin grammar, but Roger must have studied the correct use of English because, after he had become a prominent man, President Timothy Dwight of Yale, commented on his accurate use of his native language. Fortunately for a boy who enjoyed study and reading, his father possessed a small library of his own, and the Stoughton church had a Harvard-trained minister, the Reverend Samuel Dunbar, a great help to the studious Sherman. The boy thus achieved some knowledge of mathematics, physics, Latin, English poetry, history, economics, logic, philosophy, and theology. All this went on in the growing years while he plowed with a yoke of oxen, did the usual farm chores, and learned shoe-making from his father. A boy with such ambition and industry was bound to go far.

When he was twenty, his father died, and young Roger was left to care for his mother and the younger sisters and brothers. His older brother William had moved away to New Milford, Connecticut, and two years later Roger followed with the family, enticed by William's letters describing the attractions of western Connecticut. For those times, this was the "call of the West." It is reported that the family went by stage, but Roger walked the approximately fifty miles, carrying his sack of cobbler's tools upon his back.

Settlers in the frontier town found living conditions primitive. Everybody did some farming. The settler had to build his own house and outbuildings. Everybody in a family helped in the work, all year round. In the summers they grew their food. In the winters, the men cared for their animals, mended fences or stone walls, and made harnesses. The women spun, sewed, knitted. They had almost no money, but paid their debts and taxes in produce. Whatever they had — food, clothing, buildings, furniture — cost them endless labor. In addition to all this hard work, Roger Sherman continued to make shoes and, because he liked it, continued to study mathematics. He had had a surveyor grandfather, from whom, perhaps, he inherited his mathematical mind. This study led to his appointment, two years later, as surveyor of New Haven County, an office which he held for several years. Since surveying paid much better than cobbling, he put aside his shoe-making and, as the years passed, made money enough to buy land — and more land.

Commissioned by a neighbor to consult a lawyer in the county seat regarding a petition before the court, Sherman wrote down the items of the plea so as to have a clear and complete reference when the time came. During the interview in New Haven, the lawyer asked to see the paper Sherman was looking at. Handing it over reluctantly, he said it was only a memorandum he had made for himself and not likely to be helpful to the lawyer. But upon reading it, the attorney said, "My friend, you should fit yourself to be a lawyer."

When the surprised young man asked why, he was told that his notes, with a few alterations in form, were as good as any the lawyer himself could have prepared.

Undoubtedly the young man went on to Stoughton, his former home-town, while on this visit to the county seat. He made other visits to Stoughton during his first years in New Milford, for he had left a girl behind him there. In November, 1749, he married Elizabeth Hartwell, daughter of Deacon Joseph and Mary Hartwell of Stoughton, and took her back to the house he had bought the year before in New Milford.

The energetic Roger Sherman became active in town and church affairs, though he had not joined a church until he was twenty-one. (Perhaps it might be well to explain here that church membership in the strict Calvinistic congregations of that day was not easy to achieve, and since the early comers to New England were people who had broken away from the Church of England at home, partly because it was not strict enough, the descendants of seventeenth-century Americans were brought up to rigid rules.)

As a boy, Roger Sherman had been used to a Sabbath which began on Saturday at sunset. Sunday morning, at the sound of drum or conch-shell, the whole family walked to the cheerless meeting-house, children following the parents "in quiet procession." Between morning and afternoon service, there was an hour for lunch. No work and no play was permitted on Sundays, not even cooking or bed-making. This was the origin of the New England pot of baked beans, always made on Saturdays to last over. And, though children attended church, they could achieve membership only after examination and a careful observation by those who were already members. Becoming a deacon was a distinct achievement, an honor so important, indeed, that a deacon always used his title.

Sherman became town clerk of New Milford, served on the school committee, and before long was chosen "agent" to the assembly on the town's business. He and his brother opened New Milford's first store, of which he later became the sole owner. Sherman's friends and acquaintances persuaded him to write an almanac because of the astronomy and mathematics he had learned in his leisure hours. In those days when towns had no newspapers and not much else to read, almanacs were important publications. Roger Sherman wrote and published a series of almanacs for eleven years, beginning in 1750.

Early in 1754 he was admitted to the Litchfield bar and the next year represented New Milford (nineteen miles from Litchfield) in the General Assembly, which appointed him justice of the peace. One thing always leads to another, and four years later, he became a justice of the county court and, except for the two following years, he was constantly re-elected to the legislature until 1761, when he was forty years old. In 1755, during the French and Indian War, Sherman served on a committee to consider the financing of the expedition against the French stronghold at Crown Point. In 1759 he was appointed commissary for the Connecticut troops.

All these experiences helped to prepare him for a legislative career during the Revolution, especially in matters touching military supply and finance; and, by the time he was forty, Roger Sherman had made himself, with no help or fortune, a man of property with a considerable political reputation. He enlarged his business enterprise to open a store in New Haven and another in nearby Wallingford. Then, in 1760, his wife died and the next year Roger Sherman took his family to live in New Haven.

He now gave up the practice of law and devoted himself to merchandizing, which in New Haven included bookselling. His house adjoined his store on what is now Chapel Street, opposite Yale College. Since he loved books and reading, his store became a kind of rendezvous for the professors and preachers and educated men of the town — a little center for those interested in cultural pursuits.

Two years after moving to New Haven, Roger Sherman married again, and his second wife, Rebecca Prescott, gave him eight more children.

During the increasingly stormy years after the Stamp Act, Sherman was treasurer of Yale. A self-taught scholar who had lifted himself into a position of prominence altogether by his own efforts, study, and industry, he was given an honorary M.A. degree in 1768. Through the 1760's and 1770's he held many public of-

fices, representing New Haven in the lower house of the legislature and then in the upper house, an office he held for nineteen
years. From May, 1766, he was judge of the Superior Court of
Connecticut and annually reappointed for twenty-three years
thereafter.

The province of Connecticut had a homogeneous population,
being then almost entirely Anglo-Saxon. There was a strong feeling against interference from without. As the years sped on into
the agitated 1770's, Sherman stood in the conservative wing of
the Revolutionary party, while denying the supremacy of the
British Parliament over the American colonies. In 1774, John
Adams wrote that Sherman thought that Parliament had authority
to make laws for America "in no case whatever." The two had
become acquainted when members of the First Continental Congress that same year.

Adams described Sherman as awkward and stiff when speaking
in Congress, rigid as "a sophomore," standing with "his hands before him, the fingers of his left hand clenched into a fist, and the
wrist of it grasped with his right." But, said Adams, "he has a
clear head and sound judgment."

Sherman developed an interest in the Susquehanna Company,
though he does not seem ever to have become a stockholder in it.
This company was an extraordinary enterprise by an adventurous
band of men who proposed to set up in Pennsylvania a new Connecticut county separated by more than a hundred miles from
Connecticut itself. This happened because King Charles II, in
granting a charter to Connecticut in 1662, had drawn its northern
and southern boundaries carefully but had given its western
boundary only as the Pacific Ocean! The king, of course, had no
idea how far away that was. Nobody did until after the Lewis
and Clark Expedition.

In 1753, a group of Connecticut men who were looking westward for land for themselves organized the company and bought
from the Indians a tract around modern Wilkes Barre, Pennsylvania, nearly as big as the whole state of Connecticut. Here they
set up a new Connecticut County. But when they tried to settle
it Pennsylvania objected, and there was a series of little wars
which the two states decided to call off as the Revolutionary War
approached. Roger Sherman was on a Committee of the State As-

sembly to cooperate with Governor Trumbull in the matter. Before the Revolution was over, the dispute was peacefully settled, and the state of Pennsylvania kept her Susquehanna Valley lands. The state of Connecticut gave up its claim on land all the way to the coast, retaining only a "Western Reserve" in Ohio. This is now that part of Ohio which contains the city of Cleveland.

Every year Congress assigned Sherman to some committee dealing with finance. For raising money, he urged high taxes by Congress and by the states. He was against weakening the new government's credit through too many loans. This took courage as the people, unused to the taxes we have now learned to accept, voiced a strong resistance to parting with their cash. His business ability was repeatedly utilized by Congress. He was on committees for purchasing supplies and provisions, and for "supplying the army with shoes, hats, and shirts." Even earlier, the year before, when on a committee for investigating army contract frauds, Sherman surprised his colleagues by his familiarity with the making and selling of shoes.

Sherman went through a period of illness in 1776 and realized that he would have to slow down the next year. He wrote Governor Trumbull of Connecticut that his constitution would not permit "so close an application to business much longer." But he stayed on until 1781, and returned to Congress again in 1783 and 1784. With Benjamin Franklin on the committee to form the Articles of Confederation, under which the government operated before the Constitution was adopted, he proposed a plan of union which John Adams said was the best liked at the time although, he added, very little was taken from it when the Constitution was finally adopted.

The years 1783 to 1787 encompassed a very critical period in American history. Though the Pennsylvania-Connecticut controversy over the Susquehanna settlements had been officially settled, other states were in conflict. Some disputed their boundaries, others quarrelled over tariffs. Pennsylvania and Delaware had commercial differences, so did South Carolina and Georgia; Virginia and Maryland disputed over Chesapeake Bay. It soon became clear that the Articles of Confederation were weak and would have to be revised. Connecticut disregarded the call for a convention to revise the Articles until the May, 1787, session of the General Court. The legislators then appointed Roger Sherman as delegate to take the place of another delegate who had resigned. Now sixty-six, Sherman was the oldest of Connecticut's delegates, and his long years of business and legal experience, his broad general knowledge, and his forcible character made him the natural leader of the delegation.

In the Constitutional convention, Sherman was one of the most frequent speakers, credited with one hundred thirty-eight speeches. He made a strong impression. One thought him "as cunning as the Devil, and if you attack him, you ought to know him well; he is not easily managed, but if he suspects you are trying to take him in, you may as well catch an Eel by the tail." Another thought Sherman had "good sense to so high a degree that it might almost be called genius." His concise speech was noted: "With more well-digested thoughts to communicate than any other member of the Convention, he used fewer words to express his sentiments than any of his compeers." Another delegate described his appearance, not altogether favorably:

> Mr. Sherman exhibits the oddest shaped character I ever remember to have met with. He is awkward and unaccountably strange in his manner. But in his train of thinking there is something regular, deep, and comprehensive; yet the oddity of his address, the vulgarisms that accompany his public speaking, and that strange New England cant which runs through his public as well as his private speaking makes everything that is connected with him grotesque and laughable; and yet he deserves infinite praise, no Man has a better Heart or a clearer Head. If he cannot embellish he can furnish thoughts that are wise and useful. He is an able politician, and extremely artful in accomplishing any particular object; it is remarked that he seldom fails."

John Adams thought him "an old Puritan, as honest as an angel and as firm in the cause of American Independence as Mount Atlas." Thomas Jefferson said that Sherman "never said a foolish thing in his life." Mr. Macon of Georgia said Roger Sherman had "more common sense than any man" he knew.

There was a strong religious side to his character. Ever interested in theology, Sherman corresponded with several New England clergymen. During his years in Congress, it was his custom to buy a new Bible at the beginning of each new session, read in it every day and, upon his return home, give it to one of his children.

When he was seventy, he was elected to fill a vacancy in Connecticut's senatorial representation, and he was a United States senator at the time of his death, two years later.

In the summer of 1793, he was stricken with typhoid, and died on July twenty-third. After a large and impressive funeral he was buried in the cemetery behind the Center Church on the New Haven Green, but when the New Haven Green Cemetery was moved in 1821, his body was taken to the Grove Street Cemetery.

Roger Sherman has the special distinction of being the only one of all the Signers who signed all four of the greatest documents in the birth of his nation: the Articles of Association in 1774; the Declaration of Independence; the Articles of Confederation; and the Constitution itself.

Samuel Huntington

Sam ᵈ Huntington

July 3, 1731 — January 5, 1796

MANY OF THE PATRIOTS who fearlessly resisted the threats and efforts of the British government to prevent the Declaration of Independence came from humble homes, yet by the vigor of their intellect and desire to learn, acquired for themselves a certain amount of education and commanded general respect. Like Roger Sherman, Samuel Huntington never had an opportunity to attend school and college.

His great-grandfather, Simon, came from England and was one of the thirty-five original proprietors of Norwich, Connecticut. After his death, his widow settled in Boston only thirteen years after the arrival of the Mayflower. Two generations later, Nathaniel Huntington was living in Windham, Connecticut, not far from Norwich, when his wife, Mehitable Thurston Huntington, gave birth to their first child, Samuel. Nine more children were to come.

Samuel grew up on his father's farm, helping with the chores as soon as he was old enough. He also helped in his father's clothing shop. Although three of his younger brothers attended Yale, Samuel had to stay on the farm until, when he was sixteen, he was apprenticed to a cooper and learned to make barrels.

However, he was studious by nature and had a desire to learn. He taught himself Latin and law, not easy subjects, and was admitted to the bar when he was twenty-seven. He had done it all himself, borrowing books to study in the hours he could snatch from farming and barrel-making. At twenty-eight, he gave up farming, entered a law office in Norwich, and soon began to win distinction in his profession. Four years later he was made King's Attorney (District Attorney) for Connecticut. But when relations became strained between the colonies and the mother country, Huntington, whose sympathies were with the patriots, resigned, feeling that he could no longer faithfully serve the king. He was conservative, however, and loyal to the mother country so long as there was hope of conciliation. When it became evident that there must be a separation, he supported the colonies.

At the age of thirty, Samuel Huntington married Martha Devotion, daughter of the Reverend Ebenezer Devotion, of Windham. Having no children of their own, they took two of Samuel's brother's children to raise, Joseph Huntington having married Martha's sister.

In the Stamp Act year, Samuel Huntington was chosen to represent Norwich in the General Assembly of Connecticut Colony, and this body appointed him a member of the committee for defense. In ten years, Samuel Huntington had made himself well enough known, liked, and respected to be elected assistant in the upper house of the legislature, to which he was re-elected every year until 1784.

Before the outbreak of the war, Huntington had been judge of the Superior Court. With General Jabez Huntington and the Honorable Benjamin Huntington, he had represented Norwich in the Connecticut Council of Safety. Three of the original nine members of this council came from Norwich and were named Huntington.

With his record it was not strange that this self-made gentleman was appointed a delegate to the Continental Congress. Samuel Huntington took his seat in 1776 with Roger Sherman, Oliver Wolcott, and William Williams, the other Connecticut congressmen. Huntington, who served on many committees, was regarded as "a sensible, candid, and worthy man."

In 1779 he was chosen President of Congress to succeed John Jay, who had been appointed minister plenipotentiary to negotiate a treaty between the United States and Spain. Two years later he had to resign because of poor health. He returned to Philadelphia and Congress in 1783.

The next year, Huntington was Chief Justice of the Connecticut Supreme Court. He then became lieutenant-governor of the state and Governor of Connecticut in 1786. Re-elected for eleven successive years, Huntington was still the governor at the time of his death in Norwich at the age of sixty-four. This self-taught man had been gratified by the honorary degree of LL.D. conferred upon him by both Yale and Dartmouth.

When George Washington and John Adams were elected to be the first President and Vice-President of our new nation in 1789, Huntington received two electoral votes for Vice-President.

With no formal education himself, he was careful to give his nephew and namesake, whom he had taken to raise, an opportunity to study at Dartmouth and Yale. This younger Samuel Huntington later moved to Ohio and became a governor of that state.

William Williams

April 8, 1731 — August 2, 1811

IN THE VILLAGE of Lebanon, somewhat east of central Connecticut, the Reverend Solomon Williams was pastor of the First Congregational Church when his wife, Mary Porter Williams, gave him the son who was to become a Signer. William was descended from Robert Williams, who came to Roxbury, Massachusetts, from Norfolk County, England, in 1637; so the family had been in America almost a hundred years.

William was given a preparatory education sound enough to enable him to graduate from Harvard at the age of twenty. Then he began to study theology with his father.

Four years later, however, having joined the staff of Colonel Ephraim Williams, his father's cousin, William served in the Lake George operations of the French and Indian War.

Returning to Lebanon after the Lake George campaign, William Williams resumed his activities in the town's affairs, became town clerk, and set himself up in business as a merchant. Judging by the number of offices he held, Williams must have been regarded as an exceedingly worthy citizen. He was town clerk for forty-four years, selectman for Lebanon for twenty-five years; he was a representative and later a councilor in the assembly for more than forty years, speaker for many years, and a colonel in the militia.

He was an ardent patriot, chosen to serve on several committees. Strong for independence, Williams not only gave money to the cause, he also wrote for it by setting down the colonists' claims in various journals, and helping to write many of the state papers of Connecticut's governor, John Trumbull, whose daughter Mary he married when he was forty years of age.

It was on Williams's promissory note that money was raised in 1775 for the cost of sending Connecticut troops to help in the capture of Ticonderoga. Appointed to represent his colony at the conferences of delegates from all the New England colonies, the next step finds him entering the national arena as delegate to the Continental Congress of 1776.

After voting for independence and signing his name to the Declaration, he helped to frame the Articles of Confederation, under which the country was governed before we had a Constitution. In 1777, he was elected to sit on the Board of War.

Throughout the struggle, Williams offered the hospitality of his house in Lebanon to any passing American soldiers, and he allowed French officers to live there when they were stationed in Lebanon through the winter of 1780–81.

After the war, Williams was a delegate to the Hartford Convention to consider Connecticut's adoption of the new Constitution of the United States. He voted in favor of it with one objection: He did not want the clause which forbade religious tests.

Another of those who served on the bench without having had legal training, William Williams was judge of the Windham County Court for many years, growing old while meting out justice.

A hardy New Englander, the old Signer lived to ripe old age, passing away on August 2, 1811, in the town where he had been born eighty years before.

Oliver Wolcott

November 20, 1726 — December 1, 1797

LIKE THE WILLIAMS FAMILY, the Wolcotts had been in the New World about a hundred years by the time Oliver Wolcott, the Signer, was born. The first Wolcott had been Henry, an Englishman of property, who had come to Connecticut in 1630 and had become one of the founders of the settlement at Windsor. He served in the first general assembly of the colony. Oliver's father was Roger, who went to work as a mechanic at the age of twelve. Industrious and thrifty, Roger acquired a considerable property and became governor in 1751. Thus, though Roger Wolcott had no formal education himself, members of his family had been serving in civil affairs and helping build up their colony since the first Henry crossed the Atlantic.

Roger married Sarah Drake, of Windsor. They had fourteen children, the youngest of whom was Oliver. He went to Yale, was at the head of his class for four years, and graduated in 1747. Before graduating he received a commission from the British Governor Clinton of New York to raise a company of volunteers. He did so and served as its captain during service on the northern frontier for some time.

After he returned home, Oliver Wolcott studied medicine with his older brother, Dr. Alexander Wolcott, intending to practice in Goshen. But in 1751, when Litchfield was organized as a county, he settled there on property his father owned. That was the year his father became governor.

Oliver was Litchfield's first sheriff and held this position for twenty years, during which time he devoted himself more and more to public life and legal affairs. Eventually he became judge of the County Court of Common Pleas and probate judge for the Litchfield district.

In 1755, he married Laura Collins, daughter of Captain Daniel Collins of Guilford, Connecticut. They had five children.

As discord between the mother country and her American colonies mounted toward open rebellion, Wolcott again engaged in military affairs. In 1771, he was made a major in the militia, in 1774 a colonel. In midsummer of the following year, after the Continental Congress had appointed him as one of the commissioners of Indian Affairs for the northern section, he traveled to Albany to a council with representatives of the Six Nations.

In October of that troubled year, 1775, he was elected to the Continental Congress and took his place among the new national figures in Philadelphia. He was now fifty.

Oliver Wolcott did not do much committee work in Congress. He joined in the early discussions about a declaration of independence and came to be recognized as a man who was not afraid to speak his mind. But by the end of June, 1776, illness forced him to leave.

Since he arrived home on the Fourth, the day of the all-important vote, Wolcott missed the chance to take part in the final great decision. Connecticut sent William Williams as a substitute and Williams cast the vote for independence that might have been Wolcott's. Later, however, both signed the Declaration.

In the next few weeks, Wolcott recovered his health. When General Washington requested more aid in the defense of New York from Connecticut's Governor Trumbull, Wolcott was able to take the field as brigadier general of the fourteen militia regiments ordered by the Connecticut governor and the Council of Safety to reinforce General Putnam on the Hudson River.

It should not be forgotten that the wives of these patriots who were eager to serve their country, did their full part in service, too. The ladies of Litchfield gathered in the rear of Wolcott's house and melted down the lead that had once formed part of King George's statue into bullets to be used against the king's redcoats. Wives are of the greatest help — or hindrance — to the public and patriotic service of their husbands. Mrs. Wolcott managed their small farm, preserved their property, and educated the children while her husband was away in the nation's service.

In October, Wolcott returned to Philadelphia and it was then, or possibly later, that he signed the Declaration. His name is at the bottom of the first column of signatures.

That winter, the members of Congress had to leave Philadelphia ahead of the invading British, and Wolcott went with them to Baltimore.

The next summer he was again active in military matters. After being in command of the sixth Militia Brigade in north-western Connecticut, he led a force of three hundred to four hundred volunteers from the brigade to join Gates against Burgoyne in September. It is said that among their supplies at this time were some of the bullets made from the melted statue of the king.

Early in 1778 Wolcott was again in Congress, now sitting in York, Pennsylvania. Elected again in 1780, he remained until 1784. For a time in 1779, however, he was once more on military service, as major general defending the Connecticut seacoast against raids by the Tory Governor Tryon, of New York. Before the war was over his eldest son, Oliver, was serving in minor campaigns.

After the peace, Wolcott resigned from Congress in order to pay more attention to the affairs of his own state. In 1784, he was commissioner at the Treaty of Fort Stanwix to make peace with the Indians of the Six Nations. Three years later he was chosen lieutenant-governor by the legislature. There were boundary disputes between New York and Vermont, and between Connecticut and Pennsylvania about the Wyoming Valley (in Pennsylvania) which he helped to settle. In 1789, he helped conclude a treaty with the Wyandottes in which they gave up their title to Connecticut lands in the Western Reserve, now part of Ohio.

Honors descended upon him. He received an honorary degree from Yale, he became President of the Connecticut Society of

Arts and Sciences and, upon the death of Samuel Huntington in
January, 1796, he became governor and was elected to the office
the following May. But his time as governor was brief and uneventful. He died while in office, at the age of seventy-one, on
December 1, 1797. Before he died, he had the opportunity to vote,
as presidential elector, for John Adams, second President of the
United States.

A description of his person makes him appear the typical Connecticut Yankee: He was tall, dignified, of dark complexion, and
with polished manners, considered to be a man of moderation,
tolerant but very wary of new political theories. He was known
for his integrity and his strong Puritan faith.

VII

RHODE ISLAND

Step Hopkins

William Ellery

Stephen Hopkins

March 7, 1707 — July 13, 1785

BY THE TIME that great year of decision came upon our country, Benjamin Franklin and Stephen Hopkins were the oldest delegates in the Second Continental Congress. Both were practically self-taught; neither had had the opportunity of attending college. Both had represented their own colonies in the first assembly in this country, the Albany Congress of 1754. Consequently, both men had, by 1776, more experience in public affairs than any of the other fifty-four engaged in desperate consideration of the most serious problem that had yet faced the thirteen colonies — whether or not to insist upon independence.

Stephen Hopkins was born in Providence, Rhode Island, to William and Ruth Wilkinson Hopkins. His great-grandfather was Thomas H. Hopkins, who, about 1636, migrated from England to Providence, where he was assigned a lot in 1638. Stephen grew up as a farmer with little schooling. His mother taught him his first lessons, and his grandfather and uncle instructed him in elementary mathematics, for which he had a decided aptitude. Like several of his forebears, he became a surveyor and was much employed in establishing both private and public boundaries. This gave him a wide acquaintance throughout his colony.

Hopkins was only nineteen when he married Sarah Scott, descended from Rhode Island's first Quaker, Richard Scott. Three of their sons died at sea, a tragic but not unusual record for a seafaring New England family. After twenty-seven years of marriage, Mrs. Hopkins died and, two years later, Stephen married Mrs. Anne Smith. Although his mother was a Quaker, Hopkins now for the first time connected himself with the Society of Friends.

Until he was thirty-five, Hopkins worked at farming and land surveying. Then he moved into Providence and took up a mercantile business with his brother. But he had begun public life ten years earlier when, at twenty-five, he was chosen as a representative to the General Assembly. Devoted to the welfare of his fellow citizens and working with tact, energy, and care for the least detail, Hopkins had other offices thrust upon him. He was town clerk, moderator of town meetings, and at the age of twenty-nine was chosen to be one of the justices of the Court of Common Pleas for Providence County.

Like other Signers from the northern colonies, Stephen Hopkins sat on the bench without having had legal training. In 1751, he became Chief Justice of Rhode Island's Superior Court. Four years later, the same year in which he married for the second time, he was elected governor, an office in which he served nine terms.

A rivalry had developed by this time between two classes in Rhode Island: the rich and aristocratic citizens of Newport, and the farmers and mechanics of the northern part of the state. Newport and Providence became rival towns. Both were leading seaports, and Newport wished to remain the capital of the state. Hopkins championed Providence as the capital, Samuel Ward, wealthy landowner in Narragansett County, represented Newport. For over a decade a feud existed between these men and their followers, especially in the contests for the governorship. But the feud ended when both Ward and Hopkins withdrew in favor of Josias Lyndon. Years later, both Ward and Hopkins were delegates to the First Continental Congress and worked there together, so that if any personal antipathy had existed, it was no longer apparent. While Stephen Hopkins was engaged in commerce and had vessels that visited many foreign ports carrying exports and imports, Providence became a great commercial port, surpassing Newport.

Stephen Hopkins also owned tracts of land in Scituate and had interests in an iron foundry where cannon were cast and iron implements were made. But he never made a fortune because he spent too much time in public activities instead of in work for his own personal gain.

Hopkins first met Benjamin Franklin when both were attending the Albany Congress of 1754. Franklin was then urging a plan for colonial union, an idea which Hopkins also favored. After the Stamp Act of 1765, he became chairman of a committee to draft instructions to the Providence deputies in the General Assembly. He was Chief Justice when some Rhode Islanders, resisting British import duties, burned the British revenue schooner *Gaspée*. The Crown instructed its governor, Joseph Wanton, to arrest the men and have them sent to England for trial. The British plan was thwarted because Chief Justice Hopkins refused to apprehend any of the offenders "by his own order, nor suffer any Executive Officers in the Colony to do it."

In 1774, Stephen Hopkins was sent to Philadelphia as a delegate to the First Continental Congress. He was now sixty-seven, one of the oldest in that important assembly. Though a definite stand on independence for the colonies was avoided throughout that term, and many did not want to take such a bold and dangerous stand, the idea was in the air. People were talking about it. Hopkins of Rhode Island was a man with enough foresight to see, as he told members of that Congress, that "powder and ball will decide this question. The gun and bayonet alone will finish the contest in which we are engaged, and any of you who cannot bring your minds to this mode of adjusting this question had better retire in time."

After this straight talk, which Paul Revere must have heard as he was present in that first Congress, and after Hopkins's prophecy had been fulfilled in Lexington on the nineteenth of April in 1775, Hopkins was sent to the Second Continental Congress.

Here he was placed on the committee making plans for a navy, and on the committee for preparing the Articles of Confederation. As early as May 4, 1776, Rhode Island renounced its allegiance to King George III, and exactly two months from that day, Stephen Hopkins had the deep satisfaction of seeing a unanimous vote for national independence. All thirteen colonies were now arrayed against the king and war was on in earnest. In August, Hopkins signed the great document. But it was a difficult thing for him to do. We can see that his handwriting was shaky. He was now suffering from palsy and it was almost impossible for him to write.

The work that Hopkins did in connection with the Articles of Confederation was his last duty in Congress. Ill health compelled him to return home. During the first war years, he worked for independence in his own state as a member of the Rhode Island General Assembly.

He had never had the advantage of a systematic education, but Hopkins was an ardent reader and had cultivated literary and scientific tastes. Though books were rare, his grandfather had a small but choice library, which gave Hopkins the English classics to read. Since he had a real desire to learn and had made himself an educated man, he was naturally deeply interested in education and the establishment of schools. Active in founding Rhode Island College — now Brown University — Hopkins was its first chancellor, an office he held as long as he lived. He had helped found the *Providence Gazette and County Journal* in 1762 as a patriotic voice against the Tory *Newport Mercury*, or the *Weekly Advertiser*. He had contributed to its columns in the 1760's when unrest was growing, and his article on "The Rights of Colonies Examined" which appeared in 1764, was later issued as a pamphlet and reprinted throughout the colonies and in England. His desire to join the Philosophical Society of Newport as an out-of-town member, and his influence, in 1769, in having a telescope erected in Providence in order to observe the transit of Venus illustrates his wide interests. His public activities were equally varied. He was a "genial, entertaining Quaker, attractive alike to young and old."

This first citizen of Rhode Island passed away at the age of seventy-eight, not long after the final Treaty of Peace. He had lived to see his country free, independent, and at peace.

William Ellery

December 22, 1727 — February 15, 1820

IT IS BELIEVED that the great-grandfather of William Ellery came to America and settled in Gloucester, Massachusetts, sometime after the mid-1600's. His son Benjamin moved to Bristol, Rhode Island, and from there went on to Newport. These early Ellerys must have been successful and enlightened men, for Benjamin sent his son, another William, to Harvard, where he graduated in 1722. William returned from college to marry Elizabeth Almy and became the father of William, the Signer. The father held several public offices, himself directed the teaching of his son until he, too, was ready for Harvard. The younger William graduated there in 1742, only twenty years after his father!

William Ellery thus had all the formal education that the Quaker Signer of Rhode Island, Stephen Hopkins, had not been given. Yet he seems never to have achieved the wide popularity that Hopkins won, perhaps because he did not follow a single career and did not give so much of his time and effort to others. After leaving Harvard, he did not know quite what he wanted to do, since he was only fifteen. He first tried being a merchant, then served a period as a "naval officer" — that is, collector of customs — of his colony, and then, for two terms, was clerk of the General Assembly. But not until he was forty-three, when he took up the practice of law, did he find his real place and achieve success.

Three years after graduating, Ellery married Ann Remington of Cambridge. Thereafter until he was eighty, William Ellery made a yearly visit to Cambridge, so warm was his attachment to the scene of his college years and his first courtship. Ann died fourteen years after their marriage, and three years later the widower married his second cousin, Abigail Cary. It was not uncommon in those days for a woman to die young, worn out with child-bearing, and for the father to marry again to have help in raising his family. By these two wives, Ellery fathered seventeen children. Two of William Ellery's grandsons became authors: Richard Henry Dana, who wrote the American classic *Two Years Before the Mast* and William Ellery Channing, the nineteenth-century clergyman, writer, and philosopher, who counted Emerson, Hawthorne, and Thoreau among his friends.

Not until three years after his second marriage did William Ellery begin to practice law. By that time, he had served as clerk of the Court of Common Pleas. Perhaps it was this experience in the court room that turned his thoughts to a legal career.

As a lawyer he was so successful that his practice soon extended beyond the boundaries of the small colony in which he lived.

From the beginning of the colonists' dissatisfaction with Britain's mounting tyranny, Ellery was a patriot. He served on local committees organized to resist it, and upon the death of Rhode Island's congressman, Samuel Ward, was chosen to take his place in the Second Continental Congress. He took his seat in mid-May, 1776.

Soon after he arrived in that all-important assembly, Congress placed him on the Marine Committee, which dealt with naval and shipping problems. During the years he was in Congress he was on many other committees and took an active part in debates. In after years he used to like to tell about the signing of the Declaration of Independence: that he stood near the table and the secretary, Charles Thomas, because "I was determined to see how they all looked as they signed what might be their death warrant." He reported that all faces showed "undaunted resolution."

It is too bad that late in life Ellery requested his friends to preserve none of his correspondence; we might have had more intimate sidelights from him that could have brought some of those moments and men in Independence Hall into focus for us now, two hundred years after.

Only about four months after the signing, the British captured Newport and began a three-year occupation. In revenge for William Ellery's patriotism, they burned his house and destroyed his property. While all this was going on, Ellery, in Philadelphia, labored on committees: of the Treasury, for establishing expresses (mail routes), for providing relief for the war-wounded, and for army purchases. In 1779, he served on the committee for foreign relations; later, he worked on the committee for public accounts. In 1785, he was zealous in advocating the abolition of slavery in the new United States.

William Ellery was a round-faced, chunky and cheerful person, genial and kindly, well-blessed with friends, for he knew how to be a friend. As he moved into his nineties, an unusually old age for those times, he was also blessed in being free from, as he said, "sickness, pain and sorrow." Without glasses, he was reading Cicero — and in small print — sitting up in bed in his home in Newport when he passed away quietly as if going to sleep, the book still in his hand.

It was the fifteenth of February, 1820; the old Signer for Rhode Island was in his ninety-third year.

VIII

NEW HAMPSHIRE

Josiah Bartlett

Wm Whipple

Matthew Thornton

Josiah Bartlett

Josiah Bartlett

November 21, 1729 — May 19, 1795

IN PRE-REVOLUTIONARY TIMES, New Hampshire colony was sparsely settled. Having very little coastline, it had none of the first settlements like those that sprang up along the Atlantic seaboard where the ships came in. It is interesting, therefore, to see the difference in background and education of those Signers who represented the two colonies that did not touch salt water, or barely touched it (Vermont and New Hampshire), from those which naturally had a closer touch with the mother-land, where the first immigrants and much of their supplies came from. None of the three New Hampshire Signers was born in the colony.

The patriot Josiah Bartlett became a Chief Justice, Governor of New Hampshire, and a physician — all without either a law or medical degree. He was the son of Stephen and Mary Webster Bartlett, born in Amesbury, Essex County, Massachusetts. His early education was at an ordinary local school, the kind usually "kept" by a parson, but he had private tuition in Latin and Greek. At sixteen, when a modern American boy would still be in high school, he began to study medicine in the office of a relative, Dr. Ordway, who lived and practiced in the same town.

Under the doctor's guidance, young Josiah Bartlett read through such medical books as he could borrow in the libraries of his own and neighboring towns and observed what went on in Dr. Ordway's office. This was the only kind of clinical study and internship that was possible locally. In five years he was equipped, by the scientific standards of the period, to hang out his shingle. In 1750, when he was twenty-one, Dr. Bartlett began practice in Kingston, New Hampshire, where he was to live for the rest of his life.

In a short time he was "the Doctor" throughout the region and acquired a large practice. Interested in experiments, he discovered a successful treatment for an obscure but common disease by the use of Peruvian bark; and eventually he came to reject accepted treatments of some other diseases to introduce his own newer ones.

When he was twenty-five, Bartlett married his cousin, Mary Bartlett, of Newton, New Hampshire. They had twelve children. Three of his sons and seven of his grandsons became doctors.

Dr. Josiah Bartlett was also much interested in public affairs. Having earned a reputation for integrity and intelligence, his fellow townsmen chose him, the year after he was married, to represent Kingston in the Provincial Assembly of 1765, and continued to re-elect him until the beginning of the war. This was his introduction into public life.

For eight years, Bartlett had been colonel of a regiment of colonial militia. But by 1774 he was known to be a patriot, and the royal governor dismissed him. He was elected to the first Provincial Congress which, in turn, chose him as one of the New Hampshire delegates to the First Continental Congress in Philadelphia.

This last honor, Josiah Bartlett had to decline because his house had recently burned down, set on fire, as the doctor believed, by spiteful Tories. He was chosen again for the Second Continental Congress in 1775, accepted, and was the first man to vote in favor of the adoption of the resolution for independence.

Bartlett was a tall man, described as having a "fine" figure. His manner was affable though dignified. Very particular about his dress, he wore his auburn hair in the queue that was the custom of the day and wore short knee breeches with long silk hose and silver buckled shoes.

Bartlett was re-elected to Congress for 1777, but he was too exhausted by his labors in Congress the year before to serve. He had been on many committees, serving constantly without a break and taking great pains, so that he had become one of the most influential members in shaping legislation. The difficulty of travel between New Hampshire and Philadelphia was also exhausting. Again in Congress in 1778, he was the first to vote for the proposed Articles of Federation and Perpetual Union. He declined re-election the following year, whereupon his state appointed the doctor Chief Justice of its Court of Common Pleas.

He was promoted Associate Justice of the Superior Court in 1782, and Chief Justice six years later. His service on the bench ended in 1790.

It seems strange to us today to think of a layman elevated to the bench. But this occurred many times in some sections of our new country. Though no lawyer, Bartlett had been in close association with important lawyers while engaged in legislative work for fifteen years. Some of the ablest attorneys have expressed the opinion that justice had never been better administered in New Hampshire than when the judges knew very little law.

Josiah Bartlett was elected in 1790 to the highest office in his state when he became the chief executive. Ill health caused him to retire at the end of his term as New Hampshire's first governor, and it was not long until he died at his home in Kingston on May 19, 1795.

William Whipple

January 14, 1730 — November 10, 1785

WILLIAM WHIPPLE was a descendant of Matthew Whipple, who had immigrated to America from Essex County, England, at a date which is not quite certain but was earlier than 1638. The Signer was born at Kittery, Maine, the son of Captain William and Mary Cutt Whipple, in the house that had been the home of his great-grandfather on his mother's side. After some years of attending local schools, William Whipple, like many other New England boys of the eighteenth and nineteenth centuries, went away to sea while still in his early teens.

When he was about twenty-one, he became master of a sailing vessel, making many voyages in the European, West Indian, and African trade. Whipple was so successful that after about ten years he had saved up a respectable fortune and at twenty-nine gave up the rigors of life at sea and formed a partnership in a mercantile business with his brother Joseph in Portsmouth, New Hampshire. There he married his cousin, Catherine Moffatt, and went to live in her father's house, later designated as Number 70 Market Street. It is said to be the first three-storey house built in New Hampshire.

Sailors' lives make them independent, and in this sea-side town revolutionary ideas sprouted early. Captain Whipple took part in the resulting disputes, in favor of the colonists. As controversy became heated in the early 1770's, he decided to give up business and enter public life.

Captain Whipple was an immediate success as a public man. His fellow townsmen, placing the highest confidence in his integrity and patriotism, elected him to one office after another. Whipple was chosen to represent Portsmouth in the Provincial Congress in 1775; he was made a member of the council in 1776 when New Hampshire assumed its own form of government, with a House of Representatives and a Council of twelve; and he was also on the Committee of Safety and closely associated with the Portsmouth patriots. It was only another step onward when he was elected to the Second Continental Congress in Philadelphia.

William Whipple arrived in Philadelphia to attend Congress on February 29, 1776. In these first months, when many of the delegates were still hoping for better treatment after their pleas to George III, Whipple was already sure that only an American success in the field could achieve freedom. He did not think victory could come from diplomatic talk abroad. He wanted "spirited measures" against the Loyalists and speculators. He urged heavy taxation in order to spread the burden of war evenly on all the people. While serving on committees, Whipple observed with disgust a lack of national spirit in some places. The greed and selfishness of political life — which shows up in the inefficient public service which we see from time to time in any country — was not wholly absent then, and Whipple, coming in contact with it during his official work, expressed his feelings strongly in his letters. He was a firm and fearless congressman. Re-elected three times, Whipple remained in Congress until 1779, except for periods when he was on active military service.

Captain Whipple, erstwhile commander of a sailing ship, now became a soldier and, as General Whipple, was one of the few

Signers who saw active service in the Revolution. As brigadier general commanding the first of New Hampshire's two brigades of militia, he took part in the expedition against the British General Burgoyne, which resulted in a decisive defeat for the British and the great American victory which really made possible the French alliance. Burgoyne, who had at first viewed the men of New Hampshire and Green Mountains with contempt, was obliged to suffer a humiliating surrender after the battles of Stillwater and Saratoga, in which the New Hampshire troops won a large share of the honor due to the American army.

During the last years of the war, Whipple was active in the affairs of his state and he, like several other Signers, became an Associate Justice of the Superior Court, without any legal training.

When he was about fifty-two he began to be afflicted with a heart condition which was not understood by medical men in those days. He continued to ride horseback on his circuits for the court, though he often fainted and fell from his horse. He died while on circuit on November 10, 1785, at the age of fifty-five.

Matthew Thornton

c. 1714 — June 24, 1803

THE THORNTONS were of English origin, though Matthew Thornton was one of the three Signers who were born in Ireland. Over the years, religious persecution had driven the Presbyterian Thorntons from one country to another. They emigrated first from England to Scotland; then, in order to escape the persecutions in Scotland under Charles I, they crossed to Ireland. Their descendants moved on to America, where they formed part of the group of immigrants known as the Scotch-Irish. This emigration began in 1717. On August 4, 1718, five small ships arrived in Boston with about one hundred twenty families, among whom was the family of James Thornton, including his small son, Matthew.

In the autumn, the Thorntons moved on again, presumably because they had nowhere to live, to Falmouth, Maine (now Portland). Here they spent an uncomfortable first winter still aboard the ship that had brought them. From the ship they moved at last to Worcester, Massachusetts, where Matthew went to school. Then, deciding to make medicine and surgery his profession, he studied under a locally eminent physician, Thomas Green of Leicester, a neighboring town.

Puritan religious intolerance drove the Presbyterian Thorntons out of Worcester, too. About a century later, the American humorist, Artemus Ward, described the Puritans as "that band of religious patriots who fled from the land of persecution to the land of freedom where they could not only enjoy their own religion but prevent every other man from enjoying his." And that was exactly the experience the Thornton family had.

Twelve years after arriving in this country, James Thornton had been able to buy a parcel of land in Worcester, but he felt so much discrimination that after ten years he sold it and moved on north with most of the Scotch-Irish families, to Pelham. His medical son, Dr. Matthew Thornton, however, decided to go still farther north and settle in the older and more thriving settlement of Londonderry, New Hampshire, where he soon established a large and profitable practice.

In 1745, during King George's War, a phase of the French and Indian War, Dr. Thornton accompanied the military expedition against the French Fort Louisburg, on Cape Breton Island. Resuming practice upon his return, he continued to be so successful that he was able to acquire a considerable estate. He bought his father's one hundred seventy acres at Pelham and three years later bought one hundred fifty acres more. Even after all this, he still continued to put money in land.

Dr. Thornton's first appearance in public affairs came in 1758, when he represented the town of Londonderry in the Provincial Legislature, serving for four years. Then he held many important offices. He was commissioned by the royal government as colonel of the Londonderry regiment of militia; became a selectman of the town, then moderator of its town meetings as the troubles with England grew worse through the early 1770's; and finally served as President of the Provincial Congress several times. In an address in 1760 before the royal governor, he expressed his desire for "fresh zeal for His Majesty's service." But within a few years he had to change his mind. In 1775, he denounced "the unconstitutional and tyrannical acts of the British Parliament." He had been revolted by the Stamp Act and joined the patriot agitators in the hue and cry which followed its enactment into law. After this, he found himself at the front of the local revolutionary party. As chairman of the local Committee of Safety and president of the Fourth Provincial Congress, Thornton inspired the people's confidence in him by his public addresses.

Many arduous duties were heaped upon him. He wrote his Committee of Safety in October, 1775, that he had not been able to take his clothes off for ten nights! After Christmas, he was appointed on the committee to draw up a plan for the government of the colony during its contest with Great Britain. The committee's report, made on January 5, 1776, was adopted the very same day. This swift action was taken without recurrence to the people's vote, so that it was "a stretch of power." But the people were satisfied, and the committee's report became a kind of constitution for New Hampshire until 1783. It was the first written constitution adopted by any of the American states.

Rather late in life, at the age of forty-eight, Thornton married Hannah Jack, of Chester, New Hampshire, who was only eighteen, and reported to be a great beauty. She, too, was of Scottish ancestry.

On the same day that New Hampshire's constitution was adopted, Dr. Thornton was elected Speaker of the House of Representatives. Within a week, he was also chosen Associate Justice of the Superior Court. After the New Hampshire House of Representatives reassembled on September 12, 1776, Dr. Thornton was chosen as delegate to the Second Continental Congress in Philadelphia. The day after he arrived, Thornton presented his credentials to Congress and signed the Declaration on November 4. He was the last to sign that year, and was one of the Signers who had not been in Congress to hear Lee's June resolution, nor the early July debates on the Declaration.

Thornton served only part of a year in Congress. Though he was appointed as delegate for 1777, he was unable to serve; for soon after he arrived in Philadelphia, he was inoculated for smallpox, which left him with such weak eyes that he was unable to work for a while. Later, he devoted his time to the affairs of his new state.

During his last years, he wrote political essays for the newspapers. His wife died in 1786, and his son the next year. These griefs and his own infirmities caused him to retire from public life.

While visiting his daughter in Newburyport, Massachusetts, in 1803, he passed away at the age of eighty-nine.

Judge Thornton was over six feet tall and of dark complexion. His manners were plain and unassuming. He was a sociable and communicative man, with a tenacious memory and a good sense of humor. John Adams wrote in a letter: "We have from New Hampshire a Colonel Thornton, a physician by profession, a man of humor. He has a large budget of droll stories with which he entertains company perpetually."

IX

MARYLAND

Charles Carroll of Carrollton

Thos. Stone

Wm Paca

Samuel Chase

Charles Carroll
of Carrollton

Charles Carroll of Carrollton

September 19, 1737 — November 14, 1832

THERE WERE SO MANY Carrolls, and even Charles Carrolls, among his relations in Maryland that the Charles Carroll who signed the Declaration of Independence habitually called himself Charles Carroll of Carrollton. His grandfather, descended from an old and noble Irish family, came to Maryland in the autumn of 1688 as attorney-general of the province. The Carroll family came to Maryland because they were Catholics who had suffered through England's religious struggles since Henry VIII's time.

Lord Baltimore, a Catholic, had founded a colony in Maryland about 1634, as a haven, not only for his fellow-Catholics but also for members of other persecuted sects — Puritans (who were being persecuted in Virginia), Presbyterians, Anabaptists, and others. Protestants then were attracted to this lovely province, and more and more came to live there. But by the time the attorney-general's son, Charles Carroll of Annapolis, was a man, Maryland's Protestants had brought their fear and hatred of the politics of the Roman Catholic Church with them and had begun a discrimination that infuriated the second Carroll, father of the Signer.

Incredible and ridiculous as it seems to us, people who had left the old country to seek religious freedom for themselves denied it to others. By the 1700's, Catholics in Maryland could neither vote nor hold public office. Catholic lawyers were not permitted to practice. Catholics could not be teachers of young children.

The Carrolls had, however, one commodity that was a great help to them, and that was money. The first American Carroll, who had been given large tracts of land, had become a successful planter. He had also had a prosperous legal practice (before discrimination became serious), had kept a store in Annapolis, and had eventually left a fortune to his son. This second Carroll was just as ambitious, but as a Catholic he was now not allowed to practice law. Instead, since he was very rich, he put his money to work for him by loaning it to reliable people on sound security and at good interest. By the time he married his beautiful cousin Elizabeth Brooke, they were the wealthiest people in Maryland, perhaps in all the colonies.

The third Charles Carroll, their only child, inherited all this wealth and used it wisely. The boy grew up in what must have been an ideal early-American environment, at the country estate of his father and grandfather, and at the town house in Annapolis. His mother taught him until he was about nine. Then he was sent to Bohemia Manor Academy, a Catholic school conducted — sub rosa — by the Society of Jesus. His cousin, "Jacky" Carroll, was there with him. But not for long. The two were soon sent to the Collège de St. Omer in French Flanders where young Charles's father had studied. The parents accepted the fact that, in order to give their son the best education, they would have to send him three thousand miles away, and that they would be separated for about fifteen years. His father asked him to write home "at least twice a year."

Charles was a good student, preferring Latin and "the maps" to "little figures" or arithmetic. He also studied dancing and, probably, fencing. After five and a half years, he studied at a Jesuit College in Rheims for a year, and then went to Paris to the Collège de Louis-le-Grand. By this time he and his cousin were no longer together, as Jacky had decided to become a priest. After about eight years' separation, Charles's father came to France and saw his son as a young adult. From Paris, Charles went to Bourges to study law, and after that he lived in London for about six years, studying law in the Temple. All this without any idea of ever practicing law. Born with a "silver spoon in his mouth," Charles Carroll never needed funds.

After sixteen years' education, he came home to Maryland in February, 1765, the Stamp Act year. His mother had said goodbye to a ten- or eleven-year-old boy. She saw him next as a man of twenty-seven or twenty-eight. His father presented his son with a ten-thousand-acre piece of land in Frederick County, at the mouth of the Monocacy river, which became the estate known as Carrollton Manor.

As a boy, Charles Carroll of Carrollton had been thin and delicate. Now a man, he was still thin, frail-looking, and small of stature, and he was always subject to chills and fevers. But he had a good figure, grace of movement, and polished, attractive manners. He made good company in the taverns, where the townsmen collected to exchange opinions on the political problems of the time. He made such good company, indeed, that he was soon invited to join the Hominy Club, to which his good friends, Samuel Chase and William Paca, and the young portrait painter Charles Wilson Peale already belonged.

Young Carroll, a new land-owner, was soon a staunch Marylander. Incensed by the Stamp Act, he described American feelings about it in a letter to a friend in London and, as early as 1767, was prophesying armed rebellion in other letters to friends across the sea.

It must have been a lovely day in Annapolis on June 5, 1768, when thirty-one-year-old Charles Carroll married his cousin Mary Darnall. She loved social affairs, and the young couple entertained constantly in their beautiful, hospitable home.

He took on the management of the family's business affairs, including the oversight and care of the vast plantations, the slaves, the sale of the tobacco they grew, the many accounts of loans and mortgages. For Carroll of Carrollton was as much of a money-maker as his father and grandfather before him.

Then came the troubled years of the 1770's. In the first November of the decade that saw the birth of a new nation, Maryland's royal governor raised the salaries for government officials. This meant more taxation of Americans without giving the taxpayers, from whom the money came, any voice in the matter.

A Tory lawyer named Daniel Dulany, a contentious man who had no sympathy at all for the patriots' feelings, began writing arguments supporting the royal governor's views on British taxation in the form of dialogues and printing them in the *Maryland Gazette*. In these dialogues, he called the first speaker, the man who posed the questions, "First Citizen." The man who answered, expressing Dulany's own views, was "Second Citizen." A month passed and still no one in the Patriot party had answered. Then articles began to appear over the signature "First Citizen," one of the names Dulany himself had used. In these, the new and different "First Citizen" took the patriots' view, attacking Dulany's statements. These articles continued in the form of letters between "First Citizen," on one side, and Dulany, who now signed himself "Antilon."

Readers of the *Gazette* were highly entertained by this battle in print, and the town buzzed with guesses as to the identity of "First Citizen." But in the clubs and taverns where he was so well known, his fellow members soon knew their man. The resulting publicity caused Charles Carroll of Carrollton to be placed on one important public committee after another.

He was now in public life: a member of the Annapolis Committee of Correspondence; of the first Maryland Convention; of the Provincial Committee of Correspondence; and the Committee of Safety. He was also teaching the province of Maryland that a Catholic could have some good ideas and might be of use to his country. He had become, in truth, the First Citizen of his region.

His father had never been able to hide the chip he carried upon his shoulder. He resented the prejudice against Catholics. He had a temper and it was galling to him that, as a Catholic, he could not vote, especially as he had always wanted to be in public life himself. His son, on the other hand, was able to appear to overlook all this. He was not looking for offense, neither was he ambitious for public office. He had an easy, delightful manner, charmed others by being a good listener, and delivered himself of positive ideas that were helpful.

By the middle of 1773, the Patriot party won a landslide victory in the local election. Carroll was publicly thanked by an open letter printed in the *Gazette*, for his "manly and spirited opposition to the arbitrary attempt of government to establish the fees of office by proclamation."

The first time Carroll was asked to be a delegate to the First Continental Congress, he refused. Though Marylanders did not admire Carroll's religion any more than they ever had, they now admired the man himself and felt that no one else could speak more ably and creditably for Maryland than he. But Carroll knew that, even if Marylanders trusted him to keep his religion in proper relation to other matters, delegates from other provinces would not feel that way. He would still have to convince them that a man's religion was his own affair. But he was too valuable a man to be left behind, and when Maryland's first congressmen set out for Philadelphia, Carroll of Carrollton went along as an unofficial member of the Maryland delegation.

The delegates told him everything that went on, and he gave them advice. He did not seem to mind this peculiar position; he was glad to serve his province even if others got the credit. But early in 1776, Congress was faced with a problem to which Maryland's "First Citizen" seemed to be the perfect answer. Hoping for an alliance with Canada, they sent a diplomatic mission consisting of Benjamin Franklin, Samuel Chase, and Charles Carroll of Carrollton. Carroll, they felt, was the ideal man to talk to the Catholic French Canadians for, of course, Carroll could speak French perfectly. He was asked to persuade his cousin, now a Jesuit priest, to accompany the mission.

This was the first American diplomatic mission to another country, and it failed. Canada preferred to remain with Mother England. But Carroll inspected forts along the way, thereby gaining military intelligence that was later valuable to Congress and to General Washington.

Returning to Philadelphia in June, Carroll was cheered to learn that Richard Henry Lee of Virginia had placed his resolution for independence before Congress. Later that month he was at the provincial convention, meeting in Annapolis, in which the important business was Maryland's decision whether to authorize her delegates in Philadelphia to vote for independence along with the other colonies. Carroll of Carrollton was the man principally instrumental in obtaining Maryland's vote for liberty.

On July Fourth, Maryland chose new delegates to Congress, and Carroll was again elected. This time he agreed to accept. Feeling that public service was a duty, and realizing that America must seek French aid, he knew he could be of special help. With the Maryland Convention still in session, it was July 18 before Carroll took his seat in Congress. He missed the early July excitement and discussions but, after all, he had wanted independence all along. He was on hand to sign the Declaration.

Charles Carroll was now a very busy man. His father was in his seventies and the care of the vast Carroll fortune and plantations fell upon the son. This in itself was a full-time job. But Carroll of Carrollton was also a leading figure in the Maryland Assembly; he was on the Board of War; he helped to draw up the Maryland Constitution; he was elected to Maryland's first Senate. But he opposed the confiscation of Tory property, deeming such action as tyrannical as the British measures Americans were fighting to be rid of.

Carroll was a stout supporter of General Washington when armchair critics raised their complaints. He was one of the committee that went to Valley Forge to investigate the sorry situation there.

Carroll was not sent on the mission to France, where he would have been of special value. Instead, the troublemaker, Arthur Lee, wanted to go, worked hard to secure the appointment, and became a member along with Dr. Franklin and Silas Deane. The French alliance was successfully consummated, without Carroll's help, in February, 1778. Carroll had already rendered very special service in Congress, even though it was not the service he had had in mind when he accepted. But when, that winter, he was asked to be President of Congress, he declined.

After the war, he represented his state in the first Federal Congress in 1789, and remained until he resigned in 1792. Sometimes he declined offers because of his health. He was always careful of his physical condition. Perhaps he had had this dinned into him when he was a puny child. He ended his political career in 1800 when he left the Maryland Senate to devote his time to the development of his estate, which had grown to gigantic proportions. He now owned between seventy thousand and eighty thousand acres of land in Maryland, Pennsylvania, and New York.

The years rolled on. One by one the Signers were dropping off. Carroll's father died; his wife died; and his son, Charles Carroll IV passed away. There was another war with England — the War of 1812 — to which Carroll was opposed, though there was nothing he could do about that. The whole country was growing and changing, and Carroll lived to see many of the changes. He was a member of the Potomac Company, which contemplated a water route to Ohio and the west; he was a member, too, of its successor, the Chesapeake and Ohio Canal Company, organized in 1823. He was on the first board of directors of the Baltimore and Ohio Railroad and laid its cornerstone amid respectful applause, on July 4, 1828, at the age of ninety-one. He saw three of the men he had known long ago in the Independence Congress become Presidents of the new nation — George Washington, John Adams, Thomas Jefferson. He went on living after they had all passed away. The time came when Carroll of Carrollton, who had always been the puny child, the small, frail man, became the sole surviving Signer!

As such, he became one of the sights to see. People made pilgrimages to Bunker Hill outside Boston, to Independence Hall in Philadelphia, and those who could went on to see the last Signer in Baltimore, just as they visited Fort McHenry. Here was a man in the flesh, who had become a national legend.

In his latter years, Carroll spent the winter months with his elder daughter Mary, who had married Richard Caton. Carroll had built a house in Baltimore for them when they were married.

Josiah Quincy, relative to John Adams, recorded visits he made in 1826: "I paid two visits to Charles Carroll (the signer of the Declaration of Independence), and dined with him . . . at Mr. Caton's, where the service, though the most elegant I had ever seen, in no wise eclipsed the conversation. . . . Old Mr. Carroll, courtly in manners and bright in mind, was the life of the party. He was then in his ninetieth year, but carried himself as if thirty years younger than his contemporary, John Adams. I have never seen an old man so absolutely unconscious of his age." When Mr. Quincy left the drawing-room, which was on the second floor, the old man jumped up and ran downstairs to open the front door. "Aghast at this unexpected proceeding," wrote Mr. Quincy, "I began to murmur my regrets and mortification in causing him the exertion."

"'Exertion!' exclaimed Mr. Carroll, 'Why, what do you take me for? I have ridden sixteen miles on horseback this morning and am good for as much more this afternoon.'"

On into his nineties, Carroll of Carrollton took his daily constitutional on horseback. He thought it was good for him, and it probably was.

He could not be idle. He set regular hours for his time, mapping out courses of reading on which he took notes. He taught French to his great-grandchildren. He still kept the "plantation books," which included a record of all the slaves on his large estates. He took care of his own charities, and of course, because he was the wealthiest man in the country, his mail was flooded with begging letters. Even so, there is no record of his having given the vast sums to the Revolutionary War program that Robert Morris did. And here it might be mentioned that his father, Charles Carroll of Alexandria, had had the reputation of being very close with his money, never mixing business with charity. But then, in his day, when Catholics were so restricted in Maryland, he realized that the only way he could overcome religious prejudice in any degree was to possess himself of great wealth. And perhaps this was just what enabled his son, equipped by that wealth and with an excellent education, to have leisure for public affairs, and to accomplish what he did.

In the Spring of 1832, one of his callers was amazed to find the ninety-four-year-old Mr. Carroll still riding horseback. They rode around Baltimore together. But the old man had aged greatly in the last two years. By the time of his ninety-fifth birthday, in September, he was really ill — just too weak and old to go on living. He weighed under a hundred pounds. But even yet he did not want to stay in bed, reclining instead on an easy-chair or upon a couch.

Two months later, he passed away during the night.

After November 14, 1832, none of the Signers of the Declaration of Independence was left. Now they all belonged to history.

Thomas Stone

1743 — October 5, 1787

THOMAS STONE'S GREAT-GREAT-GRANDFATHER, William Stone, who came to America from Northamptonshire, England, landed in

Maryland in 1628, only a few years after the Mayflower adventurers reached Plymouth in 1620. He became Maryland's third "Proprietary Governor," that is, the governor representing Lord Baltimore, the proprietor who actually owned the colony, which had been given to him by the king.

His descendant, Thomas, the Signer, was born at Poynton Manor, Charles County, Maryland, in 1743, the eldest son of David and Elizabeth Jennifer Stone. He was taught by a Scottish school-master before he went to Annapolis to study law in the office of Thomas Johnson. Admitted to the bar in 1764, he began to practice in Frederick, Maryland.

Four years later he married Margaret Brown, who brought him a fine dowry of £1000, an enormous sum in those days and more than many newlyweds have today. The young pair bought land in Charles County near Port Tobacco and built a beautiful house, a stately dwelling that today is still considered one of the finest examples of colonial architecture in Maryland. They were settled and living in it about 1771.

When trouble with England came, Stone's sympathies were with the colonists, though he favored a mild course. Elected to Congress, he took his seat in mid-May of 1775. Thomas Stone seldom spoke in Congress, and as few of his letters remain, he is the least known nowadays of the Maryland Signers. His most important work in Congress was his service on the committee that later framed the Articles of Confederation. He voted for Independence and signed the Declaration when he was only thirty-three. He hated the thought of war, however, and was hoping, as late as September, 1776, that the Americans could still treat with Admiral Lord Howe for peace. But it was too late then to stop the war that had already begun a year and a half earlier at Lexington and Concord.

In 1783, Stone was again elected to Congress and, toward the end of this season, served as chairman, but he declined re-election thereafter and returned to his law practice. Later, when elected to the Constitutional Convention in Philadelphia, he declined because his wife was ill and he would not leave her. When she died in June, 1787, Stone was overwhelmed with grief.

He gave up his work and decided to take a trip to England, but he never got there. He was waiting in Alexandria for a ship when he died, at the age of forty-four, four months after he had lost his wife.

William Paca

October 31, 1740 — October 13, 1799

LITTLE IS KNOWN of the forebears of Signer William Paca, though the name appears in America as early as the latter 1600's and may perhaps be Italian. The family were already prosperous planters when William was born to John and Elizabeth Smith Paca on their plantation near Abingdon, Harford County, Maryland. He was given sound early schooling, probably by tutors, including a good grounding in the classical languages, before he was sent to the College of Philadelphia at the age of fifteen. By the time he was nineteen, he had received an M.A. degree and went to Annapolis to study law in the office of Stephen Bordley.

Annapolis was Maryland's chief city in those days, fashionable and entertaining. Here Paca met two other future Signers, then also apprentices in the law. Samuel Chase, a year younger than he, was reading law in the office of Hammond and Hall; and Thomas Stone, three years younger, came to Annapolis to read law in the office of Thomas Johnson. All three of these young lawyers were to be chosen as Maryland's delegates to the Congress at Philadelphia and would sign the Declaration of Independence.

Before seeking admission to the bar, William Paca went to London to complete his legal training at the Inner Temple. Then, after some foreign travel, he came home and married Mary Chew, daughter of wealthy Samuel Chew of Annapolis.

In the next few years, he earned a reputation as a lawyer and, five years after he was married, entered public life as a member of the Provincial Legislature.

With Samuel Chase, Paca held the view that the royal governor's proclamation regulating the fees of civil officers should be recalled. In this, they thought, the king's representative was going too far. Proclamations such as this were becoming more frequent and were antagonizing the freedom-loving colonists. When a poll tax was arbitrarily to be collected from all Marylanders for the support of the clergy of the Church of England only, William Paca led the opposition. After all, the very first people to come to America left England to get away from that kind of interference in their personal affairs. And it was obviously wrong to tax all voters for the benefit of one religious denomination only.

It was during this controversy that Paca, Chase, and Thomas Johnson wrote an article in reply to one signed by the Tories Daniel Dulany and James Holliday defending the tax. This was reprinted in London, and of course brought the names of Paca and the other two protesting Whigs into prominence. Paca became the local leader of the patriot cause, as the Revolution came to a boil in the 1770's.

While serving on the Maryland Committee of Correspondence, he was elected to the First Continental Congress in June, 1774. After his sojourn in Philadelphia, he was back in Annapolis in the autumn, serving as one of the city's representatives in the Provincial Congress. Also elected to the Second Continental Congress, he remained a delegate until 1779.

In Congress, William Paca was numbered among the quiet ones. Dr. Benjamin Rush called him "a good tempered worthy man, with a sound understanding which he was too indolent to exercise, and hence his reputation in public life was less than his talents." But Rush added, "He was beloved and respected by all who knew him, and considered at all times as a sincere patriot and honest man."

After the war started, William Paca, as a member of the Maryland Council of Safety, spent several thousand dollars of his own money outfitting troops. He was also a member of the convention that framed a constitution for his new state and was elected one of the first of Maryland's state senators when the new state government was established.

In 1777 he married again, his first wife having died in 1774. But his second wife, Anne Harrison of Philadelphia, was to live only three years longer. She saw her husband appointed Chief Justice of the Court of Appeals in Admiralty and Prize Cases; but she did not live to see him elected Maryland's third governor. Unanimously re-elected twice, he finished his last term in 1785. As governor, he paid much attention to the welfare of soldiers returning from the war.

In 1789, George Washington appointed Paca Federal District Judge, but this judicial service was short, for the next year, at the age of fifty, he died at "Wye Hall," his country estate in Talbot County.

Samuel Chase

Samuel Chase

April 17, 1741 — June 19, 1811

THE REVEREND THOMAS CHASE, father of Samuel, the Signer, came to America from England. His wife did not live long after the birth of their son in Somerset County, Maryland, and he moved to Baltimore to become the rector of St. Paul's Church. A classical scholar himself, he took charge of his son's education until the boy, at eighteen, went to Annapolis to study law. Two years later, Samuel Chase was admitted to practice.

He was twenty-one when he married Anne Baldwin of Annapolis, and twenty-three when, elected to the Maryland Assembly, he began his public career of twenty years' service to Maryland.

From the beginning, Samuel Chase was opposed to the irritating measures of the royal governor and, as the turbulent 1760's wore on, this young patriot was always an active leader in insurrection. After he had taken part in a demonstration against the Stamp Act, the mayor and aldermen of Annapolis denounced him as a "busy, restless incendiary, a ringleader of mobs" and "an inflaming son of discord." Chase replied that his critics were "despicable tools of power," and pointed out that what they called "mobs" were actually "men of reputation and merit."

By the time he was thirty-three, each colony had organized its Committee of Correspondence. Samuel Chase was on the Maryland committee and was sent as a delegate to the First Continental Congress. Throughout the next year or so, the busy lawyer was also serving on the Council of Safety, was a member of the Maryland Convention, and attended the Second Continental Congress in Philadelphia, where he urged a total embargo on trade with Great Britain.

In the cold February of 1776, he was appointed, with Benjamin Franklin and Charles Carroll, to go to Canada to ask for Canadian support for the colonies. When the Canadians declined, Chase returned to carry on in Maryland a vigorous agitation that was badly needed, because Maryland, like other middle colonies, was undecided. As a result of Chase's campaign, Maryland rescinded previous instructions to the delegates and at last advised them to vote for independence. Vastly relieved, though still anxious, Samuel Chase rode one hundred fifty miles in two days to get to Philadelphia in time for the final vote.

On the morning of July 1, thanks to Chase's efforts, the unanimous vote of Maryland's Convention was read before Congress. Busy as a hive of bees, Congress prepared for the final vote to make the United States of America one nation of its own.

A few days later, in a letter to John Adams, Samuel Chase wrote, "Oppression, Inhumanity and Perfidy have compelled Us to it," and asked: "How shall I transmit to posterity that I gave my consent?"

His chance came on August 2 when the Declaration had been engrossed and was ready for signatures. Seeing how strongly he felt, he must have been a happy man when he wrote down his name for posterity. He was then thirty-five and he had been working for this moment for over ten years.

Like Washington, Chase was a very tall man, over six feet tall and large in proportion. His appearance was striking, and his broad face was ruddy — so much so that some of his colleagues in the Maryland bar called him "Bacon face." We can just imagine how red he became when he was condemning British oppression.

This ardent patriot was reappointed to the Congress for two more years. He served on numerous committees, perhaps the most important of these being the one consisting of himself, Richard Henry Lee, and Gouverneur Morris, to prepare a paper discrediting British peace proposals in 1778. This document is supposed to have been largely Chase's work.

When intrigues against General Washington flared up in Congress, Samuel Chase strongly and steadfastly opposed them, and Washington always remembered this.

Maryland sent Chase to England in 1783 to recover, from two fugitive Loyalists, bank stock that had belonged to the state when it was a Crown colony. Chase started suit in the British Court of Chancery, which has always had a reputation for prolonged delays. The case dragged on and on for years, but it was ultimately settled in Maryland's favor — not by Chase himself but by William Pinckney, whom Chase had encouraged to study law and taken into his own office as a student. While he was in London, Chase met the English statesmen William Pitt, Charles Fox, and Edmund Burke, Whigs who had done their best for America before the Revolution.

Toward the end of the war, his friends urged him to move to Baltimore, where he eventually became Chief Judge of the Criminal Court and later Chief Judge of the General Court. In 1795, President George Washington received a letter from his friend Joseph McHenry, suggesting Chase for Federal office. Washington intended to appoint him attorney general, but in January, 1796, nominated him instead to the United States Supreme Court. Chase's judicial opinions while on the Supreme Court bench showed his intellectual caliber, and many of them are cited to this day. His performance on the bench was notable.

It is the more astonishing, then, to learn that his political opponents, led by John Randolph of Virginia, managed to secure Chase's impeachment. But Chase was acquitted, resumed his seat, and remained until his death. It is remarkable that Thomas Jefferson in part instigated the charge against his fellow Signer.

Samuel Chase's forceful manner of speaking earned him the title of the "Demosthenes of Maryland." Of the four Maryland Signers, it was he who was most instrumental in bringing about the unanimity of Maryland's vote on independence in those first July days of 1776. Dr. Rush noted that Samuel Chase "rendered great services to his country by awakening and directing the public spirit of his native state in the first years of the Revolution."

As Samuel Chase grew older and as his thick hair became white, one man thought he was the living image of Dr. Samuel Johnson, "in person, in manners, in unwieldy strength, in severity of reproof, in real tenderness of heart, and above all in intellect."

The years passed on, and the old judge began to suffer from gout. Ill health prevented him from serving on the bench during the 1806 term, and no court was held at all the year of his death, 1811, when he was seventy.

X

DELAWARE

Casar Rodney

Tho M:Kean

Geo Read

Caesar Rodney

[signature: Caesar Rodney]

October 7, 1728 — June 26, 1784

WILLIAM RODNEY, GRANDFATHER OF THE SIGNER, came to America about 1681 and settled in Kent County on the beautiful Delaware River. Here, during his lifetime, he built up a considerable estate, which was inherited by his son Caesar.

Caesar Rodney married a daughter of the Reverend Thomas Crawford, who had been the first missionary sent to Dover, Delaware, by the Society for the Propagation of the Gospel in Foreign Parts. This pair had eight children. The eldest was the second Caesar Rodney, who was to play a dramatic part in his colony's vote for independence.

Signer Rodney was born on his father's farm near Dover, Delaware. Since theirs was a cultivated home, his parents no doubt taught him his first lessons and perhaps sent him to the local parson's school, but there is no record of his having done any formal advanced study. Since his father died when the boy was only seventeen, Caesar had to be placed under the guardianship of Nicholas Ridgely, the clerk of the peace of Kent County. As the eldest child, he is supposed to have remained at home, helping his mother manage the plantation.

The young man's guardian seems to have led him into public life, which began with his being commissioned high sheriff of Kent County in 1755 when he was only twenty-two. During the next few years, he served his county as register of wills, recorder of deeds, clerk of the orphan's court, clerk of the peace, and justice of the peace. He was thirty when he was elected for the first time as delegate from Kent County to the colonial legislature at New Castle, and he served continuously — with the exception of the assembly of 1771 — for fifteen years. During four of those years he was speaker, and he held that post until the end of colonial government under the Crown in 1776.

Rodney was chosen representative of Kent County to the Stamp Act Congress, together with Thomas McKean, another of Delaware's Signers. George Read, Delaware's third Signer, was designated, along with Rodney and McKean, to form a Committee of Correspondence and they were instructed to prepare an address to the king.

In the summer of 1774, Caesar Rodney organized a meeting to protest British aggression and, at this time, the three men were chosen as Delaware's delegates to the First Continental Congress in Philadelphia.

On September 5, the First Congress in America assembled in Philadelphia. After Caesar Rodney and John Adams of Massachusetts were introduced to each other, Adams described Rodney in his diary as the "oddest looking man in the world; he is tall, thin and slender as a reed, pale; his face is not bigger than a large apple, yet there is sense and fire, spirit, wit, and humor in his countenance."

One can imagine with what eagerness these men, all of whom were regarded as the most influential personalities in their own colonies, anticipated meeting each other: to see what manner of men they were; to hear how they talked; to listen to their views on the most critical issues touching their country and their very lives.

During those 1770's, when the colonies' political pot was coming to a boil, there was a steady crescendo of excitement and activity. It was in 1774 that Caesar Rodney became colonel of the "Upper" regiment of the Kent County militia, and in September of 1775 he was made brigadier-general of that militia and of the western battalion of Sussex County. He was returned to the Second Congress, along with McKean and Read. These were the three Delaware representatives whose signatures are preserved for all time on the famous document of 1776.

In June of 1776, however, Rodney was presiding over the colonial assembly in New Castle, which gave new instructions to the three Delaware congressmen, authorizing them to cooperate with the other colonies. Often, as in this case, active patriots found they really ought to be in two places at the same time. Rodney was one of these, only this time his predicament was more serious than usual. On the twenty-second, he hurried to Sussex County on receiving news of a threatened Loyalist uprising. The Tories there were holding up Delaware's consent for independence. Upon his return home, he received an "express" (a message sent "expressly" by a messenger on horseback) from McKean, urging him to hasten to Philadelphia at once, as his vote was required on Richard Henry Lee's resolution for independence. McKean was voting for it. Read, still influenced by Tory sentiment and hoping for reconciliation, was *not* voting for it. Therefore the third Delaware vote was necessary to overcome the tie, and make it possible for Delaware to vote independence.

July 2 dawned cloudy and dark after a night of rain. It is thought that Rodney received McKean's message sometime in the night and started off at once. Heavy rain developed before ten in the morning, but Rodney pushed on traveling the eighty miles on horseback, and arrived in the afternoon, drenched and weary, but in time to cast his vote for independence. Rodney was present in Congress, then, while the Declaration was being discussed on the third and fourth of July, and he voted for its adoption in the afternoon of the Fourth.

Later in July, after all the excitement in Congress, Rodney was back in New Castle, presiding over the last session of the colonial assembly, which he himself had called for the purpose of fixing a date for Delaware's constitutional convention and arranging for the election of delegates. Thus engaged, he was unable to give time to his own political endeavors and was defeated as a delegate to the new convention, and also to the first state legislature.

Outwardly undisturbed by this show of ingratitude, Caesar Rodney's patriotic ardor turned again to military affairs. In November of 1776, he was made chairman of the Kent County branch of the Council of Safety. The next month, when Washington was retreating across New Jersey before turning suddenly to capture the Hessians at Trenton, and when Congress had fled to Baltimore, Rodney was busily recruiting Kent County militia and sending soldiers on to aid Washington. He was placed in command of the post at Trenton after Washington's main army had gone into winter quarters at Morristown. The Signer was in command of the Delaware militia with the rank of brigadier general when the

British invaded the state in September, 1777. All this time he kept in close touch with General Washington. Only a few days later, Thomas McKean, acting governor of the state, commissioned Rodney as major general of the Delaware militia.

By this time, Caesar Rodney was known to be the best man to depend on when danger threatened. His political star rose once more, and in December, 1777, he was again elected to Congress. In the Spring, he was elected "President" of his state for a three-year term.

As wartime excecutive, Rodney furnished the state's quota of troops, making sure they were clothed and armed. He also raised money and supplied provisions to meet a series of distressing appeals from General Washington for aid to his hungry and poorly clad soldiers. Even in 1780, Washington was still writing Rodney: "The army is again reduced to an extremity of distress, for want of provision — we have *this* day but *one* day's supply (of flour) in camp."

While he was laboring at all his tasks, Rodney was far from well himself. He suffered recurrent attacks of asthma, and he had a cancerous growth on his face that had been sapping his strength since the 1760's. He had consulted physicians in Philadelphia and submitted to an operation in 1768. Had he gone to England for treatment as he had then been advised, he might have been helped. But having received temporary relief, and being caught up in the war, he had put it off, and by the time the Americans began to win, it was too late to make the journey.

When, in 1782, he was again chosen as a delegate to Congress, he declined. His health was deteriorating, and he was now having to hide his disfigured face behind a green silk veil. He sought medical and surgical aid in Philadelphia, but nothing could be done.

Caesar Rodney was still serving, however, as speaker in the upper house of his state's legislature when, at the age of sixty-five, he died in June, 1784. His grave remained unmarked for about a hundred years, when a small stone was placed over it. In 1888, the body was moved to Christ Episcopal Churchyard in Dover, and on July 4, 1923, an equestrian statue was unveiled in Rodney Square, Wilmington, by the citizens of his state.

Thomas McKean

[signature: Tho M'Kean]

March 19, 1734 — June 24, 1817

THOUGH HE REPRESENTED the province of Delaware in both Continental Congresses, Thomas McKean was later to become both chief justice and governor of his native state, Pennsylvania, and to command Pennsylvania troops.

He was descended from William McKean, of Argyllshire, Scotland, who moved a little to the westward when he went to Londonderry, Ireland, about 1674. The Signer's father, another William, was brought as a child farther west across the ocean and became a tavern keeper in Chester County, Pennsylvania. He married Letitia Finney of a prominent and wealthy Scotch-Irish family who had also settled in Pennsylvania. The second son of this pair was Thomas.

After his first lessons, learned as a child at home, Thomas and his older brother, Robert, were sent to the Reverend Francis Allison's Academy at New London, Pennsylvania, where Thomas remained for seven years. He must have known another future Signer, George Read, very well indeed, since they were both schoolboys at the academy at the same time. When he was through at the Allison school, Thomas McKean went to New Castle, Delaware, to study law under his cousin, David Finney.

His legal studies seem to have given McKean the idea that he would like to hold office. Apparently he had very little trouble getting started and, once he had his foot on the ladder, he rose rapidly. First he became a junior clerk in the office of the Prothonotary of New Castle County, Delaware. (In Delaware, Pennsylvania, and some other states, the register or chief clerk of a court is called the prothonotary, a late Latin word, first used by the Church to mean a chief notary, or clerk.) He was only eighteen when he was appointed deputy prothonotary and recorder for probate of wills in the county. Two years later he was admitted to the bar in the Lower Counties of Delaware, then became deputy attorney general and clerk of the Delaware Assembly. At twenty-four he was admitted to practice before the Supreme Court of Pennsylvania. In 1758, he went to London to round out his legal studies. After that, for ten years, he practiced law in the three provinces of Delaware, Pennsylvania, and New Jersey, and for a time was enrolled in "Richard William's company" of infantry, in Newcastle County.

His growing prominence, his success in the law, and his various public offices naturally roused jealousies. But McKean had no time for these petty feelings. He only studied harder.

In October of 1762, McKean was elected a member of the assembly from Newcastle County. The people liked him so well, they elected him every year for the next seventeen years, though during the last six years of that time he lived in Philadelphia. He kept his house in Newcastle probably because his business frequently called him back. He declined further re-election on October 1, 1779.

At the age of twenty-nine, he married Mary Borden, eldest child of Colonel Joseph Borden, of Bordentown, New Jersey. Thomas McKean's connection with this prominent and wealthy family at once broadened his political horizon and influence. After ten years of marriage, Mary McKean died, not long after the birth of her sixth child. A year and a half later, McKean married Sarah Armitage, of New Castle, and moved to Philadelphia.

Thomas McKean's second marriage was solemnized in September, 1774, and by that time the political troubles of the colonies had become so serious that there was much correspondence between local committees and also between influential local leaders. In Delaware, McKean led the movement for a colonial congress. When this met, it selected him as one of its delegates to attend the First Continental Congress in Philadelphia on the first Monday of September, 1774. Caesar Rodney and George Read were the other Delaware delegates, and these three again took their seats when the Second Continental Congress met in May, 1775. McKean served on over thirty committees, including the five standing committees. He was regarded as particularly useful on the Secret Committee.

Strongly in favor of Richard Henry Lee's resolution for independence, McKean was horrified to find, at the last moment, that his vote for it would mean nothing without Caesar Rodney, who was in New Castle investigating Tory activity there. George Read, the third Delaware delegate, opposed independence and meant to vote against the Declaration, thereby canceling McKean's vote. When the date was set for the final vote, McKean sent an express at his own expense, asking Rodney to return.

Though he was a resident of Delaware, McKean had also put his name down among the persons dwelling in the middle ward of Philadelphia who were "able and willing to bear arms." The moment the Independence vote was won, Colonel Thomas McKean rushed off to command a group of Pennsylvania "Associators," at Perth Amboy, New Jersey. For this reason he was not able to sign the Declaration when it was engrossed and ready for signatures in early August.

Long after the war, McKean wrote in a letter to John Adams: "After the 4th July I was not in Congress for several months, having marched with a regiment of associators as colonel, to support General Washington. . . . When the associators were discharged, I returned to Philadelphia, took my seat in Congress and signed my name to the Declaration on parchment," probably in January, 1777.

In the autumn of 1776, he helped to frame Delaware's first constitution. Well-known as a rebel, McKean failed re-election to Congress at this time because of Tory opposition, and worked in his state's assembly, instead. But his interests had been steadily turning to Philadelphia, where his home now was, and in 1777 he became Chief Justice of Pennsylvania, while remaining active in Delaware politics. He held offices in both states for six years. This was bound to create jealousies.

On Christmas, 1780, McKean wrote a letter to the Delaware legislature, saying that both his health and his fortune were impaired by his constant attention to public business and asking to be excused from attending Congress. But this modest request was refused. Against his will, he was kept on until the preliminary agreement of peace was signed in 1783.

McKean's political enemies had been jealously protesting his two positions, wanting him to relinquish either the Pennsylvania chief justiceship or the Delaware seat in Congress. But his friends in both states claimed him. He wrote to John Adams that he was "hunted like a fox by the enemy — compelled to remove my family five times in a few months, and at last fixed them in a little log-house on the banks of the Susquehanna . . . and they were soon obliged to move again on account of the incursions of the Indians."

After the war, McKean, as a Federalist, worked for the ratification of the Federal Constitution in the Pennsylvania convention of 1787. He thought this frame of government "the best the world has yet seen." As the years passed, he became much less "liberal" in his views, and his much more conservative decisions as Chief Justice, a position he held for twenty-two years, brought about some conflicts either with the assembly, or the council, or with the military authorities. Nevertheless, his decisions went to the heart of the matter and revealed his honesty and his high sense of justice. Even his enemies had to admit his honesty, ability, fairness and frankness.

In manner, Judge McKean was somewhat harsh and domineering, according to some observers, but he had many admiring friends. Among these was the Massachusetts Signer John Adams, who once described McKean as one of the three men in Congress who "appeared to me to see more clearly to the end of the business than any others of the whole body."

After 1792, McKean became a Jeffersonian. He could not accept Federalist foreign policy, for he was a friend to France and never got over his aversion for England. In 1800, he warmly embraced Thomas Jefferson's election to the presidency.

Throughout his life McKean held many high offices and he was also a recipient of many honorary degrees, diplomas, and other honors. As a member of the American Philosophical Society, he must have known Benjamin Franklin well before they met in Congress.

When he died in June of 1817 at a ripe old age, only a very few Signers were left. Though some of the Signers lost everything they had during the revolutionary struggle, some were imprisoned, and some left with broken health, Thomas McKean was fortunately still possessed of large tracts of Pennsylvania land.

George Read

September 18, 1733 — September 21, 1798

THE FATHER OF GEORGE READ was John, born in Dublin, Ireland, sixth in descent from Sir Thomas Read, of Berkshire. John Read came to America after the sudden death of the girl he loved; and amid new scenes and people, in the province of Maryland near the head of Chesapeake Bay, he found another girl, Mary Howell, daughter of a planter of Welsh descent. They were married and to them were born six sons, the first being George, the Signer.

Soon after George's birth on the family farm near North East, in Cecil County, Maryland, his parents moved to New Castle County, Delaware, and George grew up on a farm that overlooked the wide and pleasant meadows and slopes beside the beautiful Delaware River.

He was sent to school first in Chester, Pennsylvania, then to an academy run by the Reverend Francis Allison in New London. Here he came to know fellow students who would later be associates in political life. In fact, the Reverend Mr. Allison taught more than one boy who was to become a Signer. George left the academy in his fifteenth year to study law in the office of John Moland, a Philadelphia attorney.

When he was twenty, George Read was admitted to the Philadelphia bar, where he began his practice. Dissatisfied when his first year's earnings proved inadequate, he moved to New Castle, drawn back to the scenes of his childhood and his father's large plantation. Here he was soon being called the "honest lawyer," and regarded as possessing "profound legal learning, clear reasoning and calm deliberation."

Though George Read at first used to say that men of ambition should never marry, he did finally take a bride when he was about thirty. She was a widow, Mrs. Gertrude Ross Till, the sister of George Ross, the Pennsylvania Signer.

That same year, George Read was appointed attorney general

of Delaware's three Lower Counties. This was his first political appointment. He held it for almost twelve years, until he resigned on being elected to the First Continental Congress. He felt he could not serve in this body of American patriots while holding office under the king, and he preferred to serve the patriots.

When New Castle heard of Boston's hardships under the Boston Port Bill, the people appointed a committee, which naturally included George Read, to raise subscriptions for relief. Boston received nine hundred dollars from this one Delaware county. Samuel Adams himself wrote a letter of thanks to Read.

The next year, 1765, Read was protesting the Stamp Act, declaring that "if this or any similar law imposing an internal tax for revenue were enforced" the colonists would fear they were about to become "slaves of Great Britain." To avoid that, they would resist. He said they would try to be "as independent of Great Britain as possible." It is not surprising that, with this attitude, he was returned to the Second Continental Congress.

Even so, Read was only a moderate Whig, cautious at first about taking the bold step of separation from the mother country. Probably because of the preponderance of Tory sentiment throughout the middle colonies, especially in Sussex County, he thought Lee's resolution for independence premature and refused to vote for it. It was this negative stand by Read that led Thomas McKean to dispatch an express to Caesar Rodney, the absent Delaware member, urging him to come quickly because his vote was needed.

After the resolution had been adopted, however, George Read at once fell in step and "zealously upheld it," later supporting the new republic at the risk of his life. In that first year of American independence, he was president of the Delaware Constitutional Convention, and a member of the committee that drafted his state's first constitution. He was thought to have more influence in his state's politics than any other member of the new government.

When the British took Wilmington in September, 1777, and captured Delaware's Governor John McKinly, Read had to assume the governor's duties. Hurrying back from Philadelphia by a roundabout route, he drove with his family along the Jersey shore of the Delaware river to Salem, as secretly as possible. But as they rowed across the river, a British man-of-war, sighting them, sent an armed barge in pursuit. At this critical moment, Read's boat grounded offshore and they were caught. Read, however, explained politely that he was a country gentleman returning home — which was true! — and the British sailors helped carry his wife, mother, and children to dry ground, unaware that the country gentleman was also an important "rebel."

As the head of his colony, Read now labored to raise troops, clothing, and provisions for the Army, and to remove a widespread disaffection to the patriot cause among the people. Gradually, he succeeded in sparking a new spirit.

Early in 1778, Read observed to George Washington in a letter, "My situation is rather an unlucky one, in a government very deficient in its laws, and those greatly relaxed in their execution." He did his best, but the next year, ill health required his resignation from the assembly and he had to decline re-election to Congress.

Three years later he was well enough to accept when Congress elected him Judge in the Court of Appeals in admiralty cases. But he was discouraged when Congress, in 1786, ordered the salaries of judges to be stopped, while keeping the court for any cases that might arise.

Read was one of his state's first United States Senators. A loyal Federalist, he supported such measures as the national bank and the excise law. Twice senator, he resigned in 1793 to become Chief Justice of Delaware, a post he held until his death in 1798.

George Read was a tall man, slight, and with fine features. Punctilious in dress — as most lawyers are — he was agreeable and dignified in manner, and a strict moralist. During the many years of his public life, he maintained his family mansion with its extensive gardens and stables overlooking the broad views of the beautiful Delaware River valley at New Castle. He was not one of the wealthy Signers, nor, on the other hand, one of those who lost vast properties and possessions during the war.

XI

NORTH CAROLINA

John Penn

Joseph Hewes,

Wm Hooper

William Hooper

Wm Hooper

June 17, 1742 — October 14, 1790

WILLIAM HOOPER was born in Boston, Massachusetts, the eldest son of Reverend William Hooper and his wife, Mary Dennie Hooper. He attended the Boston Latin School and then entered Harvard as a sophomore, graduating at eighteen. The next year he began to study law under James Otis, one of the first and most ardent of the revolutionaries. In such close contact with his legal instructor's patriot ideas, William Hooper's thoughts were now being shaped. He soon became a stout patriot, though his family remained loyal to the king throughout the Revolution. After he was admitted to the bar, Hooper left home, perhaps to rid his parents of the embarrassment of having a patriot son, and went south to Wilmington, North Carolina. Here, in 1764, he set up his law practice.

Hooper was a handsome young man whose cultivation, brilliance, and agreeable manner soon won him acceptance in the Lower Cape Fear region, a congenial community of strongly patriotic views. Three years later he married Anne Clark, a daughter of Thomas Clark, one of the early settlers of Wilmington.

Hooper's troubles began when he was appointed deputy attorney general.

William Tryon, the royal Governor of North Carolina, was a brutal and domineering man whose administrative officials oppressed landholders with false and exorbitant fees. This led to the organization of a group called "Regulators," who rose in protest, violent and otherwise. Mobs of Regulators grew bold enough to enter courtrooms and manhandle attorneys, and William Hooper suffered some rough treatment at their hands, simply because of the official position he held. When Governor Tryon led a military expedition against the Regulators in 1771, Hooper was a member of the expedition. He was, after all, one of Tryon's officials. The Regulators were crushed, but their discontent and bitterness remained. The heavy hand of the royal governor was felt out in the backwoods, and the great frontiersman, Daniel Boone, in his home on the Yadkin River, shared this discontent though he had no part with the Regulators. He preferred to go farther away — far beyond to the free and beautiful land of Kentucky where he would meet nothing but wild animals and Indians.

Two years later Hooper was elected to the assembly, where he remained until the royal government was overthrown, but by this time he was taking the side of the North Carolina colonists. Josiah Quincy, of Boston, who had come south to help set up patriot Committees of Correspondence, was at a dinner party for twenty people at Hooper's home in March of 1773. Afterward he noted in his diary that Hooper was now "apparently in the Whig interest" and had "taken their side in the House" — in spite of his Tory ancestry.

The dark clouds were gathering fast. Hooper soon achieved a place of leadership among the patriots and was placed on the Committee of Correspondence. He presided over the meeting that appointed the committee to call the first Provincial Congress and was, of course, himself elected. By this congress, he was chosen to attend the First Continental Congress in Philadelphia. Foreseeing the trouble with England, he had already written in a letter of April, 1774, that the colonies were "striding fast to independence, and ere long will build an empire upon the ruins of Great Britain."

In Congress, Hooper served on many committees and took part in many debates. In fact, John Adams considered him an orator comparable to Richard Henry Lee and Patrick Henry. Though Hooper remained a member of Congress until 1777, he was absent in July, when the vote on independence was taken, but he was back again in time to sign the Declaration.

Resigning from Congress in the Spring of 1777, Hooper returned to "Finian," his home on Masonboro Sound near Wilmington. He had lost his private income through his public service and wished to return to his remunerative law practice.

About five years later, when it looked as if Wilmington might be captured by the enemy, Hooper was forced to flee. He left his family at home, fearing the consequences to them if he were caught and they were with him. There followed a period of intense anxiety and distress, during which he became dangerously ill of malaria. In the end, his family was restored to him, but much of his property was destroyed, and his health was permanently damaged.

In 1782, William Hooper moved to Hillsboro and two years later was again a borough member in the House. He strongly advocated gentle treatment of the Loyalists, no doubt thinking of his Tory family in the North, or perhaps remembering that he, too, had once been an official of the king's government. Thomas Jefferson once remarked: "We had not a greater tory in Congress than Hooper." But this was not quite fair. Hooper was a patriotic American who made many sacrifices for his country. But he did fear the too rapid rise of the power of the masses in a democratic state.

Hooper was never a popular leader. He was too plainly the aristocrat, unable to approach the people easily, holding himself aloof from all except intimate friends who understood him. He was not a strong character and, under the blows of personal misfortune, became discouraged. No doubt recurring attacks of malaria caused his latter years of painful physical decline.

William Hooper died when he was only forty-eight years old, but he had lived to see the Constitution ratified.

Joseph Hewes

Joseph Hewes,

January 23, 1730 — November 10, 1779

THE NORTH CAROLINA SIGNER Joseph Hewes was born in Kingston, New Jersey, of Quaker parents, Aaron and Providence Worth Hewes. After his school years, he was apprenticed to a Philadelphia merchant, in whose office he spent several years learning business methods. At the age of thirty, he was able to establish a mercantile and shipping business of his own in Edenton, North Carolina.

With him, he took a nephew, Nathaniel Allen, Jr., son of his older sister, Sarah Hewes Allen. Nathaniel later became a partner and eventually inherited much of his uncle's fortune. For, though successful in business, Joseph Hewes had suffered a tragedy in his private life. He had become engaged to Miss Isabella Johnston, a sister to Samuel Johnston, president of the North Carolina Provincial Assembly and later governor, but a short time before they were to have been married, she died. Hewes never married.

A few years after he became a North Carolinian, he started his public career by winning election to the colonial assembly in 1766. He served until the royal government ended in 1775. A member of the Committee of Correspondence, he was appointed delegate to the newly organized Provincial Congress. The next step was his election to the First Continental Congress in 1774.

It is not hard to see why Hewes won political office so quickly and so easily. He had a pleasant disposition and an agreeable manner which made his fellow-townsmen in Edenton think him "one of the best and most agreeable men in the world." And, though he hesitated over voting for independence, he was an out-and-out patriot from the beginning. "I consider myself now head and ears in what the ministry call rebellion," he said in 1775. And he added that he felt no compunction "for the number of our enemies lately slain in the battle at Bunker Hill." He hoped to be there himself "next campaign." Not bad for a Quaker pacifist! No wonder Hewes was one of a small group specially denounced by the king's governor.

His service in the Continental Congress consisted mostly of committee work. He did not make speeches or take part in discussions, but his committee work was endless. One of his letters explained that he could not return to North Carolina to attend the Provincial Congress because he was attending sessions of the Continental Congress every day and working on committees every night. He often worked twelve hours a day without stopping, the result being that he began to feel the effects on his health.

Though he was well aware that a policy of non-importation of

British goods would be disastrous to his own business, Hewes, as a patriot, supported the policy. He also helped prepare the statement of colonial rights in the first session of Congress. He remained a year in Philadelphia and later returned for the Second Continental Congress. Hewes was one of many sincere patriots who did not, at first, want a break with England. He simply wanted more freedom in making the colonies' laws. This was the reason why he held back his support of Lee's resolution for independence, even against the views of his own Provincial Congress. What finally persuaded him was the great speech of John Adams in early July. Then, seeing that the popular opinion, as shown by documents received from all the thirteen colonies, was for independence, Hewes cried out:

"It is done! and I will abide by it."

John Adams was to say, years later, "The unanimity of the States finally depended upon the vote of Joseph Hewes, and was finally determined by him." This is his special distinction.

His experience in private life as a ship-owner naturally caused him to be placed at the head of the committee to fit armed vessels; to be chairman of the committee of marine; and to be the first executive head of the United States Navy. In North Carolina he had known John Paul Jones, and it was he who brought Jones into the Navy and found a ship for him.

Joseph Hewes and John Penn voted for North Carolina in favor of independence. In early August together with William Hooper, they signed the Declaration. When it was proclaimed in Halifax, North Carolina, on August 1, the crowd that had assembled to hear it broke out in a surge of rejoicing and prayer.

Hewes kept at the committee work as long as he could. He paid for gunpowder and other war supplies to be sent to the troops. For this he was afterwards reimbursed by Congress. Absent for a time, he returned when he was again elected and took his seat in 1779. But not for long. His health had been ruined by overwork and irregular bachelor hours. In November of that year, he suddenly collapsed and died soon afterward. He was only forty-nine.

Hewes was buried in the Christ Church cemetery in Philadelphia.

John Penn

Sohn Penn

May 6, 1740 — September 14, 1788

JOHN PENN WAS BORN in Caroline County, Virginia, the only child of Moses and Catherine Taylor Penn. At the time of his father's death, he was eighteen and had had only a few years at a country school. But after inheriting his father's comfortable fortune, he was able to concentrate on study. He applied himself diligently in the excellent library of his relative, Edmund Pendleton, mastered the books on law he found there, and was licensed to practice at the age of twenty-one.

Two years later, he married Susannah Lyme and for about twelve years practiced law successfully in Virginia. Then, in 1774, he moved to Granville County, North Carolina, where many of his relatives had preceded him.

John Penn is said to have possessed an attractive personality and to have been a good speaker (though Benjamin Rush said later that Penn seldom addressed Congress). As he began to take part in North Carolina's public affairs, he soon made it clear that his personality attracted and influenced the local voters and that, as a political orator, he was able to win their agreement to his way of thinking. Penn quickly became a leader in his new community and, only a year after his arrival in the colony, was chosen to attend the Provincial Congress. Here he served on many committees and was noted for tireless attention to his work. In less than a month, the Provincial Congress elected him to the First Continental Congress in Philadelphia.

In those early days, when overland travel was by horse only, and nobody traveled very much, it was a wonderful new experience for those leaders in their own communities to come together, see each other, and exchange ideas. Listening to the discussions and reports of the representatives from the other colonies, John Penn soon abandoned any thought of their ever being able to work with the royal government. He had written a letter from Philadelphia as late as February, 1776, in which he said: "My first wish is that America may be free; and second that she may be restored to Great Britain in peace and harmony and upon Just terms." But now he knew that tyranny had gone too far and realized that a return to the Empire was beyond hope.

Like the rest of those men in the Revolutionary Congress, Penn served at great personal sacrifice. They all had to give up their own private businesses, had to let their properties and estates deteriorate while, away from home, they gave their time and their effort to establishing their country's liberty, and risked complete destruction of their homes by British troops.

In April of that significant year, both Penn and Hooper were in Halifax, North Carolina, attending the Provincial Congress and urging a vote for independence. Joseph Hewes, the other North Carolina congressman, was in Philadelphia, but he was still opposing the stand for independence. By July, Penn and Hooper had returned to Congress; and Hewes, at last persuaded by John Adams's great speech, joined the others in voting for independence. In early August, all three North Carolinians signed their names on America's birth certificate.

John Penn remained in Congress until 1777. Elected again the following year, he served until 1780.

While he was in Philadelphia, Henry Laurens, the President of Congress at that time, challenged Penn to a duel. It so happened that both men were boarding at the same boarding-house and thus took breakfast together on the morning of the day set for the duel. They decided to walk together to the meeting place and, starting off, found they had to cross a difficult spot in the street. It may have been snow drifts or rain puddles, or the dirt street may have been pock-marked with holes. At any rate, the younger man, Penn, assisted his opponent across the street.

After negotiating the crossing, Penn suggested they drop the idea of fighting a duel. It did seem rather foolish, since he had just been helping his antagonist. The older man agreed and, in better spirits, they turned back. The duel never took place.

No one knows what this quarrel was about. But Laurens, though he disapproved of duelling on principle, had a savage tongue, which several times led to challenges. He accepted the challenges but seems usually to have fired his pistol in the air. At least once he stood to be shot at, but himself refused to fire at all.

In 1780, Penn became a member of the Board of War. Within the next year or so, he declined a judgeship because his health was failing. What time he had for work, he devoted to his law practice. But in September, 1788, he died at the early age of forty-eight. Not one of the North Carolina Signers ever lived to see his fiftieth birthday.

XII

SOUTH CAROLINA

Edward Rutledge J.
Thos Heyward Junr.
Thomas Lynch Junr.
Arthur Middleton

Thomas Heyward, Junior

July 28, 1746 — March 6, 1809

THOMAS HEYWARD was designated "Junior" because there were other Thomases in the family, though his father was Colonel Daniel Heyward. The colonel was one of the wealthiest of the South Carolina planters. He and his wife lived at Old House plantation, in what is now St. Luke's Parish, South Carolina, where their eldest son, Thomas, was born.

The boy was given the usual preparatory education that became the son of a gentleman of means and, again like many other boys whose fathers could afford it, was shipped off to London to study law. He was admitted to the Middle Temple, and after five years was called to the bar. The next year, 1771, upon his return home, he was also admitted to the bar in the province of South Carolina.

Given his education and social position, it was natural that the young lawyer should enter public life. In September of the next year, he was elected one of three members from St. Helena's Parish to the Commons House of Assembly. At that time, in South Carolina as in other colonies, there was a bitter controversy between the Commons and the royal governor over taxation by the British Parliament. A revolutionary party, once formed, grew so swiftly that within two years it was in political control of the colony.

When the news that the British had closed the port of Boston reached South Carolina, a convention of the people of the province was called. A general committee of this convention ordered an election to be held for delegates to a Provincial Congress to meet in Charleston, January, 1775; and Heyward was voted a delegate. The new Provincial Congress took over government of the colony, replacing the old royal British government.

South Carolina and Virginia were the two southern colonies most disturbed by British treatment of Massachusetts, and in the former, Thomas Heyward was an important and busy worker. As the year 1775 drew to a close, it became clear to all patriots that the colonies would have to set up new constitutions on which to base new governments of their own. Heyward was on the committee to prepare the new constitution for South Carolina, and in February, 1776, he was elected delegate to the Second Continental Congress in Philadelphia. After the General Assembly adjourned in April, Heyward went at once to Philadelphia and was there during the deliberations on independence and the final vote on July Fourth. He was just turned thirty when he signed the Declaration of Independence.

Re-elected more than once, Heyward served in Congress until the end of 1778. After that he returned home and became a circuit judge.

As we are indebted to John Adams and Dr. Benjamin Rush for writing down their impressions of some of the Signers and so giving us a glimpse of them, it is well to note what was recorded of Thomas Heyward. Dr. Rush found him a "firm Republican of good education and most amiable manners," who "possessed an elegant poetical genius, which he sometimes exercised . . . upon the various events of the war."

When the operations of war moved into the South, Heyward, in common with all other citizens between the ages of eighteen and forty-five, became a member of his state's militia. He was captain of a battalion of artillery in Charleston. This battalion fought in Moultrie's defeat of the British on Port Royal Island, where Heyward was wounded. He was able to take part in the defense of Charleston the next year, but when the city fell on May 12, 1780, Heyward found himself a prisoner of war. Although he was paroled at first, Sir Henry Clinton soon recalled the paroles of many militia officers and state officials and sent them to prison. Heyward was held at St. Augustine, Florida, until exchanged in July, 1781. He filled in his time by composing patriotic verses to British tunes. The British, meanwhile, plundered his beautiful plantation, "White Hall," and took away his slaves.

After he returned home, Thomas Heyward represented Charleston in the legislature for two more years before resuming his work as circuit judge until 1789. Then he retired in order to devote his whole time to agriculture and to rebuilding White Hall.

In 1773, Heyward had married Elizabeth Mathewes. She died some years later, and in 1786 he married Elizabeth Savage.

In his sixty-third year, Thomas Heyward, Jr., died and was buried in the family burial ground on his father's plantation, Old House, where he had spent his childhood. In this quiet spot, there stands a lonely monument to the "patriot, statesman, soldier, jurist."

Arthur Middleton

June 26, 1742 — January 1, 1787

THE MIDDLETONS had been a family of inherited wealth for generations before Arthur Middleton signed the Declaration of Independence. The first American Middleton was an Edward who, having inherited much property in England, traveled with his brother Arthur to Barbados, and from there to Carolina in 1678. Edward obtained a large grant of land in Berkeley County, North Carolina, where he at once entered local politics.

Edward's grandson, Henry, inherited both the family fortune and the desire to build up the new country. He was the father of Arthur, the Signer. Henry and his wife, Mary Williams Middleton, were living at Middleton Place on the Ashley river, near Charleston, South Carolina, when Arthur was born.

When he was twelve, Arthur was sent away to study in England. After a total of nine years abroad, during which he studied at Westminster School (associated with Westminster Cathedral in London), at St. John's College, Cambridge, and at the Inner Temple, London, the young American rounded off his education with a two-year tour of Europe before returning to his native land. He arrived at Charleston on the ship *Nancy*, the day before Christmas, 1763. Twelve years old when he sailed away, he was twenty-one when he returned, ready to think about finding a wife and entering local politics.

In mid-August, 1764, after his return, Arthur Middleton mar-

ried Mary Izard of Cedar Grove, St. George's Parish, Dorchester.
He had come home when Americans were everywhere becoming
embroiled in political conflict. Even his conservative father was
exerting his influence in persuading the colony to embrace the patriot cause. Holding the same opinion, Arthur found himself
chosen, the next year, a member of the committee which was to
correspond with the colony's London agent. This led to his decision to travel to England again and, with a party of relatives and
friends, Mr. and Mrs. Middleton sailed in May, 1768, on the *Nancy,*
the same ship that had brought him home four years before.

The Middletons traveled in England and southern Europe for
three years. In Rome, the young husband indulged in a study of
music and painting, for he was fond of the fine arts and literature.
After their return in September, 1770, they went to live at Middleton Place, the large estate which Arthur inherited through his
mother.

While Arthur was studying abroad, his father was as active in
the political life of the king's government in South Carolina as
he later became in resisting the royal government, though he was
never a believer in independence. Under the king, Henry Middleton was a member of the Commons House of Assembly, its
speaker in 1747, 1754, and 1755, and a member of His Majesty's
Council for South Carolina. But conservative though he was, he
resigned from the Council in 1770 to lead the opposition to the
British.

Arthur Middleton returned from abroad the same year that
saw his father take a stand with the patriots. He followed his
father's example of activity in the American cause, and wrote
political essays on the questions of the hour. He signed them
"Andrew Marvel." A year after his return, he was elected to the
House of Assembly and, a few months later, to the first Provincial
Congress representing Charleston. When, in June, 1775, the assembly decided to place the province in a position to resist oppression, three regiments were recruited and a Council of Safety organized. Middleton was active in this work and, as one of three
chosen for the Council of Safety, he advised some very bold
moves including one which apparently frightened the new royal
governor, Sir William Campell, into seeking protection from angry
rebels by boarding a British ship.

Early in 1776, Middleton was appointed one of a committee of eleven to prepare a constitution for South Carolina. His father had been chosen as the state's representative in the First Continental Congress in 1774. But as he felt American sentiment sweeping on toward independence, he resigned and let his son, who was much more radical, succeed him as a South Carolina delegate in the Second Continental Congress. Being duly elected, Arthur Middleton departed for his new duties after the adjournment of the General Assembly.

The Pennsylvanian Dr. Benjamin Rush has left us a bit of description of Middleton. From this, one gathers that he was rather a snob, an attitude all too easy to fall into when one has always been surrounded by the elegance of inherited wealth. Rush considered him a "man of cynical temper, but of upright intentions towards his country." He points out that Middleton was a critical Latin and Greek scholar, and liked to read Horace and other "classicks" during recesses from Congress. Middleton spoke often in Congress, Rush says, and "always with asperity or personalities." Middleton refused to serve on the Committee of Accounts because he said he hated accounts, never kept his own, and knew nothing about them. He of course was always able to pay someone else to attend to this uninteresting side of his business. Middleton sat in Congress during the deliberation preceding the Fourth, voted on that day for Independence, and later signed the Declaration. He served until the end of 1777.

When Charleston was besieged by the British in the Spring of 1780, Middleton fought in the state militia, to which he, in common with all men of military age, belonged. When the city fell, on May 12, he was paroled as a prisoner of war. But the parole, with those of many others of the civil and militia officers, was soon revoked by Sir Henry Clinton, and Middleton was sent to prison in St. Augustine, Florida. In the general exchange of July, 1781, he was released and resumed his duties in Congress. The war was coming to an end.

After the surrender at Yorktown, Middleton proposed to Congress that Lord Cornwallis should not be exchanged but rather be regarded as a "barbarian who had violated all the rules of modern warfare and had been guilty of innumerable cases of wanton cruelty and oppression." Congress did not pass this resolution.

Having seen the ugly devastation the British left behind them in South Carolina, Middleton could not help but feel bitter. His own beautiful family estate, Middleton Place, was on the enemy line of march, and of course they occupied it. The buildings did not suffer, but the Signer's rare collection of paintings was damaged.

In 1782, Middleton was again elected to Congress.

When the Constitution was adopted, he was appointed to a committee to prepare a seal for the state of South Carolina. He personally drew the reverse side of the design that was adopted and is still official — mute evidence, perhaps, of his art study in Italy as a young man.

At the age of forty-five, Arthur Middleton died at his home on Goose Creek when his younger son was only two years old.

Edward Rutledge

November 23, 1749 — January 23, 1800

EDWARD RUTLEDGE was only twenty-seven when he went to Philadelphia as congressman from South Carolina.

His father, Dr. John Rutledge, had come from Ireland in 1735 and married Sarah Hext when she was a mere slip of a girl. Their oldest son, John, was born when Sarah was only fifteen, and she was twenty-seven when her husband died, leaving her with seven children. Edward, the youngest, was then just a year old.

The boy was taught his school lessons by the Anglican minister of Christ Church and learned the Greek and Latin classics from a tutor in Charleston. Later he was sent, like his brother John, to England to finish his education by studying law at the Middle Temple in London. He was admitted to Middle Temple at eighteen and five years later was called to the bar. He returned the following year.

He had been home a year and had been admitted to the bar of South Carolina when his public and his married life began. In 1774, he married Henrietta Middleton, sister of the Signer; and when she died, eighteen years later, he married Mary Shubrick Eveleigh, a widow. Edward Rutledge's public life began when he was elected on July 7, 1774, to the First Continental Congress. He had made himself popular by instituting legal proceedings to protect the publisher of *The South-Carolina Gazette*, Thomas Powell, who had been imprisoned for printing his *Gazette* on unstamped paper, thereby violating the much resented Stamp Act.

Edward Rutledge's older brother John was also a delegate to the First Continental Congress. Both took part in heated discussions there, young Edward upholding his brother's arguments; in fact, the two Rutledges talked and argued so much in the debates that John Adams became impatient. He thought "young Ned Rutledge" was "a peacock" who wasted time debating upon "points of little consequence." Adams considered Edward Rutledge an "uncouth and ungraceful speaker; he shrugs his shoulders, distorts his body, nods and wiggles with his head, and looks about with his eyes from side to side, and speaks through his nose." Dr. Rush, however, thought Edward was a "sensible young lawyer," very useful in Congress, but he, too, remarks upon the young man's "great volubility in speaking." Still, allowances must be made. Edward Rutledge was then only twenty-seven, raw and green compared to many of the other delegates. Young Rutledge was no doubt very pleased with himself, to be included in that group of very important men from all over the thirteen colonies.

In February, 1776, he was again elected by the Provincial Congress to the Second Continental Congress, so that he was present, and a staunch supporter of the Declaration, in July. His brother was also re-elected, but he left Philadelphia and returned home to be on hand there for the discussions being considered in the Provincial Congress. Through the hot debates that went on during June about the question of independence, Edward Rutledge held off action, restrained by the indecisiveness of his constituents at home, while John was there talking for independence. Finally, on July 2, after the votes from the home parishes had come in "yea," the South Carolina delegates could at last take a stand in favor of the Declaration of Independence. Edward signed the document when it was prepared.

In November, 1776, Rutledge went home to take part in the defense of his new state. He belonged to the Charleston Battalion of Artillery, in which he was soon made a captain. He participated in General Moultrie's defeat of Major Gardiner on Port Royal Island in February, 1779.

In the autumn of that year, he was returned to Congress to fill a vacancy. But early in 1780, when the British commenced a third invasion of South Carolina, Captain Rutledge was back at this post, taking part in the defense of Charleston, until it fell to the enemy in May. He was captured and sent to St. Augustine, Florida, as prisoner of war and, like Middleton and Heyward, exchanged in July, 1781.

At the beginning of 1782, Edward Rutledge was back in his state's legislature, where he drew up the bill proposing the confiscation of the properties of all Loyalists, feeling this measure was necessary to repair the enemy destruction in the state.

Honors in public life and success in his law practice came in the post-war years. From 1782 to 1796, he represented Charleston again in the House. He was an efficient worker and at one point was chairman of nineteen committees!

Rutledge was a stiff conservative, and as an influential Federalist, he was a presidential elector in 1788, 1792, and again in 1796 when, Federalist or not, he voted for Thomas Jefferson for President.

He was elected to the state Senate twice, and in 1798 he became Governor of South Carolina. By this time, however, his health was poor, and he was performing his duties under physical distress. Within a year of the end of his term, Governor Rutledge, next youngest of the Signers, died in Charleston on January 23, 1800, at the age of fifty-one.

Thomas Lynch, Junior

August 5, 1749 — c. 1779

SOUTH CAROLINA'S DELEGATES to the 1776 Congress were all from wealthy families; their fathers were planters or country-gentlemen;

they all went to England to round off their educations; and they all studied law.

Thomas Lynch, the only son of Thomas and Elizabeth Allston Lynch, born in Prince George's Parish, Winyaw, South Carolina, was the youngest man to sign the Declaration. He was not quite twenty-eight at the time. His grandfather had come from Ireland to South Carolina soon after the first settlement was started there. His son Thomas, the Signer's father, discovered a method of growing rice on the lowlands, which were periodically covered by tidal water. By taking grants for large tracts of tidal areas on the North and South Santee rivers, Thomas, Senior, laid the foundation of a fortune.

His son, Thomas, Junior, received the education, probably by tutors, that country gentlemen usually gave their sons, and when he was fifteen, he was sent to Eton College in England. After two years there, he entered Gonville and Caius College, Cambridge, and topped off his studies with the law at Middle Temple in London. He came home again in 1772. The boy of fifteen returned a man of twenty-three.

Now that he was home, however, young Thomas Lynch did not want to carry on in the legal profession. His father good-naturedly allowed him to drop it, gave him Peach Tree plantation, and urged him to enter public life. On May 14, 1772, Thomas, Junior, married Elizabeth Shubrick, and the young pair settled at Peach Tree in St. James Parish on the North Santee River.

Since his wealthy and patriotic father was active in politics, Thomas, Junior, had little difficulty winning the offices for which he was a candidate. He was a member of the First and Second Provincial Congresses and a member of the First General Assembly of his state. In June of 1775, the Provincial Congress appointed him a captain in the First South Carolina Regiment. In July, he went to North Carolina to recruit a company and there contracted "swamp fever," or malaria, which affected him for the rest of his short life.

Under the constitution which the younger Lynch had helped to draft in the General Assembly, he was elected to the Second Continental Congress.

The Thomas Lynches, father and son, were the only such pair in the Second Continental Congress, though the elder Lynch did not live to become a Signer. Thomas Lynch, Senior, had been elected to both the First and Second Congresses, but a stroke of paralysis rendered him nearly helpless early in 1776. His son was elected as a sixth South Carolina delegate, in part at least so that he might care for his father.

Unhappily, the younger Lynch's health was also deteriorating, and he was too feeble to expend effort in public concerns though he was on hand at the July meeting to vote for Independence and, later, to sign the Declaration.

One may notice a space left open for another signature among the South Carolina names on the Declaration of Independence. This is a mute and pathetic reminder that it was hoped the older Lynch would live to sign.

But it was soon evident that the two Lynches could not remain in Philadelphia. The father had had a slight recovery, and doctors hoped that he might live to reach the home where he longed to be. The son tried to arrange a journey southward by easy stages for his father, and the two sick men set off together. But at Annapolis, Maryland, the father had a second stroke which killed him. The unhappy son, after burying his father there, continued his journey, reaching home with not much hope for a long life of his own.

After two years of illness, he and his wife took passage for a voyage to the West Indies, in the hope that he might regain his health in that benign climate. From the West Indies they shipped, as they intended, for the south of France, but their ship was never heard of again. All on board were probably lost at sea.

This was in 1779. Thomas Lynch, Junior, rich, well-educated, the young Signer who had everything but health, was thirty years old when he vanished.

XIII

GEORGIA

Button Gwinnett

Lyman Hall

Geo Walton.

Lyman Hall

Lyman Hall

April 12, 1724 — October 19, 1790

THIS SIGNER FOR GEORGIA, acknowledged as the most powerful factor in persuading his colony to independence, was born and spent half of his life in Connecticut. In the charming town of Wallingford, which still has over a hundred pre-Revolution houses, Lyman Hall was born on April 12, 1724.

He was the son of John and Mary Street Hall. His first New England ancestor was another John Hall, who came from Coventry, England, to Boston in 1633, moved on to New Haven, Connecticut, and finally settled in nearby Wallingford. The Signer's mother, Mary Street, was a Wallingford girl whose grandfather, the Reverend Samuel Street, was the first pastor in Wallingford.

Lyman Hall prepared for college with his uncle, the Reverend Samuel Hall, a Yale graduate of 1715. He himself went to Yale and graduated in 1747. After that, he studied theology under this same uncle and was ordained by the Fairfield West Consociation, the local church organization. Trouble developed in the congregation, however, and Hall was dismissed, though he continued preaching by filling vacant pulpits. But the ministry was not for him. When he left it to study medicine, Dr. Hall was on the road to success and prosperity.

In 1752, he married Abigail Burr, of Fairfield, but she lived only a year after her marriage. Two or three years later, Hall married again. His second wife was Mary Osborn, another Fairfield girl, daughter of Samuel and Hannah Osborn.

In the stories of the South Carolina Signers, we have mentioned the migration of New England settlers to the South. Lyman Hall may have thought that he could build up a practice more quickly in a newly settled part of the country; he may have liked the prospect of having milder winters; or he may have wanted to venture into a different region. At any rate, he moved south to

Dorchester, South Carolina, when he was thirty-two. About the time the Halls joined the colony, earlier settlers were moving on farther south. Lyman Hall was among the group who followed on to Georgia and founded the town of Sunbury in the Midway Settlement. This was in the parish of St. John, where patriot feeling became so strong that it was known as the Southern Cradle of Liberty.

The country thereabouts was densely wooded and abounded in game. The settlers made clearings and planted corn, potatoes, and peas in the uplands; but there were many swamps that had to be ditched and drained for the cultivation of rice, and where there are swamps, there are mosquitoes that carry malaria. The doctor was in demand. He soon had a big practice and wealth enough to buy a plantation.

Of all the thirteen colonies, Georgia had been granted the mildest treatment by the mother country. England had sent the settlers there large sums for silk culture and similar purposes. Consequently, as rebellion spread throughout colonies to the north in the 1760's, there existed a great difference of opinion in Georgia. The people of St. John's Parish naturally were deeply interested in the events that were taking place in the northern colonies of their birth. When seeds of revolt began to sprout in Georgia, the royal governor reported that the head of rebellion could be located in St. John's Parish, where the descendants of New England Puritans were asserting their strong feelings. The "Puritan element" were the first Georgia patriots, and Dr. Lyman Hall was the leader.

In July, 1774, the patriotic groups called a meeting — in opposition to the royal governor of the province — at the Liberty Pole at Tondee's tavern in Savannah. Dr. Hall, who of course represented St. John's Parish, and many of the others, had hoped that a majority of the parishes would unite with them in sending deputies to Congress. But this proposal met no response.

Dr. Lyman Hall, "being blessed with the art of oratory to an unusual degree," spoke far and wide and, in March, 1775, succeeded in persuading his neighbors to elect him a delegate to the Continental Congress. When he left for Philadelphia, he took with him, as a gift from his people to the suffering Massachusetts patriots, one hundred sixty barrels of rice and £50 sterling. He presented his credentials on May 13, 1775, and was unanimously admitted as a delegate from the Parish of St. John in the Colony of Georgia, but the colony of Georgia as a whole was not represented in the First Continental Congress. Dr. Hall therefore could not vote, since all questions were decided by vote of the colonies. He took part in debates, however, declaring "that the example which had been shown by the parish which he represented would be speedily followed and that the representation of Georgia would soon be complete." His prediction came true two months later when, in July, 1775, Georgia's Provincial Congress voted to join the confederated colonies in the cause of liberty. In this decision, the influence of Dr. Lyman Hall was of great weight.

The following February, Hall was elected again and sent to attend the Second Continental Congress. By this time, his neighbor, Button Gwinnett, a warm personal friend, arrived in Philadelphia as a second Georgia delegate.

These two, with the third Georgia delegate, George Walton, were on hand to vote for the Declaration of Independence and to sign it.

It was natural that Dr. Hall, in Philadelphia, should associate with the representatives of his native state. He and Roger Sherman became friends. Later — for Dr. Hall was elected to Congress for three successive terms — their opponents complained that "Georgia always votes with Connecticut." Hall declined a fourth nomination to Congress.

When, in December, 1778, Savannah fell and the entire coastal region of Georgia came under British hands, Dr. Hall's residence and rice plantation were destroyed. He moved his family north for the duration, visiting relatives in Wallingford. On his return in 1782, he settled in Savannah, resumed his medical practice, and was elected Governor of Georgia. He made an impressive and dignified chief executive, for he was six feet tall, with polite manners and easy deportment.

During his one term as governor, the northern boundary of Georgia was adjusted, the public debt arranged, land offices established, and treaties made with the Cherokee Indians. Hall's recommendation that a parcel of land be set aside for the endowment of an institution of higher learning led to one of the first state-supported colleges in America, Franklin College, the heart of what is now the University of Georgia.

Dr. Hall bought a plantation in Burke County when he retired in 1790, but he was not given much time to build up his new estate. In October of that year, he died, in the sixty-seventh year of his age.

Button Gwinnett

c. April, 1735 — May 16, 1777

BECAUSE HE WAS BAPTIZED in St. Catherine's Church, Gloucester, England, on the tenth of April, 1735, it is supposed that Button Gwinnett was born in that month. He was named Button for his godmother, Miss Barbara Button, descended from Sir Thomas Button, admiral and arctic explorer.

The name Gwinnett, pronounced with the accent on the last syllable, Gwin-*nett*, was originally the Welsh, *Gwynedd,* the name of the northern part of Wales.

The home of the Buttons, however, was in Glamorganshire, in South Wales. Miss Barbara Button never married, and having inherited wealth, was able to do much for her cousin, Anne Emes Gwinnett, who, no doubt as a mark of appreciation, named her second son for her cousin.

Samuel Gwinnett, the father of the Signer, entered the church, and in 1727 was given a living at Down Hatherly. He married Anne Emes of Twyning and brought his bride to the vicarage, where they lived for more than forty years. Here was born their second son, Button, who was to become a Signer of the Declaration of Independence in far-off America.

Nothing is recorded of the boy's education. His older brother Samuel became a clergyman and married Emilia Button. When the future American, Button Gwinnett, was twenty, his godmother died, leaving him £100. He is thought to have started his business career in Bristol under the guidance of his uncle, William Gwinnett, a Bristol merchant.

At the age of twenty-two, he married Ann Bourne, of Wolver-hampton, and for some time worked in partnership with his father-in-law, Aaron Bourne. He became interested in exporting goods to America and, for a time, was the sole owner of the brig *Nancy*. Though he carried on extensive mercantile operations, they were not successful, and his debts to a Bristol firm lost him the *Nancy*, which was seized under an attachment and sold by the sheriff to liquidate his indebtedness. Debts were to plague Button Gwinnett all his short life.

It is not known just when Button Gwinnett arrived in Savannah, Georgia — certainly after his three daughters were born, since their births are recorded in the registry of the Collegiate Church in Wolverhampton. The last date recorded is 1762. But by October, 1765, Gwinnett had secured a store property in Savannah and had begun to advertise, in the *Georgia Gazette,* his recently exported merchandize.

Not long after his own advertisement appeared, he saw one that took his fancy: St. Catherine's Island was for sale.

All along the coastline of Georgia runs a line of islands, sepa-rated from the mainland by winding waterways, salt marshes, and bays, into which Georgia's rivers empty into the sea. Between the mouth of the Medway and Sapelo Sound River lies St. Catherine's Island, about ten and one-half miles long and three and one-half miles wide at its widest part. Looking across to the mainland, less than ten miles away, one could see in Gwinnett's time the busy town and harbor of Sunbury, rival port of Savannah, some forty miles to the north. Sunbury was the home of Lyman Hall, who became a warm friend to Gwinnett and also a Signer. Sun-bury was Gwinnett's landing place on the mainland, his base of supplies, and his refuge when British war vessels and patrols came too near his island home.

It was in the Stamp Act year of 1765 that Button Gwinnett bought the island with high hopes of becoming a planter. Having become the owner of vastly more than the required fifty acres of land needed to qualify as an elector of the province, Gwinnett was commissioned His Majesty's Justice of the Peace for the par-ishes of St. John and St. Andrew. Within the next few years he was becoming better known, with the result that he was appointed to more and more committees dealing with public affairs. After his work in the Common House of Assembly, Gwinnett seems to have dropped out of public life for a time. His own personal affairs were probably too demanding.

Neither he nor the colony of Georgia took an early interest in colonial independence. Georgia was the youngest, the most remote and sparsely settled of the thirteen colonies. Moreover, her governor, Sir James Wright, was an able, sympathetic, and wise administrator. Under his guidance the province had prospered, and the British Parliament had given her many thousands of pounds, so that Georgia was more contented than her sister colonies to the north, which were being exasperated, then harassed, and finally outraged by tyrannical acts of Parliament. For this reason Georgia was the last to join her sister colonies in the common cause of the 1770's. Gwinnett himself had been rooted in England for almost thirty years before being transplanted to American soil.

New Englanders had been migrating to Georgia, bringing news of the troubles in the North, but not until July, 1774, did Georgia make her first remonstrance against the treatment of the colonies by Great Britain. This was at an open meeting held on the twenty-fourth at the Liberty Pole at Tondee's tavern in Savannah. Dr. Lyman Hall of Sunbury was there, but not many attended, and most of those present were from the two parishes of Christ Church and St. John. They tried for a more representative meeting the next month, at which resolutions were passed reciting a long list of colonial grievances, but few of them applied to Georgia. Georgia was the only one of the thirteen colonies not represented at the First Continental Congress in Philadelphia, though Dr. Lyman Hall was there as an observer.

Probably through his friendly association with Hall, Gwinnett became a Whig. In January, 1776, he attended one of the weekly meetings of the Georgia Council of Safety in Savannah. Though he may not have been a member at the time, he attended to report that British warships were lying off the coast. At Georgia's Second Provincial Congress, he was elected as a delegate to the Second Continental Congress.

Just before this, Gwinnett had been a candidate for the command of Georgia's battalion of eight companies. He very much wanted to see active service. But a popular Savannah merchant,

Samuel Ebert, also an aspirant for the colonelcy, had had some military training. As there was some opposition to Gwinnett, it was agreed that, for the sake of keeping harmony, both should withdraw, whereupon Lachlan McIntosh was chosen as a compromise. Ebert was made lieutenant colonel, and Gwinnett was sent to Congress.

The appearance of five British ships off the coast, followed by an attack on Savannah in March and the consequent swift movement of events, delayed the departure of the delegates, and not until May 20, 1776, could Gwinnett and Hall take their seats in Congress.

When writing his autobiography, John Adams remembered that Hall and Gwinnett were both intelligent and spirited men, "who made a powerful addition to our Phalanx." In a letter to Roger Sherman, Dr. Hall wrote, "Gwinnett is, if possible, a Whig to excess." Gwinnett must have been thrilled with the mounting excitement in Congress that preceded the great Fourth.

Button Gwinnett was appointed to serve on several of the important committees. He seldom spoke in public and wrote very little. His name in his handwriting on the Declaration of Independence is the only thing that draws our attention to him now — two hundred years later. Were it not for that, his amusing name would be lost in the mists of time.

After having served ten weeks in Congress, Gwinnett left Philadelphia and was back home in Georgia by late August, headed for trouble. He never returned to Congress.

A patriot who had wanted to be a soldier, Gwinnett hoped to be a general of Georgia troops, but he never achieved his desire. Instead, he was elected speaker of the Georgia Assembly and, though he was re-elected as delegate for the Fall term to the Continental Congress, there is no record of his attendance.

In the Georgia Assembly, Gwinnett helped draft Georgia's first constitution and also helped to defeat schemes for South Carolina to absorb Georgia. In the Spring of the following year, 1777, upon the death of Governor Archibald Bulloch, Gwinnett was made governor of the new state of Georgia and, of course, commander in chief of its army. He held these positions for only two months.

The Georgia patriots were disturbed by British forces so near in

East Florida. On the same day, March 4, 1777, that Button Gwinnett was chosen to be governor, he was directed by the Council
of Safety to draft militia and volunteers for a campaign against
the British in which they were to cut off all supplies for the
garrison at St. Augustine. Little more than a week later, Gwinnett
received the letter that was to raise the curtain on the final tragic
act.

The letter was from none other than John Hancock, President
of the Continental Congress then sitting in Baltimore, dated January 8, 1777. It said:

> "I have the honour to inclose you a copy of an intercepted
> letter from the Governour of East-Florida to Lord George Ger-
> maine, containing, among other things, the most convincing
> proof of the treasonable conduct of Mr. George M'Intosh of
> your State. This Gentleman it seems, is a Member of the
> Congress in Georgia, and under that character is secretly sup-
> porting, by every act in his power, the designs of the British
> King and Parliament against us.
>
> The United States of America have hitherto suffered ex-
> tremely from the misrepresentations of their enemies, but much
> more from the baseness and perfidy of their pretended friends.
> I have it therefore in command from Congress to request, that
> you will cause the said George M'Intosh to be immediately
> apprehended, and take every other step in this matter which
> shall appear to you to be necessary for the safety of the United
> States of America. . . ."

The intercepted letter referred to here was from Governor Patrick Tonyn of East Florida, reporting to Lord George Germaine
on receiving supplies of rice from the rebel colony of Georgia.
Tonyn said that he expected one thousand more barrels to arrive
and that Mr. Panton (a Georgia Tory) executed the business and
was greatly assisted by Mr. George McIntosh "one of the Rebel
Congress of Georgia."

George McIntosh was a brother of General Lachlan McIntosh
who had allied himself with the conservative section of the Whig
party, and had received the command of the First Battalion — a
post Gwinnett had wanted — after which he was made brigadier
general in command of the Georgia brigade. Button Gwinnett
had achieved his high mark in politics. His office as governor and

commander in chief of Georgia's army placed him above General McIntosh, a bitter pill for the general to swallow. Thus rivalry between the conservative Whig whose brother was in disgrace and the extreme Whig who was now ordered to arrest him had already begun. It is very likely that Gwinnett may have had his suspicions. Both the McIntosh brothers had been members of Georgia's First Provincial Congress, and George had even been a member of the Council of Safety, sitting in that body with Gwinnett many times. They were neighbors whose two parishes adjoined. Gwinnett's appointments had not only been great honors but showed that he had won the public's confidence in his integrity and ability. The McIntoshes probably hated Gwinnett, envious of his success.

As Governor of Georgia, Gwinnett did as he was ordered to do by Congress. George McIntosh was charged with treason against the United States and placed in irons. But the McIntoshes had their friends, too, and, as people did not know everything about the case, opinions were aired in a badly divided community.

Then came the East Florida expedition in the Spring of 1777, and it was bungled. General McIntosh ordered Colonel Ebert to lead the ill-fated expedition. But even though he had not himself led it, a large part of the people of Georgia lost confidence in General McIntosh's loyalty and integrity. When an inquiry followed in the assembly and the question was raised whether it was civil authority that had hampered military authority, or vice versa, McIntosh's hot temper flared. For this raised the question of whether Gwinnett as governor and commander in chief was to blame or whether it was the fault of General McIntosh.

The inquiry upheld Gwinnett.

General McIntosh, enraged, cried out before the assembly that Gwinnett was a "scoundrel and a lying rascal."

The insult was not to be borne. Gwinnett promptly challenged McIntosh to a duel. He was certainly no coward to take on a general with pistols.

The duel took place the following morning, just outside the town of Savannah. Both men hit their marks and both were wounded. The general recovered, but Gwinnett died three days later.

The burial place of Signer Button Gwinnett is unknown, and

there is no reliable picture of him. Though he had daughters, there are no descendants living to this day, so far as is known.

Only one thing remains of this Georgia Signer — his handwritten signature on the Declaration of Independence, and thirty-six other signatures, most of them owned by research libraries, universities, and historical societies. Gwinnett's are the rarest of Signer signatures and correspondingly expensive. One Gwinnett document alone brought $28,000 at an auction in 1926. Another sold in 1927 for $51,000, though that was also signed by John Hancock, Robert Morris, and others.

George Walton

Geo Walton.

c. 1741 — February 2, 1804

THE FIRST AMERICAN WALTON of George Walton's family was his grandfather, who emigrated from England in 1682; and the emigrant's son, Robert, was living near Farmville, Prince Edward County, Virginia, when his own son, George, was born in 1741. Both parents died while their boy was very young, and the child was taken to live with an uncle. When he was old enough, the uncle apprenticed him to a carpenter.

The carpenter seems to have seen qualities that had escaped the uncle. Impressed by George's intelligence and character, he released him from apprenticeship so that he could go to school, while giving him a portion of his wages. But even so, the boy had so little formal schooling that he is said to have been practically self-taught.

Nothing more of his early life is known until, at the age of twenty-eight, he moved to Savannah, Georgia, and began to study law. He was admitted to the bar in 1774 when he was thirty-three years old and the next year married Dorothy Camber, herself a patriot, though daughter of a loyal British subject.

In Savannah, Walton fell in with the local Whigs and must soon have become acquainted with Lyman Hall and Button

Gwinnett. He took part in the first meetings called by the patriot party that same summer, served on committees, and vehemently condemned British colonial policy. He was one of the group that called the meeting at the Liberty Pole at Tondee's tavern, which was the beginning of the Georgia Provincial Congress.

Chosen unanimously to be the secretary of this body, George Walton was then elected president of the newly formed Council of Safety. When the Provincial Congress met in February, 1776, to elect delegates to the Second Continental Congress, Walton was one of the men elected. The exact date of his arrival in Philadelphia is not known, but it was probably about June 29, though the journals of Congress do not mention him until July 17.

George Walton showed himself a strong advocate of independence, noted for his ability and zeal. Perhaps he had, at times, too much zeal — which can cause trouble. In Congress, Walton took an interest in Indian affairs and went to Easton, Pennsylvania, in January, 1777, when a treaty was negotiated with the Six Nations of the Iroquois.

Back in Georgia by spring, he was one of the "Conservative Whigs" who made life hard for Button Gwinnett. He was, in fact, the leader of the opposition to Gwinnett, and a friend of the firebrand, General McIntosh, who was later responsible for Gwinnett's untimely death. During the next two years, the patriot party in Georgia was itself divided by dissension.

In January, 1778, George Walton was commissioned colonel of the Georgia militia's First Regiment. During the siege of Savannah his leg was broken by a cannon-ball, he fell from his horse, and was captured by the British. The next year, he was exchanged and sent home in time to be elected governor, a position which he held for only two months.

This little man, small of stature, but good-looking, impressed others as being haughty, dignified and stern. This impression was not altogether fair, for though Walton did have a violent temper, he could be counted on to do what he said he would do, which is not always true of politicians. Bitter with his enemies, he was warm with his friends. Unfortunately, he chose to hate his colleague, Button Gwinnett, and to be friendly with Gwinnett's enemy, General McIntosh. Going to the extent of sending a doubtful letter to Congress in trying to defend McIntosh after the general had killed Gwinnett in the duel, Walton was censured by the legislature in 1783. This forced the attorney general to bring charges against him. But Walton had his backers and, of the three Georgia Signers, he served longest in the Second Continental Congress. Except for the years 1778 and 1779, when he was first fighting the British, then held as a British prisoner, he appeared regularly in Congress until 1781.

He was commissioned in 1783 to negotiate a treaty with the Cherokees in Tennessee, after which he served six years as Chief Justice of Georgia. In 1789, he was a presidential elector and was for the second time elected governor.

During this term a new constitution for Georgia was established, the capital was definitely located at Augusta, and after many frontier difficulties, the Creek Indians were pacified.

The next year, in 1790, Walton retired to his estate, "Meadow Garden," but was soon called back to public life as judge of Georgia's Supreme Court.

In 1795, he built a new home which he called "College Hill," but he was not given time to enjoy it long. Within a few months, he died there at the age of fifty-four. He was buried in Rosney Cemetery nearby. For the 1848 celebration of the Day of Independence, however, citizens erected a new monument in Augusta to the three Georgia Signers, and the bodies of Lyman Hall and George Walton were reinterred there.

BIBLIOGRAPHY

Adams, Charles Thornton. *Matthew Thornton of New Hampshire*. Philadelphia: Dando Printing and Publishing Company, 1903.

Allan, Herbert S. *John Hancock, Patriot in Purple*. New York: The MacMillan Company, 1948.

Biddle, Honorable Edward W. *James Wilson, James Smith, and George Ross, Three Signers of the Declaration of Independence who were members of the Cumberland County Bar*. Historical address delivered in the Court House, Carlisle, Pennsylvania, April 4, 1902.

Boardman, R. S. *Roger Sherman, Signer and Statesman*. Philadelphia: University of Pennsylvania Press, 1938.

Buchanan, Roberdean. *McKean Family of Pennsylvania*. Lancaster: Inquire Printing Company, 1890.

Burlingham, Charles C. *Francis Lewis*. Philadelphia: Historical Sketch read at the Sesqui-Centennial International Exposition, September 20, 1926.

Butterfield, L. H., ed. *Letters of Benjamin Rush*. 2 volumes. Princeton: Princeton University Press, 1951.

The Adams Papers. Diary and Autobiography of John Adams. 4 volumes. New York: Atheneum, 1964.

Carroll, Charles. *Journal During His Visit to Canada in 1776*. Baltimore: John Murphy for the Maryland Historical Society, 1876.

Corner, George W., ed. *The Autobiography of Benjamin Rush*. Princeton: Princeton University Press, 1948.

Drake, Francis. *Dictionary of American Biography*. 2 volumes. Gale, 1879.

Fay, Bernard. *Franklin, the Apostle of Modern Times*. Boston: Little Brown & Company, 1929.

Franklin, Benjamin. *Autobiography*. Art-Type edition. New York: Books, Incorporated.

Gurn, Joseph. *Charles Carroll of Carrollton*. New York: P. J. Kennedy and Sons, 1932.

Hart, Ann Clark. *Abraham Clark*. San Francisco: The Pioneer Press, 1923.

Historical Society of Delaware. *A Biographical Sketch in Letters to and from Caesar Rodney*. Philadelphia: University of Pennsylvania Press, 1933.

Huntington, Susan D. "Samuel Huntington." *The Connecticut Magazine*. Volume 6, Number 4, May–June, 1900.

Jenkins, Charles Francis. *Button Gwinnett*. Garden City: Doubleday, Page and Company, 1926.

Lee, Richard H. *Memoir of the Life of Richard Henry Lee*. 2 volumes. Philadelphia: H. C. Carey and I. Lea, 1825.

McGee, Dorothy Horton. *Famous Signers of the Declaration*. New York: Dodd, Mead, and Company, 1955.

Shewmake, Oscar L. Esquire. *The Honorable George Wythe*. Delivered before the Wythe Law Club of the College of William and Mary, Williamsburg, Virginia, 1921.

Smith, Ellen Hart. *Charles Carroll of Carrollton*. Cambridge: Harvard University Press, 1942.

Thoms, Herbert, Dr. *Lyman Hall, Physician, Patriot, Signer*. President's Address, New Haven County Medical Association, New Haven, Connecticut, April 28, 1927.

Van Doren, Carl. *Benjamin Franklin*. New York: Viking Press, 1938.

Whipple, William. *Collections and Proceedings of the Maine Historical Society*. Series 2, Volume VI. Portland, 1895.

Woods, David Walker Jr. *John Witherspoon*. London: Fleming H. Revell Company, 1906.

Young, Eleanor. *Forgotten Patriot*. New York: The MacMillan Company, 1950.

Profiting from the Bank
and
Savings & Loan Crisis

ALSO BY STEPHEN PIZZO AND PAUL MUOLO

Inside Job (with Mary Fricker)

Profiting from the Bank and Savings & Loan Crisis

How Anyone Can Find Bargains
at America's Greatest Garage Sale

Stephen Pizzo and Paul Muolo

HarperBusiness
A Division of HarperCollins*Publishers*

PROFITING FROM THE BANK AND SAVINGS & LOAN CRISIS. Copyright © 1993 by Stephen Pizzo and Paul Muolo. All rights reserved. Printed in the United States of America. No part of this book may be used or reproduced in any manner whatsoever without written permission except in the case of brief quotations embodied in critical articles and reviews. For information address HarperCollins Publishers, Inc., 10 East 53rd Street, New York, NY 10022.

HarperCollins books may be purchased for educational, business, or sales promotional use. For information, please call or write: Special Markets Department, HarperCollins Publishers, Inc., 10 East 53rd Street, New York, NY 10022.

FIRST EDITION

Designed by Irving Perkins Associates

Library of Congress Cataloging-in-Publication Data

Pizzo, Stephen.
Profiting from the bank and savings & loan crisis : how anyone can find bargains at America's greatest garage sale / Stephen Pizzo and Paul Muolo. — 1st ed.
p.   cm.
Includes index.
ISBN 0-88730-596-2
1. Real estate investment—United States.   2. Government sale of real property—United States.   3. Savings and Loan Bailout, 1989–
4. Resolution Trust Corporation (U.S.)—Information services.
5. Federal Deposit Insurance Corporation—Information services.
I. Muolo, Paul.   II. Title.
HD1382.5.P585   1993
332.67'24'0973—dc20   92-53369

93   94   95   96   97   PS/HC   10   9   8   7   6   5   4   3   2   1

For the nation's taxpayers

Contents

· ·

Introduction 1

1: The FDIC and RTC: The Terminators 13

2: Dialing for Dollars 28

3: Finding Home Sweet Home 53

4: Look Before You Leap 95

5: Hey Buddy, Can You Spare a Loan? 123

6: Crunching the Numbers 132

7: Do I Hear a Bid? 148

8: Buying Paper 174

9: The Flea Market of the Century 203

10: Help Wanted—Inquire Within 216

Conclusion 247

Glossary of Terms 249

Yellow Pages 277

Index 299

vii

Introduction

· ·

Anybody who buys from the Resolution Trust Corporation is going to make a profit.

—ALBERT CASEY,
RTC chief executive officer

During the past decade the gap between rich and poor widened to an unbridgeable chasm. The traditional bridge over that gap—the American middle class—shrank while the number of millionaires doubled. Some of the luckier ones made it across the middle-class bridge into the "Promised Land" of the 1980s, but many more were left behind to worry about how they were going to afford housing, medical care, food, and education for their children. Economists are now concerned that this polarity between rich and poor could become permanent and upset the delicate social chemistry that sustained a once robust American economy—an economy predicated on the promise of upward mobility.

But for those who despair that this bleak prediction might be true, and for those who missed the 1980s gravy train, we have some very good news. The train is back. But don't miss it again, because it very well might be the last good ride for a very long time. This gravy train isn't operated by savings and loan high flyers or Wall Street insider traders. This is a government-controlled railroad called the RTC & FDIC. The

1

RTC (Resolution Trust Corporation) sells assets of failed savings and loans. The FDIC (Federal Deposit Insurance Corporation) sells the assets of failed banks. And both agencies have billions of dollars worth of real estate, loans, and other assets to sell.

The financial meltdown of America's savings and loans, as well as its banks, has been catastrophic for our society. Together, the two debacles will sap much-needed taxpayer resources well into the twenty-first century. But for investors who know how to use the system, this cloud has a $400 billion silver lining: dirt-cheap homes, apartment buildings, timeshares, office buildings, raw land, automobiles, office equipment— all of which can be purchased without limit by just about anyone. In the pages ahead we will tell you how to tap into this gold mine.

So if you were among those left behind in the 1980s and don't have a lot of money to invest, or if you have money and want terrific investment bargains, this book is for you.

Come On In, the Water's Fine

John Lewis, a renter all of his life, knew exactly which house he wanted to buy. It was the one he was already renting with his wife, Lula, and their three children in suburban Pensacola, Florida. The three-bedroom home was owned by Citizens and Builders Savings Association, a local S&L that had taken title to the house after its previous owner stopped making mortgage payments. The Lewises rented the house from Citizens for $300 a month and even made a bid to buy it in 1989, offering $22,000 for the home, which had been listed at $35,000. The thrift[1] rejected their bid.

In early 1991 Citizens and Builders Savings was shut down by federal S&L regulators and the Lewises' home was taken over by the Resolution Trust Corporation (RTC), the government agency created in 1989 to clean up and sell the nation's insolvent S&Ls.

In late 1991 the Lewises learned that the RTC would sell their home at public auction to the highest bidder. The family was there the day the bids were taken, and when the auctioneer's gavel fell the home had

---

[1] "Thrift" is a synonym for S&L—as in it used to be "thrifty" to save so people placed their money in a savings institution or "thrift."

new owners—the Lewises. And much to their delight, they paid just $11,500 for it, about a third of what it was worth.

To sweeten the deal further, the RTC even loaned the couple the money to buy the home. The Lewises only had to put down $500 in cash, and the rest was financed by the government. Today their monthly mortgage payment is just $125 a month—less than half their rent.

Frederick E. Miles of Marblehead, Massachusetts, was shopping for a bargain. Mr. Miles had heard that the government was chin-deep in assets from failed S&Ls and banks. For months he and his wife, Jean, had shopped for just the right deal by attending public real estate auctions held by the Resolution Trust Corporation (RTC) and the Federal Deposit Insurance Corporation (FDIC). Serious investors, at one point in their search the two almost bought a Sheraton Hotel in Cypress Gardens, Florida, that was once listed for $8 million. By the time they decided to make a bid the Sheraton had already sold—for $948,000, about an eighth of its original asking price.

But the couple's perseverance finally paid off in December of 1991 when they paid the FDIC $625,000 for the Chamberlain Resorts Hotel, a 20-room hotel with two-bedroom suites located near Bethel, Maine, in the heart of prime ski area. Not only did they acquire a "turn key" spanking-new resort complex, but along with the package came 215 acres of riverfront property, a heated outdoor pool, and a picture-postcard view of the Longfellow Mountains ski area. The hotel had been the property of the failed First Mutual Bank of Boston in Massachusetts, which had lent a developer $2.09 million to build the resort in 1989. When the developer failed to make his loan payments, the bank foreclosed. The bank itself fell on hard times and was "foreclosed" on by the FDIC, the government agency that regulates and insures the nation's banks. The FDIC paid off the bank's insured depositors and acquired title to all its real estate holdings.

Local real estate agents in nearby Hanover, Newry, and Bethel were shocked at how little the Mileses paid for the resort hotel. The township had just reassessed the property at $1.3 million. Even with the regional recession, the local ski economy remained strong and was

anticipating 600,000 ski visits to the area for the 1992 season—
meaning the hotel would probably do a brisk business.

The FDIC had hoped to get as much as $750,000 for the Chamberlain. But when only eight bidders showed up for the auction the FDIC quickly had to decide just how much it wanted to be in the ski resort business. The answer was: We're the government; we don't want to be in the ski business. So the FDIC accepted the Miles's bid, which was the highest.

Miles, a retired auto dealer, put $161,000 down and financed the balance of the purchase price through the FDIC with a seven-year loan at 8.8 percent.

When Joseph and Millie Smith of Sacramento, California, heard that S&Ls were dropping like flies in Texas they decided to investigate what sounded like a real opportunity. The couple had been investing in real estate on a small scale for years, building a portfolio of low- to moderate-income rental units near their home in Sacramento.

The couple discovered that for about $150 they could buy an RTC catalog of available S&L assets. The evening the catalog arrived they pulled their chairs up to the fireplace and began thumbing through it. The sheer number of properties available was numbing. They decided to narrow their search and started "clipping" catalog listings for any homes that cost $10,000 or less. By the time they reached the end of the catalog Millie had gone through five boxes of paper clips.

The couple telephoned the real estate brokers the RTC had hired to sell the properties and began making offers. A few months later the Smiths had purchased at least 50 properties from bankrupt S&Ls controlled by the RTC and from shaky S&Ls.[2]

Because of tax breaks offered by the federal government, wealthy

---

[2] Revlon is known for its manufacture of cosmetics and hair and skin care products for women. Perelman, the chairman of Revlon, used his investment company, MacAndrews & Forbes, to buy a handful of Texas S&Ls from the government in 1988. The amalgam of thrifts he acquired is known today as First Gibraltar Bank, FSB, Dallas, Texas. The U.S. Government granted Perelman $1.8 billion in federal tax breaks and gave him $9.5

S&L investors, such as Revlon chairman Ronald Perelman, were allowed to sell foreclosed homes and other assets at steep discounts. Why? Desperate to unload these bankrupt S&Ls, the federal government promised these investors that no matter what price they sold a piece of real estate for, the government would make up the difference on the loss! (Generous with our money, aren't they?) Therefore, Perelman and others could sell their S&L assets to anyone they wanted and Uncle Sam would pick up the cost.

The months that followed were good to the Smiths. They were in constant contact with Texas realtors with RTC properties, and the deals began to pour in. The Smiths were getting first crack at houses selling for $500, $800, and $1,200. They couldn't believe their good fortune. "In real estate, generally, you make a low-ball offer with the anticipation that it will be rejected and then a counteroffer will be given so you have grounds for negotiation," said Millie Smith. "And when they [the RTC] just accepted our opening bids we were really amazed. We thought they might accept 1 or 2 of them but not all 32."

By early 1992 the Smiths had purchased more than 300 properties from the RTC, FDIC, or directly from ailing banks and thrifts that were anxious to unload their foreclosed properties at any cost. They fixed some of the homes up, selling them quickly for two, three, or four times what they paid for them. A house they bought in Fort Worth, Texas for $1,750, they sold a week later for $7,500 simply by nailing up a hand-painted "For Sale by Owner" sign. They hadn't done a thing to the house—not even cut the lawn.

---

billion (yes, billion) in federal assistance over 10 years to take these problem S&Ls off its hands. Since he took control, First Gibraltar has been profitable—thanks to all the billions of dollars in assistance from the government. As an incentive to get MacAndrews & Forbes to buy these bankrupt S&Ls, the government allowed them to use "past" losses of the S&L to shelter future earnings. In other words, if the "old" First Gibraltar had lost $1 billion over five years, then the new First Gibraltar would not have to pay any income tax on its first $1 billion in earnings. What's so amazing about all this is that these tax losses could be used to shelter earnings by Revlon.

* * *

What these investors have in common is that they each quickly recognized the enormous opportunity created by the meltdown of this nation's banking and savings and loan industries. What most Americans saw as a national disaster, these people saw as a once-in-a-lifetime opportunity to buy real estate cheaply.

These are just selected examples of the kind of real estate opportunities available from the RTC and FDIC, the two government agencies responsible for liquidating and selling the nation's insolvent savings and loans and banks. We could fill a book with just such success stories.

CLOSE, BUT NO FREE LUNCH

But we want to stop right here and make the following point—this is *not* a "get rich quick" book. The only easy way to make money is to inherit it or win the lottery. The only completely safe way to double your money is to fold it in half and put it back in your pocket. All other routes to riches, including those in this book, involve work, commitment, patience, and risk. This book is designed to guide you to the greatest investment opportunity in decades—the government's enormous portfolio of properties inherited from some 2,000 failed banks and savings and loans across America. Once we get you there and show you the ropes, the rest is up to you. If you play your cards right you will be able to parlay your modest savings into a highly profitable investment, as the three examples above prove. But in the process you will also experience your share of frustration and will invest as much "sweat equity" as real money.

A BOOK FOR THE PRO AND NOVICE ALIKE

We have structured this book to be a useful tool for experienced investors as well as for those who have never attended an auction or purchased a piece of real estate. For beginners we delve into details professionals will find obvious. For the professional the most important sections of this book are those dealing with how the RTC and FDIC are structured, who to call for specific types of assets, inside information from the RTC's own policy manuals on how it appraises and values properties, and how the RTC and FDIC analyze bids. We also offer information on how to buy homes from a third government agency, the Department of Housing and Urban Development, which sells about 70,000 homes each year.

THE RTC AND FDIC: OPPORTUNITIES OF A LIFETIME

Thanks to the meltdown of the savings and loan and banking industries, opportunity isn't just knocking right now, it's pounding on your door. Two elements have coincided to create this extraordinary window of opportunity:

1) A slow economy combined with a temporary oversupply of real estate has created the softest real estate sales market since World War II. As sellers, the RTC and FDIC are anxious—and on occasion, desperate. The two agencies are accepting offers far lower than they ever would have considered previously, further driving the cost of real estate down for the first time in decades. It's an aberration, and it won't last. Keep in mind that each year government agencies—including the RTC and FDIC—sell 200,000 units of housing, everything from single-family homes to apartment buildings. Those who buy now will reap the benefits of renewed inflation when the market turns around.

2) As if that weren't enough, bank and thrift regulators have been ordered by Congress to sell repossessed bank and savings and loan properties—*$400 billion worth*—into this already soft market. Doing so creates a vicious cycle. First, the government has to accept lower prices because of the already soft market. Second, dumping more properties on that market softens it further because it creates an even greater oversupply, depressing prices.

It's a terrible time to be a seller, but a marvelous time to be a buyer.

THE SYSTEM WORKS—SO WORK IT

Since 1989 the authors have been investigating and reporting on the RTC and FDIC, and we've discovered something remarkable—the government liquidation system is now working. These two agencies still have flaws, but despite what you may have read, they're actively selling real estate every day of the week and buyers are getting terrific deals.

In late 1991, plagued by complaints that the RTC was an unmanageable bureaucracy (and it was!), Congress radically reorganized the agency, stripping away layer after layer of inefficient management. By the fall the RTC was a lean machine and finally began functioning as Congress had originally intended. Private-sector professionals were brought into the management loop as properties for sale were listed with real estate brokers rather than handled by bureaucrats in Washington. Also, both the RTC and FDIC began to computerize, putting their asset inventory "on-line." The only thing you need today to tap into this inventory is a telephone and a personal computer. We'll explain how later. With the touch of a button you have access to thousands of pages of listings of homes, apartment buildings, motels, and other types of available properties, all across the nation.

When it comes to computerized listings of properties, the RTC is particularly well organized. By early 1992 the agency had installed banks of toll-free 800 lines and hired private telemarketing companies that you can call to request asset-specific searches—for a single-family house, a two-family rental unit, an apartment building—for whatever you want. Both agencies also installed public-access computer data bases so prospective buyers could search for properties nationwide from the comfort of their own computer terminals.

By mid-1992 all these changes were in place, changes that finally placed within reach of the average citizen this $400 billion inventory of assets—everything from $500 homes to $100 million resorts. But, despite all the time, money, and energy spent putting these systems in place, all of this remains the best-kept secret in town to the average investor. Potential buyers continue to hold on to the misconception that they don't have a chance against the "inside the Beltway" crowd or "good ol' boy" network of professional real estate investors. Nothing, however, could be further from the truth.

Adding to this public misperception is the tendency of Congress to drag the RTC out of the closet twice a year for a public flogging. The RTC is not perfect, but it now functions more efficiently than Congress. But politicians, looking for someone besides themselves to blame for the

$400 billion mess they made by deregulating S&Ls and banks, use the RTC as their scapegoat. You should pay absolutely no attention to such political grandstanding. Whatever mistakes the RTC may be making have little to do with your ability to buy property from it. Let the Beltway crowd argue over policy while you get great deals.

NO SHORTAGE OF DEALS

Literally billions of dollars in assets are up for sale. In the case of the RTC, about $300 billion worth of real estate, loans, and other assets will be sold during the coming years. The FDIC, which supervises the nation's banks, will have to sell at least $60 billion in assets and maybe as much as $100 billion. If the economy stays weak that number could easily grow to $150 billion. HUD sells at least $3 billion worth of homes per year and will continue to do so for the next several years.

And these assets are everywhere. No longer do buyers have to relocate down south to find a good buy. In the beginning a large portion of what the government had to sell was concentrated in Colorado, Florida, Louisiana, Oklahoma, and Texas. But as the thrift crisis rolled across the country, finally reaching both coasts—and with the banks joining the S&Ls in the federal scrap heap—the inventory is now spread across all 50 states as well as Puerto Rico and Guam.

Besides real estate, both agencies have loans secured (collateralized) by real estate that they would like to sell. At the beginning of 1992, for example, the RTC had about $150 billion or so in "performing and nonperforming" loans available for sale. The FDIC had about $6 billion in real estate available for purchase and about $12 billion worth of performing and nonperforming loans. These numbers will grow as the FDIC takes over more ailing banks in the months and years ahead.

As a general rule at least half of what these two agencies have to sell is in the form of loans or mortgages. These loans and mortgages are backed by real estate and offer to the investor another way of acquiring that real estate. If you buy the loan you can foreclose on a defaulted borrower and acquire the property in that manner. We'll discuss how to do this later.

How long it takes these two agencies to sell all of its billions of dollars in assets is anyone's guess. Some experts think that if a strong economic recovery sweeps the nation the job might be finished by 1996 or 1997. Others, less sanguine about today's plodding economy, are predicting a financial mess that will last for a decade—at least. Pessimists believe the nation's financial institutions are experiencing a period of "correction" that could last well past the year 2000. It's safe to say that no one—no matter how good a salesperson—can peddle $400 billion worth of estate and other assets very quickly, whether it's boom times or not. Expect the RTC, FDIC, and HUD to be offering billions of dollars worth of real estate and loans at discount prices for some time to come.

For now and the foreseeable future the pickings being offered by these government agencies will be plentiful. Every type of real estate asset imaginable is available for purchase: homes, hotels and motels, industrial warehouses, office buildings, raw land, strip shopping centers, even parking lots. Loans that are collateralized or backed by real estate also can be purchased from the government. Also available at fire sale prices are airplanes, appliances, artwork, cars, calculators, computers, furniture, junk bonds, loans and mortgages, rugs, yachts—even businesses like fast food franchises, horse farms, and hot tub spas. Failed American Savings and Loan Association of Irvine, California, even had an operating bordello in Nevada that the government had to sell.

For investors with money this is an opportunity to make a lot more money. For those with little or even no money, the liquidation programs of the RTC and FDIC offer a genuine opportunity to acquire a first house, a duplex, or maybe a small apartment building.

If you are a person with low to moderate income (meaning that you make 115 percent or less than the area median income, median being the middle point where half the salaries are larger and half smaller), you can get even better bargains. Congress has mandated that those who qualify under the RTC and FDIC Affordable Housing Program must get first crack at lower-priced houses and cooperatives and condo units.

If you buy a piece of real estate from the RTC—with a few exceptions—the agency will loan you the money to acquire it. The FDIC, on the other hand, will only loan you money if the property you're buying costs $500,000 or more. However, this rule is likely to change as more banks fail and the FDIC's inventory of real estate grows. When the RTC first began selling assets its seller financing limit was also $500,000, but in 1992 it was lowered to $100,000 in order to increase the number of potential buyers. The ins and outs of real estate financing available from the RTC and FDIC will be explained at length in later chapters.

Paul Miedens and his wife bought a two-bedroom and loft condominium in suburban Perrysburg, Ohio, from the RTC for $92,000. A few months before the Miedens bought their home, an almost identical unit in the same neighborhood sold for $111,000—22 percent more. The family had viewed six repossessed homes before buying the almost new condo. Along with two bedrooms, the Miedens got a loft, a fireplace, and two baths.

In December 1991 General Electric Capital Corp., a financial services conglomerate based in Stamford, Connecticut, bought 26 apartment buildings—20 of which were in Texas—from the RTC for $75 million. The number of rental apartments totaled 5,590. The cost per apartment unit was just $13,416. At an average rent of $400 per unit—excluding maintenance costs and taxes—GE will make its money back on the investment in less than three years. According to a study done by the Government Accounting Office, the auditing arm of Congress, the RTC is selling assets at an average cost of 60 cents on the dollar. This means that buyers are getting real estate discounts of around 40 percent. Depending on the physical condition of a property, discounts can range as high as 80 percent and 90 percent, but keep in mind you may have to put additional money into the property to make it habitable. In some cases, mostly in Texas and the Southwest, the RTC has simply *given away* homes and apartment buildings to charities and nonprofit groups that have agreed to rent them out to low-income families or fix them up while teaching job skills to unemployed and disadvantaged workers.

The nation's insolvent S&Ls and banks will cost the nation's taxpayers a whopping $600 billion (yes, billion) over the next 30 years. Taken separately or together, the S&L and banking debacles represent the greatest financial disasters in history. Never before has there been a multibillion dollar drain on the nation's economy like this. The Vietnam War, for example, in today's dollars, would cost only $160 billion. And the Marshall Plan, rebuilding all of western Europe after World War II, would cost only $60 billion today.

Not only has the S&L mess created investment opportunities in real estate, but it also has fueled job opportunities, as the government hires professionals to help manage and dispose of this enormous inventory— accountants, appraisers, auctioneers, lawyers, paralegals, real estate management specialists, security guards, and others are being hired at private-sector salaries by the government. Construction jobs are also being created as the RTC and FDIC move to repair and complete unfinished real estate projects left idle by bankrupt developers who borrowed heavily from these federally insured financial institutions. Professionals of all types can work for the FDIC and RTC as third-party contractors, or they can be hired on as staff professionals by these agencies. We'll tell you how to find and qualify for those jobs.

These real estate and employment opportunities will not last forever. As we noted earlier, the window of opportunity could start to close in 1996. This book is a wake-up call to investors and home buyers, to alert them to this terrific opportunity. It is designed to guide you through the federal government's enormous portfolio of properties inherited from some 2,000 failed banks and savings and loans across America.

Happy Hunting.

Chapter One

. . . .

The FDIC and RTC: The Terminators

BILLIONS OF DOLLARS IN ASSETS WITH ORDERS TO SELL IT ALL

A spot check by Congress in January 1992 showed that the Resolution Trust Corporation (RTC), created to sell assets of failed thrifts, had tens of thousands of single-family homes and apartment buildings on its shelves. The General Accounting Office's computers stopped counting at $27.3 *billion* in real estate—mostly homes, apartments, and office buildings that were available for purchase. That was *after* subtracting the $8.9 billion in homes and apartments the RTC had already sold—some 28,000 properties. And the party is just beginning.

In 1992 the RTC took over another 175 failed S&Ls. In 1993 the RTC will inherit at least 100 more dead thrifts, each one bulging at the seams with properties and other assets that will have to be sold to the public at fire sale prices. The sheer volume of RTC assets takes on almost metaphysical proportions. A glance at the RTC at the beginning of 1992 showed the following inventory: $27 *billion* in real estate, $70 *billion* in performing mortgages, and $30 *billion* in delinquent loans, just to name a few asset categories.

As if that weren't enough, close on the RTC's heels comes the FDIC, the federal agency that sells the assets of failed banks. Between these two agencies there is something for everyone up for sale anywhere in

13

the United States at virtually any point in time. If a failed bank or S&L had an asset that could even *remotely* secure a loan, even a bad loan, the RTC and FDIC now have it in their inventory. During the go-go years of financial deregulation—which led to the S&L and banking messes—borrowers put up everything imaginable as security for loans: real estate, racehorses, rare paintings, vintage cars, hunting lodges, even casinos.

The RTC and FDIC also own all the "stuff" purchased by wild and crazy thrift and bank owners during the time they had the combination to the vault. Some of their buying habits made Imelda Marcos look like she took an oath of poverty. They bought fleets of cars, jets, yachts, expensive art, fine china, even a mechanical gorilla and a magic museum—most of which the government now has to sell.

After the RTC took over Columbia Savings and Loan in Beverly Hills it had to sell the dead thrift's brand-new headquarters building. To say it was not your run-of-the-mill S&L branch would be an understatement. Columbia's former owner, Thomas Spiegel, had been very security conscious. The building had bulletproof glass, a computer system that tracked terrorist activities worldwide, and an executive bathroom that had a bulletproof shower stall. Inside the shower were secret panels that opened to reveal a cache of assault rifles. In one of life's ironies, the RTC sold the building to the talent agency that represented "Terminator" actor Arnold Schwarzenegger.

The FDIC and RTC classify their assets into specific categories under which are subcategories. It's a *$400 billion garage sale* with something for just about every size pocketbook. The two agencies are a lot alike, but they differ in several key ways. Let's start off with a brief look at each.

THE RTC

Since the RTC was formed by Congress in August 1989, it has taken over more than 650 S&Ls with $300 billion in assets. Most experts agree that the RTC will continue taking over sick thrifts through 1995. At that point the number of insolvent or bankrupt S&Ls will be slowing to a trickle. By the time the S&L carnage is over in 1995, about 1,500 S&Ls will still be in existence, but that number too is likely to shrink as strong and healthy institutions merge with each other and form multi-state unions in which one institution will have hundreds of branches in many different regions. Consequently, there will be billions of dollars worth of S&L assets to purchase for years to come.

By the time the RTC is done with its mission it will have used up at least $160 billion in Treasury Department funds, plus another $150 to $200 billion in "interest" on the $160 billion it borrowed so taxes will not have to be raised. The grand total: at least $350 billion—and maybe more.

When the RTC was created in 1989 it was placed under the control of the FDIC. But the arrangement proved unworkable. A gigantic bureaucracy grew around the RTC until it was immobilized. Trying to deal with the avalanche of S&L assets pouring into the RTC also put an unworkable strain on the FDIC. So in late 1991 Congress stripped away the FDIC's authority over the RTC and made it a separate agency. Appointed to head the RTC was a single chief executive officer, Albert Casey, a former chairman of American Airlines.

The chief executive is responsible for overseeing the day-to-day operations of the RTC. Albert Casey brought a "real world" perspective to the RTC. He had served as chairman of American Airlines from 1974 to 1985. Casey also was president of the Times Mirror Company of Los Angeles, chief executive of First Republic Bank, and Postmaster General.

Congressional passage of the Resolution Trust Corporation Refinancing, Restructuring and Improvement Act of 1991 marks the moment from which the RTC actually began to function as intended. It also created an environment in which regular taxpayers and investors—not just the rich and their well-heeled lawyers—could, for the first time, begin profiting from the S&L mess. Under the new structure the RTC functions more like a private-sector corporation than a government agency. Had this structure been chosen sooner, we might not have had the opportunity to write this book, and you might not have had so many properties to chose from.

It didn't take long for the RTC to capitalize on its newfound freedom of action. A month after the bill's passage the RTC held an auction of homes in Roswell, New Mexico, that was a smashing success—for both the RTC and home buyers. One of the projects the RTC inherited was the old, abandoned U.S. Air Force base outside Roswell. On the base were some 225 single-family homes that had once housed the base's officers and enlisted families.

The property had been neglected and the homes were quickly deteriorating in the hot desert sun. The RTC decided it wanted a quick and clean sale. About 200 people showed up to bid, and when the gavel fell for the last time that day every home had sold. Final sales prices ranged from a high price of $10,700 to a low of $1,700. First-time home buyer Rose Expinoza paid $5,500 for a three-bedroom, one-bath home. Investor Ray Sisneros purchased two homes that he planned to fix up and rent. Even in a soft real estate market he will be able to pocket a nice return on his investment by renting the property. When the market finally turns around he expects to sell the homes at a very nice profit.

But more than cheap homes are up for grabs in this giant garage sale. In fact, there is something in this grab bag for just about every size checkbook. There is definitely room here for the rich to get richer. In 1991 Denver billionaire Philip Anschutz became just a little richer when he purchased a downtown Denver skyscraper for a quarter of what it had sold for 25 years earlier. The building sold for $9 million in 1966. In 1982 it sold for $26 million. But when its owner defaulted on the loan the property joined the ranks of empty office space on the Denver market. Anschutz purchased the building from the RTC for just $2.25 million.

If it's land you want to invest in, the government has plenty. In fact, they have so much raw (undeveloped) land the RTC has said it will bend over backwards to make deals work and to speed sales. Under its streamlined land sales guidelines the RTC can sell real estate for *half* its appraised value! When was the last time anyone in America saw half-price land? And when will we ever see it again?

RTC's STRUCTURE

As we've said, the RTC is now structured much like a private corporation. It has its own board of directors that oversees its operations. Originally the RTC had two different boards, but they were combined and streamlined to cut down on bureaucratic red tape. Today the RTC board consists of the RTC chief executive, the chairman of the FDIC, the Federal Reserve chairman, the director of the OTS, and two private-sector public interest directors appointed by the President of the United States.

Headquartered in Washington, D.C., the agency further streamlined its departments in February 1992 to facilitate quicker sales and reshape policies and procedures. Four senior vice president positions were created to serve as The Four Horsemen of the S&L Apocalypse Committee. The four divisions are Legal, Planning and Corporate relations, Operations and Sales, and Asset Management and Sales. The RTC also has an inspector general's office, which investigates internal and external matters at the agency, including third-party contractors who work for the agency. Third-party contractors include, among others, real estate managers and brokers.

Although its central nervous system is in Washington, the RTC created consolidated offices in various regions of the country whose job it is to market and sell assets directly to the general public. If you are buying real estate or loans from the RTC, 9 times out of 10 you will be dealing primarily with an RTC consolidated office—not Washington. Most likely your first contact will be a real estate broker who is a contract employee of an RTC consolidated office.

WHAT'S FOR SALE?

Because it has so many different property types to sell, the RTC sorts them into different categories. Investors looking to buy properties can choose from the following categories (see the Yellow Pages for a full listing of the RTC Consolidated Offices).

Residential Real Estate

1) Single-family homes, duplexes, triplexes, and fourplexes, condominiums, and cooperatives.
2) Individual residentially zoned lots.
3) Affordable Housing Program: Single-family homes (1 to 4 units) appraised at $67,500 or less. These homes are first offered to low- and moderate-income buyers at preferential terms.

Multifamily Income Property

1) Apartment complexes (more than four units) and condominium and townhouse developments. Generally sold on a sealed-bid basis at public auctions.
2) Affordable Housing Program: Some multifamily apartment projects are placed in the Affordable Housing Program by the RTC and offered to buyers on favorable terms but under the condition that 35 percent of the units are maintained at reduced rents for low- to moderate-income tenants for 40 years.

Commercial and Industrial

1) Office buildings
2) Shopping centers
3) Former thrift and bank branch office buildings
4) Warehouses
5) Industrial complexes
6) Business parks
7) Motels, hotels, resorts
8) Developed recreational facilities
9) Mobile home parks

(See Chapter 6.)

Land

1) Undeveloped residential subdivisions
2) Commercial or industrially zoned parcels
3) Farmland and pasture land
4) Undeveloped recreational properties

(See Chapter 6.)

Environmentally Unsound Properties

These properties are generally put up for auction in segregated groups. The properties have been found to have certain environmental problems such as asbestos contamination, underground gas tanks, contaminated soil, and so on. The value of these properties has been greatly reduced by the RTC, taking into account the cleanup costs for the next owner. Buyers of environmentally unsound properties are required to complete cleanup before title can change hands.

Special Significance Properties

1) Environmentally significant (e.g., wetlands, wilderness areas)
2) Culturally significant (e.g., old Indian burial grounds)
3) Historically significant properties (e.g., the Alamo)

Special significance properties are further divided by their "value."

NATURAL VALUE. Properties of special significance are identified as properties within or adjacent to national landmarks, national or state parks, wilderness areas, wildlife refuges, areas identified by the U.S. Fish and Wildlife Service as "critical habitats," or other special natural features that include wetlands, ocean and lake shores, caves, dunes, coastal barrier islands, and estuaries.

RECREATIONAL VALUE. Properties of recreational special significance are identified as properties that are within or adjacent to existing public recreation areas or adjacent to rivers, oceans, or lakes.

SCIENTIFIC VALUE. These properties have special scientific significance or archaeological importance.

HISTORICAL OR CULTURAL VALUE. Properties of special cultural significance, based on criteria established by the National Register of Historic Places. Properties in the historic category refer to those built before 1941 that have special significance in American history, architecture, archaeology, engineering, and culture and that have buildings, structures, and objects that possess integrity of location, design, setting, materials, workmanship, feeling, and association and that

• are associated with events that have made a significant contribution to the broad patterns of our history or

- are associated with the lives of persons significant in our past or
- embody the distinctive characteristics of a type, period, or method of construction, represent the work of a master, possess high artistic values, or represent a significant or distinguishable entity whose components may lack individual distinction or
- have yielded, or may be likely to yield, information important in prehistory or history

Buyers acquiring historical property in any one of these designations will most likely find restrictions in the deed that limit the kinds of use the property can be put to and what can be built on it. These limitations will be compensated for by a lower asking price, but if they make the property useless to you, no price can be low enough.

Non–Real Estate Assets

Besides real estate and loans, the RTC has a lot of personal property for sale as well.

FURNITURE, FIXTURES, AND EQUIPMENT (FF&E)

1) Office furniture and equipment
2) Computers
3) Phone systems
4) Cars, boats, and planes
5) Fine (and not-so-fine) art
6) Miscellaneous personal property

See Chapter 9.

LOANS

1) Performing loans (secured loans that are not delinquent or delinquent less than 90 days)
   a) Delinquent up to 30 days
   b) Delinquent 30 to 90 days
2) Nonperforming loans (loans that are more than 90 days behind in payments)

Loans are also designated by quality as good, fair, poor, and distressed. See Chapter 8.

FAILED BANKS AND THE FDIC

The U.S. has about 12,000 banks currently open and operating. This figure includes small community banks, as well as large "money center" banks such as Citicorp in New York and NationsBank in Charlotte, North Carolina.

Banks didn't begin to die off as early as thrifts. While S&Ls began dropping like flies in 1985, serious trouble didn't hit the banking industry until three years later. But when it hit, it hit with a vengeance. More than 1,000 banks have failed in recent years—the same number of failures experienced by the thrift industry—and the end appears nowhere in sight. Even banking industry leaders admit that the American banking industry will shrink by several thousand more banks before this period of "consolidation" is over. In March 1992 the Office of Management and Budget had to admit that in the coming year even some giant money center banks faced failure and predicted that a single large failure could cost the FDIC an *additional* $4 billion. Bad news for the country, but it also means more bank assets up for sale to the public for years to come.

Besides the banks that have already failed, 1,081 banks were on the FDIC's so-called problem bank list at the beginning of 1992, an increase from 1991 when 1,033 banks were on the list. Not all the listed banks will fail. Some will be able to pull their chestnuts out of the fire, but even so, new ones will go on the list to replace them. Government economists estimate that at least 200 banks are likely to fail in 1993, with another 150 or so in 1994. The FDIC's own economists say that, though the number of banks that fail may get smaller each year, the problem will not be completely under control until the end of the century. In the meantime the FDIC must take control of these insolvent institutions, appraise their assets, and sell them to the highest bidder as quickly as it can. That means more assets available to you, the investor or home buyer.

THE FDIC'S STRUCTURE

Like the RTC, the FDIC has its own chair and a board of directors to oversee its vast operations. Up until a few years ago the FDIC was not in the asset liquidation business. Over the years the FDIC sold bits and pieces of insolvent banks but for the most part sold them "whole" to other banks looking to expand franchise and market share. When the trickle of bank failures turned into a tidal wave, the FDIC set up a separate department inside the agency called the Division of Liquidation to sell assets (real estate and loans mostly) from failed banks.

The FDIC also has regional and consolidated offices through which it sells assets. The FDIC regional and consolidated network breaks down as follows:

The Chicago Regional Office liquidates bank assets in Alabama, Arkansas, Delaware, District of Columbia, Florida, Georgia, Illinois, Indiana, Iowa, Kansas, Kentucky, Louisiana, Maryland, Michigan, Minnesota, Mississippi, Missouri, Nebraska, North Carolina, North Dakota, Ohio, South Carolina, South Dakota, Tennessee, Virginia, West Virginia, and Wisconsin. The Chicago regional office has consolidated offices in

- Atlanta, Ga.
- Knoxville, Tenn.
- Orlando, Fla.
- Rosemont, Ill.
- Shreveport, La.

The Dallas Regional Office liquidates bank assets in Oklahoma and Texas. The Dallas regional office has consolidated offices in

- Addison, Tx.
- Dallas
- Houston
- Midland, Tx.
- Oklahoma City
- San Antonio

The New York Regional Office liquidates assets in Connecticut, Maine, Massachusetts, New Hampshire, New Jersey, New York, Pennsylvania, Rhode Island, Boston, Vermont, Puerto Rico, and the Virgin Islands. The New York regional office has consolidated offices in

- South Brunswick, N.J.
- Hartford, Conn.
- Franklin, Mass.

The San Francisco Regional Office liquidates assets in Alaska, Arizona, California, Colorado, Guam, Hawaii, Idaho, Montana, Nevada, New Mexico, Oregon, Utah, Washington, and Wyoming. The San Francisco regional office has consolidated offices in

- Anchorage
- Denver
- Irvine, Calif.
- San Jose, Calif.

The FDIC also has special "Owned Real Estate" (ORE) centers in Atlanta, Dallas, Denver, Franklin, Irvine, and Orlando to sell real estate assets that have been appraised at $1 million or more to investors. (For the addresses of the regional, consolidated, and sales centers, see our Yellow Pages.)

When it comes to selling assets the FDIC works much like the RTC. As with the RTC, if you want to buy a piece of real estate, you will not be dealing with Washington but with the FDIC consolidated office in charge of that asset.

The FDIC also has a computer data base called the ORE Bulletin Board (private investors and bankers use the more common REO, or Real Estate Owned, rather than ORE) where you can access all of its available assets through a personal computer. However, at this writing, unlike the RTC, the FDIC does not have a dedicated toll-free telephone number from which you can request any type of asset. The FDIC will provide you with a list of available assets, but you will have to call the consolidated office in the area in which you want to invest. We suspect that as its caseload grows it will only be a matter of time before the FDIC sets up a toll-free nationwide specific asset inquiry service like the RTC's. We cover both agencies' computer data bases later in the book.

AFFORDABLE HOUSING

One pleasant by-product of the S&L and banking debacles is the opportunity for people with low and moderate incomes to finally become homeowners. When Congress was asked to vote tens of billions of dollars to bail out depositors of failed thrifts and banks, they imposed a condition: Make some of these assets available to low- and moderate-income Americans. This was not a request, it was an order.

In response, both the FDIC and the RTC established their own separate affordable housing programs, also known as AFH programs. We believe these programs are so important and the opportunities so great that we will cover these programs in great detail later in the book. In short, the AFH programs offer the first genuine opportunity in a very long time for low- and moderate-income families and individuals to own their own homes. It's an opportunity waiting for people to act.

OTHER GOVERNMENT AGENCIES AND COMPANIES THAT SELL REAL ESTATE

HUD: THE DEPARTMENT OF HOUSING AND URBAN DEVELOPMENT

Banks and savings and loans weren't the only institutions abused during the 1980s. Republican insiders turned the Department of Housing and Urban Development (HUD) into their own personal pork barrel during the Reagan administration. Instead of building low-income housing, HUD officials handed out fat contracts to fat cat friends for upscale housing developments, recreational facilities, even an off-track betting complex—everything but housing for the economically disadvantaged.

When they did hand out a contract to build an apartment building with affordable rents, developers often pocketed the development fees and then defaulted on their obligations to HUD, and the agency got stuck with the real estate. As a result, HUD had the distinction of being the largest seller of single-family homes during the last decade as it tried to shed its growing inventory of repossessed properties.

HUD was chartered fifty years ago to promote housing affordability and to make decent housing available to lower-wage Americans who were priced out of the home market for one reason or another. The Federal Housing Authority (FHA), which is part of HUD, insures billions of dollars in single-family mortgages so lenders will make the loans. When an FHA-guaranteed loan goes into default it is HUD's job to foreclose and sell the homes.

Unfortunately for the government, HUD and FHA didn't do such a great job of underwriting home mortgages during the late 1970s and 1980s, resulting in tens of thousands of foreclosures. In 1990 HUD sold 80,179 homes, followed by 73,178 in 1991. HUD has also sold a few hundred or so apartment buildings—and there's more where these came from.

Like the RTC and FDIC, to a certain degree HUD is decentralized. You won't have to go to Washington to buy a home from the agency. HUD maintains ten regional offices that oversee eighty field offices that sell these homes. HUD regional offices are in the following cities:

- Boston
- New York
- Philadelphia
- Atlanta
- Chicago
- Ft. Worth, Tx.
- Kansas City, Mo.
- Denver
- San Francisco
- Seattle

In our section on affordable housing we will discuss buying HUD properties in greater detail.

FANNIE AND FREDDIE

The Federal Home Loan Mortgage Corporation (FHLMC), also known to investors as Freddie Mac, and the Federal National Mortgage Association (FNMA), or Fannie Mae, are two publicly traded financial institutions that buy mortgages from S&Ls, mortgage bankers, and banks. Chartered by Congress to make mortgage money more available to homeowners and to provide liquidity to the home mortgage market, these two companies have been extremely profitable during the last several years. Fannie and Freddie purchase mortgages originated by S&Ls, banks, and other lenders and package them into securities that are then sold on Wall Street. In the past few years Fannie Mae has made $1 billion per year while Freddie Mac has made about $500 million per year.

Despite their phenomenal success, they occasionally get stuck with bad loans and must foreclose. Once they foreclose they must sell the homes. In 1990, for instance, Fannie Mae seized 9,034 single-family homes and 25 apartment buildings. Once it takes control of these properties it must resell them. Besides buying from the RTC, FDIC, and HUD, investors may want to consider buying properties from these two agencies as well.

Fannie Mae has regional offices in

- Chicago
- Philadelphia
- Atlanta
- Dallas
- Pasadena

Freddie Mac has regional offices in

- Arlington, Va.
- Chicago
- Atlanta
- Sherman Oaks, Calif.

(For full listings see the Yellow Pages.)

If you want to buy a home from either agency, the place to start is the regional offices. The nice thing about dealing with Fannie Mae and Freddie Mac is that they are extremely professional and move houses at a much quicker pace than the RTC, FDIC, and HUD. Despite some defaults, their loans tend to be of a higher quality than the government's, which means the properties are likely in better physical shape. The downside is that since they are in better shape, they will cost more than government-owned real estate.

IN SUMMARY

The RTC got off to a jerky start when it was formed in 1989 to sell off S&L assets. It made a lot of mistakes and a lot of enemies during those early days. Though all that changed in 1991 after a major Congressional overhall, the reputation has lingered, keeping a lot of would-be investors away.

On the heels of the S&L mess came the banking industry crisis, resulting in the failure of hundreds of banks and piling even more assets into the laps of federal regulators, this time the FDIC. It too is now peddling these assets right alongside the RTC.

As if that were not enough, in 1988 the sins of those who mismanaged HUD came home to roost as well, burdening that organization with tens of thousands of repossessed housing units—all of which have to be sold.

Taken all together it's the biggest garage sale in history—homes, condos, office buildings, commercial space, office equipment, cars, boats, planes—if a bank or S&L or their customers could dump money into it, it's for sale today through one of these federal agencies. So, as you can see, there is no shortage of assets for sale from these government agencies. For the ordinary American the meltdown in ethics and common sense during the 1980s has created the best real estate buying opportunity probably since the end of WWII. In the pages ahead we will show you the ropes.

Chapter Two

....

Dialing for Dollars

How to Access the System without
Even Leaving Home

Dealing with government agencies, whether it's the Postal Service, the IRS, Congress, the RTC, or the FDIC, can be a once-in-a-lifetime experience—you try it once and then promise never to put yourself through such an ordeal again.

Prior to 1991, investors trying to buy repossessed real estate from bank and thrift regulators had a tough time of it. Telephone calls went unreturned, asset lists were not available or slow in coming, properties listed for sale had actually been sold long ago to someone else, and so on. But things began to change in mid-1991 when RTC and FDIC officials finally realized they had to look and act like a private company, not a government bureaucracy. Otherwise, they knew that they would be stuck with their billion-dollar inventories until doomsday.

To accomplish this, the bureaucrats swallowed hard and turned to the private sector, that is, nongovernmental contractors and consultants who sell real estate and other assets for a living. After studying the RTC's sales efforts, these consultants concluded what every businessperson already knew: The most important contact with a prospective customer is the initial contact. If a customer's first impression is a bad one, then the relationship tends to end right there.

For those with no experience whatsoever in buying assets from the government, there are a few different ways to get started:

1) Watch the newspaper for RTC and FDIC auction notices
2) Call the RTC or FDIC consolidated office nearest you and ask for a real estate or loan account executive
3) Call a realtor who specializes in RTC and FDIC properties or
4) Tap the two agencies' easily-accessible computer data bases of available properties

In this chapter we will concentrate on the last option. Only by being the first to get your hands on the inventory list will you be able to beat the competition. The best way to do this is by tapping the RTC's data base of available real estate and loans. By doing so you can quickly and easily discover what properties are available in your area—hopefully before others do. At that point you can buy a property from the government[1] before it goes to auction. Though circumstances differ, chances are you will be able to buy a home, apartment building, or whatever cheaper than if you wait for a public auction.

THE RTC: DIALING FOR INFO

You don't need a computer to tap into the RTC's computer data base, just a touch-tone telephone. (If you do have a computer there is an even better way to get information. We will explain how to conduct an RTC computer search with your home computer later.) The RTC has estab-

---

[1] Throughout this book you will come across the terms *RTC, FDIC*, and *government*. For the most part these terms are interchangeable. Although the RTC only sells S&L assets and the FDIC only sells bank assets, they both use similar policies and methods. Where they do not, it will be noted. Both, of course, are government agencies.

lished a half-dozen different toll-free 800 lines staffed by professional telemarketers who give clear instructions and bend over backwards to provide you with any information you need.

There are a number of 800 numbers you can call to get different kinds of information. (All are listed in the Yellow Pages in the back of this book.) The most important 800 line you will use is the asset specific inquiry (ASI) line. The number is 1-800-RTC-3006 (1-800-782-3006).[2] To access the RTC's data base with just a phone call you will need to have a touch-tone telephone. Old rotary phones *will not* work. The asset specific inquiry data base operates through a computerized voice mail system that does not respond to rotary signals.

Once you get into the system by dialing the telephone number given above, an electronic salesperson will offer you several numbered choices. The choices change occasionally, depending on what kind of special programs the RTC has going at the time. Still, one of the choices will always connect you to a telemarketing service that will mail at your request a computer printout of property for sale in your area. This is called the **Real Estate Asset Specific Program** and it is touch-tone choice number 1.

After pushing 1 you will be given more choices, one of which will again be a list of specific properties for sale. Take your time. This is a toll-free number—it costs you nothing, so feel free to do a little browsing with your ear. Each time you call, pick a different asset category and get to know your way around the system. You should find it an efficient and user-friendly environment in which you can never wear out your welcome.

One of the choices offered allows you to order an RTC catalog of auctions that the agency provides to callers at no cost. The ordering process is completely automated, utilizing the touch-tone features on your telephone. You will be asked to punch in your zip code, then your daytime telephone number. You then will be asked to clearly speak your name and address at the sound of a tone. This will be recorded. About five days later your RTC catalog will arrive in your mailbox. If General Motors operated this well the Japanese would be in serious trouble.

---

[2] This telephone number was current at the time of publication. Though we don't expect it to, the telephone number could change for one reason or another. If it does, call the RTC in Washington to get the new telephone number.

If, when you were given all these choices, you selected the "Asset Specific" choice, you will finally be connected to a live person who will explain what kind of information you can receive from them. These operators sit at a terminal connected directly to the RTC's computers and will conduct up to five computer searches for you on any one phone contact and will mail you a computer printout of properties in your area that conform to your personally requested criteria. This service will cost you only 10 cents per property listed, with a $5 minimum. The only acceptable form of payment is by Visa, MasterCard, or American Express, so as they say, "have your credit card ready." If you find 100 properties that fit your geographical, price, and size needs, you'll be charged $10 on your credit card. (There is no charge if you do not ask that the list be mailed to you.)

The RTC operator will first ask you a few questions to help you narrow down your search. The operator will ask what kind of properties you're interested in and will offer various searchable categories, including single-family residential, duplexes, apartments, commercial, and offices. After you pick a category the operator will ask what part of the country you want searched. They can search by town, city, state, or by the first three numbers of a specific zip code area.

Once the operator has this information the search takes only about 30 seconds. The operator will tell you how many properties there are currently for sale in your category and target area. The operator will then ask if you want a printout of the properties mailed to you. Again, the list takes about five working days to arrive. The operators *will not* give you information over the telephone on these properties. The only information they are allowed to give over the phone is how many properties the computer found that fit your criteria. They are not trying to be unreasonable. These operators are professional telemarketers, not licensed real estate agents. Giving out details of properties over the phone would put these operators in conflict with state laws requiring that only licensed realtors can market real estate to the general public.

The RTC asset specific computer list you receive will provide limited information about the property, including its asking price, size, and type. (Exhibit 1 is an example of an RTC computer printout.) That's all you need to get started. The asset specific computer list will include the name and telephone number of the realtor (or asset manager, as the

RTC calls them) handling the marketing of the property for the agency. If you like, call the realtor and arrange to view the desired property.

If for any reason the realtor gives you the runaround, you should then call the consolidated office in charge of that property (that number will also be listed on the printout) to complain or arrange a viewing. The realtors are contract employees of the RTC. Most of the time you will be dealing with the realtor. The RTC picks these realtors from those who apply for RTC listings. The RTC likes to hear feedback, good or bad, about the kind of service you get from these realtors. With an estimated 80,000 realtors handling RTC and FDIC listings nationwide, they won't know if a realtor is doing a bad job unless you tell the regional office.

Unless you're investing in large commercial properties costing $25 million or more, you won't be dealing directly with the RTC consolidated office at all. The properties are offered through realtors who collect the offers and forward them to an RTC account executive at the local consolidated office in charge of the property who selects the winning offer.

The RTC updates its computer files on a regular basis. Keep in mind that the agency is a big bureaucracy and hasn't worked out all the bugs in its computer and telephone systems just yet. Chances are they never will. So don't be surprised if you find that a property listed on your printout has already been sold or that a sale is pending on it when you call the realtor. Sometimes the computer lists you receive can be up to 30 days old at any one time. If you contact the realtor listed on the asset printout—even if the property has been sold—you will not have wasted your time because you've just met someone important—an approved RTC asset manager, who most likely will be getting more RTC listings in the weeks and months ahead. Because the realtor is paid a commission when the property sells, he or she has every reason in the world to give you a call when new listings arrive.

OTHER TOLL-FREE SERVICES

Asset Inventory Publications, 1-800-431-0600. Through this number you can order and have mailed to you a six-volume set of books that lists every single asset the RTC has for sale. The books are updated every six months and cost $100.

You can also order just the commercial property listing volume

```
                    Residential - Single Family - 1 Family
                        Selected City: San Francisco
Asset Type/Number        : RES SINGLE FAM DET. 1 FAM / 7285
Broker Name/Number       : (000)
RTC Contact Name/Number: PENA, HENRY (714) 631-8600

Address          : 49      MINERVA      ST  Total Square Feet : 1671
                   SAN FRANCISCO, CA   94112
List Price       : $.00                     Year Built        : 1976
Condition        :                          Construction Type : WOO
Bedrooms         : 3                        No. Fireplaces    : 1
Bathrooms        : 2                        Garage            : 2
Heat             : GAS                      Air Condition     : NON
Amenities        :
------------------------------------------------------------------------

Asset Type/Number        : RES SINGLE FAM DET. 1 FAM / 7285
Broker Name/Number       : (000)
RTC Contact Name/Number: PETERSON, MARTHA (415) 391-4742

Address          : 763     31ST         AVE Total Square Feet : 0
                   SAN FRANCISCO, CA   94121
List Price       : $.00                     Year Built        : 0000
Condition        :                          Construction Type :
Bedrooms         : 0                        No. Fireplaces    : 0
Bathrooms        : 0                        Garage            : 0
Heat             :                          Air Condition     :
Amenities        :
------------------------------------------------------------------------

Asset Type/Number        : RES SINGLE FAM DET. 1 FAM / 7828
Broker Name/Number       : (000)
RTC Contact Name/Number: BILL KIRWIN (714) 852-7700

Address          : 1043    HOLLISTER    AVE Total Square Feet : 816
                   SAN FRANCISCO, CA   94124
List Price       : $.00                     Year Built        : 1905
Condition        : FAIR                     Construction Type : STU
Bedrooms         : 3                        No. Fireplaces    : 0
Bathrooms        : 1                        Garage            : 0
Heat             : ELE                      Air Condition     : NON
Amenities        :
------------------------------------------------------------------------
```

EXHIBIT 1.   When you call the Asset Specific line and order a computer printout of properties for sale near you, this is what you will receive. Note the $0 prices. This was an early problem with the system and is supposed to be history by the time this book reaches you.

for $25, the four residential volumes for $15 each, or the land volume for $15. If you don't want to spend that kind of money for information that could be months old, you can look at these volumes free of charge at your nearest Federal Depository Library (FDL). The RTC asset inventory publications operator will tell you where the closest FDL is located.

Portfolio Sales, 1-800-348-1484. Operators on this line will tell you about "pools" of property. A pool of similar properties might include a half dozen or so apartment buildings or condo units sold as a single asset—one bid takes all. Sometimes the agency will offer in one package an apartment building, a few office complexes, and a portfolio of nonperforming loans collateralized by small shopping centers. Occasionally the FDIC and RTC might mix and match properties in the same package. Other times it will keep the package to "like-kind" properties only. It all depends on which properties the government can get title to prior to a scheduled offering. These types of packages often are sold through a sealed bid auction in which you will have to compete against other bidders. This number will plug you into the portfolio sales calendar of events.

Contractor Line, 1-800-541-1782. If you're a licensed real estate broker looking for listings, this is the number to call. It will connect you to the Contracting Division of the RTC, where 80,000 real estate brokers have preceded you, and many are now representing the agency.

Seller Financing, 1-800-533-8951. If you need a loan and don't want to go through a bank or S&L or tried and were rejected, this is the number to call. It offers up-to-date information about RTC financing, loans, and terms.

The above numbers will get you started. Feel free to test these telephone numbers until you get a solid sense of how the RTC is structured. Most operators are a wealth of information and the automated lines are easy to use. You should order every brochure and schedule they offer. Not only will the brochures be informative, but the RTC's computer has a wonderful memory and once you enter your name and address the computer keeps it on file. That means that the next time you call in and ask an operator to send you something your information will already be on file.

The RTC also uses this information as a mailing list. If the agency is planning a big event in your area you'll be on their mailing list.

LET YOUR FINGERS DO THE TALKING

If you want to buy more than one piece of property from the RTC, the best favor you can do for yourself is to sign on to RTCNET. This is a private, computerized data base accessible over standard telephone lines with a personal computer. It was created and is maintained for the RTC by Business Information Network (BIN), a private provider of on-line computer data bases. BIN is headquartered in Fort Washington, Maryland.

Once you become a BIN subscriber and are assigned an RTCNET password by BIN you can literally browse the entire current RTC asset portfolio—nationwide—from the comfort of your own home or office through your personal computer. BIN has developed a sophisticated yet simple system for the RTC. RTCNET strikes a balance between the search and retrieval requirements of the sophisticated commercial computer data base user with the needs of the novice. The system is quick, powerful, and simple to use.

BIN updates its RTCNET data base weekly directly off the RTC's own mainframe computer system, called REOM or Real Estate Owned Management system. The RTC's computer system has garnered some criticism from the General Accounting Office because of its lack of timeliness. Our tests of the system turned up a number of properties listed for sale that had already sold. This can be a common problem when dealing with computer data bases for which the data is provided by the federal government.

The time lag is caused by the bureaucratic constraints placed on RTC asset managers. When an RTC asset manager sells a piece of real estate the manager cannot directly update the listing on the computer but must send the sales verification material to an RTC consolidated office, where it must be reviewed and then approved by RTC personnel. Only once all the documentation is found to be in order (and the money is in the bank) does the RTC remove the listing from its REOM system. Only then does the RTC let BIN update the data on RTCNET. This can take up to 45 days in some cases.

Being told a property has already sold when you call can be a disappointment, but we consider this to be a relatively small flaw. It in no way diminishes the value of RTCNET to the serious investor. The good news is that the RTC has been made aware of this problem and has begun a crash program to reduce the lag time involved in updating its system.

But most important to you is the contacts, broker names, and telephone numbers you can extract from RTCNET. Even if a particular listing is sold, the realtor (an approved private-sector RTC asset manager) you telephoned will most likely be handling new RTC listings soon. Tell the realtor what sort of properties you're interested in. Often realtors know about new listings before they hit RTCNET. Developing a personal relationship with several RTC asset managers will give you a leg up. "I have properties all the time that I know I can sell but can't get listed on the REOM computer until all the paperwork is done," says Maryland asset manager Larry Ashbury, whose company manages hundreds of RTC properties. Once RTCNET puts you in touch with people like Larry, you will be alerted to deals even before they hit the computer.

RTCNET EQUIPMENT REQUIREMENTS

To use RTCNET you will need only the simplest computer equipment. Here is the minimum system required:

- An IBM-compatible computer, IBM PS/2, or an Apple Macintosh with minimum 256K of memory
- Either floppy or hard disk drives (hard is much better)
- A modem of any kind 300-9600 baud (Hayes compatible is best)
- A computer printer—any kind

If you don't already own a computer, we suggest you buy an IBM compatible—at least 640K memory with at least a 20-megabyte hard disk and a 1200/2400 baud Hayes or Hayes-compatible internal modem card. A color monitor is nice, easy on the eyes, but not mandatory. A monochrome monitor will work just fine. If you shop around you can purchase a nice 286 IBM compatible with the above minimum requirements for around $1,000. You can buy computers with 386 and even 486 microprocessors now, but a 286 will be plenty fast and a lot cheaper. As for the choice of a printer, you can pay as little as $199 for a cheap dot matrix printer or up to $1000 or more for a laser printer. Your choice depends more on what other plans you have for your printer besides printing out RTC property listings. RTCNET supports any kind of printer.

HOW TO SIGN UP

Subscribing to RTCNET is easy. Simply dial 1-800-366-9246. Again, have your Visa, MasterCard, or American Express card ready because that's all they take. The operator will sign you up. Subscription fees are quite reasonable. You will be charged an annual subscription fee of $192, and a one-time software fee. The software fee is $48 if your computer is an IBM or IBM compatible, and $113 if you own an Apple Macintosh.

BIN will mail you their proprietary communications software on either 5¼″ or 3½″ disk—whichever your machine uses. You will not need to buy a separate communications program. BIN developed its own communications software in order to address two basic problems. First, it did not want computer "hackers" using their own sophisticated communications software to crash into BIN's data base and cause havoc. To access BIN, users must use BIN's own communications program, which identifies the user as a BIN member. BIN's software also allows the "computer-challenged"—techno-peasants—to use its system successfully. About all you have to know is how to turn on your computer. BIN's software takes care of the rest.

When you subscribe to RTCNET on BIN you also become a BIN member. This allows you access to a number of non-RTC data bases that also list properties for sale.

BIN ON-LINE CHARGES

Because BIN uses an 800 number to access its on-line service, you will not be charged for a toll call for connecting to the system even though BIN's computer is in Maryland. But once you are on the system you will be charged connect time fees. It will cost 41 cents per minute (32 cents if you are in Maryland) for the on-line charge. BIN recently examined the billings for its three thousand subscribers and said that the average RTCNET user runs up about $13 a month in on-line charges.

SIGNING ON TO THE NET

When your BIN software disk arrives in the mail, just slip it into your disk drive and type INSTALL. The software does virtually all the rest. It first probes the guts of your computer, analyzing your communication and graphic systems. This takes about 30 seconds.

When the grand tour is finished the software will offer a list of modems on your screen to choose from and ask which one comes closest to yours. If your particular modem is not listed, or you don't have a clue, select "Hayes Compatible." The computer will then ask if your telephone system requires a prefix when dialing out. Some company phone systems require that you dial an 8 or 9 prefix to get an outside line. If your modem is hooked to such a line choose "yes" and type the prefix. If you have a call waiting service, the next choice allows you to disable it while using RTCNET. Do so. Incoming calls on call waiting will scramble data coming in from RTCNET.

When all these changes are made the program searches your disk and creates a subdirectory called CALLBIN. All the modified files will be copied to this subdirectory, leaving your original files untouched. Once everything is completed the software will modify itself to fit your machine. This includes setting itself to the maximum baud speed of your modem. You will be able to modify baud speed in later sessions but for now don't worry; all is as it should be.

DIALING FOR DOLLARS

You are now ready to access the on-line RTCNET program. Using your hard disk or C-drive, enter the CALLBIN directory by typing CALLBIN. Your computer screen will tell you that the software is configuring your modem for the call. Then you will hear it dial and connect to BIN. You will know you are connected because a large "BIN" appears on your screen against a blue background (if you have color). The system will ask for your log-in code, which should have come with your software. Type the four-digit log-in code and hit enter.

You will then be asked to type your secret log-in ID number, usually a five-digit code. Don't worry if you can't see it on the screen as you type.

For security reasons only asterisks appear in case someone's looking over your shoulder. You get three cracks at this before the system disconnects you. If that happens redial and try again. Because they can't see the ID code they're typing, some new users get nervous and make mistakes. Keep trying. Type carefully, and don't give up.

Once you pass through this electronic checkpoint you're all set. The RTC's vast inventory will be an open book. Select "RTCNET" from the BIN main menu and you will get the RTC main menu. Here you get several choices:

1) NEWS: Calendar of auctions, upcoming sales events, and current RTC press releases announcing special sales events
2) USERS MANUAL: Relevant excerpts from the RTC policy manual on bid and sales procedures
3) SILVER LINING: Full text of the RTC's Affordable Housing Program newsletter
4) RTC DATA BASE: Available assets for sale nationwide

THE DATA BASE

This is the heart of RTCNET. When you select this choice a "drop down" menu will appear, giving you three further choices:

- Residential
- Commercial
- Land

Whichever you choose, a new menu will appear at the top of the computer screen. This is the meat and potatoes of RTCNET. Let's assume you picked the residential category. You now will see a residential SEARCH menu that allows you to conduct a broad search (for example, all single-family homes under $20,000) or a narrow search (all single-family homes in Dogpatch, Idaho, listed for under $20,000 that have an acre of land, a pool, four bedrooms, and a two-car garage). The SEARCH menu looks like this:

SEARCH	PropType	City	State	Region	Zip Code
Style	Bedrooms	TotRooms →		Amenities Price	
IntSqFt	Instit#	EDIT	Srch →	CLEARSrch	

PropType: If you choose this a drop down menu will give you a number of choices. In this case you will be asked to choose between:

Single-family residential
Single-family duplex
Single-family quadruplex
Single-family attached townhouse
All of the above
Single-family attached condominium
Single-family attached co-op
Single-family attached timeshare
Multifamily—5 + units
Mobile home

City: Type the name of any city. Spelling is important. New York could become Newark.

State: Displays a listing of all states. Pick the one or ones you want.

Region: Lists the RTC's regions: Eastern, Southwestern, Western, and North Central.

Zip Code: The system can search by the entire zip code or by partial zip codes. You might want to try several areas covered by different zip codes: for example 95466, 95472, 95401, 95404, or 95407—all are within one geographical area but each represents different small towns or suburbs. By entering the 954 prefix you will get any available property listed in that area. (This is the smartest way if you are interested in a distinct area and those touching on its main zip county boundary.)

Style: What kind of architecture do you like? Do you want single story or multistory?

Bedrooms: Tell the system how many you want.

TotRooms: How many rooms do you want in your new house?

Amenities: Want a pool? Other choices include laundry room, exercise facility, clubhouse, tennis, playground, storage, and security systems.

Price: Set your upper limits. If you select this option the computer will allow you to specify your price range by selecting: >$xxx,xxx and <$xxx,xxx. For example, you might want to set your upper limit at homes selling for no more than $99,000 but don't want to look at homes selling for less than $65,000. In such a case you would answer the computer's query with: <$99,000 (properties listed for less than $99,000) and >$65,000 (properties listed for more than $65,000). The computer will then cull out all properties above and below your two limits and give you only those which fall between these two parameters.

Lot Size: Want some acreage or just a large back yard?

IntSqFt: How many internal square feet do you need?

Instit#: Institution number. If you want to buy real estate from a specific failed S&L that was once near and dear to your heart, here's your chance. S&L assets listed on RTCNET are in the process of being liquidated or sold by the RTC or might be open to the public under a "conservatorship," which is sort of like an orphanage system for wayward thrifts.

EDIT Srch: Each time you choose search criteria the BIN program keeps tabs on your choices by listing them on screen in a small separate "dialogue box." This way you can always see the choices you've made so far. If you change your mind about a choice, just hit the EDIT function and the program will allow you to change one or more of your choices.

CLEAR Srch: At the end of each search the program will still retain all your search instructions. Select this option to clear those criteria before you start a new search.

MainMenu: Returns you to the RTCNET main menu.

You can choose as many search criteria as you desire. The more you choose the narrower the search and the fewer properties will pop up. Mix and match to your heart's content. The more specific you get the less you will be bothered with listings that don't suit your investment needs.

Once you select all your search criteria move the cursor to the word SEARCH on the menu and hit ENTER. Within seconds you will see the first listings scrolling across your computer screen. A counter on the top of the screen will tick off listings as the computer finds them. When it stops changing you know that the computer has found everything close to your search criteria.

Each listing is comprised of four "pages" or screens of data. (See Exhibit 2). You can use your F keys to move through the data. F2 will take you to page two, F3 to page three, and F4 to page four. Moving the cursor to NEXT will take you to the next listing.

Each residential property listing on RTCNET will contain the following information:

- Property address
- Institution number (failed institution)
- Property type
- Asking price
- Status of legal title
- Acquisition date
- Ownership (full or partnership or joint venture)
- Occupancy status (occupied or unoccupied)
- Year built
- Style
- Total number of lots
- Number of floors
- Number of bedrooms
- Type of heating and air conditioning
- Types of amenities (pool, sauna, etc.)
- Zoning
- Construction type (wood, frame, brick)
- Condition of property (good, fair, poor)
- Total number of rooms
- Total square footage (inside)
- Number of outbuildings

         Copyright (c) 1991 Business Information Network, Inc.
                         1-800-366-9246

                        Residential Database

          Asset Name:
    Property Address: 18475 WEXFORD
    City, State, Zip: DETROIT, MI   48234-
  Institution Number: 7194   REO Number: 12517127
       Property Type: SINGLE FAMILY RESIDENCE
               Price: $750   Ownership: FULLY OWNED
         Legal Title: Occupancy: UNOCCUPIED
    Acquisition Date: 09/28/90

                 ZDDDDDDDDDDDD Contact DDDDDDDDDDDD?
                 REO DEPARTMENT
                 (215) 650-8500

  ZDDDDDDD RTC Asset Manager DDDDDDDD?   ZDDDDDDDDDDDDDDD Broker DDDDDDDDDDDDDD?
  RTC SALES CENTER   RTC SALES CENTER
  (800) 782-6326   (800) 782-6326

  ZDDDDDDDD Property Manager DDDDDDDD?   ZDDDDD Contract Asset Manager DDDDD?
  RTC SALES CENTER   RTC SALES CENTER
  (800) 782-6326   (800) 782-6326

              Affordable Housing Eligibility: NO
         Year Built: 1928   Construction Type: BRICK FRONT
              Style: COLONIAL   Condition: POOR
       Total # Lots: 1   Total Rooms: 10
    Land (in Acres): 0.10   Total Square Feet: 1862
           # Floors: 2   # OutBuildings: 0
         # Bedrooms: 4   # Bathrooms: 2.0
     Size of Garage: 0.0   Size of Carport: 0.0
       Type of Heat: GAS   Type of A/C: NONE
               Pool: NO   Jacuzzi: UNKNOWN
             Tennis: UNKNOWN   Fireplace: NO
       Zoning Class: RESIDENTIAL
        Description: CONVEYANCE. REQUIRES MAJOR REPAIRS

    Institution Name: EMPIRE FEDERAL SAVINGS BANK OF AMER
             Address: 1000 ADAMS AVEN
                    : NORRISTOWN, PA 19401-
             Contact: REO DEPARTMENT
             Phone #: (215) 650-8500

  Search criterion:
  Typecode EQUALS All Above: Single, Duplex, Tri, Quad, Townhouse
  Price LESS THAN 20000

EXHIBIT 2.   When you pull a residential property file off RTCNET and print them
out on your own home computer printer, this is what they look like.

- Size of garage or carport
- Fireplace
- General description
- RTC asset manager contact (person and phone number)
- Name of failed institution from which asset was acquired
- RTC consolidated office telephone number and contact person responsible for this particular asset

RETRIEVING AND PRINTING RTC DATA

The search criteria you choose might result in a lot of "hits." But don't use expensive on-line time to read them all—you will want a physical record for reference. Here again BIN has made life easy for you. A search we conducted of the RTC's residential data base for "all homes under $20,000" resulted in 1,661 available listings! At four pages each that meant scrolling through 6,644 pages of text. But that's a waste of time and money. Just hit the F5 button and the computer will ask if you want to print the listings out on your printer or save them to disk. Unless it's only a few pages of text, we recommend saving to disk. Before printing you may want to edit the list down to just the useful information. When you choose the disk option the system will ask you for a file name and path, for example, C: RTC HOMES. This saves the file, called HOMES, on your hard disk or C-drive. (You can name the file whatever you like. We chose HOMES as an example.)

When you name the file, a small bar graph will appear on screen, telling you how much data has been transferred and how much is yet to come. When the transfer is complete, sign off RTCNET. You can then view the captured data at your leisure rather than running up on-line computer charges. We found that the best way to view data is to load it into your word processor. If you have a word processor that can handle ASCII text files (like WordPerfect), just load the file like any DOS text file. You will have some line spacing but it's not that big a deal; hit your DELETE button to kill the spaces. (You can save yourself a lot of work in this regard by simply resetting your word processor's margins from the standard default setting of 1" to .5". That's how BIN configures the data when it transmits it to you.)

COMMERCIAL REAL ESTATE ON RTCNET

If under "PropType" you selected COMMERCIAL you will have the following choices to select from:

- Mobile home park
- Office complex
- Retail
- Time share—resort
- Storage facilities/mini warehouse
- Industrial parks/warehouses
- Restaurant
- Hotel/motel
- Marina/boat yard
- Parking garage/lot
- Medical facility/private hospitals
- Nursing/retirement homes
- Resort/golf courses
- Recreation/athletic club
- Churches
- Schools
- Other commercial
- 5+ unit apartment and condo projects
- Office condos

Each commercial property listing on RTCNET will contain the following information, again in four screens (see Exhibit 3):

- Property address
- Property type
- Total number of rental units
- Asking price
- Acquisition date
- Ownership status
- Occupancy status

Copyright (c) 1991 Business Information Network, Inc.
1-800-366-9246

Commercial Database

```
           Asset Name: 1923 N. PAN AM
       Property Address: 1923 N PAN AM
       City, State, Zip: SAN ANTONIO, TX  78208-
    Institution Number: 7334                   REO Number: 32373953
          Property Type: 5+ APARTMENTS & CONDOMINIUM PROJECTS
       Number of Units: 8
                 Price: $42,000
           Legal Title:                    Ownership: FULLY OWNED
      Acquisition Date: 06/29/90           Occupancy: UNOCCUPIED
```

```
                         ZDDDDDDDDDDDD  Contact DDDDDDDDDDDD?
                         NANCY DENNIS
                         (303) 573-5959

ZDDDDDDD RTC Asset Manager DDDDDDDD?    ZDDDDDDDDDDDDD Broker DDDDDDDDDDDDD?
LEE SANDERS                             LEE SANDERS
                                        15505 SPUR CLIP
        -                               HELOTES, TX 78023-
(512) 695-2424                          (512) 695-2424

ZDDDDDDDD Property Manager DDDDDDDD?    ZDDDDD Contract Asset Manager DDDDD?
LEE SANDERS                             NANCY DENNIS
                                        1515 ARAPAHOE STRE
        -                               DENVER, CO 80202-
(512) 695-2424                          (303) 573-5959
```

```
                   Affordable Housing Eligibility: NO
           Year Built: 1930  # of Buildings: 1      # of Units: 8
            # of Lots: 1     # of Floors: 2   Land (in acres): 0.00
                Style: CONTEMPORARY           Construction: WOOD FRAME
           Total SqFt: 8405              Net Rentable SqFt: 5356
            Avg. Rent: $0                 Avg. Net Income: $0
   Avg. Total Expenses: $0
      1 Bedroom Units: 6                      Average SqFt: 0
      2 Bedroom Units: 2                      Average SqFt: 0
      3 Bedroom Units: 0                      Average SqFt: 0
      4 Bedroom Units: 0                      Average SqFt: 0
   Studio/Effic. Units: 0                     Average SqFt: 0
   # Uncovered Parking: 0               # Covered Parking: 0
            Elevators: NO        Pools: UNKNOWN    Storage: UNKNOWN
          Playgrounds: UNKNOWN  Tennis: UNKNOWN   Exercise: UNKNOWN
    Laundry Facilities: UNKNOWN Security: NO     Clubhouse: UNKNOWN
            Condition: FAIR
               Zoning: D
          Description:
```

```
    Institution Name: TRAVIS SAVINGS & LOAN ASSOC
             Address: 10100 REUNIO PLACE
                    : SAN ANTONIO, TX 78216-
             Contact: PAT KITTELL
             Phone #: (512) 841-8281
```

EXHIBIT 3.   When you pull a commercial property listing off RTCNet, this is the imformation you receive.

46

- Year built
- Style
- Total square footage
- Average rents
- Average expenses
- Number of 1-bedroom units
- Number of 2-bedroom units
- Number of 3-bedroom units
- Number of 4-bedroom units
- Studio/efficiency units
- Number of parking spaces (uncovered and covered)
- Elevators
- Playgrounds
- Laundry facilities
- Physical condition
- Zoning
- Lot size
- Construction type
- Net rentable square footage
- Average net rents
- Average unit square footage
- Amenities (pool, exercise rooms, etc.)
- RTC contract asset manager and phone number
- RTC consolidated office and contact name and phone number

LAND ON RTCNET

If you select LAND your search choices will be:

- Unimproved residential
- Residential developments
- Commercial developments
- Agricultural
- Ranch/pastures
- Oil and gas developments
- Mining

"Development," as used by the RTC when it sells land, often means these properties are unfinished, which is why they are listed in the raw land section. This means that someone started something they couldn't finish. Streets and utilities may be incomplete, which means you will have to do the rest. In many cases streets and sidewalks will be as far as they got before going belly up.

Features in the raw land data base are similar to those listed above for commercial properties. "Number of units," for example, will mean the number of units the land is zoned or approved for, not necessarily how many units exist. So don't get too excited if you see a parcel listed for $40,000 that shows "53 units."

If you are buying an uncompleted subdivision you more than likely will be required to meet all the preconditions imposed on the original developer by the local zoning authorities. The purchase price may seem cheap, and maybe it is, but you could be subject to zoning requirements that will cost you more later.

For example, the property may have been approved as a low-income rental project, meaning you *must* set aside a certain number of units for low- to moderate-income renters. Or you might be assuming the responsibility for repaying municipal bonds that were used to finance infrastructure such as sewers, sidewalks, and street lighting. The only place these conditions will appear is in the RTC due diligence package, which is available from RTC asset manager. We will discuss bid packages and due diligence later. If you're still in doubt, call the RTC account executive at the consolidated office who is in charge of the property.

Anyway, be careful when searching through the RTCNET commercial data base. Things are not as they may appear. We did a search with a criteria of "Residential developed in Arizona costing less than $100,000." The computer spit out a number of tantalizing leads. It told about an uncompleted 57-unit townhouse development outside Tempe, Arizona, that was available for just $8,500. It sounded too good to be true—it was.

With a little more research we discovered that when the RTC lists a townhouse development it first lists each lot separately. In this case the project had 57 "lots." We mistakenly assumed the price for just one lot was the price for the entire development. The $8,500 price was listed on the computer without explanation after the address. The $8,500 was the value of just that one lot, which the RTC calls a "sub-asset classification." The entire development later sold for $1.1 million. If you have any questions ask the asset manager (realtor) if the listing you are interested in is a major or sub-asset. Under some conditions the RTC will sell a sub-asset separately, but most of the time they will not want to, shall we say, break up a set.

SHOPPING FOR A LOAN?

If you want to invest in loans that are being offered by the RTC, RTCNET has a LOANS menu selection. This gives you a complete list of loan packages and pools that are available to bid on. However, you cannot search this data base. It lists all the loan pools currently available in one large file. Each listing contains the following information:

- Collateral for the loan, listed by residential, commercial, consumer, and multifamily
- Total dollar amount of the loans
- Yield
- Geographical distribution
- Number of loans in the pool
- Issuing S&L
- Contact person for bid information
- Bid deadline

OTHER RTC INFORMATION ON RTCNET

Besides searching the RTC's data base for specific assets, RTCNET provides other useful investor information. For those interested in keeping abreast of the Affordable Housing Program, selecting SILVER LINING from the RTCNET menu will allow you to read the RTC's own Affordable Housing newsletter. SILVER LINING contains stories about people who successfully purchased homes, condos, or apartment buildings from the RTC. It also posts recent changes in AFH policy and pending legislation. Back issues also are available. Again, the best and cheapest route is to download the whole thing onto your hard disk, print it out, and read it.

RTCNET also offers subscribers the complete Affordable Housing Disposition Directory. This directory lists the names and direct-dial phone numbers of RTC staff in each RTC consolidated office responsible for making this program work for you. The numbers are all toll-free 800 lines. In case you don't get satisfaction from the regional representatives, the directory also gives the names and direct-dial phone numbers of their bosses in Washington.

RTCNET has also added the RTC's *National Investor Newsletter* to its on-line service. The newsletter is put out by the RTC to reach large investors interested in multimillion-dollar assets. The newsletter includes a calendar of major asset sales, including loan pools, commercial projects such as office buildings, and large multifamily residential projects. The newsletter is of little interest to small investors, unless they simply want to see how the other half lives.

NON-RTC DATA BASES ON BIN

BIN contracts data base services with other vendors besides the RTC. All these services are available to BIN subscribers. Access fees vary, and you are warned about them before being granted access. Among the more useful services to real estate investors are:

- **National Foreclosure Data Base.** Lists over 16,000 properties for sale directly from banks and thrifts. These are properties banks and thrifts acquired through foreclosure when borrowers failed to make their mortgage payments. This service will cost you a 55 cents per minute on-line charge.
- **Real Estate Reporter.** Tracks over 80,000 foreclosures nationwide. Also offers investment information for investors who specialize in buying property at foreclosure sales. This service incurs a 55 cents per minute on-line charge.
- **Thrift Liquidation Alert.** A newsletter that specializes in reporting on recently closed thrifts. On-line fee is 49 cents per minute. (*The Resolution Trust Reporter*, another private newsletter that tracks the RTC, is available on the Lexis/Nexis computer network.)
- **Electronic Mail.** BIN offers subscribers, individuals, and com-

panies custom electronic mail services. To get your own BIN electronic mailbox you simply have to ask.

- **Private Networks.** BIN custom designs and operates private networks for corporations, associations, and other organizations. Access to private networks requires special authorization. RTCNET is a private network designed for BIN's client, the RTC.

SUMMARY

The RTC is part of a giant bureaucracy and has built-in inefficiencies. It's not surprising to find that some of its on-line computer information is outdated and occasionally inaccurate. What amazes us is that RTCNET works well despite the formidable odds against it working at all.

For the serious investor, RTCNET is a required tool. Your chances of making serious money off this huge inventory will be greatly enhanced by mastering this data base. It's expected that over time the RTC will increase the accuracy of data on RTCNET. But even as it is now, it's well worth the $250 to $300 a year it costs to use. If the data base does nothing more than introduce you to asset managers around the country who sell for the RTC, it will have paid for itself.

For the noninvestor who is simply looking for a single piece of investment property or a home or an affordable housing opportunity, the system may still be worth the cost. This is particularly true if you are not married to a specific town and are casting your net statewide or regionally. RTCNET can save you a lot of long-distance toll calls trying to find just the right property.

As of this writing Business Information Network is the only public computer access to the RTC portfolio. They are doing a good job and it is unlikely the RTC will contract with another provider. But before subscribing to BIN you might ask your closest RTC consolidated office if they are still the only show in town.

THE FDIC'S DATA BASE

As we went to press the FDIC's computer data base was still a primitive affair. The agency only had a funky computer bulletin board available through its Dallas regional office that performed like it had been designed by someone's brother-in-law. To say it's marginally useful would be an overstatement.

The FDIC says it intends to get its digital act together in 1993, but for now we can't recommend the FDIC's system, which is called the ORE Bulletin Board. ORE stands for *owned real estate*. The system is being developed in-house by the federal agency, which explains why it doesn't work. It's expected, hopefully, that the FDIC will wake up and smell the coffee and hire someone in the private sector such as Business Information Network, CompuServe, or Nexis/Lexis to help them bring their asset data base into the twentieth century. There was talk at press time that the FDIC would contract with a private-sector firm like BIN to manage its data base as well. Another option being explored took the process one step further—using Prodigy Information Network to supply information to would-be investors right in their homes, reducing the cost to the Prodigy fee of $12 per month.

IN SUMMARY

Though the FDIC lags a bit behind the RTC in the "reach out and touch someone" department, both agencies have become increasingly user-friendly. The toll-free phone numbers listed here and in our Yellow Pages will plug you directly into agencies. This may well be the first time in history that such giant bureaucracies have tried to make themselves so accessible to the ordinary citizen.

So you can ease into this process. Start by calling the RTC toll-free lines and order manuals and computer printouts. They have created a nonthreatening environment in which "no salespeople will call" if you change your mind. Go as far as you like, and stop when you like.

The ability to search RTC's data base with your home computer represents a real opportunity for the serious investor.

In short, anyone who tells you that you can't deal with the FDIC or RTC hasn't tried recently.

Chapter Three

....

Finding Home Sweet Home

AFFORDABLE HOUSING OPPORTUNITIES FROM THE RCT, FDIC, AND HUD

Eva Garcia was fed up with New York City. In 1991, after her divorce was final, she needed a more spacious and liveable place to raise her two children. After hearing that the Resolution Trust Corporation was holding an affordable housing auction in Toledo, Ohio, she packed her two children into the family car and drove all night, arriving at the auction an hour before it started. With her kids in tow, Eva bid on every large condominium offered that day until finally she realized that the auctioneer who was shouting "SOLD" was pointing at her. She had just bought a spacious condominium in Stoney Creek, a condo project in suburban Toledo, for $33,500—less than some people pay for an automobile.

Prices for single-family homes and condominium units that day ranged from a low of $2,000 up to a high of $96,000. Eva, a nurse in training and first-time home buyer, couldn't have been happier. She had long ago given up any hope of ever owning her own home.

53

Eva is not alone. Every week the RTC and FDIC quietly sell homes to thousands of citizens who once thought they were locked out of the housing market. Both agencies have portfolios bulging with residential properties, ranging from "fixer uppers" to luxury mansions.

For low- to moderate-income Americans the S&L and banking disasters have been good news. (The low- to moderate-income label applies to any citizen who makes 115 percent or less of an area's median income. Median is the middle point where half the people earn more and half earn less.) Congress has ordered both the FDIC and RTC to make a portion of their repossessed residential properties available to low- and moderate-income families and individuals. This doesn't make up for the eight years of Reagan administration insiders looting the Department of Housing and Urban Development (HUD), but it offers a great opportunity to those who act now. Together the two agencies will dispose of tens of thousands of single-family homes over the next few years. Some will be earmarked for the Affordable Housing Program; others will be sold on the open market to anyone who makes the highest offer. Each program serves a different pool of potential buyers.

BUILDING PERSONAL WEALTH

Frankly, a penny saved is an underachieving penny. The only reason to save money is in order to collect enough of it to invest in "equities"— real estate or stocks. Only by acquiring property with growth potential (equity) can you break the cycle of wage-slavedom and gain independent wealth.

A family earning $40,000 a year will earn about a million dollars in wages over a twenty-five-year working lifetime. That's a lot of money. Unfortunately, by the time it's over, you'll have precious little left. State and federal taxes will relieve you of at least 25 percent of that, leaving $750,000, and living expenses such as rent or mortgage payments, car payments, food, and utilities will consume most of the rest. If you are lucky enough to save 5 percent of your after-tax earnings (a high percentage by American standards), that means you will have put aside a measly $37,500 (not counting interest)—hardly enough to fund a golden retirement in the Caribbean.

The only way to acquire real wealth and to secure your retirement is by investing in equities *now*. But what equities? Though over the long term the stock market historically far outstrips the inflation rate, individual stocks can plunge without warning—maybe the week before you retire. The trick is to pick stocks that always increase in value. Good luck if you choose that route, and if you figure out how to do it, give us a call.

Since the beginning of time the safest and best investment has been real estate. The reason is obvious: They just don't make the stuff anymore. It's a simple case of supply and demand. There will always be stock splits and new stock issues. But there will *never* be any new real estate. What there is, is already there. And if you own a piece of it you are a fortunate soul indeed. If you don't, the government's Affordable Housing Program is a rare chance to make that giant leap.

THE AFFORDABLE HOUSING PROGRAM

The Affordable Housing Program (AFH) is a program mandated by Congress whereby the RTC and FDIC must first offer to low- and moderate-income residents of a given area homes that are "moderately" priced. For the RTC this means homes appraised at under $67,500.[1] This includes everything from condos and townhouses to mobile homes, single-family houses, and one- to four-family apartment buildings. As of September 30, 1991, 13,000 families had already purchased homes through this program.

Don't be put off by the mistaken belief that this is a program for just the "poor." This is one of the greatest fallacies of the RTC and FDIC's affordable housing effort and has caused countless qualified buyers to turn their noses up at the program. A family of four in Dallas that earns $50,000 annually can easily qualify to buy a home under this program.

Besides the single-family cap of $67,500, the RTC places a price cap on two-family, three-family, and four-family homes that can be purchased through the AFH program. The two-family (or duplex) cap is $76,000; the three-family (triplex) cap is $92,000; and the four-family

---

[1] The $67,500 is likely to be lifted or increased, probably in early 1993 as the RTC comes under increasing pressure to sell off its large inventory of real estate.

(fourplex) cap is $107,000. When it comes to condos or co-ops, a studio, one-, two-, or three-bedroom unit is considered a single-family unit.

WINDOW OF OPPORTUNITY

Prior to the S&L and banking debacles not many working-class Americans could find properties as cheaply as the one Eva Garcia bought in Toledo. Real estate values—especially homes that moderate-income Americans could afford—were soaring through the roof during the mid- to late 1980s. The S&L and banking disasters that followed changed all that. Today, by law the RTC must make available first to low- and moderate-income residents all residential properties that are appraised for $67,500 or less. The property spends its first thirty days on the market priced at 70 percent of its appraised value. If it doesn't sell, the property is marked down to 40 percent of appraised value and offered for another sixty days. After that, if it still hasn't sold it is removed from the Affordable Housing Program and sold in a multiproperty auction to the highest bidder on a "no-minimum bid" basis. The FDIC goes one step further than the RTC. Realizing that some areas like New York and Los Angeles have very few "affordable" housing units priced at $67,500, Congress mandated that the FDIC establish an affordable housing price cap tied to the median price of a given geographical area.[2]

Median home price is the "middle" point where half the homes cost more and half cost less. In the Washington, D.C., area, for example, the median home price is about $152,000. The affordable housing cap of $67,500 does little for the first-time home buyer. But under its AFH program the FDIC can raise that cap, allowing more properties to be made available to low- and moderate-income taxpayers. Using its discretion, the FDIC can include $120,000 homes (or higher) in its affordable housing auctions. This is a major advantage for moderate-income families in high-priced housing markets such as Boston, Los Angeles, San Francisco, New York, and Washington, D.C.

---

[2] In December 1991 the FDIC was forced into creating an affordable housing program after Congress voted to provide the FDIC with $70 billion in borrowing authority from the U.S. Treasury Department.

HANDYMAN SPECIALS

AFH properties, like all government-owned real estate, are sold by the RTC and FDIC "as-is," which translates into: What you see is what you get. For a low- and moderate-income home buyer who is also handy with tools or has construction skills, buying a two-, three-, or four-family unit could be a gold mine. The worse the physical shape of the house, the cheaper you can get it. If you can fix it up yourself and rent out the other units you can do quite nicely.

KEY INFORMATION. *Although the RTC cap of $67,500 sounds too low for buyers in some metropolitan areas, the auctions are worth checking out anyway. There have been many instances in which homes that were once valued at $100,000 to $150,000 were dropped into the AFH program and slashed down to the AFH limit. Also, if a home doesn't sell after thirty days its price can be reduced even further by the RTC and FDIC.*

Just how low will the government go to make some housing affordable to qualified buyers? How does *free* sound? It may sound unbelievable, but the RTC and FDIC have given AFH properties away. In 1991 alone, 380 properties were simply given away by the RTC—an average of more than one a day. Most giveaways by the two agencies are to charitable, nonprofit organizations that have an Internal Revenue Service tax exempt identification number. Giveaways must be approved by the local government where the house is located. Church groups with social outreach programs can pick up properties for their local homeless programs or battered women's shelters or to fix up and sell in order to raise hard cash.

AFH: WHO QUALIFIES?

The RTC and FDIC place an income cap on families who are allowed to purchase properties (one- to four-family homes) from the government through the AFH program. The cap is pegged to the median income of the area in which the house is located. The way the law is written, any family that earns 115 percent or less of the area median income is allowed to buy a home that has been placed in the AFH program. If you make between 80 percent to 115 percent of the area median income you are considered a moderate income resident. If you make less than 80 percent of the median income you are considered a low-income resident. In Denver, for example, a family of four that earns $41,400 or less can qualify for the AFH program. A single home buyer in Denver who earns $38,755 or less can qualify as well.

The RTC, FDIC, and local realtors selling AFH properties all provide charts that rank an area's median income. Any local Chamber of Commerce office also carries median income data. However, COCs tend to paint a rosier picture of reality, and their figures can lead you astray. When in doubt telephone the RTC or FDIC consolidated office nearest you and ask what the median figure is for the area you're interested in.

KEY INFORMATION. *If you live in a high cost-of-living area such as New York, San Francisco, or Los Angeles and you barely qualify under the 115 percent of median income rule, your best bet might be to wait for an FDIC auction where the available AFH homes will be tied to the area's median home price and not the RTC cap of $67,500. There is a risk in waiting, though. Some states weren't as hard hit by the S&L and banking messes as other states, and the number of AFH opportunities will be limited.*

Before purchasing a home from the government you will have to fill out a bidder qualification form to show the RTC and FDIC that you make 115 percent or less of the area's median income. This form must be completed before you bid on a property at auction. The government will use this form to determine if you qualify to purchase a home.

Your median income will be calculated by the number of people and dependents in your family. The RTC and FDIC will deduct amounts from your gross income depending on the number of children in your family. Remember, gross income is what you earn, not what you take home each week. The agencies will subtract $480 from your gross income for each family member who is under the age of 18. They will also subtract $400 from the total if you're an "elderly" family whose members are 62 or older. If you have a child who is under 18 and working you *do not* have to count his or her income on your bidder qualification form. Both agencies will count your liquid assets toward the overall income calculation. Assets that you are required to list include checking accounts, savings accounts, certificates of deposit, rental property, and stocks and bonds. If you have a certificate of deposit (CD) of $10,000 sitting in a bank account somewhere, the RTC will take 5 percent of the $10,000 and add it to your gross income. However, if you have less than $5,000 in liquid assets the RTC *does not* require that you take 5 percent of their value and add it to your gross income. If you have handicapped children and receive public assistance you *do not* have to include it as part of your gross income.

Question: What if I make less than 115 percent of the area median income and I suddenly inherit a lot of money or my spouse dies and I receive a large insurance settlement—do I have to include it as annual income?

Answer: Yes. RTC and FDIC rules are explicit on this. However, government rules allow you to exclude "temporary, non-recurring or sporadic income including gifts." This area could be tricky. If a relative or friend gives you $1,000, technically you don't have to declare it on your gross income qualification statement.

Other forms of income that you *do not* have to declare include:

- relocation pay
- payments you may have received for volunteer work (this is an odd exclusion since most volunteers don't receive pay)
- foster care payments
- reimbursements from medical costs and any combat pay to a family member serving in the Armed Forces (this of course would apply to Desert Storm and Vietnam veterans)

If you happen to be a retiree, the government will count your pension income and social security payments. Again, they will include 5 percent of your liquid assets toward calculating gross income.

FIGURING OUT YOUR INCOME

Each city and town has its own median income. New York, Los Angeles, and Chicago have the highest median incomes of any city. Each year the median could rise or fall, depending on the local economy, so ask the RTC or FDIC what figure they are using before you get too far. Because median incomes change based on shifts in the local economy, we offer, as an example, what the caps were on the qualifying median incomes in Texas at the beginning of 1992:

	Family of		
City	One	Two	Four
Austin	$33,000	$37,700	$47,150
Dallas	$35,300	$40,350	$50,450
Ft. Worth	$31,300	$35,750	$44,700
Houston	$33,150	$37,900	$47,350

Before you are allowed to bid at auction the RTC and FDIC will pre-screen you to make sure you qualify. If after calculating your AFH income you still have doubts, just pick up the telephone and call the RTC or FDIC consolidated office that is holding the auction. Most AFH experts can tell you on the spot whether you qualify—but keep in mind they're going by what you tell them. If you "cheat" a little and shave a few thousand off your income, remember the agency will later require a signed financial statement. Filing a false financial statement is a crime. If caught, you'll have to explain your math to a judge. Despite impressions that the RTC is a bureaucratic nightmare where a little fudging will go unnoticed, we've found the AFH program to be well managed, thorough, and staffed by competent professionals.

ARE YOU "TOO RICH"?

If you're a real estate investor looking for bargains, don't let all this low income talk turn you away from the Affordable Housing Program. There's room for you in this program too. The government offers no income limits on AFH buildings that have five or more rental units. In fact, buying an apartment building under the RTC or FDIC's affordable housing programs could be one of the best investments you've ever made. Depending on where the property is, its condition, and how good a manager you are, you could do quite well. The RTC will even lend up to 85 percent of the purchase price to help you buy an apartment building. Detailed information on how real estate investors can make money through the AFH program appears later in this chapter.

GETTING STARTED AND FINDING WHAT'S AVAILABLE

For one- to four-family homes, the first step is to telephone the RTC or FDIC consolidated office nearest you. (Consult the Yellow Pages to find the RTC or FDIC office closest to you or the region in which you wish to buy.) You also can start by calling the RTC's Affordable Housing hot line (1-800-624-HOME).[3]

In general the RTC has a better-organized affordable housing program than the FDIC. The FDIC is moving in the same direction and should be offering affordable housing opportunities in a "user-friendly" environment shortly. Keep in mind that once the RTC winds down its sales effort around late 1996 the FDIC will still be humming along, because the banking crisis followed the S&L meltdown by almost four years. Therefore, the FDIC will be selling billions of dollars worth of land, homes, and commercial properties until the end of the decade.

Because the S&L and banking crisis hit hardest in the Southwest, most of the properties first offered have been in Arizona, Louisiana, Texas, and New Mexico. But the real estate recession in America is a "rolling" recession, meaning it's been rolling around on the nation's deck like a loose cannon. Though Texas was deep in recession by 1988, the New England states didn't feel the full bite until 1990, and California didn't go into serious recession until 1991. Except for Hawaii, very few areas have been unaffected by the real estate recession.

[3] Or you can do your own search using the RTC's "RTCNET" computer data base, which you can access with a personal computer. See Chapter 2. Properties in the AFH program are clearly designated as such on the computer printout.

Hot affordable housing markets. As the banking crisis in America worsens, banks of all sizes will fail in cities and states previously untouched by this financial plague. Because New England has been hit like a sledgehammer by the recession, some of the best bargains under the AFH program might be found in Connecticut, Maine, Massachusetts, and Rhode Island.[4]

The Midwest, Illinois, Minnesota, Michigan, and other "rust belt" states are areas to keep an eye on. Parts of southern California and the Pacific Northwest have their share of bargains as well. Be patient and be flexible. So far most of the heavy AFH action has been concentrated in Arizona, Florida, Louisiana, Oklahoma, and Texas. In 1993 the RTC will offer at least eighteen thousand single-family AFH homes, condos, and townhouses and two hundred or more apartment buildings with thirty thousand apartment units under its Affordable Housing Program. The pickings should be good and the geographical spread should include most regions.

WHAT ARE PRICES LIKE?

In Texas the average sales price of an AFH home is around $28,000. Houses haven't sold this low since the 1960s. These are not "fixer uppers." Many are nice suburban homes, townhouse units, or condos built during the mid-1980s. Developers overbuilt with S&L and bank money, and now there's a glut. It's as simple as that. The best news for first-time buyers is that most properties in the AFH program are selling at sizeable discounts compared to nongovernment-owned homes.

In Dallas, for example, the median home price is $90,000, compared to the RTC AFH average in Texas of $28,000. We're not inferring that

---

[4] Interestingly, Vermont has escaped much of the financial damage suffered by other New England states, perhaps because of a perception by some builders during the go-go 1980s that the state wasn't "user-friendly." For much of the decade Vermont's largest city, Burlington, had a socialist mayor, Bernard Sanders, who later was elected to Congress. Sanders was viewed by some in the real estate industry as being anti-development and pro-rent control, which reduced development and therefore overbuilding. Also, tough environmental laws in the state prevented rampant development of ski resorts.

the $90,000 home is in the same condition or part of town as the AFH home. Some AFH properties have been vacant for months and need a bit of TLC. Still, AFH properties represent a terrific opportunity for low- and moderate-income families. A first home is the first rung on the equity ladder—a rung that until now has been too high for many to reach.

HOW TO ACT

There are two ways to buy AFH houses from the government. You can take the passive approach and just check the real estate section of your local newspaper for an announcement of an upcoming affordable housing auction, or you can get serious and call the nearest RTC or FDIC consolidated office and ask it for a list of available properties and upcoming auctions.

KEY INFORMATION. *By contacting the RTC or FDIC first before an auction takes place, you can beat the competition and avoid the auction process, which tends to drive prices up.*

Typically the RTC offers AFH properties with selected local real estate brokers for sixty days. The homes are advertised and listed just like any other home but are designated as "Affordable Housing" properties, the sale of which is limited to those who qualify. If after sixty days the property hasn't sold the RTC will then take the property listing back and try to sell it through a public auction. Ask the realtor how long he or she has had the listing, or ask to see a copy of the listing agreement with the RTC to see the date. If the realtor won't give you this information, call the RTC regional office and ask them when they gave out the listing. Also in the back of multiple listing books is a list of properties that includes a "days on the market" column. Ask to see the most recent Multiple Listing Service (MLS) book.

INVESTOR TIP. *If you want to gamble, wait until the property has been returned to the RTC unsold. Then contact the RTC consolidated office and make a bid. Because the RTC takes its costs into considera- tion when analyzing a bid, you can point out to an agency account executive that the RTC is now saving the 5 percent real estate commis-*

sion. Under its pricing guidelines, because the home has not sold the RTC can now sell it for 40 percent of its appraised value. This is the perfect time for you to make a lowball offer. The consolidated office will have to balance your offer against the costs involved in holding the property longer. The account executive might turn you down. If so, you'll get another crack at the public auction.

As with other RTC real estate, buyers can use their own real estate broker to buy an AFH property. And the listing broker must present all offers made, no matter how low, to the RTC. If the buyer has his or her own realtor, the commission will be split between the RTC broker and the buyer's broker. The RTC pays a 5 percent commission.

If you, as a buyer, use your own realtor, the listing agent will be less than pleased to split the commission. But this shouldn't hurt your chances. The listing broker must submit all bids to the RTC and the RTC (and FDIC) must accept the highest bid, regardless of who made it. Still, the listing broker has subtle advantages that give him or her a leg up. The listing broker's regular customers will certainly get a phone call the day listings arrive and will get first crack at these properties. This is a good reason to find and cultivate a relationship with a realtor who is an approved RTC contractor and gets listings on a regular basis.

AFFORDABLE HOUSING AUCTIONS

The RTC is increasingly using public auctions to sell its affordable housing properties. Some of these properties had been listed with realtors but did not sell. Others are put in the auction program immediately, without first being exposed to the market. These judgment calls are made by account executives at the RTC consolidated office handling the asset.

Buying through an auction has its good and bad points. The worst part about an auction is that you're competing against an unknown number of other bidders—which means the price of a house or condo, if there's more than one bidder, can be driven out of your reach. On the other hand, auctions can accomplish just the opposite—if few show up to bid, prices will drift lower than you expected. It's a crapshoot.

Many of the professional auction firms hired to dispose of these properties are top-notch marketing experts and publish full-color brochures of the available properties. Since the RTC pays for marketing costs, these auction companies will be more than happy to mail you a complete auction package. The nice thing about the auction process is that you can view hundreds of properties without spending a nickel.

Occasionally the RTC and FDIC will auction AFH homes together with homes that exceed the AFH price limit. AFH homes will clearly be marked in the brochures with an "A" while the other homes will be marked "G," meaning "general" or non-AFH auction. If you qualify as an AFH bidder you can still bid on the non-AFH homes at bid levels that meet your budget. Who knows, you might get lucky. But if you do not qualify as an AFH bidder you *cannot* bid on "A" designated properties. Before bidding you will have to prequalify as an AFH bidder. The prequalification sessions are held at the auction or beforehand at the RTC or FDIC consolidated office sponsoring the auction.

KEY INFORMATION. *A pre-bid qualification session will be held before the auction. If you are going to bid on an AFH property you are required to bring the following information:*

- The name and address of your employer
- A copy of your most recent pay stub and last year's W2 statement
- If you are self-employed, personal and business tax returns for the last two years
- Your bank and savings account statements showing current balances and account numbers
- A statement showing your current monthly expenses, including rent, car payments, student loans, and any other outstanding debts

The information that you bring to the prequalification session will remain confidential. The information will only be used to determine your ability to bid on affordable housing and qualify for a loan. If you qualify as a bidder but for one reason or another can't get a bank loan, the RTC will use the information to see if you qualify for an RTC loan.

THE BIDDER'S CONFERENCE

Several weeks before a public AFH auction the RTC often arranges a "Buyer Awareness Seminar" (also known as a "Bidder's Conference"). Here financial counselors will explain the auction process, how to bid (though not "what" to bid), how to get an RTC loan, financing terms, "good faith" deposit requirements (generally, the agencies require a $500 to $1,000 good faith deposit in the form of a cashier's check to bid), and the general guidelines of the AFH program. Sometimes these conferences are advertised in local papers. But to be certain you don't miss such an announcement your best bet is to simply phone the RTC hot line and select the choice for auctions. After you get the list of upcoming auctions, phone either the RTC regional office in charge of the auction or the auction house listed, and ask if they plan to hold a bidder's conference, and if so, when and where.

The RTC and FDIC also work closely with State Housing Finance Agencies (SHFAs) and local nonprofit organizations to counsel first-time buyers on the rudiments of homeownership.[5] The counselors, some of whom work for nonprofit housing advocacy groups, can provide information on which lenders in town have the best interest rates. The RTC and FDIC consolidated offices can provide the names and telephone numbers of SHFAs.

BIDDING

The RTC uses two types of auctions: "oral outcry" (or "open-cry"), in which bids are shouted out to an auctioneer, and "sealed bid" in which offers are submitted in sealed envelopes.

When it comes to oral outcry auctions, keep a few things in mind. First, people tend to get carried away at open-cry auctions. RTC statistics show that the average price of a home sold at oral outcry auctions averaged $5,000 higher than the price of homes sold through sealed bid

[5] SHFAs are state-operated organizations that provide housing and homeownership assistance to citizens through public grants and mortgages that usually carry below-market interest rates.

auctions where everyone stays quiet and calm. Sealed bid auctions are less emotional than oral outcry auctions. Either way, be careful. Set your limits before you bid and then don't go beyond them. Calculate the total price you're willing to pay. Factor in your cash down payment, monthly mortgage payment, and monthly expenses. If your monthly mortgage and related expenses (such as utilities) exceed 35 percent of your monthly take-home pay, keep your hands in your pockets and let the bidding roll on by.

INVESTOR TIP. *You can "ballpark" a monthly mortgage payment (interest, principal, and insurance) by multiplying the number of thousands in the loan by $10 (e.g., a $50,000 loan = 50 thousands × $10 = $500 a month payment). This gives you a rough estimate of what your monthly payments will be.*

If this is your first taste of high finance you should consult a social service counselor before the auction. If you win the bidding on a house you cannot afford, the first thing the government will ask is, where are you going to get the extra money to make these payments? If you don't have a good answer, the property will be offered to the runner-up bidder.

Before the auction begins each home or condo is assigned a lot number, which is used by the auctioneer to refer to that particular property. If you attend an oral outcry auction it will sound something like this: "On lot number 22 we're starting at $30,000. Do I hear $30,000? (Someone makes a bid.) Okay, do I hear $32,000?" And so on and so on.

KEY INFORMATION. *Remember to add 10 percent to the price of your bid. Auction houses are not charities. They earn their money by charging both the seller and the buyer a 10 percent commission. If you bid $30,000 that means you will actually pay $33,000.*

If you want to bid, raise your hand and loudly yell out your bid. It's as simple as that. Because it's a government auction, you won't have to worry about shills or decoys in the audience bidding the prices up. The government wants to get rid of this stuff.

HOW LOW WILL THE GOVERNMENT GO?

KEY INFORMATION. *Whether you bid at auction or contact the RTC directly, keep in mind the government has certain value schedules to follow that limit how cheaply it can sell a piece of property at any one time.*

When it first markets a property the RTC sets a minimum bid price that, rest assured, it will not share with you. If you "lowball" a bid you run the risk of falling below the RTC set minimum and your bid will simply be rejected. If the property has not sold after being on the market for a while, the RTC will begin an orderly process of lowering the price until it attracts a buyer.

As we said earlier, before a property ends up at auction the RTC and FDIC generally list all AFH homes with local real estate brokers. During the first 30 days the house (or any one- to four-family residence) is listed with a broker, you can walk into the realtor's office and make any sort of bid you like. The broker won't tell you yes or no because he or she doesn't have the authority to accept or reject an offer. Instead the broker will call the RTC account executive at the consolidated office in charge of that particular home and relay your bid.

KEY INFORMATION. *What the broker will not tell you is that during the first thirty days the house is on the market the RTC is allowed to accept a bid as low as 70 percent of "appraised" price! This represents an immediate savings to you of 30 percent. Consider it a future, built-in profit!*

LOW AND GOING LOWER

Another thing the RTC won't tell you is that if an AFH house has been on the market from thirty-one to sixty days the RTC is allowed to accept direct bids from buyers of just *40 percent of the current appraised value!* In other words, if a home is listing for $67,000 you might be able to get it for half that if it hasn't sold during the first 60 days on the market. If an AFH house has been on the market for more than sixty days and hasn't sold, then that piggy is sent to market and is auctioned to the highest bidder.

DEALING DIRECTLY WITH AN S&L

Question: Can I go directly to a failed S&L that is still being operated by the government and buy a low-priced house directly from them?

Answer: Yes. When the government moves against an insolvent S&L it first places that institution into a "conservatorship." The S&L remains open to the public while the RTC tries to sell its assets and find a buyer for its deposits. (Usually another bank or S&L buys the deposits.) While an S&L is in conservatorship you can approach it directly and make a bid on any of its real estate holdings. All of the institution's REO, or real estate owned, will be listed with the local consolidated office. If you need a list, start there. As with "receiverships," which are S&Ls that are no longer open to the public, all homes priced at $67,500 or less are placed in the RTC's Affordable Housing Clearinghouse. The clearinghouse is simply a computer listing of all AFH homes available from RTC receiverships and conservatorships.[6]

Conservatorships, which are staffed by RTC-approved employees, are a good place to pick up deals. The RTC wants to get rid of as much REO as it can, as quickly as possible. REO is real estate that has been foreclosed on by the S&L. Where did the REO come from? From the previous management, who made bad loans and has since been booted by the RTC.

KEY INFORMATION. *Although one- to four-family units owned by an S&L in federal conservatorship are subject to the AFH guidelines, low-priced apartment buildings owned by conservatorships are not subject to the AFH guidelines. Only when low-priced apartment buildings, of five units or more, move from conservatorship to receivership do they come under the AFH guidelines. (Again, a receivership occurs when the RTC closes an S&L and begins to sell all of its*

---

[6] For a short while in 1991 there was a loophole in the law under which homes valued at $67,500 that were owned by conservatorship S&Ls were not subject to the AFH guidelines—meaning anyone, no matter how much they earned—could buy low-priced homes. That loophole was closed in the spring of 1991.

remaining assets. At this point the apartment building will move into the RTC's Affordable Housing Program and become subject to that program's rules and limitations.)

FINANCING

Not only is the government selling these AFH homes at bargain basement prices, but it will even loan you the money to buy that house or condo. In some cases it'll even pay your closing costs. Ideally, the government would rather have you go out and get a loan on your own, but since it wants to sell houses as quickly as possible, the RTC, for all intents and purposes, is in the loan business. So is the FDIC, but to a lesser extent.

When you fill out the bidder qualification form, the RTC is doing two things: First it's making sure you don't exceed the income cap, and second—at the same time—it's trying to get enough information to qualify you for a mortgage. When the government sells homes at auctions it has professional loan underwriters (loan officers) on hand who will take your mortgage application the same day.

Sometimes when auctions are held, the government will distribute information lists on where you might be able to get below-market interest rate mortgages, or state or federal grants to fix up your home. The money comes from a variety of sources, including state and local housing finance agencies, nonprofit pro-housing organizations, and private foundations. The best place to get a mortgage is from a bank, S&L, mortgage banking company, or credit union.

Banks and thrifts. Even though you are a low- to moderate-income buyer you can still qualify for a bank loan. Community Reinvestment Act (CRA) laws passed by Congress require banks and S&Ls to make a certain percentage of loans in lower-priced neighborhoods. CRA laws are enforced by the FDIC, Federal Reserve, and Office of Thrift Supervision (OTS), a federal agency that regulates only S&Ls. Banks and thrifts don't like the law, but most of them work hard to meet their quotas.

Mortgage bankers and credit unions. Mortgage banking companies are independently owned businesses that only make mortgages. They do not take deposits. For many years credit unions were not in the mortgage business but now are making home loans. Not all credit unions make home mortgages. If you have any questions check with your credit union.

OTHER MORTGAGE-RELATED ITEMS TO KEEP IN MIND

Mortgage insurance. Most conventional lenders require a cash down payment of at least 10 percent, but will accept 5 percent if you purchase private mortgage insurance (PMI). Private mortgage insurance is an insurance policy that a borrower takes out to "insure" that you won't default. The premium is figured into your monthly payment and can cost as much as $50 per month, depending on your loan size.

FHA and VA loans. If you qualify you can also get a mortgage from the Federal Housing Administration (FHA) or Veterans Administration (VA). Both will lend on RTC and FDIC properties. FHA and VA loans typically require 3 percent down if you're borrowing $25,000 or less, and 5 percent down if you're borrowing more. Although the borrowing guidelines changed in the summer of 1991, you can still finance up to 57 percent of your closing costs with an FHA or VA loan.[7] Previously, borrowers could finance up to 100 percent of the closing costs. By "finance" we mean that the closing costs—the points, fees, title, and escrow charges—are added onto your overall mortgage amount, costing you nothing up front. However, the FHA and VA *will not* lend you money on a condo or a co-op unless 51 percent of the building's units are owner-occupied—meaning the owner must live there. No renters. FHA and VA loans are available from banks, S&Ls, and mortgage banking firms. Mortgage banking firms tend to specialize in this type of business.

THE RTC WILL EVEN LOAN YOU THE MONEY

The RTC has its own lending guidelines, which we cover in detail in Chapter Five. Briefly, the RTC will make thirty-year loans to qualified buyers of single-family homes who cannot get financing elsewhere.

---

[7] Previously a borrower could finance up to 100 percent of his or her closing costs. It is anticipated that the 57 percent cap will be overturned sometime in the next year or so.

FINANCING FOR RENTERS OF GOVERNMENT-OWNED PROPERTIES

If you currently rent a condo or co-op owned by a failed S&L, you can buy that apartment with an RTC-financed loan. For renters the mortgage down payment is just two months' rent. There is a catch. The program is available only to those who earn 80 percent or less than the area median income. If you make 80 to 115 percent of the area median income, the government will still lend you the money, but only up to 95 percent of the loan amount.

In some areas of the country the government might be your only source of funding on a condo or co-op, because as we noted earlier, the FHA and VA will not extend you a mortgage unless 51 percent of a building's units are owner-occupied. RTC seller financing tends to go smoothly because all parties want the same thing—a completed sale.

RTC FINANCING ON ONE- TO FOUR-FAMILY AFH PROPERTIES

Lending terms offered to low- and moderate-income buyers of RTC AFH properties are better than those offered to higher-income buyers. RTC mortgages on AFH properties are for fixed-rate terms of either fifteen or thirty years. Rates tend to be slightly lower than the prevailing market rate and the RTC does not require private mortgage insurance (PMI).

If the home you're buying costs less than $50,000 the RTC will lend you up to 97 percent of the purchase price, bringing your cash down payment to just $1,500—less than the first and last month's rent for a good apartment! Remember, though, these terms apply only to people who make less than 80 percent of the area median income. If you make 80 to 115 percent of the area median income you have to put at least 5 percent down. If the home costs more than $50,000, the RTC requires a down payment of at least $750 plus 5 percent of the sales amount that exceeds $25,000. On a home price of $51,000 that translates into $750 plus $1,300 (5 percent of $26,000), which comes to a grand total of $2,050.

The RTC places only a few restrictions on these generous AFH loans:

- The buyer/borrower must live in the home for at least one year
- The loan cannot be assumed by a third party
- The RTC loan is due and payable upon the sale of the property

KEY INFORMATION. *Depending on what your personal finances are—and how desperate the government is to unload a house—the RTC will pay a portion, or even all, of your closing costs. Circumstances vary from state to state. As one RTC official told us: "We're more likely to pay closing costs on a house in Texas than in California." That's because the RTC is up to its neck in cheap houses in Texas but doesn't have as many in California. But even in states where properties are more scarce, the RTC will bend over backwards to place a house with a low-income family. The lower your income, the more likely the government will pay your closing costs.*

After you make a bid on a home, ask an RTC account executive or asset manager or realtor in charge of the sale about the closing cost option. The fewer bidders there are, the better your chances of getting government assistance at closing time. Also, your financial statement will have to reflect a level of "poverty" that would support such an act of "charity."

ONE WARNING

Be straight on your AFH financial statement. The entire S&L and banking mess was created by liars and cheats who received million-dollar loans from lenders with phony financial statements. Understandably, Congress is in a nasty mood. Lawmakers have instructed the Justice Department (read: FBI) to have zero tolerance for anyone, even AFH buyers, who doctor their financial statements. The Justice Department will prosecute. The RTC and FDIC have plenty of AFH and non-AFH properties available for purchase. Cheating is not worth it. You just might turn out to be the poor sucker they decide to make an example of.

CAVEATS AND RESTRICTIONS ON AFH HOUSES, CONDOS, AND CO-OPS

Question: If I buy an AFH home from the RTC or FDIC can I fix it up and sell it a few months later at a profit?

Answer: No. If you qualify to buy a home under the affordable housing program the government requires that you live in it for at least one year. This is called the owner occupancy rule. But the day after a year is up, you can do whatever you like with the property—rent it, lease it, or sell it.

Question: Can I fool the government into thinking I live there when I really don't?

Answer: Only at your own risk. From time to time the RTC does follow-up occupancy checks. If you rent it out and you're caught the agency can fine you or have the Justice Department (in extreme cases) prosecute you. Again, it's just not worth the risk.

Question: What if I buy an AFH home and then find I have to move or sell it before a year is up?

Answer: If you sell before a year is up the RTC will step in and claim 75 percent of any profit you make. If you spent money remodeling you will not be able to recoup it.

The government makes exceptions to the one-year rule—in the case of a job transfer or genuine family crisis. The emphasis here is on the word "crisis." The RTC does not consider your need to raise money to pay last year's taxes a "crisis." The agency leans more toward "an act of God" definition of crisis.

Question: As an investor can I use friends or relatives who qualify under the AFH income guidelines to buy a house where I really own it?

Answer: Only if you want to share a jail cell with Charlie Keating. The person whose name appears on the bidder qualification form will be given legal title to the house. You can give him or her "gift" funds toward buying an AFH home but that person must own the property and pay for it. Using a "front" or "straw" buyer to hide true ownership is a federal felony. The Justice Department will indict. Bet on it.

RICH GET RICHER DEPARTMENT— INVESTOR OPPORTUNITIES

Just because the RTC's AFH program focuses its energies on low- to moderate-income buyers, that doesn't mean well-heeled investors are shut out. The opposite is true. For apartment building investors the AFH program can be a golden opportunity.

In December 1991 the RTC sold 26 apartment buildings through the AFH program—20 of which were in Texas—to General Electric Capital Corporation, a conglomerate based in Stamford, Connecticut. The sale price was $75 million. The number of rental units in those 26 properties totaled 5,590. The unit cost on those 5,590 properties came to just $13,416 per apartment (divide $75 million by 5,590.) You can't even buy a decent mid-sized new car for $13,000.

General Electric—not exactly a poverty case—made a killing. And it's not the only one profiting from the AFH program. Since the RTC was created in 1989 the agency has been selling apartment buildings at per unit costs far below market value. G.E. represents an example of a large corporate investor. For the small to mid-sized investor—developers, contractors, doctors, lawyers, and other professionals—opportunities abound in the AFH program.

Here's a sample of AFH apartment buildings (five or more units) that were available from the RTC in Texas in early 1992:

City	Units	Asking Price	Per unit cost
Austin	578	$4,100,000	$7,093
Corpus Christi	40	$500,000	$12,500
Dallas	72	$510,000	$7,083
Dallas	46	$210,000	$4,565
Houston	164	$2,700,000	$16,463

Keep in mind these are asking prices. The final sales price could be as low as 45 percent of the initial asking price. In 1992 the average cost of constructing just one rental unit of public housing from scratch was $78,000. But apartment buildings in the RTC's AFH program were selling at an average per unit cost of between $10,000 and $11,000!

The quality of the apartment buildings offered through the AFH multi-family program ranges from poor to excellent. Why would the RTC put perfectly good apartment buildings into its AFH program? Answer: overbuilding. During the 1980s S&Ls were practically giving money away to developers. It was a "lend now, worry later" atmosphere. Too many apartment buildings were built too quickly, forcing prices down. Because the per-unit asking prices are so low, the buildings must—by law—be offered through the AFH program. As a result, excellent bargains in apartment buildings will be plentiful through at least 1995 in the AFH program. After that, economists predict, prices will begin to stabilize and rise. By mid-decade, as populations continue to swell—especially in Texas, Florida, and California—experts predict that well-built apartment buildings will become cash cows and will remain so for many years to come.

By late 1991 the RTC had almost 15,000 single-family properties and 1,000 apartment buildings available through the AFH program. That inventory will rise and fall depending on sales and future S&L failures. For investors looking to get in at rock-bottom prices, Colorado, Florida, Oklahoma, and Texas remain your best bets. The good buys of the future, however, are likely to be found in New England, New York, New Jersey, and the Midwest. As the FDIC's caseload of insolvent banks reaches critical mass over the next two years, more and more apartment buildings will be coming to market. The greater the pressure from Congress to sell these buildings, the more the prices will be slashed. Watch for the investor focus to switch from the Southwest to these largely untapped regions of the country.

EVERY SILVER LINING HAS A CLOUD

Buying an apartment building through the AFH program, though a great opportunity for investors, does have its drawbacks. First there's the question of eligibility. As we noted earlier, it doesn't matter how much money you make—as long as you're buying an apartment building of five or more units. But not all government-owned apartment buildings are placed in the AFH program. Some are sold at RTC commercial property auctions open to all bidders. An apartment building placed in the AFH program will carry certain burdens. If an apartment building has five or more units it cannot be offered through the AFH program if its studio apartments are valued at $29,500 or more; one-bedroom units at $33,816 or more; two-bedroom units at $41,120 or more; three-bedroom units at $53,195 or more; and larger units at $58,392 or more.

(All values based on current market analysis appraisals by RTC approved appraisers.) The per unit values are reached by prorating the building's appraised value among its individual units. The formula stated above applies only to RTC properties. The FDIC has more discretion to set its own AFH caps, which tend to be more generous to investors.

One negative in buying an apartment building through the AFH program is the federal "set-aside" requirement. Because you're buying the building so cheaply, the RTC requires that you rent at least 35 percent of its units to low-income residents. The low-income set-aside requirement will be written right into the deed. You cannot escape it. Worse yet, the condition encumbers the property for forty years from the date of the sale.

The RTC, not the buyer, decides what the term "low-income" means. The rent formula for low-income units is pegged to the "adjusted" income of a family as determined by its gross income, not take-home pay. Low-income families are allowed to deduct amounts from the gross similar to the deductions allowed buyers of AFH one- to four-family homes. The rent investors can charge low-income residents can be no more than 30 percent of their gross income. For example, if their monthly adjusted gross income is $1,000 you cannot charge a low-income resident more than $300 a month for rent. Is this condition a problem for real estate investors? Yes and no. On the rental end it may be less a problem than it appears. The property manager—not the government—chooses the tenants. Depending on where the apartment building is located, the rent charged on these "set-aside" units may not be too much lower than what you were hoping to charge for rent anyway.

KEY INFORMATION. *Remember—if you buy a low-priced apartment building from a conservatorship S&L and not a receivership you can escape the 35 percent low-income rental set-aside. This loophole could change, but for now, investors are safe.*

DAVID VERSUS GOLIATH

Right now some healthy competition exists for these cheap rental units. Corporate investors like General Electric, as well as pension funds and insurance companies, are showing increasing interest in these RTC and

FDIC apartment buildings. They realize that below replacement cost per-unit prices of $10,000 don't come along everyday. In other words, they know a good deal when they see one—deed restrictions and all. The good news is that these big investors only want the larger, prime apartment buildings with 300 or more units. For the small- to mid-sized investor this is a welcome bit of knowledge. Some of the best deals available from the government are on apartment buildings of six to sixty units. These complexes are not moving as quickly as the others—and since the demand is less, discounts abound.

Question: Can a buyer "flip" an AFH apartment building within a few months after buying it?

Answer: Yes. AFH apartment properties (five units or more) *are not subject to the same one-year rule that burdens the one- to four-unit AFH program.* If you can sell it two weeks later for twice what you paid, more power to you. Uncle Sam will not be around for his share. The RTC can do nothing to you. Remember, though, the 35 percent rent set-aside for low-income residents applies to the next owner—and lasts for forty years from the date of the original RTC sale.

Question: Can a sharp lawyer get the deed restriction quietly removed?

Answer: A lawyer can try but we don't recommend such a strategy. As one RTC contractor who deals extensively with the AFH multifamily program told us, "You'd be looking for trouble if you tried to remove that deed restriction. The RTC would have you in court overnight and I think most judges would be very unsympathetic to your cause."

INVESTOR TIP. *If you buy more than one AFH apartment building at a time you can play around with the 35 percent set-aside rule. For example: You purchase three AFH apartment buildings, each with 100 rental units. Two of the buildings can have set-asides of just 10 percent each while the third has an 85 percent set-aside. It's all legal. By law, if you buy apartment buildings "in-bulk," meaning more than one at a time, you are allowed to make the low-income rent set-aside as low as 10 percent in any one building, but you will have to make up for it with more units in the other buildings.*

For a while there was a loophole in the law whereby you could shift all of the low-income set-asides to one building and have none in the others. GE did this with its bulk purchase of twenty-six apartment buildings. Unfortunately for other investors, the publicity following what GE did killed the loophole. Also, you can only play with the set-asides if you buy more than one building at a time. If you buy one AFH apartment building one month and another the next, you cannot after-the-fact alter the set-aside. You have to buy the two at the same time and tell the RTC up front what the set-asides are going to be in each apartment building.

INVESTOR TIP. *If you're afraid of the forty-year deed restriction that mandates you set aside 35 percent of the rental units for low-income residents, then the best way to buy an apartment building is not through the AFH program but to buy a delinquent or defaulted loan that the RTC has in its inventory of available assets. The RTC is dying to get rid of these loans and would be more than happy to sell them to you. After acquiring the loan you can foreclose on the building and become its owner. (See Chapter 8 on buying loans.)*

BUYING AN AFH APARTMENT BUILDING: THE SEALED BID PROCESS

When it comes to purchasing an apartment building through the AFH program, you will not be doing so at an open-cry auction. AFH apartment buildings are sold through the sealed bid process. This means that any apartment building that falls under the AFH guidelines will first be offered to the public for ninety days. During this three-month period you can view the property by filling out a "notice of inspection" form with the consolidated office. The form is a technicality and allows you access to get a closer look.

If you decide to bid you will have to wait until the ninety-day period ends. The RTC marketing material provided lists the official bid date. After you submit a formal bid the RTC allows another thirty days to conduct an in-depth inspection of the property. If you are not a seasoned real estate investor you may want to hire a structural engineer or contractor to determine the condition of the building. During this thirty-day period the RTC will examine all the bids it received to determine which gives the government the highest present dollar return. Whether you win or lose, your bid will be kept confidential. One caveat here. Not only will the government ask how much you are willing to pay, but they want to know how many of the units you will rent to low-income tenants. Even though 35 percent is the law, they will give preference to higher set-asides. If you bid $400,000 for a building and offer to rent out 35 percent (the minimum) to low-income residents and the Dallas Housing Finance Authority bids $375,000 but offers to rent out 75 percent of the units to low-income residents, the DHFA will probably get the property.

If you manage a nonprofit organization, this is good news. "For-profit" investors should view the consideration like a golf handicap. In late 1991, when Congress voted to allocate $70 billion for the ailing FDIC to prop up the nation's ailing banks, it passed several amendments to the AFH program. One amendment grants the RTC the right to negotiate *exclusively* with nonprofit organizations, cutting for-profit investors out of the loop.

Still, many investors do not see this as that big a deal. Nonprofits have limited resources. Also, the policy is not cast entirely in stone and clashes with the RTC's mandate to sell real estate at the "highest return to the taxpayer." As of this writing the exclusivity clause had not been used, or even tested for that matter. We mention it as a precaution. Of the 115 apartment buildings sold through the AFH program as of year-end 1991, only twenty had been acquired by nonprofit groups or state or local housing finance agencies.

BUDDY, CAN YOU SPARE A LOAN?

FINANCING FOR INVESTORS

Even in the AFH program "cash is king." In other words, the RTC and FDIC will take an all cash bid before they take an offer that requires financing. Having your financing locked in before you go to bid allows you to offer the RTC, in essence, "all cash." If you don't have all cash and need a loan to make a sale happen, you have two ways to go. Try a local bank or S&L for a loan. Don't be surprised if they beg off. Banks and thrifts are under a lot of pressure to reduce their loan exposure on investment real estate.

Still, if you're a regular bank customer, and haven't already borrowed to the hilt, you might get the financing—it all depends—as long as the loan doesn't look too risky. "Too risky" in regulatory-speak translates into owner equity in the venture. In other words, are you, the borrower, able and willing to make a substantial cash down payment of at least 25 percent? Also, does the appraisal show the project is worth what you're willing to pay? Will the rent proceeds allow you a good profit? If the answer to all these questions is "yes," you have a shot at getting a loan from your bank or S&L. Also, try the aforementioned mortgage companies. Mortgage bankers make large apartment building loans as well. If a bank or S&L is in no-loan mode, a mortgage company might have a stable of private investors willing to take you on.

Because you're buying your AFH apartment building at substantial discount, obtaining financing should not be a major roadblock as long as you're willing to make a down payment of at least 25 percent.

RTC SELLER-FINANCING

If you can't get (or you don't want to get) outside financing, don't worry. The RTC will lend you up to 85 percent of the purchase price on an apartment building. The terms are often better than what you can get on the open market. The catch is that the loans offered are only seven-year balloons, which means you'll have to get new financing in, yes, seven years.

KEY INFORMATION. *Although the government would prefer at least 20 percent down, RTC rules (which also apply to the FDIC) state that a down payment of 15 percent is the "absolute minimum" the government will accept. The RTC ties its mortgage interest rate to the weekly Treasury Bill Index published in the* Wall Street Journal. *Again, the loan term is for seven years, but is amortized using a thirty-year schedule—that means you're paying all interest and little or no principal.*

If you're a nonprofit group, the RTC will lend you 95 percent of the purchase price to buy an AFH apartment building. The agency also will make you a longer-term loan—fifteen years rather than seven years. Again, the loan will be amortized using a thirty-year schedule.

THE FDIC'S AFFORDABLE HOUSING PROGRAM

As we've already noted, the FDIC's AFH program is nearly identical to the RTC program. The FDIC's AFH program was late in getting under way and has learned from the RTC's early mistakes. The major difference between the two programs is that the FDIC asked for and received the authority to establish a price cap on one- to four-family units based on a particular area's cost of housing. This is good news for home buyers in high-priced housing markets such as Boston, Los Angeles, New York, and San Francisco, where even a vacant lot often sells for more than the normal $67,500 AFH cap.

Another difference between the RTC and FDIC involves seller financing. Although the RTC offers liberal seller financing on AFH properties, the FDIC offers limited financing. This is likely to change over time. When in doubt ask an account executive at the closest FDIC consolidated office. As the FDIC liquidation process gathers steam, this agency will learn the same thing the RTC learned a couple of years ago: Seller financing moves property.

Otherwise the programs are much the same and you can deal with the FDIC as you do the RTC. Instead of starting out by telephoning the RTC's consolidated offices for AFH properties, you will be calling the FDIC's consolidated offices, which are listed in our Yellow Pages. As with the RTC, you can check out the FDIC's AFH opportunities on your home computer by accessing its computer network, which is called the ORE (Owned Real Estate) Bulletin Board.

AFFORDABLE HOUSING SUMMARY

- The Affordable Housing Program is not just for the poor and disadvantaged. It's also for the most often forgotten Americans—the working middle-class who've been priced out of the housing market. For them, Ronald Reagan's "trickle down" theory of economics is based on the belief that the best way to feed the birds is to first give grain to the horses.

- The RTC has set a cap of $67,500 on homes that can be sold under the AFH program. The cap is adequate for cheaper markets but does nothing for higher-priced areas such as Chicago, Los Angeles, and New York. The FDIC—whose AFH program is similar to the RTC's—can raise the $67,500 cap at its discretion. If you live in a high-priced region, your best affordable housing bet will be with the FDIC.
- Both agencies have become "user friendly." You can access their AFH inventory through a computer or telephone.
- Real estate investors can make money with the AFH program as well. Now's the time to buy. Per unit costs of $4,000 to $16,000 abound. You will not see these prices again.
- When it comes to buying AFH apartment buildings, "cash is king." If you don't have cash or you're having difficulties obtaining financing from a bank or S&L, the RTC will lend you up to 85 percent of the purchase price.

NON-AFFORDABLE HOUSING OPPORTUNITIES

Besides AFH opportunities for investors and low- to moderate-income home buyers, the RTC and FDIC have billions of dollars' worth of residential real estate for sale that does not fall under any AFH restrictions or conditions. Investors can buy anything from suburban homes to mansions, from condos to townhouses. Whatever you desire, chances are good the RTC or FDIC has it—and you won't have to worry about a bunch of guidelines and rules. As with real estate purchases, though, it helps if you have financing lined up.

As explained in Chapter Two, if you're buying from the RTC, start by telephoning its Asset Specific 800 number (1-800-RTC-3006) or by accessing its RTCNET data base with your home computer. When your search is complete you will have a list of properties that fit your price, location, and habitat needs.

Real estate listings mailed to you by the agency will include a telephone number of the RTC asset manager and the listing real estate broker assigned to that property. Call the real estate agent listed. Only call the RTC asset manager if you have a problem reaching the real estate agent. The realtor will arrange to show you the property. After you've seen the property, make an offer through the realtor. The realtor *must* present all offers to the RTC consolidated office—no matter how low those offers might be.

As with any real estate transaction, the RTC will either accept your offer, reject it, or make you a counteroffer. The RTC's response will be communicated to you through the listing realtor. If you require RTC financing, be sure to tell the agency when your offer is made. (See Chapter 5 for RTC financing terms.) The RTC so far has been authorized to make $7 billion in loans. More than $250 million has been earmarked for loans on one- to four-family homes. The RTC has been authorized to make an additional $4.25 billion in loans if the demand is there. If you've already been approved for a bank loan, obtain a letter of credit from the lender. Include it with your offer.

If a non-AFH house has not sold after being on the market for thirty days, the RTC will instruct the realtor to reduce the price. If after ninety days the house still hasn't sold the RTC will take the listing away from the realtor and offer it through a general auction at which it will be sold with other non-AFH homes to the highest bidder.

Purchasing a non-AFH property from the RTC is a straightforward process. You just have to know what's for sale and who to call. Then make an offer. When buying from the FDIC, start by calling the closest consolidated office in the area in which you want to invest. You can also tap into its computer data base, the ORE Bulletin Board, and start that way. Either way, after that the process is the same.

OTHER GOVERNMENT HOMES FOR SALE

BUYING A HUD HOME OR APARTMENT BUILDING

The RTC and FDIC are not the only federal agencies struggling with the residue of the 1980s. When it comes to buying cheap real estate, one of the best bargains around—besides the RTC and FDIC—is the Department of Housing and Urban Development, commonly known as HUD. Created in 1934, HUD's mission in life is to promote home ownership and affordable housing. HUD also is in charge of the nation's public housing stock and is responsible for building new public housing, as well as promoting single-family ownership among low- to moderate-income Americans.

To say HUD lost sight of its mission during the eight years Ronald Reagan occupied the White House would be an understatement. While occupying itself with arranging lucrative development contracts for Republican Party insiders like former Interior Secretary James Watt, the agency paid little attention to its low- to moderate-income federal loan guarantee program operated by the Federal Housing Administration (FHA).

The FHA makes loans to individuals who for one reason or another cannot get a loan from traditional sources such as a bank or S&L. Guaranteed by the federal government, the FHA requires as little as 5 percent down. If a borrower defaults, HUD repossesses the house and then tries to sell it.

Unfortunately for taxpayers, the FHA didn't do a very good job of underwriting the millions of mortgages it insured. This included mortgages on one- to four-family homes as well as entire apartment buildings. When lenders incurred a loss on a bad home mortgage it was a little like the S&L crisis: "Heads we win, tails the government loses." The FHA picked up the tab, not the lender.

FHA loans are available from most lenders—including banks and S&Ls. Interestingly, lenders will make FHA-insured loans to the financially disadvantaged, but not other types of loans. The key, of course, is the word "insured." In making FHA loans lenders earn money by charging the borrower points and loan application fees.

Tens of thousands of FHA-insured mortgages went bad during the 1980s, leaving HUD no other choice but to foreclose. Because the FHA insured billions of dollars' worth of mortgages, it was just a matter of time before the agency started accumulating thousands of single-family properties. And once it repossessed these properties HUD had to sell them—fast. The result has been a bargain market. Over the past two years the average sales price of a home sold by HUD has been around $40,000, leaving HUD with an average loss of $20,000 to $23,000. For buyers that means getting a home for about one-third of what it normally might have sold for had it not been owned by Uncle Sam, who is now forced to sell at fire sale prices.

Property Types Available

HUD sells single-family homes, duplexes, triplexes, fourplexes, single condominium units and cooperatives, and townhouses. It also has apartment buildings available. The homes come in all shapes and sizes and are in almost all fifty states. They have garages, patios, driveways, and some are relatively new.

In 1990 and 1991 HUD foreclosed on 72,092 and 66,648 homes, respectively. During those two years it sold a total of 153,357 homes. In 1992 and 1993 HUD expects to foreclose on at least another 140,788 homes, while anticipating sales of 159,171. These are Bush administration numbers buried in the 1993 budget, which means they are certainly on the "optimistic" side. The number of foreclosures may well be much higher.

Despite HUD's huge inventory of single-family homes each year, it only has a hundred or so multifamily units (apartment buildings) available for sale. In 1991, for example, HUD sold about one hundred apartment buildings with one thousand four hundred rental units. So when it comes to apartment buildings the RTC has a lot more to offer in the way of inventory, while HUD will generally have more single-family units available at any one time. But HUD isn't under pressure from Congress to unload these properties at fire sale prices, so you can still get your best single-family property deals from the RTC. Also RTC and FDIC single-family properties are more varied and include luxury amenities and residences, unlike HUD homes, which tend to be more spartan.

KEY INFORMATION. *HUD homes are most plentiful in the Southern and Southwestern sections of the country. In 1991, for example, HUD sold twenty thousand homes in metropolitan areas such as Albuquerque, Fort Worth, Little Rock, New Orleans; and San Antonio. Southern cities such as Atlanta, Birmingham, Coral Gables, Florida; Greensboro, North Carolina; Louisville, Nashville, and Tampa, also are chock-full of available HUD homes.*

As of the beginning of 1992 the New England area had the least amount of homes available to purchase, but that situation could change as the economy continues to scrape along the bottom in Connecticut, Rhode Island, and other states.

We expect that by mid-decade HUD's inventory of good deals will begin to decline. As far as Western markets are concerned, Fresno, Phoenix, and Tucson have more to offer in the way of available HUD homes than other metropolitan areas.

WHO CAN BUY A HUD HOME?

Unlike homes sold through the RTC or FDIC Affordable Housing Programs, which cater to low- and moderate-income buyers, there are no income limitations whatsoever on who can buy a HUD home. In any city in any state anyone can walk off the street and make a bid on a home owned by the agency. The only individuals barred from buying HUD properties are employees of the agency and members of their immediate families and anyone who has defaulted on an FHA mortgage.

GETTING STARTED

Querying HUD is not as easy as dealing with the RTC. As we noted in earlier chapters, the RTC's multibillion dollar inventory of loans and real estate can be easily accessed via computer or by dialing a toll-free asset specific inquiry telephone number that gives you tailor-made lists of available properties. HUD, unfortunately, is not quite so user friendly. HUD has no computerized real estate data base that is available to the public.

HUD has ten regional offices and eighty field offices. It also has a special Indian Programs office in Phoenix that provides housing assistance to American Indians. The ten field offices are in charge of selling foreclosed homes to the general public.

The 10 regional offices are located in the following cities:
- Boston (Region I)
- New York (Region II)
- Philadelphia (Region III)
- Atlanta (Region IV)

- Chicago (Region V)
- Ft. Worth (Region VI)
- Kansas City, Mo. (Region VII)
- Denver (Region VIII)
- San Francisco (Region IX)
- Seattle (Region X)

Each regional office has a number of field offices. The field offices break down as follows:

Boston: Bangor, Me.; Burlington, Vt.; Hartford, Conn.; Manchester, N.H.; Providence, R.I.

New York: Albany and Buffalo, N.Y.; Camden and Newark, N.J.; San Juan, P.R.

Philadelphia: Baltimore, Md.; Charleston, W. Va.; Pittsburgh, Pa.; Richmond, Va.; Washington, D.C.; Wilmington, Del.

Atlanta: Birmingham, Ala.; Columbia, S.C.; Greensboro, N.C.; Jackson, Miss.; Coral Gables, Orlando, Tampa, and Jacksonville, Fla.; Knoxville, Memphis, and Nashville, Tenn.; Louisville, Ky.

Chicago: Cincinnati, Cleveland, and Columbus, Ohio; Detroit, Flint, and Grand Rapids, Mich.; Indianapolis, Ind.; Milwaukee, Wisc.; Minneapolis, Minn.; Springfield, Ill.

Fort Worth: Albuquerque, N.M.; Dallas, Houston, San Antonio, and Lubbock, Tex.; Little Rock, Ark.; Oklahoma City and Tulsa, Okla.; New Orleans and Shreveport, La.

Kansas City: Des Moines, Iowa; Omaha, Neb.; St. Louis, Mo.; Topeka, Kan.

Denver: Casper, Wy.; Fargo, N.D.; Helena, Mont.; Salt Lake City, Utah; Sioux Falls, S.D.

San Francisco: Honolulu, Hawaii; Phoenix and Tucson, Az.; Reno and Las Vegas, Nev.; Sacramento, San Diego, Santa Ana, Fresno, and Los Angeles, Calif.

Seattle: Anchorage, Alaska; Boise, Idaho; Portland, Ore.; Spokane, Wash.

For a complete listing of addresses and telephone numbers for the regional offices see our Yellow Pages.

Like the RTC and FDIC, HUD to a certain degree is decentralized, meaning that authority to buy the homes is granted by the field and regional offices, not HUD headquarters in Washington. Realtors list the properties for sale and are paid a standard sales commission for selling the homes—up to 6 percent. In general HUD pays brokers the going rate in the local market. If it's 5 percent then the realtor gets 5 percent. (If you're a realtor this is good news because no matter who buys the home you get paid a commission—that is, as long as you're the listing agent.)

HOW HUD HOMES ARE SOLD

All HUD homes are sold through an auction process. That means if you're an investor you cannot negotiate with the agency or the realtor to try to get it to whittle down the price. Besides appearing in the MLS (multiple listing service) book, homes available for sale by HUD are listed in local newspapers (both weeklies and dailies) in the city in which the house is located. Typically, new listings are advertised in the real estate section of the local newspaper on a Friday. All HUD listings are posted on Sundays.

Auctions of HUD homes are listed when the agency amasses enough properties to make an auction cost-effective. All auctions are advertised and are held on weekends in order to maximize attendance. If there are not enough homes to hold an auction, HUD will list the individual properties with real estate agents.

If you want to bid on a home you have two weeks to do so from the time the house first goes on the market. Yes, this is a very short period of time. If you see a good property and blink you could miss it entirely.

The newspaper advertisements taken out by HUD and local realtors typically state the address, a few characteristics about the property, and the asking price.

HUD sets a "bid date" for its sealed bid auction. Anyone can bid. After contacting the listing broker and viewing the home, you submit your sealed bid to the listing broker. Along with your bid you must post an earnest-money deposit of $500. (For particularly expensive properties the earnest money could be as high as $2,000, but not more.) The listing agent will place that deposit in an escrow account for you until all the bids are unsealed. A bid date will be established by HUD and the bids will be collected. HUD then has two business working days to review the bids and choose a winner. HUD rules are cut and dry: Whoever bids the most wins. The winning bid is picked by the regional or field office that has been assigned that foreclosed home. If you do not win the bid your money will be returned to you by the listing realtor.

Unlike the RTC, HUD has not been very willing to share with the public how it determines a minimum "strike" price on a home it wants to sell. If a home is listed for $30,000 HUD may take as little as $25,000. Unlike the RTC it has not disclosed publicly what percentage of the asking price it will accept. (The RTC has already let the world know that it will accept a bid that is 95 percent of the fair market value.) But making a wild lowball offer is not likely to work with HUD. Its strike price is not likely to be less than 90 percent or so of the asking price. If the house checks out, make a reasonable but conservative bid. If a home fails to attract bids, HUD will then remarket the property, likely reducing its price.

BUYING GUIDELINES:
INVESTORS VERSUS OWNER-OCCUPIERS

Although HUD was chartered to promote home ownership among low- and moderate-income families, the agency will sell its repossessed homes to anyone—even investors. But HUD is willing to accept less of a down payment from owner-occupiers than investors. If you're a buyer planning on living in the home, HUD will accept a down payment of less than 2 percent. If you're an investor who is going to rent that home out,

HUD requires that you put down at least 25 percent. Investors who buy single-family homes from HUD can rent them out to whomever they like at whatever price they want. The government imposes no limits on this.

Unlike the RTC, HUD won't loan anyone a dime to buy one of their properties. However, buyers can always obtain an FHA-insured mortgage on a HUD home even though the previous owner defaulted on an FHA loan. FHA loans are arranged through banks and thrifts. Contact one in the general area and tell them you plan to bid on a particular FHA property and want to get prequalified for a loan. Since the house already passed FHA muster once, it is likely to easily do so again. The FHA requires a house to meet some basic structural requirements such as adequate insulation, foundation, and electrical.

In the summer of 1991 Congress passed legislation tightening the FHA's loan underwriting guidelines. Those changes are still in effect today. The changes prohibit borrowers from financing more than 57 percent of their closing costs. Prior to the change a borrower could finance up to 100 percent of closing costs and then add that amount to the overall loan. This was great news for first-time home buyers, but for the FHA it posed a great risk: If a home buyer lost his or her job, or the home went down in value, the buyer could just walk away from the loan and not lose any equity because the entire purchase price as well as the points and other closing costs were financed and "insured" by the FHA (a.k.a. Uncle Sam).

If the property costs $50,000 or more, HUD now requires that the buyer put down at least 2.25 percent of the purchase price. Homes that cost less require a minimum 1.25 percent down payment—compared to the 10 percent to 20 percent required by your friendly neighborhood bank or S&L. Besides the low down payment, the FHA requires that you pay a small up-front mortgage insurance premium of 3.8 percent and an annual mortgage insurance premium of .5 percent. On a $50,000 loan this would mean $1,900 at closing, plus an extra $250 per year, or about $20 a month in mortgage insurance premiums. Considered high by some, the mortgage insurance premiums are scheduled to be reduced to 2.25 percent at closing and .55 percent per year in 1995. (It is always possible that Congress could once again change these FHA underwriting guidelines.)

BUYING APARTMENT BUILDINGS FROM HUD

Buying HUD apartment buildings can be a lot trickier than buying buildings from the RTC or FDIC. For starters, about half of all apartment buildings offered by the agency were built with federal "Section 8" grants. That means that if you're the new owner you *must* rent the units out to low- and moderate-income tenants. (As defined in our Affordable Housing section, low- and moderate-income residents make 115 percent or less of the area median income. Median is the middle point where half the people make more and half make less.)

This iron-clad requirement is going to hold down the value of these multifamily properties. If you get the property cheaply enough, you may want to go ahead. But HUD multifamily properties are better left to nonprofit groups, community organizations, and tenant groups who band together to buy and manage a project themselves. However, because Section 8 housing is so heavily subsidized by the federal government, landlords of Section 8 housing do not need to worry about tenant rents.

BIDDER INFORMATION

Auctions of HUD properties are advertised in local, and sometimes national, newspapers a minimum of sixty days before the sale date. All HUD apartment buildings are sold by federally appointed auction commissioners chosen by HUD. The auction commissioner has the discretion on what type of auction to hold—either an oral outcry, in which buyers shout out their bids, or sealed-bid, in which offers are quietly collected in envelopes. Most HUD apartment building auctions are done through oral outcry.

When bidding on an HUD multifamily property the buyer must post an earnest-money deposit. The amount of this deposit varies from region to region and is determined by the sales manager at each office. In general, anticipate that you will have to post at least 10 percent of the purchase price as a good faith deposit. As with other government auctions, the money is returned if you're not the winning bidder. HUD apartment buildings are auctioned on the courthouse steps of the county seat where the building is located. Sometimes HUD auctions buildings that are still in foreclosure. This means you may not have much of a chance to perform any significant due diligence work on the property. It's not likely that the owner who is being foreclosed on by the government will give you a walking tour of the facility. In some cases the landlord might be an absentee landlord who is less than reputable.

Keep in mind that many HUD multifamily properties are dilapidated and need extensive work. If you buy one you will be subject to HUD maintenance guidelines. After years of abuses HUD frowns upon slumlords and will levy sizeable fines if you buy a Section 8 property and decide to simply collect the subsidized rents and let the property go to seed.

LOANS

If you plan to ask for seller financing, don't bid on HUD multifamily properties. HUD is not RTC or even the FDIC. It doesn't offer any seller financing. HUD wants cash at closing. You will have to get your own loan. If you're buying a Section 8 property that needs repairs, HUD requires that you post a letter of credit to facilitate repairs. No letter of credit means no sale.

MAKING A BID

HUD regional offices will not negotiate directly with investors on the sale of apartment buildings. Buyers have to bid through the auction commissioner. If your bid is accepted you will have thirty days to close the sale. The only time HUD deals directly with buyers is when the purchaser is a nonprofit organization that has pledged to keep the building a rental project for low- to moderate-income residents.

If you have any questions about how HUD works, we advise you to call the regional and field offices. Despite Jack Kemp's housecleaning of HUD, little has been done to improve the quality and responsiveness of HUD's public affairs staff in Washington. From what we found, it often takes days for telephone calls to be returned, and responses to buyer inquiries are less than satisfactory. However, we found sales executives at the regional offices to be well versed in the rudiments of buying and selling properties. Start there.

IN SUMMARY

There are a lot of reasons people give for not buying their own home:

- I don't have enough for a down payment
- I can't qualify for a loan
- I don't make enough money
- I can't afford the price of a home in my area

But with the creation of the FDIC and RTC's Affordable Housing Programs and the sale of HUD properties, such excuses no longer hold water. Now down payments are flexible, low-income people qualify *because* they have low incomes, and the prices can't be beat. Due to congressional pressure to do something about the nation's housing crisis, these agencies are under the gun and eager to deal with the very people banks have traditionally shunned and locked out of the home market. For those who thought they would never own their own home, these programs offer a once-in-a-lifetime opportunity. This is one government program that is working.

Chapter Four

....

Look Before You Leap

How to Assess Properties Before You Bid

Like most things in life, investing in real estate is not as complicated as it may appear once you understand the basics. The fundamentals of investing are just that—fundamental. Nevertheless, industry jargon and terminology can be intimidating, leading the novice investor to believe he or she doesn't have a chance of working through what appears to be a dense bureaucracy (which, as we've already explained, really isn't). The better you can function on your own, without getting outside help from a lawyer, for instance, the greater the return on your investment. If you're a seasoned real estate investor you'll probably want to skip this chapter and go on ahead to the next one.

By following the advice given in previous chapters, you should have found more than enough properties to pique your interest. The question then will be, which one and at what price? To get the answers to those questions you first have to do some research.

LOCATION, LOCATION, LOCATION

After you've researched what the RTC and FDIC have to sell in your area and you've chosen a few target properties, your first job is to inspect the property's physical location. It's a cliché, but true, that the three most important factors affecting the value of a piece of real estate are location, location, location.

In some cases you will be familiar enough with the target area to know what parts of town are on the "right" side of the tracks and what parts are on the "wrong" side of the tracks. But just because a property is in a good part of town, that does not mean its location is automatically going to work for you. Neighborhoods undergo demographic and zoning changes constantly. Before investing you will have to inspect what kinds of social and governmental forces are at work in the area that you've targeted.

A FEW TIPS

* Drive around the property's neighborhood ten blocks in each direction. Do you like what you see? Look at the properties 5 blocks away. Are they being renovated? Can you tell if the renovation trend is moving towards your property? Or do the properties look increasingly neglected as you drive? Is this trend moving your way? Is the property you're considering a rental property rather than your personal residence? If yes, then don't apply your standards to the surroundings or neighbors. You are not going to live there. What you want to consider is, can the property be rented to the kind of people you want as tenants?
* Go to your county or city building department and check out the zoning for the area. Ask if any zoning variances have been applied for in your target area. If you discover that the county or city has just granted a variance for someone in the residential neighborhood to run a kennel, you may want to reconsider. Ask if the area has been the subject of any zoning hearings or if any zoning changes are anticipated.
* As you drive around the area, determine your target property's proximity to conveniences such as shopping, mass transit, and schools. If the property is a commercial project, does its location facilitate such critical factors as customer traffic, parking, and convenient shipping and receiving access?
* If the property is an apartment building or a small commercial

complex, check with a commercial realtor in the area to see what the local vacancy rate is.

These site appraisals should be your first considerations. Once the property's location passes muster, and only then, move on to the next consideration.

KICKING THE TIRES

Although the property inspection process differs for residential and income properties, both have common elements.

- How old is the structure or structures? An old building with a lot of "deferred maintenance" will cost you money for new appliances, updating electrical services, paint, and so on. If this is going to be your personal residence, this extra money will come right out of your pocket. If it's a duplex or fourplex rental unit that will be used to help meet the mortgage payment, then the repairs can be written off against that rental income, thereby reducing your tax liability. If this is the case, your tenants and the government, in essence, help pay for the repairs.
- What's the condition of the structure and what will it cost to fix it up? If you do not have the background or experience to make cost estimates, hire a home inspection service in the area. Fees for inspections can cost from $150 to $250. Make it clear to the inspecting contractor that you will not be hiring the contractor to do any of the repair work. This way you can be reasonably sure the estimate you are given is close to reality (see Exhibit 4). If you intend to do the work yourself, tell the inspector so the estimate doesn't include labor, just materials.

  If the inspection report is bad you may be able to use it to lower the seller's asking price. This may not always work when buying from the government because many of its properties are sold "as is" through a sealed bid process. But for RTC and FDIC properties listed with a realtor you at least have an opportunity for direct, one-on-one negotiations. A bad inspection report can result in the government accepting a lower price. An inspection report signed by a licensed contractor estimating that the property needs $25,000 in repairs, material, and labor can become a powerful negotiating tool.

Repairs and maintenance are key considerations in determining what kind of bid you should make to the RTC, FDIC, HUD, or other agencies.

The Do-It-Yourself Inspection

If you don't want to spend the money for an inspection service and you can trust your own powers of observation—which is what most small-time investors do—here are the key things to watch for.

Foundation

Start at the bottom. Does the house have a perimeter concrete foundation that raises the house at least a foot off the ground? Or does it have an old "post and pier" foundation? The answer is important if you want a bank loan. Banks love perimeter concrete foundations and they hate post and pier. A house on post and pier is one that does not have a cement skirt around it on which the perimeter of the house rests. Instead it has concrete blocks on the ground onto which wooden 4 × 4 posts are nailed. Floor joists are then laid across these posts. In essence, the house sits on short "stilts." If your target property is post and pier, figure in the cost of installing a perimeter concrete foundation. In many cases a bank will add the cost of the foundation into its loan and will require proof that the foundation has been installed. Also, if the house is in an earthquake zone be sure it not only has a perimeter concrete foundation but that it is bolted to the foundation.

Beams

Inspect the basement. While you are under the house bring a screwdriver and poke it into supporting beams. Don't stab, just firmly poke. The screwdriver should dent, but not penetrate, the beam. If the screwdriver cuts into the beam like a hot knife through butter, it means the house has dry rot, termites, or both.

BUG BUSTERS, INC.
4910 SONOMA HWY., STE. F
SANTA ROSA, CA 95409   (707)538-1080

PRICE ESTIMATES FOR RECOMMENDED WORK

THE FOLLOWING PRICE ESTIMATES ARE GIVEN FOR WORK RECOMMENDED ON THE STANDARD

STRUCTURAL PEST CONTROL INSPECTION REPORT ISSUED FOR 4980 VINE HILL RD.

  SEBASTOPOL   . DATE OF INSPECTION 4-7-89 . COMPANY REPORT NO. A-2699

STATE STAMP NO. 1966423P .

1. $50.00
*1A. $985.00
2.   Referred to other crafts
*4.   Time and material approximately $1250.00
6. $45.00
9.   Referred to owner
9A.   Referred to owner

* COMPLETION OF THESE RECOMMENDATIONS WILL BE NECESSARY FOR A STANDARD STRUCTURAL
  PEST CONTROL CERTIFICATION.

FOR FURTHER INFORMATION, PLEASE CONTACT BUG BUSTERS, INC. AT (707)538-1080.

THANK YOU,

EXHIBIT 4.   Termite inspection report and repair estimate.

Floors

Once past the foundation, jump on the floors. Do the floors "trampoline"? In other words, are they springy? Though your kids might like this effect, the message is a bad one. It means the floor stringers are too far apart, and you will have to reinforce them.

Walls and Ceilings

Now to the vertical structures. Are the walls plaster or Sheetrock? Are they cracked? Can you see the taped seams of the 4' × 8' sheetrock sections? Cracks and seams mean a lot of messy scrapping, taping, and repairs. Separated Sheetrock seams also can indicate that a house is shifting on its foundation. The condition of plaster and Sheetrock walls can also tell you a lot about potential moisture damage inside the walls. Constant moisture will show in the form of black mildew blotches, usually in the corners or where the wall meets the floor or ceiling. In really bad cases you'll have no doubts because paint and wallpaper will no longer stick to the wall.

Even though you can't see through walls, you can get a peek into them by removing plug switch and wall socket covers. This will tell you if the walls have insulation. If the house is in a flood zone, taking off a plug switch will show if the house has ever flooded. Mud or silt in the plug housings is a dead giveaway.

Doors and Windows

A lot can be told about a house by how well its doors and windows operate. Open and close all doors, including closets and kitchen cabinets. Do they swing easily, or do they jam? If they jam it could mean the foundation has shifted or is sinking, thereby throwing the door and window jambs out of square. It also can indicate the house has a moisture problem that has swollen the windows and doors.

Attic

Is it insulated? Most codes used to require R19, which is a six-inch thick piece of Fiberglas. Today R30 is recommended, which is twelve inches thick.

The attic is one of the few places in a house where you can get a good look at the electrical wiring. Is it modern Romex-type wiring,[1] or is it the old-fashioned wiring hanging from ceramic insulators? You don't need to be an electrical engineer here. If you wouldn't let your cat walk around in the attic for fear it would get electrocuted, the wiring needs to be replaced. (Cremated mice remains are another ominous sign of electrical problems.)

While inspecting the attic, take a look up. Are there leaks in the roof? Look for water stains on the beams and roof boards. Inspect areas around the chimney closely. It could be prone to leakage.

Roof

Same as the floor. Is it springy? It shouldn't be. What do the shingles look like? A roof that is flat will have a shorter life span than a steep roof. It's a simple concept: Water runs off a steep roof faster than a flat one. A composition (tar or Fiberglas shingle) roof has an average life span of twenty to twenty-five years. If the house has a wood shingle (shake) roof, you may want to replace it regardless of condition. Insurance companies hate wood roofs for obvious reasons, and if you insist on keeping it you will pay more for fire insurance. The best roofs (if supported properly) are tile or concrete tile roofs. They last forever.

Neighbors

While checking out the roof, you should use this lofty perch to spy on the neighbors. Are the adjoining yards a mess? Do they have packs of snarling pit bulls running up and down the fence line? Are old cars piled

---

[1] Romex-type modern wiring encloses the positive, negative, and ground wires all within a single, usually white, plastic sheathing.

up like cordwood in the yard? From the roof you can tell a lot about the neighborhood. If you don't like what you see, then pass.

Parking

How is the parking situation? Land in cities and even most suburbs now sells at such a premium that little room may have been allocated for parking. In some metropolitan areas curbside parking has been outlawed where streets are too narrow or curbside services, such as street cleaning and mechanized trash collection services, need easy access.

Sewage

If a property is in a rural area not served by a public sewer, you will have to become acquainted with the mysteries of septic tanks. Does the property have a septic tank or a cesspool? Of the two, a septic tank is preferred. A cesspool is a big covered hole in the ground where household sewage flows. The solids are supposed to decompose into fluids and seep into the ground. Depending on soil type, cesspools often don't work as well as septic tanks.

A septic tank is usually a buried tank built of either redwood, cement, or Fiberglas. Connected to the tank is a system of buried perforated pipes. The sewage flows into the tank. The fluids go off down the pipes (called "leach lines") and are absorbed by the earth. The solids are broken down by bacteria and turn into fluids. Septic tanks are engineered taking into account the absorption factor of the property's particular soil. The less the soil can absorb, the longer the leach lines. County building records contain information about a property's septic system. If you have a question, ask the realtor.

Sometimes it's easy to tell when a septic tank or cesspool isn't working properly. *The Grass Is Always Greener Over the Septic Tank* is the title of an Erma Bombeck book about moving to the country. Well, it shouldn't be. A big square or roundish patch of lush tropical rain forest in an otherwise barren backyard is a solid clue that the septic tank needs attention. Even the best-engineered septic tanks need to be pumped out after time. Occasionally the solids get ahead of even the hungriest bacteria. Some tanks go three years between pumpings. Others go twenty years. It all depends on the soil and how well the system is designed. Pumping can cost anywhere from $300 to $500. Not a big deal.

If you think a tank needs more than just a pumping, it might pay to have a septic tank service inspect the system. To do this a service digs down to the lid of the tank and opens the disgusting thing up. I've seen it done many times, and it has fundamentally changed my vision of Hell. Still, the exercise could be worth the cost and trauma. I once sold a house to a man who had never lived in a rural area before. Because the house had not been occupied for several months, I had no clue about the condition of its septic system. The owner vouched for the system, so we passed on an inspection. A week after he moved in I got a call from the buyer. On Sunday he had dressed for church and decided to take a stroll in his new backyard before leaving. Inspecting a patch of stunningly healthy roses, the man was swallowed by the gates of Hell. The wooden lid of the old cesspool collapsed and the man found himself shoulder deep in a well-aged brew. It turned out the whole tank had rotted through and needed to be replaced. Ditto for his Sunday suit. In this case the buyer was lucky. The seller paid the cost of both. But when the seller is a desperate and broke federal agency, the story may end very differently.

Water

If the house isn't on city water it will have a well. Wells come in two categories: trouble and trouble free. There seems little in between. You have to be concerned about three things with a well. First, how is the water? Is it hard or soft? And how does it taste? Some water is so saturated with iron that it tastes like it was run through a bucket of rusty nails before it reached your glass. If the water is hard you will need a water softener.

Second, how much water is there? Wells are tested by well and pump services for a small fee (see Exhibit 5). They will come out and "bail" your well. The process involves running the pump for a specified period of time at a specified number of gallons per minute. They do this until they figure out how many gallons per minute your well can run before it runs dry. Generally, counties like to see evidence of at least two gallons per minute flow before they will issue a building permit.

Finally, how is the pump? There are two kinds of pumps, surface

STATE OF CALIFORNIA
THE RESOURCES AGENCY
DEPARTMENT OF WATER RESOURCES
WATER WELL DRILLERS REPORT

Do Not Fill In

Nº 141566

State Well No._____

Other Well No._____

(1) OWNER:

Name Jim Dykstra

Address 4990 Vine Hill Road

Sebastopol, California 95472

(2) LOCATION OF WELL:

County Sonoma   Owner's number, if any 76-06-6

Township, Range, and Section

Distance from cities, roads, railroads, etc. Same

(3) TYPE OF WORK (check):

New Well ☒   Deepening ☐   Reconditioning ☐   Destroying ☐
If destruction, describe material and procedure in Item 11.

(4) PROPOSED USE (check):   **(5) EQUIPMENT:**

Domestic ☒ Industrial ☐ Municipal ☐   Rotary ☒
Irrigation ☐ Test Well ☐   Other ☐   Cable ☐
                                           Other ☐

(6) CASING INSTALLED:

STEEL: ☒   OTHER:_____
SINGLE ☒ DOUBLE ☐ _____

If gravel packed

From ft.	To ft.	Diam.	Gage or Wall	Diameter of Bore	From ft.	To ft.
0	186	6 5/8"	.156	12.	0	186

Size of shoe or well ring:_____ Size of gravel: Fine Pea

Describe joint Welded

(7) PERFORATIONS OR SCREEN:

Type of perforation or name of screen Torch

From ft.	To ft.	Perf. per row	Rows per ft.	Size in. x in.
153	186	1	4	3/16 x 6

(8) CONSTRUCTION:

Was a surface sanitary seal provided? Yes ☒ No ☐ To what depth 24 ft.

Were any strata sealed against pollution? Yes ☐ No ☐ If yes, note depth of strata

From _____ ft. to _____ ft.

From _____ ft. to Sand seal at 139+
Method of sealing concrete and float cement on pack

(9) WATER LEVELS:

Depth at which water was first found, if known _____ ft.

Standing level before perforating, if known 50 ft.

Standing level after perforating and developing _____ ft.

(10) WELL TESTS:

Was pump test made? Yes ☒ No ☐ If yes, by whom? Bail

Yield: 45 gal./min. with 80 ft. drawdown after _____ hrs.

Temperature of water cool Was a chemical analysis made? Yes ☐ No ☒

Was electric log made of well? Yes ☐ No ☒ If yes, attach copy

(11) WELL LOG:

Total depth 186 ft. Depth of completed well 186 ft.

Formation: Describe by color, character, size of material, and structure

ft. to	ft.	
0	1	Topsoil
1	42	Tan sand
42	61	Yellow sand
61	68	Orange sand w/ stks black sand
68	100	Clayee yellow and orange sands
100	131	Cemented tan sand
131	133	Sandy blue clay
133	140	Sandy brown clay
140	142	Sandy blue clay & shells
142	186	Cemented clayee blue sand w/ hard ledges and stks shells

Work started 3-8-76 19___ , Completed 3-9-76 19___

WELL DRILLER'S STATEMENT:

This well was drilled under my jurisdiction and this report is true to the best of my knowledge and belief.

NAME Weeks Drilling and Pump Company
(Person, firm, or corporation) (Typed or printed)

Address 6100 Sebastopol Road
Sebastopol, California 95472

[SIGNED] Gerald O. Thompson

by Gary L. Thompson (Well Driller)

License No. 177681 Dated March 9, 1976 , 19___

SKETCH LOCATION OF WELL ON REVERSE SIDE

DWR 188 (REV. 9-68)

EXHIBIT 5.   Example of well test report.

104

pumps and submerged pumps. The surface pump is the easiest to access because it's right there to see. Submerged pumps require an act of faith, since they are deep in a hole. These pumps cost anywhere between $350 and $500 to replace.

You should ask if a well inspection report is available on the property you are inspecting. Most counties require such reports to be put on file after the well is drilled and approved.

Inspection Tools

When inspecting a property yourself, bring the following items:

- A good flashlight with fresh batteries for attic and basement inspections
- A screwdriver to unscrew light switch and plug covers and to check beams for rot
- A twenty-five-foot tape measure to draw out a rough floor plan for your records
- A small carpenter's level to check floors and windowsills to see if the house is level
- If you're inspecting many different properties, you will want to keep them straight in your mind. Bring a Polaroid camera to take pictures of each. Keep a separate file for each property you intend to bid on. A picture of a property's problems can soften the government's bargaining position.

A building's physical condition can be both a curse and blessing. A property in A-1 condition will be priced accordingly and the investor will have little opportunity to inject sweat equity into the project. On the other hand, a building that needs too much "deferred maintenance" can be a real money pit that will bleed you white. The best thing to do is find a building that needs mostly cosmetic repairs rather than structural.

If you feel you can do your own inspection, it can save some money. But if you don't feel comfortable doing this kind of hands-on work, then hire a professional contractor. Consider it "cheap" insurance against an investment disaster.

Some of the best investments are so-called fixer-uppers. A coat of paint inside and out, floor coverings, and landscaping can result in returns of $5 to $10 for every dollar spent. This can be a very profitable way for beginning investors to spend their weekends. Bring a friend and pack a lunch.

NEXT STOP: THE PUBLIC RECORD

If you plan to bid on RTC or FDIC properties, one of the best ways to spend your research time is getting acquainted with the local county recorder's office. At the recorder's office you can find the accumulated knowledge of every single parcel of land in a given county. Real estate professionals call it the legal chain of title. Think of it as a property's family tree. If you want to avoid investing in a lemon, get well acquainted with the county recorder's office.

A recorder's office is to real estate what a library is to books. County documents allow you to trace any property's ownership back through the decades, even centuries. I've done searches that included references to original treaties between Indian tribes and white settlers, Spanish land grants, and presidential gifts to Civil War heroes. Each time a large parcel of land is divided or "split," a new piece of property is "created." It then gets its own deed and that deed is recorded in the appropriate county recorder's office. Each transfer of that parcel is recorded along with any new restrictions or encumbrances that are tied to the use of the land.

GETTING STARTED

Clerks at county recorder's offices are like librarians. They can help you record or find any document you need. Go to the counter and introduce yourself. Don't pretend to be anything but what you are—ignorant. They will guide you through the process.

Computerization has been slow to come to some offices. The ones that are computerized can be a pleasure. Investors can sit at a terminal and type in a property's address or "assessor's parcel number," and all the data will be on a computer screen. Still, most recorder's offices remain in the dark ages of paper. In many, land documents are filed by book and page number. The recorder will show you how to find what you want. After a while you should get the drift of it. It's not complicated, just slow. Most offices keep information on microfilm, which is helpful. With microfilm you can sit at a microfiche machine, and instead of viewing the file on paper you view it on film. It's like a mini-slide projector. Documents are numbered in sequence. You can fast forward or go in reverse. If you want a copy of the document you can put a dime in the machine or ask the clerk to make a copy. It shouldn't cost you more than two bits per document.

LOOKING UP A PROPERTY

Most recorder's offices use the same kind of cross-reference system. If you know the property's address you can find it in the recorder's "address directory," which will list the property's assessor parcel number or AP number. For recording purposes this is the only number that really counts. The AP number is your property's "real" name. Write it down. Take the AP number over to the microfiche machine and begin examining the property's chain of title. *Always* begin with the most recent document filed in the chain of title and then work your way back through time.

Most offices use a seven-digit filing system: 90-04560, for example. The first two digits mark the year the document was recorded. The rest of the numbers are sequential from the first document recorded in that year to the last one. The digits are printed in large letters in the upper corner of each document. Every now and then you may want to stop fast forwarding to see how close you're getting to your target document.

WHAT TO LOOK FOR

By searching through the county recorder's office you can discover a number of things.

Who currently owns the property? Just because the government is selling the property doesn't mean it actually owns it—yet. The RTC may be in the process of foreclosing, which means the property is still in the name of the borrower. Or the property may have been foreclosed on by a now-defunct savings and loan. The last person listed in county records as the title holder is, for all intents and purposes, the current owner. The person's name and mailing address will be listed there as well. If you like, give them a telephone call. Ask about the property's pros and cons. You can go back even further and ask other previous owners.

How much did the last owner pay for the property? This is key information, especially if it's a recent purchase. Recorders charge a "documentary transfer fee" when a property changes hands. The fee is based on a factor per thousand dollars of the sale price. In California the document transfer fee is $1.10 per thousand dollars. The fee, when paid, is embossed on the top of the recorded deed. If you see a stamp fee of $341 in California that means the house sold for $310,000. Ask the clerk what the documentary transfer fee is in your area. Also, look at selling prices of other properties in the same neighborhood. This is another clue to value.

Are there any property tax liens filed against the property? If the property taxes have not been paid, the county will have filed a lien against the property. Before the property can be sold this tax lien must be paid.

Are there any other tax liens? If the prior property owner ran afoul of the IRS, federal tax liens may have been filed against the property to secure payment.

Are there mechanics' liens filed? When professional contractors do extensive work on a property they often file a mechanic's lien to insure payment. When the work is finished a notice of completion is filed and the lien is removed. If a contractor has not been paid the mechanic's lien will stay on the property. The lien will have to be removed (paid) before the property can be sold again.

Are there any easements burdening the property? The property you're inspecting may have once been part of a larger property. When it was divided the prior owner may have granted certain access rights to neighboring properties—such as a common driveway or stairs. These access rights can sometimes constitute a real pain in the neck for future owners. All easements will be described and listed on the deed. Look for the word *excepting*. This is how easements and other rights are described.

Utility easements for telephone and electrical lines are commonplace and should not be a great concern. Watch for any easements having to do with roads. Also, there can be some real zingers from left field. Inspect the language carefully. One property I purchased had an easement dealing with the property's only well. It turned out that a prior owner had deeded 25 percent of the well's water to a neighbor fifty years ago. Only by questioning why the easement existed did I learn of the water deal.

Take a look at the deeds to the adjoining parcels. Read the written description that is called "metes and bounds." Look at the "plat map," the parcel's survey map filed at the county recorder's office (see Exhibit 6). Plat maps show easements as broken lines and mark the width and length. Plat maps also contain information on mineral rights that may not belong to the same person who owns the land.

How is the property being taxed? County assessment rolls show how a property's value, for tax purposes, is split in two. One value is assigned to the land and the other to the building and improvements. (This is done because buildings depreciate while land does not.) The combined total is the taxable value of the property.

Are loans encumbering the property in default? If a property owner defaults on a loan or loans secured by the property, the lender will file a notice of default. The borrower then has a set amount of time to cure that default (make the loan or loans current) or face foreclosure. If the RTC or FDIC is foreclosing on a property you will want to know if there are any junior lien holders. This typically involves a second mortgage. If there is more than one junior lien, junior lien holders could wind up bidding against each other for the property to protect their interests.

Were all prior loans properly reconveyed? When a loan is paid off the lender files a deed of reconveyance, which reflects the fact that the loan no longer encumbers the property (see Exhibit 7). It's a good idea to check back through a couple of past sales to make sure all the reconveyances are there. It's not difficult, but if one is missing you will have "a cloud on title" that could be discovered later on, causing problems when you try to resell.

Are there any "CC&Rs" filed on the property? CC&Rs are Covenants, Conditions, and Restrictions. CC&Rs are draconian little documents created when a subdivision is built. Some very old CC&Rs, for example, prohibit land from being sold to blacks or Jews. Recorded fifty to one hundred years ago, these restrictions have since been ruled unconstitutional. When former Lincoln Savings and Loan owner Charles Keating, Jr. developed the Estrella housing subdivision in Phoenix, his

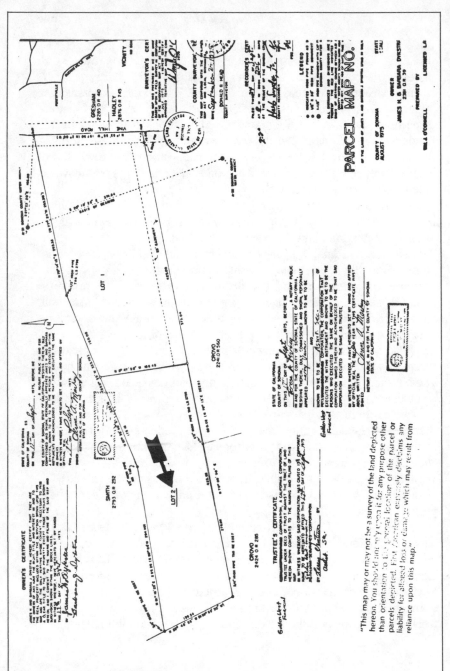

Exhibit 6.   A property parcel map. Notice the easement through Lot 1 to serve Lot 2. The large black arrow indicates that the map was "pulled" for the information of Lot 2's buyer or owner.

CC&R prohibited home buyers from viewing pornographic material on their properties or having abortions! When the press reported these patently unconstitutional conditions, Keating was forced to remove them. Still, many CC&Rs are perfectly constitutional and bind every owner of the property forever. Some CC&Rs micro-manage every aspect of life in a subdivision, from the height you can build a fence to the kinds of trees you can plant. All CC&Rs have to be recorded and noted on the deed. CC&Rs are very common in condominium projects and planned unit developments for which the care and costs of common areas need to be memorialized.

A FINAL WORD

Get comfortable with your recorder's office. It's a nice place to spend an afternoon browsing through microfilm files for nuggets of information. Before you plan to spend a day there, collect a few property prospects. Bring the addresses. As long as you're at it, poke into the history of the neighboring properties. You can learn volumes from public records— just ask any private eye.

If you really want to be nosy, take the names of your prospective neighbors and look them up in the superior court file down the hall. Are they the subject of a pending civil or criminal case? Did one just get busted for running a crack house?

Don't make an offer or bid without taking a long look at the property's plat map. Check for liens of all types. Check those easements. Look at your recorder's office visit as an "ounce of prevention."

BE YOUR OWN APPRAISER

Before bidding on RTC or FDIC properties you will need to get a grip on what your target property is really worth. This can be done in a number of ways. Some are more accurate than others. The purpose here is not to turn you into a professional appraiser but to arm you with some handy "rules of thumb" for measuring local property values. Don't skip this section. Appraising is an important skill, and it's not as mysterious as some real estate professionals would like you to believe.

Don't be overly concerned with making a mistake in your appraisal.

1991 0043772

OFFICIAL RECORDS OF
SONOMA COUNTY
BERNICE A. PETERSON

FIRST AMERICAN TITLE
AT REQUEST OF 05/14/1991   08:00:00
FEE: $ 5.00   PGS: 1
TT : $ .00

Space above this line for Recorder's use

DEED OF RECONVEYANCE

(Escrow No. 85469-GR(PAT.)   )

WHEREAS, the indebtedness secured by the Deed of Trust executed by   STEPHEN P. PIZZO and

SUSAN E. PIZZO, his wife,

to **NORTHWESTERN TITLE SECURITY CO.** as Trustee

for   PAUL PIZZO and ANITA PIZZO, husband and wife, as Community Property,

as Beneficiaries,

dated   August 18th   , 19 86 , and recorded on   September 15th , 19 86   in Book   n/a   ,

Page n/a   , Recorder's Serial No.   86072350   , Official Records of the Office of the County
Recorder of Sonoma County, State of California, has been fully paid.

NOW THEREFORE, the present Trustee under said Deed of Trust does hereby reconvey unto the parties
entitled thereto all right, title and interest which was heretofore acquired by said Trustee under said Deed of Trust.

NORTHWESTERN TITLE SECURITY COMPANY

Dated this 19th   day of   April   , 19 91   By
Patricia Smith, Asst.   Vice President

By
Marie Chandler, Asst.   Secretary

STATE OF CALIFORNIA
COUNTY OF SONOMA   } SS. On   April 19th   , 1991 , before me, the undersigned, a Notary
Public in and for said County and State, personally appeared
Patricia Smith   and   Marie Chandler
proved to me on the basis of satisfactory evidence or known to me to be the   Asst.   Vice President and
Asst.   Secretary respectively of the Corporation that executed the within instrument on behalf of the
Corporation therein named, and acknowledged to me that such Corporation executed the same.

FOR NOTARY SEAL OR STAMP

OFFICIAL SEAL
NOTARY PUBLIC - CALIFORNIA
Alice M. Barbe
PRINCIPAL OFFICE IN
SONOMA COUNTY
Commission Expires June 30, 1993

Signature
Notary Public in and for said County and State

Northwestern Title Security Company
439 College Avenue — Santa Rosa, California

EXHIBIT 7.   A deed of reconveyance.

Unless you're paying all cash for a property, the lender, whether it's a bank, the RTC, or FDIC, will serve as a backup. During loan processing the lender's own professional appraiser conducts a formal appraisal, so you'll get a chance to see how close you came. If your bid is too high the lender will sober you up by refusing to fund a loan that is in excess of the property's value. (This assumes of course that your cash down payment is no more than 10 to 20 percent of the sales price and the bank is being asked to provide the remaining 80 to 90 percent.)

WHAT IS VALUE?

When purchasing anything you have to divide the concept of value into two categories: market value and emotional value. If you buy for investment purposes you should eliminate the emotional value and rely totally on profitability. This is business, not pleasure.

When a person finds his or her "dream home," emotions can often distort reality, resulting in "real" value being totally thrown out the window. A couple we knew moved to northern California from Los Angeles, where prices were unconscionably high and living conditions (for them) unbearable. In Santa Rosa they found the quality of life to be idyllic compared to L.A. They found a house on two acres, with a creek, fruit trees, and within walking distance of the local grammar school.

Locals knew the house had been on the market a long time. The seller was in no hurry to sell and had put a high price on the place. A similar home in L.A. would've sold for $350,000. The L.A. couple saw Shangri-La and paid the asking price of $165,000 without quibbling. At the time comparable homes in the neighborhood were selling for $125,000. A few weeks later they moved in. "I went to town and dropped into the local greasy spoon," the husband told me. "During lunch I noticed that the waitress and some of the customers were whispering and looking at me. Pretty soon she came over and said, 'Excuse me, but are you the fellow who bought the Fuller home?' I proudly said I was. The next thing I know they're all slapping each other on the back and laughing. I asked her what was so funny. She stopped laughing just long enough to ask me—'Did you really pay $165,000 for that place?' "

There are no secrets in a small town.

If you're buying for investment you will want to avoid such mistakes.

Rule number one in buying investment real estate is to *never* fall in love with a target property. Eliminate, as much as possible, the emotional component of the valuation process. The only value you want to establish is the property's approximate current market value. Forget how you *feel* about a property until after you've established its market value.

To help with your appraisal, we offer the California Supreme Court's definition of "current market value":

> The highest price, estimated in terms of money, that a property will bring if exposed for sale in the open market allowing a reasonable length of time to find a buyer who buys with full knowledge of all the uses to which the property is adapted and for which it is capable of being used.

TYPES OF APPRAISALS

Professional appraisers use three universally recognized types of appraisal forms. Many busy lenders only require that appraisers submit the *Short Form Appraisal* (SFA). This is a checklist on which an appraiser notes the property's various attributes, amenities, and standard characteristics, like building materials—brick, stucco, or wood. After completing the form, the appraiser makes his or her best estimate of what the property is worth based on the checked categories.

The second is the *Letter Form Appraisal* (LFA). This is generally used when an investor hires an appraiser to do a market analysis of a property. The appraiser writes the customer a letter that gives a brief description of the property, its present condition, and other important observations. The appraiser then gives his or her opinion of its value.

The most extensive type is the *Narrative Appraisal Form* (NAF). Like the letter form, the narrative is written but reads more like a report than a letter. It is extensive, covers local zoning matters, and includes graphs and charts. NAFs generally are required by banks that are lending on income or commercial properties.

For the novice, we introduce a much simpler form: The *Between-the-Ears-Appraisal Form*. We have named it such because that's the only place you should use it. In your head.

If the property you're purchasing is worth more than $15,000, chances are good that it was appraised soon after the government repossessed it. The RTC is required to hire a state-licensed appraiser if a property is considered to be worth more than $15,000. If a property is thought to be worth $15,000 or less, the RTC only needs to obtain a local real estate broker's "opinion of value."

But never mind. You can learn a great deal by doing your own market analysis. First, never accept the seller's appraisal as fact, even if the seller is Uncle Sam. The government's job here is to get back as much money as possible for the taxpayers or, to use its own terminology, "maximize the government's return on seized assets." As fiscally laudable as this may sound, this certainly is not your goal as an investor.

Your goal is to *minimize* the cost of acquisition. Therefore, the only appraisal you should feel comfortable with is your own. It's been said that you don't know a person until you live with them. Any married couple can tell you this. It's also true that you don't really know a property until you've done your own appraisal. The appraisal you do depends on the property type. If you want to purchase single-family or one- to four-family residential homes, the analysis process is straightforward.

Market Data Approach (MDA)

The Market Data Approach uses the appraisal concept of "substitution." Substitution asks, what are other, similar properties selling for in the same neighborhood? Not a tough question to get answered. The easiest way to get this information is through a local realtor. (We have more to say about using realtors later in this chapter.) Most realtors today subscribe to a Multiple Listing Service or MLS, which tracks all current listings, pending sales, and completed sales in a geographical area, usually a county, town, or city. Many realtors also subscribe to a computerized on-line data base that also tracks properties.

Ask the realtor about your target area. Have the realtor pull a list of at least five "comps" off the MLS computer. A comp is a comparable property that has sold during the past six months in the same part of town. Make sure the comps have the same key features: number of bedrooms, baths, lot size, and amenities. The emphasis here should be on "sold," not "listed." You are not interested in what people wish they can get for their homes but what the market actually pays.

If your local MLS is not computerized, then ask the realtor if you can thumb through the latest MLS book. Usually in the back of each book are listed all the recently sold properties. The listings show the asking price, selling price, and how long they were on the market before they sold. If the listing period is long and the property has not sold, it likely means market conditions are soft. A desperate seller is likely to make large concessions. The longer the listing period, the more a seller might give. Such a soft market is bad news for the RTC and FDIC but good news for you.

If you don't have access to a realtor, your job gets a bit more complicated. You can try to use the realtor the RTC hired to market the house, but remember, that realtor is working for the RTC, not you. The more a property sells for, the more he or she makes for a commission. The more a realtor makes for the government the greater likelihood the RTC will want to use that realtor more often. Still, give it a try. The RTC contract realtor can answer questions and might even give you access to raw MLS information without first censoring it.

If you decide to go it alone you'll need to develop a few new skills. To find recent sales you'll have to tap the county recorder's office, which we mentioned earlier. Look up the latest sales price of a property. Inspect the building's county property tax. The most important thing you should remember is this: You can punch your pocket calculator until the cows come home but the ultimate measure of value is what someone is willing to pay for a piece of real estate on the open market. *Therefore, your first step will be to collect at least five comparable properties that closely match your target property in size, condition, and location.* You can stop right here if you feel this process has given you a solid sense of what your target property should fetch on the open market. If you think you need more technical information, here's a few techniques to follow.

Replacement Cost Approach (RCA)

Not as good as the market data approach, estimating the replacement cost of a property can nonetheless be valuable. Telephone a local contractor and tell the contractor you're thinking about having your dream home built. Ask how much the charge per square foot would be. Is it $50, $60, or $100 per square foot? This gives you a sketch of what it costs for labor and materials. Amenities are extra.

Then go visit your RTC or FDIC target property. Get a rough estimate on square footage. Multiply it by the replacement estimates you received from the contractor. From this you should get an estimate on what it would cost to build a new house. Add in the cost of the underlying lot or acreage. This will give you a ballpark value.

The replacement cost approach gives you a sense of what the property, as a physical object, is worth. Depending on market conditions, the actual value of a property might exceed the replacement cost. The opposite also could be true. Here's how an RCA calculation works:

Your target property is a 2,050-square-foot single-story home on a 100' × 100' lot. Construction costs run about $55 per square foot. $55 × 2,050 = $112,750 to build that house today. Through a realtor or independently you discover that 10,000-square-foot lots in that part of town are selling for $25,000 or so. Added to the construction cost of $112,750, this gives you a total replacement cost of about $137,750.

The replacement cost approach can at least give you a general idea of what the property is worth. But it doesn't mean you should offer this amount. However, if the RTC is asking, say, $98,000 for the property, then you know right away you could be onto a potential nugget.

The market data and replacement cost approaches are the two main tools you need to evaluate residential property. If your market analysis approach does not satisfy you completely, then try the replacement cost approach and see what you get. Together they should give you a good idea of what the property might be worth. Along the way you will learn more than you ever wanted to know about your local real estate market. If you intend to keep looking in the same market area at the same basic property type, after a while doing quick appraisals will become second nature. By then you should have sufficient knowledge about the local market to do the calculations in your head.

INCOME PROPERTY

If the residential property you've targeted also has income potential (a duplex or fourplex), the process becomes more involved. Besides getting to know your market, you'll need to get better acquainted with your pocket calculator.

Investors like income property because it produces two returns for them rather than just one: appreciation and rental income. With a few geographical exceptions, real estate appreciation in America has outstripped the inflation rate. Ask the vast majority of homeowners and they'll tell you real estate has been the best investment they ever made. Investors in income property want one thing and one thing only—to make money. Investors in income properties want to know what kind of return or income stream can be made from a property. When analyzing income property the first rule is not to count your chickens before they hatch. *Do not* figure future appreciation into your calculations!

If it's apartments you're looking at, figure what the rents will produce. The idea is to make more money in rents than you're paying out in mortgage and maintenance. If it's a commercial property, such as an office building, find out what kind of leases and how much money commercial landlords are getting per square foot. Some of this should be done when doing a market analysis of the property. (See "Analyzing Income Property" for a full explanation of appraising income properties.)

HOW THE RTC APPRAISES

Because it's the seller, the RTC is doing its appraisal for the opposite reason you're doing yours. The RTC began its bureaucratic life sporting an inflated opinion of the properties it had inherited from failed S&Ls. As a result, it spent the first year of its existence turning up its nose at realistic offers made by eager buyers. More than once buyers were referred to as "vultures" because, in the mind of the RTC, they wanted to "steal" properties at the expense of the taxpayer. Buyers told the agency to take a flying leap, and they stayed away from its auctions. When properties didn't sell as well as anticipated, Congress addressed the problem in 1991 with a major reorganization of the agency. One thing Congress changed was how the RTC marked down properties that didn't sell. In short, the RTC became a deep discounter of properties, a sort of Wal-Mart of real estate.

The markdown process works like this: After obtaining a market value appraisal on the property, the RTC immediately trims between 5 and 10 percent off the asking price. If the property does not sell after a few months, it can be marked down by the RTC consolidated office by as much as 20 percent. We'll be dealing more extensively with the markdown process later.

THE RTC VALUATION PROCESS

To give you an edge over other buyers, it helps to know how the RTC's property valuation process works. If you had the time you could read the agency's policy manual, but it's long and arduous reading. Instead, we've read it for you and reduced the RTC-ese to English. The agency uses three very different measures of value when assessing a property. They are:

Appraised Value—the current "as is" value, determined by an independent appraisal.

Adjusted Appraisal Value—the revised estimated value of a property if it has not sold at the appraised value after six months on the market (four months for single-family homes.) The adjusted appraised value must always be at least 80 percent of the appraised value. And the adjusted appraised value can only be reduced by 15 percent of the appraised value at any one time.

Market Value—This represents the appraised value or adjusted appraised value modified to reflect projected holding costs. Because holding costs eat into a property's value, the RTC lowers the price to reflect this dilemma. Overseen by an RTC consolidated office, this new calculation becomes the market value. The actual sales price of a property more than likely will be closer to market value than to the other two.

We offer an expanded overview of RTC pricing strategies in Chapter 7.

OTHER RESOURCES

Investing in real estate is not the cold, cruel world that some think it is. For the novice, many resources are available to help you along the way.

REALTORS

A good local real estate agent can be your most important asset. The secret is to control the relationship and maintain the upper hand. Realtors have access to updated market data through the MLS guide and data base. MLS data is only available to licensed realtors. Regular folks cannot purchase an MLS guide. Only licensed realtors who are members of the MLS can get this information.

Getting free and unlimited access to the MLS is your goal here. Get cozy with your realtor, but don't mislead him or her. Good realtors know when they're being used. Keep in mind that you can use a realtor to represent you, the buyer. This is becoming more commonplace, especially in soft markets. Good realtors will bend over backwards to develop promising clients. If you're looking to invest, interview several local realtors.

If the RTC has already mailed you a list of prospective properties you will notice that many of the listings are with the same realtor. Start with him or her. Because realtors make a commission only when the property is sold, they'll want to work with you. Also, the realtor wants the repeat business when you cash in on your investment.

If you can't find an RTC realtor, then as we mentioned earlier, get a realtor to represent you, the buyer. Don't mislead the realtor. Tell him or her your investment goals and indicate that if all goes as planned you will need a realtor to represent you. The realtor will know that even if he or she doesn't get a commission right away, there may be one down the road when you begin buying and selling properties.

When I was a realtor one of my best clients was a small investor who began investing in real estate for himself and some of his friends. In the beginning our relationship was very one-sided. I provided him with all kinds of information about the area: property values, sales, the "good" parts of town, vacancy rates, rental prices, and the like. Based on this information he acquired a number of properties directly from sellers. But within a couple of years he and his friends were sellers, not buyers. I got the listings, and the sales commissions more than made up for all that "free" advice.

Don't be discouraged if some realtors seem cold to the idea of answering all your questions during the acquisition phase of your program. You don't want a relationship with a realtor who sees you only as a current prospect. Successful realtors cultivate long-term relationships. In time you'll find one of these successful realtors. When you find a realtor willing to work hard for you, show that person some degree of loyalty. Bring properties to him or her. Let that realtor present your offer to the RTC listing broker. In time your realtor will be functioning like a secretary of sorts. If you bring the realtor enough business he or she'll be more than happy to handle loose ends in the paperwork, which frees you up to concentrate on other properties.

TITLE COMPANIES

Title companies are another terrific resource. If you've purchased a home, chances are you've already met your first title officer.

A title company performs three major services for buyers of real estate:

1) It searches the title to determine if the property is encumbered in any way and provides a report to the buyer, seller and lender.
2) It provides title insurance to insure the lender against any undiscovered defects in title.
3) It handles all the paperwork for the buyer and seller and disburses all monies to the proper parties.

Title company employees who manage escrows are called "title officers." Cultivating a personal relationship with a good title officer can save you a lot of work and headaches. A seasoned title officer can manage any title quirks that come along and can research and extract essential information on particular properties for you.

Most big title companies maintain their own computerized property records. They can research almost any property you want using nothing more than an address or assessor's number. Good title companies have what they call a "title plant," which is an in-house collection of regularly updated property records and recorded documents.

Because title companies earn their keep by charging escrow fees and writing title insurance, like realtors they will want to develop a long-term relationship with anyone who conducts a lot of real estate business. Though less likely than a realtor to answer a bunch of questions, they can be useful for certain kinds of problems. For example, say you've completed your own title search on a property and can't find evidence that an old loan was ever repaid. With a good title company you can ask to have their title plant research for a "deed of reconveyance." If they can't find it, the company can tell you how to cure this cloud on the title. Realtors depend heavily on their favorite title officers. Ask your realtor who he or she can recommend.

Other Resources

Besides those listed here, there are other places you can turn for help. As we said in the introduction, this book is not intended to be a complete guide to real estate investing. Many excellent books have been published on the subject and are available at your bookstore.

IN SUMMARY

Real estate is just another commodity, like a car, a washing machine, or a home computer system. But the same consumers who think nothing of reading up on something like a home computer system before buying one avoid doing the same thing with real estate. Somehow real estate has become, in some people's minds, a commodity like stocks and bonds that only experts can understand.

But as we've seen in this chapter, there are no real mysteries about real estate and no codes to break in order to become a knowledgeable buyer. It's just common sense. Follow the instructions in this chapter, and in short order you'll be making your own decisions about real estate investments.

Just remember to keep your pocket calculator at hand and to listen to it rather than your beating heart. "Do the numbers" should be the mantra of every novice real estate investor. Do you have enough income to service the loan? Do you have enough money to make the necessary repairs? What about taxes and insurance? Whatever your heart has to say about a property is only relevant after these questions are answered to your calculator's satisfaction.

That's it—all you need to get started. If you follow these guidelines the process should go smoothly. Only fear of failure now stands between you and some great real estate deals.

Chapter Five

....

Hey Buddy, Can You Spare a Loan?

How to Get Government Financing to Buy Government Property

Okay, so you've found the perfect property. You had it appraised, you inspected it, and finally you've reached a conclusion on bid price. Now it's time to worry about financing. Just how are you going to finance this purchase? In most cases, if you can't get a bank loan the RTC will loan you the money. The RTC can extend credit on any sale over $100,000. In this case, obtaining a government loan can be a pretty good deal.

Congress has authorized the RTC to provide seller financing when appropriate to facilitate the sale of real estate assets. (The RTC and FDIC, however, will not provide financing to buy loans.) Both agencies offer financing on the following: residential, commercial and industrial, raw land, and Affordable Housing Program properties.

RTC LOAN TERMS

DOWN PAYMENT AND INTEREST RATE

The RTC pegs the interest rate charged on its mortgages to the weekly U.S. Treasury Note Constant Maturity Index. This index can be checked by reading the Treasury note and bond tables published in the *Wall Street Journal*. The rate is pegged to whatever the rate was on the previous Wednesday before the auction or contract date.

If you don't read the *Wall Street Journal*, telephone the RTC asset manager handling the auction or sale. He or she will tell you that week's rate. Once you have the rate, the math is easy. The actual interest rate charged depends on the size of your down payment. The RTC prefers 25 percent cash down, but will accept as little as 15 percent. The rate on your mortgage will be a number of percentage points (or basis points) above the Treasury index. One percentage point equals 100 basis points—like a dollar is equal to 100 cents. If someone says a rate is "1.50 percent over the prime rate" the same thing can be expressed as "150 basis points above prime." In this example, if prime is 6.00 percent the rate charged would be 7.50 percent.

In any case, the rate you pay on an RTC loan depends on how much cash you have to put down. The RTC has a sliding scale to determine your rate:

- If you make a cash down payment of 30 percent or more, the RTC loan interest rate charged will be the Treasury Index Rate plus 150 basis points (TIR + 1.5%).
- If you make a cash down payment of 25 to 29 percent, you will be charged the Treasury Index Rate plus 187.5 basis points (TIR + 1.875%).
- If you make a cash down payment of 20 to 24 percent, you will be charged the Treasury Index Rate plus 225 basis points (TIR + 2.25%).
- If you make a cash down payment of 15 to 19 percent, you will be charged the Treasury Index Rate plus 262.5 basis points (TIR + 2.625%).

Example

You want to offer $125,000 for a property. You have $30,000 cash to put down and want the government to carry the balance of $95,000 as a loan. What would your interest rate be on that loan?

> Look in the *WSJ*. That week's Treasury Index Rate was 6.25 percent (or 625 basis points). Your $30,000 cash down represents a 24 percent down payment. 625 basis points + 225 basis points = 850 basis points or 8.5 percent. You will pay the government an interest rate of 8.5 percent on your $95,000 loan.
>
> Get an amortization table from your realtor. Look up the 8.5 percent table on a 30-year loan. You will see that your monthly mortgage payment would be $716.

The RTC can be extremely flexible on the subject of down payments. The guidelines given by the RTC to field supervisors reveal just how creative they can be:

> While an equity commitment of 15% is the absolute minimum, in certain situations this 15% commitment may be allocated between down payment and a funded escrow to be used solely for capital improvements on the property. While important, down payments should not be viewed mechanically without reference to the overall economics of the transaction. In some cases . . . investment of time and expense by the purchaser may be more relevant than the percentage of down payment. In other cases, especially property sales involving syndication of tax benefits, "equity" may represent only a share of the developer's fee generated by the public subsidy (for low income housing) and not necessarily indicate a serious financial stake in the project.

Talk about wiggle room! As you can see, the RTC is giving its field supervisors a great deal of latitude in deciding how much of a down payment is considered enough.

Unless it's a loan to purchase an AFH unit, single-family residential mortgages made by the RTC that have less than a 20 percent down payment will require private mortgage insurance (PMI). For borrowers that means a few extra bucks a month included in the monthly payment to pay the insurance premium. The amount of premium declines each year along with the outstanding loan balance. (RTC residential loans are made at fifteen-year and thirty-year terms.)

In case you're wondering, these mortgages are not "held" by the government. In other words, you won't be making out your monthly mortgage to Uncle Sam. The RTC will place your loan into a "pool" of similar loans that it will then sell to investors in the form of mortgage-backed securities. As a mortgagor (one who pays a mortgage) you might find that the right to "service" your loan will be sold or transferred to another company. This will not affect your loan payment or terms. From time to time when a loan changes servicers, the paperwork gets messed up, though it's a rare occurrence.

TERMS OF RTC LOANS

Only residential loans made by the RTC have terms of fifteen and thirty years. Almost all other loans carry terms of only seven years. On a seven-year loan the monthly payment is still calculated off a thirty-year amortization schedule. That means that in seven years you'll have to pay the full loan amount or get a new mortgage. When you have a seven-year loan most of your payments are for interest—that means the principal is hardly reduced.

When you make a bid you can ask for a longer-term loan, but you'd better have a good reason. The RTC can grant a loan extension of up to three additional years. The agency is not crazy about doing this. The decision to grant a longer-term loan is made based on market conditions only—not the needs of the borrower. If an extension is granted the RTC requires a 10 percent principal reduction in each of the three extension years. No interest-only loans are allowed on residential and commercial properties.

Raw land is the hardest asset for the RTC to sell, so it bends over backwards to accommodate prospective buyers. Therefore, RTC loans on raw land are a different matter. Here the RTC will break its own rule against interest-only loans and allow interest-only payments on raw land loans. However, before such a loan is made the borrower must agree to make periodic principal payments at set intervals during the life of the loan.

LIEN PRIORITY

The RTC always wants to be the first mortgage (or lien) holder on the property it sells to you when it's providing the financing. However, even here there is some flexibility. If a bank is providing most of the loan amount, the RTC will consider making a small second mortgage on the property. However, the combined loans cannot exceed 85 percent of the sales price.

KEY INFORMATION. *If the RTC makes you a first mortgage, you cannot go out later and get a second mortgage on the property without the agency's permission. If you get a second mortgage without the RTC's permission and they find out, your RTC loan could be called due at the RTC's discretion.*

ASSUMABILITY

All RTC loans are "due on sale." This means RTC loans cannot be assumed by subsequent buyers. If you sell the property, the loan has to be repaid in full.

PREPAYMENT TERMS

As we noted earlier, the RTC wants to sell your loan into the secondary market. Investors who buy securities backed by home mortgages like certainty and dislike the prospect of having the loans paid off early and therefore having their anticipated return diminished. (A prepayment occurs when you sell the home or pay it off early.) If mortgage borrowers pay off a loan before maturity, the investor in that loan loses all the future interest payments. To protect mortgage securities investors from "prepayment shocks," lenders can impose a prepayment fee on borrowers that can sometimes get costly.

The RTC does not always insist on a prepayment fee. Like everything else, it's negotiable. Still, the agency tells its field supervisors to impose the fee when it can get away with it because it increases the marketability of the loans on the secondary market. RTC prepayment fees are as follows: 5 percent of the principal balance if the loan is prepaid in the first year, 4 percent in the second year, and so on down the line. When you make your offer on the property, designate in your offer that you want an RTC loan without a prepayment fee clause.

PERSONAL LIABILITY

If you borrow from the RTC, you are personally liable for fraud, misrepresentation, waste, enforcement costs, real estate taxes, and environmental indemnifications. If you lied on your loan application and doctored your financial statement to qualify for the loan, the RTC will fine you or take the house away. If you destroy the RTC property you bought (without first paying off your RTC mortgage) or you dump toxic waste in your backyard or build a nuclear reactor (you get the message), the RTC will hold you personally, and legally, responsible forever—and a day.

COMMERCIAL PROPERTY DEBT-SERVICE RATIOS

The RTC is idealistic when it comes to debt-service ratios. In a good debt-service ratio situation the rents on a property meet or exceed the monthly mortgage payment, insurance, taxes, and maintenance costs. When this happens the lender can rest easily.

Unfortunately, the RTC does not often find itself in this sort of good situation. Even in its own policy manuals, the RTC admits to field supervisors that "many RTC properties are leased well below traditional break-even levels at 75% of financing."

Therefore, when it comes to making loans the RTC has to be flexible. When it appears that a debt-service ratio is going to be low—meaning rents may not right away cover the mortgage payment—the RTC looks away from the property and to the financial strength of the borrower for added comfort. If the property *and* the borrower are weak, the likelihood of a meeting of the minds is low.

INSURANCE

The RTC, like all lenders, requires the borrower to have fire, liability, comprehensive, and general liability insurance on the property it acquires. The RTC remains as the property's co-beneficiary until the loan is repaid.

RELEASE PRICE

Let's say you purchase a townhouse development from the RTC and the RTC makes you one blanket loan covering the whole asset. Then six months later you sell half the development to someone else. If you want to release a portion of a real estate development from an RTC blanket loan, the RTC requires 105 percent of the pro rata debt allocated to the released collateral. In other words, if the RTC loan was $200,000 and you sold half the project, the RTC would require that you pay the loan down by $105,000, and then the RTC will continue to carry the balance of $95,000.

COMMERCIAL LOAN FEE

When it makes commercial property loans the RTC charges a $\frac{1}{10}$ of 1 percent application processing fee with a floor of $1,500 and a ceiling of $7,500. The fee is due when the application is submitted and is non-refundable.

BRIDGE LOANS

The RTC will provide a temporary "bridge" loan to facilitate a sale as long as you can get financing elsewhere shortly after the deal closes. Bridge loans are available on commercial property and carry a maximum term of 18 months. A 25 percent cash down payment is required to get a bridge loan.

If these RTC loan terms don't thrill you, then shop around for a better deal. We doubt there's one out there. Conventional lenders—banks and S&Ls—will nick you for appraisal fees, document preparation fees, extra points, and so on, which the RTC does not charge for.

But the RTC doesn't care who lends you the money. The agency just wants to sell as much real estate as quickly as it can. If they have to lend you the money to make that happen, they'll do that at pretty fair terms. The worst thing about an RTC loan is that it's not assumable. If you sell the property a year after you buy it from the RTC, the new buyer cannot assume (begin paying) your RTC loan. The new buyer will have to get his or her own bank loan. It's a minor point, but one worth mentioning.

Anyway, after your RTC loan actually closes, you can always shop around for a better loan later on. Once the property becomes yours you have seven long years to play the interest rate waiting game. When rates dip to a low point, you can refinance the property.

MULTIPLE PROPERTY PURCHASES

What if you want to buy four separate RTC properties? Will the RTC still provide financing? Will it roll the total amount into one big loan covering all the properties? The answer is yes and no. Yes, the RTC will provide financing on the four properties, but no, it will not issue a blanket loan on all four. Instead the RTC will handle each as a separate sale. Each is eligible to get its very own RTC loan.

Again, remember the RTC motto: Cash is king. In its policy manuals, the RTC tells its field supervisors: "If there is an all-cash offer on the table, it may be considered advantageous for the RTC to accept the offer even if the sales price is less than the terms sale alternative." In other words, if you bid $25,000 for a property and want the RTC to make you a $20,000 loan, and then someone comes along and offers $21,500 in cash, you will probably lose that fight.

If you can arrange your own financing before making a bid you will be better off. This way the RTC can "cash out" and be done with the property, hopefully forever. If you arrange for outside financing, make sure you have something to show the RTC that documents this fact when you make your offer. A loan commitment letter signed by your banker is the preferential way to handle this.

Still, it's nice to know that during times of tight credit you won't be closed out of the game. If no one else will, both the RTC and FDIC can make you the loan you need.

RAW LAND LOANS?

Few lenders will make loans on raw land, and often those that do will not lend more than 50 percent of the purchase price. Not the RTC. Beginning in 1992 the agency adopted a policy where it will loan any purchaser up to 85 percent of the purchase price for fifteen years.

IN SUMMARY

The RTC provides seller financing on all sorts of real estate: residential, commercial, multifamily, and raw land. Terms differ for each, but it's an easy and straightforward way to buy. Later you can shop for permanent financing at your leisure.

Only loans on single-family homes made by the RTC have terms of 30 years. Most other loans carry seven-year terms. That means you have seven years before the loan is due. Because you have no points or other fees to pay on an RTC loan, government financing is a good deal—particularly if you intend to sell the property before the loan is due.

The one downside to requesting RTC financing is that when it takes bids the agency will give first consideration to all-cash offers. If you request RTC financing you may never make it to the final round of bidding. That's the risk you run. If you can't get financing anywhere else, then that risk doesn't seem so bad.

Chapter 6

....

Crunching the Numbers

Analyzing and Buying Income Property

The RTC and FDIC have a bellyfull of income properties. To say the least, high-flying bank and thrift owners were the world's biggest optimists. Failed banks and thrifts financed everything from office buildings and shopping centers to apartment complexes and health spas—you name it. And they built these projects whether they were needed or not. Former FDIC Chairman Bill Seidman once said his "favorite" piece of FDIC-owned property was a "spec airport"—an airport built in the middle of nowhere by a developer who was anticipating urban sprawl. When the government seized Charles Keating, Jr.'s palatial Phoenician Hotel resort in Phoenix, an FDIC official remarked that the landscaping was "very nice." A loyal Keating employee shot back, "Nice? Let me tell you, sir, that's the way God would have done it—if He'd had the money."

Well, they had the money—yours and mine—and now the RTC and FDIC own their thousands of pet projects. Not all of the income properties built (hotels, malls, luxury housing developments) were pipe dreams, though. In fact, most are properties with great long-term potential just looking for a new owner. The reasons these projects ever worked are many. Unscrupulous developers skimmed money out of the construction loans and into their own pockets, leaving the projects with insufficient funds to be completed or marketed properly, or money was diverted in the form of kickbacks to crooked loan officers. But often the problem was only that during the 1980s banks and S&Ls got a little carried away and over-lent to developers, creating a glut of properties.

Some income properties should never have been built because no one needed them. But demographics will eventually cure that problem as the marketplace absorbs these excess units. Other projects were poorly designed for the purpose for which they were built. But such buildings can often be adapted to other purposes. All these income properties are creations of value simply waiting for the right time, the right use, and the right owner.

Buying income property from the government is radically different from buying government-owned residential property. Income property, for the most part, is a lot more expensive and the risk of loss is much greater—but so are the potential gains. When purchasing a home, your criteria are personal and emotional as well as financial. Investors in income property buy for one reason only: to make money and benefit from the income a property produces. The trick is to be able to calculate your risks and income opportunities for a given property before you bid. Analyzing income property is not as arcane as you think. There are no mysteries or hidden formulas. Done right, the math is simple and straightforward, and you don't need an MBA to reach an informed investment conclusion.

INCOME PROPERTY GIVES A DOUBLE WHAMMY

If you already own a home, any additional real estate you purchase will likely be income property. What you're doing here is investing—hoping to make money on the rent or down the road through appreciation. That's the "double whammy" of income property: *appreciation and income.* Appreciation is realized when you sell or refinance income property years from now. In the meantime, rental income gives an immediate return and helps pay the mortgage and—hopefully—most other costs.

At its best, rents can provide regular added monthly income and cover carrying costs.

A well-chosen income property should at least cover your total mortgage payments, insurance costs, and taxes. "Great" income properties yield a positive cash flow—covering all your mortgage and operating costs and leaving you a little extra (or a lot extra) each month, called "net spendable income." Good positive cash flow properties became increasingly rare during the 1980s. But thanks to the S&L and banking disasters, positive cash flow properties are again available in the form of apartment buildings, strip shopping centers, warehouses, and even office buildings, though you'll have to be extra careful with the latter due to severe oversupply in many areas.

WHY INCOME PROPERTY IS SUCH A GOOD INVESTMENT

In 1976 my wife (Susan Pizzo) and I had saved about $8,500. The money sat in a bank account earning about 8 percent interest, which meant with compounding it would about double in ten years. At the time inflation was running in the double digits and we wanted this money to work a bit harder than that.

We had already purchased our own home, and so we began looking for a small piece of investment real estate. The property we finally decided on was an unassuming twenty-five-year-old wood-frame duplex in a small rural town sixty-five miles north of San Francisco. The town was changing from an old resort community to a year-round suburb of growing Santa Rosa, California, 12 miles to the east. Since this little town was rapidly becoming a bedroom community to Santa Rosa, we decided it would be a good idea to buy some bedrooms.

The absentee owner of the duplex had tired of maintaining a property eighty miles away and listed the property for $36,000. We offered $29,000 with $7,500 down, and asked that the seller carry the balance at 7 percent. He countered at $31,500 with $7,250 down. He would carry the balance, $24,250 at 8 percent. Our payments would be $175 per month. We accepted. Averaging income and expenses for the period owned, here's how that little investment has worked for us:

Gross Rents:	$1,000/mo.
Annual Gross:	$12,000
Less Annualized Expenses:	
Mortgage:	$ 2,100
Insurance:	$ 250
Maintenance:	$ 850 (avg.)
Property Taxes:	$ 934
Utilities	$ 0 (Tenants Pay)
Total Expenses:	$ 4,134
Net Rents:	$ 7,866
(Or $655.50 per month net spendable income)	

For simplicity purposes we will not discuss here depreciation, mortgage interest, and capitalized deductions taken for tax purposes. Such deductions reduce your taxes on this income, and we'll cover them later.

Now, let's see how that investment compares with a simple savings account. If we had left our $7,250 in the bank for the same fifteen years, drawing an average 8 percent interest, compounded it would have increased to $23,975. By comparison our little duplex did much better than that. The net rent collected over fifteen years was $62,010. Annualized, that comes to a return on our cash investment of $7,250 of 57 percent a year! ($62,010/15 = $4134, $4134/$7250 = .57).

In the meantime, the building increased in value significantly, further compounding our gain. We bought the building for $31,500 in 1976. In 1991 it was worth $145,000, a gain in value of $113,500, or an additional annual gain of $7,567 on top of rents. With net rents of $4,134, plus appreciation of $7,567, we were really earning $11,701 per year on our little $7,250 cash investment, or a return of 160 percent—just a bit better than the 8.32 percent compounded rate of return we would have earned at the bank.

By the time our first son is ready for college in 1996, the duplex will have plenty of equity. We can either sell the property or borrow against it to cover his tuition and that of his younger brother four years later. By then the building should be worth at least $200,000—or $25,000 per year per kid for four years. Thanks to this little building my wife and I do not lie awake nights worrying about how we are going to pay for our kids' college education.

That investment, made fifteen years ago, was the best decision we ever made. It opened our eyes to the compounding gains that can be had by investing in real estate, particularly income-producing property. Since then we have purchased other properties, even a "fixer upper" operating dairy farm in Wisconsin. All of our real estate investments have produced wonderful returns and a peace of mind that comes only from financial security. That little duplex was not our last income property investment, but the one that most clearly answers the question, "Why should we buy real estate?"

HOW TO ANALYZE INCOME PROPERTY

Using such arcane phrases as "uneven cash flow analysis," "present value of future dollar calculations," and "sinking funds," professional real estate investors can make income property analysis look like quantum physics. The pros find great comfort in these calculations, but for the novice or small investor they can often be just a frustrating waste of time. The small to mid-sized investor needs to know one thing only: After my down payment, will the rental income on the property exceed my monthly mortgage and holding costs? (In a nutshell, this is what the pros want to know too, but they couch it in more sophisticated terms.)

ANALYZING RTC OR FDIC PROPERTIES

Case Study

(Property description of a sample RTC listing)

Asset Name: **Broadmore Manor Apartments**
Property Address: 1111 Broadmore St.
City, State, Zip: Walnut Hill, CA 92401
RTC Asking Price: $200,000

Occupancy: Fully rented
Condition: Good

Number of Units: 4 (Two 2-bdrs, two 3-bdrs)
Year Built: 1984
Acquisition Date: 08/14/91
Construction: Stucco
Total Square Footage: 5,436

ANALYSIS PROCESS OF PROPERTY

Vacancy Factor

Your first task is to establish the local vacancy ratio. Your goal is to keep the four units fully rented. But if the local vacancy ratio is 50 percent, you're going to have a problem. Before making an investment decision and calculation you first need to know what the vacancy rate actually is.

There are a few different ways to go about this. Contact a professional property management company in the area. Tell them what you have in mind and ask if they can provide any hard data on the local rental market. Property managers make their living by managing other people's income properties. Once they hear you're considering a property—and because they will want to manage your property—they might paint a rosier picture of the rental market than what really exists. Keep this in mind. On the other hand they won't exaggerate too much, because if they wind up managing your property and rentals don't match their predictions they run the risk of losing your business. Property managers can be found in your telephone book in the real estate listings section.

A simpler way to get a feel for the rental market is to drive by similar apartment buildings in the neighborhood early in the morning on a weekday. We mean EARLY! We're talking 3 A.M.—before anyone leaves for work. Check out the parking areas. Are they full of cars or half empty? If you see lots of empty spaces there might be trouble. Weekends are not a good time to check for vacancy because people might simply be away.

If the property has a rental history and current tenants, the RTC will include this information in the property's due diligence package. Due diligence packages are available at RTC and FDIC auctions or are given to serious bidders who show they have at least enough money for a down payment. The income history of a property tells you the current rent, the occupancy ratio (how many of the units are now rented) and which renters are in arrears (behind in their rent.)

If the building is vacant—which is not the case in our above example, but is sometimes the case with RTC properties—then you need to investigate similar buildings in the neighborhood.

If you discover the local vacancy factor is much higher than 10 percent and your target property has a vacancy rate of that or higher, you may want to pass. Even if the building you are considering is fully rented, for purposes of this analysis, assume a 5 percent vacancy factor—meaning your units will be empty 5 percent of the year, and you will not receive any rental income.

Establish Rents

Next, investigate what rents are in the immediate area. How much will your apartments fetch each month when compared to similar units? Drive around and copy telephone numbers off "Apartment for Rent" signs. Call landlords. Tell them you want to rent a place. See how willing they are to dicker. In a strong rental market no one dickers.

Now that we've established the vacancy ratio and the rental price, it's time to do our first calculation. We've discovered that the two 2-bedrooms in Walnut Hill rent out for $500 each. That comes to $1,000. The two 3-bedrooms rent out at $700 each. That's $1,400. Together, all four rent for $2,400. Now subtract the vacancy calculation of 5 percent. This represents the property's Gross Operating Income or GOI. To summarize:

- Total rents: $2,400/month or $28,000 per year
- Vacancy ratio: 5%, or $1400/year
- Gross Operating Income = $26,560

We now have the first element in our income analysis. Write that figure down and let's move on.

The next calculation we need to do is the property's estimated Net Operating Income (NOI). This is an easy calculation, but requires some research. First list the property's annual operating expenses, *excluding* the loan payments. If you're lucky the RTC or FDIC asset manager might have a breakdown handy, but don't count on it. Do your own anyway. And be conservative, not liberal. You can't fool yourself into making a profit.

Annual operating expenses

- Property Taxes: $2,000
- Fire and liability insurance: $1,000
- Utilities: $0 (tenants pay)
- Sewer assessment: $950
- Maintenance (5% of gross income): $684 (unless the building and its systems are old and break down a lot)
- Advertising and misc.: $1,800 (including a sinking fund for appliance and floor covering replacement, etc.)

Total Operating Expenses = $6,434

Next, subtract the annual operating expense of $6,434 from your gross operating income of $26,600. You should arrive at $19,354.00. This is your net operating income. The end is now in sight. There's just one more calculation to make. In a moment you will subtract your estimated financing costs (monthly mortgage payment) from the NOI. But before you do, there are a few important things to consider:

- What is the most you are willing (or able) to pay for this property? The government is asking $200,000, but during inspection you concluded it needs $20,000 in repairs.
- You decide to offer no more than $150,000. For your down payment you have only $10,000 cash. You will have to borrow the rest, including the $20,000 needed to remodel. You already know the RTC will finance an 80 percent mortgage that amortizes on a thirty-year schedule. More than likely you'll be getting an RTC seven-year balloon mortgage. If you can swing it, a bank or S&L might offer you an 80 percent loan that also amortizes on a thirty-year schedule but is not due in seven years. Either way, you'll need a $120,000 mortgage (80% + $150,000 = $120,000).

If you've done this simple math correctly, you will learn that you're about $20,000 short. Don't forget the repairs. Also, factor in closing costs, which will be at least another $5,000. So in total, you're $25,000 short. The solution (for this example) is to take out a "second" mortgage from a source who agrees to be junior (subordinate) to the bank or RTC loan. (If the RTC is making the first loan, you will need its permission to get a second.) Let's assume you find private-sector lenders willing to make both loans on the following terms:

The bank loan: $120,000 at 9 percent interest for twenty-five years = $985 per month.[1]

A second mortgage of $25,000 at 10 percent for ten years (interest only) = $208 per month.

Total monthly loan service = $1,194

Total annual loan service = $14,328

Now subtract the annual loan service from your NOI to get your Net Spendable Income (NSI): $19,354 − $14,328 = $5,026 NSI.

Even with your second mortgage this property has positive cash flow. If the RTC takes your bid, you're all set.

After completing these sorts of calculations a few times it should become second nature. There's no magic to it, no hidden tricks. Just simple math and common sense. You don't have to be a rocket scientist. Still, we recommend that before you spend thousands of dollars on an investment property you first spend $29.95 and purchase a *business* pocket calculator. Prices for these little wonders range from under $20 to more than $150. For most small investors the Texas Instruments BA-35 calculator is more than adequate and priced at under $30. The BA-35 will calculate loan payments, balloon payments, compound interest calculations, present- and future-value calculations, loan balances, and many other commonly used business formulas. You don't need to learn the mathematical formulas that make it all happen. Just tap in the appropriate information and the machine coughs up the answer you need.

[1] All figures are rounded.

APPRAISING INCOME PROPERTY

As we noted earlier, compared to residential real estate, the stakes are higher when it comes to investing in income property. To separate the "dogs" from the "cash cows" there are a few different quick calculations you can do that will tell you if an income property is a waste of time. Some short cuts are more useful than others, but we'll briefly touch on them all.

PRICE PER UNIT METHOD (PPUM)

Take the per-unit price attributed to the units by local real estate experts and multiply it by the number of units in the building. A marginally useful tool, this gives you a theoretical value of the property. For example, if local experts are using a $40,000 per unit factor, then your four-unit property could be worth $160,000, not the $200,000 the RTC is asking.

The flaw with the price per unit method is that it does not differentiate between different-sized units. A studio apartment is given the same value as a three-bedroom unit. PPUM is often used by large investors who control one hundred or more rental units in the local market. They often figure lump sum costs on all holdings and then divide by the number of units they control. Included as lump sum costs are such factors as maintenance, expenses, and taxes. Considered a "broad stroke" technique, PPUM reflects a certain degree of reality, but it is not perfect. It's useful for quick "on-the-run" calculations for which you can divide the asking price by the number of units in a building.

Before you can make this calculation, you'll need to know what the average cost of rental units is in your particular area. Commercial real estate managers should have those figures readily handy and be happy to share them with you.

GROSS MULTIPLIER METHOD (GMM)

The GMM method is slightly more precise than the unit price approach. It uses a "rent multiplier" to gauge value. (Again, local realtors can tell you what rent multiplier is being currently used in your area.) For example: The gross rent multiplier in your area is 7. The apartment complex you're considering produces gross annual rents of $28,000. Multiply 7 × $28,000 = $196,000. Theoretically your target property is worth $196,000.

The weakness with GMM is that it does not take into account any property's expenses. Still, it can be used to determine if the seller's asking price is above or below the local norm.

NET OPERATING INCOME METHOD (NOIM)

One of the more accurate gauges of value, NOIM deducts property expenses from gross rents and factors in the vacancy ratio. (However, it does not take into consideration mortgage payments.) If your property produces $28,000 in gross rents and has $8,646 a year in expenses, then your NOI is $19,354. Ask a local realtor or two what the rent multiplier is in your target area. For sake of argument, one tells you it's 10 and another says it's 11. Split the difference at 10.5. Then multiply 10.5 × $19,354 = $203,217. Theoretically, that's now the value of your property.

CAPITALIZATION RATE METHOD (CRM)

This method takes you down to the bottom line right away. When you open a savings account you want to know what your rate of return (the interest rate paid by the bank) will be. The same holds true when investing in income property. Instead of interest income you'll be receiving rental income. Like a passbook account, rental income can be calculated as a rate of return to determine what a particular property might be worth.

Ask a commercial realtor what the current "cap rate" is. The realtor replies that it's 10. A 10 means that before investors buy they'll demand at least a 10 percent return from a building's net operating income. Keep in mind that income properties must compete against other investments such as stocks, bonds, and Treasury notes. Using the cap rate method we're trying to compare the property's investment value in the current investment climate.

Cap rates rise and fall with the condition of the local market and are often based on anticipated price appreciation. Take the cap rate and multiply it by your net operating income (NOI). For example, your property's net operating income is $19,354. The cap rate, according to your realtor is 10. Multiply the 10 by $19,354. Your investment value is $193,540.

The higher the cap rate demanded by investors, the lower it drives the value of an income property. It's common sense: The more investors demand in return on an asset's value, the less they'll pay for it based on a given net income stream.

Seasoned investors routinely use these shortcuts when analyzing income property. For the most part these methods are quick, easy, and, more often than not, come close to the mark. As you may have noticed we used the same NOI figure in all these examples and the values we came up with did not vary greatly. Nevertheless, don't rely exclusively on these shortcuts. Always complete your full-blown market value analysis and get comps.

Again, there are plenty of different ways to calculate the value of income property. Bookstores are full of them. But for making a bid on RTC or FDIC properties, the examples given above are enough to get you in the neighborhood. If you bag an investment property a good tax advisor can tell you all about depreciation schedules and how they're used to lower your investment income for tax purposes. Don't worry. It's just more good news.

With income property the biggest mistake you can make is to let your emotions overrule your calculations. No matter how much your eyes and heart love a property, you must be able to put those considerations aside and follow the simple steps above. Your heart will lie to you. Busy divorce courts are a testament to that truth. It's a cliché, but *numbers* don't lie. Numbers have no feelings, and they don't care. Numbers always tell the truth. We will say it over and over: *do the numbers*. Better that you let the numbers break your heart than to let your heart break your bank account.

SOME THOUGHTS ON BEING A LANDLORD

Many hardball real estate investors will advise you not to fall in love with your rental properties. They also warn you not to get too chummy with tenants. Both are sound pieces of advice but should be taken in moderation.

Your investment is going to be someone else's "home sweet home."

Treat it accordingly. You may have reached a point in your life where you can live in a better property than the one you're renting—that's all well and good. In fact, that's the whole point of this book—to raise your standard of living. But when buying and operating rentals, always ask yourself: Would I put my family, or for that matter my mother, in one of these units? If the answer is no, then calculate the cost of upgrading the rental in your cost estimates before you bid. You don't have to love your income property, but you should still be able to love yourself after you cash your tenant's rent check.

Do not purchase residential rental units unless you are prepared to become that building's superintendent or are prepared to hire a super to perform regular maintenance. Water heaters and plumbing are the two most frequent problems you'll have. Early on Thanksgiving Day I was called by a tenant because the element went out in her oven just when she put the turkey in. Guests were coming and all repair services, of course, were closed. I contacted another tenant who was having Thanksgiving at a relative's home and got permission for the woman to cook the turkey in her oven. That's the lot of the landlord.

If you don't like being bothered by other people's problems, then find a more passive investment. Also, it's better that you not think of your renters as "tenants." You'll do a lot better in this business if you consider them to be what they really are—your *customers*. Treat them accordingly. I have sometimes felt uncomfortable in the role of landlord. Having control over a family's hearth and home is a unique responsibility. Too many landlords abuse it. If you've never been a landlord, remember that you may own the building, but always remember also, you are a guest when in your tenant's home.

COMMERCIAL AND INDUSTRIAL INCOME PROPERTY

Commercial and industrial property investing is a venue in which you can lose serious money fast. A lot of losers have preceded you. A large chunk of the real estate being offered by the RTC and FDIC is the direct by-product of those earlier follies. On the other hand, the opportunities for gain are equally large.

Commercial and industrial properties are generally rented by the square foot. Calculations you make on square foot income are the same as on the rental and lease income we discussed above. Find out what the square foot rate is for the kind of property you're considering. Then apply the cap rate method to the result.

Commercial and industrial property investments are not for the faint-hearted or the amateur investor. A glut of office space exists in most major markets—we're talking double-digit vacancy ratios in such previously hot markets as Los Angeles, New York, and even the formerly recession-proof Washington, D.C. Double-digit vacancy ratios will remain in most major office markets through 1995 as both the RTC and FDIC dump more real estate at fire sale prices.

A small retail shop across the street from a regional shopping center may look like a real buy. But if half the shops across the street are vacant, your square footage estimates will be theoretical at best. Do your homework. National commercial real estate companies such as JBS Associates in Chicago and Cushman and Wakefield in Los Angeles spit out commercial vacancy rate data every month. National real estate companies track vacancy trends in—usually—the fifty largest markets. The National Association of Realtors in Washington also has readily available residential and commercial vacancy data.

Most vacancy studies conducted by these large organizations are free for the asking. Watch the business or real estate section of your local newspaper—firms like Cushman and Wakefield regularly supply vacancy data tables to business and real estate editors hungry for easy copy. The graphs are simple to read. At the bottom of the graph or list of statistics the paper will credit the company or organization that provided the numbers. Give them a call and ask for a copy of the full study.

Cushman and Wakefield data can be extremely useful to an investor thinking of purchasing an RTC office building because it compares a city's vacancy ratio over the past years with its current vacancy ratio. Investors should look to see if the vacancy trend is headed up or down. For example, in 1991 in Washington, D.C. the office vacancy rate was 12 percent, compared to 8.9 percent in 1988. This is a sign that vacancies are increasing, not a bullish indicator. (The only ones renting new office space these days are the RTC and FDIC.) In San Francisco, the vacancy ratio on office space in 1988 was 15.3 percent. In 1991 the vacancy ratio had fallen to 13.2 percent—a good sign. Unless you can get office buildings for a song, stay away from Los Angeles office properties. In

1988 the city had an office vacancy ratio of 16.5 percent—which was horrible. Nevertheless, some fools, flush with easy S&L and bank loans, kept building anyway and by 1991 the vacancy rate had jumped to 25.2 percent, creating what locals have dubbed "see-through office buildings." Clearly, it's going to be a decade before L.A. stabilizes.

Investment returns on commercial property can be handsome when the property is researched and purchased properly—as long as favorable market conditions provide renters. Unless you're buying office space for your own company for the long haul, make sure you understand the market. Otherwise, you will be just the latest in a long line of fools who thought it would be a real ego trip to own an office building or a complex of shops or a small shopping center. Megalomaniacs are poorly suited to be real estate investors.

IN SUMMARY

As you gain experience analyzing income properties, you'll soon be doing the calculations in your head. You'll know you are getting better at it when you can glance down a list of properties for sale and eliminate most of them without even leaving home or picking up the telephone.

But when a property makes its way onto your short list it's time to put the mental calculator away and take out the silicone brain in your desk drawer. Open a file on the prospective property. Start crunching the numbers—expenses, taxes, mortgage payments, the real vacancy factors. Start narrowing things down. Always do the numbers. Always.

Commercial real estate may be too much of a leap for first-time buyers. But it shouldn't be avoided. There are plenty of small—two-to four-unit—properties that are both residential and income properties wrapped in one. Buyers can live in one unit and rent out the others.

For the professional investor, now is a great time to buy apartment buildings. Immigrants are pouring into America throughout the Southwest. In California alone, more than 800,000 new households were formed in 1991, but only 500,000 housing units were built. What does that tell you as an investor? Fewer and fewer Americans can afford their own home and must rent. All this adds up to a very bright future for landlords.

The commercial and industrial real estate glut is concentrated in certain big cities, the Southwest and the Northeast. But throughout Main Street America thousands of government-owned commercial properties are available and remain a solid value. A lot of them are former S&L and bank branches, and if you don't mind having a Ft. Knox vault in the middle of your building, you can get them cheap. Turn the vault into a wine cellar, or rent out space to other businesses that have security needs that can't be filled by a bank safety deposit box. If nothing else, it's a great conversation piece.

Income property that can carry its own debt load and expenses is a terrific investment. It will appreciate in time while costing you virtually nothing to own. If it also throws off net spendable income, so much the better. Income property is where you find serious investors because it's where you can make serious money.

Chapter 7

....

Do I Hear a Bid?

How to Bid at Government Auctions

When the S&L mess first reared its ugly head, the government tried, without much luck, to sell repossessed assets itself. But would-be real estate buyers were unanimous in their conclusion that "You just can't do business with these people."

Ironically, federal bank and thrift regulators—who spent the 1980s in a near coma while their wards were being looted—swung suddenly to the other extreme, becoming overdiligent, hyperactive watchdogs when it came to peddling the real estate they ended up owning. Prospective buyers were treated rudely, calls went unreturned, and good offers were often ignored. Instead of being welcomed with open arms, private-sector investors were treated as "vultures" looking for a free lunch at the government's expense. Rather than welcoming their interest in these assets, bank and thrift regulators showed them the door.

Yes, a few vultures certainly flew among the flock, but most of the prospective customers were just real estate professionals trying to buy something at a good price—hardly an un-American inclination. Instead of working with these buyers, government "liquidation specialists" drove them away through inattention and distinctly unprofessional conduct. That was the past—but a past that continues to haunt the RTC.

148

Though the RTC has ironed out most of its operating wrinkles, to this day those early buyers will not go anywhere near another government property sale. That's bad news for taxpayers, but good news for investors just discovering the RTC, FDIC, and HUD. Old rumors die hard, however. During your initial search phase don't be surprised if fellow investors warn that, "You can't deal with the RTC or FDIC." Our message couldn't be clearer: Those rumors are no longer true.

What happened to change things? By the end of 1990 Congress was up to its neck in complaints about the RTC. Constituents kept telling elected officials that RTC account executives wouldn't return telephone calls, that someone else bought the property they wanted but at a lower price, and on and on. Congress,[1] which holds the purse strings to the S&L bailout, told the RTC to fly right, or the ball game was over—no more money.

With a new chief executive, Albert Casey, appointed in mid-1991, the RTC began to get its sales act together and was up and running. It hired outside private-sector sales and computer experts to organize and manage its real estate and loan portfolios. In time the RTC (as well as the FDIC) was actually advertising in the *Wall Street Journal*, trying to get the word out to the investing public.

ROUND THEM UP—HEAD THEM OUT

As we noted earlier, when the RTC takes over a savings and loan it usually leaves the S&L open for a time through a conservatorship. Old management is replaced and the RTC tries to sell the thrift to a new owner. But even if successful in this effort, nine times out of ten the new buyer doesn't want all the real estate, loans, and other assets left behind by the prior owners. To accommodate a new buyer, the RTC will take over those assets and place them into a separate receivership through which it will market them to the public.

Rather than repeat old mistakes, the RTC does not try to sell these assets themselves. The RTC lists these properties with approved asset

---

[1] Congress must approve all taxpayer funding of the savings and loan bailout. After an RTC funding bill is approved by Congress it must be signed by the President.

managers. Approved asset managers manage properties for the government under what is known as a Standard Asset Management and Disposition Agreement, or SAMDA. Managers who have these contracts are known as SAMDA contractors. Today, thousands of different firms manage, auction, and sell properties for the RTC through a SAMDA contract. Some national firms just manage, some just auction, and some just sell. Many, like the Los Angeles-based Cushman and Wakefield and the Alexandria, Virginia-based J.E. Robert & Co., do all three.

Often the RTC or FDIC will hire a SAMDA contractor like C&W or J.E. Robert to sell assets "in bulk" at large public auctions. Most of the assets sold at these large bulk sale auctions are income properties such as apartment buildings, hotels, offices, shopping centers, and warehouses.

HOW THE AUCTION AND BULK-SALE PROCESS WORKS

In general, auctions are advertised at least sixty days ahead of time in large national newspapers such as the *Wall Street Journal* and the *New York Times*, as well as in local newspapers. If you miss an auction notice you can always call the RTC auction hot line (1–800–RTC–3006). A prerecorded message will tell you about all upcoming RTC auctions. The hot line recording gives the name, address, and telephone number of the SAMDA contractor in charge of the auction. Auction information is also listed on RTCNET, the agency's computer data base. The FDIC does not yet have an auction hot line, but information about upcoming auctions can be obtained by calling the consolidated office nearest you. Both the RTC and FDIC encourage their asset managers to advertise auctions aggressively.

When the RTC hires a SAMDA contractor to conduct an auction, the asset manager always sets up a toll-free number that you can call for further information. (In early 1992 when C&W was auctioning off $180 million worth of RTC commercial real estate properties, it assigned 120 of its employees to work exclusively on just that auction.) Operators should be able to answer most of the basics. One of the primary responsibilities of the operator is to mail out auction catalogs to interested investors. The catalog should arrive on your doorstep within five working days at the most.

Most of the catalogs put together by the SAMDA contractors come in an 8″ × 11″ color format. Auction catalogs carry a photo of each property, its address, a description, zoning, listed price, and the name and telephone number of the SAMDA contractor, or asset manager,[2] in charge of the property.

If a property catches your eye, don't rely solely on what's in the catalog. Catalogs give a thumbnail sketch of a property but fall short of what you'll need to make an informed bid. If you like the property call the asset manager and ask for its due diligence package—which is a detailed, blow-by-blow description of the property's key features and credit history.

At this point the free ride is over. The SAMDA contractor will charge you a fee of between $15 to $25 for the detailed due diligence package. But for anyone seriously thinking of making a bid on a property the price is cheap. In return for your $15 to $25 you will receive an information-packed ringbinder that will tell you more than you ever need to know about an RTC property.

Inside the due diligence package you should find the following information:

• A detailed description of the property
• The property's income history (if it's income property)
• A list of all current tenants, their names, rent amounts, and overdue rents
• The property's expense history, including utility expenses, taxes, and special assessments
• Notice of any special environmental concerns, including notifications (if there are any) about possible toxic contaminations or easements
• A current demographic breakdown of the surrounding area
• A property type vacancy ratio analysis for real estate in that particular area
• A trend analysis for the area showing increases or decreases in occupancy, rents, and employment
• A traffic analysis for both auto and foot traffic (if commercial)

---

[2] For discussion purposes, *SAMDA contractor* and *asset manager* are considered to be one and the same.

- An overview of area amenities, including parks, schools, and public transportation
- A demand analysis showing the current marketability and rentability of similar property types
- An analysis of the area's employment picture (jobs, job type, major employers, employment trends)

As you see, the modest cost of this due diligence package is money well spent—cheap at many times the price. Due diligence packages contain the kinds of income analysis and demographic information on a property that are usually only available to well-heeled professionals. If you paid for these studies yourself, the cost would easily run into thousands of dollars for each property.

The due diligence package contains all the information you'll need to make an intelligent bid. *Keep in mind that SAMDA contractors are employed by the RTC only to market the property.* Although you will mail your bid to them, they do not become involved in the bid consideration process. The SAMDA contractor forwards your *sealed* bid envelope to the RTC consolidated office overseeing the auction. Your sealed bid is then opened by RTC personnel on the day after the bid deadline.

Think of SAMDA contractors as a convenience provided to you by the RTC. They are required to bend over backwards to help you. Besides studying their due diligence package, you can contact the SAMDA contractor to arrange a physical inspection of the property. SAMDA contractors hold open houses on all properties that are being offered. Most open houses are held at least a month before the bid date. (Besides viewing the property, it might be a good idea to take a quick trip down to the county recorder's office to get a look at the property's title and zoning histories. Also take a look at the title and zoning history of neighboring properties. The SAMDA contractor will be of no help here. You have to do this on your own.)

PUTTING MONEY WHERE YOUR MOUTH IS

After inspecting the property, its due diligence package, and its title history, you should by now have a rough idea what you're going to bid. The next step will be to telephone the RTC consolidated office in charge of the auction and request what is known as a *Direct Bid Brochure*. This package is free and contains specific instructions on bid procedures. Also ask for a copy of the agency's booklet, *General Terms & Conditions*. This booklet contains a lot of "contract-ese" and boilerplate jargon, but slog through it anyway. Buried in all the grey text may be some "need to knows."

The bidding process itself is cut and dried.

WHO CAN BID?

Anyone over eighteen years of age can bid, regardless of sex, race, citizenship, or marital status. Before bidding, though, you must submit proof to the RTC that you are financially capable of coming up with the purchase price. If you offer to put $25,000 cash down, bank statements showing that you indeed have $25,000 will be required along with your bid. If you state in your offer that you plan to borrow the balance from a certain lender, then a signed loan commitment letter from that lender is required. A general financial statement showing your current assets and liabilities may also be required, particularly if you are asking the RTC to carry the loan.

CASH DEPOSIT

When you submit your completed bid form, attach a personal check for 1 percent of the price you bid. If you offer $55,000 for a property, enclose a check for $550. This deposit check will not be cashed unless yours is the winning bid. If you win the bid, not only will your check be cashed, but you will be required to cough up another 4 percent, bringing your total deposit to 5 percent. You have *three working days* to come up with the 5 percent. If you fail to do so, the RTC will discard your bid and accept the next best bid.

The RTC does not fool around. It will not give you additional time to "come up with the rest of the money." Despite what some members of Congress may think, the agency is not in the business of providing social services. If you make a bid, have the money in hand. The RTC has a good computer system that tracks all registered bidders. If the agency pegs you as a flake, chances are that any future bids you make will get short shrift.

UNACCEPTABLE BID TERMS

The RTC *does not* accept bids that request option agreements, creative financing schemes, or lot splits. The agency does not like to divide parcels of land. It's all or nothing. The lot-splitting process takes too much legal work and time. The government also ignores requests by bidders that the RTC repair property defects prior to closing. All properties sold by the RTC and FDIC are on an "as is" basis. Don't even bother asking. Keep your bids simple and straightforward.

ACCEPTABLE FINANCING TERMS

The RTC likes all-cash bids. Aside from that, the RTC will also entertain bids calling for seller financing. The whole purpose of an auction is to make the *government's* life easier, not yours. Still, as we detailed in earlier chapters, the government will extend seller financing to eligible buyers. Except for loans on single-family residences, most of the mortgages offered by the government are seven-year balloons. After seven years you'll have to find another loan.

BROKER COMMISSIONS

A licensed real estate broker representing a buyer can receive a sales commission from the RTC and FDIC. But before the broker can receive his or her cut, the buyer has to fill out and submit with the sealed bid a signed "Purchaser/Co-broker Certificate." Included in the bid package, the form must be signed by both the buyer and the broker. (See Exhibit 8.)

If a bid is accepted, the broker receives half the sales commission, for which he or she will be most grateful to the buyer. The RTC pays the same commission amount whether or not you have a broker representing you. Having a broker will not prejudice your chances of winning a bid. RTC and FDIC commissions begin at 5 percent for most residential properties, but decrease for large commercial properties as the selling price climbs into the millions. When in doubt, ask the SAMDA contractor what the broker commission will be on a given property.

Resolution Trust Corporation
Comprehensive Advertising and Marketing Program

Direct Bid Offering
California Commercial Properties
Winter 1991 - 1992

BID FORM

PLEASE NOTE: THIS BID FORM AND ATTACHED PURCHASER/CO-BROKER CERTIFICATE (IF
APPLICABLE) ARE THE ONLY DOCUMENTS TO BE COMPLETED BY BIDDERS. HOWEVER, ALL
BIDDERS SHOULD CAREFULLY REVIEW THE FORM OF PURCHASE AGREEMENT TO BE
USED, AND ALL EXHIBITS TO THE PURCHASE AGREEMENT.

Dated: _____

To:
Cushman & Wakefield
300 South Grand Avenue, Suite 3750
Los Angeles, California 90071
Attention: Direct Bid Offering

      Re: Resolution Trust Corporation
              Comprehensive Advertising and Marketing Program
              Direct Bid Offering - Property No. _____
Gentlemen:

The undersigned Bidder hereby submits the following Bid, in accordance with the Resolution Trust
Corporation ("RTC") Direct Bid Offering Instructions. If RTC accepts Bidder's bid, Bidder agrees to be bound
by the terms and conditions of the Purchase and Sale Agreement and Joint Escrow Instructions in the form
previously furnished to the undersigned (the "Purchase Agreement"), and to execute five (5) copies thereof,
duly completed by RTC with the particulars of this transaction, promptly upon receipt. Bidder acknowledges
that it has reviewed a copy of the form of the Purchase Agreement, including all exhibits thereto and the
documents to be executed for Seller financing, if applicable, and Bidder approves of their respective terms and
conditions.

1. Direct Bid Offering Property Number: _____

2. Property Address: _____

    _____

3. Purchase Price: _____

    _____ ($ _____)

4. Seller Financing Requested: Yes _____ No _____

EXHIBIT 8.   Five-page RTC real estate bid form for sealed-bid auctions. These
forms are included in the auction bid package. They must be returned to the asset
management firm in a *sealed* envelope.

5. Amount of Financing Requested: $_____

6. Percentage of bid amount to be financed (not more than eighty-five percent (85%)):_____%

7. Name of Bidder: _____

8. Type of Entity, e.g., Corporation, Partnership, Trust, etc.: _____

9. Bidder's Taxpayer Identification Number:_____

10. Bidder's Address for Notices: _____

11. Bidder's Telephone Number: _____

12. Bidder's Fax Number:_____

13. Name and Title
    of Bidder's Contact Person: _____

    _____

14. Bidder hereby submits with this bid the following items:

    A.   A check in the amount of $_____, representing one percent (1%)
            of the Purchase Price (the "Bid Deposit").

    B.   If Bidder is represented by a co-broker, a fully-executed Purchaser/Broker Certificate in the
            form of Exhibit "1" to this Bid Form.

    C.   Financial statements or evidence of ability to close the transaction, as follows (check if
            applicable):

            (i)   __   A copy of the Bidder's latest personal and/or corporate tax return;

            (ii) __   A letter addressed to RTC from the Bidder's institutional lender, or bank, on that
                       institution's letterhead, stating the bidder's financial capabilities;

            (iii) __   Identification of any equity partners and such partner's financial capabilities;

            (iv) __   Financial statement that sets forth in detail the Bidder's assets and liabilities;

            (v)   __   Other (Explain)   _____

                       _____

    The undersigned Bidder agrees to furnish any additional evidence of financial capability that may be
    requested by RTC or the DBO Underwriter, and acknowledges that if this bid is conditionally accepted
    and Bidder has made a request for Seller financing that RTC recommends to the DBO Underwriter,
    the undersigned shall be obligated to pay a NON-REFUNDABLE underwriting fee equal to one-tenth
    (1/10) of one percent (1%) of the loan amount, with a minimum fee of One Thousand Five Hundred
    Dollars ($1,500) and a maximum fee of Ten Thousand Dollars ($10,000), within seven (7) days after

Broker identified above, if any, for commissions or other reimbursement arising in connection with any sale of the Property to the undersigned by RTC.

2. CO-BROKER CERTIFICATE.

The undersigned Co-Broker hereby certifies, represents and warrants to RTC that it has not associated with any other broker other than Broker in connection with the interest of the above named Purchaser in purchasing the Property from RTC. Co-Broker acknowledges and agrees that: (a) Co-Broker's commission shall be paid by Broker, rather than RTC, through the escrow process directly and solely to the undersigned Co-Broker; and (b) RTC shall have no liability to pay a commission to Co-Broker. RTC shall have no liability to pay a commission to any Co-Broker. The undersigned Co-Broker hereby agrees to indemnify, defend and hold RTC harmless from and against the claims of any other Co-Broker who claims that it was acting by or through the undersigned Co-Broker in connection with any such sale to the above-named Purchaser.

The undersigned Co-Broker hereby agrees that it shall be entitled to fifty percent (50%) of the gross commission paid by RTC in connection with the sale of the Property to the above-named Purchaser. The commission shall be paid only upon full and complete closing of sale and payment of such purchase price in full to RTC (for the purpose hereof, the purchase price shall include the amount of any financing provided by RTC in connection with such sale).

The undersigned Co-Broker agrees and acknowledges that no commissions will be paid by RTC to a broker, which directly or indirectly acquires any interest in the Property being purchased or otherwise financially participates in the purchase of the Property in any way. The undersigned Co-Broker hereby certifies he/she is serving in this transaction only as a broker and not as a principal or direct or indirect owner, lender, or other financial participant.

IT IS UNDERSTOOD THAT A COMMISSION FROM RTC SHALL NOT BE PAYABLE TO ANY CO-BROKER UNLESS THIS PURCHASER/CO-BROKER CERTIFICATE IS EXECUTED BY THE PURCHASER AND CO-BROKER AND SUBMITTED TO BROKER ON OR BEFORE 5:00 P.M. P.S.T., JANUARY 30, 1992.

PURCHASER:

Date:_____   _____

_____

By:_____

Name:_____

Title:_____

CO-BROKER:

Date:_____   _____

_____

License #:_____

By:_____

Name:_____

Title:_____

1823BID.WXT   xi

157

RTC has indicated its conditional acceptance of this Bid. This underwriting fee shall not be applied toward the Purchase Price.

(If applicable): Bidder is making multiple bids and the Bidder's financial information is submitted with the Bid Form for DBO Property Number _____.

15. Bidder acknowledges it is not relying on any legal or tax advice from RTC in connection with the transactions contemplated by this Bid.

16. The undersigned Bidder understands that properties may be withdrawn from the Direct Bid Offering at any time prior to closing, and that if the undersigned becomes the successful Bidder, the undersigned will not have the right to assign or transfer its right to purchase the property covered by this Bid.

17. The undersigned Bidder represents that the execution and delivery of this Bid have been authorized by any and all necessary parties.

18. Bidder is not acting as a nominee, agent, or trustee for any person or entity who will be the true or beneficial owner of the property that is the subject of this Bid; and Bidder is purchasing the property for its own account and not with the intent of selling the property to, or exchanging the property with, any other person or entity who has requested or arranged with Bidder to enter into the Purchase Agreement for such purpose. There are no agreements, written or oral, express or implied, between (i) Bidder or any of the persons executing the Purchase Agreement on behalf of Bidder and (ii) the previous owner of the property or any person or entity affiliated or connected with the previous owner of the property (collectively, the "Previous Owner") for the payment of any additional amounts to the Previous Owner in connection with the sale of the property or which contemplate the retention by or conveyance to the Previous Owner of any interest in the property or any interest in any entity which may own or hold title to the property, including, without limitation, Bidder.

IN WITNESS WHEREOF, the undersigned hereby submits this Bid.

_____

By: _____

Name: _____

Its: _____

158

RESOLUTION TRUST CORPORATION
COMPREHENSIVE ADVERTISING AND MARKETING PROGRAM
DIRECT BID OFFERING

PURCHASER/CO-BROKER CERTIFICATE

NAME OF
PURCHASER: _____

PURCHASER'S
ADDRESS: _____

_____

PURCHASER'S
TELEPHONE
NUMBER: _____

NAME OF
CO-BROKER: _____

NAME OF SALES
PERSON, IF OTHER
THAN CO-BROKER: _____

CO-BROKER'S
ADDRESS: _____

_____

CO-BROKER'S
TELEPHONE NUMBER: _____

PROPERTY
NUMBER: _____

PROPERTY
ADDRESS: _____

_____

1. **PURCHASER CERTIFICATE.**

The undersigned Purchaser hereby certifies, represents and warrants to the Resolution Trust Corporation ("**RTC**") and Cushman & Wakefield ("**Broker**"), acting as RTC's exclusive agent, that the above-named Co-Broker is the sole Co-Broker through whom the undersigned has considered and shall consider the Property described above (the "**Property**") for purchase from RTC. The undersigned Purchaser hereby agrees to indemnify, defend and hold RTC harmless from and against any and all claims of brokers, other than the Co-

BROKER-BUYERS

A licensed real estate broker can purchase properties from the government but don't expect the RTC to pay that broker a commission. If you're a licensed real estate broker bidding for yourself don't count on the commission to reduce your down payment.

BROKER-NONBROKER PARTNERSHIPS

If you and a broker friend decide to invest together in RTC properties it might be wise if the broker remains just that—a broker—during the acquisition phase. After you receive full title there's nothing to stop the broker from using his or her commission to buy into the property with you as a partner.

RETRACTING A BID

In some cases the RTC will ask you to bid on a property without fully inspecting it or, for that matter, having a chance to see a title report. Therefore the RTC allows for a thirty-day inspection period that begins *the day after* your bid is accepted. During this thirty-day period you can bail out of the property without penalty by submitting a "termination notice" to the consolidated office. After the thirty-day period expires, your deposit becomes nonrefundable.

ACCESS TO THE PROPERTY

Initially you may have had limited access to the property during an open house. After your bid is accepted the RTC allows expanded access, which gives you the opportunity to bring in a site engineer. Before bringing in an engineer the RTC requests that you give "reasonable" notice so they can make arrangements with the asset manager and tenants. Before being granted access to the property you must accept personal liability for injury or damage done during the inspection. Depending on just how much poking around you intend to do, the RTC may require that you provide proof of liability insurance.

Besides allowing you to inspect the physical property, the RTC also grants unlimited access to the building's books, records, leases, and contracts.

CLOSE BIDS

Until title changes hands, you will have no way of knowing how close your bid was to the winning bid. After closing you can visit the county recorder's office to see how much the winner paid. The RTC will not disclose to anyone what the winning bidder paid. However, if your bid and the winning bid are close the RTC will hold your bid during the thirty-day inspection period. If the winner bails out or cannot perform under the contract, the RTC will award the property to you—if you still want it. You then have to increase your deposit to 5 percent. If you don't want it, the next closest bidder gets the property.

RTC BID ANALYSIS

Once the bid deadline passes, you will have to wait. It takes the RTC about thirty days to choose a winner. This is not just a "red tape" delay. The RTC brings in a staff of private accountants to analyze each individual bid to determine which bid nets the RTC the most money in today's dollars.

This bid opening and analysis process is not open to the public. And the RTC will not disclose what formula it uses to judge bids. The only thing they tell bidders is the oft repeated: Cash is king. In fact, the RTC accountants are simply holding each bid up to a standard net present value analysis that you can do on your own business calculator. Nothing mysterious here. The only thing the government wants is to return as much money to the taxpayers as possible.

Still, the behind-closed-doors process upsets some bidders who wonder if, perhaps, someone's brother-in-law isn't getting a sweet deal at their expense. Actually the process is kept confidential for a number of sound reasons:

- The RTC does not want to encourage expensive lawsuits by litigious bidders. By opening up the process the agency could find itself in the middle of constant arguments between bidders who for one reason or another claim their bid is superior even though on the surface everything looks equal. Such litigation could tie up a sale for months, or worse, years. Multiply that times the thousands of properties the RTC has to sell and you can understand its worst nightmare.

If all bids were cash this would not be a problem, but rarely are all bids cash. In most cases bids are a combination of cash plus financing. Therefore the need for accountants to calculate the net present value of each, based on the unique details of the offers.

- If successful bids were made public, a sore loser with time to spare might try to halt the sale by filing a lawsuit. Such suits often result in a "leis pendens"—legal notice filed at the recorder's office that someone else has a claim against the property. Once the property is so encumbered, no one will buy it, and the winning bidder (as well as the taxpayers) will be left twisting in the wind. Under the present system, the burden of proof is on the plaintiff, not the RTC. It is much harder to reverse a sale than to stop one.

As working journalists the authors have a built-in dislike and suspicion of anything the government does behind closed doors. It's certainly not outside the realm of possibility that on occasion favoritism may have been given to certain bidders. But from what we've seen, the process—for the most part—has been fair. Because the RTC—not the SAMDA contractor—decides who gets the property, there is little chance that an asset manager's favorite client (or brother-in-law) will be given the inside track during the bid consideration process. Moreover, RTC personnel operate under strict conflict of interest rules that can land them in jail if they show any form of favoritism to a buyer. In case you were wondering, RTC employees and their relatives are prohibited from purchasing any assets from the agency. It's a felony.

If you were treated unfairly in an RTC or FDIC asset sale, both agencies have an office of inspector general in Washington, D.C. that investigates such matters. Solid evidence helps, but at the very least you can file a letter of complaint. If you lose a property through favoritism, still, it might be best to simply move along to another property. As long as you get your bid money back, squabbling over a lost property usually turns out to be a major waste of time. There's plenty of fish in the government pond.

KEY INFORMATION. *Your bid must arrive at the real estate manager's office in its original* sealed *envelope. It is* extremely important *that you write on the outside of your bid envelope on both the front and back in large readable letters:* Bid Enclosed. *If you don't, the SAMDA contractor has no way of distinguishing your bid from all other mail coming into the office. If your bid letter is opened by accident, the real estate manager must return it, which means you'll have to submit it all over again. If this happens the day before bid deadline you could miss the boat.*

When deciding what to bid, once again review all that's available: the due diligence package provided by the RTC, your own income property and market analysis, and your financial statements, and then figure out what you're willing to pay. One of the most useful pieces of information to keep in mind is how the RTC appraises and values property and adjusts it downward during the marketing phase.

It's rare, if not unheard of, for sellers to disclose so much about how they value assets, but the RTC is just such a seller. When the RTC began seizing S&Ls in late 1989 it quickly learned that establishing a value on properties is not easy. Many S&L properties had been valued by appraisers who were "on the take." During the mid- to late 1980s some appraisers were taking kickbacks to inflate their appraisals. These artificially inflated appraisals allowed crooked developers and bankers to skim loan proceeds and embezzle money out of loan proceeds. Compounding the RTC's problems, the national real estate economy went into a tailspin in 1991, dragging the value of already overvalued assets down even further.

After several fits and starts the RTC finally got serious about helping its field personnel reappraise properties by issuing a set of government-backed appraisal guidelines. The RTC also created bid acceptance rules, giving its employees a set of parameters to follow if bids fall short of appraised values. Here's an inside view of how the RTC appraises its properties:

When the asset is acquired by the RTC:

1) The agency's asset managers order a new appraisal on the property using an RTC-approved appraiser.
2) The appraisal is reviewed by asset managers at the closest RTC consolidated office to see if it follows agency guidelines.
3) The real estate broker chosen by the RTC to market the property is then asked to comment on the appraisal.
4) If all passes muster the new appraisal becomes the RTC's "starting point" on value.
5) From that value, the RTC then subtracts estimated holding costs and sets a new value.
6) The property is listed on the open market through a broker, asset manager, or SAMDA contractor at the new, adjusted value. RTC personnel monitor the property closely and if it doesn't sell, consider a price reduction.

If a property does not sell at its adjusted appraised value within a specific time frame, the consolidated office in charge of that asset has been given the power to reduce the asking price. There are limits to how much a property can be reduced at one time, but some reductions can be substantial. Two events can trigger a price reduction:

- A property has been aggressively marketed for six months (four for residential properties) and no offers are received or
- Offers are received but are significantly below the property's appraised value.

If either occurs the consolidated office can lower the asking price, with certain limitations:

- A property's asking price cannot be lowered more than 15 percent at one time.
- A second price reduction can occur only after the property has been exposed to the market for another three months.
- If a property's asking price has been reduced by more than 20

percent of its original asking price, further reductions cannot occur without first obtaining a new appraisal on the property.

EXAMPLES OF RTC APPRAISALS

The following are based on actual examples given by the RTC to its field personnel.

Example 1. A single-family residential home on the outskirts of Houston, Texas

- Appraised value: $100,000
- Date of appraisal: 1/1/90
- Estimated marketing period: 6 months
- Average holding costs for area: $200 per month (taxes, insurance, maintenance)
- RTC's current cost of money: 9% (based on current one-year Treasury bond yield)

Date: 4/1/90

Scenario: The property is listed with a broker for $100,000. During its first three months on the market the RTC has received only one bid, for $89,000.

Is this an acceptable bid by RTC guidelines?

No. When the bid is received the RTC immediately calculates the property's *present value*. The present value is used to measure all offers and gives the RTC a clear picture of what a property is worth at any time during the sales process.

The RTC sets a present value formula that assumes the property will sell six months from the appraisal date. It then prorates holding costs, which in this case come to $591 for three months' time:

- Future Value: $100,000 in three months
- Current discount rate: 9% annualized
- Holding costs subtracted from asking price: present value of $97,783

The result is a new present value (as of 4/1/90) of $97,192.[3] With only three months on the market, the RTC cannot yet sell this property for less than 95 percent of the property's adjusted value. That means the lowest bid the RTC can accept at this point is $92,332.

Date: 5/1/90

Scenario: The property still has not sold and the highest bid is still $89,000. Even though the RTC asset manager now has the right to lower the price 15 percent, in his opinion an 8 percent reduction should do the trick. He then decides to lower the asking price to $92,000. The RTC then adjusts the current value downward by again subtracting holding costs and calculating present value based on a two-month holding period. (Remember the original estimated holding period was for six months.)

- Future value: $92,000 in two months
- Discount rate: still 9%
- Present value: $90,635
- Minus two months' expenses of $395.54

New adjusted market value (AMV) = $90,239. Because the RTC can only accept bids that are at least 95 percent of its adjusted market value, the new asking price translates into a minimum acceptable bid of $85,727.

The RTC now decides to take the $89,000 offer.

Example 2. An office building in North Dallas, Texas

- Appraised Value: $1 million
- Date of appraisal: 1/1/90
- Estimated marketing period: 12 months
- Income generated: $40,000 per month

[3] The property is assumed to sell at the appraised value of $100,000 six months from the appraisal date, or in three months from 4/1/90 at a 9 percent discount rate. Subtracting three months' remaining holding costs of $591 gives a present value of $97,192.

- Expenses: $50,000 per month
- RTC current cost of money: 9% (based on current one-year Treasury note rate)

Date: 5/1/90
Scenario: The office building has been marketed extensively and the best offer received is $850,000. Should it be accepted? RTC officials at the consolidated office get out their calculators and figure:

- The building's present value is determined to be $941,975. This figure is achieved by taking the $1 million appraised value and calculating its future value eight months from now at the 9 percent discount rate.
- Then the RTC subtracts from the present value the anticipated building income for the next eight months. (This income would not be realized by the agency if it accepts the offer.) The value of that "missed" income comes to $309,464, which is achieved by calculating a present value of this cash flow stream, discounted at the 9 percent annual rate.
- The agency also subtracts the building's holding costs, which, if it accepts the offer, it will not have to pay. The anticipated holding costs = $386,609. Again the present value of expenses ($50,000 per month) is discounted at the 9 percent annual rate.

The result is an adjusted market value of $864,609. This means the minimum acceptable bid (95 percent of AMV) is now $821,379.

Example 3: Same as in Example 2, but let's change the circumstances. Let's say the RTC never received the $850,000 bid, and the property stays on the market.

Date: 7/1/90
Scenario: The property has been for sale for a full six months without receiving an acceptable offer. Six more months remain in the original marketing period. Based on a market analysis and an examination of low bids already received, the RTC asset manager decides a full 15 percent

reduction in the asking price is justified. The property's new adjusted market value becomes *$850,000*.

Date: 8/1/90
Scenario: The RTC receives a bid of $650,000 from a qualified buyer. Five full months remain on the marketing period. Does the offer have a chance? The RTC first determines the property's present market value:

- $850,000 for five months at the 9 percent discount rate equals a present value of $818,830
- Plus PV of income (five months at $40,000 lost) = $195,000
- Subtract PV of holding expenses ($50,000 × 5 months) = $244,472

The result gives the agency a new present value of $769,936. The minimum acceptable bid (95 percent of value) is now *$731,439*. Therefore a bid of $650,000 is deemed unacceptable.

Date: 10/1/90
Scenario: The property still hasn't attracted acceptable bids, and the RTC asset manager orders an additional 5 percent reduction in the asking price. Since the property was first listed for sale, its price has been reduced by 20 percent to $800,000.

Date: 11/1/90
Scenario: The RTC receives a new bid for $700,000. Two months remain in the original marketing period. What chance does this offer have? Let's look:

- PV of adjusted appraised value = $788,134
- Plus PV of holding period income = $79,109
- Minus PV of holding costs = $98,886

This gives us a new present market value of $768,357. The minimum acceptable bid (95 percent of PMV) is now *$729,939*.

But the RTC asset manager is concerned that a 20 percent price reduction may not be enough and on November 15 orders a new appraisal, which is required when a manager seeks a reduction of greater than 20 percent. (The bidder would not know this.) During the newest appraisal roof damage of $50,000 is discovered.

Date: 12/1/90
Scenario: The RTC receives a new offer of $675,000 from the same bidder who made the rejected $700,000 offer a month earlier. The bidder knows the property hasn't sold for almost a year and decides to make a lowball offer. The RTC calculates present market value:

- PV of adjusted appraised value of $800,000 = $794,045
- Plus PV of holding income = $39,702
- Minus PV of holding expenses = $49,628
- Roof repair costs (which have been disclosed to the bidder) = $50,000

New present market value = $734,119. Therefore the new minimum acceptable bid is *$697,413*.

If the RTC is selling this property through a real estate broker and is paying a 4 percent commission, this offer would be unacceptable. But because it's saving $27,000 on commissions by marketing the property itself, the $675,000 offer is deemed acceptable based on a minimum PV price of $670,413.

Example 4. A 100-acre tract of raw land outside Tucson, Arizona

- Appraised Value: $650,000
- Date of appraisal: 1/1/90
- Estimated marketing period: 24 months
- Holding costs: $2,000 per month
- RTC's current cost of money: 8% (based on current two-year Treasury yield)

Date: 6/1/90
Scenario: The property has been marketed, and the best offer received to date is $400,000. Can the RTC accept this offer?

- PV of appraised value = $572,908
- Minus PV of holding expenses = $35,572

Present market value = $537,336, and the minimum acceptable bid is $483,602.

Date: 8/1/90
Scenario: After seven months on the market the RTC asset manager adjusts the appraised value down 15 percent. The new adjusted appraised value is $552,500.

Date: 10/1/90
Scenario: A bid of $420,000 is received. Will it fly? Let's see:

- PV of adjusted appraised value = $500,090
- Minus PV of holding expenses = $28,452

Present market value = $471,637, and the minimum acceptable bid is $424,475. Though this bid doesn't quite meet RTC guidelines, it's off by only $4,475. The RTC would more than likely make the buyer a counter-offer and a happy ending for all would be reached.

As you can see, it's worth your time to learn the marketing history of an asset you're bidding on. Investors looking for a great deal can afford to wait six months and gamble that the price will be reduced another 15 percent. However, if there's a particular property you really want and it's in good shape, playing the waiting game can sometimes lead to disappointment. The property might be sold the first month it's out for bid.

The guidelines illustrated above show how hemmed in asset managers can be. Managers at the RTC consolidated offices often lack authority to go outside the guidelines. On the other hand, these guidelines also show that the RTC is ready and able to reduce its asking prices when the marketplace is telling it that the price is too high. Also, on properties that are difficult to sell, good faith offers that fall short of the guideline limits are often taken "upstairs" by the consolidated office to Washington, where regional RTC officials will go to bat for a bidder if they believe the bid is in good faith and that market conditions are such that they may later regret rejecting the bid.

"Our policy of disclosing our pricing strategy caused a lot of controversy in the marketplace to begin with," said RTC Southwest Regional Manager Carmen Sullivan. "But instead of holding all this information to our vests, which inhibits buyers from negotiating, we just lay it all out in front of everyone."

As an investor, your "bottom line" bid should fit *your* bottom line, not the government's. It pays to do the math. The above examples should give you a leg up on the competition. When playing poker, if you can see someone else's cards your chances of winning are greatly improved.

WINNER TAKES ALL

If your sealed bid is accepted, the RTC likes to close the sale quickly—within sixty days. From the moment you achieve a meeting of the minds on a bid, the buyer and seller have clearly designated responsibilities.

CLOSING COSTS

The RTC pays half the escrow costs and the buyer pays the other half. The purchaser pays all prorated property and transfer taxes and title insurance premiums.

RENTS

Rents are prorated to the day of closing. Any portion of rents due to the RTC but collected after closing must be paid by the seller to the RTC.

OPERATING EXPENSES

If the sale closes before maintenance expenses for the month have been determined, the RTC will estimate those expenses for the month. After closing the two parties will compare the estimate to actual expenses and balance the account.

DELIVERY AND POSSESSION

The RTC transfers title to the buyer through the use of a quitclaim deed. A quitclaim deed gives the buyer all the seller's rights to the property, though the RTC makes no warranties as to precisely what those rights might be. In essence, a quitclaim deed conveys property without guaranteeing that it is "free and clear"—that no one else has some right or interest in it. The RTC uses quitclaim deeds because it's the quickest and cleanest way for *them* to transfer a property without incurring any future liabilities should the title be marred, but both the RTC and FDIC are very good at "clearing title" before putting properties up for sale. This makes it even more imperative that the buyer conduct his or her own title search. Don't be lazy. Get down to that courthouse. At closing the RTC turns over the keys to the property and the sale, as they say, "is a done deal." At that moment the buyer becomes responsible for all valid leases and contracts encumbering the property.

FAILING TO PERFORM ON THE BID

If a purchaser makes a bid, it's accepted, and then the bidder fails to come through on the purchase price, he or she is then considered "in default." The RTC and FDIC can then legally keep whatever deposit money was posted (as we noted earlier, usually 5 percent). The greater the bid, the larger your loss if you fail to follow through.

If the RTC fails to perform on any part of its agreement with the buyer, the contract states that the RTC's only responsibility to the purchaser is to return the deposit money. The RTC bid contract shields the agency from any legal damages for failure to perform.

IN SUMMARY

Bidding at an auction can be intimidating the first time. It's sort of like audience participation in a play or nightclub act. But once you get in the swing of it, it's a lot of fun. And the feeling of bagging a great deal at an auction can only be compared to reeling in a big one when fishing.

Bidding at a sealed-bid auction is less exciting than attending an open-cry auction. But statistics show that buyers get better deals at sealed-bid auctions. Open-cry auctions create a frenzied atmosphere in which buyers tend to get carried away. Sealed-bid auctions are quiet, dignified affairs. You submit your bid from the privacy of your own office or home any time prior to the bid deadline. Then you wait. Within thirty days you'll get an answer. If your bid gets chosen, expect a telephone call, followed by a request to increase your deposit to 5 percent. If you lose a bid, the consolidated office will send back your 1 percent deposit in the mail within thirty days.

Remember, you control the process. Before you make a bid imagine that your bid was accepted and you now have to perform (i.e., cough up the money). How would you feel? If the answer is "delighted," submit your bid and hope for the best.

Chapter 8

....

Buying Paper

Buying Good and Bad Loans from the RTC and FDIC

Who in their right mind would want to buy a delinquent loan?

Many investors will argue that if an obligation is "delinquent" it must be worthless. But savvy investors know that one person's shipwreck is another's sunken treasure. If purchased intelligently, buying a delinquent or "late" mortgage loan or note from the government can yield healthy returns for investors. However, keep in mind that buying a loan or a group of loans (called a "pool") from the RTC and FDIC is not without risk. You can make some expensive mistakes investing in "paper."

But investing in delinquent loans is no longer uncharted territory. In fact, it's catching on as more and more investors come to understand the opportunities underlying these ugly duckling loans. As one RTC official told us, "We're seeing a lot of new faces at our loan auctions. It's no longer the select group it used to be." Buying loans is unfamiliar territory for most Americans, but it's not as complicated as some of the terminology would lead one to believe. We'll try to demystify the process while also explaining the rewards and risks involved.

174

UGLY IS ONLY SKIN DEEP

Together the RTC and FDIC hold about $400 billion in assets. About 60 to 75 percent of what the two have to sell start out as loans. Some stay loans while others are foreclosed on and the underlying real estate sold. Knowing how to buy a delinquent loan from the government gives you another avenue to purchase assets at a discount.

Loans come in all shapes, sizes, and conditions. Some are delinquent, some are not. Some are secured, some are not. Just because an S&L failed doesn't necessarily mean all of its loans are bad. To sort out this diversity the RTC and FDIC divide their loans into four basic categories.

1) Good Quality Loans (GQL). Also known as "current" loans— the borrower is paying the loan on time and the loan has no apparent problems. Because the loan is in good shape, the RTC doesn't offer much of a discount. If it's a large loan (over $50,000), the RTC tells its asset managers to hold any discounts offered to buyers to 5 percent of the loan's outstanding balance. (On smaller-performing loans the RTC will offer discounts of up to 10 percent of the loan balance.) The only time that discount will be increased is if interest rates begin rising or falling rapidly. If rates go up quickly, then the loan (by comparison) will yield a lower return than competing interest-paying investments (i.e., newer mortgage loans being sold on the secondary market). If rates fall by more than two percentage points, then the likelihood that borrowers will pay off their loans early increases greatly, which in turn decreases the loan's value. When such shifts in the market occur, the RTC will increase its discount to match market conditions.

2) Fair Quality Loans (FQL). FQLs generate sufficient cash flow to cover at least 75 percent of the outstanding principal balance should the loan go into default. On FQLs that are $50,000 to $250,000 in size, the RTC will offer discounts of up to 90 percent. On loans smaller than $50,000 the RTC will offer larger discounts.

3) Poor Quality Loans (PQL). PQLs in general are considered "delinquent," meaning the borrower is not paying. Once these loans go into default the RTC expects to recover 25 to 75 percent of the outstanding balance. Some PQLs are, or could become, the subject of litigation. The RTC will dump these loans at 85 percent of their outstanding balance. But keep talking. PQLs are a major headache and the agency is open to all sorts of offers.

4) Distressed Loans (DLs). DLs are in default or just about to go into default. At best the government may recoup 25 percent of the loan's outstanding principal. DLs that have balances of $50,000 or less can be sold by the consolidated office for 75 percent of the Estimated Cash Recovery (ECR). ECR is not the same thing as "the outstanding balance." ECR is a much lower value—often a fraction of the outstanding loan balance.

DLs are only for investors with strong stomachs and stout nerves. You can get them cheap enough, but you're buying a real pig in a poke. If you can work with delinquent borrowers to turn loans around or are emotionally prepared to foreclose on someone's house, you can do well buying DLs. Otherwise, it's best to leave these opportunities to others.

DELINQUENT LOANS

WHY INVEST IN A DELINQUENT LOAN?

Investing in delinquent loans sold by the RTC isn't as crazy as it sounds. In one regard it can be viewed as an "alternate route" to gaining title to the underlying real estate. With delinquent loans you have several possible plays:

- Buy at discount a loan that's "just a little delinquent" and then work with the borrower to bring the note current. If you are successful, you can sit back and collect interest, knowing that the discount has boosted your effective yield well beyond the interest rate being charged the borrower.
- Buy a deeply delinquent loan at a steep discount. Work with the borrower to either bring the loan current, or ask the borrower to relinquish a portion of the property's ownership to you in return for renegotiating the terms and balance of the loan. In this case you

become a partner in the property with the borrower, gaining an equity interest as well as retaining a portion of the original loan.
• Buy a deeply delinquent loan at discount and foreclose on the underlying property.

CAVEATS

Buying troubled loans is a lot more stressful than buying real estate. The potential profits are larger, but so are the headaches. When you purchase a delinquent loan you acquire someone else's problems—the borrower's. Unless you hire an attorney (and attorneys can get expensive), you will have to personally contact the debtor to inform him or her of the wonderful news that you now own the loan. As we noted, purchasing delinquent loans is not for the fainthearted. Every default brings with it a tearjerking explanation. If you're a bleeding heart, turn the page. This part of the book is not for you. On the other hand, if you can maintain an emotional distance from other people's problems and keep a cool business head, buying troubled loans is a terrific way to make money. It can also be a way to get property cheaper than if you wait for the RTC or FDIC to foreclose and sell it: As soon as the borrower goes into default, you can foreclose.

Example. The RTC is selling a troubled loan on a duplex in your neighborhood.

• Original loan amount: $108,000
• Original down payment: $27,000
• Principal paid so far: $1,330
• Outstanding balance: $106,670
• Original appraised value: $135,000
• Monthly mortgage payment: $830
• Terms: 8.50%, 30-year, fixed-rate

The borrower kept the loan current for two years and then stopped making payments. He is three months late. To get rid of the loan quickly, the RTC sells it to you at 90 percent of its outstanding balance. You pay around $96,500. The borrower (also known as mortgagor) lives in one of a duplex's two rental units and leases out the other. After researching the property you find that similar units will produce gross rents of about $925 per month.

You have two scenarios to analyze before deciding whether to bid. First, what if the borrower reinstates the loan by making all of his past overdue payments? How does this affect your investment? This consideration relies on probability. Statistics culled by the National Association of Realtors show that the average life of a California mortgage loan is six to seven years. (The borrower might move or refinance—that's why very few thirty-year mortgages ever really last that long.) The loan you bought is already two years old. Chances are the borrower will not stay for twenty-eight more years. It's a gamble, but not a particularly risky one, according to the statistics. If the loan becomes current—meaning the borrower is now paying on time—you can feel satisfied because you bought the loan at a 10 percent discount and you're gaining monthly income—at least 8.50 percent worth. Prevailing CD rates (in 1993 for example) are under 4 percent. You're making at least 4.50 percent more than what the bank is offering. The now-current debtor probably will repay the loan within five years, returning most of your principal. If that occurs the combination of the discount you got buying the loan from the RTC, together with the loan's higher interest rate, could combine to give you an effective return well into the double digits.

But even better is scenario number two. The borrower continues to miss loan payments. As the loan's new owner you decide to get the property appraised and come up with a minimum value of $135,000, the original purchase price. You foreclose on the property. If you gain title you will have successfully acquired a $135,000 property for $96,000. You just made $39,000.

Or you might consider playing landlord, renting the property out after you gain title. You already know that the units can bring in gross rents of $925, which comes to $11,100 a year. Subtract estimated expenses of 25 percent of gross rents ($2,775), which leaves you with a yearly net operating income of $8,325. On top of this income you will also garner whatever market appreciation occurs during your period of ownership.

As you can see, a rotten loan can be converted into a very sweet investment.

To figure out which of these two scenarios is the most likely to occur, you need to do a little sleuthing at your county recorder's office. Look at the property's title. Are there any other liens filed against the property or its owner? Are there mechanics' liens and tax liens filed against the property? If there are, it means the borrower is in deep over his head and is unlikely to pull out of this tailspin.

Loans come in all sizes, secured by all kinds of real estate, and you don't have to be a high roller to play in this league. I once advised a client who bought a $9,500 note for just $7,125—a hefty 25 percent discount. The loan was collateralized by a subdivision lot in Clearlake, California, a rural area being settled by soon-to-be-retired "grey-collar" aerospace industry workers. Because of the cyclical nature of the aerospace industry, similar loans had become late but were usually "cured" or brought current before foreclosure. After first inspecting the lot (a nice corner lot near the lake), I advised my client to go ahead.

The borrower was late with his payment a few times, but paid a 10 percent late fee without complaint, further increasing my client's return. Everything was fine for a while. Then the borrower defaulted—three months went by without payment. My client and I moved into action, instructing the title company trustee to file a Notice of Intent to Foreclose. To fend off foreclosure, the borrower immediately cured the default, bringing the loan current. In addition, he paid all foreclosure costs and still more late fees. Then, just two years into a ten-year note, he suddenly paid the loan off in full.

It was a profitable experience. The interest rate on the note was 9 percent on a $9,500 balance. But my client had purchased the note at a discount, paying just $7,125. Between interest payments and late fees the total annualized return on the investment approached 30 percent.

As you can see, buying loans can be a terrific way to diversify your investment portfolio and boost the effective yield. The trick is knowing when to buy and when to pass, when to hold them and when to fold them.

ARE THERE MANY LOANS AVAILABLE?

When most Americans read or see news accounts about the RTC, they incorrectly believe that most of what the government is selling is real estate—usually raw land or office buildings in Texas. But actually, as of the beginning of 1992, 55 percent of what the RTC had to sell was in the form of loans—both performing and nonperforming. The loans that are available for purchase are located in virtually every part of the country.

As we've noted, not all the loans the RTC and FDIC sell are bad loans. Some 45 percent of what the RTC has to sell includes "performing" loans backed, or "collateralized," by one- to four-family homes and commercial construction projects such as shopping centers and office buildings. The borrowers are making all their loan payments on a regular basis. Loans in this category will be of little interest to you. In fact, unless you are a Wall Street broker, you're out of this game entirely. Performing loans are packaged together in pools and sold to Wall Street firms, pension funds, and institutional investors in $100 million-plus pools.

That's not to say you can't buy a performing loan from the RTC or FDIC. Both agencies have loans they call "nonconforming loans," which are difficult to sell to institutional buyers because they don't fit the narrow standard secondary-loan market criteria. If you are interested in performing loans tell the regional RTC or FDIC loan representative and the representative will contact you when he or she gets a small nonconforming loan that fits your needs. But the pickings are more plentiful over in the nonperforming loan arena. That's where the real action is.

INVESTOR TIP. *About 15 percent of the RTC's $300 billion in assets is in the form of nonperforming loans—that translates into $45 billion in available product over the next five years—and that doesn't even count what the FDIC will acquire from the avalanche of failing banks. About 4 percent of the RTC's $45 billion in nonperforming loans (almost $1 billion) is collateralized (secured) by one- to four-family residences, a prime target for the small investor.*

FIRST MORTGAGES

Depending on how delinquent the loan is, nonperforming first mortgages can be purchased from the RTC for 10 to 90 cents on the dollar. That means if you purchase a delinquent loan from the RTC that has an original mortgage amount of $100,000, you can acquire the loan from the government for $10,000 to $90,000. The cheaper you can buy the loan, the higher the risk that you'll never recover your money. That's how the game is played.

SECOND MORTGAGES

Delinquent second mortgages on one- to four-family homes, shopping centers, office buildings, and raw land also are available for purchase from the RTC and FDIC. But "seconds" mean just that—you will be in second position if the borrower defaults. Someone else has a first mortgage in front of yours on the same property. As the second lien holder, if the borrower defaults on the first you will have to step in and keep the first mortgage current. If not, the first lien holder can foreclose and wipe you out. Once you reinstate the first loan, you then foreclose on the second (your loan) and take control of the property, subject to the first. You will gain title to the property but you now will be responsible for the first mortgage.

When buying seconds, make sure the property has some equity left in it. At the very least the property should be worth more than the first and second mortgages combined. A minimum of 20 percent more is a good cushion because it allows you to absorb foreclosure costs and legal expenses tied to the default.

Do not get lax with seconds. Perform your due diligence. Go down to the county recorder's office and make sure that you file a "Request for Notice of Default." This document requires the recorder to notify you if the borrower defaults on the first loan and is being foreclosed on by the lender. When a notice of default is filed on the first, be prepared to pounce. If you fail to do so the first lien holder can foreclose, take the property, and wipe you out. Once the property is in the first lien holder's name your second mortgage becomes worthless, since he or she has no obligation to you whatsoever.

Besides firsts and seconds on real estate, the RTC and FDIC offer a wide array of other types of nonperforming loans: consumer loans, credit card loans, student loans, automobile loans, mobile home loans, loans secured by furniture, and construction and land loans. Construction and land loans account for about 7 percent of all RTC assets.

Timeshare loans on vacation properties also are available—and plentiful. Each type of loan brings its own opportunities and risks. Be certain you understand both before jumping into these waters.

GETTING STARTED

The quickest way to discover what sort of loans the RTC has to sell is to pick up your telephone and call the RTC consolidated office nearest you. As you may remember from earlier chapters, the RTC and FDIC have consolidated offices in every region of the nation—even in such formerly robust economic markets as Southern California, New England, and the New York/New Jersey metropolitan area. If you're looking to buy a nonperforming loan in Florida, for example, you would call the RTC's consolidated office in Tampa.

Each consolidated office holds regular auctions of nonperforming loans. There are two types of auctions: closed, or "sealed," bids, and oral outcry. (More on that later.) Besides being offered through the RTC's consolidated offices, delinquent loans are auctioned—on the RTC's behalf—to the highest bidder by national loan auction companies such as Hudson & Marshall in Macon, JBS Associates in Chicago, and Ross-Dove & Co. in San Francisco. Each auction company has a toll-free telephone number and will gladly mail you a brochure or list of loans that are available. (Consult our Yellow Pages for these numbers.)

INVESTOR TIP. *When inquiring about a loan or loan package, you should ask for the loan number (or the loan pool number), what the loan was yielding in terms of interest when it was performing, the outstanding balance on each loan, and how long the loan has been delinquent. (Believe it or not, some borrowers stopped paying their loans after their bank or S&L went out of business because they didn't know who to direct the payments to.)*

FINDING OUT ABOUT LOAN AUCTIONS

Announcements of auctions of nonperforming loans (and real estate) are advertised regularly in the *Wall Street Journal* and business trade publications such as the *National Mortgage News* and *American Banker* as well as in local newspapers. But spotting such ads leaves too much to chance. Instead of relying on the media, call the closest consolidated office or telephone the RTC hot line (1-800-RTC-3006) and listen for the updated calendar of auctions. All upcoming RTC loan auctions are also listed on-line on RTCNET, the agency's computer data base.

FINDING A GOOD BAD LOAN

Typically, loans are sold in pools that are groups of loans. If you want to buy just one loan that is collateralized by a single-family house, you will have a tougher time of it. Still, some single nonperforming home loans are available for purchase—usually on large luxury properties. If you're a capital-rich investor in search of a larger home, buying a delinquent mortgage on an upscale property will be cheaper than buying that same home through your friendly neighborhood realtor. (Your play here is to buy the loan, foreclose, and then take over the house.)

Single delinquent loans are plentiful on commercial properties such as office buildings, "strip" shopping centers, hotels, motels, warehouses, and even raw land.

At auctions sometimes the loan is big and the price small. At an RTC auction in Denver one investor bought a delinquent business loan with a face value of $1.8 million for just $30,000. Now all the investor has to do is figure out how to collect.

BUYING PERFORMING LOANS

Many of the RTC and FDIC's performing single-family loans are packaged into securities and sold through Wall Street to financial companies or wealthy investors. These loans tend to be "vanilla" in nature—that is, they all have the same loan maturity, terms, down payment, and so on.

If you want to buy just one vanilla performing loan, forget it. The government won't bother selling it to you. But both the RTC and FDIC have a number of small performing (or "good quality") loans whose terms are so weird or awkward nobody else wants them. These loans have earned the nickname of PITA loans (Pain-in-the-Ass loans). The reason they're a pain is because they're difficult to service. For example, instead of paying monthly a PITA loan might have a semiannual or an annual payment term. Because they're so odd, PITA loans foul up a bank's loan servicing department, where computers are programmed only to handle standard loans.

Typically, PITA loans were originated by a small-town S&L or bank that tailored mortgages to the specific needs of individuals. They range in size from $5,000 to $30,000. PITA loans may not even be listed for sale by the government because they're too odd and puny. Other times they might be packaged with a group of other "nonconforming" loans and sold in bulk. But one thing is for certain—the government hates these small performing loans and likes to get rid of them as soon as possible. The smartest thing an investor can do is call the closest RTC or FDIC consolidated office and let them know you're in the market for these "oddball" loans. The government would love to hear from you. As one FDIC official put it: "Small, nonvanilla loans are just impossible to handle. It costs money to service them and because of their size few big bidders want them. We'd like to get them out of our hair as soon as possible."

Go in and meet with an RTC account executive in charge of loan sales in your region. Tell him or her what you have in mind and how much you are willing to pay. Keep in mind that because these are performing loans you won't be able to purchase them at particularly deep discounts. Government regulations mandate that the RTC should try and sell performing loans at 90 percent or so of the outstanding balance. For investors that still represents a 10 percent discount, which increases the effective yield. If you bid close to 90 cents on the dollar, the government probably will take the offer.

KICKING THE TIRES

Once you decide to bid on a loan or a loan pool, the first order of business is to analyze the loan file. When bidding on loans you will be dealing with either the RTC or FDIC consolidated office or the auction company charged with selling that particular package of loans. Loan files are available for review at the consolidated offices and can be examined free of charge. At this point investors will not have to post any sort of good faith money, but they must fill out an investor survey. (For a copy of what's on the investor survey, see Exhibit 9.) The investor survey will ask you, the potential purchaser, a number of general questions, including what type of loans you're interested in, who you're investing for, what type of loans you want, what part of the country you're interested in, and so on.

KEY INFORMATION. *Interested bidders in RTC loans also must complete a "fitness" certification survey. Although filling out the form is mandatory, there are only six questions, which are short and to the point. Among the questions asked are whether you've ever been convicted of a felony or defaulted on any loans that caused $50,000 or more in damages to a federally insured bank, S&L, or credit union. (Convicted felons who have caused a loss of $50,000 or more at a federally insured bank or thrift might be more interested in the authors' previous book,* Inside Job: The Looting of America's Savings and Loans. *You might even be in it.*)

For larger RTC loan auctions, loan files can often be reviewed either on microfiche or "in the flesh," which means you'll be reviewing the original loan files. The RTC and FDIC will not mail investors copies of the loan files. It is against the law to do so. Loan files are the key to unlocking the quality of your investment and determining how much to bid.

KEY INFORMATION. *The loan file should give you the following:*

- The borrower's annual income and current address
- The latest appraisal on the property
- The payment history of the loan
- Remaining unpaid balance and the interest rate
- The loan's origination date
- A credit report and financial statement on the borrower
- A current title report showing other liens against the property

All are essential in determining whether you want to buy a loan. Review the information carefully. Ask about missing data.

By the way, before the RTC or FDIC lets investors review a loan file they must sign a confidentiality agreement. Loan files contain some very private information, such as the borrower's income. The confidentiality

OMB No. 3064 - 0089
Expiration Date 6/30/94

FEDERAL DEPOSIT INSURANCE CORPORATION
DIVISION OF LIQUIDATION - ASSET MARKETING DEPARTMENT

INVESTOR SURVEY - LOAN SALES

INSTRUCTIONS: PLEASE PRINT OR TYPE

NAME (Last, First MI) ☐ MR. ☐ MRS. ☐ MS.	TITLE

COMPANY NAME	AREA CODE & TELEPHONE NUMBER

STREET/P.O. BOX NUMBER

CITY	STATE	ZIP CODE	FAX: AREA CODE & NUMBER

COUNTRY (If other than the United States)	S.S. #:

(CHECK THE APPROPRIATE BOXES BELOW)

SURVEY COMPLETED FOR:	HOW DID YOU HEAR ABOUT FDIC SALES?	
☐ CORPORATION ☐ PARTNERSHIP	☐ FDIC ADVERTISEMENT	☐ CONTACTED BY FDIC
☐ BROKER ☐ INDIVIDUAL	☐ BROKER	☐ OTHER

TYPE OF LOANS DESIRED

☐ ACCOUNTS RECEIVABLE, LOANS SECURED BY	☐ INVENTORY, LOANS SECURED BY
☐ AGRICULTURAL	☐ JUDGMENTS
☐ AUTOMOBILE LOANS	☐ LEASES
☐ BANKRUPTCY, LOANS IN	☐ LOAN SERVICING RIGHTS
☐ CHARGED - OFF LOANS	☐ MOBILE HOME LOANS
☐ COMMERCIAL - SECURED	☐ MORTGAGE (COMMERCIAL) - 1ST LIEN ONLY
☐ COMMERCIAL - UNSECURED	☐ MORTGAGE (COMMERCIAL) - ALL OTHER LIENS
☐ CREDIT CARDS	☐ MORTGAGE (MULTI-FAMILY) - 1ST LIEN ONLY
☐ ENERGY RELATED	☐ MORTGAGE (MULTI-FAMILY) - ALL OTHER LIENS
☐ GOVERNMENT GUARANTEED - SBA	☐ MORTGAGE (RESIDENTIAL) - 1ST LIEN ONLY
☐ GOVERNMENT GUARANTEED - OTHER THAN SBA	☐ MORTGAGE (RESIDENTIAL) - ALL OTHER LIENS
☐ INSTALLMENT - SECURED	☐ PARTICIPATED LOANS
☐ INSTALLMENT - UNSECURED	☐ STUDENT LOANS
☐ INTERNATIONAL	☐ TIMESHARES

LOAN QUALITY DESIRED	PAYMENT RATE DESIRED
☐ CURRENT	☐ FIXED RATE
☐ DELINQUENT OR NONPERFORMING	☐ ADJUSTABLE RATE

PORTFOLIO BOOK VALUE DESIRED		LOAN SIZE DESIRED WITHIN PORTFOLIO	
☐ UNDER $2.5 MILLION	☐ $10 MILLION - $25 MILLION	☐ UNDER $25,000	☐ $250,000 - $500,000
☐ $2.5 MILLION - $5 MILLION	☐ OVER $25 MILLION	☐ $25,000 - $100,000	☐ $500,000 - $1 MILLION
☐ $5 MILLION - $10 MILLION		☐ $100,000 - $250,000	☐ OVER $1 MILLION

GEOGRAPHICAL AREAS DESIRED

☐ ALABAMA	☐ FLORIDA	☐ KENTUCKY	☐ MONTANA	☐ OHIO	☐ TEXAS
☐ ALASKA	☐ GEORGIA	☐ LOUISIANA	☐ NEBRASKA	☐ OKLAHOMA	☐ UTAH
☐ ARIZONA	☐ GUAM	☐ MAINE	☐ NEVADA	☐ OREGON	☐ VERMONT
☐ ARKANSAS	☐ HAWAII	☐ MARYLAND	☐ NEW HAMPSHIRE	☐ PENNSYLVANIA	☐ VIRGINIA
☐ CALIFORNIA	☐ IDAHO	☐ MASSACHUSETTS	☐ NEW JERSEY	☐ PUERTO RICO	☐ VIRGIN ISLANDS
☐ COLORADO	☐ ILLINOIS	☐ MICHIGAN	☐ NEW MEXICO	☐ RHODE ISLAND	☐ WASHINGTON
☐ CONNECTICUT	☐ INDIANA	☐ MINNESOTA	☐ NEW YORK	☐ SOUTH CAROLINA	☐ WEST VIRGINIA
☐ DELAWARE	☐ IOWA	☐ MISSISSIPPI	☐ NORTH CAROLINA	☐ SOUTH DAKOTA	☐ WISCONSIN
☐ DISTRICT OF COLUMBIA	☐ KANSAS	☐ MISSOURI	☐ NORTH DAKOTA	☐ TENNESSEE	☐ WYOMING

FDIC 7240/01 (8-91)   **SEE REVERSE FOR MAILING INSTRUCTIONS, PRIVACY ACT STATEMENT, AND BURDEN STATEMENT**

EXHIBIT 9. Survey form used by the FDIC and RTC for loan sales. Those filling out these forms will be notified when the agencies have loans fitting their needs available.

PRIVACY ACT STATEMENT

The primary purpose of this information is to match qualified prospective investors with specific loan portfolios for sale. Furnishing the information is voluntary; failure to furnish all or part of the information may result in the prospective investor not receiving notice of the availability of a portfolio. Information may be disclosed to other federal or state agencies that also have loans for sale; to appropriate federal, state, or local agencies for law enforcement purposes; to persons involved in the conduct of judicial or administrative proceedings; and to a congressional office in response to an inquiry made at the individual's request. The information is collected pursuant to 12 U.S.C. 1819, 1821, and 1823.

BURDEN STATEMENT

Public reporting burden for this collection of information is estimated to average 15 minutes per response, including the time for reviewing instructions, searching existing data sources, gathering and maintaining the data needed, and completing and reviewing the collection of information. Send comments regarding this burden estimate or any other aspect of this collection of information, including suggestions for reducing this burden, to the Assistant Executive Secretary (Administration), Office of the Executive Secretary Room F-400, FDIC, Washington, D.C. 20429; and to the Office of Management and Budget, Paperwork Reduction Project (3064-0089), Washington, D.C. 20503.

RETURN TO:

F.D.I.C
PO BOX 802090
DALLAS TX 75380
ASSET MARKETING DEPARTMENT

agreement is your promise not to blab the information all over creation. If you do and you're caught, you will be fined.

INVESTOR TIP. *The riskier a loan file looks, the lower you should bid. The amount depends on the condition of the underlying collateral (property). When in doubt, drive by the property and take a look. Ask yourself: How would I feel about owning this? If the property and its loan file make you queasy, pass. Then again, you could bid next to nothing—and win.*

First-time investors should only consider a loan, or loans, whose collateral is in your own backyard—so you can keep an eye on it. Knowing that your collateral (a house or apartment unit) is within "checking out" distance lets you sleep easier at night. It also allows you to review (or perform due diligence) on the loan before bidding on it.

Buying delinquent loans is a specialized investment, but it is not as complicated as it sounds. However, it takes hard work, diligence, and a willingness to work with troubled borrowers. If you have the capital to invest, but not the expertise, keep in mind that the expertise can be bought—by hiring a collection agency, collection specialist, or a consulting real estate lawyer who specializes in working with troubled borrowers. However, hiring someone else will increase your overhead without necessarily increasing your return. Be careful who you choose. It will be the difference between making a killing and getting killed.

When an auction is announced and a bid date is established, you will have anywhere from three to four weeks to review a loan file. So will your competitors. Don't rely solely on the offering circular and brochure put out by the marketing company hired by the RTC. It's the company's job to try to sell you. Alone, this will not provide enough detailed data to allow for an intelligent bid.

The condition of the loan files can vary. Depending on how well managed the bank or S&L was, the loan file may be void of appraisals, credit history, and other key data. Expect the worst. After all, if the loans had been well managed, the S&L might not have failed in the first place. Study all information in the loan file carefully, paying special attention to the borrower's income and where the collateral is geographically located. Verify as much of this information as you can.

KEY INFORMATION. *Investors in loans can also order from the RTC that loan's due diligence bid package. The cost is about $50. The bid package provides you with essential information such as loan balance, rates, delinquencies, and so on. When ordering the bid package, you still will need to complete a confidentiality agreement and investor fitness certification form.*

Depending on the size of the loan auction, loans may be ranked by interest rate, age of delinquency, location of collateral, or location of lender. Concentrate on the features you find most attractive. Again, if you're just getting into this ball game, select a loan whose collateral is nearby.

LOAN AUCTIONS

The RTC and FDIC hold two types of loan auctions: sealed-bid or closed auctions and oral outcry or open-cry auctions.

SEALED-BID AUCTION

At a closed or sealed-bid auction investors submit bids on a form provided by the RTC or the marketing company. Along with a 5 percent down payment check (which is refundable), the form is then handed over to the marketing company, which forwards the sealed envelope to the consolidated office sponsoring the auction. *Remember to write* Bid Enclosed *on the outside of your envelope.* Your bid and everyone else's will be opened together on a specified day. The final decision on who gets the loan or loan package is made by the RTC and FDIC, not the auction company.

ORAL OUTCRY AUCTION

Like cattle at a ranch auction, here the loans are trotted out one at a time before an assemblage of bidders. The auctioneer will identify the loan or pool by a specific loan number, which corresponds to the number in the auction catalog. The auctioneer then starts the bidding by saying, "This pool is starting out at $10,000. Do I hear $10,000?"

The bidding has officially begun. The auctioneer then asks for bids from the room. Most government auctions take place in hotel ballrooms. If you want to bid just shout it out. After registering, you will be awarded a little stick with a number on top. Just raise your stick and you'll be in the game.

Bidding on loans at auction will cost you earnest money up front. As with other RTC auctions, if you don't win your money is returned. Before bidding, investors must present the auction company or RTC with a cashier's check to establish a good faith relationship. The requirement keeps out charlatans, dilettantes, and nonserious bidders.

The size of the good faith deposit is determined by the size of the loans the government is trying to auction. At some auctions the government sells as much as $200 million in nonperforming loans. If it's a multimillion-dollar bulk sale your good faith deposit might be as high as $10,000 to $20,000, maybe even more depending on the size of the auction. At smaller auctions the good faith deposit will be less, maybe as little as a couple thousand dollars. Once you know what size loan or pool you want, check with the auction house about the deposit size. Again, you will need a cashier's check. The RTC does not accept personal checks at auctions.

KEY INFORMATION. *If you win the bid your good faith deposit is applied toward the purchase price. You then have twenty-four hours to bring your total deposit up to a minimum of 10 percent of the purchase price. You have seven business days to come up with the balance and close the transaction. At closing you must provide the balance before the government turns over the loan portfolio. You are now the owner of a second-hand loan or loans.*

All sales are "nonrecourse," which means if you don't like what you bought, too bad. Neither the RTC nor the FDIC make refunds.

SELLER FINANCING ON LOANS

Unlike its policy on real estate or its affordable housing program for low- to moderate-income home buyers, the RTC *rarely* provides seller financing on loans or loan pools. Only when large financial companies or Wall Streeters are bidding (and usually if the loans are delinquent) will the RTC provide any form of seller financing. When it does, the loans made to buyers are usually five-year or seven-year balloons.

Most investors, whether they're bidding on a $100,000 loan or a $1 million loan, will have to come up with their own financing. As we've often said: Cash is king. The government does not look kindly upon bidders who come up short on closing day. Depending on the circumstances, if you welsh on a bid you could lose your deposit money.

TAKING THE COLLATERAL

Once you become the proud new owner of a nonperforming loan, the real work begins. Because many nonperforming loans sold by the RTC and FDIC are backed by real estate, you just foreclose and take the real estate. But keep in mind that foreclosure laws differ from state to state. You may have to wait up to 120 days after the first loan payment is missed before you can foreclose. There are also redemption periods in some states, which allow defaulted borrowers up to one year to redeem their property. But to do so they have to pay all that is owed, all costs, and accrued interest. Most states have straightforward foreclosure laws. After gaining title to the loan you can use the loan's trustee (usually a title company) to foreclose on your behalf.

If the loan never had a trustee, or the borrower files bankruptcy, you may need an attorney to sort matters out. A good real estate lawyer can cut through the red tape of bankruptcy and foreclose quickly. The faster you gain control of property, the sooner you can sell it or rent it out to gain rental income.

Once a borrower learns the loan has been sold to an investor and that he or she is no longer dealing with some impersonal bureaucracy, the borrower may bring the loan current. On the other hand, the borrower may say, "I don't have any money" and offer to give or sell you the property. When this happens you can take the property through a "deed in lieu" of foreclosure.

A deed in lieu has advantages: It's fast, cheap, a foreclosure isn't involved, and nine times out of ten you won't need a lawyer. But never be too quick to accept a desperate borrower's offer. A formal foreclosure process wipes out all liens on the property, while a deed in lieu allows liens to "run with the property." A hard-pressed borrower might offer a deed in lieu to escape contractor bills and other obligations. As the new owner through a deed in lieu you will be on the hook for these debts unless they are removed before you take title.

The RTC loan file may not list any junior liens. Be careful. If the property is large enough, it's worth a trip to the county recorder's office. Examine the chain of title and look for mechanics' liens. Again, a foreclosure wipes out any junior liens, a deed in lieu does not.

NON-REAL ESTATE LOANS

AUTO LOANS

Only specialists should consider buying paper secured by anything on wheels. Car loans can be tricky. When analyzing auto loan files, make sure the cars still exist and aren't sitting in a "chop shop" somewhere up in the Bronx or East L.A.

Most auto loans are sold by the government in pools. In late 1991, for example, the RTC's Denver office sold a pool of nonperforming car loans with an outstanding balance of $56,000 for just $35,000, leaving the investor with a potential profit of $21,000—if the investor can find the cars and their owners. Car loans are a nice niche for someone already in the car loan servicing business.

STUDENT LOANS

Uncollateralized, student or college loans can be highly risky. There's nothing "physical" backing these up. Do not acquire from the government *any* student loans taken out to attend a vocational institution (e.g., a beauty academy, truck driving school, or air-conditioning maintenance college). Although many vocational schools are legitimate, these loans have been subject to considerable fraud—especially in Florida. Consumers have been enticed into taking out student loans through various "incentives" programs in which cash gifts or kickbacks are offered. The student is then told by the vocational school that he or she does not have to repay the loan because it's "government guaranteed." Such fly-by-night vocational schools don't care if the student drops out or finishes the course because the school has the money even before the semester starts. Only after borrowing the money does the student discover the school is less than what he or she thought, and the student drops out, thinking—incorrectly—that the loan does not have to be repaid.

Trying to collect on a student vocational loan is like waiting for Godot. If you decide to focus on this area, stick to loans written on four-year accredited colleges and universities. Today a lot of confusion surrounds student loans. As noted, some young borrowers think they don't have to repay their college loans. They're wrong, but do you really want to be the person to tell them that?

The richer the student or parents (who may have co-signed the loan), the better the chance you'll get repaid. Analyzing the risks here requires more resources than the casual investor possesses. But again, any company with easy access to credit reporting services and collection agencies can make a profitable sideline out of chasing down delinquent student loans.

TIMESHARE LOANS

Be careful here, too. One $489,000 package of timeshare loans was sold by the RTC Valley Forge consolidated office for just $97,800—that's about 20 cents on the dollar. Not bad if the new owners can collect 30 cents or more on the dollar. But the timeshare marketplace is notoriously cyclical, with long periods of decline marked by brief flurries of interest.

The key to timeshare loans is rental income and "tradeability." With a timeshare you "own" anywhere from three weeks to three months of a single unit, usually a studio or one- or two-bedroom apartment. You can either live in the timeshare for that period, trade it for time somewhere else (in Hawaii, for example), or rent it out, pocketing the income.

Timeshares in popular vacation spots such as Hawaii, Florida, and California and Colorado ski areas more than likely will hold value as long as the project is well maintained. If the timeshare can be traded for two weeks in Europe or the Caribbean, all the better. But during the 1980s unscrupulous developers borrowed tens of millions of dollars to finance timeshare developments in places such as Georgia and Tennessee.

Developers misled investors into thinking these units were readily tradeable. When buyers discovered that no one wanted to spend time in their backwoods timeshare unit, they defaulted.

If the unit is located in a popular region, the next thing to look at is the unit's rent potential. If you foreclose on a timeshare without incurring a lot of legal costs and the property is a good rental vehicle (a timeshare in Honolulu or on Maui would of course be ideal), you can do well. Professional timeshare management companies in the area can give you a good overview of the local market.

Investigate timeshare projects thoroughly. Some have been rife with fraud, not just misrepresentation. Projects can be "oversold," meaning that two people show up for the same week only to discover that they own the same share. As you might recall, this sort of "double selling" landed televangelist/developer Jim (as in Jim and Tammy) Bakker in the Big House for forty years (the sentence has since been reduced). It's sort of like that scene from Mel Brooks's *The Producers* where Zero Mostel sells 25 percent interest in his play to one hundred different people. Each person owns one-quarter of the whole only to find out that ninety-nine other people do also.

Home mortgages, apartment loans, loans on raw tracts, and office building loans are all a lot less speculative than timeshare loans. Still, the higher the risk, the cheaper you can buy.

MORTGAGE SERVICING RIGHTS

Here's an interesting idea: How would you like to own a failed bank or S&L's mortgage servicing rights? The buying and selling of mortgage servicing rights is a booming business that the general public knows virtually nothing about. Investors in RTC and FDIC servicing rights have experienced returns on their investments of 20 or 30 percent and even higher.

But what is a servicing right? A servicing right is a legal contract whereby a company or person is responsible for "servicing" a loan—that is, collecting the interest and principal on a loan from the borrower. Why would someone want to service a loan? Because you can make money doing it. Let's say a homeowner takes out a home loan from ABC Bank and begins paying $1,000 per month. Unbeknownst to the borrower, a certain portion of that $1,000 payment is given to the servicer who keeps tabs on that loan. A mortgage servicer's job is to make sure the home-owner pays the loan on time and then pass on the principal, interest, and tax payments to the proper parties. In a nutshell, the servicer is the bill collector on that loan.

On a monthly mortgage payment, the servicer might receive any-where from .28 percent to .57 percent of the interest charge to service that loan. This is peanuts, you might think, but when you're handling thousands of loans per month—even hundreds of thousands of loans per month—it becomes a tidy little business. (The mortgage servicing busi-ness in the United States is a multibillion-dollar-per-year business. Just think of all the mortgages out there: homes, condos, coops, apartment buildings, shopping centers, and warehouses, to name a few. The larger the dollar amount of the loan, the larger the servicing fee. However, the servicing cost of a $100,000 loan is the same as for a $500,000 loan.)

S&Ls, banks, and mortgage banking firms (mortgage banking com-panies make only mortgages but unlike banks and S&Ls do not accept deposits) regularly service mortgages. For some it's the only way they can make any money. Servicing rights are bought and sold like any financial commodity and the RTC and FDIC have billions of dollars' worth of mortgage servicing rights to sell. Mortgage servicing rights available from the government can be bought at steep discounts. Small investors should ignore this business unless they have extensive mortgage servic-ing experience and a good computer operation to keep track of the loans.

However, investors with money—doctors, lawyers, and other professionals—have banded together to form partnerships to buy the expertise and hire professionals who service loans for a living. Even foreign investors from Europe and Hong Kong have grouped together to buy servicing rights from the RTC and FDIC. Buying servicing rights can be one of the best "silver linings" of the S&L and banking messes.

KAMIKAZE INVESTING

INVESTING IN UNSECURED LOANS

Besides the loans we have already discussed, the RTC also has scores of "signature" loans available. A signature loan is secured by just that—the borrower's signature and little more. It's a plain old-fashioned personal loan where a borrower walked into an S&L, filled out a loan form, and strolled away with the money—no down payment, no equity, no nothing. During the "wild and crazy" 1980s—and thanks to S&L deregulation—these loans sprouted like weeds after a spring shower. Every S&L owner had friends who they believed were "as good as their signature"—but weren't.

By their very nature, unsecured signature loans are *highly* speculative. They can also yield large returns—as long as the buyer knows what he or she is doing. The key to collecting on a signature loan is the borrower's financial condition. By purchasing at steep discounts, an experienced collection agency that specializes in collecting unpaid debts from deadbeats can make a killing buying signature loans from the government. As one RTC official told us, "You put your money down and take your chances. This kind of loan is not for the amateur."

JUNK BONDS

Junk bonds. Just hearing these two words can turn many a stomach. When people think of junk bonds they think of convicted Wall Street felon Michael Milken and his "den of thieves" at Drexel Burnham Lambert.

Technically, a junk bond is a high-yield, high-risk debt issued by a corporation. Think of it as a very risky loan. Companies that issue junk bonds include upstarts, firms with bad or poor credit, or businesses that don't like the loan terms being offered by commercial banks. Junk bonds can be broken down into $1,000 denominations and sold on a retail basis to small investors. Savings and loans bought more than $14 billion in junk bonds, a healthy portion of which is now in the hands of the RTC. (By law banks were never allowed to invest in junk bonds. Only S&Ls had—but no longer have—this authority.)

Normally the RTC does not offer these bonds to the little guy. The agency sells junk bonds in bulk to Wall Street firms such as Merrill Lynch, Saloman Brothers, and First Boston, which in turn offer them to institutional investors and wealthy individuals. If you have money to burn and feel lucky, start with Wall Street. All the major investment banking houses—Bear Stearns, Donaldson Lufkin & Jenrette, Merrill, Morgan Stanley, Smith Barney, to name a few—sell junk bonds. A word of warning, though: Most of the better-quality S&L junk bonds have already been scooped up by savvy Wall Street investors. What's left can be best termed "toxic waste." If you're a real bottom fisher and know the junk bond market, you can still find bargains here. And the RTC will be glad to hear from you.

REAL ESTATE INVESTMENT TRUSTS (REITs)

Small investors who don't want to mess with collecting on delinquent loans can invest in an REIT, or Real Estate Investment Trust, sponsored by the RTC. Investing in a REIT is a lot like investing in a stock or bond. Depending on how the REIT is structured, it's akin to a mutual fund. But instead of investing in companies, you invest in delinquent loans collateralized by real estate. RTC REITs invest in what the agency calls sub- or nonperforming loans.

In the real world REITs—in general—are collateralized by real estate—hence the name "real estate investment trust." Some REITs invest in certain types of projects such as nursing homes or apartments, while others invest in a wide array of properties. Sold in denominations of $1,000 or more, REITs often are marketed to middle-class and upper-middle-class investors.

Beginning in late 1992 the RTC began to offer REITs to the general public for the first time, in an effort to dispose more quickly of its nonperforming loan portfolio. Under its new Multiple Investor Fund program (MIF) the RTC lumps nonperforming loans into large pools, divides the pool into affordable slices, and offers these slices to the general public. The pool is then managed by professional loan workout specialists, and if the pool performs better than expected the investors pocket the profits. Under the RTC's MIF program, the general public, rather than institutional investors, will get first crack at each REIT pool.

The RTC offers these REITs through "sponsors." Instead of the government, you'll be working with investment firms like Merrill Lynch. Phone your consolidated office and you will be told which brokerage firm near you is handling its REIT sales. If the RTC REIT program takes off, expect the FDIC to follow suit with its nonperforming real estate.

REITs are not without risk. RTC REITs are, after all, collateralized by pools of nonperforming loans it could not otherwise market. If an

REIT is not managed properly, your investment could head south. On the other hand, if it's well managed, investors can do well. The key is the REIT's manager, so ask about the sponsor or management team the RTC has selected for the REIT you are interested in investing in.

These REIT pools are a nice way to take a chance on the RTC's nonperforming loans without having to actually get your hands dirty. You just put your money down and let the REIT managers deal with the defaulted borrowers and foreclosures and resales. If they do well—you do well.

BUYING LOANS FROM THE FDIC

As far as selling loans and real estate is concerned, the RTC and FDIC—as already explained—are sister organizations. The FDIC handles bank assets; the RTC, S&L assets. Their sales methods are similar but not identical. As with the RTC, investors looking to buy loans from the FDIC should first approach the consolidated office nearest them. (Again, check our Yellow Pages.)

As the RTC's caseload of assets begins to shrink in 1995, the FDIC's inventory of available products will be increasing and may not peak until some time in 1997 or a bit later. In 1992, for example, the FDIC had available for purchase $2.1 billion in performing loans and $9.1 billion in nonperforming loans. Those numbers could double each year, depending on the depth of the nation's banking crisis.

There are two major differences when it comes to purchasing loans from the FDIC. First, the FDIC doesn't rely as heavily on "open-cry" auctions. That means if you want to buy loans from the FDIC you'll be doing so through the sealed-bid process. As with the RTC, you will have three to four weeks to review the loan file before making a bid. More times than not an auction house will not be involved in the process. You will deal directly with FDIC account executives who take your sealed bid along with all the others.

Another key difference is that unlike the RTC, the FDIC's consolidated office does not require a good faith or earnest money deposit. This is a plus for bidders who don't want to hassle with the formality of obtaining a cashier's check. However, if you win a sealed-bid auction for loans you have twenty-four hours to post a down payment (usually 10 percent). You then have ten business days to close the deal. Most FDIC sealed-bid loan auctions involve large pools of loans. If you want just a few loans you'll have a tougher time of it. Still, FDIC account executives in charge of selling loans are more than happy to talk to you about buying small loans with balances of $20,000 or less. Like the RTC, the FDIC wants to get rid of the "small stuff" as soon as possible. Tell the FDIC account executive what you want. With a little luck you might be able to work out a deal without going through an auction process.

MORE CAVEATS

DUE DILIGENCE

The most important piece of advice to keep in mind when buying nonperforming loans is that it takes hard work and due diligence. Sure, you can acquire some loans for five or ten cents on the dollar—but will you know how to collect on those loans to make it worth your while? More so than buying real estate, acquiring delinquent loans takes a great deal of time and research. With real estate you size up the building. With a loan investors need to analyze the underlying property *plus* the entire loan file.

Purchasing loans from the government can be a profitable business. But go over the loan files with a fine-tooth comb. Get to know the collateral. Bargains abound, but so do black holes. "If you run a tight ship and watch the overhead you can make this business work for you," says Roland Russell, vice president of National Asset Management Corporation in Dallas, a specialist in nonperforming loans. The key word here is "work." Doctors and lawyers looking for a killing—listen up. You may be cash-rich but more than likely you don't have the expertise to buy delinquent loans. If that's the case, hire someone who does and factor the cost into your anticipated yield. Cash-rich doctors tend to be some of the worst investors we've ever met.

BANKRUPTCY

Another concern to loan investors is the bankruptcy court. With a simple wave of the pen, any citizen who has more debts than liquid assets can file a petition in the nearest federal courthouse, declaring him- or herself bankrupt and asking for court protection from creditors. By filing for bankruptcy, individual citizens, companies, or partnerships can obtain temporary relief from paying their bills—including loans.

For loan investors, bankruptcy filings can turn into major headaches, driving up legal bills. If you're functioning as your own lawyer, this won't be as great a concern, but it can delay resolution of the loan. The RTC or FDIC loan file should tell you whether the borrower is operating under bankruptcy protection. If a delinquent borrower has filed for bankruptcy, the court will prevent creditors (you, the loan investor) from foreclosing until a judge can better analyze the debtor's financial situation. In time a trustee is appointed by the court to oversee the estate or holdings of the person or company filing for bankruptcy protection.

Investors in delinquent loans can sometimes be broadsided by a bankruptcy filing. After reviewing a loan file you may think: "No way this guy's going to file for bankruptcy. He has too many assets." Then a couple of days after you buy the loan and send the debtor his first warning notice—lo and behold, he files for bankruptcy. However, just because a debtor has filed for bankruptcy, it doesn't mean a deal can't be worked out. If the loan is secured by something tangible, such as a car or house, you're considered a "secured" lender, and you still might make out. If you bought a delinquent unsecured personal line of credit or student loan, you're likely to have a tougher time of it.

Types of Bankruptcy Filings

There are a number of different types of bankruptcy filings: Chapter 7, Chapter 11, and Chapter 13.

Most individuals file for Chapter 13, which is for people with small amounts of debt. Chapter 13 cases often move quickly and can be resolved within a relatively short period of time. If someone has $100,000 or less in liquid assets he or she can file for Chapter 13. If the debtor has more, he or she has to file Chapter 11 (reorganization) or Chapter 7 (liquidation).

Chapter 11 is commonly used by struggling companies that for one reason or another are having severe problems paying their bills. Chapter 11 means the company is going to reorganize its operations by cutting staff and by trying to get you, the creditor, to accept less for the note you hold. Depending on what type of loan you hold—and how much you paid for it—this might not be so bad. Again, if the loan is collateralized by real estate, the debtor might just hand the property over and be rid of the headache. Then again, he may want to reduce the amount of money he's paying you every month—which isn't so good.

Chapter 7 means the debtor's problems are so bad that the debtor is going to sell everything (liquidate) and give whatever proceeds are raised to all the people he or she owes money. Again, this isn't good news to an investor who has just bought a loan from the RTC or FDIC. Still, if the loan is secured by real estate your chances of collecting are better than if there's no collateral backing the loan.

As in all bankruptcy cases, you can always work out a deal to foreclose on the loan with the trustee, creditor, or the creditor's lawyer.

The Dreaded Cramdown

Cramdowns or pushdowns occur most frequently in cases where individuals and companies have filed for bankruptcy and have tried to get the mortgage amount they owe reduced by petitioning the court. Debtors ask the court to reduce the size of their outstanding mortgage by arguing that land prices have decreased so much that they, the debtor, have no chance of emerging from bankruptcy unless the court allows their mortgage to be legally reduced.

In other words, they're trying to reduce, or "cramdown," the debt they owe to the mortgage holder. This is a serious concern when it comes to large commercial mortgages on hotels, shopping centers, and raw land but less of a concern when it comes to residential and other types of mortgages. (Very few individuals filing for personal bankruptcy bother going this route.)

However, on a positive note, the courts have ruled against cramdowns. In fact, in early 1992, the Supreme Court ruled that companies and individuals liquidating their assets in bankruptcy court cannot reduce their mortgage debt just because the market value of their property has fallen. This is good news for lenders and investors in delinquent loans. Still, it remains a volatile issue that may not go away. It also is a highly technical issue. Any loan investor who gets entangled in a cramdown case should consult a lawyer and read very carefully the Supreme Court ruling (Dewsnup *v.* Timon, January 1992).

IN SUMMARY

Buying loans from the RTC or FDIC, though not for everybody, can be quite rewarding financially. But as we've said, it's not a sure thing—no free lunch here. As with buying real estate, it's essential that you do your homework and look before leaping. Sometimes you can make a killing; other times—watch out. If you don't have the expertise, either get it or hire it. If you don't have enough money to buy the type of loans you want, form a pool with other investors.

Carefully review the loan files. Employed debtors with steady incomes are safer bets than someone teetering on the edge of bankruptcy. The deeper the discount offered by the RTC or FDIC, the less the likelihood of repayment. If you're a novice, stick to buying delinquent loans collateralized by something tangible and within close physical proximity to where you live or work. You'll want to keep an eye on your investment.

If you're a small investor with not much to play with, contact an RTC or FDIC account executive in the consolidated office nearest you and tell him or her you're only interested in small loans of $20,000 or less (or whatever your range is). Performing loans are available to small investors—but again you'll have to approach the FDIC and RTC and ask for them by name. Both agencies like to get rid of the small stuff first and tend to package them in pools.

When it comes to performing loans, be prepared to pay close to par. Deep discounts won't be as plentiful as with delinquent loans.

If you want to avoid dealing with auctions and regulators, your best bet might be to approach an ailing bank before the FDIC or RTC moves in. Ask it about its bad loans. By purchasing bad loans before the government moves in, you can avoid competitive bidding and save thousands of dollars—millions even, depending on what type of investor you are.

Chapter 9

....

The Flea Market of the Century

*Buying Non-Real Estate Property from
the RTC and FDIC*

The RTC and FDIC call the stuff "FF&E" short for "furniture, fixtures, and equipment." But don't let these three narrow categories fool you. Besides selling billions of dollars' worth of real estate and loans, the government has millions of dollars' worth of "hard" assets to sell: artwork, adding machines, cars, computers, couches, microwaves, stereos, and the list goes on and on. It's a virtual treasure trove, a bargain hunter's ultimate dream—it's the flea market to end all flea markets.

FF&E property is taken right out of the corporate offices of the nation's failed banks and S&Ls. Once the government seizes an insolvent institution, it compiles an inventory of all property at all the branches of every failed financial institution. Its goal? To sell anything that isn't nailed down. Everything must go and almost any offer will be considered, because the longer the government has to maintain this stuff the more it costs the taxpayers.

203

WHERE DID ALL THIS STUFF COME FROM?

When S&Ls were deregulated by the government in 1982 some bankers read it as a sign to buy now (using the S&L's money) and worry about paying later. Having the combination to the vault transformed some bankers into world-class shoppers. Miami S&L owner David L. Paul (indicted in 1992) used CenTrust Savings's money to purchase a $12 million oil painting by Flemish artist Peter Paul Rubens and then took the painting home to hang over his fireplace. Paul claimed the humidity in the office would harm the artwork.

Other high-flying thrift owners used their institutions' federally insured deposits to buy yachts, planes, fleets of expensive cars, crystal, silverware, sculptures, antiques—all in the name of doing good business. The booty now belongs to Uncle Sam, who must sell it through auction.

Every few weeks, anywhere in America, the RTC or FDIC holds an FF&E auction. The goal is to sell everything, even the tables the merchandise sits on. Nearly every auction has at least a few truly unique items. Try these on for size: a mechanical gorilla, a magic museum, a racehorse—just a few actual items sold at RTC auctions in recent months. However, much of this FF&E inventory is banking-related office furniture and equipment. For anyone setting up a new business or expanding an old one, an RTC or FDIC auction is a great opportunity to get equipped on the cheap. You need copy machines? Uncle Sam has them. A PBX phone system? Yep. Need a forest of filing cabinets? A sea of desks? A fireplace for the corporate office? Some Western art? How about some power tools for the maintenance department? RTC and FDIC auctions have all this and much, much more.

At a single FDIC auction in early 1992 the auctioneer sold the remnants of eight failed northeastern banks. In all they sold 1,493 "lots"— items or groups of items. This included: thirty-one Olympia electric typewriters that went out the door for $5 apiece; a Karex Lektreiver for $200; a Micro Design microfiche reader for just $75; a $15,000 safe for $1,600. A Canon 450 FAX machine went for $400 and a complete Epson IBM-compatible desktop computer system sold for just $475. A professional bank electronic security system, which had cost its former owner several thousand dollars, went for just $75. As the auctioneer's gavel slammed down on each item an FDIC observer sat grim-faced, shaking his head in glum resignation as one item after another went for next to nothing—such as the multiplex telephone system with twelve extensions that sold for just $650. The FDIC official just shrugged his shoulders. With more than 150 people attending, everything sold that day, even the old teller cages that the auctioneer claimed were worth at least $15,000. In the end, though, he accepted $1,575 for them.[1]

WHEN THE RTC GOES TO AUCTION

The RTC requires its consolidated offices to use the auction process to dispose of FF&E property when:

- a wide variety of assets are available for sale. By combining FF&E into a single auction, the government strives to create buyer "frenzy," which it hopes will increase prices. From what we've found, this is not always the case.
- "difficult to sell" assets do not sell. When this happens, the RTC combines these assets (for example, the mechanical gorilla) with other more desirable assets (such as office computers), hoping that someone will want the computers enough to take the gorilla as well.
- all other attempts to sell FF&E have failed. On occasion the RTC may try to offer FF&E to a wholesaler before going to auction. Side deals can be worked out—as long as you have cash. If FF&E can't be sold to a wholesaler (like a used office equipment retailer), then it's time to hold an auction.
- holding assets begins costing the conservatorship or receivership a lot of money through maintenance and upkeep. This happens with cars, cattle, produce, and so on.

TYPES OF AUCTIONS

When selling FF&E the RTC utilizes two auction methods: absolute and reserve price. Absolute auctions are also known as "everything must go" auctions. FF&E is auctioned and sold without regard to any mini-

---

[1] Alan Wade, "Bidding for the Bones." *United States Banker*, January 1992, 11.

mum price. This is where you can pick up a used microwave oven for $5. At reserve price auctions, the RTC sets a minimum sales price for certain FF&E items (a car, for instance) and refuses to go below that minimum. Usually found in the classified section of your local newspaper, the posted auction notice will specify that the RTC or FDIC *reserves the right to accept or reject any bid* that is less than its minimum reserve price for that item. If a reserve price is established the auctioneer will advise buyers prior to the start of bidding.

Depending on circumstances, it's possible that the RTC and FDIC might use both absolute and reserve prices in the same real estate auction. If that's the case the assets will be clearly marked accordingly. However, with commercial real estate and bare land values still in flux, anticipate that many upcoming auctions will involve absolute sales. Also, it is more likely that absolute bids will be used when selling single-family residences and condos, as opposed to office buildings and shopping malls.

GETTING PLUGGED IN:
FINDING OUT ABOUT AUCTIONS

Investors have a few different ways to get plugged into the RTC auction circuit. The quickest way is to telephone the RTC asset hotline (1-800-RTC-3006) and use the voice mail system. One of the choices listed is for the RTC's "Auction Calendar," which posts every auction event for that particular month. (Subscribers to RTCNET on the Business Information Network can also learn about auction dates and locations by accessing the agency's on-line computer data base. You'll need a personal computer to do so. See Chapter 2.) Using the toll-free number is the easiest way to get information quickly without having to explain yourself to a real human being. However, the asset hotline requires a touch-tone telephone. As already noted, a rotary won't work.

If you have a rotary telephone or don't want to talk to a machine, you can call the RTC Auction Center or the RTC National Sales Center in Washington, D.C. Both will supply you with the necessary information—dates, places, times, and the telephone number of the auction house in charge of the sale. In general, telephone operators and sales executives in Washington are knowledgeable, helpful, and polite. Both offices are particularly useful if you are looking for something unique, such as fine art or antiques.

If you want detailed information on what exactly is being offered, you have to call the auction house hired by the RTC. All FF&E is sold through private auction contractors who specialize in squeezing the most out of auction items. Free of charge, auction companies will mail you a list of *everything that is being offered* that day. If you have a FAX machine, most will fax you a list. (The ones we contacted did.)

KEY INFORMATION. *The RTC and FDIC do not auction FF&E themselves. However, if you're looking to buy office equipment in bulk, you can approach the consolidated office and make a bid for equipment, desks, or filing cabinets (whatever) without going through the auction process. RTC regulators allow the agency to sell FF&E to anybody at any time as long as they pay "fair market value." RTC personnel are in charge of determining fair market value.*

Middendorf & Co., a Washington, D.C. investment banking firm operated by former Navy secretary and ambassador J. William Middendorf, approached the RTC in March 1992 about buying office furniture for a new business. The firm walked away with dozens of desks, chairs, and a conference table, all for $3,780. This may sound like a lot of money until you learn that the original cost of the conference table alone was $7,000.

What other gems does the government have to offer? When we called the Regenhold Auction Consultants, Inc., in Clearwater, Florida, they immediately faxed us a list of items appearing in its next RTC auction:

- Sony color televisions
- Compaq and IBM computers
- IBM electronic typewriters
- Filing and storage cabinets
- Casio and Sharp desk calculators
- Microwave ovens
- Refrigerators and freezers
- Conference tables

- Secretarial chairs, armchairs, and couches
- Bruning blueprint machine
- Drafting tables
- Modular workstations
- Desks
- Credenzas
- Lamps
- Paper cutters
- Clocks
- Paymaster checks
- Coffeemakers
- Paper shredders

FF&E offered by the RTC and FDIC tend to be similar. Because S&L crooks were more colorful than bank looters, the RTC is the best place to shop if you're looking for something that might sell at Abercrombie and Fitch rather than Office Furniture USA.

Both the RTC and FDIC regularly advertise FF&E auctions at least two to four weeks ahead of time. Most of the ads appear in the classified section of your local daily newspaper (see Exhibit 10). But it is best not to leave things to chance. You may or may not spot an auction ad. Your best bet remains calling the RTC hotline and getting a schedule of auction events on a regular basis.

HOW THE GOVERNMENT APPRAISES FF&E

As with valuing real estate, the RTC has a system to evaluate the worth of FF&E. If an S&L has FF&E thought to be worth $5,000 or more, the RTC must get an independent appraisal on all items that will be sold. If the failed institution's FF&E is believed to be worth $250,000 or more, two appraisals are required.

If the S&L has a certain valuable item (e.g., a Ming Dynasty vase), the RTC will request that the auctioneer set it aside and offer it later in the auction, setting a "floor" or "reserve" price. If the floor isn't met the fixture will be taken back, reappraised, and offered again at a later date.

PREVIEWING THE MERCHANDISE

A few days before an auction occurs, the private auction house allows bidders to preview all the merchandise that will be offered. The viewing period usually lasts for only a few hours. If the merchandise you are interested in buying is mechanical, the auction house will allow bidders to check it out within certain limits. If it's an electrical appliance they will supply electrical hookups so you can see if the appliance operates. If it's a car or truck, chances are they'll let you run the engine, but they probably won't allow you to take it for a spin.

EXHIBIT 10.   A typical advertisement for an RTC auction.

Generally the auction company will hand you an asset list with a box next to each asset up for bid. Each FF&E item is assigned a lot number. Bring a pencil and a notebook. Write down the lot numbers you're interested in bidding on. If it's a copy machine you want, plug it in and test it out. At some of the auctions we attended the copiers ranged in quality from poor to excellent. Usually there are plenty of copiers to choose from.

At the preview, take as much time as they allow. Take notes on everything. If you don't get one item, you might get the next. Once an auction gets rolling the bidding becomes fast and furious. One trip to the restroom and you can miss half a dozen items. If the S&L had a sea of filing cabinets the auction house might sell them all in one lot. As many as twenty cabinets might make up that lot. The auction house will first try to sell the lot as a "whole." If it doesn't sell, then they will begin spinning individual items out of the lot for bid.

We cannot emphasize enough: Take special care to inspect every item you're bidding on. Why? Because nothing you buy from the government can be returned. All sales are FINAL. Also, if it's broken or won't work right, guess what? It's your problem after that gavel drops on your winning bid. Before auction the RTC and FDIC will hand out fliers. Read them carefully. This is what you'll see:

NOTICE

THE PROPERTY IS BEING SOLD "AS IS," "WHERE IS," AND "WITH ALL FAULTS," WITHOUT ANY REPRESENTATION OR WARRANTY WHATSOEVER AS TO ITS CONDITION, FITNESS FOR ANY PARTICULAR PURPOSE, MERCHANTABILITY OR ANY OTHER WARRANTY, EXPRESS OR IMPLIED. SELLER HAS ONLY LIMITED KNOWLEDGE OF ITS CONDITION. BUYER WILL PURCHASE THE PROPERTY BASED SOLELY ON ITS OWN INDEPENDENT INVESTIGATION AND INSPECTION OF THE PROPERTY AND NOT IN RELIANCE ON ANY INFORMATION PROVIDED BY SELLER, ITS AGENTS, OR CONTRACTORS. SELLER WILL NOT REPAIR OR IMPROVE THE PROPERTY PRIOR TO SALE. THE PROPERTY WILL BE SOLD SUBJECT TO RENTAL AGREEMENTS -OR OTHER CONDITIONS, IF ANY. THE PROPERTY MAY BE WITHDRAWN WITHOUT NOTICE AT ANY TIME PRIOR TO SALE.

BIDDING AT AUCTION AND HOW TO BID

Most auction houses function by the same house rules. Before being allowed to bid you will have to post a deposit, usually $50 to $100. (It's refundable if you don't buy. If you do buy, it's applied to the purchase price.) Registration takes place early that morning or the day before. We advise that you go the day before and beat the crush.

When you arrive the day of the auction, an auction company employee will assign you a bidder's number, which is usually printed on a wooden ping-pong-like paddle. When you want to make a bid you hold up your paddle. Do not keep your paddle in the air for longer than it takes to gain the auctioneer's attention. The auctioneer will keep rattling off a new, higher asking price, and if your arm remains in the air he will interpret that as a sign that you want to bid even more. If this occurs you might top your own bid. We saw this happen at an RTC auction in Alexandria, Virginia. A young man kept his paddle in the air and wound up paying $400 more for a truck than he had intended.

Instead of using paddles, some auction houses use strips of cardboard with a number printed on the end. Others use nothing, but request that you raise your hand and shout out your bid registration number. If you don't want to bid, don't say a word and don't raise your arm. This is known as "sitting on your paddle."

Most auctions occur in the auctioneer's warehouse. But others are held right at the former S&L's headquarters or in a hotel ballroom—whichever can hold the most merchandise and is conveniently located to parking. Most auctions occur on a Saturday and begin at 9:00 or 10:00 in the morning. In general, one auctioneer does all the selling, aided by one or two assistants. Each company has "criers" (or spotters) who prowl through the audience watching for bids. When a bid is made a spotter will point to the bidder and issue forth a hearty—though often undiscernable—shout. At the more aggressive auction houses spotters will also prod bidders to bid, pointing at them as if to say, "Was that the thought of a bid I just saw cross your mind?" This is all part of the show and meant in good humor, so don't let yourself be bullied into a bid.

Before the auction actually starts, the auctioneer will take about twenty minutes to once again explain the rules. Then all the bidders gather around the item for sale (or it is placed on a stage in front of bidders seated in bleachers). The auctioneer starts the bidding, sells the item, and moves to the next item.

If you've never been to an oral outcry auction, treat yourself and go, even if you're not going to purchase anything. Auctioneers are a lot like politicians: real hams who like to put on a show. A good auctioneer knows how to stimulate bidding. By the expression on your face he knows if you're going to bid or not. Investors who frequent auctions learn early how to maintain a poker face. But don't be surprised if the auctioneer or one of his criers decides to confront you—"Well, ya gonna just sit on that paddle all day long or you gonna bid?" Don't be taken aback or embarrassed. Part of the show, it's all done with a sense of humor. (And no, you don't have to bid if you don't want to.)

Every auctioneer has a different style—from the "big city" auctioneer with his dignified ways to the "country bumpkin" who likes to regale the audience with stories about how he just sold a new Mercedes to his "rich uncle who just got out of the poorhouse." Some auctioneers still use the old-fashioned rolling fast-talk, which newcomers find colorful but impossible to understand. If you're not sure what he's saying, don't bid. When in doubt, ask one of his assistants to translate.

KEY INFORMATION. *Before bidding, keep in mind that you will be charged a 10 percent auction fee—in addition to the purchase price. If you buy a copier for $100 the final price will be $110. Then add in that state's sales tax. If it's Florida, for example, the final price on the copier is $117 (based on Florida's state sales tax of 7 percent).*

PAYMENT: CASH AND CARRY

If you win the bid, a spotter puts your registration number on the item and forwards the information to the bookkeeper. You have until the end of the auction to settle with the bookkeeper. At day's end you must pay up. Auction companies often require a certified check and tend to be annoyed with anything less. Other forms of acceptable payment include cash, cashier's check, travelers check, or a money order. Company or personal checks are accepted only when accompanied by a letter from your bank guaranteeing payment. Checks are made payable to the auction company, which then forwards the proceeds to the RTC or FDIC.

KEY INFORMATION. *Once you've settled it's up to you, not the auction company, to cart the item away. If you purchase a large conference table, make sure you have the means to carry it away. Unless it's a Van Gogh, the government never wants to see this stuff again.*

SEALED BID AUCTIONS

On occasion the RTC or FDIC will hold its own sealed-bid auction for certain specialty FF&E items—usually artwork. During its first year of operation the RTC lumped artwork in with its regular FF&E auctions. This led to allegations by art experts that the government was selling "fine art" at "decorative art" prices.

Where did this fine art come from? From S&L owners who used the thrift's money to buy whatever they wanted. These guys had plenty of money, but were a bit short on taste. Sometimes S&L owners bought pure schlock, other times they did not—like David Paul of failed Cen-Trust Savings of Miami. Through Sotheby's Paul paid $12 million for Rubens's original *Portrait of a Man as Mars*, painted in the seventeenth century.

When the RTC seized Columbia Savings and Gibraltar Savings, both of California, it sold most of their artwork on a sealed-bid basis. The RTC produced glossy full-color catalogs, highlighting each piece. Art experts agreed that most of the paintings had little value, *but* a dozen were found to be "significant" contemporary works. By attending sealed-bid auctions, or getting a look at the catalog, investors who "know art when they see it" may find a few diamonds tucked away beneath the sofas and Xerox copiers.

In Phoenix in early 1992 the RTC sold 600 pieces of Western art acquired from failed thrifts. The works ranged from $10 prints to a $35,000 oil painting by Olaf Wieghorst. The agency said the auction was "just the beginning" of its sealed-bid sales effort, noting that it has hundreds of other pieces of artwork stored, but yet to be cataloged.

Under the category of "artwork" the RTC includes paintings,

antiques, photographs, prints, and sculpture. All items are appraised for the agency by art dealers, consultants, and other experts. Once an artwork is appraised and identified by a dealer as "fine art," the RTC establishes a minimum "reserve price" or "minimum acceptable bid" price of 70 percent of the appraised value. This applies to all fine art appraised at $5,000 or more. The RTC says it will not sell for less than that, and it will remove the item from the auction if bids come up short. Whether it sticks to its threat is another story. But if you see a piece you really want, bid anyway. After all, even at the reserve price of 70 percent you've just gotten a 30 percent discount. If you're speculating and don't care if you get the piece or not, go ahead and lowball your bid. See what happens. Desperate sellers can be unpredictable.

The RTC follows a set of predetermined guidelines for establishing reserve prices on FF&E artwork:

- If the item is worth $1,000 or less the agency does not have to establish a reserve price.
- If the item is appraised at $1,000 to $5,000, the reserve price cannot be less than 50 percent of that value.
- If the piece is worth $5,000 or more the reserve price can be no less than 70 percent of that value.

DIRECT SALE OF FF&E

As we noted earlier, the two agencies can avoid the FF&E auction process and sell directly to any buyer. These buyers might include a professional wholesaler or a business looking to buy in bulk (such as in the case of Middendorf & Co.). When this happens it's called a "direct sale."

When a direct sale occurs the inventory is sold directly from a failed thrift or bank. How can an investor determine whether the FDIC or RTC is willing to make a direct sale? The answer is simple: Just ask. If a failed bank or thrift was large and had many different branches and corporate headquarters, chances are better that the agencies will try to sell much of the FF&E on site through direct sales. But they will not advertise the fact. It's up to the aggressive buyer to inquire. Do so as soon as the agency places a bank or thrift into either a conservatorship or receivership. That fact, at least, will be in the local papers. Call the closest RTC or FDIC consolidated office and ask what plans it has for the FF&E. If you're told it's too soon to say, leave your name and number. But don't count on the RTC or FDIC calling you. Check on a weekly basis.

IN SUMMARY

When regulators close a bank or savings and loan and take it over, they inherit everything not human. If you can imagine it, the FDIC and RTC have either sold it or eventually will. It's easy to become an auction junkie the same way some people get hooked on garage sales. Once you get plugged into the FDIC and RTC auction circuit your biggest problem is going to be explaining to your spouse why a bank vault, a complete PBX phone system, or a crate containing two desktop computers and eighty staplers was a "great buy."

The whole trick to bidding at auction is to first inspect the merchandise. Kick the tires, open the hood, whatever. Don't get caught up in the feeding frenzy and overbid. Everything from cars to fireplaces, copiers to desks, is available from both the RTC and FDIC. This garage sale will be going on for at least the next couple of years. Call the closest consolidated office or check your local newspaper. Remember it's cash and carry and they don't deliver—so bring a pickup truck.

Chapter 10

....

Help Wanted—Inquire Within

Contracting and Employment Opportunities with the RTC and FDIC

One of the least-known benefits of the banking and S&L debacles is the job opportunities created by these scandals. If you're not looking to invest in real estate or loans, getting a government-related job or management contract is yet another way to profit from this financial meltdown.

WHAT'S AVAILABLE?

The amount of money up for grabs here is truly phenomenal. J.E. Robert Co., a real estate management and sales firm based in Alexandria, Virginia, is expected to make *$55 million* in fees by working for the RTC over the next few years. Its task? To manage, auction, and sell for the government $3.1 billion worth of assets—mostly real estate and loans.[1] IBM, the computer conglomerate, is expected to make $51 million from the RTC for developing and maintaining the agency's computer network.

[1] The J.E. Robert contract estimate is based on public contracting data issued by the RTC in early 1992.

216

Northcorp Realty Advisers, Dallas—which is classified as a "woman owned business" (WOB)—will earn $30 million in fees from the RTC by managing and selling real estate and loans.

J.E. Robert, IBM, and Northcorp are all RTC "contractors"— private-sector companies that have been contracted to do certain tasks for the RTC. Although it issued each of these firms a multimillion-dollar contract, the RTC—and FDIC—has thousands of other, smaller tasks that cannot be done "in-house" and must be assigned to private-sector firms. There's plenty of room here for the "little guy," especially small-town real estate brokers and appraisers.

The majority of the FDIC and RTC's contracts are to manage and sell real estate and loans. These contracts are called Standard Asset Management and Disposition Agreements, or SAMDA contracts. SAMDA contractors generally receive a negotiated fee to manage property and then are given a disposition fee once that property is sold. Real estate brokers that list and sell houses for the government are SAMDA contractors. The agency also assigns Standard Asset Management Agreement contracts, or SAMAs, where an asset manager receives management fees for overseeing and managing a property, but does not receive a disposition fee once that asset is sold.

If you're looking for work there are two ways to go here: Either become an RTC contractor or hire on with a firm that is already an RTC contractor. The RTC and FDIC need the following services:

- accountants
- appraisers—real estate, loans, securities, FF&E, and artwork
- attorneys and paralegals
- auction companies—for real estate, loans, and FF&E
- computer management, hardware, and software companies
- construction and demolition—to finish or destroy selected real estate projects
- investment banking firms (brokerage houses)—to manage and sell mortgage-backed securities and junk bonds
- marketing and advertising firms
- mortgage loan servicers
- private investigators
- printing companies

- real estate managers and realtors
- real estate and loan appraisers
- security companies—to guard half-finished real estate projects and other valuable items
- title companies and services

As of 1992 the RTC had already awarded 15,000 contracts with estimated fees totaling more than *$1 billion*.[2]

BECOMING A GOVERNMENT CONTRACTOR: GETTING STARTED

Like most government contracting work you must bid competitively against other companies or individuals. And before you can even bid you must register with the government so it can determine whether you're an eligible bidder.

As with most RTC and FDIC business, the best way to start is at an agency consolidated office. If you're based in Dallas but you want to bid on job contracts offered by the RTC's Newport Beach office in California, telephone Newport Beach, not the Dallas consolidated office. Upon request any consolidated office will mail you a contractor registration packet. Packets also are available by calling the RTC National Sales Center in Washington. It should take five to seven working days to get one. (The one we requested took four days to get to us.)

The contractor registration packet is 27 pages long, including instructions. Among the questions asked are the standard name and address questions. You will be asked what kind of work you're interested in. Some of the choices offered include:

- Leasing
- Security service
- Evictions
- Property maintenance

[2] *Source*: RTC Office of Inspector General semiannual report, released December 1991.

- Property management
- Real estate brokerage
- Broker's opinion
- Marketing/sales
- Marketing/promotion
- Securities (portfolio analysis)
- Loans (the form asks what loan size you want to manage)
- Construction
- Environmental consulting
- Tax consulting

And the list goes on for several more pages. Each category includes several employment subcategories. Almost every type of real estate and banking job is represented—and there's even a few you might not expect. Try these subcategories:

- Armored vehicle services
- Boat and airplane maintenance
- Expert witness (for RTC and FDIC civil lawsuits against alleged banking wrongdoers)
- Industrial hygiene survey
- Soils engineering

Your completed form should be mailed to the RTC's Contract Registration Department in Washington. Each of the consolidated offices will keep their own master list of "registered" contractors. To bid with different offices you will have to get on each office's master list. Each consolidated office relies on its own registered contractor or "source" lists to pick winning contractors. It costs nothing to register with the RTC or FDIC. It is anticipated that the contracting process will be streamlined in the coming year or two, making it even easier for individuals and firms to get work with these agencies.

A key part of the registration package you will complete is a Fitness and Integrity Certification form (see Exhibit 11). Among the questions asked:

SECTION VII

FITNESS AND INTEGRITY CERTIFICATIONS

QUALIFICATIONS OF CONTRACTOR (Sections 1606.4 & 1606.5)

Information and certifications required on this form will be used in determining contractor's fitness and integrity for entering into contracts with RTC as provided by Part 1606 of RTC's Rules and Regulations—Regarding Qualification of, Ethical Standards of Conduct for, and Restrictions on the Use of Confidential Information By Independent Contractors. **Please refer to those regulations for policies and procedures to be followed by both Contractors and RTC. The definitions of the terms used in this form are contained on page 20.**

If the answer to any of the questions in Parts B and C is "Yes," please provide RTC with a statement describing the past history of the situation and the matter's present disposition. RTC retains the right, in its sole discretion, to qualify or disqualify a Contractor.

	YES	NO
PART A: Each of the following questions must be answered. If the answer to any of these questions is "YES," RTC is prohibited from hiring you.		
1. Is the Contractor an individual who has been convicted of a felony?		
2. Has the Contractor been removed from, or prohibited from participating in the affairs of, any insured depository institution pursuant to any final enforcement action taken by any federal banking agency?		
3. Is the Contractor in default on two or more obligations to pay principal or interest to insured depository institutions in an aggregate amount in excess of $50,000 (which is defined in the regulation as constituting a pattern or practice of defalcation)?		
4. Has the Contractor caused a substantial loss to any federal deposit insurance fund?		
5. Is the Contractor currently in default on an obligation to FDIC, FSLIC or RTC?		
PART B: Each of the following questions must be answered. If the answer to any of these questions is "YES," RTC may decide, in its sole discretion, to qualify or disqualify a Contractor.	YES	NO
1. Has the Contractor (if not an individual) or any of the Contractor's related entities been convicted of a felony?		
2. Has any related entity been removed from, or prohibited from, participating in the affairs of any insured depository institution pursuant to any final enforcement action taken by any federal banking agency?		
3. Is any related entity in default on two or more obligations to pay principal or interest to insured depository institutions in an aggregate amount in excess of $50,000 (which is defined in the regulation as constituting a pattern or practice of defalcation)?		
4. Has any related entity caused a substantial loss to any federal deposit insurance fund?		
5. Have any of the following failed to pay an obligation to pay principal or interest at its full value owed to any federal deposit insurance fund, FSLIC, or RTC: (a) The Contractor or any related entity of the Contractor.		
(b) An entity that, during the past five years was a related entity of the Contractor.		
(c) An entity that, during the past five years, was a related entity of any individual or entity that now controls the Contractor.		
6. Is any related entity currently in default on an obligation to FDIC, FSLIC, or RTC?		

RTC 10400/01 (8-90)

EXHIBIT 11.   Two-page RTC Contractor fitness and integrity questionnaire.

QUALIFICATIONS OF CONTRACTOR (Sections 1606.4 & 1606.5) (Continued:)

PART C: The following questions relate to the Contractor and its related entities. If the answer to any of these questions is "YES," RTC may decide at its sole discretion, to qualify or disqualify a Contractor.	YES	NO
1. Is the Contractor or any related entity a party to an administrative or judicial proceeding in which any of them is alleged to have engaged in fraudulent activity or has been charged with the commission of a felony or which seeks a remedy that would prevent or materially interfere with its ability to perform on the contract?		
2. Is the Contractor or any related entity subject, to their knowledge, to an administrative or criminal investigation relating to fraudulent activity or the commission of a felony?		
3. Has the Contractor or any related entity, during the past 5 years been held liable for fraud, dishonesty, misrepresentation, or breach of fiduciary duty?		
4. Is either the Contractor or any related entity currently excluded from federal procurement or nonprocurement programs?		
5. Is the Contractor or any related entity subject to an unsatisfied final judgment in favor of FDIC, FSLIC or RTC?		
6. Is the Contractor or any related entity a party to a lawsuit in which the FDIC, FSLIC or RTC is seeking recovery in excess of $50,000 from the Contractor or its related entities?		

PART D: Does the Contractor agree that he/she will not employ any individual or subcontractor to directly perform work on the contract who:	YES	NO
(a) has been convicted of a felony?		
(b) has been removed from, or prohibited from participating in the affairs of, any insured depository institution pursuant to any final enforcement action by any federal banking agency?		
(c) has demonstrated a pattern or practice of defalcation?		
(d) has caused a substantial loss to federal deposit insurance funds? or		
(e) is currently in default on any obligation to FDIC, FSLIC, an insured depository institution or RTC?		

NOTICE: An individual who acts on behalf of RTC pursuant to a contract or any other agreement is deemed a public official, therefore is subject to federal bribery and graft rules as set forth in Title 18 U.S.C.

CERTIFICATION

In signing this certification I represent and warrant that I have the authority to execute this certification on behalf of the firm represented. I further certify that the above answers are true and correct and that all attached information provided to RTC is true and correct.

Signature of Principal Officer   Name and Title of Principal or Officer (Please print or type)

Firm's Name (Please print or type)   Date Signed

19

221

- Are you a convicted felon?
- Are you in default on loans exceeding $50,000 at any insured S&L, bank, or credit union?
- Have you caused any type of loss to the Federal Deposit Insurance Corporation fund (which insures bank and S&L deposits)?
- Have you been banned by the government from working at a bank or S&L?

A "yes" response to any of these questions will automatically eliminate you from ever working for the RTC or FDIC. This also applies to *any* of your employees.

A note here: The government relies solely on your responses to these questions. After filing a contract registration form you will not be investigated. However, once you bid on a contract and become a finalist then the government will actually investigate the veracity of your answers. If you lie on the registration form, the RTC will boot you automatically. Just ask the Ralph Edgar Group Inc., in Lake Geneva, Wisconsin. A real estate manager, REGI had been an RTC contractor for about six months. When the RTC inspector general's (IG) office began auditing the firm it discovered that REGI had allegedly caused an $80,000 loss at a failed S&L. This alleged indiscretion was not listed on the company's registration form and REGI was shown the door.

In another case in 1992 the giant real estate management firm of Cushman & Wakefield was barred for six months from doing any work for the RTC after it was learned that one of its contract appraisers had once had a brush with a failed thrift. Everyone agreed that the use of the appraiser was an oversight and that otherwise Cushman & Wakefield had an unblemished record with the RTC. Nevertheless, the sentence was carried out—no new RTC contracts for six months.

Slow to get started, the RTC's Office of Inspector General (IG) is now up and running. Its goal is to audit and investigate as many RTC contractors as possible. So take the disclosure process seriously. The RTC sure does.

Question: What if I fill out the contract registration form honestly, win a contract, and then later on I discover one of my employees was responsible for a bad loan at a failed S&L?

Answer: In the RTC's eyes ignorance is not an excuse. If you're thinking of contracting with either agency, screen all your employees for their ties to any failed S&Ls or banks. Remember Cushman & Wakefield.

The only way to please the RTC when it discovers that one of your employees is an alleged S&L wrongdoer is to dismiss that person immediately. Then and only then can you apply for reinstatement as a contractor.

BIDDING ON CONTRACTS

When an RTC consolidated office needs a job done that it cannot accomplish with its own staff it sends out a Solicitation of Service (SOS) to every contractor on its regional contractor source list (see Exhibits 12–18). If you have not registered with that particular consolidated office or did not check off the box for that particular job category, you will not receive an SOS. (Previously the RTC had a national contractor data base but it was scrapped in favor of having each consolidated office keep its own local list.)

By law the RTC must use competitive bidding when selecting contractors. To date there has been little evidence of favoritism in the contracting process. There have been lots of cases of sour grapes when someone loses a bid but little in the way of proof that someone's brother-in-law was awarded a sweetheart contract. When sending out an SOS the RTC must solicit at least ten qualified contractors for bids. Many SOS's will also appear in the *Wall Street Journal* classifieds.

WHAT TO BID? HOW MUCH CAN I MAKE?

There is no easy answer to the question: How much can I make? The RTC does not reveal how much it's willing to pay for you to manage, say, a hotel or a portfolio of loans. The agency generally asks for a flat fee bid, or on smaller jobs, a time and materials bid. If your bid is the lowest it doesn't necessarily mean you win the SAMDA contract. The RTC awards contracts based on cost, but it also analyzes a registrant's experience and technical skills. Supposedly, both are weighted equally. (Prior RTC experience is not a prerequisite for bidding.)

```
                    RESOLUTION TRUST CORPORATION

              SOLICITATION OF SERVICES NO. _____

                              [Date]


Attention:_____
_____
_____


         Re:    Solicitation of Services for
                Asset Management and Disposition


Dear Prospective Offeror:


         Resolution Trust Corporation ("RTC") is seeking proposals from
qualified respondents to assist in the management and disposition of certain
assets owned by RTC.  Your firm has been selected among others to submit a
proposal in a competitive format, as outlined in the enclosed Solicitation of
Services.  The Solicitation is non-transferable.

         If your firm wishes to participate in this Solicitation, please
execute and return the enclosed Confidentiality Agreement on or before
_____ to:

             Resolution Trust Corporation
             A t t e n t i o n:    _____
             _____
             _____


If RTC receives your executed Confidentiality Agreement on or before that
date, it will send you confidential materials describing the Initial Pool of
Assets in the portfolio as to which services are requested.   Proposals
responsive to this Solicitation must be received by Noon, Eastern Standard
Time, _____.

                         RESOLUTION TRUST CORPORATION


                         By:_____
                         Title:_____

Enclosures
```

EXHIBIT 12.   Sample Asset Management Application Form.

224

RESOLUTION TRUST CORPORATION

SOLICITATION OF SERVICES
TO ASSIST IN
ASSET MANAGEMENT AND DISPOSITION

I. INTRODUCTION

A. Overview. Resolution Trust Corporation ("RTC") is soliciting proposals from qualified respondents to assist in the management and disposition of certain assets owned by RTC. The services RTC requires are described in RTC's Asset Management and Disposition Agreement (the "Agreement"), which is attached as Exhibit 1 to this Solicitation. If you submit a proposal, you must accept the Agreement in its entirety, without modification, and the terms of your proposal will be incorporated by reference in the Agreement. By submitting a proposal, you agree to perform the Agreement according to its terms if RTC accepts your offer during the Acceptance Period defined below.

B. Amendments to Solicitation. You should acknowledge receipt of any amendments to this Solicitation by (a) signing and returning a copy of the amendment to the RTC office publishing this Solicitation; or (b) by acknowledging receipt of the amendment by letter or telegram. RTC must receive the acknowledgement of any amendment by the time specified for receipt of proposals.

C. Offerors Conference. This Solicitation provides you with sufficient information to prepare a proposal. In order to provide a forum for questions and to ensure equal opportunity and knowledge for all offerors, RTC will hold an Offerors Conference at _____ on _____, 199_ at ____.m. ("Conference"). You and other offerors are limited to two attendees per firm at the Conference. If you wish to attend the Conference, please submit the names of the attendees from your firm to _____ by _____, 1990.

RTC will respond to questions or requests for clarification regarding the engagement only at the Conference. Please submit any questions or clarifications you wish to have addressed at the Conference in writing to _____ at the above address by _____, 199_. RTC will respond to additional questions at the Conference.

You should be aware that an RTC Specialist familiar with the Assets subject to the Agreement will attend the Conference to explain the bases for the Estimated Recovery Values established for Assets in the Initial Pool of Assets. If you elect not to attend the Conference, you will be deemed to have waived any objection based on your not having had access to information provided at the Conference.

TO:

FROM:

DATE:

RE: Conflict of Interest Guidance for SOS No._____

In the interest of maintaining complete objectivity in this
evaluation proceeding, I need to be sure that you do not have
interests which might conflict with your duties in connection
therewith.

You should keep in mind that a conflict of interest situation may
exist where your private interests (including previous employment)
conflict or raise a reasonable question of conflict with your
duties and responsibilities. The potential conflict is of concern
whether it is real or apparent.

The purpose of this memorandum is to request that you review on a
continuing basis your situation and if you identify any financial
and/or employment interest related to yourself, your spouse, minor
child or dependent(s) which may create a conflict of interest or
the appearance thereof in the context of your duties and
responsibilities as a member or advisor to this panel, you should
notify the chairperson immediately. In reviewing your situation,
you should ask yourself the following questions:

1. Have I, or my spouse, minor children, or dependent(s)
    (hereinafter "family"), been connected as an employee,
    officer, owner, director, member, trustee, partner, advisor,
    or consultant to any of the organizations to be solicited or
    those who submit proposals, or do I, or my family, have any
    continuing financial interests through a pension or retirement
    plan, shared income, or other arrangement as a result of any
    current or prior employment or business or professional
    association?

2. Am I or my family now negotiating or do I or my family have
    any arrangement concerning prospective employment with any
    proposer?

3. Do I or my family have any financial interest through the
    ownership of stock, stock options, bonds, securities, or other
    arrangements including trust, in any proposer?

EXHIBIT 13.   Sample Conflict of Interest Memorandum.

226

4. The undersigned as a member of the Technical Proposal Evaluation Committee, hereby acknowledges the notification that he/she is subject to Federal statutes relating to conflicts of interest and the regulations promulgated thereunder, as more particularly set out at Part 336, FDIC Circular 2410.2, entitled "Employees Responsibilities and Conduct" and 18 U.S.C. 201-209.

If you believe that no present conflict of interest exists, please complete the attached agreement and return it to the chairperson promptly.

```
              SUMMARY RATING SHEET FOR SOS NO._____

                             ENTITLED

              _____

        Proposer:_____ Evaluator:_____ Date:_____


Evaluation Criteria:  Element Weight x Numerical Rating = Points Rating


A.   Technical Performance of the Process   (30%)

     1.   Adequacy of management personnel to
          effectively supervise the professional
          staff.                                  10% x _____ = _____

     2.   Adequacy of professional staff to perform.   7% x _____ = _____

     3.   Adequacy of support personnel to effectively
          perform the required work.              6% x _____ = _____

     4.   Adequacy of clerical staff to support
          technical and management personnel.     3% x _____ = _____

     5.   Acceptability of proposed management system
          to timely resolve problems.             2% x _____ = _____

     6.   Adequacy of supporting equipment to perform
          over the entire duration of the contract.   2% x _____ = _____

B.   Soundness, Completeness, and Thoroughness of the
     Proposal in Complying with the Major Tasks of the
     Statement of Work (20%)

     Project planning, engineering and design,
     procurement placement, installation and shakedown,
     test plan formulation, test plan implementation/
     process operation, process evaluation, and
     equipment and process removal. ·             20% x _____ = _____
```

EXHIBIT 14.   Sample Evaluation Form. From time to time management contractors will be evaluated by the RTC. This form helps the agency determine the quality of the work being performed by contractors.

C. Key Personnel, Project Management, Corporate
Resources, and Related Corporate Experience
as They Pertain to This Project (50%)

    1.   Qualifications and experience of key personnel
        to be assigned to the project and the
        effectiveness of the proposed project
        management system.   25% x _____ = _____

    2.   Corporate resources and related corporate
        experience of the proposing organization
        in related projects.   25% x _____ = _____

    TOTAL   100% x _____ = _____

D. Bonus Points for M/WOB   _____ = _____

    SEE SCORING PLAN FOR EXPLANATION OF NUMERICAL RATINGS.

```
TO:         Technical Evaluation Panel Members

FROM:

DATE:

RE:         Confidentiality Agreement - Proposal Evaluation for
            SOS No._____

In order to ensure the confidentiality of financial and technical
data which may be submitted by proposers under the subject
solicitation, you are requested to sign the following agreement and
promptly return this memorandum to the chairperson of your panel.


                              AGREEMENT


In anticipation of my participation as a member of, or advisor to,
the panel formed to evaluate proposals submitted in response to
SOS, I agree that I will not disclose any information during the
proceeding of the evaluation concerning the evaluation to anyone
who is not also participating in the same proceedings and then only
to the extent that such information is required in connection with
such proceedings. Subsequent to the conclusion of the panel's
activities, I further agree not to disclose any information in
connection with said proceedings except as authorized and/or
permitted by RTC concerning this action on the panel's composition
and activities direct to me from any source outside the panel.




_____          _____
Date                                Name/Title
```

EXHIBIT 15.   Sample Confidentiality Agreement. Before you can bid on a government contract the RTC or FDIC will ask that you sign a confidentiality statement. The statement helps the government maintain the integrity of the contracting process and protect the asset(s) you might manage.

AGREEMENT

This is to advise that to the best of my knowledge and belief,
I have no current conflict of interest which may interfere
with my assignment and I agree to report promptly any such
conflict of which I become aware.

_____   _____
Date   Name/Title

```
XYZ Management
Attention_____
Address
City, State, Zip Code

        Re:  Proposal for Property Management Services
             (Receivership)/(Property Name)
             RTC Asset No. _____

Dear _____:

RTC appreciates the time you have taken to prepare and submit your recent
proposal to provide property management services for the referenced asset.
After reviewing all the proposals submitted, a decision was made to select
another contractor.

Although RTC attempts to include as many firms in its contractor selection
process, obviously, only one contractor can be selected.  If you want to
'iscuss the basis of our selection, please send a written letter to my
attention within three business days upon receipt of this letter.  Upon
receipt of your written request, we will schedule a conference to review your
proposal and our selection process.

Since our firm remains on our contractor data base as a potential contractor,
you may receive solicitations of services on other properties.  Your future
participation will very much be appreciated.

Thank you for your interest in working with RTC.

Sincerely,

RESOLUTION TRUST CORPORATION



By: _____
       Regional Contract Specialist

cc:  RTC Representative
```

EXHIBIT 16. Sample Letter for Unsuccessful Proposals. If you are rejected after bidding on an RTC contract the agency will send you a rejection notice. The notice is merely a formality. After being rejected you can bid again on other contracts.

PURPOSE

The Resolution Trust Corporation's (RTC) Contractor Selection and Engagement policy and procedures are intended to provide every contractor with a fair and equal opportunity to provide contract services relating to RTC assets. One important aspect of the policy is that contract awards are made on the basis of competitive proposals solicited from several interested contractors, spreading the proposal opportunities among as many different qualified contractors as possible. Because each asset is uniquely different, the expertise and qualifications required for a specific assignment may vary greatly. Our experience, however, shows that most contractors while promoting themselves as a full service firm, have limited areas of true expertise. Many of the contractors interested in providing services to RTC are unfamiliar with the federal procurement process or with the selection process used by RTC. Because of their unfamiliarity, many of these contractors believing they are the most qualified for the engagement, assume the selection was made on grounds other than expertise and qualifications. So that these contractors do not become frustrated or disgruntled with RTC, it is important that they fully understand the process used to evaluate their proposal. For such contractors, a debriefing conference is the best is the best way to explain this selection process and offer comments and suggestions for improving future contracting opportunities.

GUIDELINES

Once a final decision is made as to who is to be awarded the contract, all other contractors submitting unsuccessful proposals should be given written notice of the contract award. The written notice should thank them for their interest in offering their services to RTC and for their time and effort in preparing their proposal. If desired, the notice can specify the contractor selected. The notice should also offer the contractor an opportunity to review, in person or by telephone, the RTC Contractor Selection Process and possible reasons why their proposal was unsuccessful. This is best accomplished by giving the contractor a set time period (within 3 days of their receipt of the notice) within which to send written notice to the RTC Regional Contract Specialist of their desire for a debriefing conference. The debriefing can then be set up to fit his or her schedule and that of the appropriate RTC Representative.

These guidelines merely establish a general frame work for a debriefing conference. There are many items which can and should be discussed with the contractor. At the same time, there are many items which clearly should not be discussed during the debriefing conference. A suggested agenda for the conference is set forth below:

EXHIBIT 17.   Guidelines for debriefing unsuccessful contractors.

233

INSTRUCTIONS FOR COMPLETING THE PROPOSAL EVALUATION WORKSHEET

SAMPLE PROPOSAL EVALUATION WORKSHEET
(ATTACHMENT 3 TO COMPETITIVE BID MEMORANDUM)

WORKSHEET FOR

OFFICIAL USE ONLY

EVALUATOR:___John Doe_____

FIRM: ABC Corporation

DATE:_____

EVALUATION CRITERA: A: Technical
Performance of the
Process (30)

EVALUATION SCORE:

(10,8,5,2,0):___300_____

Strengths: (1) Excellent upper management;

(2) Demonstrated understanding of the statement of work;

(3) Unique methodology

Weaknesses: (1) Workflow monitoring not indicated;

(2) No discussion of emergency handling;

(3) Minor training deficiencies of key personnel.

Correctable Weaknesses: (1) Request work flow chart;

(2) How will emergency situations be processed?;

(3) Schedule training for key personnel.

Uncorrectable Weaknesses: None

Desired Clarification or Substantiation: (1) Provide detailed work flow

with names and responsibilities;

(2) Provide written procedures for emergencies along with alternates who

are responsible;

(3) Provide details of training; i.e., inhouse, outside source, when,
course description, etc.

EXHIBIT 18.   RTC personnel are asked to use this form as guidance in evaluating
contract bids.

234

What you eventually bid on a contract depends on your assessment of your hourly costs and other overhead. During the RTC's first two years some contractors walked away with fat contracts that allowed them huge profit margins. With the agency's IG office watching every penny now and Congress just waiting for news that someone got rich off the RTC, pork barrel contracts are becoming rare. But there is plenty of honest work out there and the RTC is prepared to pay an honest wage.

There are a number of ways to make these contracts work for you or your company. Some SAMDA contractors decide to break even on the management part of the contract and to make their profit on the disposition fee when the property is sold, since they can receive fees for *both* management and disposition functions. Ideally you should be able to make a profit on both. It all depends on who you are bidding against and what their bidding strategy is. Don't underbid. You could wind up losing money, or at best breaking even. Remember, SAMA contractors do not get a disposition fee. All their money is made on management fees. If you are only bidding to manage RTC properties, bid accordingly. You will not make any disposition income to compensate for management losses.

The amount of money you can make depends on the size and type of the asset. Here's a sampling of contractors, the fees they make, and the book value of assets under management. (Book value is what an asset is listed for on the balance sheet of an insolvent institution. Market value is often significantly *lower.*)

Company	Fees	Book Value of Asset
J.E. Robert	$55 million	$3.12 billion
Coopers & Lybrand	$32 million	$753 million
Northcorp Realty	$30 million	$1.285 billion
FGB Realty	$16 million	$1.091 billion

Many contractors that work for the government are privately held and are not listed on any public stock exchanges. Therefore it is impossible to tell you how much of a profit they are making off their RTC contracts because neither they nor the RTC will disclose that information. Still, the estimated contractor fees available from the RTC in the agency's public reading room in Washington, D.C., reveal that as of the beginning of 1992, of more than one hundred major RTC contractors reviewed each was making $3 million or more in fees from the government.

It is assumed that the larger a contract the greater the economy of scale involved. Companies that manage and service loans know that it takes the same number of computers and personnel to manage one thousand loans as it does five thousand loans. Realtors that list properties for the RTC can receive up to a 5 percent commission on one- to four-family residences. On large commercial properties for which the sales price runs into the millions, sales commissions as a percentage of the sales price are scaled back as the price goes up.

A rare glimpse of how much a contractor can make comes from a Government Accounting Office (GAO)[3] audit done on the RTC's Denver office. In 1991 the RTC hired the Financial Management Task Force (FMTF), a Denver consulting firm specializing in audits of financial institutions, to audit the assets of ninety-two failed S&Ls. The RTC paid FMTF $51 per hour to audit the financial records and books of the ninety-two institutions. In turn FMTF paid its ninety-eight employees hourly rates of $14 to $45. According to the GAO, ninety-three of the ninety-eight (95 percent) employees were paid hourly rates of $25 or less.

FMTF's total take on the contract? More than $20 million. Its gross profit, according to GAO, was almost 30 percent. GAO wasn't crazy about this and neither was Congress, but FMTF certainly was. Are more great deals like this available? Here and there, perhaps, but the RTC has tightened up its cost accounting and contracting procedures and "killings" like this are now few and far between. But contractors we talked to said you can still make a healthy profit from the RTC. The key is watching your costs and not underbidding.

In case you're wondering, the RTC will reimburse contractors for all travel and travel-related expenses tied to the job. Have receipts available and be prepared to prove that such travel is related to your contract with the government. On one RTC contract a New York accounting firm billed the government $662,000 for travel. Another firm, based in South

---

[3] GAO is the auditing arm of the Congress of the United States.

Bend, Indiana, billed the agency $690,000. The bills were paid, but were later scrutinized by the IG's office.

When the RTC puts out a call for help with an SOS the process starts with the RTC consolidated office. When a given RTC consolidated office needs something done it calls RTC headquarters in Washington. Washington then sends out a notice to all available contractors that a contract is available and describes the work. Qualifying contractors are invited to make a bid for the job.

Most of the time the winning bidder is chosen by the consolidated office who "let" the contract. Each contract's guidelines can differ, but at last check, if a contract's dollar value is $100,000 or less the consolidated office can approve it without referring the matter to Washington. Larger winning contract bids are sent to Washington for approval. Most multimillion-dollar contracts will wind up on the desk of the Chair of the RTC.

It should take a maximum of ninety days to approve a contract. If you win a contract your paycheck will come directly from the RTC in Washington even though the work is being done for one of the consolidated offices.

WHAT'S AN MWOB AND WHY SHOULD YOU CARE?

MWOB stands for Minority or Woman Owned Business and offers such businesses a leg up on the competition. The Financial Institutions Reform, Recovery and Enforcement Act of 1989 (FIRREA), which bailed out the S&L industry, mandated that the agency be more progressive in giving women and minorities a chance to compete with the J.E. Roberts and IBMs of the world, akin to affirmative action hiring. So far no one has raised a big stink about the MWOB program. And it became the law of the land when President Bush signed FIRREA into law.

MWOBs are automatically awarded extra points that count toward the RTC's decision to hire a contractor when several bids are close. As noted, all contracts are determined by cost and technical skill of the firms bidding. But right from the start an MWOB firm receives 5 additional points on the RTC's cost evaluation and ten additional points on the technical evaluation. All contracts are awarded on a point system in which points are given based on experience and bid cost. The more points a company gains, the greater its chance of winning a contract.

To achieve MWOB status a firm must be at least 51 percent owned by a minority or a woman. If you fake it or lie and get caught by the IG's office you lose your contract instantly. It has already happened once to a firm "controlled" by the wife of its true owner.

CONTRACTOR TIP. *MWOBs that don't have all the skills needed to contract with the government can form a joint venture with a non-MWOB firm and bid on work together. The RTC awards joint ventures extra points toward contract consideration as long as the MWOB partner manages 25 percent of the joint venture's business.*

Who in the RTC's eyes is a minority? According to its own regulations any American who is of African, American Indian, Asian, Hispanic, Alaskan Native, or Pacific Islander descent is a minority for MWOB purposes. When in doubt, ask the consolidated office. Gays are not considered minorities.

THE FDIC AND CONTRACTING

The FDIC's contracting office functions in a similar manner but so far hasn't had the kind of need for contractors as the RTC. This too is changing as more banks fail. If you find RTC contracting too competitive you might consider trying the FDIC. Your chances of winning and obtaining a better deal could be greater.

Currently the FDIC awards most of its contracts through its headquarters in Washington. But the agency is trying to decentralize and by the time you read this many of its smaller contracts will be awarded by its regional and consolidated offices. (Remember, under the FDIC's structure the regional offices oversee the consolidated offices.)[4]

When the FDIC needs a contractor it sends out a nationwide Request

---

[4] Real estate brokers trying to get listings from the FDIC should approach the agency's consolidated offices. The commission paid is negotiable but should be similar to what the RTC is paying. (As we noted in an earlier chapter, HUD pays real estate brokers up to a 6 percent commission on single-family homes.)

for Proposal, or RFP. The RFP is akin to the RTC's solicitation of services request. The FDIC has a central source list of contractors it draws on to send RFPs. On occasion it coordinates with the RTC's contracting office on projects. But for the most part you must reregister with the FDIC to bid on its contracts. Just because you're an RTC-approved contractor doesn't mean your name automatically goes into the FDIC's data base. It's a pain, but if you want its business, register.

FIRST, WE HIRE ALL THE LAWYERS

Shakespeare may not have liked lawyers very much, but the government apparently loves them. The S&L and banking bailouts may be the best thing to happen to the legal profession since the invention of the United States judicial system. The S&L bailout bill, FIRREA, is often mockingly referred to as the "Lawyers Relief Act of 1989" because of all the job opportunities it created for the legal community. In 1990 and 1991 the RTC and FDIC paid private law firms more than $1.5 billion (yes, *billion*) in fees to handle a variety of chores. About thirty different law firms made $2.5 million dollars or more in fees from the two agencies in 1991 alone. What are these law firms doing for the government? Everything from foreclosures and asset seizures to investigations and civil complaints. The biggest profit center, though, is clearly in the area of civil litigation.

When an S&L or bank fails the RTC or FDIC hires a private law firm to see if it can sue any of the S&L's former officers or directors for negligence, fraud, dereliction of duties, and so on. Since 1985 the government has filed hundreds of lawsuits against alleged S&L and bank wrongdoers for contributing to the failure of a financial institution. Thousands of former S&L managers, and even real estate developers, have been targeted for damages by private law firms working for the RTC and FDIC.[5]

---

[5] The government has promised to leave no stone unturned in the S&L and banking debacles. Even Neil Bush, the son of President Bush, and Arizona Governor Fife Symington—both former S&L directors—have been sued for their alleged roles in savings and loan failures. Lincoln Savings former owner Charles Keating is being sued for over $1 billion by the law firm of Morrison & Hecker, which is working for the FDIC.

HOW MUCH CAN I MAKE AS A CONTRACT LAWYER?

The most profitable area for contract lawyers is in civil litigation. As a rule the RTC and FDIC hire entire law firms, rather than individual attorneys. Litigation cases are labor-intensive and take up hundreds, even thousands, of work hours. However, one lawyer working as a litigation specialist can find work with either agency working on fairly narrow cases or cases involving very small institutions, chasing down deadbeats, or unscrambling contract disputes.

The RTC and FDIC will pay hourly rates of anywhere from $100 to $400 to bring deadbeats and wrongdoers to the bargaining table—or to justice—whichever comes first. The New York law firm of Cravath Swaine and Moore made $12 million in one year pressing the RTC and FDIC's civil case against former Drexel Burnham Lambert junk bond king Michael Milken. (Cravath's regular hourly rate is $600, but the FDIC reportedly negotiated the price down to $450 per hour, offering the firm incentive clauses on the amount of money the government recovered in the case.)

Currently both agencies cap the annual fees a law firm can charge the government at $2.5 million. Waivers are frequently granted, especially if your firm is handling a large damage claim as in the government's case against Milken or former Lincoln Savings owner Charles Keating, Jr.

If you're a lawyer and civil litigation is your forte, the RTC and FDIC can keep you gainfully employed for the next decade. Although 90 percent or so of all civil defendants settle out of court with the government, cases must be investigated and lawsuits must be filed. (The government has to sue before it can settle.) Most RTC and FDIC cases last anywhere from two to five years, some even longer, depending on the complexity of the charges.

Private investigators that work for law firms can do quite well by latching on to FDIC and RTC work. Who do you think does all the dirty work for lawyers? You think well-dressed lawyers sit in a car staking out a subject's recoverable assets? No way. That's "PI" work—short for private investigator. Ditto goes for paralegals. Lawyers don't do the grunt work. Paralegals, also known as legal assistants, are the ones with the dirt under their nails.

To become a contract lawyer you must first be approved by the agencies' Washington offices. Most of the usual contracting and conflict of interest rules that apply to other contractors apply to lawyers as well—even more so. If your law firm or any of its partners or associates have been sued by the government for contributing to an S&L or bank failure, close the book right here. You are disqualified. Besides former officers and directors, the government is going out of its way to sue law firms and accountants that aided and abetted S&L and bank criminals.

All civil litigation work is approved by the RTC or FDIC in Washington. The consolidated offices do not play much of a role in overseeing civil litigation. Lawyers who specialize in real estate foreclosure matters and the seizing of assets will be subject to a certain degree of oversight from the closest consolidated office.

A note to minorities and women: If your law firm is 51 percent owned by a woman or minority, the RTC offers extra points toward qualifying you for government legal work. The RTC program for lawyers is called MWOLF, meaning your shop is a Minority or Woman Owned Law Firm. Most of the rules that apply to the MWOB program apply here.

CAN I GET A "STAFF" JOB WITH THE RTC OR FDIC IN MY AREA?

The news here isn't as promising. Staff jobs working directly for the RTC or FDIC are becoming harder to come by. As part of its effort to cut down on bureaucratic red tape, the RTC is trying to use as many private-sector firms as possible to manage and sell assets, eliminating the need for staff employees. Ditto for the FDIC.

If you're looking for S&L and bank cleanup related employment your best bet is to latch onto a firm that is already doing contract work for the government. Some government-approved contractors subcontract certain chores such as security jobs or construction. You can also form your own company and register with the RTC and FDIC to find work that way. (The irony of working for the RTC and FDIC in liquidations is that the better the job you do the quicker you'll be out of work.)

In March 1992 the RTC decided to cut more government red tape and announced plans to eliminate its four regional offices, while maintaining most of its fourteen consolidated offices. (Consolidated offices are localized to handle assets in their immediate region.) Stripping away another level of bureaucracy is good news for buyers of government-owned real estate and loans but not such good news for those looking for staff jobs. It's good news for SAMDA contractors, though, because stripping away another level of government increases the likelihood that more contractors will be used. (Choose your silver lining.)

The RTC currently has about seven thousand full-time employees. This includes its Washington staff and all of its field offices. In the hope of cutting down on red tape, the RTC will have consolidated its operations into six field offices nationwide by the end of 1993 (see our Yellow Pages). There will be ongoing job opportunities with the RTC due to attrition, and the RTC has authority to hire up to 2,000 more people if needed, though don't expect staffing to go much above current levels.

In the name of fiscal conservatism, the President and Congress do not want the RTC's staff to grow any more than it has to. Using more and more private contractors is the wave of the future. If anything, Congress wants the RTC to begin downsizing. When exactly that will happen is anyone's guess. On the positive side, more private contractors will be hired to do piecework for the RTC. This allows the RTC to get the job done without increasing permanent staff.

A word of warning: Congress hates the RTC with a passion. Because Congress—along with Presidents Bush and Reagan—created the S&L mess by deregulating the industry, it now wants nothing to do with the agency except to grandstand when it finds something wrong with it. (The last thing in the world you will see is a member of Congress saying what a great job the RTC is doing.)

Staff positions at both agencies pay well. Here's a sampling of job openings with the agencies in 1992:

Job Title	Agency	Salary Range
Associate Director of Resolutions (Washington, D.C.)	FDIC	$88,000 to $99,000
Site Sales Coordinator (Somerset, N.J.)	RTC	$77,000 to $88,000
Freedom of Information Act Specialist (Atlanta)	RTC	$41,000 to $53,000

See anything you like? There's plenty more, but as we said the job security isn't what it used to be. Your best bet for full-time employment with the agency is at a large consolidated office or at headquarters in Washington, D.C. That most likely means relocating. Now more than ever the two agencies are watching every nickel, and they are less likely to hire now than two years ago. Still, employees leave and must be replaced.

Both agencies hire Government Grade (GG) and Liquidation Grade (LG) employees. If you have a choice—and you probably won't—try to get a job as a GG employee. In five years both agencies will be downsizing, the RTC more than the FDIC. LGs (those more directly involved with liquidations) will be laid off first. GGs are less likely to be fired and are considered career employees who have the option of retiring with the agency if they so choose.

A lawyer likely can make more money in financial-institution-related work in the private sector, but the RTC and FDIC offer decent pay and excellent benefits, including paid medical and dental. A child care program is being considered as well. This is, after all, a government job.

REAL ESTATE AGENTS

The RTC already employs thousands of real estate agents across the country. These agents are given listings of RTC properties in their area to expose these properties to the open market. Realtors are paid a 5 percent sales commission if the property sells during the listing period.

To get on the RTC's list of approved real estate agents you must first fill out the RTC registration form and mail it back to Washington. After that is done you should call the consolidated office near you and make personal contact to let them know you are registered and eager to do a good job for them.

The RTC also uses real estate brokers when they need an independent assessment of value for a property. These "opinions of value" are issued by realtors rather than licensed appraisers, and the RTC will pay you for writing up such an opinion of value.

APPRAISERS

If you've read much of this book, you already know that the RTC's rules require it to perform *a lot* of appraising. To get all these appraisals done in a timely manner the RTC needs to hire private-sector appraisers. The government now requires appraisers doing work for federally insured financial institutions and federal agencies to be certified in the state in which they work. If you have not gotten your certification yet don't even apply to the RTC. Do that first, then fill out the RTC registration form and send it to Washington along with a copy of your state certification. Also contact your nearest consolidated office and make personal contact.

CERTIFIED PUBLIC ACCOUNTANTS

The RTC and FDIC use outside accountants to help analyze bids submitted in sealed-bid offerings. Accountants are hired to do net present value analysis of each bid and compare the results with other similar bids in order to advise the RTC and FDIC on which of similar bids offers the agency the most cash value.

LICENSED CONTRACTORS

Not all the properties the RTC and FDIC end up with are ready for the market. Some are projects that have either fallen into serious disrepair or were never completed to begin with. In such cases the RTC may decide it is in its best interest to complete the project before trying to market it and will hire a contractor to do the work. In other cases contractors are hired to simply maintain large projects while they are being marketed.

LAW ENFORCEMENT

The S&L scandal has created job opportunities for law enforcement officials. Approved by Congress and signed by President Reagan in 1982, S&L deregulation[6] legislation led to the white-collar looting of many of the nation's S&Ls. Real estate and loan scams that occurred as

[6] The S&L industry was deregulated by passage of the Garn–Germain Act of 1982. The landmark legislation allowed S&Ls to go outside their traditional turf of home mortgage lending. Many of the new powers granted facilitated risky and fraudulent lending.

far back as five years ago are just now being investigated by the Federal Bureau of Investigation and Justice Department. The statute of limitation on these cases runs for ten years.

Currently there are more than nine thousand open cases of S&L and bank fraud being pursued by the FBI and a backlog of some twenty-eight thousand criminal referrals yet to be investigated. If you're an accountant and don't want to work for the RTC or FDIC, try the FBI. Congress has allocated millions of extra dollars per year to prosecute S&L and bank wrongdoers. The FBI is literally drowning in bank fraud cases. If there was ever a career opportunity, this is it. Congress has allotted an additional $70 million to the FBI specifically targeted at bank fraud investigations. The agency is actively recruiting accountants and lawyers to follow paper trails and question suspects. The maximum age of applicants is thirty-five because the agency has a mandatory retirement age of fifty-five.

Special bank fraud task forces have already been formed in Boston, Dallas, Los Angeles, and Tampa. New task forces in other cities will be formed during the next two years. In particular New England, Southern California, and Washington, D.C., are expected to be "hot spots" for FBI hiring.

A FEW THINGS TO THINK ABOUT

As more banks fail, the FDIC's caseload of real estate and loans will grow as the RTC's declines. As we noted, the FDIC has its own liquidation staff and contractor network to handle its assets. Both agencies are moving toward employing more and more private contractors. If you are in real estate management or sales, no time has been better to land government work than now. Legal work is plentiful and available. If you like to sue people, working for the RTC or FDIC is a dream come true.

Because the FDIC regulates and insures banks (besides liquidating assets), it will always be around, but by law the RTC is scheduled to "sunset" by the end of the decade. Yes, the RTC will not be around forever—or will it? Even though Congress has shown nothing but animosity toward it, there has been talk in Washington of using the agency to liquidate other types of government assets. For instance, the RTC might be used to foreclose on delinquent Small Business Administration[7] loans, selling the collateral to the highest bidder. Or the RTC could be used to auction the nation's closed military installations. Or to sell real estate properties for HUD. Take your pick. This agency isn't dead yet.

IN SUMMARY

Job availability with the RTC will decline over the next three years because the agency is supposed to sell itself out of existence. But at the same time the FDIC will be forced to hire people to handle its still increasing caseloads as more and more troubled banks fail.

Physical assets such as hotels, homes, resorts, and office buildings deteriorate and need maintenance while the agencies seek a buyer. Contractors will be hired to handle such ongoing maintenance. Sometimes the properties will be incomplete and contractors will be hired to finish the work.

Accountants will be used to analyze bids, appraisers will be hired to set asking prices, and of course lawyers will be needed. Aren't they always.

---

[7] The Small Business Administration (SBA) is a government agency that loans money to start up businesses. When those businesses fail it's up to the government to collect on whatever collateral was posted for the loan.

Conclusion

• •

Now you know more than you ever thought you'd care to know about buying assets from failed banks, S&Ls, and HUD. The purpose of this book is to demystify the process and to unlock this opportunity for every size investor—from the average citizen with little to invest up to the wealthy entrepreneur or portfolio manager. After all, each of us is paying the tab for the disaster; we should all have an equal crack at profiting from it as well.

Of course the old adage "Those who got, am those who get" will continue to function despite this book. The rich will get richer off the bank and S&L mess—which, ironically, some of those very tycoons helped create. But never mind, life has never been fair and it's not getting any better. But the fat cats are not interested in the small properties that clutter the RTC and FDIC's portfolio. They will continue to gobble up the multimillion-dollar resorts, golf courses, hotels, apartment complexes, and shopping centers. That will leave the individual homes, building lots, small farms, small shops, duplexes, fourplexes, sixplexes, and so on for you. And since the big investors aren't buying these properties, the RTC, FDIC, and HUD have little choice but to deal with you.

These two giant bureaucracies—the FDIC and RTC—are forever reshuffling their organizational cards, so things will change from time to time. For example, just before publication the RTC decided to consolidate about ten of its small regional offices into larger consolidated offices. The FDIC will inevitably become more and more like the RTC as time goes on. If you call a number in our Yellow Pages only to find the number disconnected, call the main toll-free number and select the asset specific line. When the human being comes on the line tell him or her what you want and you'll be told what consolidated office to call. This isn't the purpose of the asset specific line, but it's the quickest way to get an answer. If that doesn't work you'll have to make a toll call to the RTC in Washington—Main Office, Public Affairs—202-416-7566.

And one last time—though this book may help you "get rich quick," we make no such claim. The deals are there, but you will work and work hard to get your hands on them. Those individuals we met who have bought several pieces of property from these agencies have dedicated nearly full time to the task, had ten disappointments for every success, and have almost thrown in the towel more than once. But they didn't. They kept calling, kept looking, and kept making bids, and eventually the law of averages worked in their favor. So think of this book as a tool chest—not a treasure chest.

Now it's up to you. You can sit around and complain about the mess politicians made of the economy, particularly the banks and thrifts, or get out there and take advantage of that mess. It's your choice—the cloud or the silver lining. Which will it be?

Good hunting and good luck!

Glossary of Terms

. . . .

(RTC and FDIC related terms in ***BOLD**.)

ACCELERATION CLAUSE: A clause in a loan document that allows the lender to call the note, requesting payment in full based on certain predefined guidelines.

ACCOMMODATION PARTY: A person who cosigns a loan but has no ownership rights.

ACKNOWLEDGMENT: A formal declaration made before a notary public or attorney by a person signing a document. The acknowledgment certifies that the person signing the document is indeed the person indicated as the signator. Acknowledgments are required on nearly all recorded documents.

AD VALOREM TAX: A tax levied by state and local governments on real estate. The tax is a factor of the value placed on the property by the taxing entity.

ADJUSTED COST BASIS: For tax purposes, adjusted cost basis is calculated by adding the amount paid for a property, plus the amount spent on improvements, less total depreciation taken against the property.

ADJUSTABLE RATE MORTGAGE (ARM): A mortgage on

which the interest rate varies based on a certain, predetermined index such as the Treasury yield.

*AFFORDABLE HOUSING PROGRAM: A special program in which the RTC must first offer all houses appraised at $67,500 or lower to low- and moderate-income home buyers. The FDIC has a similar program but has the discretion to raise the cap according to local housing prices. A low- to moderate-income home buyer makes 115 percent or less of an area's median income.

ALL-INCLUSIVE DEED OF TRUST: Also known as an all-inclusive mortgage, it "wraps" two or more mortgages against a property into one larger loan. See *Wrap-around Mortgage*.

ALTA TITLE INSURANCE POLICY: A comprehensive title insurance policy that protects the lender from unknown defects in title, such as mechanics' liens. ALTA is an abbreviation for American Land Title Association. Lenders generally require the borrower to pay the one-time cost for this coverage.

AMENITIES: Features that make a home or property desirable. A brick fireplace, a large backyard, good location, and a swimming pool all are amenities.

AMORTIZATION: A loan is considered amortizing if its payment schedule results in repayment of the loan, interest, and principal in equal installments over a set period of time.

ANNUAL PERCENTAGE RATE (APR): The true interest expense to the borrower per year. Federal law requires interest charged on loans to be disclosed as an annual percentage rate.

ANNUITY: A sum of money paid or received annually or at other fixed periods.

APPRAISAL: The estimate of a property's current market value. Also an estimate of value at a specified time or under specified circumstances.

*APPRAISED VALUE: As used by the RTC and FDIC, appraised value represents the most current value of an asset as reflected on a failed institution's balance sheet. In ordinary real estate terms the appraised value of a property is the value placed on it by a professional appraiser.

ASSESSED VALUE: Not to be confused with appraised value. The assessed value of a property is determined by a local tax assessor. It never equals the market value figure. Market value is almost always much greater than the assessed value. Buyers are forewarned that most assessors immediately reassess a property following its sale, raising the assessed value based on the new sales price. This results in increased property taxes.

*ASSET ACQUISITION DATE: Found on RTC and FDIC asset forms, it indicates the date the agency took the asset over from a failed institution.

*ASSET CODE: A three-digit number used by the FDIC and RTC to identify property taxes. The codes are used to choose the appropriate contractor or vendor to dispose of the property.

*ASSET LOCATION: The specific address of an asset (usually real estate), which is cataloged by the RTC by separate "fields" for street, city, county, state, and zip code. RTC asset searches on a personal computer can narrow a search by selecting any combination of these fields.

*ASSET NUMBER: Every individual asset acquired by the RTC is assigned its own asset number. Referring to an asset by its specific number assures that you and the RTC are talking about the same property.

*ASSET OWNERSHIP: On its asset forms the RTC breaks down ownership into several different types: 100 percent owned by the agency; sub-owned by a failed institution's affiliate; J/V-owned, meaning it was held by a joint venture in which the institution had a share; or other, for complex types of mixed ownership.

APPURTENANCE: Anything located on or belonging to the land: a building or road, for example.

ASSESSMENT: Fees placed on real property by local and county governments to pay for sewer, sidewalks, street lighting, roads, and other services. Some assessments are permanent, while others are one-time only charges called "special assessments."

ASSETS: Personal and real property owned.

ASSIGN: To transfer ownership or title in an asset to another party. When a person signs over his or her rights to a note, loan, or property, he or she "assigns" those rights to another.

ASSIGNEE: The person to whom title or ownership is transferred.

ASSIGNOR: The person transferring (giving up) the title or ownership.

ASSIGNMENT OF RENTS: Future rents from a piece of property can be assigned to a lender as additional security for a loan. Assignments are often added to the property's deed for security in the event of a default.

ASSUME: When a buyer accepts the loan obligations of the seller. When a buyer agrees to this he or she signs an assumption agreement with the lender acknowledging responsibility for the loan.

ATTORNEY IN FACT: Anyone legally authorized to conduct certain business in another's name.

*AVAIL: Abbreviation used on RTC and FDIC asset forms indicating that a property is still available.

*AUCT: Indicates that an RTC asset will be sold at auction.

BALANCE SHEET: A financial statement listing a person or company's assets and liabilities and showing net worth.

BALLOON PAYMENT: A short-term loan—usually five or seven years—on which the principal amount owed is due in one lump sum. Most payments on a balloon loan are interest only, with no principal paid.

BENEFICIARY: The person legally entitled to certain benefits. On a trust deed or note the beneficiary is a creditor (usually the lender) who is secured by the property.

BILL OF SALE: A document that transfers ownership or title of personal property in the same manner that a deed transfers title to real estate.

BLANKET MORTGAGE: A loan secured by more than one piece of property. Blanket mortgages or blanket loans often are used in subdivisions or when a certain property of a borrower is inadequate to secure a loan.

BOND: Both the government and corporations issue bonds. When a municipality issues a bond to pay for streets or other infrastructure costs, residents pay for the bonds through (usually) higher taxes.

*BOOK VALUE: The value of an asset as carried on the books of a financial institution. Book value may not equal market value, which may be higher. When the RTC and FDIC use this term they employ a narrow definition: "Gross value as of three months prior to the semiannual report date as stated on the trial balance sheet of the (failed) institution." (Go figure.)

BROKER: A person licensed by the state to sell real estate. Loan brokers offer mortgages to home buyers. Real estate brokers sell real estate.

*BULK: Indicates that the RTC has decided to include a particular asset in a bulk sale with other assets. Loans are often sold in this manner.

BUSINESS OPPORTUNITY: A legal term describing a business that is for sale. A business opportunity may or may not include real property. A business opportunity without real estate is appraised according to its income potential.

CALL: To declare a loan due and payable in full.

CAPITAL: Also called "net worth." A person or company's capital or net worth is calculated by adding all assets and subtracting all liabilities. The resulting figure is capital.

CAPITAL GAIN: The profit received after selling an asset (real estate, for example) after subtracting cost and improvements from the sales price.

CAPITALIZATION: A technique used to appraise income property by multiplying the estimated net income by an "x factor" representing the desired rate of return.

CASH FLOW: The difference between a property's total income and its total expenses, including mortgage payments. When the result is negative this is known as "negative cash flow."

CEASE AND DESIST ORDER: A legal order issued by the government ordering a property or business owner to cease an activity—such as polluting ground water. C&Ds, as they are known, are sometimes used when a property owner has violated zoning restrictions.

CERTIFICATE OF DISCHARGE: A written document signed by the lender discharging the security when the debt (loan or note) is satisfied. Also known as a release of mortgage.

CERTIFICATE OF SALE: A document issued to a buyer of property purchased at a court-ordered execution sale or judicial foreclosure. The holder can redeem it for a deed in the property if the owner of the property fails to redeem it within one year.

CHATTEL MORTGAGE: A mortgage on personal property (rather than real estate). Today the chattel mortgage has been largely replaced by security agreements.

CLOSING STATEMENT: A statement given to both buyer and seller by an attorney or escrow agent accounting for all monies involved in the sale, including fees, charges, cash down payments, and loans.

COLLATERAL: Any kind of property used to secure a loan.

*COMMERCIAL ASSET DESCRIPTION: RTC and FDIC data elements listed for commercial asset listings. This includes year built, land size, zoning, parking information, present rental or lease status, number of units, floors, elevators, and a short narrative description.

COMMITMENT: A promise by a lender to make a loan on a property. Commitments come in many forms: a firm commitment, a standby commitment, and a conditional commitment. A conditional commitment is a promise to make a loan if specified guidelines are met. A standby loan commitment is a written commitment made by a lender to fund a loan up to a certain limit if the borrower should need such a loan for a specified reason or property during a specified time period at predetermined terms.

COMMUNITY PROPERTY: Property jointly owned by a husband and wife. Community property does not belong to one or the other but to both.

COMPOUND INTEREST: Interest calculated on the outstanding principal and interest already accumulated.

CONDEMNATION: The government has the power to condemn private property under a variety of circumstances. This is called the "power of eminent domain." When the government condemns a property it takes it for some public purpose, such as the construction of a highway.

CONDITIONAL SALE CONTRACT: A contract in which the seller retains title to the property until the full purchase price is paid.

CONDOMINIUM: Ownership in a single unit or apartment with shared ownership in common areas, such as swimming pool, lawns, and parking areas.

*CONSERVATORSHIP: An S&L or bank that has been taken over by the government but remains open to the public. Conservatorships are considered "wards" of the government. Even though it is insolvent, a conservatorship still makes loans and takes deposits. Conservatorships are run by government-appointed managers.

CONSIDERATION: In real estate, consideration is another term for money or something else of value given to induce another to enter into a contract.

*CONSOLIDATED OFFICE: A localized office of the RTC or FDIC. One consolidated office covers many states. The RTC's mid-Atlantic consolidated office, for instance, sells assets in Georgia, Maryland, North Carolina, South Carolina, Tennessee, Virginia, West Virginia, and Washington, D.C.

CONSTRUCTION LOAN: A construction loan is a short-term loan that generally lasts for a year or so. Once the building is complete, the lender, or another party, replaces the construction loan with long-term financing, called a "take out loan."

CONTINGENCY: Any condition placed on a contract. Contingencies must be met before a contract becomes binding.

CONVENTIONAL LOAN: A loan made without government insurance or government guarantees.

CONVEYANCE: A document that transfers title or some other interest in property.

COOPERATIVE APARTMENT: A "co-op" is an investment in which the buyer owns a share in an apartment house and the right to occupy, rent, or resell a specific apartment unit or units.

COSIGNER: A person, not the borrower, who also signs on a note, thereby accepting joint responsibility for its repayment. A cosigner is used when the borrower's income or assets are not enough to qualify or secure the desired loan.

COST APPROACH: An appraisal technique that uses the cost of replacement to determine the value of a property.

COVENANT: A promise in a contract. Covenants and conditions

are often also part of a subdivision approval and bind future owners.

CREATIVE FINANCING: When a property cannot be sold through conventional means the buyer and seller often find creative ways to close the deal—such as having the seller carry the loan and then selling the loan to an investor later. The permutations are endless. If you resort to creative financing to buy or sell a property you may want to consult an attorney.

CREDITOR: The person to whom a debt is owed.

*CULTURAL VALUE: Some RTC properties are considered to have special cultural value. To attain this classification a property must have been built before 1941 and have some special significance to U.S. history, architecture, archeology, engineering, or culture.

*DATE OF CONSTRUCTION: The RTC and FDIC include approximate dates or construction on all their improved property asset forms.

DEBENTURES: Bonds not secured by mortgages or liens.

DEBT SERVICE: The amount of money the buyer will need each month to make interest or interest and principal payments on a loan.

DEBTOR: The person who owes a debt.

DEED: That instrument that transfers title in property from one person to another.

DEED OF RECONVEYANCE: A deed of trust that releases a lien once the loan is paid in full, conveying full title.

DEED OF TRUST: Transfers title in a property to a trustee who holds it until the loan is paid in full.

DEFAULT: Failure to repay an obligation or perform as agreed.

DEFERRED MAINTENANCE: Maintenance and repairs on a

property that are required but not completed. A lot of RTC properties suffer from some degree of deferred maintenance.

DEFICIENCY JUDGMENT: A court-ordered judgment for obligations not fully covered by the sale of the underlying security.

DEPARTMENT OF HOUSING AND URBAN DEVELOPMENT (HUD): A federal agency created to promote affordable housing. HUD also oversees the Federal Housing Administration, which insures mortgages for low- and moderate-income home buyers. HUD forecloses on delinquent FHA loans and sells the underlying collateral—a house.

DEPOSIT RECEIPT: A document used by real estate agents that functions as a temporary contract for the purchase and sale of real estate.

DEPRECIATION: The loss of value in an asset for any reason. Depreciation is a concern to income property owners who use it as a tax reduction tool.

DISCOUNT: Buying a note for less than its current unpaid balance is called buying a note at discount. Doing so can greatly increase the note's effective rate of return for the buyer.

DISCOUNT POINTS: Points or fees are charged by lenders to either offset a low interest rate or to boost the loan's effective yield. One point represents one percent of the principal amount of the loan.

DISCOUNT RATE: The interest rate charged by the Federal Reserve Bank for money borrowed by its members (banks). When the discount rate decreases it allows banks to lower rates for home loans and other consumer credit.

DUE-ON-SALE CLAUSE: A clause in a loan contract that allows the lender to require that a loan be paid in full when the property collateralizing it is sold.

*DUE DILIGENCE PACKAGE: A package of documents distributed by the RTC or its asset managers that gives bidders detailed information about a loan or piece of real estate.

EASEMENT: An interest one piece of property has in another property for a specified use. For example, a parcel may require a road or "right of way" through an adjoining parcel.

ECONOMIC LIFE: The period of time over which a property will yield a return on an investment.

ECONOMIC OBSOLESCENCE: When certain properties, particularly commercial and industrial properties, lose value over time due to decreased desirability or usefulness.

EFFECTIVE AGE: A judgment of age determined by the condition of a property rather than its chronological age. A poorly built "young" building can have a higher effective age than a well-built older structure.

EFFECTIVE INTEREST RATE: The actual interest rate paid by a borrower.

ELIGIBLE SINGLE-FAMILY PROPERTY: A home that is a one- to four-family property. Five or more units connotes multi-family status.

EMINENT DOMAIN: See *Condemnation*.

ENCUMBER: To place obligations (encumbrances) against a piece of property.

ENCUMBRANCE: Anything that limits the ownership in a property. This includes loans secured by the property, liens, easements, or any kind of restriction that runs (remains with) the property.

ENDORSEMENT: The signature on the back of a note or check that transfers ownership.

EQUITABLE TITLE: A state of ownership the buyer possesses

after he or she has contracted to buy a property but before legal title has been conveyed.

EQUITY PARTICIPATION: When a lender takes partial ownership in a project on which it lends.

EQUITY: The value of the owner's interest in excess of all debt against a property.

ESCALATION CLAUSE: A clause in a loan that calls for the interest to increase over a period of time.

ESCROW: Payments and fees on a piece of property that are temporarily held until certain conditions are met—such as the sale of a piece of property. In the past attorneys acted as "escrow agents" in real estate transactions. Today this service is mostly performed by escrow and title companies.

EXTENSION AGREEMENT: An agreement to extend the original terms of a contract. For example, an extension may be granted by a lender extending the term of a loan. A seller may extend a sales contract, extending the time allowed for the deal to close.

*FEDERAL DEPOSIT INSURANCE CORPORATION (FDIC): The regulatory agency and insurance fund that oversees the nation's banks. The FDIC administers the Bank Insurance Fund (BIF) and Savings Association Insurance Fund (SAIF), which insure deposits at banks and S&Ls up to $100,000 per account.

FEDERAL HOME LOAN MORTGAGE CORPORATION (FHLMC): Also known as Freddie Mac. Chartered by Congress, the publicly owned company buys mortgages in the "secondary" market from banks, mortgage bankers, and S&Ls. An extremely profitable company, it occasionally sells foreclosed homes.

FEDERAL HOUSING ADMINISTRATION (FHA): A government agency charged with insuring loans for low- and moderate-income home buyers.

FEDERAL NATIONAL MORTGAGE ASSOCIATION: Also

known as Fannie Mae. Like Freddie Mac, Fannie Mae buys loans from banks, S&Ls, and mortgage bankers. It too is quite profitable but occasionally forecloses on homes and sells them.

*FF&E: "Furniture, Fixtures & Equipment"—property seized from failed banks and S&Ls and auctioned to the highest bidder.

FIDUCIARY: A person in a position of trust. An attorney has a fiduciary responsibility to the client, for example.

FINANCE CHARGE: Points, interest, and other fees paid in connection with a loan. Truth-in-lending laws require that lenders inform all borrowers in advance about all charges associated with a mortgage.

FINANCIAL STATEMENT: A complete accounting of a person's assets and liabilities. A financial statement is reflective of a person's financial condition.

FINANCING STATEMENT: A document filed with a county recorder or secretary of state giving notice that a security interest exists on a specified property.

FINDER'S FEE: A fee paid to someone who locates for another a desired property or who brings a buyer to a seller. The fee is generally a percentage of the sales price and is paid upon consummation of the sale.

FIXTURE: When a building is sold it is sold with fixtures. Fixtures are anything attached to the building. Unattached items are considered personal property.

FORECLOSURE: When a lender takes control of a property through a legal action. The RTC and FDIC often foreclose on delinquent loans to secure the underlying collateral—usually real estate.

FORECLOSURE SALE: When the trustee for the lender sells a foreclosed property at auction. The lender can bid on the outstanding balance in order to seize control of the property.

FORFEITURE: The loss of a right or interest because of default.

FREE AND CLEAR: To owe nothing on a property is to own it free and clear.

GOVERNMENT NATIONAL MORTGAGE ASSOCIATION (GNMA): A government agency that buys from lenders loans insured by the VA and FHA.

GRANT: To transfer real property. See *Grant Deed*.

GRANT DEED: Deed which transfers ownership in Real Estate.

GRANTEE: The person to whom property is granted.

GRANTOR: The person granting or conveying a property.

GROSS INCOME: Total income before expenses.

GROSS RENT MULTIPLIER: A rule-of-thumb method to determine the approximate value of a rental property. Ask a local realtor for the current gross multiplier and then multiply gross rents by that number. The resulting figure should approximate the value of the property.

GROUND LEASE: A long-term lease on vacant land. Ground leases are made with the understanding that the tenant will build on the site.

GROUND RENT: Rent charged on a ground lease.

HARD MONEY: Cash loaned, as opposed to credit extended, which is called soft money.

HAZARD INSURANCE: Insurance covering a property against damage. A lender always requires the borrower to carry insurance for at least the amount owed.

HOLDER IN DUE COURSE: A person who takes possession of a negotiable instrument, such as a note in good faith.

HYPOTHECATION: Putting up property, real or personal, as security for a loan without giving up possession.

IMPOUND ACCOUNT: An account set up as a trust account by the lender to collect monies needed to pay taxes and insurance on a property.

*INAC: An RTC abbreviation, it indicates that a property is currently inactive or not available for sale at this time.

- **INCOME APPROACH:** A way to appraise income properties by capitalizing their income.

INCOME RATIO: A ratio of the borrower's income and housing expense. Used by lenders to determine eligibility.

INSTALLMENT NOTE: A note that is paid off in regular installments.

INSTALLMENT SALE: A method of selling property by spreading out the gain or profit over many years for income tax purposes.

INSTITUTIONAL LENDER: A lender that originates loans. Banks, savings and loans, and credit unions are all institutional lenders.

JOINT NOTE: A note that has two or more signatories who share liability.

JOINT VENTURE: When two or more people join together in a single project for profit. Unlike a partnership, a joint venture is created for investment in a single project only.

JUDGMENT: A decision made by a court. Usually the term applies to monies payable from one party to another.

JUNIOR LIEN: A loan secured by a property that already has a loan against it. The new loan is then referred to as a "second mortgage." A junior lien is subordinate to the senior, or first, mortgage.

LAND CONTRACT: A contract between a buyer and seller. The buyer contracts to pay the purchase price in regular installments. The seller contracts to sign over legal title of the property when the full purchase price has been paid.

LATE CHARGE: A penalty fee charged a borrower when the monthly payment is late.

LEASEHOLD: A property interest created by a lease agreement.

LEGAL DESCRIPTION: A description of a given property as it appears in county records.

LESSEE: The tenant under a lease agreement.

LESSOR: The landlord under a lease agreement.

LEVERAGE: A method of investing whereby the investor uses money borrowed at rates lower than the effective income a property can produce.

LIEN: An unpaid obligation against a property. Liens can be filed against a property by unpaid contractors or others with a valid claim. A court judgment is a lien.

LIEN RELEASE: A document signed by a lienholder releasing the property from the lien.

LIMITED PARTNERSHIP: A legal partnership consisting of different investors and managed by one "general" partner. Limited partnerships often are formed to invest in real estate or other businesses.

LIQUIDATION: The complete sale of a business or asset during which everything connected to that asset is sold. Insolvent S&Ls are often liquidated by the government.

*LIST PRICE: The asking price in U.S. dollars of an RTC or FDIC asset. If the RTC or FDIC has not completed its appraisal, "TBD" (to be determined) will be typed next to "Listing Price."

LOAN BROKER: Brokers who find lenders for borrowers and receive a fee for the service.

LOAN COMMITTEE: A committee at an institutional lender that reviews and approves loan applications.

LOAN CORRESPONDENT: A loan broker or agent used by a non-local lender to originate loans in a certain area.

LOAN PACKAGE: The file of documents created by, and required in, the loan approval process. Documents include the loan application, the appraisal, financial statements, and employment verifications.

LOAN-TO-VALUE RATIO: The value of the loan as a percentage of a property's price. On new loans the down payment is subtracted from the purchase price to achieve a loan-to-value ratio. When a buyer makes a 20 percent down payment the loan-to-value is said to be 80 percent. Most lenders prefer 20 percent down but will accept less if a borrower takes out a private mortgage insurance policy.

LOCK-IN CLAUSE: A clause in a mortgage that prohibits the early repayment of a loan.

*LOW- AND MODERATE-INCOME HOME BUYERS: Home buyers who earn 115 percent or less of an area's median income, the median being the point where half the people earn more and half earn less. Low- and moderate-income buyers are eligible to purchase homes from the RTC and FDIC's Affordable Housing Programs.

MAI: A professional designation for appraisers. The letters stand for Member American Institute.

MARKET PRICE: The price paid for a property on the open market by a buyer without regard to motives, market pressures, or sophistication.

MECHANIC'S LIEN: A judgment filed by a contractor to encumber a property. Mechanics' liens are filed to ensure that a contractor is paid in full. If a lien is on a house, then that home cannot be sold. When the contractor is paid, the lien is removed.

*MEDIAN HOME PRICE: The middle point where half the homes cost more and half less.

*MEDIAN INCOME: The middle point where half the people make more and half make less.

*MINORITY OR WOMAN OWNED BUSINESS (MWOB): Companies that are 51 percent minority or woman owned. MWOBs receive special consideration when bidding on RTC contracts.

*MINORITY OR WOMAN OWNED LAW FIRM (MWOLF): Same as above but for law firms.

MORTGAGE: A lien or note secured by real property—a home or office building, for example.

MORTGAGE BANKER/MORTGAGE COMPANY: A person or company that originates mortgages but does not take deposits. A mortgage company is usually "funded" by a bank or a group of investors and then immediately sells the loans into the secondary mortgage market.

MORTGAGE POOL: More than one mortgage. A series of mortgages make up a mortgage pool. Also known as a loan pool.

MORTGAGEE: The person (lender) to whom the mortgage is given.

MORTGAGOR: The borrower or person who executes the mortgage.

*MULTIFAMILY PROPERTY (MFH): FDIC and RTC-speak for an apartment building with five or more units.

NARRATIVE APPRAISAL: A descriptive appraisal that divulges details about a property, its amenities, and the reasoning behind those values.

*NATURAL VALUE: Properties considered by the RTC to have natural values or environmental or cultural significance. These include natural landmarks, wilderness areas, wildlife refuges, and wetlands, among others.

NEGOTIABLE INSTRUMENT: A check is a negotiable instrument. So is a note. Negotiable instruments can be transferred (sold) to others who then obtain their benefits.

NET SPENDABLE INCOME: That which is left from gross income after operating expenses, loan payments, and taxes are deducted.

NET WORTH: The financial worth of an individual after liabilities are deducted from gross assets.

NOMINAL INTEREST RATE: The interest rate that appears on the note or loan documents. Not to be confused with an "effective" or "true" interest rate, it does not include fees and points and other actual costs charged to the borrower.

NONJUDICIAL FORECLOSURE: A foreclosure that is effected without recourse to the courts. A foreclosure under a trust deed, which is carried out by the trustee, is a nonjudicial foreclosure.

NONPERFORMING LOAN: A mortgage that is not current—the borrower is behind in payments. Also known as a delinquent loan.

NOTARY PUBLIC: A public official who is empowered to witness signatures and administer oaths. Most recorded documents need to be signed before a notary.

NOTE: A promise to repay a loan. In a note the borrower promises to pay the beneficiary a set amount of money over a set period of time.

NOTICE OF DEFAULT: A notice filed by a lender, declaring a loan in default. Before a lender can foreclose and sell the property the notice must be published in a general circulation and the borrower informed.

OBLIGEE: The person to whom a legal obligation is owed.

OBLIGOR: The person who owes another person a legal obligation.

OFFEREE: The person to whom an offer is made.

OFFEROR: The person making an offer.

ORIGINATION FEE: A fee paid by a borrower to the lender to obtain a mortgage.

OWNER-OCCUPIED UNIT: A home or condo unit in which the mortgagor actually lives (as opposed to renting it out.)

PARTIAL RECONVEYANCE: A reconveyance that releases part of a property or subdivision as security for a loan.

PARTICIPATION: Certificates that sell like securities. Each certificate represents an interest (a participation) in a loan or venture.

PAYEE: The person to whom a note is payable.

PAYOR: The person who agrees to pay on a note. (Also known as the "maker.")

*PARTICIPATION STATUS: Often banks and S&Ls sell part of large commercial loans to other institutions in order to spread out the risk. These parts are called participations. Sometimes participations are sold in large joint venture projects. The RTC and FDIC indicate the participation status of an asset as "LD" for lead participation or "JR" for junior participation.

*PEND: Indicates that there is a pending sale on a specific asset. A pending sale is not a sale. Many pending sales fall apart before they can close. So if you are interested in a particular property that is listed as "pend," keep in touch with the RTC or FDIC until the sale closes.

PERFORMANCE BOND: A bond posted by a contractor that guarantees completion of a project according to pre-agreed-upon conditions.

PERSONAL PROPERTY: Property that is not real property. Personal property is movable and is also called "chattel."

*PITA LOANS: Pain-in-the-ass loans—usually small or odd loans that are difficult for the RTC or FDIC to service. The government wants to get rid of these as soon as possible.

PMI: Private Mortgage Insurance.

POINT: One percent of the principal amount of a loan charged by the lender to increase the effective interest rate of the loan. Points are charged when a loan is made or renewed.

POWER OF ATTORNEY: A document authorizing one person to act for another.

POWER-OF-SALE CLAUSE: The clause in a trust deed mortgage that gives the trustee authority to sell a property that is security for a loan in the event of default.

PRELIMINARY TITLE REPORT: A report, generally required by lenders, that shows the condition of a property's title, including all liens.

PREPAYMENT CLAUSE: A clause in a mortgage that allows the borrower to pay the loan off before its due date without penalty.

PREPAYMENT PENALTY: A clause in a mortgage that charges the borrower a penalty for paying a loan off early.

PRIVATE MORTGAGE INSURANCE: An insurance policy taken out by a borrower to insure that he or she will not default on a high loan-to-value ratio mortgage.

PROGRESSION: An appraisal concept that says a building of lower value can be increased in value by its proximity to a higher-quality building.

PROMISSORY NOTE: A promise to pay back a specified loan amount on specified terms at a specified time. This note may be secured or unsecured. If secured by real estate it will be secured by a trust deed.

*PROPERTY CONDITION: The FDIC and RTC describe on their asset lists a property's physical condition. The condition is listed as P for poor, F for fair, G for good, and E for excellent. On newly acquired assets this information may not be available. In such cases the agencies may default to a simple n/a rating.

PRORATION: If you buy a property three months into a tax year the property taxes will be "prorated" to reflect this. The seller will pay for the three months of the year it owned the property and you will pay for the remaining nine months. This is how prorating works. It applies to many period costs associated with a property. Not only taxes can be prorated, but loan payments, insurance, annual condo maintenance fees, and so on.

PURCHASE MONEY DEED OF TRUST: This is a mortgage. In some states, such as California, the law protects a borrower from "deficiency judgments" when money is borrowed under a purchase money deed of trust to buy real estate.

QUIET TITLE ACTION: For many reasons a property's chain of title may have a "cloud" over it. This means that somewhere along the line of ownership somebody either forgot to file a document clearing an old loan or easement or ownership. The people who need to sign to clear up such a defect may be long dead or otherwise unavailable. To clear up such a cloud on title you file a court action called a "quiet title action." You should require the seller to do this at his or her expense before you buy the property. Lenders will not loan on a property with a defective title.

REAL ESTATE SETTLEMENT PROCEDURES ACT: Professionals refer to this federal law simply as RESPA. The law requires a number of things and forbids others. For example, it forbids lenders paying realtors kickbacks for sending borrowers to them. It also requires lenders to provide borrowers with specific information about their loan.

REAL ESTATE INVESTMENT TRUST: An investment fund collateralized by real estate or loans. The RTC plans to offer REITs to investors beginning sometime in 1993.

REALTOR: Another name for a real estate broker.

RECAPTURE: The time it takes for an investor to "recapture" an initial investment in income property.

*RECEIVERSHIP: An RTC receivership consists solely of all assets from a failed S&L or bank that have been slated for liquidation. Receiverships are closed to the public and, unlike conservatorships, do not take deposits.

RECONVEYANCE DEED: When you pay off a note secured by a trust deed, the lender files a "deed of reconveyance." This reconveys the title in the property from the trustee to you and acknowledges to the public record that the loan has been paid in full.

RECORDATION: Any document recorded for the public record at the county recorder's office.

REDEMPTION: When a property is foreclosed on, the owner has a "redemption period"—a period of time during which he or she can bring the loan current, including penalties, and redeem the property.

REFINANCE: To take out a new mortgage on an existing property that you already own.

REGRESSION: The opposite of progression. If you build an expensive house in a neighborhood where other homes cost less, the other homes reduce the value of your home.

REINSTATEMENT: Curing a default under a deed of trust.

RELEASE CLAUSE: A clause in a deed of trust that allows for the release of portions of a property upon the meeting of specified conditions. Release clauses are often used in subdivisions.

RELEASE OF MORTGAGE: Also called a "certificate of discharge." It releases a lien or mortgage on a property.

REPLACEMENT COST: An estimate of what it would cost to reproduce an existing structure. Replacement cost is used as part of the appraisal process.

REQUEST FOR PROPOSAL (RFP): A notice sent by the FDIC to registered thirty-party contractors when the agency solicits work that it cannot do in house. The RTC equivalent is an SOS, or solicitation of services.

REQUEST FOR RECONVEYANCE: A request made by a

trustee under a deed of trust for a reconveyance from the lender when a loan is repaid.

*RESOLUTION TRUST CORPORATION (RTC): The federal agency created by Congress in 1989 to resolve and sell the nation's insolvent S&Ls (thrifts). RTC assets are overseen and sold by its fourteen consolidated offices.

*RTC CONTRACTOR OR ASSET MANAGER: A third-party, nongovernment company that performs contract work for the RTC or FDIC—usually real estate or loan managers. Also known as a "contract agent."

*RTCNET: The RTC's on-line computer data base. Anyone with a personal computer can access information on available real estate and loans.

*SAMDA: Standard asset management and disposition agreement.

*SAMDA CONTRACTOR: Thirty-party contractors that manage and sell real estate and loans for the government are known as SAMDA contractors.

*SAMA: Standard asset management agreement.

*SAMA CONTRACTOR: SAMA contractors are paid only to manage, not sell, RTC assets.

SALE-LEASEBACK: When a property owner sells his or her property and then leases it back from the new owner.

SATISFACTION: When a party to a contract performs on all terms of the contract, the party is said to have "satisfied" his or her obligation.

*SCIENTIFIC VALUE: RTC properties of scientific significance or archeological importance.

SEASONED LOAN: A loan that is more than five years old is considered seasoned. Most have a steady payment history and are desirable to companies that service loans.

SECONDARY FINANCING: A junior loan, usually a second mortgage.

SECURITY: Collateral that is pledged to secure a loan.

SECURITY AGREEMENT: A document securing interest in personal, rather than real, property.

SECURITY DEPOSIT: A sum of money put up by a tenant to secure the condition of the property or terms of a lease.

SHORT-FORM APPRAISAL: An appraisal that uses a check-off sheet rather than a running commentary.

SIGNATURE LOAN: A loan secured only by a borrower's signature.

SIMPLE INTEREST: Interest paid only on the principal, not on accrued interest already paid or owed—as opposed to compound interest.

SOCIAL OBSOLESCENCE: Also known as "economic obsolescence." Refers to a structure that has outlived its social or economic usefulness. A blacksmith's shop would be a good example.

SOFT MONEY LOAN: When a portion of the loan is held by the seller to facilitate the sale of a property. If the seller provides cash it as known as a hard money loan.

*SOLICITATION OF SERVICES (SOS): A notice sent to registered third-party contractors when the RTC needs work done by a private management firm—usually for real estate or loan management services. (See Standard Asset Management Disposition Agreement and Request for Proposal.)

*SPEC: An RTC abbreviation on property listings that indicates that a particular asset has "special significance," meaning it could be environmentally sensitive or have some type of cultural or scientific value.

STRAIGHT NOTE: A note under which the principal amount is due in a lump sum at a specified time rather than in periodic payments.

SUBJECT TO: If you acquire a property with existing financing, then you are acquiring the property "subject to" existing obligations. A property may be subject to many forms of encumbrances, such as easements, besides financing.

SUBORDINATE: If you have a first loan on a property and agree to allow the buyer to bring a new first loan in front of your loan, you have agreed to "subordinate" your loan to the new one. Your loan will still be secured by the property but will be junior to the new first.

SUBSTITUTION: An appraisal term that says if you have two identical properties the one sporting the lowest price will receive the greatest demand. The buyer will "substitute" the cheaper one for the more expensive property.

SUBSTITUTION OF MORTGAGOR: Where a lender agrees to allow a buyer to assume an existing loan.

TAKE-OUT LOAN: Permanent financing for a property. A construction loan is a short-term loan. When a property is completed the owner then seeks long-term financing, called a take-out loan.

TAX-FREE EXCHANGE: If you sell a property at a profit you will be taxed on that profit as ordinary income. But if you swap the property for one of a "like kind" (an apartment house, for example), you will not be taxed on the exchange value.

TERM: The length of a loan, contract, or lease.

TERMINATION STATEMENT: A release of lien on personal property.

TIMESHARE: Instead of owning a property outright, timeshares allow you to own anywhere from two weeks to two months of a single unit—usually an apartment unit. These apply strictly to resort and vacation properties.

THRIFT INSTITUTION: Another name for an S&L.

TITLE INSURANCE: Protects the buyer and lender against unknown defects in title.

TRADING ON EQUITY: Borrowing against a property at rates lower than your anticipated net income from the property.

TRUSTEE: A person who holds title to real property until the loan is paid off.

TRUSTEE'S SALE: The sale of a property at foreclosure under a trust deed.

TRUSTOR: The person conveying property to a trustee.

UNLAWFUL DETAINER ACTION: A legal action taken to quickly recover possession of real property. It is used by landlords, for example, when a tenant fails to pay rent and refuses to leave.

VETERAN'S ADMINISTRATION LOAN: A loan backed by the Veteran's Administration. The government guarantee is reflected by a lower interest rate.

VARIABLE INTEREST RATE: Same as an Adjustable Rate Mortgage. The interest rate increases or decreases according to a predetermined index.

VESTING OF TITLE: Taking or receiving title to a property.

VOLUNTARY LIEN: A lien placed against a property intentionally by its owner to secure an obligation.

WAIVE: To give up something. To waive a right or privilege.

WRAP-AROUND LOAN: A loan in which two or more mortgages—usually a seasoned loan and a newer one—encumber a property and are wrapped into one. This is often done when a seller does not want to pay off a first mortgage because it may carry a big prepayment penalty. Instead the seller creates a new loan, leaving the old one intact. The seller continues to make payments on the first from payments he or she receives from the buyer on the new note.

YIELD: The interest rate earned by a lender on a mortgage. It also applies to the interest rate an investor receives on a note or investment.

Yellow Pages

· ·

THE RESOLUTION TRUST CORPORATION

Resolution Trust Corporation, Washington, D.C.
(Main headquarters)
801 17th St. N.W.
Washington, D.C. 20434

(202) 416-7600
(202) 416-7566 (public affairs)

CONSOLIDATED AND REGIONAL OFFICES OF THE RTC (AS OF 1/93)

Western Region

Intermountain Consolidated Office
1515 Arapahoe St.
Tower 3, Suite 800
Denver, CO 80202

(303) 556-6500
(303) 556-6552 (FAX)

Territory: Utah, Colorado, New Mexico

Central Western Consolidated Office
2910 North 44th Street
Phoenix, AZ 85018

(602) 224-1766
(602) 954-9059 (FAX)

Territory: Arizona, Nevada

Coastal Consolidated Office
400 MacArthur Blvd.
Newport Beach, CA 92660

(714) 852-7700
(714) 852-7775 (FAX)

Territory: California, Hawaii

Southwestern Region

Gulf Coast Consolidated Office
2223 West Loop South
Houston, TX 77027

(713) 888-2700
(713) 888-2720 (FAX)

North Central Region

Minneapolis Consolidated Office
3400 Yankee Drive
4th Floor
Eagan, MN 55122

(612) 683-4400
(612) 683-0858 (FAX)

Territory: Alaska, Idaho, Iowa, Minnesota, Montana, Oregon, Nebraska, North Dakota, South Dakota, Washington, Wisconsin, Wyoming

Kansas City Consolidated Office
Board of Trade Building II
4900 Main Street
Kansas City, MO 64112

(816) 531-2212
(816) 531-3017 (FAX)

Territory: Arkansas, Kansas, Missouri

Chicago Consolidated Office
25 Northwest Point Blvd.
Elk Grove Village, IL 60007

(708) 806-7750
(708) 806-7789 (FAX)

Territory: Kentucky, Illinois, Indiana, Michigan, Ohio

Consolidated Offices of the Eastern Region

Northeast Consolidated Office
Valley Forge Corporate Center
1000 Adams Avenue
Valley Forge, PA 19482

(215) 650-8500
(215) 650-8550 (FAX)

Territory: Connecticut, Maine, Massachusetts, New Hampshire, New Jersey, New York, Pennsylvania, Rhode Island, Vermont

Mid-Atlantic Consolidated Office
Colony Square
Building 100, Suite 2300
Atlanta, GA 30361

(404) 881-4840
(404) 881-4999 (FAX)

Territory: Alabama, District of Columbia, Georgia, Maryland, North
Carolina, South Carolina, Tennessee, Virginia, West Virginia

Metropolitan Consolidated Office
300 Davidson Ave.
Somerset, NJ 08873

(908) 805-4000
(908) 805-5986 (FAX)

Territory: Metropolitan New York, New Jersey

NATIONAL RTC AND REGIONAL SALES CENTERS

The RTC has centralized sales centers that provide investors with
information and assistance on large commercial properties and loan
sales and auctions.

National Sales Center
1133 21st Street, N.W.
Washington, D.C. 20036

(202) 416-4200

RTC consolidated offices in Baton Rouge, Eagan, Elk Grove,
Kansas City, Phoenix, Tampa, and Valley Forge also function as
regional sales centers where large loan and real estate auctions take
place.

Additional Sales Center Locations

Houston Sales Center
10000 Memorial Drive
Houston, TX 77024

(800) 879-8492

Dallas (Southwestern) Regional Sales Center
300 North Ervay
24th Floor
Dallas, TX 75201

(214) 953-4673

Denver (Western Regional) Sales Center
1225 17th St.
Suite 3200
Denver, CO 80202

(303) 291-5700
(303) 556-6500

RTC AFFORDABLE HOUSING CONTACTS

The following telephone numbers are for RTC affordable housing specialists who work out of the agency's regional and consolidated offices. These specialists will tell you what properties are being offered for sale and whether you qualify for any of the available units. They also can inform you about the different types of financing that are available.

Arizona
(602) 224-1776 (Phoenix)
(800) 937-7782

California
(714) 631-8600 (Costa Mesa)
(800) 283-9288

Colorado
(303) 556-6500 (Denver)
(800) 873-5815

Florida
(813) 870-7000 (Tampa)
(800) 283-1241

Georgia
(404) 225-5600 (Atlanta)
(800) 628-4362

Illinois
(708) 806-7750 (Elk Grove Village)
(800) 526-7521

Louisiana
(504) 339-1000 (Baton Rouge)
(800) 477-8790

Minnesota
(612) 683-4400 (Eagan)
(800) 873-5815

Missouri
(816) 531-2212 (Kansas City)
(800) 365-3342

New Jersey
(908) 805-4000 (Somerset)
(800) 431-0600

Oklahoma
(918) 587-7600 (Tulsa)
(800) 456-5382

Pennsylvania
(215) 650-8500 (Norristown)
(800) 782-6326

Texas
Dallas
(214) 443-2300
(800) 782-4674

Houston
(713) 888-2700
(800) 782-4221

San Antonio
(512) 524-4700
(800) 388-4254

Washington, D.C. (RTC Main Headquarters)
801 17th St.
6th Floor
Washington, D.C. 20434

(202) 416-6995
(202) 416-7219

"QUICK-DEX": COMMONLY CALLED RTC TELEPHONE NUMBERS

National Sales Center, Washington, D.C. (202) 416-4200

Real Estate Information Center and Orders for Asset Inventory (800) 431-0600

Asset Specific Inquiry Service (800) 732-3006

Bulk Sales Information (800) 782-8806

Sales of Mortgage and Investment Securities (202) 416-7544

Office of Third Party Contracts (800) 541-1782

Contracting Information Packets (202) 416-6940

Office of Contractor Oversight (202) 416-7592

Contract Administration (202) 416-2192

Low Income and Affordable Housing Information (202) 416-7348

Public Affairs and Media (202) 416-7566

FEDERAL DEPOSIT INSURANCE CORPORATION

Like the RTC, the FDIC has regional offices, and each regional office also has its own "consolidated" offices.

REGIONAL OFFICES OF THE FDIC

Chicago Regional Office (Alabama, Arkansas, Delaware, District of Columbia, Florida, Georgia, Illinois, Indiana, Iowa, Kansas, Kentucky, Louisiana, Maryland, Michigan, Minnesota, Mississippi, Missouri, Nebraska, North Carolina, North Dakota, Ohio, South Carolina, South Dakota, Tennessee, Virginia, West Virginia, Wisconsin)
30 South Wacher Drive
32nd Floor
Chicago, IL 60606

(312) 207-0200

Dallas Regional Office (Oklahoma, Texas)
1910 Pacific Ave. #1700
Dallas, TX 75201

(214) 754-0098

New York Regional Office (Connecticut, Maine, Massachusetts, New Hampshire, New York, Pennsylvania, Rhode Island, Vermont, Puerto Rico, Virgin Islands)
452 5th Avenue—21st Floor
New York, NY 10018

(212) 704-1200

San Francisco Regional Office (Alaska, Arizona, California, Colorado, Guam, Hawaii, Idaho, Montana, Nevada, New Mexico, Oregon, Utah, Washington, Wyoming)
25 Ecker St., Suite 1900
San Francisco, CA 94105

(415) 546-1810

CONSOLIDATED OFFICES OF THE **FDIC**

Consolidated Offices of the Chicago Regional Office

Atlanta Consolidated Office
285 Peachtree Center Avenue NE
Marquis Building Tower II, Suite 300
Atlanta, GA 30303

(404) 880-3000

Bossier City Consolidated Office
6001 Financial Plaza
Shreveport, LA 71129

(318) 686-6700

Knoxville Consolidated Office
800 South Gay Street
Knoxville, TN 37902

(615) 544-4500

O'Hare Consolidated Office
9525 West Bryn Mawr
Suite 300
Rosemont, IL 60018

(708) 671-8800

Orlando Consolidated Office
5778 South Semoran Blvd.
Orlando, FL 32822

(407) 273-2230

Consolidated Offices of the Dallas Regional Office

Addison Consolidated Office
14651 Dallas Parkway
Suite 200
Dallas, TX 752450

(214) 239-3317

Houston Consolidated Office
7324 Southwest Freeway
Suite 1600
Arena Tower #2
Houston, TX 77074

(713) 270-6565

Dallas Consolidated Office
5080 Spectrum Dr.
Suite 1000E
Dallas, TX 75248

(214) 701-2400

(Note: The Dallas Consolidated Office sells assets from failed S&Ls. These assets were given to the FDIC to sell prior to the creation of the RTC in August 1989.)

Midland Consolidated Office
N. Petroleum Building
303 Air Park Dr.
Midland, TX 79705

(915) 685-6400

Oklahoma City Consolidated Office
999 N.W. Grand Blvd.
Oklahoma City, OK 73118

(405) 842-7441

San Antonio Consolidated Office
4440 Piedras Dr. South
San Antonio, TX 78228

(512) 731-2000

Consolidated Offices of the New York Region

South Brunswick Consolidated Office
Cornwall Rd.
Jersey Center Metroplex
Monmouth, NJ 08852

(201) 422-9000

Franklin Consolidated Office
124 Grove St.
Franklin, MA 02038

(508) 520-7250

Hartford Consolidated Office
111 Founders Place
East Hartford, CT 06108

(203) 244-4571

Consolidated Offices of the San Francisco Regional Office

Irvine Consolidated Office
3347 Michelson Dr.
Irvine, CA 92715

(714) 975-5400

San Jose Consolidated Office
2870 Zanker Rd.
Suite 200
San Jose, CA 95134

(408) 434-0640

Denver Consolidated Office
707 17th St.
Suite 3000
Denver, CO 80202

(303) 296-4703

Anchorage Consolidated Office
440 East 36 Avenue
Anchorage, AK 99503

(907) 261-7400

FDIC ORE (OWNED REAL ESTATE) SALES CENTERS

The FDIC has six regional sales centers that market and sell commercial real estate valued at $1 million or greater. They are located at the consolidated offices based in Atlanta; Franklin, Massachusetts; and Orlando for the Eastern U.S.; Dallas for the Southwestern part of the country; Denver for the Mountain states; and Irvine, California for the West Coast. These offices are similar in nature to the RTC national and regional sales centers.

FDIC AFFORDABLE HOUSING PROGRAM (AFH)

The FDIC AFH program is still in its infancy. Initial inquiries should be made to the FDIC headquarters in Washington at:

550 17th St. N.W.
Washington, D.C. 20429

(202) 393-8400

NATIONAL AUCTION COMPANIES THAT SELL LOANS AND REAL ESTATE FOR THE RTC AND FDIC

Hudson & Marshall
717 North Avenue
Macon, GA 31298

(912) 743-1511 (Macon)
(800) 842-9401 (Atlanta, toll free)

JBS Associates
200 North LaSalle St.
Chicago, IL 60601

(312) 701-0777

Ross-Dove & Co.
330 Hatch Drive
Foster City, CA 94404

(415) 571-4700

Yellow Pages note: All auction companies offer free brochures on real estate, loans, and furniture, fixtures, and equipment (FF&E) that is available to purchase. To get a listing, just pick up the telephone (most auction companies have toll-free telephone numbers) and ask. Auction companies are more than happy to supply you with listings.

REAL ESTATE

The listing below is alphabetical. Some companies, acting as "realtors" for the RTC, just sell properties; some companies just auction, while others do both. Many real estate and auction companies working for the RTC and FDIC offer properties on a national basis, meaning that a Virginia-based company can offer properties located in Southern California, Texas, Louisiana, or elsewhere.

There are thousands of realtors who sell properties for the RTC and FDIC. We decided to limit our listing to the large regional and national realtors and auction firms. We list only their corporate headquarters.

REAL ESTATE AND AUCTION COMPANIES

Atlanta Auctions Inc.
20 Park Ave.
Baltimore, MD 21201

(410) 752-5300 (Baltimore)
(800) 345-2628 (toll free)

Century 21
2601 East Main Street
Irvine, CA 92714

(714) 553-2100

Coldwell Banker
1953 Gallows Road
Suite 340
Vienna, VA 22182

(703) 556-6100

Cushman & Wakefield
300 South Grand
Suite 3750
Los Angeles, CA 90017

(800) 676-6798

Grubb & Ellis
One Montgomery St.
Ninth Floor
San Francisco, CA 94104

(415) 433-1050

J.E. Robert & Co., Inc.
11 Canal Center
Alexandria, VA 22314

(703) 739-4440

NRC Auctions
720 North Franklin St.
Suite 400
Chicago, IL 60610

(312) 642-7900

RE/MAX
5445 DTC Parkway
Suite 1200
Englewood, CO 80111

(303) 770-5531

Sheldon Good & Co.
333 West Wacker Dr.
Chicago, IL 60606

(312) 346-1500

DEPARTMENT OF HOUSING AND URBAN DEVELOPMENT (HUD)

HUD sells foreclosed homes, condos, co-ops, and apartment buildings through its 10 regional and 80 field offices. Most of the action is at the regional level.

REGIONAL OFFICES

Boston Regional Office
Thomas P. O'Neill Federal Bldg.
10 Causeway St., Room 375
Boston, MA 02222

(617) 565-5234

New York Regional Office
26 Federal Plaza
New York, NY 10278

(212) 264-8068

Philadelphia Regional Office
105 South Seventh St.
Philadelphia, PA 19106

(215) 597-2560

Atlanta Regional Office
Richard B. Russell Federal Building
75 Spring St. S.W.
Atlanta, GA 30303

(404) 331-5136

Chicago Regional Office
626 West Jackson Blvd.
Chicago, IL 60606

(312) 353-5680

Fort Worth Consolidated Office
1600 Throckmorton
P.O. Box 2905
Ft. Worth, TX 76113

(817) 885-5401

Kansas City Regional Office
Professional Building
1103 Grand Ave.
Kansas City, MO 64106

(816) 374-6432

Denver Regional Office
Executive Tower Bldg.
1405 Curtis St.
Denver, CO 80202

(303) 844-4513

San Francisco Regional Office
405 Golden Gate Ave.
P.O. Box 36003
San Francisco, CA 94102

(415) 556-4752

Seattle Regional Office
1321 Second St.
Seattle, WA 98101

(206) 442-5414

FEDERAL NATIONAL MORTGAGE ASSOCIATION—FANNIE MAE

FNMA—Fannie Mae as it is known—is a large, well-operated congressionally chartered company that buys mortgages from S&Ls and banks.

Although it is quite profitable, it too gets stuck with millions of dollars worth of bad loans that it must foreclose on and sell. Anyone with cash or financing is eligible to buy real estate from Fannie Mae. The same holds true of the Federal Home Loan Mortgage Corporation (FHLMC), commonly referred to as Freddie Mac.

Main Headquarters
3900 Wisconsin Ave. N.W.
Washington, D.C. 20016

(202) 752-8400

Midwestern Regional Office
One South Wacker Dr.
Suite 3100
Chicago, IL 60606

(312) 368-6201

Northeastern Regional Office
510 Walnut Street
16th Floor
Philadelphia, PA 19106

(215) 575-1421

Southeastern Regional Office
950 East Paces Ferry Road
Atlanta, GA 30326

(404) 365-6079

Southwestern Regional Office
Two Galleria Tower
13455 Noel Road
Suite 600
Dallas, TX 75240

(214) 770-7663

Western Regional Office
135 North Los Robles Ave.
Suite 300
Pasadena, CA 91101

(818) 568-5170

FEDERAL HOME LOAN MORTGAGE CORPORATION—FREDDIE MAC

Main Headquarters
8200 Jones Branch Drive
McLean, VA 22102

(703) 903-2000

Northeast Regional Office
2231 Crystal Dr.
Suite 900
Arlington, VA 22202

(703) 685-4500

North Central Regional Office
333 West Wacker Drive
Suite 3100
Chicago, IL 60606

(312) 407-7400

Southeast/Southwest Regional Office
2839 Paces Ferry Rd. N.W.
Suite 700
Atlanta, GA 30339

(404) 438-3800

Western Regional Office
15303 Ventura Blvd.
Suite 200
Sherman Oaks, CA 91403

(818) 905-0070

FEDERAL HOME LOAN BANK SYSTEM

The FHLB system consists of 12 Federal Home Loan Banks. It was chartered by Congress during the Depression to provide liquidity to the savings and loans. Although it does not sell real estate, it provides financing to home buyers and investors who purchase affordable housing units from the RTC and FDIC.

PUBLICATIONS

A number of news organizations cover the RTC and FDIC on a regular basis. Some, including the *Bank Resolution Reporter, Resolution Trust Reporter*, and *Thrift Liquidation Alert* regularly list available properties and auction dates. Among the best ones:

SPECIFIC COVERAGE

Bank Resolution Reporter (26 issues per year)
Dorset Group Inc.
225 West 34th St.
Suite 918
New York, NY 10122

(212) 563-4405
(212) 564-8879 (Fax)

Price: $348 to $398 per year

Resolution Trust Reporter (26 issues per year)
The address, phone, and price are the same as above

Thrift Liquidation Alert (50 issues per year)
One Riverfront Plaza
Suite 1480
Newark, NJ 07102

(201) 596-1300
(201) 596-0148 (Fax)

Price: $629 per year

GENERAL AND OCCASIONAL COVERAGE

American Banker (daily newspaper, except weekends and holidays)
One State Street Plaza
New York, NY 10004

(212) 943-6700

National Mortgage News
212 W. 35th St.
Suite 1300
New York, NY 10001

(212) 563-4008

Wall Street Journal (daily newspaper except weekends and holidays)
200 Liberty Street
New York, NY 10281

(212) 416-2000

Index

Absolute auctions, 205–6
Accountants, job opportunities, 244
Adjusted Appraisal Value, 119
Affordable Housing Clearinghouse, 69
Affordable Housing Disposition Directory, 50
Affordable Housing Program (AFH), 10, 17, 24, 55–83
  auctions of, 56, 63–68
    bidder's conference, 66
    bidding, 66–67, 79–80
    how low will the government go, 68
    prebid qualification session, 65
  caveats and restrictions on, 73–74
  dealing directly with an S&L in, 69–70
  FDIC compared with RTC, 82
  financing and, 70–73
    apartment buildings, 80–82
    banks and thrifts, 70, 80–81
    FHA and VA loans, 71–72
    mortgage bankers and credit unions, 70–71
    RTC, 71–73
  getting started and finding what's available in, 61–62
  giveaways and, 57
  handyman specials and, 57
  hot housing markets in, 62
  income and, 57–60
    figuring out, 60
    qualifications, 57–59
  multifamily apartment projects in, 18
  price caps and, 55–58
    geographical variations, 56
  real estate brokers and, 64
  real estate investors and, 60–61, 74–82
    deed restriction, 78–79
    drawbacks, 76–77
    reselling, 78
    sealed bid process, 79–80
  RTCNET and, 61
  warning about, 73
  as window of opportunity, 56–57
Affordable housing programs (AFH programs), 53–94. *See also* Affordable Housing Program
  HUD and, 24–25
  low- to moderate-income label and, 54–55
American Savings and Loan Association, 10
Anschutz, Philip, 16
Apartment building investors
  AFH program and, 75–82
  "set-aside" requirement, 77–79
  financing for, 80–82
  HUD and, 92
Appraisals, 111–19
  for furniture, fixtures, and equipment (FF&E), 208
  for income property, 117–18

Appraisals (*cont.*)
  Market Data Approach (MDA) to, 115–16
  Replacement Cost Approach (RCA) to, 116–17
  RTC, 118–19
    bidding compared with, 165–71
    valuation process, 119
    types of, 114–15
    value and, 113–14
Appraised Value, 119
Appraisers, job opportunities for, 243–44
Appreciation, 133
Artwork, 213–14
Ashbury, Larry, 36
Assessor parcel number (AP number), 107
Asset Inventory Publications, 32–34
Asset specific inquiry (ASI) line, 30–32
Attic, inspection of, 101
Auctions. *See also* Furniture, fixtures, and equipment (FF&E) auctions; Loan auctions
  AFH, 56, 63–68
    bidder's conference, 66
    bidding, 66–67, 79–80
    prebid qualification session, 65
  bidding at. *See* Bidding
  catalogs for, 150–51
  FDIC, 3–4
  HUD, 90
  RTC, 2–3, 15–16
  workings of, 150–52
Auto loans, 192

Bakker, Jim, 194
Bank failures
  effects of, 2, 11–12, 21
  FDIC and, 21
  sale of assets after. *See* Federal Deposit Insurance Corporation
  in Southwest, 61
Bankruptcy
  buying paper and, 199–202
  cramdowns or pushdowns and, 201–2
  types of, 200–201
Banks, AFH program financing and, 70, 80–81
Beams, inspection of, 98

Between-the-Ears-Appraisal Form, 114
Bidder's conference, 66
Bidding, 148–73
  acceptable terms and, 154
  access to the property and, 160–61
  AFH apartment buildings and, 79–80
  broker-buyers and, 160
  broker commissions and, 154
  broker-nonbroker partnerships and, 160
  cash deposit and, 153
  close, 161
  on contracts, 223–38
    evaluation form, 234
    Solicitation of Services (SOS), 223–35
  due diligence packages, 151–52
  failing to perform and, 172
  forms for, 156–59
  at furniture, fixtures, and equipment (FF&E) auctions, 211–12
  HUD properties and, 89–90, 92–93
  real estate brokers and, 154, 160
  requirements for, 153
  retracting and, 160
  RTC analysis of, 161–65
  RTC appraisals and, 165–71
  unacceptable terms and, 154
BIN. *See* Business Information Network (BIN)
Bonds, junk, 196–97
Broadmore Manor Apartments, analyzing, 136–37
Brokers. *See* Real estate brokers
Brooks, Mel, 194
Bush, George, 242
Bush, Neil, 239n
Business Information Network (BIN), 35.
  See also RTCNET
  installation of, 38
  non-RTC data bases on, 50–51
  on-line charges and, 37

California
  current market value in, 114
  document transfer fee in, 108
CALLBIN, 38
Capitalization Rate Method (CRM), 142–43

Casey, Albert, 1, 15, 149
Cash deposit, bidding and, 153
Cash flow, income property and, 134
Catalogs
    RET, 4
    RTC, 30, 150–51
CC&Rs (Covenants, Conditions, and
    Restrictions), 109, 111
Ceilings, inspection of, 100
CenTrust Savings, 204
Certified public accountants, job
    opportunities for, 244
Cesspools, 102
Chamberlain Resorts Hotel (near Bethel,
    Maine), 3
Chapter 7 bankruptcy, 200–201
Chapter 11 bankruptcy, 200–201
Chapter 13 bankruptcy, 200
Chicago Regional Office, FDIC, 22
Citizens and Builders Savings
    Association, 2
Civil litigation, 240
Close bids, 161
Closings, 171–72
    cost of, 171
    delivery and possession and, 172
Collateral, taking, 191–92
Columbia Savings and Loan, 14, 213
Commercial and industrial property
    as income property, 144–46
    of RTC, 18
    RTCNET, 45–49
    RTC loan fees for, 129
    on RTCNET, 48–49
Commissions, bidding and, 154
Community Reinvestment Act (CRA), 70
Computer data base
    in county recorder's office, 106
    FDIC, 51–52
    of FDIC, 23
    Multiple Listing Service, 115
    of RTC, 8, 23. *See also* RTCNET
    telephone access, 29–35
Confidentiality Agreement, 230–31
Conflict of Interest Memorandum, 226–
    27
Congress, U.S., 7–11, 54–56, 242, 244–
    45
    AFH and, 55–56

amendments, 80
    FHA and, 91
    financing and, 70
    RTC created by, 14–15
    RTC reorganized by, 8, 15, 149
Contractor line, 34
Contractors (contracts)
    bidding on, 223–38
    evaluation form, 234
    Solicitation of Services (SOS), 223–
        35
    FDIC and, 238–39
    getting started as, 218–23
    for lawyers, 239–41
    licensed, 244
    SAMAs. *See* Standard Asset
        Management and Disposition
        Agreements
Covenants, Conditions, and Restrictions
    (CC&Rs), 109, 111
Cravath Swaine and Moore, 240
Credit unions, AFH program financing
    and, 70–71
CRM (Capitalization Rate Method), 142–
    43
Current owners, 107–11
Cushman and Wakefield, 145, 150
Customers, renters as, 144

Dallas Regional Office, FDIC, 22
Deed restriction, AFH program and, 78–
    79
Deeds
    in lieu, 191–92
    quitclaim, 172
    of reconveyance, 109, 112
Delivery and possession, 172
Direct Bid Brochure, 153
Direct sale of furniture, fixtures, and
    equipment (FF&E), 214–15
Distressed Loans (DLs), 176
Documentary transfer fees, 108
Doors, inspection of, 100
Down payments, 125
Drexel Burnham Lambert, 240
Due diligence, 151–52, 199

Earnest-money deposits, 90
Easements, 108–10

800 numbers
　FDIC's lack of, 23
　Resolution Trust Corporation (RTC), 8,
　　29–35
　　AFH program, 61
　　Asset Inventory Publications, 32–34
　　asset specific inquiry line, 30–32
　　auction hot line, 150
　　contractor line, 34
　　seller financing of, 34
　　subscription, 37
Electronic Mail, 50–51
Emotional value, 113–14
Environmentally unsound properties of
　RTC, 18–19
Equipment requirements for RTCNET,
　36–38
Estimated Cash Recovery (ECR), 176
Evaluation Form, 228–29
Expinoza, Rose, 16

Fair Quality Loans (FQL), 175
Fannie Mae. *See* Federal National
　Mortgage Association
FDIC. *See* Federal Deposit Insurance
　Corporation
Federal Bureau of Investigation (FBI),
　245
Federal Deposit Insurance Corporation
　(FDIC), 1–15, 21–29
　affordable housing programs of. *See*
　　Affordable Housing Program (AFH)
　auctions of, 3–4
　buying loans from, 198–99
　buying non-real estate assets from. *See*
　　Furniture, fixtures, and equipment
　buying paper from. *See* Loan auctions;
　　Paper, buying
　computerized asset listings of, 23, 51–
　　52. *See also* Owned Real Estate
　　(ORE) Bulletin Board
　contracting and, 238–39
　Division of Liquidation of, 22
　failed banks and, 21
　HUD compared with, 86, 89
　income property of. *See* Income
　　property
　job opportunities and. *See* Contractors;
　　Job opportunities

nonaffordable housing opportunities of,
　83–84
　RTC compared with, 23
　RTC controlled by, 15
　seller financing of, limit on, 10
　structure of, 21–23
Federal Depository Library (FDL), 34
Federal Home Loan Mortgage
　Corporation (FHLMC; Freddie
　Mac), 25–27
Federal Housing Administration (FHA),
　mortgages of, 71–72, 85, 91
Federal Housing Authority (FHA), 25
Federal National Mortgage Association
　(FNMA; Fannie Mae), 25–27
Federal Reserve, 70
Financial Institutions Reform, Recovery
　and Enforcement Act (FIRREA),
　237, 239
Financial Management Task Force
　(FMTF), 236
Financing. *See also* Seller financing
　AFH program and, 70–73
　apartment buildings, 80–82
　banks and thrifts, 70, 80–81
　FHA and VA loans, 71–72
　mortgage bankers and credit unions,
　　70–71
　renters of government-owned
　　properties, 72–73
　RTC, 71–73
　HUD properties and, 93
FIRREA (Financial Institutions Reform,
　Recovery and Enforcement Act),
　237, 239
First Gibraltar Bank, 5
First mortgages, buying, 180–81
Fitness certification surveys, 185
Fitness and integrity certifications form,
　219–22
Fixer-uppers, 105–6
Fixtures. *See* Furniture, fixtures, and
　equipment
Floors, inspection of, 100
Foreclosure, 191–92
Forms
　bid, 156–59
　fitness and integrity certifications, 219–
　　22

Foundation, inspection of, 98
Freddie Mac. *See* Federal Home Loan
    Mortgage Corporation
Free property, AFH, 57
Furniture, fixtures, and equipment
    (FF&E), 203–15
    appraisals for, 208
    auctions, 205–14
        bidding at, 211–12
        finding out about, 206–9
        payment at, 212–13
        previewing the merchandise and,
            209–10
        sealed-bidding, 213–14
        types of, 205–6
        when the RTC goes to, 205
    definition of, 203
    direct sale of, 214–15
    of RTC, 20

Garcia, Eva, 53
Garn-Germain Act (1982), 244*n*
General Accounting Office (GAO), 9, 11,
    35, 236
General Electric Capital Corp., 11, 75,
    77–79
General Terms & Conditions, 153
Gibraltar Savings, 213
GMM (Gross Multiplier Method), 141–42
GOI (Gross Operating Income), 138
Good Quality Loans (GQL), 175
Government Grade (GG) employees, 243
Gross Multiplier Method (GMM), 141–42
Gross Operating Income (GOI), 138

Historical or cultural value, 19–20
Home inspection services, 97–99, 103–5
Housing and Urban Development
    Department, U.S. (HUD), 7, 9–
    10, 24–27, 84–94, 246
    apartment building investors and, 92–
        93
    bidder information and, 92–93
    buying guidelines and, 90–91
    FDIC compared with, 86, 89
    financing and, 93
    investors versus owner-occupiers and,
        90–91
    property types available from, 86–87

Reagan administration looting of, 54,
    85
    regional and field offices of, 87–89
    RTC compared with, 86–87, 89–90
    sales procedures for, 89–90
    who can buy from, 87
Hudson & Marshall, 182

IBM, 216–17
Income
    Gross Operating (GOI), 138
    median, 57–60
    Net Operating (NOI), 138–39, 142–43
    rental, 133–34
Income cap, AFH program and, 57–60
Income property, 117–18, 132–47
    analyzing, 136–40
        rents, 138
        vacancy factor, 137–38
    appraisals for
        Capitalization Rate Method (CRM),
            142–43
        Gross Multiplier Method (GMM),
            141–42
        Net Operating Income Method
            (NOIM), 142
        Price Per Unit Method (PPUM), 141
    commercial and industrial, 144–46
    double whammy of, 133–36
    as investment, 133–36
    property assessment for, 117–18
Industrial property. *See* Commercial and
    industrial property
Inspection reports, 97–99, 103–5
Inspection tools, 105–6
Insurance
    mortgage, 71
    RTC financing and, 128
Insurance companies, 77–78
Interest rates, RTC and, 123–25
Investment, 54–55. *See also* Apartment
    building investors; Commercial and
    industrial property; Income
    property; Paper, buying; Real
    estate investors
    HUD properties and, 90–93
    income property as, 133–36
    savings compared with, 135
Investor surveys, 184–87

JBS Associates, 145, 182
J.E. Robert & Co., 150, 216, 218
Job opportunities, 12, 216–48. *See also*
    contractors (contracts)
    for appraisers, 243–44
    for certified public accountants, 244
    for lawyers, 239–41
    for real estate brokers, 243
    "staff," 241–43
    what's available in, 216–18
Junk bonds, 196–97
Justice Department, U.S., 73–74, 245

Keating, Charles, Jr., 109, 111, 132,
    239n, 240
Kemp, Jack, 93

Land
    of RTC, 16, 18
    RTCNET, 47–48
    RTC financing for, 130–31
Landlord, thoughts on being a, 143–44
Law enforcement, job opportunities and,
    244–45
Lawyers, job opportunities for, 239–41
Letter Form Appraisal (LFA), 114
Letter for Unsuccessful Proposals, 232
Lewis, John, 2
Licensed contractors, job opportunities
    for, 244
Lien priority, RTC financing and, 126–
    27
Liens
    mechanic's, 108
    tax, 108
Lincoln Savings and Loan, 109, 111
Liquidation Grade (LG) employees, 243
Loan auctions
    finding out about, 182–83
    types of, 189–90
Loans. *See also* Financing; Mortgages;
    and specific types of loans
    buying. *See* Paper, buying
    property assessment and, 109
    RTC, 9, 20–21. *See also* Resolution
        Trust Corporation, seller financing
        of
    on RTCNET, 49
    security for, 14

Location, property assessment and, 95–
    97
Low-income, definition of, 77
Low- to moderate-income, definition of,
    54–55

MacAndrews & Forbes, 5
Market value, 113–14, 119
Mechanics liens, 108
Median income, AFH program and, 57–
    60
Median price, definition of, 56
Middendorf, J. William, 207
Middendorf & Co., 207, 214
Miedens, Paul, 11
Miles, Frederick E., 3
Miles, Jean, 3
Milken, Michael, 196, 240
Minority or Woman Owned Business
    (MWOB), 237–38, 241
Minority or Woman Owned Law Firm
    (MWOLF), 241
MLS (Multiple Listing Service), 115–16
Morrison & Hecker, 239n
Mortgage banking companies, AFH
    program financing and, 70–71
Mortgage insurance, 71
Mortgage servicing rights, 194–95
Mortgages, 9. *See also* Federal Home
    Loan Mortgage Corporation;
    Federal National Mortgage
    Association
    "ballpark" payment of, 67
    buying
        first, 180–81
        second, 181
    FHA, 71–72, 85, 91
    Veterans Administration, 71
Multifamily income properties. *See also*
    Apartment building investors
    of RTC, 18
Multiple Investor Fund Program (MIF),
    197
Multiple Listing Service (MLS), 63, 115–
    16
Multiple property purchases, RTC
    financing and, 130
MWOB (Minority or Woman Owned
    Business), 237–38, 241

MWOLF (Minority or Woman Owned Law Firm), 241

Narrative Appraisal Form (NAF), 114
National Association of Realtors, 145
National Foreclosure Data Base, 50
National Investor Newsletter, 50
National Register of Historic Places, 19
Natural value, 19
Neighbors, inspection of, 101–2
Net Operating Income (NOI), 138–39, 142–43
Net Operating Income Method (NOIM), 142
New England
 AFH program in, 62
 HUD properties in, 86–87
New York Regional Office, FDIC, 22–23
NOI (Net Operating Income), 138–39, 142–43
NOIM (Net Operating Income Method), 142
Nonprofit organizations
 AFH program and
  financing, 81–82
  RTC negotiations, 80
 free property for, 57
Non-real estate assets, 9, 174–215. *See also* Furniture, fixtures, and equipment; Paper, buying
 of Resolution Trust Corporation (RTC), 20–21
 types of, 10, 14
Non-real estate loans, 192–95
 auto, 192
 mortgage servicing rights, 194–95
 student, 192–93
 timeshare, 193–94
Northcorp Realty Advisers, 217

Office of Management and Budget, 21
Office of Thrift Supervision (OTS), 70
On-line charges, BIN, 37
Operating expenses, closings and, 171
Oral outcry auctions, 189–90
Oral outcry (open-cry) bidding, 66
Overbuilding, AFH program and, 75–76

Owned Real Estate (ORE)
 Bulletin Board, 23, 52, 82
 centers, 23
Owner occupancy rule, 74, 78
Owners, current, 107–8

Paper, buying, 174–202. *See also* Loan auctions
 amount available, 179–82
  first mortgages, 180–81
  second mortgages, 181
 analyzing loan file and, 184–89
 basic categories and, 175–76
 caveats, 177–79, 199–202
  bankruptcy, 199–202
  due diligence, 199
  from FDIC, 198–99
  getting started, 182
  investor surveys and, 184–87
  junk bonds, 196–97
  non-real estate, 192–95
   auto, 192
   mortgage servicing rights, 194–95
   student, 192–93
   timeshare, 193–94
  performing loans, 183–84
  reasons for, 176–77
  risks of, 174
  seller financing and, 190–91
  signature loans, 195–96
  taking the collateral and, 191–92
Parking, inspection of, 102
Paul, David L., 204, 213
Payment, at furniture, fixtures, and equipment (FF&E) auctions, 212–13
Pension funds, 77–78
Perelman, Ronald, 4, 5n
Performing loans, buying, 183–84
Personal liability, RTC financing and, 128
Pizzo, Susan, 134
Plat maps, 109–10
Poor Quality Loans (PQL), 175–76
Portfolio sales, 34
Portrait of a Man as Mars (Rubens), 213
PPUM (Price Per Unit Method), 141
Prebid qualification session, 65
Prepayment terms, RTC financing and, 127

Price Per Unit Method (PPUM), 141
Private mortgage insurance (PMI), 71
Private Networks, 51
Problem bank list, 21
Prodigy Information Network, 52
Producers, The, 194
Property assessment, 95–122. *See also*
    Appraisals
  for income property
    Capitalization Rate Method (CRM),
      142–43
    Gross Multiplier Method (GMM),
      141–42
    Net Operating Income Method
      (NOIM), 142
    Price Per Unit Method (PPUM),
      141
  inspections and
    attic, 101
    beams, 98
    do-it-yourself, 98–106
    doors and windows, 100
    floors, 100
    foundation, 98
    neighbors, 101–2
    parking, 102
    professional, 97–99, 103–5
    roof, 101
    sewage, 102–3
    tools, 105–6
    walls and ceilings, 100
    water, 103–5
  location and, 95–97
  public records and, 106–12
    assessor parcel number, 107
    what to look for, 107–12
  realtors and, 120–21
  title companies and, 121–22
Property parcel map, 109–10
Public records and, 106–12
  assessor parcel number in, 107
  what to look for in, 107–12
Pumps, 103, 105

Quitclaim deeds, 172

Ralph Edgar Group Inc. (REGI), 222
Reagan, Ronald, 82, 242, 244
Real Estate Asset Specific Program, 30

Real estate brokers
  AFH program and, 64
  bidding and, 154, 160
  commissions of, 154
  job opportunities for, 243
  property assessment and, 120–21
  RTC and, 34
Real Estate Investment Trusts (REITs),
  197–98
Real estate investors, AFH program and,
  74–82
  deed restriction, 78–79
  drawbacks, 76–77
  reselling, 78
  sealed bid process, 79–80
Real Estate Owned (REO) Bulletin Board,
  23
Real Estate Owned Management system
  (REOM), 35
Real Estate Reporter, 50
Recession, "rolling," 61
Reconveyance, deeds of, 109, 112
Recreational value, 19
Regenhold Auction Consultants, Inc., 207
REITs (Real Estate Investment Trusts),
  197–98
Renovation trend, property assessment
  and, 96
Rent
  income from, 133–34
  property analysis and, 138
Rents, closings and, 171
Replacement Cost Approach (RCA), 116–
  17
Request for Proposal (RFP), 238–39
Reselling, AFH program and, 73–74, 78
Reserve price auctions, 206, 214
Residential property of RTC, 17–18. *See
  also* Affordable Housing Program
  (AFH)
  RTCNET, 39–44
Resolution Trust Corporation (RTC),
  1–21, 23–84
  Affordable Housing Clearinghouse of,
    69
  amount of assets for sale by, 9, 13
  Auction Center of, 206
  auctions, 2–3, 15–16
  catalogs of, 4, 30

computerized asset listings of, 8. *See also* RTCNET
telephone access, 29–35
Contract Registration Department of, 219
contracting division of, 34
creation of, 14–15
800 numbers. *See* 800 numbers of RTC
FDIC compared with, 23
HUD compared with, 86–87, 89–90
National Sales Center of, 206, 218
nonaffordable housing opportunities of, 83–84
Office of Inspector General (IG) of, 222
property assessment of, 118–19
reorganization of, 8, 15, 149
seller financing of, 3, 123–31
  AFH program, 81–82
  assumability, 127
  bridge loans, 129
  commercial loan fee, 129
  commercial property debt-service ratios, 128
  down payments, 125
  800 numbers, 34
  insurance, 128
  interest rates, 123–25
  land, 130–31
  lien priority, 126–27
  limit, 10–11
  multiple property purchases, 130
  personal liability, 128
  prepayment terms, 127
  release price, 129
  terms, 126
structure of, 16–17
types of property of, 17–21. *See also* Affordable Housing Program
  commercial and industrial, 18
  environmentally unsound properties, 18–19
  income. *See* Income property
  land, 18
  loans, 16
  multifamily income, 18
  non-real estate assets, 9, 20–21. *See also* Furniture, fixtures, and equipment; Loan auctions; Paper, buying

residential, 17–18
special significance properties, 19–20
Resolution Trust Corporation Refinancing, Restructuring and Improvement Act (1991), 15
Resolution Trust Reporter, 50
Retracting bids, 160
Revlon, 4–5
Roof, inspection of, 101
Ross-Dove & Co., 182
Roswell, New Mexico, RTC auction in, 15–16
RTCNET, 35–51
  accessing, 38–39
  retrieving and printing, 44
  AFH program and, 61
  auction information on, 150
  commercial and industrial property on, 45–49
  warning, 48–49
  equipment requirements for, 36–38
  furniture, fixtures, and equipment (FF&E) auctions and, 206
  land on, 47–48
  loans on, 49
  other RTC information on, 49–50
  residential property on, 39–44
Rubens, Peter Paul, 204, 213
Russell, Roland, 199

SAMAs (Standard Asset Management Agreements contracts), 217, 235
San Francisco Regional Office, FDIC, 23
Sanders, Bernard, 62
Savings, investment compared with, 54, 135
Savings and loans (S&Ls)
  AFH program financing and, 70, 81
  conservatorships of, 69, 149
  dealing directly with, 69–70
  deregulation of, 244–45
  effects of financial meltdown of, 2, 11–12
  future of, 14–15
  Reagan administration looting of, 244–45
  sale of assets of. *See* Resolution Trust Corporation; RTCNET
  in Southwest, 61

Schwarzenegger, Arnold, 14
Scientific value, 19
Sealed-bid auctions, 189
  for furniture, fixtures, and equipment
    (FF&E), 213–14
Sealed bids, 66–67
  AFH apartment buildings and, 79–
    80
  forms for, 156–59
  HUD and, 90
Second mortgages, buying, 181
Seidman, Bill, 132
Seller financing
  of FDIC, limit on, 10
  HUD and, 93
  of loans, 190–91
  RTC, 123–31
    AFH program, 71–73, 81–82
    assumability, 127
    bridge loans, 129
    commercial loan fee, 129
    commercial property debt-service
      ratios, 128
    down payments, 125
    800 numbers, 34
    insurance, 128
    interest rates, 123–25
    land, 130–31
    lien priority, 126–27
    limit, 10–11
    multiple property purchases, 130
    personal liability, 128
    prepayment terms, 127
    release price, 129
    terms, 126
Septic tanks, 102–3
"Set-aside" requirement, AFH program
  and, 77–79
Sewage, inspection of, 102–3
Sheraton Hotel (Cypress Gardens,
  Florida), 3
Short Form Appraisal (SFA), 114
Signature loans, 195–96
SILVER LINING, 49
Sisneros, Ray, 16
Small Business Administration (SBA),
  246
Smith, Joseph, 4–5
Smith, Millie, 4–5

Solicitation of Services (SOS), 223–
  34
  Confidentiality Agreement and, 230–
    31
  Conflict of Interest Memorandum and,
    226–27
  Evaluation Form, 228–29
  Letter for Unsuccessful Proposals and,
    232
Sotheby's, 213
Southwest, AFH opportunities in the,
  61
Special significance properties of RTC,
  19–20
Spiegel, Thomas, 14
"Staff" jobs, 241–43
Standard Asset Management and
  Disposition Agreements
  (SAMDAs), 150–52, 154, 162–64,
  217, 235, 242
Student loans, 192–93
Sullivan, Carmen, 171
Supreme Court, California, 114
Supreme Court, U.S., 201–2
Symington, Fife, 239n

Tax liens, 108
Taxes, property, 109
Telephone numbers. *See* 800 numbers
Texas, AFH program in, 62–63, 75
35 percent low-income rental set-aside,
  AFH program and, 77–79
Thrift Liquidation Alert, 50
Thrifts. *See* Savings and loans (S&Ls)
Timeshare loans, 193–94
Title companies, property assessment
  and, 121–22
Tools, inspection, 105
Treasury Department, U.S., 15, 56
Treasury Note Constant Maturity Index,
  U.S., 123–24
"Trickle down" theory, 82

Unsecured loans, 195–96
Unsuccessful contractors, guidelines for
  debriefing of, 233

Vacancy factor, property analysis and,
  137–38

Vacancy rates
  commercial, 145
  property assessment and, 97
Value
  market vs. emotional, 113–14
  RTC's assessment of, 119
  special significance properties and, 19–20
Vermont, 62–63
Veterans Administration (VA) mortgages,
    71–72

Wall Street Journal, 124
Walls, inspection of, 100
Water, inspection of, 103–5
Watt, James, 85
Wealth, building, 54–55
Wells, 103
Wieghorst, Olaf, 213
Windows, inspection of, 100

Zoning, 96